© Greg Martin

Thomas L. Friedman has won the Pulitzer Prize three times for his work at *The New York Times*, where he serves as the foreign affairs columnist. He is the author of three previous books, all of them bestsellers: *From Beirut to Jerusalem*, winner of the National Book Award for nonfiction; *The Lexus and the Olive Tree: Understanding Globalization*; and *Longitudes and Attitudes: Exploring the World After September 11*. In 2005 *The World Is Flat* was given the first Financial Times and Goldman Sachs Business Book of the Year Award, and Friedman was named one of America's Best Leaders by *U.S. News & World Report*. He lives in Bethesda, Maryland, with his family.

ALSO BY THOMAS L. FRIEDMAN

From Beirut to Jerusalem (1989)

The Lexus and the Olive Tree (1999)

Longitudes and Attitudes (2002)

THE WORLD IS FLAT

THOMAS L. FRIEDMAN

THE WORLD IS FLAT

A Brief History of
the Twenty-first Century

**FURTHER
UPDATED AND EXPANDED**

Picador / Farrar, Straus and Giroux
New York

For information on Picador Reading Group Guides, please contact Picador.
Phone: 646-307-5259
Fax: 212-253-9627
E-mail: readinggroupguides@picadorusa.com

Grateful acknowledgment is made to the following for permission to reprint excerpts of their work: the Associated Press; *Business Monthly*; *BusinessWeek*; *City Journal*; Discovery Channel / Discovery Times Channel; *Education Week*, Editorial Projects in Education; *Fast Company* / Mansueto Ventures; *Forbes*; *New Perspectives Quarterly*; John Seigenthaler; the International Finance Corporation and the International Bank for Reconstruction and Development / World Bank; and YaleGlobal Online (http://yaleglobal.yale.edu/). Excerpts from articles from *The Washington Post* are copyright © 2004. Reprinted with permission.

Book design by Jonathan D. Lippincott

Library of Congress Control Number: 2007929112
ISBN-13: 978-0-312-42507-4
ISBN-10: 0-312-42507-4

First edition published in 2005 by Farrar, Straus and Giroux
First updated and expanded edition published in 2006 by Farrar, Straus and Giroux
First Picador Edition: August 2007

1 3 5 7 9 10 8 6 4 2

To Matt and Kay
and to Ron

Contents

Introduction to the Paperback Edition / ix

How the World Became Flat

One: While I Was Sleeping / 3
Two: The Ten Forces That Flattened the World / 51
  Flattener #1. 11/9/89
  Flattener #2. 8/9/95
  Flattener #3. Work Flow Software
  Flattener #4. Uploading
  Flattener #5. Outsourcing
  Flattener #6. Offshoring
  Flattener #7. Supply-Chaining
  Flattener #8. Insourcing
  Flattener #9. In-forming
  Flattener #10. The Steroids
Three: The Triple Convergence / 200
Four: The Great Sorting Out / 233

America and the Flat World

Five: America and Free Trade / 263
Six: The Untouchables / 278
Seven: The Right Stuff / 308
Eight: The Quiet Crisis / 337
Nine: This Is Not a Test / 374

Developing Countries and the Flat World

Ten: The Virgin of Guadalupe / 403

Companies and the Flat World

Eleven: How Companies Cope / 441

You and the Flat World

Twelve: Globalization of the Local / 477
Thirteen: If It's Not Happening, It's Because
  You're Not Doing It / 489
Fourteen: What Happens When We All Have Dog's Hearing? / 515

Geopolitics and the Flat World

Fifteen: The Unflat World / 533
Sixteen: The Dell Theory of Conflict Prevention / 580

Conclusion: Imagination

Seventeen: 11/9 Versus 9/11 / 607

Acknowledgments / 637
Index / 641

Introduction to the

Paperback Edition

Why go through all the trouble of writing a second expanded and updated version of *The World Is Flat* only a year after the first expanded version was published and a mere two years after the original? I can offer a very brief answer: because I could and because I had to. Precisely because of the powerful technological forces detailed in this book, the publishing industry has sped up and it is now possible to revamp a whole book relatively easily. That is what I mean when I say I could. The reason I must do it is fourfold. First, the forces flattening the world didn't stop when the first edition of this book was published in April 2005, and I wanted to keep tracking them and weaving them into my overall thesis. Second, I wanted to answer one of the questions I was asked most often by parents while I was traveling around the country to speak about the book: "Okay, Mr. Friedman, thank you for telling us that the world is flat—now what do I tell my kids?" In the 2.0 edition, I added a lot more material on the subject of what is the "right" education to access the new middle-class jobs, and I have added still more in this 3.0 edition. Third, I found many of the comments from readers and reviewers both thoughtful and useful, and I wanted to absorb some of the best of them into the book. And finally, in this 3.0 edition, I have added two new chapters to deal with themes related to the flat world that were not apparent to me before but now seem extremely important. One deals with how to be a political activist and social entrepreneur in a flat world. The other deals with a more troubling phenomenon—how we manage our reputations in a world where we are all becoming publishers and therefore all becoming public figures.

This book has triggered a cottage industry of articles with variations on the title "The World Is Not Flat." I have two reactions to these: (1) No kidding. (2) Whenever you opt for a big metaphor like "The World Is Flat," you trade a certain degree of academic precision for a much larger degree of explanatory power. Of course the world is not flat. But it isn't round anymore, either. I have found that using the simple notion of flatness to describe how more people can plug, play, compete, connect, and collaborate with more equal power than ever before—which is what is happening in the world—really helps people who are trying to understand the essential impact of all the technological changes coming together today. Not only do I make no apologies for it, I think that with every passing year, it becomes more true and more useful in explaining in a simple way what is happening. My use of the word "flat" doesn't mean equal (as in "equal incomes") and never did. It means equalizing, because the flattening forces are empowering more and more individuals today to reach farther, faster, deeper, and cheaper than ever before, and that is equalizing power—and equalizing opportunity, by giving so many more people the tools and ability to connect, compete, and collaborate. In my view, this flattening of the playing field is the most important thing happening in the world today, and those who get caught up in measuring globalization purely by trade statistics—or as a purely economic phenomenon instead of one that affects everything from individual empowerment to culture to how hierarchical institutions operate—are missing the impact of this change.

At some point I will stop writing this book. But for now, I am just enjoying the chance to keep sharing what I am learning—and am thankful that the flattening of the world makes doing so easier than ever.

Thomas L. Friedman
Washington, D.C.
April 2007

How the World
Became Flat

ONE

While I Was Sleeping

Your Highnesses, as Catholic Christians, and princes who love and promote the holy Christian faith, and are enemies of the doctrine of Mahomet, and of all idolatry and heresy, determined to send me, Christopher Columbus, to the above-mentioned countries of India, to see the said princes, people, and territories, and to learn their disposition and the proper method of converting them to our holy faith; and furthermore directed that I should not proceed by land to the East, as is customary, but by a Westerly route, in which direction we have hitherto no certain evidence that anyone has gone.

— Entry from the journal of Christopher Columbus on his voyage of 1492

No one ever gave me directions like this on a golf course before: "Aim at either Microsoft or IBM." I was standing on the first tee at the KGA Golf Club in downtown Bangalore, in southern India, when my playing partner pointed at two shiny glass-and-steel buildings off in the distance, just behind the first green. The Goldman Sachs building wasn't done yet; otherwise he could have pointed that out as well and made it a threesome. HP and Texas Instruments had their offices on the back nine, along the tenth hole. That wasn't all. The tee markers were from Epson, the printer company, and one of our caddies was wearing a hat from 3M. Outside, some of the traffic signs were also sponsored by Texas Instruments, and the Pizza Hut billboard on the way over showed a steaming pizza, under the headline "Gigabites of Taste!"

No, this definitely wasn't Kansas. It didn't even seem like India. Was this the New World, the Old World, or the Next World?

I had come to Bangalore, India's Silicon Valley, on my own Columbus-like journey of exploration. Columbus sailed with the *Niña,* the *Pinta,* and the *Santa María* in an effort to discover a shorter, more direct route to India by heading west, across the Atlantic, on what he presumed to be an open sea route to the East Indies—rather than going south and east around Africa, as Portuguese explorers of his day were trying to do. India and the magical Spice Islands of the East were famed at the time for their gold, pearls, gems, and silk—a source of untold riches. Finding this shortcut by sea to India, at a time when the Muslim powers of the day had blocked the overland routes from Europe, was a way for both Columbus and the Spanish monarchy to become wealthy and powerful. When Columbus set sail, he apparently assumed the earth was round, which was why he was convinced that he could get to India by going west. He miscalculated the distance, though. He thought the earth was a smaller sphere than it is. He also did not anticipate running into a landmass before he reached the East Indies. Nevertheless, he called the aboriginal peoples he encountered in the new world "Indians." Returning home, though, Columbus was able to tell his patrons, King Ferdinand and Queen Isabella, that although he never did find India, he could confirm that the world was indeed round.

I set out for India by going due east, via Frankfurt. I had Lufthansa business class. I knew exactly which direction I was going thanks to the GPS map displayed on the screen that popped out of the armrest of my airline seat. I landed safely and on schedule. I too encountered people called Indians. I too was searching for India's riches. Columbus was searching for hardware—precious metals, silk, and spices—the sources of wealth in his day. I was searching for software, brainpower, complex algorithms, knowledge workers, call centers, transmission protocols, breakthroughs in optical engineering—the sources of wealth in our day.

Columbus was happy to make the Indians he met his slaves, a pool of free manual labor. I just wanted to understand why the Indians I met were taking our work, why they had become such an important pool for the outsourcing of service and information technology work from

America and other industrialized countries. Columbus had more than one hundred men on his three ships; I had a small crew from the Discovery Times channel that fit comfortably into two banged-up vans, with Indian drivers who drove barefoot. When I set sail, so to speak, I too assumed that the world was round, but what I encountered in the real India profoundly shook my faith in that notion. Columbus accidentally ran into America but thought he had discovered part of India. I actually found India and thought many of the people I met there were Americans. Some had actually taken American names, and others were doing great imitations of American accents at call centers and American business techniques at software labs.

Columbus reported to his king and queen that the world was round, and he went down in history as the man who first made this discovery. I returned home and shared my discovery only with my wife, and only in a whisper.

"Honey," I confided, "I think the world is flat."

How did I come to this conclusion? I guess you could say it all started in Nandan Nilekani's conference room at Infosys Technologies Limited. Infosys is one of the jewels of the Indian information technology world, and Nilekani, the company's CEO, is one of the most thoughtful and respected captains of Indian industry. I drove with the Discovery Times crew out to the Infosys campus, about forty minutes from the heart of Bangalore, to tour the facility and interview Nilekani. The Infosys campus is reached by a pockmarked road, with sacred cows, horse-drawn carts, and motorized rickshaws all jostling alongside our vans. Once you enter the gates of Infosys, though, you are in a different world. A massive resort-size swimming pool nestles amid boulders and manicured lawns, adjacent to a huge putting green. There are multiple restaurants and a fabulous health club. Glass-and-steel buildings seem to sprout up like weeds each week. In some of those buildings, Infosys employees are writing specific software programs for American or European companies; in others, they are running the back rooms of major American- and European-based multinationals — everything from computer maintenance to specific research projects to answering customer calls routed there from all over the world. Security is tight, cameras monitor the doors, and if you are working for American Express, you cannot get into the building that is managing services and research for General Electric. Young Indian engineers, men and women, walk briskly from building to building, dangling ID badges. One looked like he could do my taxes. Another looked like she could take my computer apart. And a third looked like she designed it!

After sitting for an interview, Nilekani gave our TV crew a tour of Infosys's global conferencing center—ground zero of the Indian outsourcing industry. It was a cavernous wood-paneled room that looked like a tiered classroom from an Ivy League law school. On one end was a massive wall-size screen and overhead there were cameras in the ceiling for teleconferencing. "So this is our conference room, probably the largest screen in Asia—this is forty digital screens [put together]," Nilekani explained proudly, pointing to the biggest flat-screen TV I had ever seen. Infosys, he said, can hold a virtual meeting of the key players from its entire global supply chain for any project at any time on that supersize screen. So their American designers could be on the screen speaking with their Indian software writers and their Asian manufacturers all at once. "We could be sitting here, somebody from New York, London, Boston, San Francisco, all live. And maybe the implementation is in Singapore, so the Singapore person could also be live here . . . That's globalization," said Nilekani. Above the screen there were eight clocks that pretty well summed up the Infosys workday: 24/7/365. The clocks were labeled US West, US East, GMT, India, Singapore, Hong Kong, Japan, Australia.

"Outsourcing is just one dimension of a much more fundamental thing happening today in the world," Nilekani explained. "What happened over the last [few] years is that there was a massive investment in technology, especially in the bubble era, when hundreds of millions of dollars were invested in putting broadband connectivity around the world, undersea cables, all those things." At the same time, he added, computers became cheaper and dispersed all over the world, and there was an explosion of software—e-mail, search engines like Google, and proprietary software that can chop up any piece of work and send one part to Boston, one part to Bangalore, and one part to Beijing, making it easy for anyone to do remote development. When all of these things suddenly came together around 2000, added Nilekani, they "created a platform where intellectual work, intellectual capital, could be delivered from anywhere. It could be disaggregated, delivered, distributed, produced, and put back together again—and this gave a whole new degree of freedom to the way we do work, especially work of an intellectual nature . . . And what you are seeing in Bangalore today is really the culmination of all these things coming together."

We were sitting on the couch outside Nilekani's office, waiting for the TV crew to set up its cameras. At one point, summing up the implications of all this, Nilekani uttered a phrase that rang in my ear. He said to me, "Tom, the playing field is being leveled." He meant that countries like India are now able to compete for global knowledge work as never before—and that America had better get ready for this. America was going to be challenged, but, he insisted, the challenge would be good for America because we are always at our best when we are being challenged. As I left the Infosys campus that evening and bounced along the road back to Bangalore, I kept chewing on that phrase: "The playing field is being leveled."

What Nandan is saying, I thought to myself, is that the playing field is being flattened . . . Flattened? Flattened? I rolled that word around in my head for a while and then, in the chemical way that these things happen, it just popped out: My God, he's telling me the world is flat!

Here I was in Bangalore—more than five hundred years after Columbus sailed over the horizon, using the rudimentary navigational technologies of his day, and returned safely to prove definitively that the world was round—and one of India's smartest engineers, trained at his country's top technical institute and backed by the most modern technologies of his day, was essentially telling me that the world was *flat*—as flat as that screen on which he can host a meeting of his whole global supply chain. Even more interesting, he was citing this development as a good thing, as a new milestone in human progress and a great opportunity for India and the world—the fact that we had made our world flat!

In the back of that van, I scribbled down four words in my notebook:

"The world is flat." As soon as I wrote them, I realized that this was the underlying message of everything that I had seen and heard in Bangalore in two weeks of filming. The global competitive playing field was being leveled. The world was being flattened.

As I came to this realization, I was filled with both excitement and dread. The journalist in me was excited at having found a framework to better understand the morning headlines and to explain what was happening in the world today. Clearly Nandan was right: It is now possible for more people than ever to collaborate and compete in real time with more other people on more different kinds of work from more different corners of the planet and on a more equal footing than at any previous time in the history of the world—using computers, e-mail, fiber-optic networks, teleconferencing, and dynamic new software. That was what I discovered on my journey to India and beyond. And that is what this book is about. When you start to think of the world as flat, or at least in the process of flattening, a lot of things make sense in ways they did not before. But I was also excited personally, because what the flattening of the world means is that we are now connecting all the knowledge centers on the planet together into a single global network, which—if politics and terrorism do not get in the way—could usher in an amazing era of prosperity, innovation, and collaboration, by companies, communities, and individuals. But contemplating the flat world also left me filled with dread, professional and personal. My personal dread derived from the obvious fact that it's not only the software writers and computer geeks who get empowered to collaborate on work in a flat world. It's also al-Qaeda and other terrorist networks. The playing field is not being leveled only in ways that draw in and superempower a whole new group of innovators. It's being leveled in a way that draws in and superempowers a whole new group of angry, frustrated, and humiliated men and women.

Professionally, the recognition that the world was flat was unnerving because I realized that this flattening had been taking place while I was sleeping, and I had missed it. I wasn't really sleeping, but I was otherwise engaged. Before 9/11, I was focused on tracking globalization and exploring the tension between the "Lexus" forces of economic integration and the "Olive Tree" forces of identity and nationalism—hence my 1999 book,

The Lexus and the Olive Tree. But after 9/11, the olive tree wars became all-consuming for me. I spent almost all my time traveling in the Arab and Muslim worlds. During those years I lost the trail of globalization.

I found that trail again on my journey to Bangalore in February 2004. Once I did, I realized that something really important had happened while I was fixated on the olive groves of Kabul and Baghdad. Globalization had gone to a whole new level. If you put *The Lexus and the Olive Tree* and this book together, the broad historical argument you end up with is that there have been three great eras of globalization. The first lasted from 1492—when Columbus set sail, opening trade between the Old World and the New World—until around 1800. I would call this era Globalization 1.0. It shrank the world from a size large to a size medium. Globalization 1.0 was about countries and muscles. That is, in Globalization 1.0, the key agent of change, the dynamic force driving the process of global integration, was how much brawn—how much muscle, how much horsepower, wind power, or, later, steam power—your country had and how creatively you could deploy it. In this era, countries and governments (often inspired by religion or imperialism or a combination of both) led the way in breaking down walls and knitting the world together, driving global integration. In Globalization 1.0, the primary questions were: Where does my country fit into global competition and opportunities? How can I go global and collaborate with others through my country?

The second great era, Globalization 2.0, lasted roughly from 1800 to 2000, interrupted by the Great Depression and World Wars I and II. This era shrank the world from a size medium to a size small. In Globalization 2.0, the key agent of change, the dynamic force driving global integration, was multinational companies. These multinationals went global for markets and labor, spearheaded first by the expansion of the Dutch and English joint-stock companies and the Industrial Revolution. In the first half of this era, global integration was powered by falling transportation costs, thanks to the steam engine and the railroad, and in the second half by falling telecommunication costs—thanks to the diffusion of the telegraph, telephones, the PC, satellites, fiber-optic cable, and the early version of the World Wide Web. It was during this era that we really saw the birth and maturation of a global economy, in the sense that there was enough movement of goods and information from continent to continent for there to be a global market, with global arbitrage in products and labor. The dynamic forces behind this era of globalization were breakthroughs in hardware—from steamships and railroads in the beginning to telephones and mainframe computers toward the end. And the big questions in this era were: Where does my company fit into the global economy? How does it take advantage of the opportunities? How can I go global and collaborate with others through my company? *The Lexus and the Olive Tree* was primarily about the climax of this era, an era when the walls started falling all around the world, and integration— and the backlash to it—went to a whole new level. But even as the walls fell, there were still a lot of barriers to seamless global integration. Remember, when Bill Clinton was elected president in 1992, virtually no one outside of government and the academy had e-mail, and when I was writing *The Lexus and the Olive Tree* in 1998, the Internet and e-commerce were just taking off.

Well, they took off—along with a lot of other things that came together while I was sleeping. And that is why I argue in this book that right around the year 2000 we entered a whole new era: Globalization 3.0. Globalization 3.0 is shrinking the world from a size small to a size tiny and flattening the playing field at the same time. And while the dynamic force in Globalization 1.0 was countries globalizing and the dynamic force in Globalization 2.0 was companies globalizing, the dynamic force in Globalization 3.0—the force that gives it its unique character—is the newfound power for *individuals* to collaborate and compete globally. And the phenomenon that is enabling, empowering, and enjoining individuals and small groups to go global so easily and so seamlessly is what I call the *flat-world platform*, which I describe in detail in this book. Just a hint: The flat-world platform is the product of a convergence of the personal computer (which allowed every individual suddenly to become the author of his or her own content in digital form) with fiber-optic cable (which suddenly allowed all those individuals to access more and more digital content around the world for next to nothing) with the rise of work flow software (which enabled individuals all over the world to collaborate on that same digital content from anywhere, regardless of the distances between them). No one anticipated this convergence. It just happened—right around the year 2000. And when it did, people all over the world started waking up and realizing that they had more power than ever to go global *as individuals*, they needed more than ever to think of themselves as individuals competing against other individuals all over the planet, and they had more opportunities to work with those other individuals, not just compete with them. As a result, every person now must, and can, ask: Where do *I* as an individual fit into the global competition and opportunities of the day, and how can *I*, on my own, collaborate with others globally?

But Globalization 3.0 differs from the previous eras not only in how it is shrinking and flattening the world and in how it is empowering individuals. It also is different in that Globalization 1.0 and 2.0 were driven primarily by European and American individuals and businesses. Even though China actually had the biggest economy in the world in the eighteenth century, it was Western countries, companies, and explorers who were doing most of the globalizing and shaping of the system. But going forward, this will be less and less true. Because it is flattening and shrinking the world, Globalization 3.0 is going to be more and more driven not only by individuals but also by a much more diverse—non-Western, non-white—group of individuals. Individuals from every corner of the flat world are being empowered. Globalization 3.0 makes it possible for so many more people to plug in and play, and you are going to see every color of the human rainbow take part.

(While this empowerment of individuals to act globally is the most important new feature of Globalization 3.0, companies—large and small—have been newly empowered in this era as well. I discuss both in detail later in the book.)

Needless to say, I had only the vaguest appreciation of all this as I left Nandan's office that day in Bangalore. But as I sat contemplating these changes on the balcony of my hotel room that evening, I did know one thing: I wanted to drop everything and write a book that would enable me to understand how this flattening process happened and what its implications might be for countries, companies, and individuals. So I

picked up the phone and called my wife, Ann, and told her, "I am going
to write a book called *The World Is Flat.*" She was both amused and curious—well, maybe *more* amused than curious! Eventually, I was able to
bring her around, and I hope I will be able to do the same with you, dear
reader. Let me start by taking you back to the beginning of my journey to
India, and other points east, and share with you some of the encounters
that led me to conclude the world was no longer round—but flat.

Jaithirth "Jerry" Rao was one of the first people I met in Bangalore,
and I hadn't been with him for more than a few minutes at the Leela
Palace hotel before he told me that he could handle my tax returns and
any other accounting needs I had—from Bangalore. No thanks, I de-
murred, I already have an accountant in Chicago. Jerry just smiled. He
was too polite to say it—that he may already be my accountant, or rather
my accountant's accountant, thanks to the explosion in the outsourcing
of tax preparation.

"This is happening as we speak," said Rao, a native of Mumbai, formerly Bombay, whose Indian firm, MphasiS, has a team of Indian accountants able to do outsourced accounting work from any state in
America and the federal government. "We have tied up with several
small and medium-size CPA firms in America."

"You mean like my accountant?" I asked. "Yes, like your accountant,"
said Rao with a smile. Rao's company has pioneered a work flow software
program with a standardized format that makes the outsourcing of tax returns cheap and easy. The whole process starts, Jerry explained, with an
accountant in the United States scanning my last year's tax returns, plus
my W-2, W-4, 1099, bonuses, and stock statements—everything—into a
computer server, which is physically located in California or Texas.
"Now your accountant, if he is going to have your taxes done overseas,
knows that you would prefer not to have your surname be known or your
Social Security number known [to someone outside the country], so he
can choose to suppress that information," said Rao. "The accountants in
India call up all the raw information directly from the server in America
[using a password], and they complete your tax returns, with you re-

maining anonymous. All the data stays in the U.S. to comply with privacy regulations . . . We take data protection and privacy very seriously. The accountant in India can see the data on his screen, but he cannot take a download of it or print it out—our program does not allow it. The most he could do would be to try to memorize it, if he had some ill intention. The accountants are not allowed to even take a paper and pen into the room when they are working on the returns."

I was intrigued at just how advanced this form of service outsourcing had become. "We are doing several thousand returns," said Rao. What's more, "Your CPA in America need not even be in their office. They can be sitting on a beach in California and e-mail us and say, 'Jerry, you are really good at doing New York State returns, so you do Tom's returns. And Sonia, you and your team in Delhi do the Washington and Florida returns.' Sonia, by the way, is working out of her house in India, with no overhead [for the company to pay]. 'And these others, they are really complicated, so I will do them myself.'"

In 2003, some 25,000 U.S. tax returns were done in India. In 2004, the number was 100,000. In 2005, it was roughly 400,000. In a decade, you will assume that your accountant has outsourced the basic preparation of your tax returns—if not more.

"How did you get into this?" I asked Rao.

"My friend Jeroen Tas, a Dutchman, and I were both working in California for Citigroup," Rao explained. "I was his boss and we were coming back from New York one day together on a flight and I said that I was planning to quit and he said, 'So am I.' We both said, 'Why don't we start our own business?' So in 1997–98, we put together a business plan to provide high-end Internet solutions for big companies . . . Two years ago, though, I went to a technology convention in Las Vegas and was approached by some medium-size [American] accounting firms, and they said they could not afford to set up big tax outsourcing operations in India, but the big guys could, and [the medium guys] wanted to get ahead of them. So we developed a software product called VTR—Virtual Tax Room—to enable these medium-size accounting firms to easily outsource tax returns."

These midsize firms "are getting a more level playing field, which they were denied before," said Jerry. "Suddenly they can get access to the same advantages of scale that the bigger guys always had."

Is the message to Americans, "Mama, don't let your kids grow up to be accountants"? I asked.

Not really, said Rao. "What we have done is taken the grunt work. You know what is needed to prepare a tax return? Very little creative work. This is what will move overseas."

"What will stay in America?" I asked.

"The accountant who wants to stay in business in America will be the one who focuses on designing creative, complex strategies, like tax avoidance or tax sheltering, managing customer relationships," he said. "He or she will say to his clients, 'I am getting the grunt work done efficiently far away. Now let's talk about how we manage your estate and what you are going to do about your kids. Do you want to leave some money in your trusts?' It means having the quality-time discussions with clients rather than running around like chickens with their heads cut off from February to April, and often filing for extensions into August, because they have not had the quality time with clients."

Judging from an essay in the journal *Accounting Today* (June 7, 2004), this does, indeed, seem to be the future. L. Gary Boomer, a CPA and CEO of Boomer Consulting in Manhattan, Kansas, wrote, "This past [tax] season produced over 100,000 [outsourced] returns and has now expanded beyond individual returns to trusts, partnerships and corporations . . . The primary reason that the industry has been able to scale up as rapidly as it has over the past three years is due to the investment that these [foreign-based] companies have made in systems, processes and training." There are about seventy thousand accounting grads in India each year, he added, many of whom go to work for local Indian firms starting at $100 a month. With the help of high-speed communications, stringent training, and standardized forms, these young Indians can fairly rapidly be converted into basic Western accountants at a fraction of the cost. Some of the Indian accounting firms even go about marketing themselves to American firms through teleconferencing and skip the travel. Concluded Boomer, "The accounting profession is currently in transformation. Those who get caught in the past and resist change will be forced deeper into commoditization. Those who can create value through leadership, relationships and creativity will transform the industry, as well as strengthen relationships with their existing clients."

What you're telling me, I said to Rao, is that no matter what your profession—doctor, lawyer, architect, accountant—if you are an American, you better be good at the touchy-feely service stuff, because anything that can be digitized can be outsourced to either the smartest or the cheapest producer, or both. Rao answered, "Everyone has to focus on what exactly is their value-add."

But what if I am just an average accountant? I went to a state university. I had a B+ average. Eventually I got my CPA. I work in a big accounting firm, doing a lot of standard work. I rarely meet with clients. They keep me in the back. But it is a decent living and the firm is basically happy with me. What is going to happen to me in this system?

"It is a good question," said Rao. "We must be honest about it. We are in the middle of a big technological change, and when you live in a society that is at the cutting edge of that change [like America], it is hard to predict. It's easy to predict for someone living in India. In ten years we are going to be doing a lot of the stuff that is being done in America today. We can predict our future. But we are behind you. You are defining the future. America is always on the edge of the next creative wave . . . So it is difficult to look into the eyes of that accountant and say this is what is going to be. We should not trivialize that. We must deal with it and talk about it honestly . . . Any activity where we can digitize and decompose the value chain, and move the work around, will get moved around. Some people will say, 'Yes, but you can't serve me a steak.' True, but I can take the reservation for your table sitting anywhere in the world, if the restaurant does not have an operator. We can say, 'Yes, Mr. Friedman, we can give you a table by the window.' In other words, there are parts of the whole dining-out experience that we can decompose and outsource. If you go back and read the basic economics textbooks, they will tell you: Goods are traded, but services are consumed and produced in the same place. And you cannot export a haircut. But we are coming close to exporting a haircut, the appointment part. What kind of haircut do you want?

Which barber do you want? All those things can and will be done by a call center far away."

As we ended our conversation, I asked Rao what he is up to next. He was full of energy. He told me he'd been talking to an Israeli company that is making some big advances in compression technology to allow for easier, better transfers of CAT scans via the Internet so you can quickly get a second opinion from a doctor half a world away.

A few weeks after I spoke with Rao, the following e-mail arrived from Bill Brody, the president of Johns Hopkins University, whom I had just interviewed for this book:

> Dear Tom, I am speaking at a Hopkins continuing education medical meeting for radiologists (I used to be a radiologist) . . . I came upon a very fascinating situation that I thought might interest you. I have just learned that in many small and some medium-size hospitals in the US, radiologists are outsourcing reading of CAT scans to doctors in India and Australia!!! Most of this evidently occurs at night (and maybe weekends) when the radiologists do not have sufficient staffing to provide in-hospital coverage. While some radiology groups will use teleradiology to ship images from the hospital to their home (or to Vail or Cape Cod, I suppose) so that they can interpret images and provide a diagnosis 24/7, apparently the smaller hospitals are shipping CAT scan images to radiologists abroad. The advantage is that it is daytime in Australia or India when it is nighttime here—so after-hours coverage becomes more readily done by shipping the images across the globe. Since CAT (and MRI) images are already in digital format and available on a network with a standardized protocol, it is no problem to view the images anywhere in the world . . . I assume that the radiologists on the other end . . . must have trained in [the] US and acquired the appropriate licenses and credentials . . . The groups abroad that provide these after-hours readings are called "Nighthawks" by the American radiologists that employ them.
> Best,
> Bill

Thank goodness I'm a journalist and not an accountant or a radiologist. There will be no outsourcing for me—even if some of my readers wish my column could be shipped off to North Korea. At least that's what I thought. Then I heard about the Reuters operation in India. I didn't have time to visit the Reuters office in Bangalore, but I was able to get hold of Tom Glocer, the CEO of Reuters, to hear what he was doing. Glocer is a pioneer in the outsourcing of elements of the news supply chain.

With 2,300 journalists around the world, in 197 bureaus, serving a market including investment bankers, derivatives traders, stockbrokers, newspapers, radio, television, and Internet outlets, Reuters has always had a very complex audience to satisfy. After the dot-com bust, though, when many of its customers became very cost-conscious, Reuters started asking itself, for reasons of both cost and efficiency: Where do we actually need our people to be located to feed our global news supply chain? And can we actually disaggregate the work of a journalist and keep part in London and New York and shift part to India?

Glocer started by looking at the most basic bread-and-butter function Reuters provides, which is breaking news about company earnings and related business developments, every second of every day. "Exxon comes out with its earnings and we need to get that as fast as possible up on screens around the world: 'Exxon earned thirty-nine cents this quarter as opposed to thirty-six cents last quarter.' The core competency there is speed and accuracy," explained Glocer. "You don't need a lot of analysis. We just need to get the basic news up as fast as possible. The flash should be out in seconds after the company releases, and the table [showing the recent history of quarterly earnings] a few seconds later."

Those sorts of earnings flashes are to the news business what vanilla is to the ice cream business—a basic commodity that actually can be made anywhere in the flat world. The real value-added knowledge work happens in the next five minutes. That is when you need a real journalist who knows how to get a comment from the company, a comment from the top two analysts in the field, and even some word from competitors to put the earnings report in perspective. "That needs a higher journalistic skill set—someone in the market with contacts, who knows who the best industry analysts are and has taken the right people to lunch," said Glocer.

The dot-com bust and the flattening of the world forced Glocer to rethink how Reuters delivered news—whether it could disaggregate the functions of a journalist and ship the low-value-added functions to India. His primary goal was to reduce the overlap Reuters payroll, while preserving as many good journalism jobs as possible. "So the first thing we did," said Glocer, "was hire six reporters in Bangalore as an experiment. We said, 'Let's let them just do the flash headlines and the tables and whatever else we can get them to do in Bangalore.'"

These new Indian hires had accounting backgrounds and were trained by Reuters, but they were paid standard local wages and vacation and health benefits. "India is an unbelievably rich place for recruiting people, not only with technical skills but also financial skills," said Glocer. When a company puts out its earnings, one of the first things it does is hand it to the wires—Reuters, Dow Jones, and Bloomberg—for distribution. "We will get that raw data," he said, "and then it's a race to see how fast we can turn it around. Bangalore is one of the most wired places in the world, and although there's a slight delay—one second or less—in getting the information over there, it turns out you can just as easily sit in Bangalore and get the electronic version of a press release and turn it into a story as you can in London or New York."

The difference, however, is that wages and rents in Bangalore are less than one-fifth what they are in those Western capitals.

While economics and the flattening of the world have pushed Reuters down this path, Glocer has tried to make a virtue of necessity. "We think we can off-load commoditized reporting and get that done efficiently somewhere else in the world," he said, and then give the conventional Reuters journalists, whom the company is able to retain, a chance to focus on doing much higher-value-added and personally fulfilling journalism and analysis. "Let's say you were a Reuters journalist in New York. Do you reach your life's fulfillment by turning press releases into boxes on the screen, or by doing the analysis?" asked Glocer.

Obviously, it is the latter. Outsourcing news bulletins to India also allows Reuters to extend the breadth of its reporting to more small-cap companies, companies it was not cost-efficient for Reuters to follow before with higher-paid journalists in New York. But with lower-wage Indian reporters, who can be hired in large numbers for the cost of one reporter in New York, it can now do that from Bangalore. By the summer of 2004, Reuters had grown its Bangalore content operation to three hundred staff, aiming eventually for a total of fifteen hundred. Some of those are Reuters veterans sent out to train the Indian teams, some are reporters filing earnings flashes, but most are journalists doing slightly more specialized data analysis—number crunching—for securities offerings.

"A lot of our clients are doing the same thing," said Glocer. "Investment research has had to have huge amounts of cost ripped out of it, so a lot of firms are using shift work in Bangalore to do bread-and-butter company analysis." Until recently the big Wall Street firms had conducted investment research by spending millions of dollars on star analysts and then charging part of their salaries to their stockbrokerage departments, which shared the analysis with their best customers, and part to their investment banking business, which sometimes used glowing analyses of a company to lure its banking business. In the wake of New York State attorney general Eliot Spitzer's investigations into Wall Street practices, following several scandals, investment banking and stockbrokerage have had to be distinctly separated—so that analysts will stop hyping companies in order to get their investment banking. But as a result, the big Wall Street investment firms have had to sharply reduce the cost of their market research, all of which has to be paid for now by their brokerage departments alone. And this created a great incentive for them to outsource some of this analytical work to places like Bangalore. In addition to being able to pay an analyst in Bangalore about $15,000 in total compensation, as opposed to $80,000 in New York or London, Reuters has found that its India employees tend to be financially literate and highly motivated as well. Reuters also recently opened a software development center in Bangkok because it turned out to be a good place to recruit developers who had been overlooked by all the Western companies vying for talent in Bangalore.

I find myself torn by this trend. Having started my career as a wire service reporter with United Press International, I have enormous sympathy with wire service reporters and the pressures, both professional and financial, under which they toil. But UPI might still be thriving today as a wire service, which it is not, if it had been able to outsource some of its lower-end business when I started as a reporter in London twenty-five years ago.

"It is delicate with the staff," said Glocer, who has cut the entire Reuters staff by roughly a quarter, without deep cuts among the reporters. The Reuters staff, he said, understand that this is being done so that the company can survive and then thrive again. At the same time, said Glocer, "these are sophisticated people out reporting. They see that our clients are doing the exact same things. They get the plot of the story . . . What is vital is to be honest with people about what we are doing and why and not sugarcoat the message. I firmly believe in the lesson of classical economists about moving work to where it can be done best. However, we must not ignore that in some cases, individual workers will not easily find new work. For them, retraining and an adequate social safety net are needed."

In an effort to deal straight with the Reuters staff, David Schlesinger, who is now the company's global managing editor, sent all editorial employees a memo, which included the following excerpt:

OFF-SHORING WITH OBLIGATION

I grew up in New London, Connecticut, which in the 19th century was a major whaling center. In the 1960's and 70's the whales were long gone and the major employers in the region were connected with the military—not a surprise during the Vietnam era. My classmates' parents worked at Electric Boat, the Navy and the Coast Guard. The peace dividend changed the region once again, and now it is best known for the great gambling casinos of Mohegan Sun and Foxwoods and for the pharmaceutical researchers of Pfizer. Jobs went; jobs were created. Skills went out of use; new skills were required. The region changed; people changed. New London, of course, was not unique. How many mill towns saw their mills close; how many shoe towns saw the shoe industry move elsewhere; how many towns that were once textile powerhouses now buy all their linens from China? Change is hard. Change is hardest on those caught by surprise. Change is hardest on those who have difficulty changing too. But change is natural; change is not new; change is important. The current debate about off-shoring is dangerously hot. But the debate about work going to India, China and Mexico is actually no different from the debate once held about submarine work leaving New London or shoe work leaving Massachusetts or textile work leaving North Carolina. Work gets done where it can be done most effectively and efficiently. That ultimately helps the New Londons, New Bedfords and New Yorks of this world even more than it helps the Bangalores and Shenzhens. It helps because it frees up people and capital to do different, more sophisticated work, and it helps because it gives an opportunity to produce the end product more cheaply, benefiting customers even as it helps the corporation. It's certainly difficult for individuals to think about "their" work going away, being done thousands of miles away by someone earning thousands of dollars less per year. But it's time to think about the opportunity as well as the pain, just as it's time to think about the obligations of off-shoring as well as the opportunities . . . Every person, just as every corporation, must tend to his or her own economic destiny, just as our parents and grandparents in the mills, shoe shops and factories did.

"THE MONITOR IS BURNING?"

Do you know what an Indian call center sounds like? While filming the documentary about outsourcing, the TV crew and I spent an evening at the Indian-owned "24/7 Customer" call center in Bangalore. The call center is a cross between a co-ed college frat house and a phone bank raising money for the local public TV station. There are several

floors with rooms full of twenty-somethings—some twenty-five hundred
in all—working the phones. Some are known as "outbound" operators,
selling everything from credit cards to phone minutes. Others deal with
"inbound" calls—everything from tracing lost luggage for U.S. and
European airline passengers to solving computer problems for confused
American consumers. The calls are transferred here by satellite and undersea fiber-optic cable. Each vast floor of a call center consists of clus-
ters of cubicles. The young people work in little teams under the banner
of the company whose phone support they are providing. So one corner
might be the Dell group, another might be flying the flag of Microsoft.
Their working conditions look like those at your average insurance company. Although I am sure that there are call centers that are operated like
sweatshops, 24/7 is not one of them.

Most of the young people I interviewed give all or part of their salary
to their parents. In fact, many of them have starting salaries that are
higher than their parents' retiring salaries. For entry-level jobs into the
global economy, these are about as good as it gets.

I was wandering around the Microsoft section around six p.m.
Bangalore time, when most of these young people start their workday to
coincide with the dawn in America, when I asked a young Indian computer expert there a simple question: What was the record on the floor
for the longest phone call to help some American who got lost in the
maze of his or her own software?

Without missing a beat he answered, "Eleven hours."

"Eleven hours?" I exclaimed.

"Eleven hours," he said.

I have no way of checking whether this is true, but you do hear snip-
pets of some oddly familiar conversations as you walk the floor at 24/7
and just listen over the shoulders of different call center operators doing
their things. Here is a small sample of what we heard that night while
filming for Discovery Times. It should be read, if you can imagine this,
in the voice of someone with an Indian accent trying to imitate an
American or a Brit. Also imagine that no matter how rude, unhappy, ir-
ritated, or ornery the voices are on the other end of the line, these young
Indians are incessantly and unfailingly polite.

Woman call center operator: "Good afternoon, may I speak with . . . ?" (Someone on the other end just slammed down the phone.)

Male call center operator: "Merchant services, this is Jerry, may I help you?" (The Indian call center operators adopt Western names of their own choosing. The idea, of course, is to make their American or European customers feel more comfortable. Most of the young Indians I talked to about this were not offended but took it as an opportunity to have some fun. While a few just opt for Susan or Bob, some really get creative.)

Woman operator in Bangalore speaking to an American: "My name is Ivy Timberwoods and I am calling you . . ."

Woman operator in Bangalore getting an American's identity number: "May I have the last four digits of your Social Security?"

Woman operator in Bangalore giving directions as though she were in Manhattan and looking out her window: "Yes, we have a branch on Seventy-fourth and Second Avenue, a branch at Fifty-fourth and Lexington . . ."

Male operator in Bangalore selling a credit card he could never afford himself: "This card comes to you with one of the lowest APR . . ."

Woman operator in Bangalore explaining to an American how she screwed up her checking account: "Check number six-six-five for eighty-one dollars and fifty-five cents. You will still be hit by the thirty-dollar charge. Am I clear?"

Woman operator in Bangalore after walking an American through a computer glitch: "Not a problem, Mr. Jassup. Thank you for your time. Take care. Bye-bye."

Woman operator in Bangalore after someone has just slammed down the phone on her: "Hello? Hello?"

Woman operator in Bangalore apologizing for calling someone in America too early: "This is just a courtesy call, I'll call back later in the evening . . ."

Male operator in Bangalore trying desperately to sell an airline credit card to someone in America who doesn't seem to want one: "Is that because you have too many credit cards, or you don't like flying, Mrs. Bell?"

Woman operator in Bangalore trying to talk an American out of her

computer crash: "Start switching between memory okay and memory
test . . ."

Male operator in Bangalore doing the same thing: "All right, then,
let's just punch in three and press Enter . . ."

Woman operator in Bangalore trying to help an American who cannot stand being on the help line another second: "Yes, ma'am, I do
understand that you are in a hurry right now. I am just trying to help
you out . . ."

Woman operator in Bangalore getting another phone slammed down
on her: "Yes, well, so what time would be goo . . ."

Same woman operator in Bangalore getting another phone slammed
down on her: "Why, Mrs. Kent, it's not a . . ."

Same woman operator in Bangalore getting another phone slammed
down on her: "As a safety back . . . Hello?"

Same woman operator in Bangalore looking up from her phone: "I
definitely have a bad day!"

Woman operator in Bangalore trying to help an American woman
with a computer problem that she has never heard before: "What is the
problem with this machine, ma'am? The monitor is burning?"

There are currently about 245,000 Indians answering phones from
all over the world or dialing out to solicit people for credit cards or
cell phone bargains or overdue bills. These call center jobs are low-wage,
low-prestige jobs in America, but when shifted to India they become
high-wage, high-prestige jobs. The esprit de corps at 24/7 and other call
centers I visited seemed quite high, and the young people were all eager
to share some of the bizarre phone conversations they've had with
Americans who dialed 1-800-HELP, thinking they would wind up talking to someone around the block, not around the world.

C. M. Meghna, a 24/7 call center female operator, told me, "I've had
lots of customers who call in [with questions] not even connected to the
product that we're dealing with. They would call in because they had lost
their wallet or just to talk to somebody. I'm like, 'Okay, all right, maybe

you should look under the bed [for your wallet] or where do you normally keep it,' and she's like, 'Okay, thank you so much for helping.'"

Nitu Somaiah: "One of the customers asked me to marry him."

Sophie Sunder worked for Delta's lost-baggage department: "I remember this lady called from Texas," she said, "and she was, like, weep-
ing on the phone. She had traveled two connecting flights and she lost
her bag and in the bag was her daughter's wedding gown and wedding
ring and I felt so sad for her and there was nothing I could do. I had no
information.

"Most of the customers were irate," said Sunder. "The first thing they
say is, 'Where's my bag? I want my bag now!' We were like supposed to
say, 'Excuse me, can I have your first name and last name?' 'But where's
my bag!' Some would ask which country am I from? We are supposed to
tell the truth, [so] we tell them India. Some thought it was Indiana, not
India! Some did not know where India is. I said it is the country next to
Pakistan."

Although the great majority of the calls are rather routine and dull,
competition for these jobs is fierce — not only because they pay well, but
because you can work at night and go to school during part of the day, so
they are stepping-stones toward a higher standard of living. P. V. Kannan,
CEO and cofounder of 24/7, explained to me how it all worked: "Today
we have over four thousand associates spread out in Bangalore, Hyder-
abad, and Chennai. Our associates start out with a take-home pay of
roughly $200 a month, which grows to $300 to $400 per month in six
months. We also provide transportation, lunch, and dinner at no extra
cost. We provide life insurance, medical insurance for the entire family — and other benefits."

Therefore, the total cost of each call center operator is actually
around $500 per month when they start out and closer to $600 to $700
per month after six months. Everyone is also entitled to performance
bonuses that allow them to earn, in certain cases, the equivalent of
100 percent of their base salary. "Around 10 to 20 percent of our associates pursue a degree in business or computer science during the day
hours," said Kannan, adding that more than one-third are taking some

kind of extra computer or business training, even if it is not toward a degree. "It is quite common in India for people to pursue education through their twenties—self-improvement is a big theme and actively encouraged by parents and companies. We sponsor an MBA program for consistent performers [with] full-day classes over the weekend. Everyone works eight hours a day, five days a week, with two fifteen-minute breaks and an hour off for lunch or dinner."

Not surprisingly, the 24/7 customer call center gets about seven hundred applications a day, but only 6 percent of applicants are hired. Here is a snippet from a recruiting session for call center operators at a women's college in Bangalore:

Recruiter 1: "Good morning, girls."

Class in unison: "Good morning, ma'am."

Recruiter 1: "We have been retained by some of the multinationals here to do the recruitment for them. The primary clients that we are recruiting [for] today are Honeywell. And also for America Online."

The young women—dozens of them—then all lined up with their application forms and waited to be interviewed by a recruiter at a wooden table. Here is what some of the interviews sounded like:

Recruiter 1: "What kind of job are you looking at?"

Applicant 1: "It should be based on accounts, then, where I can grow, I can grow in my career."

Recruiter 1: "You have to be more confident about yourself when you're speaking. You're very nervous. I want you to work a little on that and then get in touch with us."

Recruiter 2 to another applicant: "Tell me something about yourself."

Applicant 2: "I have passed my SSC with distinction. Second P also with distinction. And I also hold a 70 percent aggregate in previous two years." (This is Indian lingo for their equivalents of GPA and SAT scores.)

Recruiter 2: "Go a little slow. Don't be nervous. Be cool."

The next step for those applicants who are hired at a call center is the training program, which they are paid to attend. It combines learning how to handle the specific processes for the company whose calls they will be taking or making, and attending something called "accent neutralization class." These are daylong sessions with a language teacher who prepares the new Indian hires to disguise their pronounced Indian accents when speaking English and replace them with American, Canadian, or British ones—depending on which part of the world they will be speaking with. It's pretty bizarre to watch. The class I sat in on was being trained to speak in a neutral middle-American accent. The students were asked to read over and over a single phonetic paragraph designed to teach them how to soften their *t*'s and to roll their *r*'s.

Their teacher, a charming eight-months-pregnant young woman dressed in a traditional Indian sari, moved seamlessly among British, American, and Canadian accents as she demonstrated reading a paragraph designed to highlight phonetics. She said to the class, "Remember the first day I told you that the Americans flap the 'tuh' sound? You know, it sounds like an almost 'duh' sound—not crisp and clear like the British. So I would not say"—here she was crisp and sharp—" 'Betty bought a bit of better butter' or 'Insert a quarter in the meter.' But I would say"—her voice very flat—" 'Insert a quarter in the meter' or 'Betty bought a bit of better butter.' So I'm just going to read it out for you once, and then we'll read it together. All right? 'Thirty little turtles in a bottle of bottled water. A bottle of bottled water held thirty little turtles. It didn't matter that each turtle had to rattle a metal ladle in order to get a little bit of noodles.'

"All right, who's going to read first?" the instructor asked. Each member of the class then took a turn trying to say this tongue twister in an American accent. Some of them got it on the first try, and others, well, let's just say that you wouldn't think they were in Kansas City if they answered your call to Delta's lost-luggage number.

After listening to them stumble through this phonetics lesson for half an hour, I asked the teacher if she would like me to give them an authentic version—since I'm originally from Minnesota, smack in the Midwest, and still speak like someone out of the movie *Fargo*. Absolutely, she said. So I read the following paragraph: "A bottle of bottled water held thirty little turtles. It didn't matter that each turtle had to rattle a metal ladle in order to get a little bit of noodles, a total turtle delicacy . . . The problem was that there were many turtle battles for less than oodles of noodles. Every time they thought about grappling with the haggler turtles their little turtle minds boggled and they only caught a little bit of noodles."

The class responded enthusiastically. It was the first time I ever got an ovation for speaking Minnesotan. On the surface, there is something unappealing about the idea of inducing other people to flatten their accents in order to compete in a flatter world. But before you disparage it, you have to taste just how hungry these kids are to escape the lower end of the middle class and move up. If a little accent modification is the price they have to pay to jump a rung of the ladder, then so be it—they say.

"This is a high-stress environment," said Nilekani, the CEO of Infosys, which also runs a big call center. "It is twenty-four by seven. You work in the day, and then the night, and then the next morning." But the working environment, he insisted, "is not the tension of alienation. It is the tension of success. They are dealing with the challenges of success, of high-pressure living. It is not the challenge of worrying about whether they would have a challenge."

That was certainly the sense I got from talking to a lot of the call center operators on the floor. Like any explosion of modernity, outsourcing is challenging traditional norms and ways of life. But educated Indians have been held back so many years by both poverty and a socialist bureaucracy that many of them seem more than ready to put up with the hours. And needless to say, it is much easier and more satisfying for them to work hard in Bangalore than to pack up and try to make a new start in America. In the flat world they can stay in India, make a decent salary, and not have to be away from families, friends, food, and culture. At the end of the day, these new jobs actually allow them to be more Indian. Said Anney Unnikrishnan, a personnel manager at 24/7, "I finished my MBA and I remember writing the GMAT and getting into Purdue University. But I couldn't go because I couldn't afford it. I didn't have the money for it. Now I can, [but] I see a whole lot of American industry has come into Bangalore and I don't really need to go there. I can work for a multinational sitting right here. So I still get my rice and sambar [a traditional Indian dish], which I eat. I don't need to, you know, learn to eat coleslaw and cold beef. I still continue with my Indian food and I still work for a multinational. Why should I go to America?"

The relatively high standard of living that she can now enjoy—enough for a small apartment and car in Bangalore—is good for America as well. When you look around at 24/7's call center, you see that all the computers are running Microsoft Windows. The chips are designed by Intel. The phones are from Lucent. The air-conditioning is by Carrier, and even the bottled water is by Coke. In addition, 90 percent of the shares in 24/7 are owned by U.S. investors. This explains why, although the United States has lost some service jobs to India in recent years, total exports from American-based companies—merchandise and services—to India have grown from $2.5 billion in 1990 to $5 billion in 2003. So even with the outsourcing of some service jobs from the United States to India, India's growing economy is creating a demand for many more American goods and services.

What goes around, comes around.

Nine years ago, when Japan was beating America's brains out in the auto industry, I wrote a column about playing the computer geography game Where in the World Is Carmen Sandiego? with my then nine-year-old daughter, Orly. I was trying to help her by giving her a clue suggesting that Carmen had gone to Detroit, so I asked her, "Where are cars made?" And without missing a beat she answered, "Japan."

Ouch!

Well, I was reminded of that story while visiting Global Edge, an Indian software design firm in Bangalore. The company's marketing manager, Rajesh Rao, told me that he had just made a cold call to the VP for engineering of a U.S. company, trying to drum up business. As soon as Mr. Rao introduced himself as calling from an Indian software firm, the U.S. executive said to him, "*Namaste*," a common Hindi greeting. Said Mr. Rao, "A few years ago nobody in America wanted to talk to us. Now they are eager." And a few even know how to say hello in proper Hindu fashion. So now I wonder: If I have a granddaughter one day, and I tell her I'm going to India, will she say, "Grandpa, is that where software comes from?"

No, not yet, honey. Every new product—from software to widgets—goes through a cycle that begins with basic research, then applied research, then incubation, then development, then testing, then manufacturing, then deployment, then support, then continuation engineering in order to add improvements. Each of these phases is specialized and unique, and neither India nor China nor Russia has a critical mass of talent that can handle the whole product cycle for a big American multinational. But these countries are steadily developing their research and development capabilities to handle more and more of these phases. As that continues, we really will see the beginning of what Satyam Cherukuri, of Sarnoff, an American research and development firm, has called "the globalization of innovation" and an end to the old model of a single American or European multinational handling all the elements of the product development cycle from its own resources. More and more American and European companies are outsourcing significant research and development tasks to India, Russia, and China.

According to the information technology office of the state government in Karnataka, where Bangalore is located, Indian units of Cisco Systems, Intel, IBM, Texas Instruments, and GE have already filed a thousand patent applications with the U.S. Patent Office. Texas Instruments alone has had 225 U.S. patents awarded to its Indian operation. "The Intel team in Bangalore is developing microprocessor chips for high-speed broadband wireless technology, to be launched in 2006," the Karnataka IT office said, in a statement issued at the end of 2004, and "at GE's John F. Welch Technology Centre in Bangalore, engineers are developing new ideas for aircraft engines, transport systems and plastics." Indeed, GE over the years has frequently transferred Indian engineers who worked for it in the United States back to India to integrate its whole global research effort. GE now even sends non-Indians to Bangalore. Vivek Paul is the president of Wipro Technologies, another of the elite Indian technology companies, but he is based in Silicon Valley to be close to Wipro's American customers. Before coming to Wipro, Paul managed GE's CAT scanner business out of Milwaukee. At the time he had a French colleague who managed GE's power generator business for the scanners out of France.

"I ran into him on an airplane recently," said Paul, "and he told me he had moved to India to head up GE's high-energy research there."

I told Vivek that I love hearing an Indian who used to head up GE's CT business in Milwaukee but now runs Wipro's consulting business in

Silicon Valley tell me about his former French colleague who has moved to Bangalore to work for GE. That is a flat world.

Every time I think I have found the last, most obscure job that could be outsourced to Bangalore, I discover a new one. My friend Vivek Kulkarni used to head the government office in Bangalore responsible for attracting high technology global investment. After stepping down from that post in 2003, he started a company called B2K, with a division called Brickwork, which offers busy global executives their own personal assistant in India. Say you are running a company and you have been asked to give a speech and a PowerPoint presentation in two days. Your "remote executive assistant" in India, provided by Brickwork, will do all the research for you, create the PowerPoint presentation, and e-mail the whole thing to you overnight so that it is on your desk the day you have to deliver it.

"You can give your personal remote executive assistant their assignment when you are leaving work at the end of the day in New York City, and it will be ready for you the next morning," explained Kulkarni. "Because of the time difference with India, they can work on it while you sleep and have it back in your morning." Kulkarni suggested I hire a remote assistant in India to do all the research for this book. "He or she could also help you keep pace with what you want to read. When you wake up, you will find the completed summary in your in-box." (I told him no one could be better than my longtime assistant, Maya Gorman, who sits ten feet away!)

Having your own personal remote executive assistant costs around $1,500 to $2,000 a month, and given the pool of Indian college grads from which Brickwork can recruit, the brainpower you can hire dollar-for-dollar is substantial. As Brickwork's promotional material says, "India's talent pool provides companies access to a broad spectrum of highly qualified people. In addition to fresh graduates, which are around 2.5 million per year, many qualified homemakers are entering the job market." India's business schools, it adds, produce around eighty-nine thousand MBAs per year.

"We've had a wonderful response," said Kulkarni, with clients coming from two main areas. One is American health-care consultants, who often need lots of numbers crunched and PowerPoint presentations drawn up. The other, he said, are American investment banks and financial services companies, which often need to prepare glossy pamphlets with graphs to illustrate the benefits of an IPO or a proposed merger. In the case of a merger, Brickwork will prepare those sections of the report dealing with general market conditions and trends, where most of the research can be gleaned off the Web and summarized in a standard format. "The judgment of how to price the deal will come from the investment bankers themselves," said Kulkarni. "We will do the lower-end work, and they will do the things that require critical judgment and experience, close to the market." The more projects his team of remote executive assistants engages in, the more knowledge they build up. They are full of ambition to do their higher problem solving as well, said Kulkarni. "The idea is to constantly learn. You are always taking an examination. There is no end to learning . . . There is no real end to what can be done by whom."

Unlike Columbus, I didn't stop with India. After I got home, I decided to keep exploring the East for more signs that the world was flat. So after India, I was soon off to Tokyo, where I had a chance to interview Kenichi Ohmae, the legendary former McKinsey & Company consultant in Japan. Ohmae has left McKinsey and struck out on his own in business, Ohmae & Associates. And what do they do? Not consulting anymore, explained Ohmae. He is now spearheading a drive to outsource low-end Japanese jobs to Japanese-speaking call centers and service providers in China. "Say what?" I asked. "To China? Didn't the Japanese once colonize China, leaving a very bad taste in the mouths of the Chinese?"

Well, yes, said Ohmae, but he explained that the Japanese also left behind a large number of Japanese speakers who have maintained a slice of Japanese culture, from sushi to karaoke, in northeastern China, particularly around the northeastern port city of Dalian. Dalian has become for

Japan what Bangalore has become for America and the other English-speaking countries: outsourcing central. The Chinese may never forgive Japan for what it did to China in the last century, but the Chinese are so focused on leading the world in the next century that they are ready to brush up on their Japanese and take all the work Japan can outsource.

"The recruiting is quite easy," said Ohmae in early 2004. "About one-third of the people in this region [around Dalian] have taken Japanese as a second language in high school. So all of these Japanese companies are coming in." Ohmae's company is doing primarily data-entry work in China, where Chinese workers take handwritten Japanese documents, which are scanned, faxed, or e-mailed over from Japan to Dalian, and then type them into a digital database in Japanese characters. Ohmae's company has developed a software program that takes the data to be entered and breaks it down into packets. These packets can then be sent around China or Japan for typing, depending on the specialty required, and then reassembled at the company's database in its Tokyo headquarters. "We have the ability to allocate the job to the person who knows the area best." Ohmae's company even has contracts with more than seventy thousand housewives, some of them specialists in medical or legal terminologies, to do data-entry work at home. The firm has recently expanded into computer-aided designs for a Japanese housing company. "When you negotiate with the customer in Japan for building a house," he explained, "you would sketch out a floor plan—most of these companies don't use computers." So the hand-drawn plans are sent electronically to China, where they are converted into digital designs, which then are e-mailed back to the Japanese building firm, which turns them into manufacturing blueprints. "We took the best-performing Chinese data operators," said Ohmae, "and now they are processing seventy houses a day."

Chinese doing computer drawings for Japanese homes, nearly seventy years after a rapacious Japanese army occupied China, razing many homes in the process. Maybe there is hope for this flat world . . .

I needed to see Dalian, this Bangalore of China, firsthand, so I kept moving around the East. Dalian is impressive not just for a Chinese city. With its wide boulevards, beautiful green spaces, and nexus of universities, technical colleges, and massive software park, Dalian would stand out in Silicon Valley. I had been here in 1998, but there had been so much new building since then that I did not recognize the place. Dalian, which is located about an hour's flight northeast of Beijing, symbolizes how rapidly China's most modern cities—and there are still plenty of miserable, backward ones—are grabbing business as knowledge centers, not just as manufacturing hubs. The signs on the buildings tell the whole story: GE, Microsoft, Dell, SAP, HP, Sony, and Accenture—to name but a few—all are having backroom work done here to support their Asian operations, as well as new software research and development.

Because of its proximity to Japan and Korea, each only about an hour away by air, its large number of Japanese speakers, its abundance of Internet bandwidth, and many parks and a world-class golf course (all of which appeal to knowledge workers), Dalian has become an attractive locus for Japanese outsourcing. Japanese firms can hire three Chinese software engineers for the price of one in Japan and still have change to pay a roomful of call center operators ($90 a month starting salary). No wonder some twenty-eight hundred Japanese companies have set up operations here or teamed up with Chinese partners.

"I've taken a lot of American people to Dalian, and they are amazed at how fast the China economy is growing in this high-tech area," said Win Liu, director of U.S./EU projects for DHC, one of Dalian's biggest homegrown software firms, which has expanded from thirty to twelve hundred employees in six years. "Americans don't realize the challenge to the extent that they should."

Dalian's dynamic mayor, Xia Deren, forty-nine, is a former college president. (For a Communist authoritarian system, China does a pretty good job of promoting people on merit. The Mandarin meritocratic culture here still runs very deep.) Over a traditional ten-course Chinese dinner at a local hotel, the mayor told me how far Dalian has come and just where he intends to take it. "We have twenty-two universities and colleges with over two hundred thousand students in Dalian," he explained. More than half those students graduate with engineering or science degrees, and even those who don't, those who study history or literature, are still being directed to spend a year studying Japanese or English, plus computer science, so that they will be employable. The mayor estimated that more than half the residents of Dalian had access to the Internet at the office, home, or school.

"The Japanese enterprises originally started some data-processing industries here," the mayor added, "and with this as a base they have now moved to R & D and software development . . . In the past one or two years, the software companies of the U.S. are also making some attempts to move outsourcing of software from the U.S. to our city . . . We are approaching and we are catching up with the Indians. Exports of software products [from Dalian] have been increasing by 50 percent annually. And China is now becoming the country that develops the largest number of university graduates. Though in general our English is not as competent as that of the Indian people, we have a bigger population, [so] we can pick out the most intelligent students who can speak the best English."

Are Dalian residents bothered by working for the Japanese, whose government has still never formally apologized for what the wartime Japanese government did to China?

"We will never forget that a historical war occurred between the two nations," he answered, "but when it comes to the field of economy, we only focus on the economic problems—especially if we talk about the software outsourcing business. If the U.S. and Japanese companies make their products in our city, we consider that to be a good thing. Our youngsters are trying to learn Japanese, to master this tool so they can compete with their Japanese counterparts to successfully land high-salary positions for themselves in the future."

The mayor then added for good measure, "My personal feeling is that Chinese youngsters are more ambitious than Japanese or American youngsters in recent years, but I don't think they are ambitious enough, because they are not as ambitious as my generation. Because our generation, before they got into university and colleges, were sent to distant rural areas and factories and military teams, and went through a very hard time, so in terms of the spirit to overcome and face the hardships, [our generation had to have more ambition] than youngsters nowadays."

Mayor Xia had a charmingly direct way of describing the world, and

although some of what he had to say gets lost in translation, he gets it—
and Americans should too: "The rule of the market economy," this
Communist official explained to me, "is that if somewhere has the richest human resources and the cheapest labor, of course the enterprises
and the businesses will naturally go there." In manufacturing, he pointed
out, "Chinese people first were the employees and working for the big
foreign manufacturers, and after several years, after we have learned all
the processes and steps, we can start our own firms. Software will go
down the same road . . . First we will have our young people employed
by the foreigners, and then we will start our own companies. It is like
building a building. Today, the U.S., you are the designers, the architects, and the developing countries are the bricklayers for the buildings.
But one day I hope we will be the architects."

I just kept exploring—east and west. By the summer of 2004, I was in
Colorado on vacation. I had heard about this new low-fare airline
called JetBlue, which was launched in 1999. I had no idea where they
operated, but I needed to fly between Washington and Atlanta, and
couldn't quite get the times I wanted, so I decided to call JetBlue and see
where exactly they flew. I confess I did have another motive. I had heard
that JetBlue had outsourced its entire reservation system to housewives in
Utah, and I wanted to check this out. So I dialed JetBlue reservations and
had the following conversation with the agent:

"Hello, this is Dolly. Can I help you?" answered a grandmotherly
voice.

"Yes, I would like to fly from Washington to Atlanta," I said. "Do you
fly that route?"

"No, I'm sorry we don't. We fly from Washington to Ft. Lauderdale,"
said Dolly.

"How about Washington to New York City?" I asked.

"I'm sorry, we don't fly that route. We do fly from Washington to
Oakland and Long Beach," said Dolly.

"Say, can I ask you something? Are you really at home? I read that
JetBlue agents just work at home."

"Yes, I am," said Dolly in the most cheerful voice. (I later confirmed with JetBlue that her full name is Dolly Baker.) "I am sitting in my office upstairs in my house, looking out the window at a beautiful sunny day. Just five minutes ago someone called and asked me that same question and I told them and they said, 'Good, I thought you were going to tell me you were in New Delhi.'"

"Where do you live?" I asked.

"Salt Lake City, Utah," said Dolly. "We have a two-story home, and I love working here, especially in the winter when the snow is swirling and I am up here in the office at home."

"How do you get such a job?" I asked.

"You know, they don't advertise," said Dolly in the sweetest possible voice. "It's all by word of mouth. I worked for the state government and I retired, and [after a little while] I thought I have to do something else and I just love it."

David Neeleman, the founder of JetBlue Airways Corp., has a name for all this. He calls it "homesourcing." JetBlue now has four hundred reservation agents, like Dolly, working at home in the Salt Lake City area, taking reservations—in between babysitting, exercising, writing novels, and cooking dinner.

A few months later I visited Neeleman at JetBlue's headquarters in New York, and he explained to me the virtues of homesourcing, which he actually started at Morris Air, his first venture in the airline business. (It was bought by Southwest.) "We had 250 people in their homes doing reservations at Morris Air," said Neeleman. "They were 30 percent more productive—they take 30 percent more bookings, by just being happier. They were more loyal and there was less attrition. So when I started JetBlue, I said, 'We are going to have 100 percent reservation at home.'"

Neeleman has a personal reason for wanting to do this. He is a Mormon and believes that society will be better off if more mothers are able to stay at home with their young children but are given a chance to be wage earners at the same time. So he based his home reservations system in Salt Lake City, where the vast majority of the women are Mormons and many are stay-at-home mothers. Home reservationists work twenty-five hours a week and have to come into the JetBlue regional office in

Salt Lake City for four hours a month to learn new skills and be brought up to date on what is going on inside the company.

"We will never outsource to India," said Neeleman. "The quality we can get here is far superior . . . [Employers] are more willing to outsource to India than to their own homes, and I can't understand that. Somehow they think that people need to be sitting in front of them or some boss they have designated. The productivity we get here more than makes up for the India [wage] factor."

A *Los Angeles Times* story about JetBlue (May 9, 2004) noted that "in 1997, 11.6 million employees of U.S. companies worked from home at least part of the time. Today, that number has soared to 23.5 million—16% of the American labor force. (Meanwhile, the ranks of the self-employed, who often work from home, have swelled during the same period—to 23.4 million from 18 million.) In some eyes, homesourcing and outsourcing aren't so much competing strategies as they are different manifestations of the same thing: a relentless push by corporate America to lower costs and increase efficiency, wherever that may lead."

That is exactly what I was learning on my own travels: Homesourcing to Salt Lake City and outsourcing to Bangalore were just flip sides of the same coin—sourcing. And the new, new thing, I was also learning, is the degree to which it is now possible for companies and individuals to source work anywhere.

I just kept moving. In the fall of 2004, I accompanied the chairman of the Joint Chiefs of Staff, General Richard Myers, on a tour of hot spots in Iraq. We visited Baghdad, the U.S. military headquarters in Fallujah, and the 24th Marine Expeditionary Unit encampment outside Babil, in the heart of Iraq's so-called Sunni Triangle. The makeshift 24th MEU base is a sort of Fort Apache, in the middle of a pretty hostile Iraqi Sunni Muslim population. While General Myers was meeting with officers and enlisted men there, I was free to walk around the base, and eventually I wandered into the command center, where my eye was immediately caught by a large flat-screen TV. On the screen was a live TV feed that looked to be coming from some kind of overhead camera. It showed some people moving around behind a house. Also on the screen, along the right side, was an active instant-messaging chat room, which seemed to be discussing the scene on the TV.

"What is that?" I asked the soldier who was carefully monitoring all the images from a laptop. He explained that a U.S. Predator drone—a small pilotless aircraft with a high-power television camera—was flying over an Iraqi village, in the 24th MEU's area of operation, and feeding real-time intelligence images back to his laptop and this flat screen. This drone was actually being "flown" and manipulated by an expert who was sitting back at Nellis Air Force Base in Las Vegas, Nevada. That's right, the drone over Iraq was actually being remotely directed from Las Vegas. Meanwhile, the video images it was beaming back were being watched simultaneously by the 24th MEU, United States Central Command headquarters in Tampa, CentCom regional head-quarters in Qatar, in the Pentagon, and probably also at the CIA. The different analysts around the world were conducting an online chat about how to interpret what was going on and what to do about it. It was their conversation that was scrolling down the right side of the screen.

Before I could even express my amazement, another officer traveling with us took me aback by saying that this technology had "flattened" the military hierarchy—by giving so much information to the low-level offi-cer, or even enlisted man, who was operating the computer, and em-powering him to make decisions about the information he was gathering. While I'm sure that no first lieutenant is going to be allowed to start a firefight without consulting superiors, the days when only senior officers had the big picture are over. The battlefield is being leveled.

I told this story to my friend Nick Burns, the U.S. ambassador to NATO and a loyal member of the Red Sox Nation. Nick told me he was at CentCom headquarters in Qatar in April 2004, being briefed by General John Abizaid and his staff. Abizaid's team was seated across the table from Nick with four flat-screen TVs behind them. The first three had overhead images being relayed in real time from different sectors of

Iraq by Predator drones. The last one, which Nick was focused on, was showing a Yankees–Red Sox game.

On one screen it was Pedro Martinez versus Derek Jeter, and on the other three it was the Jihadists versus the First Cavalry.

FLATBURGERS AND FRIES

I kept moving—all the way back to my home in Bethesda, Maryland. By the time I settled back into my house from this journey to the edges of the earth, my head was spinning. But no sooner was I home than more signs of the flattening came knocking at my door. Some came in the form of headlines that would unnerve any parent concerned about where his college-age children are going to fit in. For instance, Forrester Research, Inc., was projecting that more than three million service and professional jobs would move out of the country by 2015. But my jaw really dropped when I read a July 19, 2004, article from the *International Herald Tribune* headlined: "Want Fries With Outsourcing?"

> Pull off U.S. Interstate Highway 55 near Cape Girardeau, Missouri, and into the drive-through lane of a McDonald's next to the highway and you'll get fast, friendly service, even though the person taking your order is not in the restaurant—or even in Missouri. The order taker is in a call center in Colorado Springs, more than 900 miles, or 1,450 kilometers, away, connected to the customer and to the workers preparing the food by high-speed data lines. Even some restaurant jobs, it seems, are not immune to outsourcing.
>
> The man who owns the Cape Girardeau restaurant, Shannon Davis, has linked it and three other of his 12 McDonald's franchises to the Colorado call center, which is run by another McDonald's franchisee, Steven Bigari. And he did it for the same reasons that other business owners have embraced call centers: lower costs, greater speed and fewer mistakes.

Cheap, quick and reliable telecommunications lines let the order takers in Colorado Springs converse with customers in Missouri, take an electronic snapshot of them, display their order on a screen to make sure it is right, then forward the order and the photo to the restaurant kitchen. The photo is destroyed as soon as the order is completed, Bigari said. People picking up their burgers never know that their order traverses two states and bounces back before they can even start driving to the pickup window.

Davis said that he had dreamed of doing something like this for more than a decade. "We could not wait to go with it," he added. Bigari, who created the call center for his own restaurants, was happy to oblige—for a small fee per transaction.

The article went on to note that McDonald's Corp. said it found the call center idea interesting enough to start a test with three stores near its headquarters in Oak Brook, Illinois, with different software from that used by Bigari. "Jim Sappington, a McDonald's vice president for information technology, said that it was 'way, way too early' to tell if the call center idea would work across the thirteen thousand McDonald's restaurants in the United States . . . Still, franchisees of two other McDonald's restaurants, beyond Davis's, have outsourced their drive-through ordering to Bigari in Colorado Springs. (The other restaurants are in Brainerd, Minnesota, and Norwood, Massachusetts.) Central to the system's success, Bigari said, is the way it pairs customers' photos with their orders; by increasing accuracy, the system cuts down on the number of complaints and therefore makes the service faster. In the fast-food business, time is truly money: shaving even five seconds off the processing time of an order is significant," the article noted. "Bigari said he had cut order time in his dual-lane drive-throughs by slightly more than 30 seconds, to about 1 minute, 5 seconds, on average. That's less than half the average of 2 minutes, 36 seconds, for all McDonald's, and among the fastest of any franchise in the country, according to QSRweb.com, which tracks such things. His drive-throughs now handle 260 cars an hour, Bigari said, 30 more than they did before he started the call center . . . Though his operators earn, on average, 40 cents an hour more than his line employees, he has cut his overall labor costs by a percentage point, even as drive-through sales have increased . . . Tests conducted by outside companies found that Bigari's drive-throughs now make mistakes on fewer than 2 percent of all orders, down from about 4 percent before he started using the call centers, Bigari said."

Bigari "is so enthusiastic about the call center idea," the article noted, "that he has expanded it beyond the drive-through window at his seven restaurants that use the system. While he still offers counter service at those restaurants, most customers now order through the call center, using phones with credit card readers on tables in the seating area."

And I kept going east, right to my living room, where one day Ann, my wife, who is a first-grade reading teacher, pointed out to me an article about how American kids and parents are now turning to Indians for online tutoring. An October 2005 Associated Press report from Cochin, India, tells the whole story:

A few stars are still twinkling in the inky pre-dawn sky when Koyampurath Namitha arrives for work in a quiet suburb of this south Indian city. It's barely 4:30 a.m. when she grabs a cup of coffee and joins more than two dozen colleagues, each settling into a cubicle with a computer and earphones. More than 7,000 miles away, in Glenview, Ill., outside Chicago, it's the evening of the previous day and 14-year-old Princeton John sits at his computer, barefoot and ready for his hour-long geometry lesson. The high school freshman puts on a headset with a microphone and clicks on computer software that will link him through the Internet to his tutor, Namitha, many time zones away.

It's called e-tutoring—yet another example of how modern communications, and an abundance of educated, low-wage Asians, are broadening the boundaries of outsourcing and working their way into the minutiae of American life, from replacing your lost credit card through reading your CAT scan to helping you revive your crashed computer. Princeton is one of thousands of U.S. high school students turning to tutors in India.

"Hello Princeton, how are you? How was your test?" Namitha asks. "Hello, yeah . . . I'm good," Princeton replies. "It was good."

Namitha works for a company called Growing Stars, based in Cochin and Fremont, California. Princeton and his 12-year-old sister Priscilla each meet with their online math teacher twice a week. The chitchat ends quickly and a geometry worksheet pops up on Princeton's computer screen. Teacher and pupil speak to one another, type messages and use digital "pencils" to work on problems, highlight graphs and erase mistakes. Princeton scrawls on something that looks like a hyped-up mouse pad and it shows up on Namitha's screen. He can also use a scanner to send copies of assignments or textbook pages that he needs help understanding. "Here we go," Princeton says, as they begin a lesson on such concepts as parallel lines and complementary angles in the quiet coziness of the family's suburban home . . .

The first e-tutoring businesses started less than three years ago, and already thousands of Indian teachers coach U.S. students in math, science or English for about $15 to $20 an hour, a fraction of the $40 to $100 that private tutoring costs in the United States . . . Princeton's mother, Bessy Piusten, is pleased with the results, saying her children have been getting all A's and B's since they started online tutoring about two years ago . . . At the end of the session, Namitha assigns Princeton problems for their next meeting. "Homework! C'mon!" Princeton protests. "Fine, fine. But without homework, life would be wonderful," he says.

Though I was already home, I kept on moving east—to downtown Washington, D.C., right next to my office. One afternoon in the fall of 2005 I walked over to interview the U.S. trade representative, Ambassador Rob Portman, whose aide, Amy M. Wilkinson, a White House fellow, told me the most unusual flat-world story. The United States and Oman had just completed negotiations on a free-trade agreement to eliminate tariffs and trade barriers between the two nations. What was unusual, though, was that Portman sealed the deal via a videoconference with

Maqbool Bin Ali Sultan, Oman's minister of commerce and industry, who participated virtually from Muscat, the country's capital.

What could be flatter, I asked myself, than a free-trade agreement sealed using flat-screen TVs? Ms. Wilkinson later filled me in: "There were approximately 30 press folks in our conference room with notebooks in hand. Ambassador Portman stood at a podium in the front of the room. His image was projected on a digital videoconference dual screen. [The] Omani minister of commerce and industry and a roundtable of Omani press were projected on the other half of the screen. Ambassador Portman gave remarks. The Omani minister gave remarks. The session was then opened for questions. The U.S. press peppered Portman with questions. We broke and asked if the Omanis had questions. They asked questions of their minister. Then the crossover began when a U.S. reporter asked both Ambassador Portman and Minister Maqbool Bin Ali Sultan a question together. The exchange continued with U.S. press asking the Omani minister questions and vice versa. The meeting ended with Portman [on one side of the screen] extending his hand in a 'virtual handshake.' The Omani minister [on the other] did the same. It looked a bit funny and got a few chuckles but seemed to work for everyone. The process included more people than if teams had traveled in either direction. Connecting digitally eliminated a tremendous amount of wear and tear and seemed to satisfy everyone around the 'virtual table.'"

I recalled that virtual deal signing one day months later when I telephoned my stockbroker, Mark Madden at UBS, and he put me on hold. While I was waiting, a commercial for UBS played over and over. It noted that global markets today were more accessible and interconnected than ever before—and that, because of this change, UBS services were now available in "only" two locations: "Everywhere, and right next to you."

As UBS explained in the commercial: "Because financial solutions have no borders or boundaries, UBS puts investment analysts in markets across the globe. We have specialists worldwide in wealth management, asset management, and investment banking. So your UBS financial adviser can draw on a network of resources to provide you with an appropriate solution—and shrink the world to a manageable size."

I loved that concept of a company with only two offices—"everywhere, and right next to you"—because it captured perfectly the way the flattening of the world allows companies to be more global than ever and, yet, at the same time, more personal than ever.

Some of the signs of flattening back home, though, had nothing to do with economics. A month before the 2004 election I had appeared on the CBS News Sunday morning show *Face the Nation*, hosted by veteran correspondent Bob Schieffer. CBS had been in the news a lot in previous weeks because of Dan Rather's *60 Minutes* report about President George W. Bush's Air National Guard service that turned out to be based on bogus documents. After the show that Sunday, Schieffer mentioned that the oddest thing had happened to him the week before. When he walked out of the CBS studio, a young reporter was waiting for him on the sidewalk. This isn't all that unusual, because as with all the Sunday-morning shows, the major networks—CBS, NBC, ABC, CNN, and Fox—always send crews to one another's studios to grab exit interviews with the guests. But this young man, Schieffer explained, was not from a major network. He politely introduced himself as a reporter for a Web site called InDC Journal and asked whether he could ask Schieffer a few questions. Schieffer, being a polite fellow, said sure. The young man interviewed him on a device Schieffer did not recognize and then asked if he could take his picture. A picture? Schieffer noticed that the young man had no camera. He didn't need one. He turned his cell phone around and snapped Schieffer's picture.

"So I came in the next morning and looked up this Web site and there was my picture and the interview and there were already three hundred comments about it," said Schieffer, who, though keenly aware of online journalism, was nevertheless taken aback at the incredibly fast, low-cost, and solo manner in which this young man had put him up in lights.

I was intrigued by this story, so I tracked down the young man from InDC Journal. His name is Bill Ardolino, and he is a very thoughtful guy. I conducted my own interview with him online—how else?—and began by asking about what equipment he was using as a one-man network/newspaper.

"I used a minuscule MP3 player/digital recorder (three and a half inches by two inches) to get the recording, and a separate small digital camera phone to snap his picture," said Ardolino. "Not quite as sexy as an all-in-one phone/camera/recorder (which does exist), but a statement on the ubiquity and miniaturization of technology nonetheless. I carry this equipment around D.C. at all times because, hey, you never know. What's perhaps more startling is how well Mr. Schieffer thought on his feet, after being jumped on by some stranger with interview questions. He blew me away."

Ardolino said the MP3 player cost him about $125. It is "primarily designed to play music," he explained, but it also "comes prepackaged as a digital recorder that creates a WAV sound file that can be uploaded back to a computer . . . Basically, I'd say that the barrier to entry to do journalism that requires portable, ad hoc recording equipment, is [now] about $100 — $200 to $300 if you add a camera, $400 to $500 for a pretty nice recorder and a pretty nice camera. [But] $200 is all that you need to get the job done."

What prompted him to become his own news network?

"Being an independent journalist is a hobby that sprang from my frustration about biased, incomplete, selective, and/or incompetent information gathering by the mainstream media," explained Ardolino, who describes himself as a "center-right libertarian." "Independent journalism and its relative, blogging, are expressions of market forces—a need is not being met by current information sources. I started taking pictures and doing interviews of the antiwar rallies in D.C., because the media was grossly misrepresenting the nature of the groups that were organizing the gatherings—unrepentant Marxists, explicit and implicit supporters of terror, etc. I originally chose to use humor as a device, but I've since branched out. Do I have more power, power to get my message out, yes. The Schieffer interview actually brought in about twenty-five thousand visits in twenty-four hours. My peak day since I've started was fifty-five thousand when I helped break 'Rathergate' . . . I interviewed the first forensics expert in the Dan Rather National Guard story, and he was then specifically picked up by *The Washington Post*, *Chicago Sun-Times*, *Globe*, *NYT*, etc., within forty-eight hours.

"The pace of information gathering and correction in the CBS fake memo story was astounding," he continued. "It wasn't just that CBS News 'stonewalled' after the fact, it was arguably that they couldn't keep up with an army of dedicated fact-checkers. The speed and openness of the medium is something that runs rings around the old process . . . I'm a twenty-nine-year-old marketing manager [who] always wanted to write for a living but hated the AP style book. As überblogger Glenn Reynolds likes to say, blogs have given the people a chance to stop yelling at their TV and have a say in the process. I think that they serve as sort of a 'fifth estate' that works in conjunction with the mainstream media (often by keeping an eye on them or feeding them raw info) and potentially function as a journalism and commentary farm system that provides a new means to establish success.

"Like many facets of the topic that you're talking about in your book, there are good and bad aspects of the development. The splintering of media makes for a lot of incoherence or selective cognition (look at our country's polarization), but it also decentralizes power and provides a better guarantee that the *complete* truth *is* out there . . . somewhere . . . in pieces."

On any given day one can come across stories like that one—stories that tell you that old hierarchies are being flattened, that the playing field is being leveled, and that people who understand this transformation can wield more power than ever. I was shuffling through the June 25, 2005, edition of the *Financial Times* when a headline caught my eye: "Google Lures More Talent." The article seemed straightforward enough, detailing how Google had managed to hire legendary technologist Louis Monier away from eBay, where he was heading advanced technology. But I was brought up short by a paragraph in the middle of the article: "Mr. Monier revealed his motives [for leaving eBay] in an e-mail exchange with blogger John Battelle, who spread the news on his website, battellemedia.com." In other words, a top blogger whose expertise is Google broke the story, and the giant *Financial Times* had to quote his one-man Web site to be on top of the story itself.

Micah L. Sifry, an expert on the interplay of politics and technology, summarized the phenomenon well in an essay in *The Nation* (November 22, 2004): "The era of top-down politics—where campaigns, institutions and journalism were cloistered communities powered by hard-to-amass capital—is over. Something wilder, more engaging and infinitely more satisfying to individual participants is arising alongside the old order."

I offer the Schieffer-Ardolino and *Financial Times* cases as just two examples of how the flattening of the world has happened faster and changed rules, roles, and relationships more quickly than social science can capture. And, though I know it is a cliché, I have to say it nevertheless: *You ain't seen nothin' yet.* As I detail in the next chapter, we are entering a phase where we are going to see the digitization, virtualization, and automation of more and more everything. The gains in productivity will be staggering for those countries, companies, and individuals who can absorb the new technological tools. And we are entering a phase where more people than ever before in the history of the world are going to have access to these tools—as innovators, as collaborators, and, alas, even as terrorists. You say you want a revolution? Well, the real information revolution is about to begin. I call this new phase Globalization 3.0 because it followed Globalization 2.0, but I think this new era of globalization will prove to be such a difference of degree that it will be seen, in time, as a difference in kind. That is why I introduced the idea that the world has gone from round to flat. Everywhere you turn, hierarchies are being challenged from below or are transforming themselves from top-down structures into more horizontal and collaborative ones.

"'Globalization' is the word we came up with to describe the changing relationships between governments and big businesses," said David Rothkopf, a former senior Department of Commerce official in the Clinton administration and now a private strategic consultant. "But what is going on today is a much broader, much more profound phenomenon." It is not simply about how governments, business, and people communicate, not just about how organizations interact, but is about the emergence of completely new social, political, and business models. "It is about things that impact some of the deepest, most ingrained aspects of society right down to the nature of the social contract," added Rothkopf. "What happens if the political entity in which you are located no longer corresponds to a job that takes place in cyberspace, or no longer really encompasses workers collaborating with other workers in different corners of the globe, or no longer really captures products produced in multiple places simultaneously? Who regulates the work? Who taxes it? Who should benefit from those taxes?"

I am convinced that the flattening of the world, if it continues, will be seen in time as one of those fundamental shifts or inflection points, like Gutenberg's invention of the printing press, the rise of the nation-state, or the Industrial Revolution—each of which, in its day, noted Rothkopf, produced changes in the role of individuals, the role and form of governments, the ways business was done and wars were fought, the role of women, the forms religion and art took, and the way science and research were conducted, not to mention the political labels that we as a civilization have assigned to ourselves and to our enemies. "There are certain pivot points or watersheds in history that are greater than others because the changes they produced were so sweeping, multifaceted, and hard to predict at the time," Rothkopf said.

If the prospect of this flattening—and all of the pressures, dislocations, and opportunities accompanying it—makes you uneasy about the future, you are neither wrong nor alone. Whenever civilization has gone through a major technological revolution, the world has changed in profound and unsettling ways. But there is something about the flattening of the world that is going to be qualitatively different from the great changes of previous eras: the speed and breadth with which it is taking hold. The introduction of printing happened over a period of decades and for a long time affected only a relatively small part of the planet. Same with the Industrial Revolution. This flattening process is happening at warp speed and directly or indirectly touching a lot more people on the planet at once. The faster and broader this transition to a new era, the greater the potential for disruption, as opposed to an orderly transfer of power from the old winners to the new winners.

To put it another way, the experiences of the high-tech companies in the last few decades that failed to navigate the rapid changes brought about in their marketplace by these types of forces may be a warning to all the businesses, institutions, and nation-states that are now facing these inevitable, even predictable, changes but lack the leadership, flexibility, and imagination to adapt—not because they are not smart or aware, but because the speed of change is simply overwhelming them.

And that is why the great challenge for our time will be to absorb these changes in ways that do not overwhelm people or leave them behind. None of this will be easy. But this is our task. It is inevitable and unavoidable. It is the ambition of this book to offer a framework for how to think about this task and manage it to our maximum benefit.

I have shared with you in this chapter how I personally discovered that the world is flat. The next chapter details how it got that way.

TWO

The Ten Forces That Flattened the World

*T*he Bible tells us that God created the world in six days and on the
seventh day he rested. Flattening the world took a little longer. The
world has been flattened by the convergence of ten major political
events, innovations, and companies. None of us has rested since, or maybe
ever will again. This chapter is about the ten forces that flattened the world
and the multiple new forms and tools for collaboration that this flattening
has created.

FLATTENER #1
11/9/89
The New Age of Creativity: When the Walls Came Down and the Windows Went Up

The first time I saw the Berlin Wall, it already had a hole in it.

It was December 1990, and I was traveling to Berlin with the reporters covering secretary of state James A. Baker III. The Berlin Wall
had been breached a year earlier, on November 9, 1989. Yes, in a wonderful kabalistic accident of dates, the Berlin Wall fell on 11/9. The wall,
even in its punctured and broken state, was still an ugly scar across
Berlin. Secretary Baker was making his first visit to see this crumbled
monument to Soviet communism. I was standing next to him with a
small group of reporters. "It was a foggy, overcast day," Baker recalled in

his memoir, *The Politics of Diplomacy*, "and in my raincoat, I felt like a character in a John le Carré novel. But as I peered through a crack in the Wall [near the Reichstag] and saw the high-resolution drabness that characterizes East Berlin, I realized that the ordinary men and women of East Germany, peacefully and persistently, had taken matters into their own hands. This was their revolution." After Baker finished looking through the wall and moved along, we reporters took turns peering through the same jagged concrete hole. I brought a couple of chunks of the wall home for my daughters. I remember thinking how unnatural it looked—indeed, what a bizarre thing it was, this cement wall snaking across a modern city for the sole purpose of preventing the people on the other side from enjoying, even glimpsing, freedom.

The fall of the Berlin Wall on 11/9/89 unleashed forces that ultimately liberated all the captive peoples of the Soviet Empire. But it actually did so much more. It tipped the balance of power across the world toward those advocating democratic, consensual, free-market-oriented governance, and away from those advocating authoritarian rule with centrally planned economies. The Cold War had been a struggle between two economic systems—capitalism and communism—and with the fall of the wall, there was only one system left and everyone had to orient himself or herself to it one way or another. Henceforth, more and more economies would be governed from the ground up, by the interests, demands, and aspirations of the people, rather than from the top down, by the interests of some narrow ruling clique. Within two years, there was no Soviet Empire to hide behind anymore or to prop up autocratic regimes in Asia, the Middle East, Africa, or Latin America. If you were not a democracy or a democratizing society, if you continued to hold fast to highly regulated or centrally planned economics, you were seen as being on the wrong side of history.

For some, particularly among the older generations, this was an unwelcome transformation. Communism was a great system for making people equally poor. In fact, there was no better system in the world for that than communism. Capitalism made people unequally rich, and for some who were used to the plodding, limited, but secure Socialist lifestyle—where a job, a house, an education, and a pension were all guaranteed, even if they were meager—the fall of the Berlin Wall was deeply unsettling. But for many others, it was a get-out-of-jail-free card. That is why the fall of the Berlin Wall was felt in so many more places than just Berlin, and why its fall was such a world-flattening event.

Indeed, to appreciate the far-reaching flattening effects of the fall of the Berlin Wall, it's always best to talk to non-Germans or non-Russians. Tarun Das was heading the Confederation of Indian Industry when the wall fell in Berlin, and he saw its ripple effect felt all the way to India. "We had this huge mass of regulation and controls and bureaucracy," he recalled. "Nehru had come to power [after the end of British colonial rule] and had a huge country to manage, and no experience of running a country. The U.S. was busy with Europe and Japan and the Marshall Plan. So Nehru looked north, across the Himalayas, and sent his team of economists to Moscow. They came back and said that this country [the Soviet Union] was amazing. They allocate resources, they give licenses, there is a planning commission that decides everything, and the country moves. So we took that model and forgot that we had a private sector . . . That private sector got put under this wall of regulation. By 1991, the private sector was there, but under wraps, and there was mistrust about business. They made profits! The entire infrastructure from 1947 to 1991 was government-owned . . . [The burden of state ownership] almost bankrupted the country. We were not able to pay our debts . . . Sure, we might have won a couple of wars with Pakistan, but that did not give the nation confidence."

In 1991, with India running out of hard currency, Manmohan Singh, the finance minister at that time (and now the prime minister), decided that India had to open its economy. "Our Berlin Wall fell," said Das, "and it was like unleashing a caged tiger. Trade controls were abolished. We were always at 3 percent growth, the so-called Hindu rate of growth—slow, cautious, and conservative. To make [better returns], you had to go to America. Well, three years later [after the 1991 reforms] we were at 7 percent rate of growth. To hell with poverty! Now to make it you could stay in India and become one of *Forbes*'s richest people in the world . . . All the years of socialism and controls had taken us downhill to the point where we had only $1 billion in foreign currency. Today we have $118 billion . . . We went from quiet self-confidence to outrageous ambition in a decade."

The fall of the Berlin Wall didn't just help flatten the alternatives to free-market capitalism and unlock enormous pent-up energies for hundreds of millions of people in places like India, Brazil, China, and the former Soviet Empire. It also allowed us to think about the world differently—to see it as more of a seamless whole. Because the Berlin Wall was not only blocking our way; it was blocking our sight—our ability to think about the world as a single market, a single ecosystem, and a single community. Before 1989, you could have an Eastern policy or a Western policy, but it was hard to think about having a "global" policy. Amartya Sen, the Nobel Prize–winning Indian economist now teaching at Harvard, once remarked to me that "the Berlin Wall was not only a symbol of keeping people inside East Germany—it was a way of preventing a kind of global view of our future. We could not think globally about the world when the Berlin Wall was there. We could not think about the world as a whole." There is a lovely story in Sanskrit, Sen added, about a frog that is born in a well and stays in the well and lives its entire life in the well. "It has a worldview that consists of the well," he said. "That was what the world was like for many people on the planet before the fall of the wall. When it fell, it was like the frog in the well was suddenly able to communicate with frogs in all the other wells . . . If I celebrate the fall of the wall, it is because I am convinced of how much we can learn from each other. Most knowledge is learning from the other across the border."

Yes, the world became a better place to live in after 11/9, because each outbreak of freedom stimulated another outbreak, and that process in and of itself had a flattening effect across societies, strengthening those below and weakening those above. "Women's freedom," noted Sen, citing just one example, "which promotes women's literacy, tends to reduce fertility and child mortality and increase the employment opportunities for women, which then affects the political dialogue and gives women the opportunity for a greater role in local self-government."

Finally, the fall of the wall did not just open the way for more people to tap into one another's knowledge pools. It also paved the way for the adoption of common standards—standards on how economies should be run, on how accounting should be done, on how banking should be conducted, on how PCs should be made, and on how economics papers should be written. I discuss this more later, but suffice it to say here that common standards create a flatter, more level playing field. To put it another way, the fall of the wall enhanced the free movement of best practices. When an economic or technological standard emerged and proved itself on the world stage, it was much more quickly adopted after the wall was out of the way. In Europe alone, the fall of the wall opened the way for the formation of the European Union and its expansion from fifteen to twenty-five countries. That, in combination with the advent of the euro as a common currency, has created a single economic zone out of a region once divided by an Iron Curtain.

While the positive effects of the wall coming down were immediately apparent, the cause of the wall's fall was not so clear. There *was* no single cause. To some degree the termites just ate away at the foundations of the Soviet Union, which were already weakened by the system's own internal contradictions and inefficiencies; to some degree the Reagan administration's military buildup in Europe forced the Kremlin to bankrupt itself paying for warheads; and to some degree Mikhail Gorbachev's futile efforts to reform something that was unreformable brought communism to an end. But if I had to point to one factor as first among equals, it was the information revolution that began in the early to mid-1980s. Totalitarian systems depend on a monopoly of information and force, and too much information started to slip through the Iron Curtain, thanks to the spread of fax machines, telephones, and, eventually, the personal computer.

Following the pioneering release of the Apple II home computer by Steve Jobs and Steve Wozniak in 1977, the first IBM PC (personal computer) hit the markets in 1981. The first version of the Windows operating system launched in 1985, and the breakthrough version that made IBM PCs much more user-friendly—Windows 3.0—shipped on May 22, 1990, only six months after the wall went down. While the fall of the wall eliminated a physical and geopolitical barrier—one that held back information, stood in the way of shared standards, and kept us from having a view of the world as a single unified community—the rise of the Windows-enabled PC, which really popularized personal computing, eliminated another hugely important barrier: the limit on the amount of information that any single individual could amass, author, manipulate, and diffuse.

"The Windows-powered PC enabled millions of individuals, for the first time ever, to become authors of their own content in digital form, which meant that content could be shared far and wide," explained Craig J. Mundie, a chief technical officer for Microsoft. Over time the Apple-IBM-Windows revolution enabled the digital representation of all the important forms of expression—words, music, numeric data, maps, photographs, and eventually voice and video. It also, said Mundie, "created an army of people able to create this digital content more easily and cheaply than ever before—from their desktops, kitchens, bedrooms, and basements—instead of being required to access a big mainframe computer that was largely restricted for business purposes." Suddenly ordinary people could get the benefit of computing without being programmers.

It is impossible to exaggerate how important this was to the flattening of the world. The rise of the Windows-enabled PC, combined with the fall of the Wall, set in motion the whole flattening process. To be sure, men and women have long been authoring their own content, beginning with drawings on cave walls up through Gutenberg and the typewriter. But the Windows-enabled PCs and Apples made it possible for individuals to author their own content right from their desktops *in digital form*. And those last three words are critical. Because once people could author their own content in digital form—in the form of computer bits and bytes—they could manipulate it on computer screens in ways that made individuals so much more productive. And with the steady advances in telecommunications, they would soon be able to disseminate their own digital content in so many new ways to so many more people. Think of what one person can do with pen and paper. Think of what one person can do with a typewriter. And then think of what one person can now do with a PC.

One of Bill Gates's early mottoes for Microsoft, which he cofounded, was that the company's goal was to give every individual "IAYF"—information at your fingertips. When I said earlier that this era of Globalization 3.0 is about individuals globalizing themselves, that was largely made possible by the Apple and Windows-enabled IBM PCs and their many clones. They are the tools that gave *individuals* the power to author, shape, and disseminate information at their fingertips.

"People said, 'Wow, there is an asset here, and we should take advantage of it,'" said Microsoft's Mundie. And the more established Windows became as the primary operating system, "the more programmers went out and wrote applications for rich-world businesses to put on their computers, so they could do lots of new and different business tasks, which started to enhance productivity even more. Tens of millions of people around the world became programmers to make the PC do whatever they wanted in their own languages. Windows was eventually translated into thirty-eight languages [with more being added all the time]. People were able to become familiar with the PC in their own languages."

In this same time period, some people other than scientists started to discover that if they bought a PC and a dial-up modem, they could connect their PCs to their telephones and send e-mails through private Internet service providers—like CompuServe and America Online. "The diffusion of personal computers, fax machines, Windows, and dial-up modems connected to a global telephone network all came together in the late 1980s and early 1990s to create the basic platform that started the global information revolution," argued Mundie. The key was the melding of them all together into a single interoperable system. That happened, said Mundie, once we had in crude form a standardized computing platform—the IBM PC—along with a standardized graphical user interface for word processing and spreadsheets—Windows—along with a standardized tool for communication—dial-up modems and the global phone network. Once we had that basic interoperable platform, then the killer applications—spreadsheets and word processing—drove its diffusion far and wide.

And once more and more people connected their Windows-enabled PCs with that global communications platform, which spread even more quickly after 1989, when the Berlin Wall came down (and China and India started opening to the global economy), there was nothing to stop the digital representation of everything—words, music, photos, data, video—and then the global exchange of all that digital information. The political constraint on individual reach collapsed with the fall of the Berlin Wall (though of course large swaths of repression still exist), and the practical constraint on individual reach collapsed with the rise of the Apple and Windows-enabled, modem-connected IBM PC. This coincidental breakthrough suddenly gave individuals in this flattening world both reach and scale—reach because they could create content in so many new and different ways and scale because they could share their content with so many more people.

As new and exciting as this breakthrough was compared to what existed before, it was nothing compared to what would come later. "This [initial] platform was constrained by too many architectural limits," said Mundie. "There was missing infrastructure." The Internet as we know it today—with seemingly magical transmission protocols that can connect everyone and everything—had not yet emerged. Back then, networks had only very basic protocols for exchanging files and e-mail messages. Yes, AOL users could communicate with CompuServe users, but it was neither simple nor reliable. People could write new applications that allowed selected systems to work together, but in general this was limited to planned exchanges between PCs within the network of a single company. As a result, said Mundie, "a huge amount of data and creativity was accumulating in all those computers," but there was no easy, interoperable way to share it and mold it.

Nevertheless, this period from 11/9 to the mid-1990s led to a huge advance in personal empowerment. Looking back, one can say that it was the age of "Me and my machine can now talk to each other better and faster, so that I personally can do more tasks" and the age of "Me and my machine can now talk to a few friends and some other people in my company better and faster, so we can become more productive."

As I said, this level of connectivity surely helped to put the nail in the coffin of communism, because the very tools that were being used to improve productivity in the West (PCs, faxes, modems), even though much scarcer in the East, vastly improved horizontal person-to-person communication there, to the detriment of top-down Communist systems.

Though we didn't notice it at the time, there was a discordant note in this exciting new era. It wasn't only Americans and Europeans who joined the people of the Soviet Empire in celebrating the fall of the wall—and claiming credit for it. Someone else was raising a glass—not of champagne but of thick Turkish coffee. His name was Osama bin Laden and he had a different narrative. His view was that it was the jihadi fighters in Afghanistan, of which he was one, who had brought down the Soviet Empire by forcing the Red Army to withdraw from Afghanistan (with some help from U.S. and Pakistani forces). And once that mission had been accomplished—the Soviets completed their pullout from Afghanistan on February 15, 1989, just nine months before the fall of the Berlin Wall—bin Laden looked around and found that the other superpower, the United States, had a huge presence in his own native land, Saudi Arabia, the home of the two holiest cities in Islam. And he did not like it.

So, while we were dancing on the Wall, savoring our Apples, opening up our Windows, and proclaiming that there was no ideological alternative to free-market capitalism, bin Laden was turning his gunsights on America. Both bin Laden and Ronald Reagan saw the Soviet Union as the "evil empire," but bin Laden came to see the United States as evil too. He did have an ideological alternative to free-market capitalism—political Islam. He did not feel defeated by the end of the Soviet Union; he felt emboldened by it. He did not feel attracted to the widened playing field; he felt repelled by it. And he was not alone. Some people thought that Ronald Reagan had brought down the wall by bankrupting the USSR through an arms race; others thought IBM, Steve Jobs, and Bill Gates had brought down the wall by empowering individuals to download the future. But a world away, in Muslim lands, many thought bin Laden and his comrades had brought down the Soviet Empire and the Wall through religious zeal, and millions of them were inspired to upload the past.

In short, while we were celebrating 11/9, the seeds of another memorable date—9/11—were being sown. But more about that later in the book. For now, let the flattening continue.

FLATTENER #2
8/9/95
The New Age of Connectivity: When the Web Went Around and Netscape Went Public

By the mid-1990s, the PC-Windows era had reached a plateau. It was wonderful that people all over the world could suddenly author their own content in digital form. But if we were really going to make the most of this breakthrough, we needed a breakthrough in connectivity—one that would allow each of us to take our digital content and send it anywhere at very little cost, so that others could share it and work on it with us. The "event" that made that happen was actually a coincidence of events that took place in the space of just a few years in the 1990s—the emergence of the Internet as a tool of low-cost global connectivity; the emergence, on top of the Internet, of the World Wide Web as a seemingly magical virtual realm where individuals could post their digital content for everyone else to access; and, finally, the spread of the commercial Web browser, which could retrieve documents or Web pages stored in Web sites and display them on any computer screen in such a simple manner that everyone would—and did—want to use it. This sudden revolution in connectivity constituted a major flattening force.

The concept of a World Wide Web—a system for creating, organizing, and linking documents so they could be easily browsed over the Internet—was developed by British computer scientist Tim Berners-Lee. Berners-Lee is someone who certainly helped to flatten the world. While consulting for CERN, the European Organization for Nuclear Research in Switzerland, he created the World Wide Web and posted the first Web site in 1991. It was part of an effort to foster a computer network that would enable scientists to share their research more easily. The telephone and the modem made it possible to establish physical connections between all the world's PCs. But all that the modem and phone line did was connect you to the Internet. Unless you knew how to manually drive around the Internet to find things, it was not all that exciting. Yes, there were emerging e-mail systems and networks to communicate with on the

Internet, but sharing data was really rudimentary—because there were no Web sites or Web pages or Web browsers to bring to life the data in other people's computers, and worse, no easy way to navigate to them.

The first big breakthrough to bring the Internet alive as a tool of connectivity and collaboration—a tool that anyone, not just computer geeks, could use—was Berners-Lee's World Wide Web. Although people often use the terms "World Wide Web" and "Internet" interchangeably, they are not the same. As Berners-Lee himself explains on his own Web site: "The Internet ('Net) is a network of networks. Basically it is made from computers and cables. What Vint Cerf and Bob Kahn [the inventors of the Internet] did was to figure out how this could be used to send around little 'packets' of information . . . That's what the Internet does. It delivers packets—anywhere in the world, normally in well under a second. Lots . . . of programs use the Internet: electronic mail, for example, was around long before the global hypertext system I invented and called the World Wide Web."

And what is the World Wide Web? What is this amazing cyberspace that has become a kind of parallel universe? Berners-Lee explains: "The Web is an abstract (imaginary) space of information. On the Net, you find computers—on the Web, you find documents, sounds, videos . . . information. On the Net, the connections are cables between computers; on the Web, connections are hypertext links. The Web exists because of programs which communicate between computers on the Net. The Web could not be without the Net. The Web made the Net useful because people are really interested in information (not to mention knowledge and wisdom!) and don't really want to have to know about computers and cables."

The first Web site Berners-Lee created (and therefore the first Web site ever) was at http://info.cern.ch and was first put up on August 6, 1991. It explained how the World Wide Web worked, how one could own a browser, how to go about setting up a Web server. *Time* magazine (June 14, 1999), in profiling Berners-Lee as one of the one hundred most important people of the twentieth century, summed up his creation of the World Wide Web this way: "Thomas Edison got credit for the light bulb, but he had dozens of people in his lab working on it. William

Shockley may have fathered the transistor, but two of his research scientists actually built it. And if there ever was a thing that was made by committee, the Internet—with its protocols and packet switching—is it. But the World Wide Web is Berners-Lee's alone. He designed it . . . And he . . . fought to keep it open, nonproprietary and free." He popularized "a relatively easy-to-learn coding system—HTML (hypertext markup language) that has come to be the lingua franca of the Web; it's the way Web-content creators put those little colored, underlined links in their text, add images and so on. He designed an addressing scheme that gave each Web page a unique location, or url (universal resource locator). And he hacked a set of rules that permitted these documents to be linked together on computers across the Internet. He called that set of rules HTTP (HyperText Transfer Protocol). And on the seventh day, Berners-Lee cobbled together the World Wide Web's first (but not the last) browser, which allowed users anywhere to view his creation on their computer screen. In 1991 the World Wide Web debuted, instantly bringing order and clarity to the chaos that was cyberspace. From that moment on, the Web and the Internet grew as one, often at exponential rates. Within five years, the number of Internet users jumped from 600,000 to 40 million. At one point, it was doubling every 53 days."

As hugely important as Berners-Lee's invention was, what really popularized the Internet and the Web as tools of both connectivity and commerce was the creation of easy-to-install and easy-to-use commercial browsers. After Berners-Lee, other scientists and academics created a number of browsers to surf this early Web, but the first widely popular commercial browser—and the whole culture of Web browsing for the general public—was created by a tiny start-up company in Mountain View, California, called Netscape. Netscape went public on August 9, 1995, and the world has not been the same since.

As John Doerr, the legendary venture capitalist whose firm Kleiner Perkins Caulfield & Byers had backed Netscape, put it, "The Netscape IPO was a clarion call to the world to wake up to the Internet. Until then, it had been the province of the early adopters and geeks."

Netscape was a huge flattening force for several reasons. To begin with, the Netscape browser not only brought the Internet alive but also made the Internet accessible to everyone from five-year-olds to ninety-five-year-olds. The more alive the Internet became, the more different people wanted to do different things on the Web, so the more they demanded computers, software, and telecommunications networks that could easily digitize words, music, data, and photos and transport them on the Internet to anyone else's computer. This demand was satisfied by another catalytic event: the rollout of Windows 95, which shipped fifteen days after Netscape took its stock public. Windows 95 would soon become the operating system used by most people worldwide, and unlike previous versions of Windows, it was equipped with built-in Internet support, so that not just browsers but all PC applications could "know about the Internet" and interact with it.

Looking back, what enabled Netscape to take off was the existence, from the earlier phase, of millions of PCs, many already equipped with modems. Those are the shoulders Netscape stood on. What Netscape did was bring a new killer app—the browser—to this installed base of PCs, making the computer and its connectivity inherently more useful for millions of people. This in turn set off an explosion in demand for all things digital and sparked the Internet boom, because every investor looked at the Internet and concluded that if everything was going to be digitized—data, inventories, commerce, books, music, photos, and entertainment—and transported and sold on the Internet, then the demand for Internet-based products and services would be infinite. This led to the dot-com stock bubble and a massive overinvestment in the fiber-optic cable needed to carry all the new digital information. This development, in turn, wired the whole world together, and, without anyone really planning it, made Bangalore a suburb of Boston.

Let's look at each one of these developments.

W hen I sat down with Jim Barksdale, the former Netscape CEO, to interview him for this book, I explained to him that one of the early chapters was about the ten innovations, events, and trends that had flattened the world. The first event, I told him, was 11/9, and I explained the significance of that date. Then I said, "Let me see if you can guess the significance of the second date, 8/9." That was all I told him: 8/9. It took Barksdale only a second to ponder that before shooting back with the right answer: "The day Netscape went public!"

Few would deny that Barksdale is one of the great American entrepreneurs. He helped Federal Express develop its package tracking and tracing system, then moved over to McCaw Cellular, the mobile phone company, built that up, and oversaw its merger with AT&T in 1994. Just before the sale closed, he was approached by a headhunter to become the CEO of a new company called Mosaic Communications, forged by two now-legendary innovators—Jim Clark and Marc Andreessen. In mid-1994, Clark, the founder of Silicon Graphics, had joined forces with Andreessen to found Mosaic, which would quickly be renamed Netscape Communications. Andreessen, a brilliant young computer scientist, had just spearheaded a small software project at the National Center for Supercomputing Applications (NCSA), based at the University of Illinois, that developed the first really effective, easy-to-use Web browser, also called Mosaic. Clark and Andreessen quickly understood the huge potential for Web-browsing software and decided to partner up to commercialize it. As Netscape began to grow, they reached out to Barksdale for guidance and insight into how best to go public.

Today we take this simplified browser technology for granted, but it was actually one of the most important inventions in modern history. When Andreessen was back at the University of Illinois NCSA lab, he found that he had PCs, workstations, and the basic network connectivity to move files around the Internet, but it was still not very exciting—because there was no simple, evocative user interface to pull up and display the contents of other people's Web sites. So, as Wikipedia recounts, Andreessen and a full-time salaried coworker, Eric Bina, started developing a user-friendly browser "with integrated graphics that would work on a wide range of computers. The resulting code was the Mosaic Web browser. Andreessen was fastidious in monitoring and responding to all user comments for suggestions and improvements to the browser, which fueled its accessibility and its popularity." Mosaic, in short, made Web sites viewable by any idiot, scientist, student, kindergartener, or grandma or grandpa. Marc Andreessen did not invent the Internet or the World Wide Web, but he certainly played a historic role in helping to bring them alive and make them easily usable tools.

"The Mosaic browser started out in 1993 with twelve users, and I knew all twelve," said Andreessen. There were only about fifty Web sites at the time and they were mostly just single Web pages. "Mosaic," he explained, "was funded by the National Science Foundation. The money wasn't actually allocated to build Mosaic. Our specific group was to build software that would enable scientists to use supercomputers that were in remote locations, and to connect to them by the NSF network. So we built [the first browsers as] software tools to enable researchers to 'browse' each other's research. I looked at it as a positive feedback loop: The more people had the browser, the more people would want to be interconnected, and the more incentive there would be to create content and applications and tools. Once that kind of thing gets started, it just takes off and virtually nothing can stop it. When you are developing it, you are not sure anyone is going to use it, but once it started we realized that if anyone is going to use it *everyone is going to use it*, and the only question then was how fast it would spread and what would be the barriers along the way."

Indeed, everyone who tried the browser, including Barksdale, had the same initial reaction: *Wow!* "Every summer, *Fortune* magazine had an article about the twenty-five coolest companies around," Barksdale recalled. "That year [1994] Mosaic was one of them. I not only had read about Clark and Andreessen but had turned to my wife and said, 'Honey, this a great idea.' And then just a few weeks later I get this call from the headhunter. So I went down and spoke to Doerr and Jim Clark, and I began using the beta version of the Mosaic browser. I became more and more intrigued the more I used it." Since the late 1980s, people had been putting up databases with Internet access. Barksdale said that after speaking to Doerr and Clark, he went home, gathered his three children around his computer, and asked them each to suggest a topic he could browse the Internet for—and wowed them by coming up with something for each of them. "That convinced me," said Barksdale. "So I called back the headhunter and said, 'I'm your man.'"

Netscape's first commercial browser—which could work on an IBM PC, an Apple Macintosh, or a Unix computer—was released in December 1994, and within a year it completely dominated the market. You could download Netscape for free if you were in education or a non-profit. If you were an individual, you could evaluate the software for free to your heart's content and buy it on disk if you wanted it. If you were a company, you could evaluate the software for ninety days. "The underlying rationale," said Andreessen, "was: If you can afford to pay for it, please do so. If not, use it anyway." Why? Because all the free usage stimulated a massive growth in the network, which was valuable to all the paying customers. It worked.

"We put up the Netscape browser," said Barksdale, "and people were downloading it for three-month trials. I've never seen volume like this. For big businesses and government it was allowing them to connect and unlock all their information, and the point-and-click system that Marc Andreessen invented allowed mere mortals to use it, not just scientists. And that made it a true revolution. And we said, 'This thing will just grow and grow and grow.'"

Nothing did stop it, and that is why Netscape played another hugely important flattening role: It helped make the Internet truly interoperable. You will recall that in the Berlin Wall–PC–Windows phase, individuals who had e-mail and companies that had internal e-mail could not connect very far. The first Cisco Internet router, in fact, was built by a husband and wife at Stanford who wanted to exchange e-mail; one was working off a mainframe and the other on a PC, and they couldn't connect. "The corporate networks at the time were proprietary and disconnected from each other," said Andreessen. "Each one had its own formats, data protocols, and different ways of doing content. So there were all these islands of information out there that were disconnected. And as the Internet emerged as a public, commercial venture, there was a real danger that it would emerge in the same disconnected way."

Joe in the accounting department would get on his office PC and try to get the latest sales numbers for 1995, but he couldn't do that because the sales department was on a different system from the one accounting was using. It was as if one was speaking German and the other French. And then Joe would say, "Get me the latest shipment information from Goodyear on what tires they have sent us," and he would find that Goodyear was using a different system altogether, and the dealer in Topeka was running yet another system. Then Joe would go home and find his seventh grader on the World Wide Web researching a term paper, using open protocols, and looking at the holdings of some art museum in France. And Joe would say, "This is crazy. There has to be one totally interconnected network."

In the years before the Internet became commercialized, Berners-Lee, Vint Cerf, Bob Kahn, and other scientists had developed a series of "open protocols" meant to make everyone's e-mail system or university computer network connect seamlessly with everyone else's—to ensure that no one had some special advantage. These mathematical-based protocols, which enable digital devices to talk to one another, were like magical pipes that, once you adopted them for your network, made you compatible with everyone else, no matter what kind of computer they were running. These protocols were (and still are, more or less) known by their alphabet soup names: mainly FTP, HTTP, HTML, SSL, SMTP, POP, and TCP/IP. Together, they form a system for transporting data around the Internet and the World Wide Web in a relatively secure manner, no matter what network your company or household has or what computer or cell phone or handheld device you are using. Each protocol had a different function: TCP/IP was the basic plumbing of the Internet, or the basic railroad tracks, on which everything else above it was built and moved around. FTP moved files. SMTP and POP moved e-mail messages, which became standardized, so that they could be written and read on different e-mail systems. HTML, as noted above, allowed ordinary people to author Web pages, and HTTP enabled people to connect to HTML documents on the World Wide Web. Finally, as people began to use these Web pages for electronic commerce, SSL was created to provide security for Web-based transactions.

As browsing and the Internet in general grew, Netscape wanted to make sure that Microsoft, with its huge market dominance, would not be able to shift these Web protocols from open to proprietary standards that only Microsoft's servers would be able to handle. "Netscape helped to guarantee that these open protocols would not be proprietary by commercializing them for the public," said Andreessen. "Netscape came along not only with the browser but with a family of software products that implemented all these open standards so that the scientists could communicate with each other no matter what system they were on—a Cray supercomputer, a Macintosh, or a PC. Netscape was able to provide a real reason for everyone to say, 'I want to be on open standards for everything I do and for all the systems I work on.' Once we created a way to browse the Internet, people wanted a universal way to access what was out there. So anyone who wanted to work on open standards went to Netscape, where we supported them, or they went to the open-source world and got the same standards for free but unsupported, or they went to their private vendors and said, 'I am not going to buy your proprietary stuff anymore . . . I am not going to sign up to your walled garden anymore. I am only going to stay with you if you interconnect to the Internet with these open protocols.'"

Netscape began pushing these open standards through the sale of its browsers, and the public responded enthusiastically. Sun started to do the same with its servers, and Microsoft started to do the same with Windows 95, considering browsing so critical that it famously built its own browser directly into Windows with the addition of Internet Explorer. Each realized that the public, which suddenly could not get enough of e-mail and browsing, wanted the Internet companies to work together and create one interoperable network. They wanted companies to compete with each other over different applications, that is, over what consumers could do *once they were on* the Internet—not over *how they got on* the Internet in the first place. As a result, after quite a few "format wars" among the big companies, by the late 1990s the Internet computing platform became seamlessly integrated. Soon anyone was able to connect with anyone else anywhere on any machine. It turned out that the value of compatibility was much higher for everyone than the value of trying to maintain your own little private network. This integration was a huge flattener, because it enabled so many more people to get connected with so many more other people.

There was no shortage of skeptics at the time, who said that none of this would work because it was all too complicated, recalled Andreessen. "You had to go out and get a PC and a dial-up modem. The skeptics all said, 'It takes people a long time to change their habits and learn a new technology.' [But] people did it very quickly, and ten years later there were eight hundred million people on the Internet." The reason? "People will change their habits quickly when they have a strong reason to do so, and people have an innate urge to connect with other people," said Andreessen. "And when you give people a new way to connect with other people, they will punch through any technical barrier, they will learn new languages—people are wired to want to connect with other people and they find it objectionable not to be able to. That is what Netscape unlocked." As Joel Cawley, IBM's vice president of corporate strategy, put it, "Netscape created a standard around how data would be transported and rendered on the screen that was so simple and compelling that anyone and everyone could innovate on top of it. It quickly scaled around the world and to everyone from kids to corporations."

In the summer of 1995, Barksdale and his Netscape colleagues went on an old-fashioned road show with their investment bankers from Morgan Stanley to try to entice investors around the country to buy Netscape stock once it went public. "When we went out on the road," said Barksdale, "Morgan Stanley said the stock could sell for as high as $14. But after the road show got going, they were getting such demand for the stock, they decided to double the opening price to $28. The last afternoon before the offering, we were all in Maryland. It was our last stop. We had this caravan of black limousines. We looked like some kind of Mafia group. We needed to be in touch with Morgan Stanley [headquarters], but we were somewhere where our cell phones didn't work. So we pulled into these two filling stations across from each other, all these black limos, to use the phones. We called up Morgan Stanley, and they said, 'We're thinking of bringing it out at $31.' I said, 'No, let's keep it at $28,' because I wanted people to remember it as a $20 stock, not a $30 stock, just in case it didn't go so well. So then the next morning I get on the conference call and the thing opened at $71. It closed the day at $56, exactly twice the price I set."

Netscape eventually fell victim to overwhelming (and, the courts decided, monopolistic) competitive pressure from Microsoft. Microsoft's decision to give away its browser, Internet Explorer, as part of its dominant Windows operating system, combined with its ability to invest more and better resources into Web browsing than Netscape, combined with a certain loss of focus at Netscape as it expanded so fast, led Netscape to steadily lose market share. In the end, Netscape was sold for $10 billion to AOL, which never did much with it. But though Netscape may have been only a shooting star in commercial terms, what a star it was, and what a trail it left.

"We were profitable almost from the start," said Barksdale. "Netscape was not a dot-com. We did not participate in the dot-com bubble. We *started* the dot-com bubble."

A nd what a bubble it was.
"Netscape going public stimulated a lot of things," said Barksdale. "The technologists loved the new technology things it could do, and the businesspeople and regular folks got excited about how much money they could make. People saw all those young kids making money out of this and said, 'If those young kids can do this and make all that money, I can too.' Greed can be a bad thing—folks thought they could make a lot of money without a lot of work. It certainly led to a degree of overinvestment, putting it mildly. Every sillier and sillier idea got funded."

What was it that stimulated investors to believe that demand for Internet usage and Internet-related products would be infinite? The short answer is digitization. Once the PC-Windows revolution demonstrated to everyone the value of being able to digitize information and manipulate it on computers and word processors, and once the browser brought the Internet alive and made Web pages sing and dance and display, everyone wanted everything digitized as much as possible so they could send it to someone else down the Internet pipes. Thus began the digitization revolution. Digitization is that magic process by which words, music, data, films, files, and pictures are turned into bits and bytes—combinations of 1s and 0s—that can be manipulated on a computer screen, stored on a microprocessor, or transmitted over satellites and fiber-optic lines. It used to be the post office was where I went to send my mail, but once the Internet came alive, I wanted my mail digitized so I could e-mail it. Photography used to be a cumbersome process involving film coated with silver dug up from mines halfway across the world. I used to take some pictures with my camera, then bring the film to the drugstore to be sent off to a big plant somewhere for processing. But once the Internet made it possible to send pictures around the world, attached to or in e-mails, I didn't want to use silver film anymore. I wanted to take pictures in the digital format, which could be uploaded, not developed. (And by the way, I didn't want to be confined to using a camera to take them. I wanted to be able to use my cell phone to do it.) I used to have to go to Barnes & Noble to buy and browse for books, but once the Internet came alive, I wanted to browse for books digitally on Amazon.com as well. I used to go to the library to do research, but now I wanted to do it digitally through Google or Yahoo!, not just by roaming the stacks. I used to buy a CD to listen to Simon & Garfunkel—CDs had already replaced albums as a form of digitized music—but once the Internet came alive, I wanted those music bits to be even more malleable and mobile. I wanted to be able to download them into an iPod. In recent years the digitization technology evolved so I could do just that.

Well, as investors watched this mad rush to digitize everything, they said to themselves, "Holy cow. If everyone wants all this stuff digitized and turned into bits and transmitted over the Internet, the demand for Web service companies and the demand for fiber-optic cables to handle all this digitized stuff around the world is going to be limitless! You cannot lose if you invest in this!"

And thus was the bubble born.

Overinvestment is not necessarily a bad thing—provided that it is eventually corrected. I'll always remember a news conference that Microsoft chairman Bill Gates held at the 1999 World Economic Forum in Davos, at the height of the tech bubble. Over and over again, Gates was bombarded by reporters with versions of the question, "Mr. Gates, these Internet stocks, they're a bubble, right? Surely they're a bubble. They must be a bubble?" Finally an exasperated Gates said to the reporters something to the effect of, "Look, you bozos, of course they're a bubble, but you're all missing the point. This bubble is attracting so much new capital to this Internet industry, it is going to drive innovation faster and faster." Gates compared the Internet to the gold rush, the idea being that more money was made selling Levi's, picks, shovels, and hotel rooms to the gold diggers than from digging up gold from the earth. Gates was right: Booms and bubbles may be economically dangerous; they may end up with many people losing money and a lot of companies going bankrupt. But they also often do drive innovation faster and faster, and the sheer overcapacity that they spur—whether it is in railroad lines or automobiles—can create its own unintended positive consequences.

That is what happened with the Internet stock boom. It sparked a huge overinvestment in fiber-optic cable companies, which then laid massive amounts of fiber-optic cable on land and under the oceans, which dramatically drove down the cost of making a phone call or transmitting data anywhere in the world.

The first commercial installation of a fiber-optic system was in 1977, after which fiber slowly began to replace copper telephone wires, because it could carry data and digitized voices much farther and faster in larger quantities. According to Howstuffworks.com, fiber optics are made up of strands of optically pure glass each "as thin as a human hair," which are arranged in bundles, called "optical cables," to carry digitized packets of information over long distances. Because these optical fibers are so much thinner than copper wires, more fibers can be bundled into a given diameter of cable than can copper wires, which means that much more data or many more voices can be sent over the same cable at a lower cost. The most important benefit of fiber, though, derives from the dramatically higher bandwidth of the signals it can transport over long distances. Copper wires can carry very high frequencies too, but only for a few feet before the signal starts to degrade in strength due to certain parasitic effects. Optical fibers, by contrast, can carry very high-frequency optical pulses on the same individual fiber without substantial signal degradation for many, many miles.

The way fiber-optic cables work, explains one of the manufacturers, ARC Electronics, on its Web site, is by converting data or voices into light pulses and then transmitting them down fiber lines, instead of using electronic pulses to transmit information down copper lines. At one end of the fiber-optic system is a transmitter. The transmitter accepts coded electronic pulse information—words or data—coming from copper wire out of your home telephone or office computer. The transmitter then processes and translates those digitized, electronically coded words or data into equivalently coded light pulses. A light-emitting diode (LED) or an injection-laser diode (ILD) can be used to generate the light pulses, which are then funneled down the fiber-optic cable. The cable functions as a kind of light guide, guiding the light pulses introduced at one end of the cable through to the other end, where a light-sensitive receiver converts the pulses back into the electronic digital 1s and 0s of the original signal, so they can then show up on your computer screen as e-mail or in your cell phone as a voice. Fiber-optic cable is also ideal for secure communications, because it is very difficult to tap.

It was actually the coincidence of the dot-com boom and the Telecommunications Act of 1996 that launched the fiber-optic bubble. The act allowed local and long-distance companies to get into each other's businesses, and enabled all sorts of new local exchange carriers to compete head-to-head with the Baby Bells and AT&T in providing both phone services and infrastructure. As these new phone companies came online, offering their own local, long-distance, international, data, and Internet services, each sought to have its own infrastructure. And why not? The Internet boom led everyone to assume that the demand for bandwidth to carry all that Internet traffic would double every three months— *indefinitely.* For about two years that was true. But then the law of large numbers started to kick in, and the pace of doubling slowed. Unfortunately, the telecom companies weren't paying close attention to the developing mismatch between demand and reality. The market was in the grip of an Internet fever, and companies just kept building more and more capacity. And the stock market boom meant *money was free! It was a party!* So every one of these incredibly optimistic scenarios from every one of these new telecom companies got funded. In a period of about five or six years, these telecom companies invested about $1 trillion in wiring the world. And virtually no one questioned the demand projections.

Few companies got crazier than Global Crossing, one of the companies hired by all these new telecoms to lay fiber-optic cable for them around the world. Global Crossing was founded in 1997 by Gary Winnick and went public the next year. Robert Annunziata, who lasted only a year as CEO, had a contract that the Corporate Library's Nell Minow once picked as the worst (from the point of view of shareholders) in the United States. Among other things, it included Annunziata's mother's first-class airfare to visit him once a month. It also included a signing bonus of two million shares of stock at $10 a share below market.

Henry Schacht, a veteran industrialist now with Warburg Pincus, was brought in by Lucent, the successor of Western Electric, to help manage it through this crazy period. He recalled the atmosphere: "The telecom deregulation of 1996 was hugely important. It allowed competitive local exchange carriers to build their own capacities and sell in competition with each other and with the Baby Bells. These new telecoms went to companies like Global Crossing and had them install fiber networks for them so they could compete at the transport level with AT&T and MCI, particularly on overseas traffic . . . Everyone thought this was a new world, and it would never stop. [You had] competitive firms using free capital, and everyone thought the pie would expand infinitely. So [each company said,] 'I will put my fiber down before you do, and I will get a bigger share than you.' It was supposed to be just a vertical growth line, straight up, and we each thought we would get our share, so everybody built to the max projections and assumed that they would get their share."

It turned out that while business-to-business and e-commerce developed as projected, and a lot of Web sites that no one anticipated exploded—like eBay, Amazon, and Google—they still devoured only a fraction of the capacity that was being made available. So when the dot-com bust came along, there was just way too much fiber-optic cable out there. Long-distance phone rates went from $2 a minute to 10¢. And the transmission of data was virtually free. "The telecom industry has invested itself right out of business," Mike McCue, chief operations officer of Tellme Networks, a voice-activated Internet service, told CNET News.com in June 2001. "They've laid so much fiber in the ground that they've basically commoditized themselves. They are going to get into massive price wars with everyone and it's going to be a disaster."

It was a disaster for many of the companies and their investors (Global Crossing filed for bankruptcy in January 2002, with $12.4 billion in debt), but it turned out to be a great boon for consumers. Just as the national highway system that was built in the 1950s flattened the United States, broke down regional differences, and made it so much easier for companies to relocate in lower-wage regions, like the South, because it had become so much easier to move people and goods long distances, so the laying of global fiber highways flattened the developed world. It helped to break down global regionalism, created a more seamless global commercial network, and made it simple and almost free to move digitized labor—service jobs and knowledge work—to lower-cost countries.

(It should be noted, though, that those fiber highways in America tended to stop at the last mile—before connecting to households. While a huge amount of long-distance fiber cable was laid to connect India and America, virtually none of these new U.S. telecom companies laid any substantial new local loop infrastructure, due to a failure of the 1996 telecom deregulation act to permit real competition in the local loop between the cable companies and the telephone companies. Where the local broadband did get installed was in office buildings, which were already pretty well served by the old companies. So this pushed prices down for businesses—and for Indians who wanted to get online from Bangalore to do business with those businesses—but it didn't create the sort of competition that could bring cheap broadband capability to the American masses in their homes. That has started happening only more recently.)

The broad overinvestment in fiber cable is a gift that keeps on giving, thanks to the unique nature of fiber optics. Unlike other forms of Internet overinvestment, it was permanent: Once the fiber cables were laid, no one was going to dig them up and thereby eliminate the overcapacity. So when the telecom companies went bankrupt, the banks took them over and then sold their fiber cables for ten cents on the dollar to new companies, which continued to operate them, which they could do profitably, having bought them in a fire sale. But the way fiber cable works is that each cable has multiple strands of fiber in it with a potential capacity to transmit many terabits of data per second on each strand. When these fiber cables were originally laid, the optical switches—the transmitters and receivers—at each end of them could not take full advantage of the fiber's total capacity. But every year since then, the optical switches at each end of that fiber cable have gotten better and better, meaning that more and more voices and data can be transmitted down each fiber. So as the switches keep improving, the capacity of all the already installed fiber cables just keeps growing, making it cheaper and easier to transmit voices and data every year to any part of the world. It is as though we laid down a national highway system where people were first allowed to drive 50 mph, then 60 mph, then 70 mph, then 80 mph, then eventually 150 mph on the same highways without any fear of accidents. Only this highway wasn't just national. It was international.

"Every layer of innovation gets built on the next," said Andreessen, who went on from Netscape to start another high-tech firm, Opsware Inc. "And today the most profound thing to me is the fact that a fourteen-year-old in Romania or Bangalore or the Soviet Union or Vietnam has all the information, all the tools, all the software easily available to apply knowledge however they want. That is why I am sure the next Napster is going to come out of left field. As bioscience becomes more computational and less about wet labs, and as all the genomic data becomes easily available on the Internet, at some point you will be able to design vaccines on your laptop."

I think Andreessen touches on what is unique about the flat world and the era of Globalization 3.0. It is going to be driven by groups and individuals, but of a much more diverse background than those twelve scientists who made up Andreessen's world when he created Mosaic. Now we are going to see the real human mosaic emerge—from all over the world, from left field and right field, from West and East and North and South— to drive the next generation of innovation. Indeed, a few days after Andreessen and I talked, the following headline appeared on the front page of *The New York Times* (July 15, 2004): "U.S. Permits 3 Cancer Drugs from Cuba." The story went on to say, "The federal government is permitting a California biotechnology company to license three experimental cancer drugs from Cuba—making an exception to the policy of tightly restricting trade with that country." Executives of the company, CancerVex, said that "it was the first time an American biotechnology company had obtained permission to license a drug from Cuba, a country that some industry executives and scientists say is surprisingly strong in biotechnology for a developing nation . . . More than $1 billion was spent over the years to build and operate research institutes on the west side of Havana staffed by Cuban scientists, many of them educated in Europe."

Just to summarize again: The Apple-PC-Windows flattening phase was about me interacting with my computer and me interacting with my own limited network inside my own company. Then came along this Internet–e-mail–browser phase, and it flattened the earth a little bit more. It was about me and my computer interacting with anyone anywhere on any machine, which is what e-mail is all about, and me and my computer interacting with anybody's Web site on the Internet, which is what browsing is all about. In short, the Apple-PC-Windows phase begat the Netscape browsing–e-mail phase, and the two together enabled more people to communicate and interact with more other people anywhere on the planet than ever before.

But the fun was just beginning. This phase was just the foundation for the next step in flattening the flat world.

FLATTENER #3
WORK FLOW SOFTWARE

I met Scott Hyten, the CEO of Wild Brain, a cutting-edge animation studio in San Francisco that produces films and cartoons for Disney and other major studios, at a meeting in Silicon Valley in the winter of 2004. I had been invited by John Doerr, the venture capitalist, to test out the ideas in this book with a few of the companies that he was backing. Hyten and I really hit it off, maybe because after hearing my arguments he wrote me an e-mail that said, "I am sure in Magellan's time there were plenty of theologians, geographers, and pundits who wanted to make the world flat again. I know the world is flat, and thank you for your support."

A man after my own heart.

When I asked him to elaborate, Hyten sketched out for me how animated films are produced today through a global supply chain. I understood immediately why he too had concluded that the world is flat. "At Wild Brain," he said, "we make something out of nothing. We learn how to take advantage of the flat world. We are not fighting it. We are taking advantage of it."

Hyten invited me to come and watch them produce a cartoon segment to really appreciate how flat the world is, which I did. The series they were working on when I showed up was for the Disney Channel and called *Higglytown Heroes*. It was inspired by all the ordinary people who rose to the challenge of 9/11. Higglytown "is the typical 1950s small town," said Hyten. "It is Pleasantville. And we are exporting the production of this American small town around the world—literally and figuratively. The foundation of the story is that every person, all the ordinary people living their lives, are the heroes in this small town—from the schoolteacher to the pizza delivery man."

This all-American show is being produced by an all-world supply chain. "The recording session," explained Hyten, "is located near the artist, usually in New York or L.A., the design and direction is done in San Francisco, the writers network in from their homes (Florida, London, New York, Chicago, L.A., and San Francisco), and the animation of the characters is done in Bangalore with edits from San Francisco. For this show we have eight teams in Bangalore working in parallel with eight different writers. This efficiency has allowed us to contract with fifty 'stars' for the twenty-six episodes. These interactive recording/writing/animation sessions allow us to record an artist for an entire show in less than half a day, including unlimited takes and rewrites. We record two actors per week. For example, last week we recorded Anne Heche and Smokey Robinson. Technically, we do this over the Internet. We have a VPN [virtual private network] configured on computers in our offices and on what we call writers' 'footballs,' or special laptop computers that can connect over any cat-five Ethernet connection or wireless broadband connection in the 'field.'

This VPN allows us to share the feed from the microphone, images from the session, the real-time script, and all the animation designs amongst all the locations with a simple log-in. Therefore, one way for you to observe is for us to ship you a football. You connect at home, the office, most hotel rooms, or go down to your local Starbucks [which has wireless broadband Internet access], log on, put on a pair of Bose noise-reduction headphones, and listen, watch, read, and comment. 'Sharon, can you sell that line a little more?' Then, over the eleven-week production schedule for the show, you can log in twenty-four hours a day and check the progress of the production as it follows the sun around the world. Technically, you need the 'football' only for the session. You can use your regular laptop to follow the 'dailies' and 'edits' over the production cycle."

Hyten has since left Wild Brain, but I am glad I visited him that day, because the company is a graphic example of the next layer of innovation, and the next flattener, that broadly followed on the Berlin Wall–Windows and Netscape phases. The fall of the Berlin Wall was a loud historic event that nobody missed. Netscape's going public was also much ballyhooed. But the rise and integration of work flow software was a quiet revolution that most people had no clue was happening. It crystallized in the mid- to late 1990s and, when it did, it had as profound an impact on the world as the first two flatteners. It enabled more people in more places to design, display, manage, and collaborate on business data previously handled manually. As a result, work started to flow within and between companies and continents faster than ever.

To get to this point took a lot of new software innovation piled on the shoulders of earlier innovations. Here's how the work flow revolution developed: When the walls went down, and then the PC and Netscape browser enabled people to connect with other people as never before, it did not take long before all these people who were connecting wanted to do more than just browse and send e-mail, instant messages, pictures, and music over this Internet platform. They wanted to shape things, design things, create things, sell things, buy things, keep track of inventories, do somebody else's taxes, and read somebody else's X-rays from half a world away. And they wanted to be able to do any of these things from anywhere to anywhere and from any computer to any computer — seamlessly.

The first big breakthrough in work flow was actually the combination of the PC and e-mail. Remember, before the diffusion of computers and the Internet, work flow consisted of your sales department taking an order on paper over the phone, walking it over to your shipping department, which shipped the product, and then someone from shipping walking over to billing with a piece of paper and instructing the billing department to churn out an invoice to the customer. But as a result of the Wall–PC–Netscape innovations, work flow took a huge leap forward. Your sales department could take an order over the phone or by mail, enter it into a computer system, e-mail the order to the shipping department within your own company, and then have the shipping department send out the product to the customer and automatically spit out a computerized bill at the same time.

In other words, the Windows-enabled PC gave everyone in the office the ability to create and manipulate digital content—words, data, pictures—at their fingertips on their desktops, which was a great leap forward from paper and typewriters. And, if your whole office was using the same hardware, software, and e-mail system, you could be even more productive, by seamlessly shooting your digitized content around your company, from department to department. But more often than not, back in the 1980s and early 1990s, companies did not run all the same software and hardware. Companies installed systems piecemeal or found that one computer-software system was good for the accounting department and another system was best for inventory management and a third was best for e-mail. Therefore, a company's sales department might be running Microsoft, while the inventory department was running Novell or IBM. As a result, they could not communicate or collaborate digitally with each other—couldn't work together on each other's digital content, or certainly not without difficulty. So while each individual department was more productive inside its own walls, because it had computers, software, and e-mail, when there was an issue between departments that needed to be resolved, someone from sales still had to walk around the wall, over to inventory, and speak to someone there. Work still did not flow digitally, and collaboration did not happen digitally, as easily as it might have. We often forget that the software industry started out like a bad fire department. Imagine a city where every neighborhood had a different interface for connecting the fire hose to the hydrant. Everything was fine as long as your neighborhood's fire department could handle your fire. But when a fire became too big, and the fire engines from the next neighborhood had to be called in, they were useless because they could not connect their hoses to your hydrants.

So while it was a big breakthrough that we standardized the ways that words, music, pictures, and data would be digitized on PCs and transported on the Internet, for work really to be able to flow seamlessly around my company, and then to other companies in my digital ecosystem, we needed two more things. We needed more magic pipes, more transmission protocols and languages, that would ensure that everyone's e-mail and software applications could connect seamlessly with everyone else's e-mail and software applications inside and outside my company—no matter what computer or software they were running. And we needed programmers to come along and write new applications—new software—that would enable us really to get the maximum from our computers as we worked with this digitized data, words, music, and pictures and shaped them into products.

The software industry did the first by creating and popularizing a protocol known as SMTP—simple mail transfer protocol—which enabled the exchange of e-mail messages between heterogeneous computer systems. So you could send e-mail to other people without having to worry about what hardware or e-mail service they had. Suddenly the world had an electronic postman who delivered the mail anywhere quickly and cheaply, despite rain, sleet, or snow.

But for your company to get really flat, e-mail was not enough. All your internal departments—sales, marketing, manufacturing, billing, and inventory—had to become interoperable, no matter what machines or software each of them was running and no matter what documents or data anyone wanted to exchange or collaborate on. That is, your sales department had to be able to send not just e-mail messages but also documents to your billing department and spreadsheets to your supplier's inventory department. And your supplier's inventory department had to be seamlessly connected to its supplier's supplier, which was a factory in China.

To work through the Tower of Babel of software and hardware speaking different languages that evolved in the 1980s and early 1990s, however, required another big breakthrough. It required electronic railroad tracks that could run between everyone's hardware, and railroad cars that could transport documents or data, in a way that could be read by anyone's software. This railroad turned out to be the protocols I mentioned above—the language of the Internet and World Wide Web. HTML was the language that enabled anyone to design and publish documents and data so that they could be transmitted to, and read on, any computer anywhere. HTTP was the computer language that described how you put this content on the Internet railroad—how you made it into a railroad car that could go anywhere. And TCP/IP (transmission control protocol/Internet protocol) was the railroad track—the transport system that took the data from your Web pages around the Internet from computer to computer and Web site to Web site. (As stepforth.com, a technology Web site, described it, TCP/IP "is based on the simple concept of breaking large chunks of data into byte-size packets, directing those packets from computer to computer through a scalable network, and reconstituting the individual packets to replicate the original document.")

"These protocols allowed people to exchange things other than standardized Word documents or e-mail," explained Craig Mundie, the Microsoft chief technical officer. "They enabled anyone to describe any kind of document they wanted—from an Amazon.com page to a credit card payment format—and transport it from machine to machine, and put it in front of your face, without any prior understanding or preparation between the person sending it and you, the person receiving it." That enabled work to really start flowing by the mid-1990s.

It sure did. Wild Brain wanted seamlessly interoperable work flow software to make animated films with a production team spread out around the world. Boeing wanted it so that its airplane factories in America could constantly resupply different airline customers with parts, through its computer ordering systems, no matter what country those orders came from, and so its designers could work on planes using airplane engineers from Russia to India to Japan. Doctors wanted it so that an X-ray taken in Bangor could be read in a hospital in Bangalore, without the doctor in Maine ever having to wonder what computers that Indian hospital had. And Mom and Dad wanted it so that their e-banking software, e-brokerage software, office e-mail, and spreadsheet software all would work off their home laptop and be able to interface with their office desktop or BlackBerry handheld device. And once everyone's applications started to connect to everyone else's applications, work could not only flow like never before, but it could be chopped up, disaggregated, and sent to the four corners of the world as never before.

"But then," added Microsoft's Mundie, "we said to ourselves, 'Geez, if we really want to automate everything, then we need to make it much easier not just for people to talk to people, but for machines to talk to machines—for machines to interact with other machines about any subject without any humans involved at all or any a priori relationship between the different companies whose machines were communicating.'" That was the next work flow breakthrough.

Technically, what made it possible was the development of a new data description language, called XML (extensible markup language) and its related transport protocol called SOAP (simple object access protocol). Together, they allow any two computer programs to exchange formatted data or documents that contain any form of information—whether billing records, financial transactions, medical records, music, pictures, bank records, Web pages, advertisements, book excerpts, Word documents, or stock sales. Microsoft, IBM, and a host of other companies contributed to the development of XML and SOAP, and both were subsequently ratified and popularized as Internet standards. This took work flow to a whole new level. Suddenly I could write my own invoice program, using XML and SOAP, and know that my computers could transmit that invoice to your computers, without any human beings involved or any a priori agreement between our two companies. The net result, added Mundie, was that "the industry created a global platform for a global workforce of people and computers."

In sum, we started in the 1980s with people being able to use PCs to author their own content in digital form, which they printed out on paper and then exchanged with others by hand or surface mail and eventually e-mail. Then we went to people being able to churn out digital content on their PCs, which they transmitted around the Internet, thanks to standardized protocols, collaborating with anyone anywhere. And finally, today, we have reached a point in work flow that machines are talking to other machines over the Internet using standardized protocols, with no humans involved at all.

STANDARDS ON TOP OF STANDARDS

Where is all this going? The great thing about HTML, HTTP, TCP/IP, XML, and SOAP is that once they were adopted as standards—and everything and everyone became increasingly interoperable and interconnected—software companies stopped competing over who got to control the fire hydrant nozzles and focused on who could make better hoses and fire trucks to pump more water. Once a standard takes hold, people start to focus on the quality of *what* they are doing as opposed to *how* they are doing it. In other words, once everyone could connect with everyone else, they got busy on the real value add, which was coming up with the most useful and nifty software applications to enhance collaboration, innovation, and creativity.

Meanwhile, more and more standards were being adopted. Work really flows when you not only get standards for the underlying pipes—so anyone can send any document, picture, or data to any other machine with any other software—but when you also start to standardize what the pipes are carrying—the documents or the business processes. So now we are not just coding documents and software applications in a standardized way—like a Word document or a Web page—that can be read by anyone else on his or her own computer or anyone else's machine, we are also standardizing the business process that those documents represent. "For example," said IBM's Joel Cawley, "when you apply for a mortgage, go to your closing, or buy a house, there are literally dozens of processes and data flows among many different companies. One bank may handle securing your approval, checking your credit, establishing your interest rates, and handling the closing—after which the loan almost immediately is sold to a different bank." Once a standard is established around all these real estate processes, the broker can focus a lot more on you and your needs, not on chasing documents. We are already seeing standards emerging around how payrolls are done, e-commerce payment, and risk profiling, around how music and photos are digitally transmitted and edited—the JPEG standard, for instance—and, most important, around how supply chains are connected.

For instance, it is great that anyone can get on eBay and become a buyer or seller from any machine using any browser, but what really made the eBay marketplace explode was when it adopted PayPal, a standard that enabled the buyer to pay the seller very easily. PayPal is a money transfer system founded in 1998 to facilitate C2C (customer-to-customer) transactions, like a buyer and seller brought together by eBay. According to ecommerce-guide.com, using PayPal, anyone with an e-mail address can send money to anyone else with an e-mail address, whether the recipient has a PayPal account or not. PayPal doesn't even care whether a commercial transaction is taking place. If someone in the office is organizing a party for someone else and everyone needs to chip in, they can all do it using PayPal. In fact, the organizer can send everyone PayPal reminders by e-mail with clear instructions as to how to pay up. PayPal can accept money from the purchaser in one of three ways, notes ecommerce-guide.com: charging the purchaser's credit card for any transactions (payments), debiting a checking account for any payments, or deducting payments from a PayPal account established with a personal check. Payment recipients can use the money in their account for online purchases or payments, can receive the payment from PayPal by check, or can have PayPal directly deposit the money into a checking account. Setting up a PayPal account is simple. As a payer, all you have to do is to provide your name, your e-mail address, your credit card information, and your billing address for your credit card.

All of these interoperable banking and e-commerce functions flattened the Internet marketplace so radically that even eBay was taken by surprise. Before PayPal, explained eBay CEO Meg Whitman, "If I did business on eBay in 1999, the only way I could pay you as a buyer was with a check or money order, a paper-based system. There was no electronic way to send money, and you were too small a merchant to qualify for a credit card account. What PayPal did was enable people, *individuals*, to accept credit cards. I could pay you as an *individual* seller on eBay with a credit card. This really leveled the playing field and made commerce more frictionless." In fact, it was so good that eBay bought PayPal, but not on the recommendation of its Wall Street investment bankers—on the recommendation of its users.

"We woke up one day," said Whitman, "and found out that 20 percent of the people on eBay were saying, 'I accept PayPal, please pay me that way.' And we said, 'Who are these people and what are they doing?' At first we tried to fight them and launched our own service, called Billpoint. Finally, in July 2002, we were at [an] eBay Live [convention] and the drumbeat through the hall was deafening. Our community was telling us, 'Would you guys stop fighting? We want a standard—and by the way, *we have picked the standard* and it's called PayPal, and we know you guys at eBay would like it to be your [standard], but it's theirs.' And that is when we knew we had to buy the company, because it was the standard and it was not ours . . . It is the best acquisition we ever made."

In the coming phase of work flow, here is how you will make a dentist appointment: First, there will be a common standard for making dental appointments with any dentist. You will instruct your computer by voice to make an appointment. Your computer will automatically translate your voice into a digital instruction. It will automatically check your calendar against the available dates on your dentist's calendar and offer you three choices. You will click on the preferred date and hour. The week before your appointment, your dentist's calendar will automatically send you an e-mail reminding you of the appointment. The night before, you will get a computer-generated voice message by phone, also reminding you of your appointment.

For work flow to keep advancing along these lines, though, and deliver the productivity enhancements we want, "we need more and more common standards," said IBM's strategic planner Cawley. "These are standards about how we do business work together." The more we connect everyone through common communication standards, like XML, and then, on top of those protocols, connect more and more people through standardized business processes, said Cawley, the easier it is to chop up work and send pieces of it to be done anywhere in the world, and the more it increases productivity and enables my whole digital ecosystem to collaborate better, cheaper, and faster, and the more energy my employees have to concentrate on the high-touch, high-value-add, customized innovation or service that differentiates one company from another. Standards don't stop innovation, added Cawley, they just clear away a lot of extraneous stuff so you can focus on what really matters.

THE LATEST ÜBERSTANDARD

As I write, work flow is about to go to yet another level. Now that we have created more and more standard ways for people and machines to describe and share documents and work together, and at least some standards for how to conduct certain kinds of commerce—like mortgages or credit card payments—another revolution is under way, made possible by an emerging new way of coding called AJAX (short for asynchronous JavaScript and XML). AJAX provides easy access to richer and more sophisticated Web-based business tools that you can use to run a whole company—online—at very low cost. When I say run a company, I mean keeping track of inventory, staying in touch with customers, recruiting, project management, product development, scheduling, budgeting, and human resources. In the Business Web, as it is being called, you access these tools on the Web, use them on the Web, and store all your business data on the Web, rather than on your own computers. Before long these Web-delivered services will likely replace some, or all, of the business software programs that you buy, load, update, upgrade, and integrate with other systems.

This constitutes a huge leap forward in work flow. Ray Ozzie, another of Microsoft's chief technical officers, calls it "the Internet services disruption." Here is how it works: Internet-based services companies are emerging today all across the Web. For a fee, these companies—Salesforce.com, for example—give you access to a library of Web-based business applications, which you can just tap into online to run your business. These applications operate like traditional software programs and can handle a wide range of business tasks. The big difference is that all these management tools, data, or even photos are not stored on your computer as software. They are stored remotely on the Salesforce.com platform. Because these tools are delivered over the Internet and written in standard Web formats, they are accessible to anyone who has an Internet connection and are easily interoperable with any business. What enables work flow at this level is AJAX, a Web development technique that allows complex Internet business applications to be embedded onto a Web page, then called up with a simple browser and accessed as easily as viewing a page on Amazon.com. AJAX, in effect, allows you to do over the Internet all the word, data, and business processing you would normally do on a PC with conventional software. You as a business pay Salesforce.com $65 per individual user per month to subscribe to its Web-based platform ($17 per user for companies of one to five people). Software becomes something you rent, instead of something you own. Somebody else takes care of the upgrading and maintenance.

"We can upgrade our service on a daily basis and, because the service is built using Web standards and delivered over the Web, upgrades are instantaneously available and can be immediately accessed by every customer around the world," said Ken Juster, Salesforce.com's executive vice president for law, policy, and corporate strategy. "We are not just trying to move information and data; we are trying to share business solutions and best practices for how things get done — within companies and across companies."

As your company uses the online business tools offered by Salesforce.com to make your work flow, your business process team may come up with a customized solution that works really well for you and your clients. You can then turn around and offer that solution back to the Salesforce.com platform as a tool others might want to use — for free, or you can get a fee for your business process innovation. That way Salesforce.com basically uses its customers and partners to grow its platform and embed itself into more and more businesses. Its customers, in effect, become part of its sales and research and development teams.

"We could never build applications for customers as quickly and easily as they can for themselves," Marc Benioff, the Salesforce.com CEO, told internetnews.com on April 12, 2005. Because a huge library of business process applications is available at Salesforce.com, they can be drawn upon by a one-person company or by IBM. Juster said one of his favorite customers using Salesforce.com's platform is a thirty-something small businessman in Shanghai, Justin Lu, and his company, Protime Consulting. Lu helps global companies which have outlets in China, like Sony, Hyatt, or Estée Lauder, with their e-marketing and Web site solutions. He now has thirty people working for him and does over $1 million in business annually. "I can run virtually my entire business on the Web using Salesforce.com," said Lu. "We've been able to grow very quickly by focusing on what's important to generating more revenue and keeping our systems costs low with Web-delivered services."

For instance, he uses Salesforce.com's online e-mail marketing system to send out mass e-mails, he uses its sales force automation system to handle all presale data, and he uses its customer relationship management system to build a corporate memory around all his customer interactions. He is getting the intellectual property from these three applications, said Juster, and they are empowering him to start a company with very little money.

I learned of a start-up that is using the Business Web to sell organic vitamins. This guy pays Yahoo! a fee every month so that any time anyone searches for the words "organic vitamins" on Yahoo!, one of his ads pops up. He then uses the Salesforce.com platform to manage his back room, and he found a manufacturer to make his own private-label organic vitamins. Boom! With virtually no money, working out of his home—but leveraging the search power of Yahoo! and the backroom power of Salesforce—he is now out there competing with major drugstore chains.

Just as the Business Web is giving small businessmen like Justin Lu easy access to some business tools that only large companies could afford a few years ago, it is also setting the stage for a revolutionary change in the balance of power among the providers of business applications. The next logical step in the evolution of the Business Web will be eBay-like marketplaces for business services. Individual developers and entrepreneurs, whether they are located in Shanghai, Bangalore, or Silicon Valley, will be able to write applications, plug their innovations into Web platforms like Salesforce.com, and leverage the marketing and distribution strength of these Web platforms to sell globally, without the heavy investment that is required today to commercialize software.

"This is just the beginning of the Business Web," argued Benioff, Salesforce.com's CEO, in a memo to his staff in November 2005. "The software industry is going through a transformation that is unlike anything it has seen in two decades, and [comparable to] the emergence of the PC itself . . . New Internet-based companies are showing how services will replace software for both consumers and corporations." As Benioff likes to put it: "Microsoft wants you to buy more software. We want to see the end of software."

Microsoft has taken notice. *The New York Times* reported on November 9, 2005, that Ray Ozzie had written an in-house memo warning senior executives that Microsoft had to fundamentally alter its business "or face being at a significant competitive disadvantage to a growing array of companies offering Internet services." A few days later, Microsoft announced that it would offer two new services—Windows Live and Office Live, which essentially are Business Web versions of two of its more popular products. A few weeks later, Google announced that it was offering a free, downloadable software bundle, with none of the programs coming from Microsoft. This is going to get interesting!

There is no question that the Business Web will challenge Microsoft. But I wouldn't short Microsoft or throw out all my software just yet. It is true we are going from a world where companies were independent systems, to a world where they became interconnected and interdependent systems, to a world where now companies large and small can assemble an interoperable system of systems on their own just by going to the Business Web and renting or assembling whatever discrete programs they would like. The virtual company is here—and it is going to be very disruptive. Because it is going to give small and medium-size businesses access to some of the powerful work flow tools that a few years ago only big companies could afford.

But remember: When you have these standardized work flow tools, so does everyone else. You still have to have a unique product or service to offer. And for that you often need to develop a unique way to apply information technologies to your core value proposition, whatever it is. It is great to be able to do your customer relationship management on the Web for a small fee, it is great to have really efficient work flow. But first you need your own customers—your own distinctive competency for your company. And that means you need proprietary insights, innovations and, yes, proprietary software tools or systems, to build your unique product or service. Your distinctive competency—the thing that will build a moat around your company—will always be created, enhanced, or embodied in some proprietary algorithm or manufacturing process or software application. You can't get everything off the shelf or off the Web—if you could, your competition could, too. If you are running a bond fund, all the standards and work flow that now exist for seamlessly trading bonds are a godsend for you. But it will be your own unique, knock-their-socks-off algorithm for when to buy and sell those bonds that will ultimately determine your success or failure. That is why there will still be a place for the big, smart traditional software companies, like Microsoft and SAP, that can create a tailored solution for each client. Also, as Microsoft has demonstrated, it too will make some of its programs available on the Business Web.

Nevertheless, this revolution in work flow that we have witnessed—from transmission protocols to standards to business processes that you can now just rent off the Web—is surely going to lead to an explosion of experimentation and innovation. And out of this whirlwind, many new products and services will surely emerge, as well as a demand for more tailored, proprietary software and IT systems to drive them forward. By the time the smoke next clears, how we think about work, how we make it flow, and even how we start a company will probably be radically transformed.

"Work flow platforms are enabling us to do for the service industry what Henry Ford did for manufacturing," said Jerry Rao, the entrepreneur doing accounting work for Americans out of India. "We are taking apart each task, [standardizing it,] and sending it around to whoever can do it best, and because we are doing it in a virtual environment, people need not be physically adjacent to each other, and then we are reassembling all the pieces back together at headquarters [or some other remote site]. This is not a trivial revolution. This is a major one. It allows for a boss to be somewhere and his employees to be someplace else." These work flow software platforms, Rao added, "enable you to create virtual global offices—not limited by either the boundaries of your office or your country—and to access talent sitting in different parts of the world and have them complete tasks that you need completed in real time. And so 24/7/365 we are all working. And all this has happened in the twinkling of an eye—the span of the last two or three years."

Genesis: The Flat-World Platform Emerges

We need to stop here and take stock, because at this point the platform for the flattening of the world has started to emerge. First, the falling of the walls, the opening of the Windows, and the rise of the PC all combined to empower more individuals than ever to become authors of their own content in digital form. Then the spread of the Internet and the coming to life of the Web, thanks to the browser and fiber optics, enabled more people than ever to be connected and to share their digital content with more other people for less money than any time before. Finally, the emergence of standardized transmission pipes and protocols that connected everyone's machines and software applications, and also encouraged the development of standardized business processes for how certain kinds of commerce or work would be conducted, meant that more people were not just seamlessly connected but also were able to seamlessly work together on one another's digital content more than ever before.

Put it all together and what you end up with is the crude foundation of a whole new global platform for collaboration. This was the genesis moment for the flattening of the world, and it came together in the mid- to late 1990s. All the elements of this new platform (such as the Business Web) would take more time to fully emerge and converge. That would happen only in the 2000s. But this moment in the mid- to late 1990s was when people first started to feel that something was changing in a big way. There was suddenly available a platform for collaboration that all kinds of people from around the globe could now plug and play, compete and connect on—in order to share work, exchange knowledge, start companies, and invent and sell goods and services. "It is the creation of this platform, with these unique attributes, that is the truly important sustainable breakthrough that made what you call the flattening of the world possible," said Microsoft's Craig Mundie. Because, as Joel Cawley, the IBM strategist, added, "We were not just communicating with each other more than ever, we were now able to collaborate—to build coalitions, projects, and products together—more than ever."

This rudimentary platform helped to spawn six more flatteners, or, more accurately, six new forms of collaboration. I call them "uploading," "outsourcing," "offshoring," "supply-chaining," "insourcing," and "in-forming." Each of these new forms of collaboration was either made possible by this emerging flat-world platform or greatly enhanced by it. And as more and more of us learn how to collaborate in these new and different ways, we are steadily flattening the world even more.

It is always dangerous to declare a turning point in history. We always tend to feel that when we are alive something really major is happening. But I am convinced that the genesis of this new flat-world platform and the six new forms of collaboration it has spawned will be remembered in time as one of the most important turning points in the history of mankind—one no less significant than the invention of the printing press or electricity. Someone had to be alive when it happened—and it happens to be you and me.

FLATTENER #4
UPLOADING
Harnessing the Power of Communities

Alan Cohen still remembers the first time he heard the word "Apache" as an adult, and it wasn't while watching a cowboys-and-Indians movie. It was the 1990s, the dot-com market was booming, and he was a senior manager for IBM, helping to oversee its emerging e-commerce business. "I had a whole team with me and a budget of about $8 million," Cohen recalled. "We were competing head-to-head with Microsoft,

Netscape, Oracle, Sun—all the big boys. And we were playing this very big-stakes game for e-commerce. IBM had a huge sales force selling all this e-commerce software. One day I asked the development director who worked for me, 'Say, Jeff, walk me through the development process for these e-commerce systems. What is the underlying Web server?' And he says to me, 'It's built on top of Apache.' The first thing I think of is John Wayne. 'What is Apache?' I ask. And he says it is a shareware program for Web server technology. He said it was produced for free by a bunch of geeks just working online in some kind of open-source chat room. I was floored. I said, 'How do you buy it?' And he says, 'You download it off a Web site for free.' And I said, 'Well, who supports it if something goes wrong?' And he says, 'I don't know—it just works!' And that was my first exposure to Apache . . .

"Now you have to remember, back then Microsoft, IBM, Oracle, Netscape were all trying to build commercial Web servers. These were huge companies. And suddenly my development guy is telling me that he's getting ours off the Internet for free! It's like you had all these big corporate executives plotting strategies, and then suddenly the guys in the mail room are in charge. I kept asking, 'Who runs Apache? I mean, who are these guys?'"

Yes, the geeks in the mail room are deciding what software they will be using—and what you will be using too, because communities of geeks are now collaborating to design new software and then to upload it to the world. It's called community developed software. But, thanks to the flat-world platform, more and more geeks on the Web are also offering up their own news and opinion pieces, cutting out the middlemen of newspapers. It's called blogging. And a community of geeks in the library is now writing its own encyclopedia entries, uploading them to the world, and cutting out the traditional book-form encyclopedias and even digital ones like Encarta. It's called Wikipedia. And the geeks in the dorm are increasingly offering up their own songs, and videos, and poetry, and rap, and commentary, to you and me and the rest of the world, cutting out the music stores and the traditional content providers. It's called podcasting. And the geeks on Amazon.com are increasingly writing their own book reviews, becoming among the most important reviewers in the world, reducing the dominance of traditional icons like *The New York Review of Books* and *The New York Times Book Review*. Soon, I suspect, Amazon will publish your whole book for you online. And the geeks on eBay are already creating their own virtual commercial community and policing themselves as to who is a trustworthy buyer or seller, by handing out stars. And the terrorist geeks in al-Qaeda are increasingly uploading their own news reports, threats, and speeches, not waiting for the BBC or CBS to come talk to them, and then they're zapping their terror messages directly into your computer, via AOL or MSN.

These are all variations of uploading. The genesis of the flat-world platform not only enabled more people to author more content, and to collaborate on that content. It also enabled them to upload files and globalize that content—individually or as part of self-forming communities—without going through any of the traditional hierarchical organizations or institutions.

This newfound power of individuals and communities to send up, out, and around their own products and ideas, often for free, rather than just passively downloading them from commercial enterprises or traditional hierarchies, is fundamentally reshaping the flow of creativity, innovation, political mobilization, and information gathering and dissemination. It is making each of these things a bottom-up and globally side-to-side phenomenon, not exclusively a top-down one. This is now true inside traditional companies and institutions as well as outside them. Uploading is, without doubt, becoming one of the most revolutionary forms of collaboration in the flat world. More than ever, we can all now be producers, not just consumers.

I got the idea of defining "uploading" (in this context) as my fourth flattener from a brilliant essay, "We Are the Web," by *Wired* magazine's cofounder and "senior maverick," Kevin Kelly (August 2005). Kelly noted that when the Internet first emerged on a mass scale in the post-Netscape era, "the bandwidth on cable and phone lines was asymmetrical: download rates far exceeded upload rates. The dogma of the age held that ordinary people had no need to upload; they were consumers, not producers. Fast-forward to today, and the poster child of the new Internet regime is BitTorrent. [BitTorrent is a Web site that allows users to upload their own

online music libraries and download other people's at the same time.] . . .
Our communication infrastructure has taken only the first steps in this
great shift from audience to participants, but that is where it will go in the
next decade." It is not impossible to imagine, added Kelly, that one day in
the future, "everyone alive will (on average) write a song, author a book,
make a video, craft a Weblog, and code a program . . . What happens
when the data flow is asymmetrical—but in favor of the creators? What
happens when everyone is uploading far more than they download?"

It was long assumed that producing any product of substance or complexity takes some kind of hierarchical organization or institution. The
assumption was that you needed top-down vertical integration to get
such things done and out into the world. But thanks to our newfound
ability to upload—which came about as a direct result of the flat-world
platform—you can now produce really complex things, as an individual
or as part of a community, with so much less hierarchy and so much less
money than ever before.

I am going to focus here on three forms of uploading: the community-
developed software movement, Wikipedia, and blogging/podcasting.

COMMUNITY-DEVELOPED SOFTWARE

The community-developed software movement, also known as the "open-
source" community, derives its identity from the notion that companies or
ad hoc communities should make available online the source code—the
underlying programming instructions that make a piece of software
work—and then let anyone who has something to contribute improve it
and let millions of others just download it for their own use. Think of
these communities as chat rooms with freelance engineers who collaborate together to produce a piece of software, with everyone contributing
improvements to the source code to make it sing and dance better, and
using it, as long as they conform to the license rules of that particular
open-source community. While these communities tend to operate along
the same lines, they are divided into two factions by one big issue. One
faction, let's call it the "intellectual commons community," basically says

that anyone in the community may use the source code as the foundation for a commercial product—as long as you always acknowledge the original group that produced it. So as that software rolls downstream into subsequent improvements, adaptations, and implementations, you have to give the original community credit each time. The other group, let's call it the "free software community," argues that if you build and distribute any derivative product on the shoulders of community-developed free software code, you need to contribute your innovation back to the community as well. That is, you need to make your product free.

Not being a computer geek, I had never focused much on the open-source movement, but when I did, I discovered it was an amazing universe of its own, with self-forming communities of online, come-as-you-are volunteers. The first community-developed software movement really to make a mark took the intellectual commons approach. It came out of the academic and scientific communities, where for a long time self-organized collaborative communities of scientists have come together through private networks (and, eventually, the Internet) to pool their brainpower or share insights around a particular science or math problem. The Apache Web server had its roots in this form of open-sourcing. When I asked a friend of mine, Mike Arguello, an IT systems architect, to explain to me why people share knowledge or work in this way, he said, "IT people tend to be very bright people and they want everybody to know just how brilliant they are." Marc Andreessen, who invented the Mosaic Web browser, agreed: "Open-source is nothing more than peer-reviewed science. Sometimes people contribute to these things because they make science, and they discover things, and the reward is reputation. Sometimes you can build a business out of it; sometimes they just want to increase the store of knowledge in the world. And the peer review part is critical—and open-source is peer review. Every bug or security hole or deviation from standards is reviewed." Some people also clearly get a buzz from trying to challenge giants, like Microsoft or IBM, by proving that they can build something better for free.

To learn more about this intellectual commons form of software development, I went exploring among the geeky guys and girls in the mailroom. Eventually, I found my way to one of their pioneers, Brian

Behlendorf. If Apache—the open-source Web server community—were an Indian tribe, Behlendorf would be the tribal elder. I caught up with him one day in his glass-and-steel office near the San Francisco airport, where he is now founder and chief technology officer of CollabNet, a start-up focused on creating software for companies that want to use an open-source approach to innovation. I started with two simple questions: Where did you come from? and How did you manage to pull together an open-source community of online geeks that could go toe-to-toe with IBM?

"My parents met at IBM in Southern California, and I grew up in a town just north of Pasadena, La Canada," Behlendorf recalled. "The public school was very competitive academically, because a lot of the kids' parents worked at the Jet Propulsion Laboratory that was run by Caltech there. So from a very early age I was around a lot of science in a place where it was okay to be kind of geeky. We always had computers around the house. We used to use punch cards from the original IBM mainframes for making shopping lists. In grade school, I started doing some basic programming, and by high school I was pretty into computers . . . I graduated in 1991, but in 1989, in the early days of the Internet, a friend gave me a copy of a program he had downloaded onto a floppy disk, called 'Fractint.' It was not pirated, but was freeware, produced by a group of programmers, and was a program for drawing fractals. [Fractals are beautiful images produced at the intersection of art and math.] When the program started up, the screen would show this scrolling list of e-mail addresses for all the scientists and mathematicians who contributed to it. I noticed that the source code was included with the program. This was my first exposure to the concept of open-source. Here was this program that you just downloaded for free, and they even gave you the source code with it, and it was done by a community of people. It started to paint a different picture of programming in my mind. I started to think that there were some interesting social dynamics to the way certain kinds of software were written or could be written—as opposed to the kind of image I had of the professional software developer in the back office tending to the mainframe, feeding info in and taking it out for the business. That seemed to me to be just one step above accounting and not very exciting."

After graduating in 1991, Behlendorf went to Berkeley to study physics, but he quickly became frustrated by the disconnect between the abstractions he was learning in the classroom and the excitement that was starting to emerge on the Internet.

"When you entered college back then, every student was given an e-mail address, and I started using it to talk to students and explore discussion boards that were starting to appear around music," said Behlendorf. "In 1992, I started my own Internet mailing list focused on the local electronic music scene in the Bay Area. People could just post onto the discussion board, and it started to grow, and we started to discuss different music events and DJs. Then we said, 'Hey, why don't we invite our own DJs and throw our own events?' It became a collective thing. Someone would say, 'I have some records,' and someone else would say, 'I have a sound system,' and someone else would say, 'I know the beach and if we showed up at midnight we could have a party.' By 1993, the Internet was still just mailing lists and e-mail and FTP sites [file transfer protocol repositories where you could store things]. So I started collecting an archive of electronic music and was interested in how we could put this online and make it available to a larger audience. That was when I heard about Mosaic [the Web browser developed by Marc Andreessen]. So I got a job at the computer lab in the Berkeley business school, and I spent my spare time researching Mosaic and other Web technologies. That led me to a discussion board with a lot of the people who were writing the first generation of Web browsers and Web servers."

(A Web server is a software program that enables anyone to use his or her home or office computer to host a Web site on the World Wide Web. Amazon.com, for instance, has long run its Web site on Apache software. When your Web browser goes to www.amazon.com, the very first piece of software it talks to is Apache. The browser asks Apache for the Amazon Web page and Apache sends back to the browser the content of the Amazon Web page. Surfing the Web is really your Web browser interacting with different Web servers.)

"I found myself sitting in on this forum watching Tim Berners-Lee and Marc Andreessen debating how all these things should work," recalled Behlendorf. "It was pretty exciting, and it seemed radically inclusive. I didn't need a Ph.D. or any special credentials, and I started to see some parallels between my music group and these scientists, who had a common interest in building the first Web software. I followed that [discussion] for a while and then I told a friend of mine about it. He was one of the first employees at Wired magazine, and he said Wired would be interested in having me set up a Web site for them. So I joined there at $10 an hour, setting up their e-mail and their first Web site — HotWired . . . It was one of the first ad-supported online magazines."

HotWired decided it wanted to start by having a registration system that required passwords—a controversial concept at that time. "In those days," noted Andrew Leonard, who wrote a history of Apache for Salon.com in 1997, "most Webmasters depended on a Web server program developed at the University of Illinois's National Center for Supercomputing Applications (also the birthplace of the groundbreaking Mosaic Web browser). But the NCSA Web server couldn't handle password authentication on the scale that HotWired needed. Luckily, the NCSA server was in the public domain, which meant that the source code was free to all comers. So Behlendorf exercised the hacker prerogative: He wrote some new code, a 'patch' to the NCSA Web server, that took care of the problem." Leonard commented, "He wasn't the only clever programmer rummaging through the NCSA code that winter. All across the exploding Web, other Webmasters were finding it necessary to take matters into their own keyboards. The original code had been left to gather virtual dust when its primary programmer, University of Illinois student Rob McCool, had been scooped up (along with Marc Andreessen and Lynx author Eric Bina) by a little-known company in Silicon Valley named Netscape. Meanwhile, the Web refused to stop growing—and kept creating new problems for Web servers to cope with." So patches of one kind or another proliferated like Band-Aids on bandwidth, plugging one hole here and breaching another gap there.

Meanwhile, all these patches were slowly, in an ad hoc open-source manner, building a new modern Web server. But everyone had his or her own version, trading patches here and there, because the NCSA lab couldn't keep up with them all.

"I was just this near-dropout," explained Behlendorf. "I was having a lot

of fun building this Web site for *Wired* and learning more than I was learning at Berkeley. So a discussion started in our little working group that the
NCSA people were not answering our e-mails. We were sending in
patches for the system and they weren't responding. And we said, 'If NCSA
would not respond to our patches, what's going to happen in the future?'
We were happy to continue improving this thing, yet we were worried
when we were not getting any feedback and seeing our patches integrated.
So I started to contact the other people I knew trading patches . . . Most of
them were on the standards working groups [the Internet Engineering
Task Force] that were setting the first standards for the interconnectivity between machines and applications on the Internet . . . And we said, 'Why
don't we take our future into our own hands and release our own [Web
server] version that incorporated all our patches?'

"We looked up the copyright for the NCSA code, and it basically just
said give us credit at Illinois for what we invented if you improve it—and
don't blame us if it breaks," recalled Behlendorf. "So we started building
our own version from all our patches. None of us had time to be a full-
time Web server developer, but we thought if we could combine our
time and do it in a public way, we could create something better than we
could buy off the shelf—and nothing was available then, anyway. This
was all before Netscape had shipped its first commercial Web server.
That was the beginning of the Apache project."

By February 1999, they had completely rewritten the original NCSA
program and formalized their cooperation under the name "Apache."

"I picked the name because I wanted it to have a positive connotation
of being assertive," said Behlendorf. "The Apache tribe was the last tribe
to surrender to the oncoming U.S. government, and at the time we worried that the big companies would come in and 'civilize' the landscape
that the early Internet engineers built. So 'Apache' made sense to me as a
good code name, and others said it also would make a good pun"—as in
the APAtCHy server, because they were patching all these fixes together.

So in many ways, Behlendorf and his open-source colleagues—most
of whom he had never met but knew only by e-mail through their open-
source chat room—had created a virtual, online, bottom-up software factory, which no one owned and no one supervised. "We had a software

project, but the coordination and direction were an emergent behavior based on whoever showed up and wanted to write code," he said.

But how does it actually work? I asked Behlendorf. You can't just have a bunch of people, unmonitored, throwing code together, can you?

"Most software development involves a source code repository and is managed by tools such as the Concurrent Versions System," he explained. "So there is a CVS server out there, and I have a CVS program on my computer. It allows me to connect to the server and pull down a copy of the code, so I can start working with it and making modifications. If I think my patch is something I want to share with others, I run a program called Patch, which allows me to create a new file, a compact collection of all the changes. That is called a patch file, and I can give that file to someone else, and they can apply it to their copy of the code to see what impact that patch has. If I have the right privileges to the server [which is restricted to a tightly controlled oversight board], I can then take my patch and commit it to the repository and it will become part of the source code. The CVS server keeps track of everything and who sent in what . . . So you might have 'read access' to the repository but not 'commit access' to change things. When someone makes a commit to the repository, that patch file gets e-mailed out to all the other developers, and so you get this peer review system after the fact, and if there is something wrong, you fix the bug."

So how does this community decide who are trusted members?

"For Apache," said Behlendorf, "we started with eight people who really trusted each other, and as new people showed up at the discussion forum and offered patch files posted to the discussion forum, we would gain trust in others, and that eight grew to over one thousand. We were the first open-source project to get attention from the business community and get the backing from IBM."

Because of Apache's proficiency at allowing a single-server machine to host thousands of different virtual Web sites—music, data, text, pornography—it began to have "a commanding share of the Internet Service Provider market," noted Salon's Leonard. IBM was trying to sell its own proprietary Web server, called GO, but it gained only a tiny sliver of the market. Apache proved to be both a better technology and free. So

IBM eventually decided that if it could not beat Apache, it should join Apache. You have to stop here and imagine this. The world's biggest computer company decided that its engineers could not best the work of an ad hoc open-source collection of geeks, so they threw out their own technology and decided to go with the geeks!

IBM "initiated contact with me, as I had a somewhat public speaker role for Apache," said Behlendorf. "IBM said, 'We would like to figure out how we can use [Apache] and not get flamed by the Internet community, [how we can] make it sustainable and not just be ripping people off but contributing to the process . . .' IBM was saying that this new model for software development was trustworthy and valuable, so let's invest in it and get rid of the one that we are trying to make on our own, which isn't as good."

John Swainson was the senior IBM executive who led the team that approached Apache (he's now chairman of Computer Associates). He picked up the story: "There was a whole debate going on at the time about open-source, but it was all over the place. We decided we could deal with the Apache guys because they answered our questions. We could hold a meaningful conversation with these guys, and we were able to create the [nonprofit] Apache Software Foundation and work out all the issues."

At IBM's expense, its lawyers worked with the Apache group to create a legal framework around it so that there would be no copyright or liability problems for companies, like IBM, that wanted to build applications on top of Apache and charge money for them. IBM saw the value in having a standard vanilla Web server architecture—which allowed heterogeneous computer systems and devices to talk to one another, displaying e-mail and Web pages in a standard format—that was constantly being improved for free by an open-source community. The Apache collaborators did not set out to make free software. They set out to solve a common problem—Web serving—and found that collaborating for free in this open-source manner was the best way to assemble the best brains for the job they needed done.

"When we started working with Apache, there was an apache.org Web site but no formal legal structure, and businesses and informal structures don't coexist well," said Swainson. "You need to be able to vet the code, sign an agreement, and deal with liability issues. [Today] anybody can download the Apache code. The only obligation is that they acknowledge that it came from the site, and if they make any changes that they share them back." There is an Apache development process that manages the traffic, and you earn your way into that process, added Swainson. It is something like a pure meritocracy. When IBM started using Apache, it became part of the community and started making contributions.

Indeed, the one thing the Apache people demanded in return for their collaboration with IBM was that IBM assign its best engineers to join the Apache open-source group and contribute, like everyone else, for free. "The Apache people were not interested in payment of cash," said Swainson. "They wanted *contribution* to the base. Our engineers came to us and said, 'These guys who do Apache are good and they are insisting that we contribute good people.' At first they rejected some of what we contributed. They said it wasn't up to their standards! The compensation that the community expected was our best contribution."

On June 22, 1998, IBM announced plans to incorporate Apache into its own new Web server product, named WebSphere. The way the Apache collaborative community organized itself, whatever you took out of Apache's code and improved on, you had to give back to the whole community. But you were also free to go out and build a patented commercial product on top of the Apache code, as IBM did, provided that you included a copyright citation to Apache in your own patent. In other words, this intellectual commons approach to open-sourcing encouraged people to build commercial products on top of it. While it wanted the foundation to be free and open to all, it recognized that it would remain strong and fresh if both commercial and noncommercial engineers had an incentive to participate.

Today Apache is one of the most successful open-source tools, powering about two-thirds of the Web sites in the world. And because Apache can be downloaded for free anywhere in the world, people from Russia to South Africa to Vietnam use it to create Web sites. Those individuals who need or want added capabilities for their Web servers can buy products like WebSphere, which attach right on top of Apache.

At the time, selling a product built on top of an open-source program was a risky move on IBM's part. To its credit, IBM was confident in its ability to keep producing differentiated software applications on top of the Apache vanilla. This model has since been widely adopted, after everyone saw how it propelled IBM's Web server business to commercial leadership in that category of software, generating huge amounts of revenue.

As I will repeat in this book: There is no future in vanilla for most companies in a flat world. A lot of vanilla making in software and other areas is going to shift to open-source communities. For most companies, the commercial future belongs to those who know how to make the richest chocolate sauce, the sweetest, lightest whipped cream, and the juiciest cherries to sit on top, or how to put them all together into a sundae. Jack Messman, chairman of the Novell software company, which has now become a big distributor of Linux, the open-source operating system, atop which Novell attaches gizmos to make it sing and dance just for your company, put it best: "Commercial software companies have to start operating further up the [software] stack to differentiate themselves. The open source community is basically focusing on infrastructure" (*Financial Times*, June 14, 2004).

The IBM deal was a real watershed. Big Blue was saying that it believed in the open-source model and that with the Apache Web server, this open-source community of engineers had created something that was not just useful and valuable but "best in its class." That's why the open-source movement has become a powerful flattener, the effects of which we are just beginning to see. "It is incredibly empowering of individuals," Brian Behlendorf said. "It doesn't matter where you come from or where you are—someone in India or South America can be just as effective using this software or contributing to it as someone in Silicon Valley." The old model is winner take all: I wrote it, I own it—the standard software license model. "The only way to compete against that," concluded Behlendorf, "is to all become winners."

The other big form of community-developed software is the free software movement. According to the openknowledge.org Web site, "The free/open source software movement began in the 'hacker' culture of U.S. computer science laboratories (Stanford, Berkeley, Carnegie Mellon, and MIT) in the 1960s and 1970s. The community of programmers was small and close-knit. Code passed back and forth between the members of the community—if you made an improvement you were expected to submit your code to the community of developers. To withhold code was considered gauche—after all, you benefited from the work of your friends, you should return the favor." The free software movement, however, was and remains inspired by the ethical ideal that software should be free and available to all, and it relies on open-source collaboration to help produce the best software possible to be distributed for free. The primary goal of the free software movement is to get as many people as possible writing, improving, and distributing software for free, out of a conviction that this will empower everyone and free individuals from the grip of global corporations.

In 1984, according to Wikipedia, an MIT researcher and ex-hacker, Richard Stallman, launched the "free software movement" along with an effort to build a free operating system called GNU. Stallman founded the Free Software Foundation and something called the GNU General Public License (GPL). The GPL specified that users of the source code could copy, change, or upgrade the code, provided that they made their changes available under the same license as the original code. In 1991, a student at the University of Helsinki named Linus Torvalds, building off Stallman's initiative, posted his Linux operating system to compete with the Microsoft Windows operating system and invited other programmers online to try to improve it—for free. Since Torvalds's initial post, programmers all over the world have manipulated, added to, expanded, patched, and improved the GNU/Linux operating system, whose license says anyone can download the source code and improve upon it, but then must make the upgraded version freely available to everybody else. Torvalds insists that Linux must always be free. Therefore, commercial software companies that sell improvements that enhance or adapt Linux have to be careful not to combine and/or distribute any of Linux's copyrighted code in their commercial products. The General Public License under which Linux code, and other free software, is written and distributed requires that if you combine new code with Linux and redistribute it, then you are obligated to make the modified or combined work available to the community for free.

Much like Microsoft Windows, Linux offers a family of operating systems that can be adapted to run on the smallest desktop computers, laptops, PalmPilots, and even wristwatches, all the way up to the largest supercomputers and mainframes. So a kid in India with a cheap PC can learn the inner workings of the same operating system that is running in some of the largest data centers of corporate America. As I was working on this segment of the book, I went to a picnic one afternoon at the Virginia country home of Pamela and Malcolm Baldwin, whom my wife came to know through her membership on the board of World Learning, an educational NGO. I mentioned in the course of lunch that I was thinking of going to Mali to see just how flat the world looked from its outermost edge—the town of Timbuktu. The Baldwins' son Peter happened to be working in Mali as part of something called the GeekCorps, which helps to bring technology to developing countries. A few days after the lunch, I received an e-mail from Pamela telling me that she had consulted with Peter about accompanying me to Timbuktu, and then she added the following, which told me everything I needed to know: "Peter says that his project is creating wireless networks via satellite, making antennas out of plastic soda bottles and mesh from window screens! Apparently everyone in Mali uses Linux . . ."

Only in a flat world would you ever hear such a comment!

The free software movement has become a challenge to Microsoft and some other big global software players. As *Fortune* magazine reported (February 23, 2004), "The availability of this basic, powerful software, which works on Intel's ubiquitous microprocessors, coincided with the explosive growth of the Internet. Linux soon began to gain a global following among programmers and business users . . . The revolution goes far beyond little Linux . . . Just about any kind of software [now] can be found in open-source form. The SourceForge.net website, a meeting place for programmers, lists an astounding 86,000 programs in progress. Most are minor projects by and for geeks, but hundreds pack real value . . . If you hate shelling out $350 for Microsoft Office or $600 for Adobe Photoshop, OpenOffice.org and the Gimp are surprisingly high-quality free alternatives." Big companies like Google, E*Trade, and Amazon, by combining Intel-based commodity server components and the Linux operating system, have been able to cut their technology spending dramatically—and get more control over their software.

Truth be told, though, while Linux and Apache began as pure forms of community-developed software, uploaded by self-generating collaborative communities, it wasn't long before Apache became a kind of "blended model," thanks to its collaboration with IBM. Some people worked on it for free and others were paid to do so by IBM, so the company could sell its own services, upgrades, and attachments around the basic software. At the same time, we are now seeing venture capitalists actually funding open-source start-ups—paying software companies to put out some program for free in the hope that a community will develop around it, so that the start-up company can sell additional bells and whistles to the community for profit. Red Hat, for instance, helps support the development of Linux and other open-source solutions and has created a business around it. Red Hat won't sell you Linux per se—that's not allowed—but for a fee it will provide support and customize Linux for your business.

These blended models are probably the future. Why? To begin with, for a complex software platform to be sustainable—that is, to be constantly freshened, debugged, and improved—there has to be an economy around it. Talented open-source community software developers have only so much time, inclination, energy, and resources to put into developing code for free. At some point, the work won't go on at the highest level if there isn't some economic incentive for someone in the community.

In the case of Linux, it is wonderful that people in Mali can download the software for free, but Linux is not really being developed for free anymore. One should not get too romantic about all this. IBM does not sell an operating system that competes with Linux. But IBM sells software that competes with Microsoft's. So IBM is very happy to pay quality software engineers to work on Linux in order to encourage its expansion as a competitor to Microsoft Windows—and thereby cut into Microsoft's profits, weakening its ability to compete with IBM in its areas of specialty. Sun Microsystems set up OpenOffice.org for the same reason. As the Sun Web site puts it: "The OpenOffice.org community was founded by Sun Microsystems in 2000. An active community, of which Sun is a key member, enhances and supports the OpenOffice.org office suite." Hey, that's business. But it *is* business. The important thing, from the consumer's point of view, is that these blended models of community-developed software are driving more competition and producing cheaper, if not free, software for the public.

Needless to say, the whole notion of community-developed software is hotly debated around Microsoft. Given the company's centrality in the software business, I thought it was important to hear its side of the story. Here's what I took away from my discussions in Redmond: In Microsoft's view, the blended model that has evolved out of the community software movement is really just a new form of commercial competition, and no one should have any illusions about it. Whatever the founders of the community-developed software movement may have intended or hoped for—in terms of profit-free community-developed software—that is not what has actually developed. Community-based software development is now a business, one that holds potential for Microsoft as for every other company.

Having said that, the Microsoft executives I spoke with still believe that this form of software has its limitations—and will not, or should not, make the traditional, commercial software industry obsolete—for several reasons. To begin with, Microsoft argues that if innovators are not going to be financially rewarded for their innovations, the incentive for path-breaking innovation will eventually dry up and so will the money for the really deep R & D that is required to drive progress in this increasingly complex field. Microsoft's success in creating the standard PC operating system produced the bankroll that allowed Microsoft to spend billions of dollars on R & D to develop Microsoft Office, a whole suite of applications that it can now sell for a couple hundred dollars. As Craig Mundie, the Microsoft chief technical officer, put it: "The virtuous cycle of innovation, reward, reinvestment, and more innovation is what has driven all big breakthroughs in our industry. The software business as we have known it is a scale economic business. You spend a ton of money up front to develop a software product, and then the marginal cost of producing each one is very small, but if you sell a lot of them, you make back your

investment and then plow profits back into developing the next generation. But when you insist that you cannot charge for software, you can
only give it away, you take the software business away from being a scale
economic business." He continued: "It is true that scientific research will
increasingly require more of a community effort, but I would argue this is
more of a requirement for multidisciplinary collaboration due to the complexity of the problems, rather than a belief that the fundamental insights
that lead to real innovation come from groups now rather than individuals. I believe that open-source will continue as a powerful trend but will
revert primarily to the intellectual commons model that has long been
with us in academia, rather than one that removes the financial incentive
to do software." As for Microsoft's founder Bill Gates, he too is obviously
convinced that the future of software is not in free. "You need capitalism
[to drive innovation]. To have [a movement] that says innovation does not
deserve an economic reward is contrary to where the world is going.
When I talk to the Chinese, they dream of starting a company. They are
not thinking, 'I will be a barber during the day and do free software at
night.' . . . When you have a security crisis in your [software] system, you
don't want to say, 'Where is the guy at the barbershop?'" Mundie also
points out that no matter what business you are in, "sooner or later you are
likely to find that without some proprietary software and IT system that
embodies and facilitates your core competency—the unique essence of
what you do—it is going to be very hard to gain and sustain an edge on
your competition in a world where everyone can get all the same free
software." Companies will want systems designed just for them that no
one else has or they will want IT tool kits to design things for themselves
that no one else has. As such, says Microsoft, there will still be plenty of
room for proprietary software systems. Finally, scale and scope do matter.
There is a big advantage to students and companies that you can go anywhere in the world today, fire up a computer, and find a standardized
Microsoft Word program to write your business report or essay on. I
would not want to have to wrestle with a different word processing program everywhere I went. That would not help work flow.

    But the reason I think community-developed software is also here to
stay is that while it may not be sustainable without an economic in-

centive at some point, as a sheer tool for making breakthroughs and spreading those breakthroughs virally, it has proved to be very powerful. Until 2004, the Linux operating system was the best-known open-source software challenging Microsoft. Then, in November 2004, the Mozilla Foundation, a nonprofit group supporting open-source software, released Firefox, a free, fast, easy-to-install Web browser loaded with features that Microsoft's Internet Explorer lacked. "Just over a month later," wrote *New York Times* technology writer Randall Stross (December 19, 2004), "the foundation celebrated a remarkable milestone: 10 million downloads." Donations from Firefox's appreciative new users paid for a two-page advertisement in *The New York Times*. "With Firefox," Stross added, "open-source software moves from back-office obscurity to your home, and to your parents', too. (Your children in college are already using it.) It is polished [and] as easy to use as Internet Explorer." By November 2005, its first anniversary, the Firefox browser had gobbled up roughly 10 percent of the worldwide browser market, most of it coming out of Microsoft Explorer's hide. One reason Firefox spread so fast is its community-development aspect: Users could contribute to how it developed, and many extensions that added specific new applications to the browser were written by users. By November 2005, a new souped-up version, Firefox 1.5, was on the march.

This explosive growth is quite amazing when you realize how Firefox came about. Firefox is actually a descendant of Mosaic and the original Netscape Navigator browser, which was overwhelmed by Microsoft Internet Explorer in 1998. While Firefox, like any other piece of open-source software, is the product of many different programmers' improvements and insights, noted *Wired* magazine (February 2005), "two people in particular are most responsible for the browser's success: Blake Ross, an angular hyper-kinetic 19-year-old Stanford sophomore with spikey black hair, and Ben Goodger, a stout, soft-spoken 24-year-old New Zealander. At age 14, Ross, logging on to his family's America Online account, started fixing bugs for the Mozilla Group, a cadre of programmers responsible for maintaining the source code of Netscape's browsers. Ross quickly became disenchanted with Netscape's feature creep [too many bells and whistles], and in 2002 he brashly decided to splinter off and develop a pared-down, fast, easy-to-use browser. Goodger . . . took the reins when Ross became a full-time college student in 2003. Goodger pulled the project's loose ends together and whipped the browser into shape for the release of Firefox 1.0 late last year [2004]."

So a nineteen-year-old from Stanford and a twenty-four-year-old from New Zealand, working in an open-source community for free, starting from two ends of the world, produced a browser that took 5 percent of the Internet Explorer market in about six months. I particularly liked what Ross told *Wired* about how it felt when he first started uploading, when he first started hacking away at Mozilla as a ninth grader: "It was incredible — just realizing that you can touch something that so many people use. It's a great feeling to make a little change to the code and then actually see the change in the window of a big famous product. You've caused something to happen in an application that's being used all over the world."

There is no better description of the allure of uploading — as opposed to just downloading.

Bottom line: The flattening of the world is producing another big shakeout in the software business. In time, I think we will see a new equilibrium emerge in which all the different forms of software will have a place: traditional commercial software, à la Microsoft or SAP, along with the Business Web model of rent-a-software, à la Salesforce.com, along with free software produced either by funded communities or by inspired individuals.

COMMUNITY-DEVELOPED ANSWERS

Brian Behlendorf, for his part, is betting his career that more and more people and companies will want to take advantage of the new flat-world platform to do community-developed innovation of all sorts of products. In 2004, he started a new company called CollabNet to promote the use of community development as a tool to drive software innovation within companies. What CollabNet does, for example, is to create a secure Web site, where those with a password can go and see the source code of the software and the defects that need to be addressed, and then participate in a discussion among engineers, product managers, and customer support on how the software should be improved. It is a totally flat, low-friction environment to enhance collaboration and overcome obstacles. "CollabNet is an arms dealer to the forces flattening the world," said Behlendorf. "Our role in this world is to build the tools and infrastructure so that an individual—in India, China, or wherever—as a consultant, an employee, or just someone sitting at home, can collaborate. We are giving them the tool kit for decentralized collaborative development. We are enabling bottom-up development, and not just in cyberspace." While CollabNet is primarily focused on how to enable a corporation to collaborate internally to produce its own open-source software and keep it fresh, there are a variety of businesses besides software that are now discovering what happens if you can tap the innovative power of the community. One creative variation on this open-source approach was the attempt a couple of years ago by a Canadian gold-mining company, Goldcorp Inc., to try to tap "all of us" to find its gold deposits. According to the June 2002 issue of *Fast Company*:

> In January 1848, a work crew at John Sutter's mill, near Sacramento, California, came across a few select nuggets of gold. Before long, a half-million prospectors arrived there seeking instant riches. The gold rush was on. Some 153 years later, another gold rush broke out at an old mine called Red Lake, in northwestern Ontario. This time, the fortune hunters wielded geological-modeling software and database mining tools rather than picks and shovels. The big winners were from Australia. And they had never even seen the mine.
>
> Rob McEwen, chairman and CEO of Goldcorp Inc., based in Toronto, had triggered the gold rush by issuing an extraordinary challenge to the world's geologists: We'll show you all of our data on the Red Lake mine online if you tell us where we're likely to find the next 6 million ounces of gold. The prize: a total of $575,000, with a top award of $105,000.

The mining community was flabbergasted. "We've seen very large data sets from government surveys online," says Nick Archibald, managing director of Fractal Graphics, the winning organization from West Perth, Australia. "But for a company to post that information and say, 'Here I am, warts and all,' is quite unusual indeed."

McEwen knew that the contest, which he called the Goldcorp Challenge, entailed big risks. For one thing, it exposed the company to a hostile-takeover bid. But the risks of continuing to do things the old way were even greater. "Mining is one of humanity's oldest industrial pursuits," McEwen says. "This is *old* old economy. But a mineral discovery is like a technological discovery. There's the same rapid creation of wealth as rising expectations improve profitability. If we could find gold faster, we could really improve the value of the company."

McEwen, a small, soft-spoken man with a neatly trimmed mustache and meticulous tailoring, had one big advantage over his slow-footed competitors: He wasn't a miner, he didn't think like a miner, and he wasn't constrained by a miner's conventional wisdom. As a young man, he went to work for Merrill Lynch, following his father into the investment business. But his father also had a fascination with gold, and McEwen grew up hearing tales of miners, prospectors, and grubstakes at the dinner table. Soon he was bitten by the gold bug too, and he hammered out a template of what he thought a 21st-century gold-mining company should look like. In 1989, he saw his chance. He stepped into a takeover battle as a white knight and emerged as majority owner of an old and underperforming mine in Ontario.

It was hardly a dream come true. The gold market was depressed. The mine's operating costs were high. The miners went on strike. McEwen even got a death threat. But the new owner knew that the mine had potential. "The Red Lake gold district had 2 operating gold mines and 13 former mines that had produced more than 18 million ounces combined," he says. "The mine next door had produced about 10 million ounces. Ours had produced only 3 million."

McEwen believed that the high-grade ore that ran through the neighboring mine was present in parts of the 55,000-acre Red Lake stake—if only he could find it. His strategy began to take shape at a seminar at MIT in 1999. Company presidents from around the world had come there to learn about advances in information technology. Eventually, the group's attention turned to the Linux operating system and the open-source revolution. "I said, 'Open-source code! That's what I want!'" McEwen recalls.

His reasoning: If he could attract the attention of world-class talent to the problem of finding more gold in Red Lake, just as Linux managed to attract world-class programmers to the cause of better software, he could tap into thousands of minds that he wouldn't normally have access to. He could also speed up exploration and improve his odds of discovery.

At first, Goldcorp's geologists were appalled at the idea of exposing their super-secret data to the world. "This is a very conservative, very private industry," says Dr. James M. Franklin, former chief geoscientist for the Geological Survey of Canada and a judge in the Goldcorp Challenge. "Confidentiality and secrecy about reserves and exploration have been its watchwords. This was a totally unconventional thing to do."

But in March 2000, at an industry meeting, McEwen unveiled the Goldcorp Challenge. The external response was immediate. More than 1,400 scientists, engineers, and geologists from 50 countries downloaded the company's data and started their virtual exploration. When the entries started coming in, the panel of five judges was astonished by the creativity of the submissions. The top winner was a collaboration by two groups in Australia: Fractal Graphics, in West Perth, and Taylor Wall & Associates, in Queensland, which together had developed a powerful 3-D graphical depiction of the mine.

For McEwen, the contest itself was a gold mine. "We have drilled four of the winners' top five targets and have hit on all four," he says. "But what's really important is that from a remote site, the winners were able to analyze a database and generate targets without ever visiting the property. It's clear that this is part of the future."

Between the new high-grade discoveries and the mine's modernized facilities, Red Lake is finally performing along the lines that McEwen had envisioned. In 1996, Red Lake was producing at an annual rate of 53,000 ounces at $360 an ounce. By 2001, the mine was producing 504,000 ounces at $59 an ounce.

As for the open-source miners who won the competition, *Fast Company* noted how much this opportunity meant for them as well:

Red Lake, Ontario and West Perth, Australia are at opposite ends of the earth. But that didn't stop Nick Archibald and his team of geologists at Fractal Graphics, an Australian geoscience consulting firm, from thinking that they could find gold in Canada.

First-place winners of the 2001 Goldcorp Challenge, Archibald and his mates shared a grand prize of $105,000 for their presentation detailing likely targets for finding gold. "I'd never been to the mine," Archibald says. "I'd never even been to Canada."

But when he learned of the contest, Archibald recognized an opportunity for his company, which specializes in the production of 3-D models of mines . . . Although the prize money, which Archibald's team shared with Taylor Wall & Associates, barely covered the cost of the project, the publicity has boosted the firm's business. "It would have taken us years to get the recognition in North America that this project gave us overnight," he says.

More important, Archibald adds, the Challenge has opened the industry's eyes to a new way of doing exploration. "This has been a big change for mining," he says. "This has been like a beacon in a sea of darkness."

BLOGGING: UPLOADING NEWS AND COMMENTARY

Soon after the community-developed software movement gained momentum, we witnessed the emergence of another bottom-up, self-organized form of uploading: blogging. I see this most vividly in my own profession, journalism, where bloggers, one-person online commentators, who often link to one another depending on their ideology, have created a kind of open-source newsroom. A blog is your own personal virtual soapbox, where you can get up every morning and, in the form of a column or a newsletter or just a screed, tell the world what you think about any subject, upload that content onto your own Web site, and then wait for the world to come check it out. If others like it, they will link to your blog from their blog or to other kinds of content, like online news articles or commentaries. I now read bloggers (the term comes from the word "Weblog") as part of my daily information-gathering routine. In an article about how a tiny group of relatively obscure news bloggers helped to blow the whistle that exposed the bogus documents used by CBS News's Dan Rather in his infamous report about President George W. Bush's Air National Guard service, Howard Kurtz of *The Washington Post* wrote (September 20, 2004), "It was like throwing a match on kerosene-soaked wood. The ensuing blaze ripped through the media establishment as previously obscure bloggers managed to put the network of Murrow and Cronkite firmly on the defensive. The secret, says [Web designer and blogger] Charles Johnson, is 'open-source intelligence gathering.' Meaning: 'We've got a huge pool of highly motivated people who go out there and use tools to find stuff. We've got an army of citizen journalists out there.'"

That army is often armed with nothing more than a tape recorder, a camera-enabled cell phone, and a Web site, but in a flat world it can collectively get its voice heard as far and wide as CBS or *The New York Times*. These bloggers have created their own online commons, with no barriers to entry. That open commons often has many rumors and wild allegations swirling in it. Because no one is in charge, standards of practice vary wildly, and some of it is downright irresponsible. But because no one is in charge, information flows with total freedom. And when this community is onto something real, like the Rather episode, it can create as much energy, buzz, and hard news as any network or major newspaper.

A new blog is created every seven seconds, according to Technorati.com, a site that tracks these easily updated Web journals. Technorati says there are more than twenty-four million blogs already, and the number is growing at about seventy thousand a day and doubling every five months—from Iraqi bloggers, who give their own take on news from the front, to bloggers who follow and critique golf course architecture, to poker bloggers, investment bloggers, to just plain you and me bloggers.

Mark Glaser, a freelance writer based in San Francisco, writing for the Web site YaleGlobal Online (July 28, 2005), noted that on July 7, the day of the London underground bombings, the BBC Web site invited viewers and listeners to send in photos of what they had seen. "In 24 hours," he wrote, "the site received 20,000 written accounts via e-mail, 1,000 photos, and 20 videos. One of the site's main images that day was an amateur photo of the scene of the double-decker bus bombing. The BBC, the *Guardian*, and MSNBC.com were among the big media sites that walked the walk of citizen journalism, allowing their readers to become contributors on a moment's notice—with zero journalistic training." The BBC was both harnessing the power of uploading and channeling it into useful editorial content.

The BBC's willingness to open itself to bloggers shows both the strength and weakness of blogging, and why it is still not clear how it will affect traditional journalism. Who can digest twenty thousand blogs in twenty-four hours? You cannot drink your news from a fire hose. It is just too overwhelming. So, as with software, what we are likely to see are more blended approaches, in which traditional news organizations absorb, filter, and select the best from the blogosphere, and blend it with their more traditionally edited news. (Today, major corporations, such as General Electric, monitor and respond daily to what the blogs are saying about them.) It is impossible to imagine what it is going to be like in ten years when virtually everyone you know has a blog. But that is where we are heading. If you look at the Facebook.com phenomenon, an online social directory spreading virally in high schools and colleges, millions of young people now have a platform for telling their own stories.

"The next generation is growing up online, rather than adapting to it in their mid-adult years," Micah Sifry, an analyst of the intersection between technology and politics, wrote in *The Nation* (November 22, 2004). "More than 2 million children aged 6–17 have their own Web site, according to a December 2003 survey by Grunwald Associates. Twenty-nine percent of kids in grades K–3 have their own e-mail address. Josh Koenig, one of the twenty-somethings who cut their teeth at the Dean campaign and now a co-founder of Music for America, says, 'We're only seeing the first drips of what is going to be a downpour.' When he told me that in most high schools in America, students are using the Web to rank their teachers, I thought that was a bit of hyperbole. But then I discovered RateMyTeachers.com, where more than 6 million ratings have been posted by students on more than 900,000 teachers at 40,000 American and Canadian middle and high schools. That's almost triple the number from one year ago, covering about 85% of all the schools in both countries . . . The future is in their hands, though the rest of us will be taken along for the ride."

The audio version of blogging, known as "podcasting," has really taken off. The phenomenon evolved with Apple's wildly popular hand-held audio player, the iPod. Podcasts involve individuals and companies producing their own audio and video files—music, commentary, books, poetry readings, singing recitals, anything you can imagine that can be done by voice or video—which can then be uploaded onto platforms, like Apple iTunes. These podcasts are then downloaded by users or subscribers, who listen to them or watch them on their computer, iPod, MP3 player, cell phone, or other portable device. Podcasting is having a big impact on traditional music and video companies and radio stations, because so many people now have the power to become video and music producers, not just passive listeners and viewers.

The video-sharing site YouTube illustrates just how popular uploading has become. YouTube was founded by some former employees of PayPal in February 2005, just after the first edition of this book was completed. In October 2006, not long after the second edition of this book came out, YouTube was sold to Google for $1.65 billion. The YouTube Web site enables users to upload, view, and share videos, parts of movies,

TV clips, music videos, lectures, or comic performances made by themselves or others. In effect, it enables any amateur to become a network or movie studio and develop a following. And, indeed, some YouTube artists now have huge audiences.

It would be impossible to catalog all the uses of YouTube (even terrorist organizations are now using it to spread their messages). My favorites are those that underscore just how much uploading is empowering the little guys and gals. Consider the following story from *The New York Times Magazine* (December 10, 2006): "As long as there have been personal fouls and holding penalties, sports fans have vilified referees for making bad calls. But in recent years, criticizing the officials of the major professional and college sports has evolved from a crude art form—'Ref, if you had one more eye you'd be a cyclops! Go back to Foot Locker!'—to an efficient science. Instant replay and multiple camera angles have exposed even the tiniest officiating errors. And with the rise of YouTube, sophisticated methods of scrutinizing, publicizing and condemning those errors have emerged. These days, just hours after the end of a game marred by questionable officiating, fans of the aggrieved team take to the Web, collecting clips of bad calls and stringing them together into short videos. Sometimes a single egregious error is isolated and repeated over and over—a shaming strategy that has a certain heavy-handed and humiliating power. Many of the clips use slow-motion analysis, a feature that led a writer at *Slate* magazine to dub the genre 'the YouTube Zapruder film.' The most persuasive videos are those that edit down the footage of an entire game to only its controversial calls. A few minutes of watching how seemingly every decision in Game 5 of the Dallas Mavericks–Houston Rockets playoff series last year was overly generous to Dallas can turn even the most indifferent observer into a conspiracy theorist. The officiating blunder that seemed to inspire the most videos this year was the fourth-quarter onside kick that helped decide the Oregon-Oklahoma football game. While Oregon was judged to have recovered the ball, the replay clearly shows that the call should have favored Oklahoma. The response on YouTube was swift and vitriolic. 'Cheaters!' was the title of one video. Another was called 'The Officiating That Changed My Philosophy on Life.' Sports leagues have started to fight back. The NFL recently asked

YouTube to take down thousands of videos containing footage of its games, including many that were critical of the officiating."

WIKIPEDIA: COMMUNITY-UPLOADED CONTENT

Another form of uploaded community development that I used regularly in writing this book is Wikipedia, the user-contributed online encyclopedia, also known as "the people's encyclopedia." The word "wiki" is taken from the Hawaiian word for "quick." Wikis are Web sites that allow users to directly edit any Web page on their own from their home computer. In a May 5, 2004, essay on YaleGlobal Online, Andrew Lih, an assistant professor at the Journalism and Media Studies Centre at the University of Hong Kong, explained how Wikipedia works and why it is such a breakthrough.

"The Wikipedia project was started by Jimmy Wales, head of Internet startup Bomis.com, after his original project for a volunteer, but strictly controlled, free encyclopedia ran out of money and resources after two years," wrote Lih. "Editors with Ph.D. degrees were at the helm of the project then, but it produced only a few hundred articles. Not wanting the content to languish, Wales placed the pages on a wiki Web site in January 2001 and invited any Internet visitors to edit or add to the collection. The site became a runaway success in the first year and gained a loyal following, generating over 20,000 articles and spawning over a dozen language translations."

How, you might ask, does one produce a credible, balanced encyclopedia by way of an ad hoc open-source, open-editing movement? After all, every article in the Wikipedia has an "Edit this page" button, allowing anyone who surfs along to add or delete content on that page. Its success starts with the fact, Lih explained, that "because wikis provide the ability to track the status of articles, review individual changes, and discuss issues, they function as social software. Wiki Web sites also track and store every modification made to an article, so no operation is ever permanently destructive. Wikipedia works by consensus, with users adding and modifying content while trying to reach common ground along the way.

"However, the technology is not enough on its own," wrote Lih. "Wales created an editorial policy of maintaining a neutral point of view (NPOV) as the guiding principle . . . According to Wikipedia's guidelines, 'The neutral point of view attempts to present ideas and facts in such a fashion that both supporters and opponents can agree . . .' As a result, articles on contentious issues such as globalization have benefited from the cooperative and global nature of Wikipedia. Over the last two years, the entry has had more than 90 edits by contributors from the Netherlands, Belgium, Sweden, United Kingdom, Australia, Brazil, United States, Malaysia, Japan and China. It provides a manifold view of issues from the World Trade Organization and multinational corporations to the anti-globalization movement and threats to cultural diversity." A *Newsweek* piece on Wikipedia (November 1, 2004) quoted Angela Beesley, a volunteer contributor from Essex, England, and self-confessed Wikipedia addict who monitors the accuracy of more than one thousand entries: "A collaborative encyclopedia sounds like a crazy idea, but it naturally controls itself."

It certainly sells itself. By the end of 2005, Wikipedia was getting 2.5 billion page views a month, which made it one of the most visited reference sites on the Web, along with Dictionary.com. I am sure you thought it was great when you were growing up and the *Encyclopaedia Britannica* salesperson came to your door, showing off those big books. I sure did. Then you really thought it was cool when you got your first copy of Encarta with Microsoft Windows and could click on to your own encyclopedia. The online ad for the latest edition of Encarta reads as follows: "Microsoft Encarta Standard 2006 is the number-one best-selling encyclopedia brand. It's a source you can trust for exploring a world of knowledge that's accurate, engaging, and up to date—with over 36,000 articles, tens of thousands of pictures and sound clips, videos, animations, games, maps, and more." Do you know how many articles there are in Wikipedia, the uploaded encyclopedia? As I write these words on November 29, 2005, the Wikipedia.org Web site reported: "In this English version, started in 2001, we are currently working on 841,358 articles"—and counting. And Wales is just getting started. He has expanded into Wiktionary, a dictionary and thesaurus; Wikibooks, digital textbooks and manuals; Wikiquote, an online "book" of quotations; Wikispecies, a cyber-directory of species; and, of course, Wikinews, the free-content news source that you can write and upload yourself.

Wikipedia, though, is not all sweetness and light, and it does not always control itself. When the people can upload their own encyclopedia, lots of things can happen, and not all of them good. Your enemies can use it as a global poster board to smear your name if they want, and it can take time to sort out. John Seigenthaler Sr., the founding editorial director of USA Today and founder of the Freedom Forum First Amendment Center at Vanderbilt University, woke up one morning and found his bio on Wikipedia as follows: "John Seigenthaler Sr. was the assistant to Attorney General Robert Kennedy in the early 1960's. For a brief time, he was thought to have been directly involved in the Kennedy assassinations of both John, and his brother, Bobby. Nothing was ever proven."

He was not amused. That bio entry was being read and repeated all over the world. On November 29, 2005, he wrote the following in an op-ed piece in USA Today:

This is a highly personal story about Internet character assassination. It could be your story.

I have no idea whose sick mind conceived the false, malicious "biography" that appeared under my name for 132 days on Wikipedia, the popular, online, free encyclopedia whose authors are unknown and virtually untraceable. There was more:

"John Seigenthaler moved to the Soviet Union in 1971, and returned to the United States in 1984," Wikipedia said. "He started one of the country's largest public relations firms shortly thereafter."

At age 78, I thought I was beyond surprise or hurt at anything negative said about me. I was wrong. One sentence in the biography was true. I was Robert Kennedy's administrative assistant in the early 1960s. I also was his pallbearer. It was mind-boggling when my son, John Seigenthaler, journalist with NBC News, phoned later to say he found the same scurrilous text on Reference.com and Answers.com.

I had heard for weeks from teachers, journalists and historians about "the wonderful world of Wikipedia," where millions of people worldwide visit daily for quick reference "facts," composed and posted by people with no special expertise or knowledge — and sometimes by people with malice.

At my request, executives of the three websites now have removed the false content about me. But they don't know, and can't find out, who wrote the toxic sentences.

I phoned Jimmy Wales, Wikipedia's founder, and asked, "Do you . . . have any way to know who wrote that?"

"No, we don't," he said. Representatives of the other two websites said their computers are programmed to copy data verbatim from Wikipedia, never checking whether it is false or factual . . .

We live in a universe of new media with phenomenal opportunities for worldwide communications and research — but populated by volunteer vandals with poison-pen intellects. Congress has enabled them and protects them.

When I was a child, my mother lectured me on the evils of "gossip." She held a feather pillow and said, "If I tear this open, the feathers will fly to the four winds, and I could never get them back in the pillow. That's how it is when you spread mean things about people."

For me, that pillow is a metaphor for Wikipedia.

I like Wikipedia. I have used it in writing this book. But I use it with the knowledge that the community is not always right, the network doesn't always self-correct—certainly not as fast as its errors can get spread. It is not an accident that IBM today has a senior staffer who polices Wikipedia's references to IBM and makes sure that everything that gets in there is correct. More young people will learn about IBM from Wikipedia in coming years than from IBM itself.

HOW FAR CAN UPLOADING GO?

My bottom line is this: Uploading, by individuals or communities, is already a huge flattener. It is spreading because the flat-world platform that makes it possible is spreading and because uploading responds to a very deep human longing for individuals to participate and make their voices heard. *New York Times* reporter Seth Schiesel wrote a telling piece in this regard (June 21, 2005), in which he noted that growing numbers of young men "would rather play a sports video game than watch the real thing on television." He pointed out that since 2000, sales of sports video games in the United States have risen by 34 percent, to $1.2 billion in 2004, while television broadcast ratings for almost all major sports have fallen among male viewers between twelve and thirty-four. But what struck me most about the article was a quote Schiesel had from a young man who loved to play the NBA-branded video basketball games, in which you can control when the players (patterned after actual NBA players) pass and shoot: "'I like Kobe, O.K.?' Albert Arce said, referring to Kobe Bryant, the Los Angeles Lakers star. 'But I like to play him because I can make him pass to the other guys. When I see him on TV, it's like he doesn't know how to pass.'"

He would rather play Kobe than watch Kobe! That attitude, says Micah Sifry, "is indicative of the larger shift in the Internet age away from a static and passive approach to media to an active and participatory approach. It is more fun to be in the game than to watch the game." Tim O'Reilly, the founder and CEO of O'Reilly Media, one of the world's premier computer book publishers, has his own way of describing the uploading phenomenon. He calls it the "architecture of participation"—systems that are designed for users to produce, not just consume. He suggests that the companies that design their software, their systems, their Web sites, and their encyclopedias to encourage participation will be the ones that draw the most users.

People like to upload, and that is why of all the ten forces flattening the world, uploading has the potential to be the most disruptive. Just how many people will exercise that ability to be in the game, and how soon, is what will determine just how disruptive uploading becomes.

"The act of participating is like a muscle you have to use," noted Sifry, "and we are so unused to being active participants in the process that even though the tools are there now many people don't use them . . . There are also still deeply ingrained habits of deference to authority and institutions." In short, the number of uploaders is still relatively small. But as the tools for individual uploading and collaboration become more diffused, and as more and more people get positive feedback from their uploading experiences, I am certain every big institution or hierarchical structure will feel the effects.

You have been warned.

FLATTENER #5
OUTSOURCING
Y2K

India has had its ups and downs since it achieved independence on August 15, 1947, but in some ways it might be remembered as the luckiest country in the history of the late twentieth century.

Until recently, India was what is known in the banking world as "the second buyer." You always want to be the second buyer in business—the person who buys the hotel or the golf course or the shopping mall after the first owner has gone bankrupt and its assets are being sold by the bank at ten cents on the dollar. Well, the first buyers of all the cable laid by all those fiber-optic cable companies—which thought they were going to get endlessly rich in an endlessly expanding digital universe—were their American shareholders. When the bubble burst, they were left holding either worthless or much diminished stock. The Indians, in effect, got to be the second buyers of the fiber-optics companies.

They didn't actually purchase the shares—they just benefited from the overcapacity in fiber optics, which meant that they and their American clients got to use all that cable practically for free. This was a huge stroke of luck for India (and to a lesser degree for China, the former Soviet Union, and Eastern Europe), because what is the history of modern India? While India certainly had natural resources to mine (coal, iron ore, diamonds), with so many mouths to feed, it couldn't just live off them—not even close. So instead India mined the brains of its own people, educating a relatively large slice of its elites in the sciences, engineering, and medicine. In 1951, to his enduring credit, Jawaharlal Nehru, India's first prime minister, set up the first of India's seven Indian Institutes of Technology (IIT) in the eastern city of Kharagpur. In the fifty-five years since then, hundreds of thousands of Indians have competed to gain entry and then graduate from these IITs and their private-sector equivalents (as well as the six Indian Institutes of Management, which teach business administration). Given India's one-billion-plus population, this competition produces a phenomenal knowledge meritocracy. It's like a factory, churning out and exporting some of the most gifted engineering, computer science, and software talent on the globe.

This, alas, was one of the few things India did right. Because its often dysfunctional political system, coupled with Nehru's preference for pro-Soviet, Socialist economics, ensured that up until the mid-1990s India could not provide good jobs for most of those talented engineers. So America got to be the second buyer of India's brainpower! If you were a smart, educated Indian, the only way you could fulfill your potential was by leaving the country and, ideally, going to America, where some twenty-five thousand graduates of India's top engineering schools have settled since 1953, greatly enriching America's knowledge pool thanks to their education, which was subsidized by Indian taxpayers.

"The IITs became islands of excellence by not allowing the general debasement of the Indian system to lower their exacting standards," noted *The Wall Street Journal* (April 16, 2003). "You couldn't bribe your way to get into an IIT . . . Candidates are accepted only if they pass a grueling entrance exam. The government does not interfere with the curriculum, and the workload is demanding . . . Arguably, it is harder to get into an IIT than into Harvard or the Massachusetts Institute of Technology . . . IIT alumnus Vinod Khosla, who co-founded Sun Microsystems, said: 'When I finished IIT Delhi and went to Carnegie Mellon for my Masters, I thought I was cruising all the way because it was so easy relative to the education I got at IIT.'"

For most of their first fifty years, these IITs were one of the greatest bargains America ever had. It was as if someone installed a brain drain that filled up in New Delhi and emptied in Palo Alto. Roughly one of four IIT grads ended up in the United States—so many that the American IIT expats have their own organization in the United States and hold an annual convention here.

And then along came Netscape, the 1996 telecom deregulation, and Global Crossing and its fiber-optic friends. The world got flattened and that whole deal got turned on its head. "India had no resources and no infrastructure," said Dinakar Singh, one of the most respected young hedge fund managers on Wall Street, whose parents graduated from an IIT and then immigrated to America, where he was born. "It produced people with quality and by quantity. But many of them rotted on the docks of India like vegetables. Only a relative few could get on ships and get out. Not anymore, because we built this ocean crosser, called fiber-optic cable . . . For decades you had to leave India to be a professional . . . Now you can plug into the world from India. You don't have to go to Yale and go to work for Goldman Sachs [as I did.]"

India could never have afforded to pay for the bandwidth to connect brainy India with high-tech America, so American shareholders paid for it. Sure, overinvestment can be good. The overinvestment in railroads turned out to be a great boon for the American economy. "But the railroad overinvestment was confined to your own country and so too were the benefits," said Singh. In the case of the digital railroads, "it was the foreigners who benefited." India got to ride for free.

It is fun to talk to Indians who were around at precisely the moment when American companies started to discover they could draw on India's brainpower in India. One of them is Vivek Paul, now the president of Wipro, the Indian software giant. "In many ways the Indian information technology [outsourcing] revolution began with General Electric coming over. We're talking the late 1980s and early '90s. At the time, Texas Instruments was doing some chip design in India. Some of their key designers [in America] were Indians, and they basically let them go back home and work from there [using the rather crude communications networks that existed then to stay in touch]. At that time, I was heading up the operations for GE Medical Systems in Bangalore. [GE's chairman] Jack Welch came to India in 1989 and was completely taken by India as a source of intellectual advantage for GE. Jack would say, 'India is a developing country with a developed intellectual capability.' He saw a talent pool that could be leveraged. So he said, 'We spend a lot of money doing software. Couldn't we do some work for our IT department here?'" Because India had closed its market to foreign technology companies, like IBM, Indian companies had started their own factories to make PCs and servers, and Welch felt that if they could do it for themselves, they could do it for GE.

To pursue the project, Welch sent a team headed by GE's chief information officer over to India to check out the possibilities. Paul was also filling in as GE's business development manager for India at the time. "So it was my job to escort the corporate CIO, in early 1990, on his first trip," he recalled. "They had come with some pilot projects to get the ball rolling. I remember in the middle of the night going to pick them up at the Delhi airport with a caravan of Indian cars, Ambassadors, based on a very dated 1950s Morris Minor design. Everyone in the government drove one. So we had a five-car caravan and we were driving back from the airport to town. I was in the back car, and at one point we heard this loud bang, and I thought, What happened? I shot to the front, and the lead car's hood had flown off and smashed the windshield—with these GE people inside! So this whole caravan of GE execs pulls over to the side of the road, and I could just hear them saying to themselves, 'This is the place we're going to get software from?'"

Fortunately for India, the GE team was not discouraged by the poor quality of Indian cars. GE decided to sink roots, starting a joint development project with Wipro. Other companies were trying different models. But this was still pre-fiber-optic days. Simon & Schuster, the book publisher, for instance, would ship its books over to India and pay Indians $50 a month (compared to $1,000 a month in the United States) to type them by hand into computers, converting the books into digitized electronic files that could be edited or amended easily in the future—

particularly dictionaries, which constantly need updating. In 1991, Manmohan Singh, then India's finance minister, began opening the Indian economy for foreign investment and introducing competition into the Indian telecom industry to bring down prices. To attract more foreign investment, Singh made it much easier for companies to set up satellite downlink stations in Bangalore, so they could skip over the Indian phone system and connect with their home bases in America, Europe, or Asia. Before then, only Texas Instruments had been willing to brave the Indian bureaucracy, becoming the first multinational to establish a circuit design and development center in India in 1985. TI's center in Bangalore had its own satellite downlink but had to suffer through having an Indian government official to oversee it—with the right to examine any piece of data going in or out. Singh loosened all those reins post-1991. A short time later, in 1994, HealthScribe India, a company originally funded in part by Indian-American doctors, was set up in Bangalore to do outsourced medical transcription for American doctors and hospitals. Those doctors at the time were taking handwritten notes and then dictating them into a Dictaphone for a secretary or someone else to transcribe, which would usually take days or weeks. HealthScribe set up a system that turned a doctor's touch-tone phone into a dictation machine. The doctor would punch in a number and simply dictate his notes to a PC with a voice card in it, which would digitize his voice. He could be sitting anywhere when he did it. Thanks to the satellite, a housewife or student in Bangalore could go into a computer and download that doctor's digitized voice and transcribe it—not in two weeks but in two hours. Then this person would zip it right back by satellite as a text file that could be put into the hospital's computer system and become part of the billing file. Because of the twelve-hour time difference with India, Indians could do the transcription while the American doctors were sleeping, and the file would be ready and waiting the next morning. This was an important breakthrough for companies, because if you could safely, legally, and securely transcribe from Bangalore medical records, lab reports, and doctors' diagnoses—in one of the most litigious industries in the world—a lot of other industries could think about sending some of their backroom work to be done in India as well. And they did. But it remained limited by what could be handled by satellite, where there was a voice delay. (Ironically, said Gurujot Singh Khalsa, one of the founders of HealthScribe, they initially explored having Indians in Maine—that is, American Indians—do this work, using some of the federal money earmarked for the tribes to get started, but they could never get them interested enough to put the deal together.) The cost of doing the transcription in India was about one-fifth the cost per line of doing it in the United States, a difference that got a lot of people's attention.

By the late 1990s, though, Lady Luck was starting to shine on India from two directions: The fiber-optic bubble was starting to inflate, linking India with the United States, and the Y2K computer crisis—the so-called millennium bug—started gathering on the horizon. As you'll remember, the Y2K bug was a result of the fact that when computers were built, they came with internal clocks. In order to save memory space, these clocks rendered dates with just six digits—two for the day, two for the month, and, you guessed it, two for the year. That meant they could go up to only 12/31/99. So when the calendar hit January 1, 2000, many older computers were poised to register that not as 01/01/2000 but as 01/01/00, and they would think it was 1900 all over again. It meant that a huge number of existing computers (newer ones were being made with better clocks) needed to have their internal clocks and related systems adjusted; otherwise, it was feared, they would shut down, creating a global crisis, given how many different management systems—from water to air traffic control—were computerized.

This computer remediation work was a huge, tedious job. Who in the world had enough software engineers to do it all? Answer: India, with all the techies from all those IITs and private technical colleges and computer schools.

And so with Y2K bearing down on us, America and India started dating, and that relationship became a huge flattener, because it demonstrated to so many different businesses that the combination of the PC, the Internet, and fiber-optic cable had created the possibility of a whole new form of collaboration and horizontal value creation: outsourcing. Any service, call center, business support operation, or knowledge work that could be digitized could be sourced globally to the cheapest, smartest, most efficient provider. Using fiber-optic-cable-connected workstations, Indian techies could get under the hood of your company's computers and do all the adjustments, even though they were located halfway around the world.

"[Y2K upgrading] was tedious work that was not going to give them an enormous competitive advantage," said Vivek Paul, the Wipro executive, whose company did some outsourced Y2K drudge work. "So all these Western companies were incredibly challenged to find someone else who would do it and do it for as little money as possible. They said, 'We just want to get past the damn year 2000!' So they started to work with Indian [technology] companies who they might not have worked with otherwise."

To use my parlance, they were ready to go on a blind date with India. They were ready to get "fixed up." Added Jerry Rao, "Y2K means different things to different people. For Indian industry, it represented the biggest opportunity. India was considered as a place of backward people. Y2K suddenly required that every single computer in the world needed to be reviewed. And the sheer number of people needed to review line-by-line code existed in India. The Indian IT industry got its footprint across the globe because of Y2K. Y2K became our engine of growth, our engine of being known around the world. We never looked back after Y2K."

By early 2000, the Y2K work started to wind down, but then a whole new driver of business emerged—e-commerce. The dot-com bubble had not yet burst, engineering talent was scarce, and demand from dot-coms was enormous. Said Paul, "People wanted what they felt were mission-critical applications, key to their very existence, to be done, and they could go nowhere else. So they turned to the Indian companies, and as they turned to the Indian companies they found that they were getting delivery of complex systems, with great quality, sometimes better than what they were getting from others. That created an enormous respect for Indian IT providers. And if [Y2K work] was the acquaintanceship process, this was the falling-in-love process."

Outsourcing from America to India, as a new form of collaboration, exploded. By just stringing a fiber-optic line from a workstation in

Bangalore to my company's mainframe, I could have Indian IT firms like Wipro, Infosys, and Tata Consulting Services managing my e-commerce and mainframe applications.

"Once we're in the mainframe business and once we're in e-commerce—now we're married," said Paul. But again, India was lucky that it could exploit all that undersea fiber-optic cable. "I had an office very close to the Leela Palace hotel in Bangalore," Paul added. "I was working with a factory located in the information technology park in Whitefield, a suburb of Bangalore, and I *could not get a local telephone line between our office and the factory.* Unless you paid a bribe, you could not get a line, and we wouldn't pay. So my phone call to Whitefield would go from my office in Bangalore to Kentucky, where there was a GE mainframe computer we were working with, and then from Kentucky to Whitefield. We used our own fiber-optic lease line that ran across the ocean—but the one across town required a bribe."

India didn't benefit only from the dot-com boom; it benefited even more from the dot-com bust! That is the real irony. The boom laid the cable that connected India to the world, and the bust made the cost of using it virtually free and also vastly increased the number of American companies that would want to use that fiber-optic cable to outsource knowledge work to India.

Y2K led to this mad rush for Indian brainpower to get the programming work done. The Indian companies were good and cheap, but price wasn't first on customers' minds—getting the work done was, and India was the only place with the volume of workers to do it. Then the dot-com boom comes along right in the wake of Y2K, and India is one of the few places where you can find surplus English-speaking engineers, at any price, because all of those in America have been scooped up by e-commerce companies. Then the dot-com bubble bursts, the stock market tanks, and the pool of investment capital dries up. American IT companies that survived the boom and venture capital firms that still wanted to fund start-ups had much less cash to spend. Now they needed those Indian engineers not just because there were a lot of them, but precisely because they were low-cost. So the relationship between India and the American business community intensified another notch.

One of the great mistakes made by many analysts in the early 2000s was conflating the dot-com boom with globalization, suggesting that both were just fads and hot air. When the dot-com bust came along, these same wrongheaded analysts assumed that globalization was over as well. Exactly the opposite was true. The dot-com bubble was only one aspect of globalization, and when it imploded, rather than imploding globalization, it actually turbocharged it.

Promod Haque, an Indian American and one of the most prominent venture capitalists in Silicon Valley with his firm Norwest Venture Partners, was in the middle of this transition. "When the bust took place, a lot of these Indian engineers in the U.S. [on temporary work visas] got laid off, so they went back to India," explained Haque. But as a result of the bust, the IT budgets of virtually every major U.S. firm got slashed. "Every IT manager was told to get the same amount of work or more done with less money. So guess what he does? He says, 'You remember Vijay from India who used to work here during the boom and then went back home? Let me call him over in Bangalore and see if he will do the work for us for less money than what we would pay an engineer here in the U.S.'" And thanks to all that fiber cable laid during the boom, it was easy to find Vijay and put him to work.

The Y2K computer readjustment work was done largely by low-skilled Indian programmers right out of tech schools, said Haque, "but the guys on visas who were coming to America were not trade school guys. They were guys with advanced engineering degrees. So a lot of our companies saw that these guys were good at Java and C++ and architectural design work for computers, and then they got laid off and went back home, and the IT manager back here who is told, 'I don't care how you get the job done, just get it done for less money,' calls Vijay." Once America and India were dating, the burgeoning Indian IT companies in Bangalore started coming up with their own proposals. The Y2K work had allowed them to interact with some pretty large companies in the United States, and as a result they began to understand the pain points and how to do business-process implementation and improvement. So the Indians, who were doing a lot of very specific custom code maintenance to higher-value-add companies, started to develop their own products and transform themselves from maintenance to product companies, offering a range of software services and consulting. This took Indian companies much deeper inside American ones, and business-process outsourcing—letting Indians run your back room—went to a whole new level. "I have an accounts payable department and I could move this whole thing to India under Wipro or Infosys and cut my costs in half," said Haque. All across America, CEOs were saying, "'Make it work for less,'" he added. "And the Indian companies were saying, 'I have taken a look under your hood and I will provide you with a total solution for the lowest price.'" In other words, the Indian outsourcing companies said, "Do you remember how I fixed your tires and your pistons during Y2K? Well, I could actually give you a whole lube job if you like. And now that you know me and trust me, you know I can do it." To their credit, the Indians were not just cheap, they were also hungry and ready to learn anything.

The scarcity of capital after the dot-com bust made venture capital firms see to it that the companies they were investing in were finding the most efficient, high-quality, low-price way to innovate. In the boom times, said Haque, it was not uncommon for a $50 million investment in a start-up to return $500 million once the company went public. After the bust, that same company's public offering might bring in only $100 million. Therefore, venture firms wanted to risk only $20 million to get that company from start-up to IPO.

"For venture firms," said Haque, "the big question became, How do I get my entrepreneurs and their new companies to a point where they are breaking even or profitable sooner, so they can stop being a draw on my capital and be sold so our firm can *generate good liquidity and returns*? The answer many firms came up with was: I better start outsourcing as many functions as I can from the beginning. I have to make money for my investors faster, so what can be outsourced must be outsourced."

Henry Schacht, who was heading Lucent during part of this period, saw the whole process from the side of corporate management. The business economics, he told me, became "very ugly" for everyone. Everyone found prices flat to declining and markets stagnant, yet they were still spending huge amounts of money running the backroom operations of their companies, which they could no longer afford. "Cost pressures were enormous," he recalled, "and the flat world was available, [so] economics were forcing people to do things they never thought they would do or could do . . . Globalization got supercharged"—for both knowledge work and manufacturing. Companies found that they could go to MIT and find four incredibly smart Chinese engineers who were ready to go back to China and work for them from there for the same amount that it would cost them to hire one engineer in America. Bell Labs had a research facility at Tsingdao that could connect to Lucent's computers in America. "They would use our computers overnight," said Schacht. "Not only was the incremental computing cost close to zero, but so too was the transmission cost, and the computer was idle [at night]."

For all these reasons I believe that Y2K should be a national holiday in India, a second Indian Independence Day, in addition to August 15. As Johns Hopkins foreign policy expert Michael Mandelbaum, who spent part of his youth in India, put it, "Y2K should be called Indian Interdependence Day," because it was India's ability to collaborate with Western companies, thanks to the interdependence created by fiber-optic networks, that really vaulted it forward and gave more Indians than ever some real freedom of choice in how, for whom, and where they worked.

To put it another way, August 15 commemorates freedom at midnight. Y2K made possible *employment* at midnight—but not any employment, employment for India's best knowledge workers. August 15 gave independence to *India*. But Y2K gave independence to *Indians*—not all, by any stretch of the imagination, but a lot more than fifty years ago, and many of them from the most productive segment of the population. In that sense, yes, India was lucky, but it also reaped what it had sowed through hard work and education and the wisdom of its elders who built all those IITs.

Louis Pasteur said it a long time ago: "Fortune favors the prepared mind."

FLATTENER #6

OFFSHORING
Running with Gazelles, Eating with Lions

On December 11, 2001, China formally joined the World Trade Organization, which meant Beijing agreed to follow the same global rules governing imports, exports, and foreign investments that most countries in the world were following. It meant China was agreeing, in principle, to make its own competitive playing field as level as the rest of the world. A few days later, the American-trained Chinese manager of a fuel pump factory in Beijing, which was owned by a friend of mine, Jack Perkowski, the chairman and CEO of ASIMCO Technologies, an American auto parts manufacturer in China, posted the following African proverb, translated into Mandarin, on his factory floor:

Every morning in Africa, a gazelle wakes up.
It knows it must run faster than the fastest lion or it will be killed.
Every morning a lion wakes up.
It knows it must outrun the slowest gazelle or it will starve to death.
It doesn't matter whether you are a lion or a gazelle.
When the sun comes up, you better start running.

I don't know who is the lion and who is the gazelle, but I do know this: Ever since the Chinese joined the WTO, both they and the rest of the world have had to run faster and faster. This is because China's joining the WTO gave a huge boost to another form of collaboration—offshoring. Offshoring, which has been around for decades, is different from outsourcing. Outsourcing means taking some specific, but limited, function that your company was doing in-house—such as research, call centers, or accounts receivable—and having another company perform that exact same function for you and then reintegrating their work back into your overall operation. Offshoring, by contrast, is when a company takes one of its factories that it is operating in Canton, Ohio, and moves the whole factory offshore to Canton, China. There, it produces the very same product in the very same way, only with cheaper labor, lower taxes, subsidized energy, and lower health-care costs. Just as Y2K took India and the world to a whole new level of outsourcing, China's joining the WTO took Beijing and the world to a whole new level of offshoring—with more companies shifting production offshore and then integrating it into their global supply chains.

In 1977, Chinese leader Deng Xiaoping put China on the road to capitalism, declaring later that "to get rich is glorious." When China first opened its tightly closed economy, companies in industrialized countries saw it as an incredible new market for exports. Every Western or Asian manufacturer dreamed of selling its equivalent of one billion pairs of underwear to a single market. Some foreign companies set up shop in China to do just that. But because China was not subject to world trade rules, it was able to restrict the penetration into its market by these Western companies through various trade and investment barriers. And when it was not doing that deliberately, the sheer bureaucratic and cultural difficulties of doing business in China had the same effect. Many of the pioneer investors in China lost their shirts and pants *and underwear*—and with China's Wild West legal system there was not much recourse.

Beginning in the 1980s, many investors, particularly overseas Chinese who knew how to operate in China, started to say, "Well, if we can't sell that many things to the Chinese right now, why don't we use China's disciplined labor pool to make things there and sell them abroad?" This dovetailed with the interests of China's leaders. China wanted to attract foreign manufacturers and their technologies—not simply to manufacture one billion pairs of underwear for sale in China but to use low-wage Chinese labor to also sell six billion pairs of underwear to everyone else in the world, and at prices that were a fraction of what the underwear companies in Europe or America or even Mexico were charging.

Once that offshoring process began in a range of industries—from textiles to consumer electronics to furniture to eyeglass frames to auto parts—the only ways other companies could compete was by offshoring to China as well (taking advantage of its low-cost, high-quality platform), or by looking for alternative manufacturing centers in Eastern Europe, the Caribbean, or somewhere else in the developing world.

By joining the World Trade Organization in 2001, China assured foreign companies that if they shifted factories offshore to China, they would be protected by international law and standard business practices. This greatly enhanced China's attractiveness as a manufacturing platform. Under WTO rules, Beijing agreed—with some time for phase-in—to treat non-Chinese citizens or firms as if they were Chinese in terms of their economic rights and obligations under Chinese law. This meant that foreign companies could sell virtually anything anywhere in China. WTO membership status also meant that Beijing agreed to treat all WTO member nations equally, meaning that the same tariffs and the same regulations had to apply equally for everyone. And it agreed to submit itself to international arbitration in the event of a trade dispute with another country or a foreign company. At the same time, government bureaucrats became more customer-friendly, procedures for investments were streamlined, and Web sites proliferated in different ministries to help foreigners navigate China's business regulations. I don't know how many Chinese actually ever bought a copy of Mao's Little Red Book, but U.S. embassy officials in China told me that two million copies of the Chinese-language edition of the WTO rule book were sold in the weeks immediately after China signed on to the WTO. To put it another way, China under Mao was closed and isolated from the other flattening forces of his day, and as a result Mao was really a challenge only to his own people. Deng Xiaoping made China open to absorbing many of the ten flatteners and, in so doing, made China a challenge to the whole world.

Before China signed on to the WTO, there was a sense that, while China had opened up to get the advantages of trade with the West, the government and the banks would protect Chinese businesses from any crushing foreign competition, said Jack Perkowski of ASIMCO. "China's entry into the WTO was a signal to the community outside of China that it was now on the capitalist track for good," he added. "Before, you had the thought in the back of your mind that there could be a turning back to state communism. With WTO, China said, 'We are on one course.'"

Because China can amass so many low-wage workers at the unskilled, semiskilled, and skilled levels, because it has such a voracious appetite for factory, equipment, and knowledge jobs to keep its people employed, and because it has such a massive and burgeoning consumer market, it has become an unparalleled zone for offshoring. China has more than 160 cities with a population of one million or more. You can go to towns on the east coast of China today that you have never heard of and discover that this one town manufactures most of the eyeglass frames in the world, while the town next door manufactures most of the disposable cigarette lighters in the world, and the one next to that is doing most of the computer screens for Dell, and another is specializing in mobile phones. The Japanese business consultant Kenichi Ohmae estimates in his book *The United States of China* that in the Zhu Jiang Delta area alone, north of Hong Kong, there are fifty thousand Chinese electronics component suppliers.

"China is a threat, China is a customer, and China is an opportunity," Ohmae remarked to me one day in Tokyo. "You have to internalize China to succeed. You cannot ignore it." Instead of competing with China as an enemy, argues Ohmae, you break down your business and think about which part of the business you would like to do in China, which part you would like to sell to China, and which part you want to buy from China.

Here we get to the real flattening aspect of China's opening to the world market. The more attractive China makes itself as a base for offshoring, the more attractive other developed and developing countries competing with it, like Malaysia, Thailand, Ireland, Mexico, Brazil, and Vietnam, have to make themselves. They all look at what is going on in China and the jobs moving there and say to themselves, "Holy catfish, we had better start offering these same incentives." This has created a process of competitive flattening, in which countries scramble to see who can give companies the best tax breaks, education incentives, and subsidies, on top of their cheap labor, to encourage offshoring to their shores.

Ohio State University business professor Oded Shenkar, author of the book *The Chinese Century*, told *BusinessWeek* (December 6, 2004) that he gives it to American companies straight: "If you still make anything labor intensive, get out now rather than bleed to death. Shaving 5% here and there won't work." Chinese producers can make the same adjustments. "You need an entirely new business model to compete," he said. China's flattening power is also fueled by the fact that it is developing a huge domestic market of its own. The same *BusinessWeek* article noted that this brings economies of scale, intense local rivalries that keep prices low, an army of engineers that is growing by 350,000 annually, young workers and managers willing to put in twelve-hour days, an unparalleled component base in electronics and light industry, "and an entrepreneurial zeal to do whatever it takes to please big retailers such as Wal-Mart Stores, Target, Best Buy and J.C. Penney."

While visiting Beijing in the fall of 2005, I met with Charles M. Martin, president of the American Chamber of Commerce for the People's Republic of China. He told me that he had just returned from visiting a sock factory in Zhejiang Province. This manufacturer produces socks and ladies' underwear for mass merchandisers around the world, as well as retailers within China. The factory owner opened a box of socks for Martin and told him that if you bought a dozen pair of these basic socks from him, you would pay 11¢ a pair—the wholesale price. But the factory owner went on to explain that even at 11¢ a pair he was becoming "uncompetitive"—his competitors were selling socks for even less. So he was planning to relocate his factory four hundred miles inland, into a poor sector of northern Jiangsu Province, where the local government had promised him still lower taxes, lower land costs, and lower labor costs.

Eventually, there will be no more inland China for factories to shift into, and China's manufacturers will not be able to lower their costs any further by just moving—but we are not there yet, which is why China is such a leveling force for manufacturing and why cutting your costs by 5 percent here or there, if you are a Western manufacturer of any basic commodity item, just won't do it. You need a whole new business model.

Critics of China's business practices say that its size and economic power mean that it will soon be setting the global floor not only for low wages but also for lax labor laws and workplace standards. This is known in the business as "the China price."

But what is really scary is that China is not attracting so much global investment by simply racing everyone to the bottom. That is just a short-term strategy. The biggest mistake any business can make when it comes to

China is thinking that it is winning only on wages and not improving quality and productivity. In the private, non-state-owned sector of Chinese industry, productivity increased 17 percent annually—I repeat, 17 percent annually—between 1995 and 2002, according to a study by the U.S. Conference Board. This is due to China's absorption of both new technologies and modern business practices, starting from a very low base. Incidentally, the Conference Board study noted, China lost fifteen million manufacturing jobs during this period, compared with two million in the United States. "As its manufacturing productivity accelerates, China is losing jobs in manufacturing—many more than the United States is—and gaining them in services, a pattern that has been playing out in the developed world for many years," the study said.

China's real long-term strategy is to outrace America and the EU countries to the top, and the Chinese are off to a good start. China's leaders are much more focused than many of their Western counterparts on how to train their young people in the math, science, and computer skills required for success in the flat world, how to build a physical and telecom infrastructure that will allow Chinese people to plug and play faster and easier than others, and how to create incentives that will attract global investors. What China's leaders really want is the next generation of underwear or airplane wings to be *designed* in China as well. That is where things are heading in another decade. So in thirty years we will have gone from "sold in China" to "made in China" to "designed in China" to "dreamed up in China"—or from China as collaborator with the worldwide manufacturers on nothing to China as a low-cost, high-quality, hyperefficient collaborator with worldwide manufacturers on *everything*. This should allow China to maintain its role as a major flattening force, provided that political instability does not disrupt the process. Indeed, while researching this chapter, I came across an online Silicon Valley newsletter called the *Inquirer,* which follows the semiconductor industry. What caught my eye was its November 5, 2001, article headlined "China to Become Center of Everything." It quoted a *China People's Daily* article that claimed that four hundred out of the Forbes 500 companies have invested in more than two thousand projects in mainland China. And that was five years ago.

Japan, being right next door to China, has taken a very aggressive approach to internalizing the China challenge. Osamu Watanabe, chairman of the Japan External Trade Organization, Japan's official organ for promoting exports, told me in Tokyo, "China is developing very rapidly and making the shift from low-grade products to high-grade, high-tech ones." As a result, added Watanabe, Japanese companies, to remain globally competitive, have had to shift some production and a lot of assembly of middle-range products to China, while shifting at home to making "even higher value-added products." So China and Japan "are becoming part of the same supply chain." After a prolonged recession, Japan's economy started to bounce back in 2003, due to the sale of thousands of tons of machinery, assembly robots, and other critical components in China. In 2003, China replaced the United States as the biggest importer of Japanese products. Still, the Japanese government is urging its companies to be careful not to overinvest in China. It encourages them to practice what Watanabe called a "China plus one" strategy: to keep one production leg in China but the other in a different Asian country—just in case political turmoil unflattens China one day.

This China flattener has been wrenching for certain manufacturing workers around the world but a godsend for all consumers. *Fortune* magazine (October 4, 2004) quoted a study by Morgan Stanley estimating that since the mid-1990s alone, cheap imports from China have saved U.S. consumers roughly $600 billion and have saved U.S. manufacturers untold billions in cheaper parts for their products. This savings, in turn, *Fortune* noted, has helped the Federal Reserve to hold down interest rates longer, giving more Americans a chance to buy homes or refinance the ones they have, and giving businesses more capital to invest in new innovations.

In an effort to better understand how offshoring to China works, I sat down in Beijing with Jack Perkowski of ASIMCO, a pioneer in this form of collaboration. If they ever have a category in the Olympics called "extreme capitalism," bet on Perkowski to win the gold. In 1988 he stepped down as a top investment banker at Paine Webber and went to a leverage buyout firm, but two years later, at age forty-two, decided it was time for a new challenge. With some partners, he raised $150 million to buy companies in China and headed off for the adventure of his life. Since then he has lost and remade millions of dollars, learned every lesson the hard way, but survived to become a powerful example of what offshoring to China is all about and what a powerful collaborative tool it can become.

"When I first started back in 1992–1993, everyone thought the hard part was to actually find and gain access to opportunities in China," recalled Perkowski. It turned out that there were opportunities aplenty but a critical shortage of Chinese managers who understood how to run an auto parts factory along capitalist lines, with an emphasis on exports and making world-class products for the Chinese market. As Perkowski put it, the easy part was setting up shop in China. The hard part was getting the right local managers who could run the store. So when he initially started buying majority ownership in Chinese auto parts companies, Perkowski began by importing managers from abroad. Bad idea. It was too expensive, and operating in China was just too foreign for foreigners. Scratch plan A.

"So we sent all the expats home, which gave me problems with my investor base, and went to plan B," he said. "We then tried to convert the 'Old China' managers who typically came along with the plants we bought, but that didn't work either. They were simply too used to working in a planned economy where they never had to deal with the marketplace, just deliver their quotas. Those managers who did have an entrepreneurial flair got drunk on their first sip of capitalism and were ready to try anything.

"The Chinese are very entrepreneurial," said Perkowski, "but back then, before China joined the WTO, there was no rule of law and no bond or stock market to restrain this entrepreneurialism. Your only choices were managers from the state-owned sector, who were very bureaucratic, or managers from the first wave of private companies, who were practicing cowboy capitalism. Neither is where you want to be. If your managers are too bureaucratic, you can't get anything done—they just give excuses about how China is different—and if they are too entrepreneurial, you can't sleep at night, because you have no idea what they are going to do." Perkowski had a lot of sleepless nights.

One of his first purchases in China was an interest in a company making rubber parts. When he subsequently reached an agreement with his Chinese partner to purchase his shares in the company, the Chinese partner signed a noncompete clause as part of the transaction. As soon as the deal closed, however, the Chinese partner went out and opened a new factory. "Noncompete" did not quite translate into Mandarin. Scratch plan B.

Meanwhile, Perkowski's partnership was hemorrhaging money—Perkowski's tuition for learning how to do business in China—and he found himself owning a string of Chinese auto parts factories. "Around 1997 was the low point," he said. "Our company as a whole was shrinking and we were not profitable. While some of our companies were doing okay, we were generally in tough shape. Although we had majority ownership and could theoretically put anyone on the field that we wanted, I looked at my [managerial] bench and I had no one to put in the game." Time for plan C.

"We essentially concluded that, while we liked China, we wanted no part of 'Old China' and instead wanted to place our bets on 'New China' managers," said Perkowski. "We began looking for a new breed of Chinese managers who were open-minded and had gotten some form of management training. We were looking for individuals who were experienced at operating in China and yet were familiar with how the rest of the world operated and knew where China had to go. So between 1997 and 1999, we recruited a whole team of 'New China' managers, typically mainland Chinese who had worked for multinationals, and as these managers came on board, we began one by one to replace the 'Old China' managers at our companies."

Once the new generation of Chinese managers, who understood global markets and customers and could be united around a shared company vision—*and knew China*—was in place, ASIMCO started making a profit. Today ASIMCO has sales of about $350 million a year in auto parts from thirteen Chinese factories in nine provinces. The company sells to customers in the United States, and it also has thirty-six sales offices throughout China servicing automakers in that country too.

From this base, Perkowski made his next big move—taking the profits from offshoring back onshore in America. "In April of 2003, we bought the North American camshaft operations of Federal-Mogul Corporation, an old-line components company that is now in bankruptcy," said Perkowski. "We bought the business first to get access to its customers, which were primarily the Big Three automakers, plus Caterpillar and Cummins. While we have had long-standing relationships with Cat and Cummins—and this acquisition enhanced our position with them—the camshaft sales to the Big Three were our first. The second reason to make the acquisition was to obtain technology which we could bring back to China. Like most of the technology that goes into modern passenger cars and trucks, people take camshaft technology for granted. However, camshafts [that part of the motor that controls the intake and exhaust valves] are highly engineered products which are critical to the performance of the engine. The acquisition of this business essentially gave us the know-how and technology that we could use to become the camshaft leader in China. As a result, we now have the best camshaft technology and a customer base both in China and the U.S."

This is a very important point, because the general impression is that offshoring is a lose-lose proposition for American workers—something that was here went over there, and that is the end of the story. The reality is more complicated.

Most companies build offshore factories not simply to obtain cheaper labor for products they want to sell in America or Europe. Another motivation is to serve that foreign market without having to worry about trade barriers and to gain a dominant foothold there—particularly a giant market like China's. According to the U.S. Commerce Department, nearly 90 percent of the output from U.S.-owned offshore factories is sold to foreign consumers. But this actually stimulates American exports. There are a variety of studies indicating that every dollar a company invests overseas in an offshore factory yields additional exports for its home country, because roughly one-third of global trade today is within multinational companies. It works the other way as well. Even when production is moved offshore to save on wages, it is usually not all moved offshore. According to a January 26, 2004, study by the Heritage Foundation, *Job Creation and the Taxation of Foreign-Source Income*, American companies that produce at home and abroad, for both the American market and China's, generate more than 21 percent of U.S. economic output, produce 56 percent of U.S. exports, and employ three-fifths of all manufacturing employees, about nine million workers. So if General Motors builds a factory offshore in Shanghai, it also ends up creating jobs in America by exporting a lot of goods and services to its own factory in China and benefiting from lower parts costs in China for its factories in America. Finally, America is a beneficiary of the same phenomenon. While much attention is paid to American companies going offshore to China, little attention is paid to the huge amount of offshore investment coming into America every year, because foreigners want access to American markets and labor just like we want access to theirs. On September 25, 2003, DaimlerChrysler celebrated the tenth anniversary of its decision to build the first Mercedes-Benz passenger car factory outside Germany, in Tuscaloosa, Alabama, by announcing a $600 million plant expansion. "In Tuscaloosa we have impressively shown that we can produce a new production series with a new workforce in a new factory, and we have also demonstrated that it is possible to have vehicles successfully 'Made by Mercedes' outside of Germany," Professor Jürgen Hubbert, the DaimlerChrysler Board of Management member responsible for the Mercedes Car Group, announced on the anniversary.

Not surprisingly, ASIMCO will use its new camshaft operation in China to handle the raw material and rough machining operations, exporting semifinished products to its camshaft plant in America, where more skilled American workers can do the finished machining operations, which are most critical to quality. In this way, ASIMCO's American customers receive the benefit of a China supply chain and at the same time have the comfort of dealing with a known, American supplier.

The average wage of a high-skilled machinist in America is $3,000 to $4,000 a month. The average wage for a factory worker in China is about $150 a month. In addition, ASIMCO is required to participate in a Chinese government-sponsored pension plan covering health care, housing, and retirement benefits. Between 35 and 45 percent of a Chinese worker's monthly wage goes directly to the local labor bureau to cover these benefits. The fact that health insurance in China is so much cheaper—because of lower wages, much more limited health service offerings, and no malpractice suits—"certainly makes China an attractive place to expand and add employees," explained Perkowski. "Anything which can be done to reduce a U.S. company's liability for medical coverage would be a plus in keeping jobs in the U.S."

By taking advantage of the flat world to collaborate this way—between onshore and offshore factories, and between high-wage, high-skilled American workers close to their market and low-wage Chinese workers close to theirs—said Perkowski, "we make our American company more competitive, so it is getting more orders and we are actually growing the business. And that is what many in the U.S. are missing when they talk about offshoring. Since the acquisition, for example, we have doubled our business with Cummins, and our business with Caterpillar has grown significantly. All of our customers are exposed to global competition and really need their supply base to do the right thing as far as cost competitiveness. They want to work with suppliers who understand the flat world. When I went to visit our U.S. customers to explain our strategy for the camshaft business, they were very positive about what we were doing, because they could see that we were aligning our business in a way that was going to enable them to be more competitive."

This degree of collaboration has been possible only in the last couple of years. "We could not have done what we have done in China in 1983 or 1993," said Perkowski. "Since 1993, a number of things have come together. For example, people always talk about how much the Internet has benefited the U.S. The point I always make is that China has benefited even more. What has held China back in the past was the inability of people outside China to get information about the country, and the inability of people inside China to get information about the rest of the world. Prior to the Internet, the only way to close that information gap was travel. Now you can stay home and do it with the Internet. You could not operate our global supply chain without it. We now just e-mail blueprints over the Internet—we don't even need FedEx."

The advantages for manufacturing in China, for certain industries, are becoming overwhelming, added Perkowski, and cannot be ignored. Either you get flat or you'll be flattened by China. "If you are sitting in the U.S. and don't figure out how to get into China," he said, "in ten or fifteen years from now you will not be a global leader."

Now that China is in the WTO, a lot of traditional, slow, inefficient, and protected sectors of the Chinese economy are being exposed to some withering global competition—something received as warmly in Canton, China, as in Canton, Ohio. Had the Chinese government put WTO membership to a popular vote, "it never would have passed," said Pat Powers, who headed the U.S.-China Business Council office in Beijing during the WTO accession. A key reason why China's leadership sought WTO membership was to use it as a club to force China's bureaucracy to modernize and take down internal regulatory walls and pockets for arbitrary decision making. China's leadership "knew that China had to integrate globally and that many of their existing institutions would simply not change and reform, and so they used the WTO as leverage against their own bureaucracy. And for the last two and a half years they've been slugging it out."

Over time, adherence to WTO standards will make China's economy even flatter and more of a flattener globally. But this transition will not be easy, and the chances of a political or economic crackup that disrupts or slows this process are not insignificant. But even if China implements all the WTO reforms, it won't be able to rest. It will soon be reaching a point where its ambitions for economic growth will require more political reform. China will never root out corruption without a free press and active civil society institutions. It can never really become efficient without a more codified rule of law. It will never be able to deal with the inevitable downturns in its economy without a more open political system that allows people to vent their grievances. To put it another way, China will never be truly flat until it gets over that huge speed bump called "political reform."

It seems to be heading in that direction, but it still has a long way to go. I like the way a U.S. diplomat in China put it to me in the spring of 2004: "China right now is doing titillation, not privatization. Reform here is translucent—and sometimes it is quite titillating, because you can see the shapes moving behind the screen—but it is not transparent. [The government still just gives] the information [about the economy] to a few companies and designated interest groups." Why only translucent?

I asked. He answered, "Because if you are fully transparent, what do you do with the feedback? They don't know how to deal with that question. They cannot deal [yet] with the results of transparency."

If and when China gets over that political bump in the road, I think it could become not only a bigger platform for offshoring but another free-market version of the United States. While that may seem threatening to some, I think it would be an incredibly positive development for the world. Think about how many new products, ideas, jobs, and consumers arose from Western Europe's and Japan's efforts to become free-market democracies after World War II. The process unleashed an unprecedented period of global prosperity—and the world wasn't even flat then. It had a wall in the middle. If India and China move in that direction, the world will not only become flatter than ever but also, I am convinced, more prosperous than ever. Three United States are better than one, and five would be better than three.

But even as a free-trader, I am worried about the challenge this will pose to wages and benefits of certain workers in the United States, at least in the short run. It is too late for protectionism when it comes to China. Its economy is totally interlinked with those of the developed world, and trying to delink it would cause economic and geopolitical chaos that could devastate the global economy. Americans and Europeans will have to develop new business models that will enable them to get the best out of China and cushion themselves against some of the worst. As *BusinessWeek*, in its dramatic December 6, 2004, cover story on "The China Price," put it, "Can China dominate everything? Of course not. America remains the world's biggest manufacturer, producing 75% of what it consumes, though that's down from 90% in the mid-'90s. Industries requiring huge R&D budgets and capital investment, such as aerospace, pharmaceuticals, and cars, still have strong bases in the U.S. . . . America will surely continue to benefit from China's expansion." That said, unless America can deal with the long-term industrial challenge posed by the China price in so many areas, "it will suffer a loss of economic power and influence."

Or, to put it another way, if Americans and Europeans want to benefit from the flattening of the world and the interconnecting of all the markets and knowledge centers, they will all have to run at least as fast as the fastest lion—and I suspect that lion will be China, and I suspect that will be pretty darn fast.

FLATTENER #7

SUPPLY-CHAINING
Eating Sushi in Arkansas

I had never seen what a supply chain looked like in action until I visited Wal-Mart headquarters in Bentonville, Arkansas. My Wal-Mart hosts took me over to the 1.2-million-square-foot distribution center, where we climbed up to a viewing perch and watched the show. On one side of the building, scores of white Wal-Mart trailer trucks were dropping off boxes of merchandise from thousands of different suppliers. Boxes large and small were fed up a conveyor belt at each loading dock. These little conveyor belts fed into a bigger belt, like streams feeding into a powerful river. Twenty-four hours a day, seven days a week, the suppliers' trucks feed the twelve miles of conveyor streams, and the conveyor streams feed into a huge Wal-Mart river of boxed products. But that is just half the show. As the Wal-Mart river flows along, an electric eye reads the bar codes on each box on its way to the other side of the building. There, the river parts again into a hundred streams. Electric arms from each stream reach out and guide the boxes—ordered by particular Wal-Mart stores— off the main river and down its stream, where another conveyor belt sweeps them into a waiting Wal-Mart truck, which will rush these particular products onto the shelves of a particular Wal-Mart store somewhere in the country. There, a consumer will lift one of these products off the shelf, and the cashier will scan it in, and the moment that happens, a signal will be generated. That signal will go out across the Wal-Mart network to the supplier of that product—whether that supplier's factory is in coastal China or coastal Maine. That signal will pop up on the supplier's computer screen and prompt him to make another of that item and ship it via the Wal-Mart supply chain, and the whole cycle will start anew. So no sooner does your arm lift a product off the local Wal-Mart's shelf and onto the checkout counter than another mechanical arm starts making another one somewhere in the world. Call it "the Wal-Mart Symphony" in multiple movements—with no finale. It just plays over and over 24/7/365: delivery, sorting, packing, distribution, buying, manufacturing, reordering, delivery, sorting, packing . . .

Just one company, Hewlett-Packard, will sell four hundred thousand computers through the four thousand Wal-Mart stores worldwide in *one day* during the Christmas season, which will require HP to adjust its supply chain, to make sure that all of its standards interface with Wal-Mart's, so that these computers flow smoothly into the Wal-Mart river, into the Wal-Mart streams, into the Wal-Mart stores.

Wal-Mart's ability to bring off this symphony on a global scale—moving 2.3 billion general merchandise cartons a year down its supply chain into its stores—has made it the most important example of the next great flattener I want to discuss, which I call supply-chaining. Supply-chaining is a method of collaborating horizontally—among suppliers, retailers, and customers—to create value. Supply-chaining is both enabled by the flattening of the world and a hugely important flattener itself, because the more these supply chains grow and proliferate, the more they force the adoption of common standards between companies (so that every link of every supply chain can interface with the next), the more they eliminate points of friction at borders, the more the efficiencies of one company get adopted by the others, and the more they encourage global collaboration.

To appreciate how important supply-chaining has become as a source of competitive advantage and profit in a flat world, think about this one fact: Wal-Mart today is the biggest retail company in the world, and it does not make a single thing. All it "makes" is a hyperefficient supply chain. As Yossi Sheffi, an expert on supply-chain management and a professor of engineering systems at MIT, likes to say, "Making stuff—that's easy. Supply chain, now that is really hard." What he means is that with today's technology it is difficult to keep intellectual property secret and thus easy to reverse-engineer any product and "make stuff" in a matter of days. However, building a process that "delivers stuff" across the globe—

involving dozens of suppliers, distributors, port operators, customs brokers, forwarders, and carriers in a finely tuned chain operating in concert—is not only difficult, it's very, very hard to duplicate.

Before looking at Wal-Mart in detail, let me make a few general
points about supply chains and why they have become so important.
When the world is flat, your company both can and must take advantage
of the best producers at the lowest prices anywhere they can be found. If
you don't, your competitors will. So global supply chains—that draw
parts and products from every corner of the world—have become essential for both retailers and manufacturers. That is the good news. The bad
news, as Sheffi suggests, is that making these chains work is much harder
than it looks and requires constant innovation and constant adjustment.
There are two basic challenges in developing a global supply chain in a
flat world, he explains. One is "global optimization." What that means is
that it doesn't matter if you can get one part cheaper in one place. The
key is that the total cost of delivering all your parts on time from all four
corners of the globe to your factories or retail outlets has to be low, and
certainly lower than those of your competitors. "If I am the transportation manager in a company, I want to do business with the cheapest
trucking company," said Sheffi. "If I am the production manager in that
company, I want to do business with the most reliable trucking company.
And they may not be the same." So the first challenge is balancing out all
these factors to get the most reliable, low-cost delivery system in place.
The second major challenge, said Sheffi, is coordinating disruption-
prone supply with hard-to-predict demand. That is, you don't want to buy
too many of one part, or one sweater—because then you will have to discount them when they pile up on the shelves of your factory or store. But
you don't want to buy too few of that part or those sweaters, either, because customers might not find what they want when they go shopping,
and you may lose not only a sale that day but a customer for life. Both
challenges are exacerbated by the short life cycle of products today, particularly fashion and consumer electronics products. Innovation is happening much faster, and so products go in and out of fashion much faster,
which makes forecasting demand much more difficult.

There are many ways that companies try to meet these challenges, noted Sheffi. One is by replacing inventory with information. This is an area that Wal-Mart pioneered. The faster you can get information from stores about what customers are buying—what products, what models, and what colors—the faster you can get that information to your manufacturers and designers and the faster they can send back down the supply chain more red sweaters and fewer yellow ones. Advanced information technology also gives Wal-Mart "visibility" into where products are at any time as they move through the supply chain. Thus, if demand is high in Texas and lower than expected in New England, Wal-Mart can redirect the flow midstream in order to ensure that products are routed to Texas, where customers want them. The Spanish fashion retailer Zara is particularly adept at this and regularly outperforms its competition. Zara lives by the motto that it is more profitable to incur shortages than overstock, and then to respond to shortages with lightning speed so you are offering customers exactly what they want with much less risk of leftovers. How do they do this?

Zara spends heavily on sophisticated information technology, "including PDA's with transmission capabilities for all store managers to monitor customer preferences and then send data directly to a central planning office," according to *Longitudes 04*, a collaborative study by Harvard Business School and UPS. "This technology has so reduced execution time that it can get a new product from design to store shelves in no more than 30 days, allowing Zara to postpone design decisions to incorporate up-to-the-minute results from its stores. By planning well to handle the day-to-day risk of fickle consumer tastes and rapidly changing style preferences, Zara is also prepared to adapt when unforeseen events occur. Immediately after September 11, Zara executives realized that consumers were in a somber mood, and within just a few weeks [Zara executives] had stocked their stores with new merchandise that was predominantly black."

This strategy is known in the business as "postponement," and the idea, explained Sheffi, whose latest work is *The Resilient Enterprise: Overcoming Vulnerability for Competitive Advantage*, is that as it becomes harder and harder to forecast demand, good companies find ways to postpone adding value to their products until the last possible moment. This

THE TEN FORCES THAT FLATTENED THE WORLD

is the genius of Dell. Because Dell has a customer for every computer before it is manufactured, Dell makes exactly the number of computers that customers want, each one exactly the way the customer wants it. It has no inventory of computers. It has a basic supply of parts and then adds value by tailoring screen size, memory, and software to the desires of each customer. "Dell can get stuck with parts that it bought on spec, but each part can be used in many configurations so it is likely to be used sooner or later," said Sheffi. "Dell can never get stuck, however, with computers that don't get bought." The bottom line, concluded Sheffi, is that in a flat world, products are turned from innovations into commodities faster than ever, competition is coming from all over the globe and is more intense than ever, and consumer demand is more volatile and informed than ever, with fads moving in and out around the globe like lightning bolts. In this world, a smart and fast global supply chain is becoming one of the most important ways for a company to distinguish itself from its competitors.

A s consumers, we love supply chains, because they deliver us all sorts of goods—from tennis shoes to laptop computers—at lower and lower prices and tailored more and more precisely to just what we want. That is how Wal-Mart became the world's biggest retailer. But as workers, we are sometimes ambivalent or hostile to these supply chains, because they expose us to higher and higher pressures to compete, and force our companies to cut costs, and also, at times, cut our wages and benefits. That is how Wal-Mart became one of the world's most controversial companies. No retail company has been more efficient at improving its supply chain (and thereby flattening the world) than Wal-Mart, and no company epitomizes the tension that supply chains evoke between the consumer in us and the worker in us than does Wal-Mart. A September 30, 2002, article in *Computerworld* summed up Wal-Mart's pivotal role: "'Being a supplier to Wal-Mart is a two-edged sword,' says Joseph F. Eckroth Jr., CIO at Mattel Inc. 'They're a phenomenal channel but a tough customer. They demand excellence.' It's a lesson that the El Segundo, Calif.–based toy manufacturer and thousands of other suppliers learned as the world's largest retailer, Wal-Mart Stores Inc., built an inventory and supply chain management system that changed the face of business. By investing early and heavily in cutting-edge technology to identify and track sales on the individual item level, the Bentonville, Ark.–based retail giant made its IT infrastructure a key competitive advantage that has been studied and copied by companies around the world. 'We view Wal-Mart as the best supply chain operator of all time,' says Pete Abell, retail research director at high-tech consultancy AMR Research Inc. in Boston."

In pursuit of the world's most efficient supply chain, Wal-Mart has piled up a list of business offenses over the years that has given the company several deserved black eyes and that it is belatedly starting to address in a meaningful way. But its role as one of the ten forces that flattened the world is undeniable, and it was to get a handle on this that I decided to make my own pilgrimage to Bentonville. I don't know why, but on the flight in from La Guardia, I was thinking, Boy, I would really like some sushi tonight. But where am I going to find sushi in northwest Arkansas? And even if I found it, would I want to eat it? Could you really trust the eel in Arkansas?

When I arrived at the Hilton near Wal-Mart's headquarters, I was stunned to see, like a mirage, a huge Japanese steak house–sushi restaurant right next door. When I remarked to the desk clerk who was checking me in that I never expected to get my sushi fix in Bentonville, he told me, "We've got three more Japanese restaurants opening up soon."

Multiple Japanese restaurants in Bentonville?

The demand for sushi in Arkansas is not an accident. It has to do with the fact that all around Wal-Mart's offices, vendors have set up their own operations to be close to the mother ship. Indeed, the area is known as "Vendorville." The amazing thing about Wal-Mart's headquarters is that it is so, well, Wal-Mart. The corporate offices are crammed into a reconfigured warehouse. As we passed a large building made of corrugated metal, I figured it was the maintenance shed. "Those are our international offices," said my host, spokesman William Wertz. The corporate suites are housed in offices that are one notch below those of the principal, vice principal, and head counselor at my daughter's public junior high school—*before it was remodeled.* When you pass through the lobby, you see these little cubicles where potential suppliers are pitching their products to Wal-Mart buyers. One has sewing machines all over the table, another has dolls, another has women's shirts. It feels like a cross between Sam's Club and the covered bazaar of Damascus. Attention Wal-Mart shareholders: The company is definitely not wasting your money on frills.

B ut how did so much innovative thinking—thinking that has reshaped the world's business landscape in many ways—come out of such a Li'l Abner backwater? It is actually a classic example of a phenomenon I point to often in this book: the coefficient of flatness. The fewer natural resources your country or company has, the more you will dig inside yourself for innovations in order to survive. Wal-Mart became the biggest retailer in the world because it drove a hard bargain with everyone it came in contact with. But make no mistake about one thing: Wal-Mart also became number one because this little hick company from northwest Arkansas was smarter and faster about adopting new technology than any of its competitors. And it still is.

David Glass, the company's CEO from 1988 to 2000, oversaw many of the innovations that made Wal-Mart the biggest and most profitable retailer on the planet. *Fortune* magazine once dubbed him "the most underrated CEO ever" for the quiet way he built on Sam Walton's vision. David Glass is to supply-chaining what Bill Gates is to word processing. When Wal-Mart was just getting started in northern Arkansas in the 1960s, explained Glass, it wanted to be a discounter. But in those days, every five-and-dime got its goods from the same wholesalers, so there was no way to get an edge on your competitors. The only way Wal-Mart could see to get an edge, he said, was for it to buy its goods in volume *directly from the manufacturers.* But it wasn't efficient for manufacturers to ship to multiple Wal-Mart stores spread all over, so Wal-Mart set up a distribution center to which all the manufacturers could ship their merchandise, and then Wal-Mart got its own trucks to distribute these goods itself to its stores. The math worked like this: It cost roughly 3 percent more on average for Wal-Mart to maintain its own distribution center. But it turned out, said Glass, that cutting out the wholesalers and buying direct from the manufacturers saved on average 5 percent, so that allowed Wal-Mart to cut costs on average 2 percent and then make it up on volume.

Once it established that basic method of buying directly from manufacturers to get the deepest discounts possible, Wal-Mart focused relentlessly on three things. The first was working with the manufacturers to get them to cut their costs as much as possible. The second was working on its supply chain from those manufacturers, wherever they were in the world, to Wal-Mart's distribution centers, to make it as low-cost and frictionless as possible. The third was constantly improving Wal-Mart's information systems, so it knew exactly what its customers were buying and could feed that information to all the manufacturers, so the shelves would always be stocked with the right items at the right time.

Wal-Mart quickly realized that if it could save money by buying directly from the manufacturers, by constantly innovating to cut the cost of running its supply chain, and by keeping its inventories low by learning more about its customers, it could beat its competitors on price every time. Sitting in Bentonville, Arkansas, it didn't have much choice.

"The reason we built all our own logistics and systems is because we are in the middle of nowhere," said Jay Allen, Wal-Mart's senior vice president of corporate affairs. "It really was a small town. If you wanted to go to a third party for logistics, it was impossible. It was pure survival. Now with all the attention we are getting there is an assumption that our low prices derive from our size or because we're getting stuff from China or being able to dictate to suppliers. The fact is the low prices are derived from efficiencies Wal-Mart has invested in—the system and the culture. It is a very low-cost culture." Added Glass, "I wish that I could say we were brilliant and visionary, [but] it was all born out of necessity."

The more that supply chain grew, the more Walton and Glass understood that scale and efficiency were the keys to their whole business. Put simply, the more scale and scope their supply chain had, the more things they sold for less to more customers, the more leverage they had with suppliers to drive prices down even more, the more they sold to more customers, the more scale and scope their supply chain had, the more profit they reaped for their shareholders . . .

Sam Walton was the father of that culture, but necessity was its mother, and its offspring has turned out to be a lean, mean supply-chain machine. In 2004, Wal-Mart purchased roughly $260 billion worth of merchandise and ran it through a supply chain consisting of 108 distribution centers around the United States, serving the some three thousand Wal-Mart stores in America.

In the early years, "we were small—we were 4 or 5 percent of Sears and Kmart," said Glass. "If you are that small, you are vulnerable, so what we wanted to do more than anything else was grow market share. We had to undersell others. If I could reduce from 3 percent to 2 percent the cost of running my distribution centers, I could reduce retail prices and grow my market share and then not be vulnerable to anyone. So any efficiency we generated we passed on to the consumer."

For instance, after the manufacturers dropped off their goods at the Wal-Mart distribution center, Wal-Mart needed to deliver those goods in small bunches to each of its stores. It meant that Wal-Mart had trucks going all over America. Walton quickly realized if he connected his drivers by radios and satellites, after they dropped off at a certain Wal-Mart store, they could go a few miles down the road and pick up goods from a manufacturer so they wouldn't come back empty and so Wal-Mart could save the delivery charges from that manufacturer. A few pennies here, a few pennies there, and the result is more volume, scope, and scale.

In improving its supply chain, Wal-Mart leaves no link untouched. While I was touring the Wal-Mart distribution center in Bentonville, I noticed that some boxes were too big to go on the conveyor belts and were being moved around on pallets by Wal-Mart employees driving special minilift trucks with headphones on. A computer tracks how many pallets each employee is plucking every hour to put onto trucks for different stores, and a computerized voice tells each of them whether he is ahead of schedule or behind schedule. "You can choose whether you want your computer voice to be a man or a woman, and you can choose English or Spanish," explained Rollin Ford, Wal-Mart's executive vice president, who oversees the supply chain and was giving me my tour.

A few years ago, these pallet drivers would get written instructions for where to pluck a certain pallet and what truck to take it to, but Wal-Mart discovered that by giving them headphones with a soothing computer voice to instruct them, drivers could use both hands and not have to carry pieces of paper. And by having the voice constantly reminding them whether they were behind or ahead of expectations, "we got a boost in productivity," said Ford. It is a million tiny operational innovations like this that differentiate Wal-Mart's supply chain.

But the real breakthrough, said Glass, was when Wal-Mart realized that while it had to be a tough bargainer with its manufacturers on price, at the same time the two had to collaborate to create value for each other horizontally if Wal-Mart was going to keep driving down costs. Wal-Mart was one of the first companies to introduce computers to track store sales and inventory and was the first to develop a computerized network in order to share this information with suppliers. Wal-Mart's theory was that the more information everyone had about what customers were pulling off the shelves, the more efficient Wal-Mart's buying would be, the quicker its suppliers could adapt to changing market demand.

In 1983, Wal-Mart invested in point-of-sale terminals, which simultaneously rang up sales and tracked inventory deductions for rapid resupply. Four years later, it installed a large-scale satellite system linking all of the stores to company headquarters, giving Wal-Mart's central computer system real-time inventory data and paving the way for a supply chain greased by information and humming down to the last atom of efficiency. A major supplier can now tap into Wal-Mart's Retail Link private extranet system to see exactly how its products are selling and when it might need to up its production.

" 'Opening its sales and inventory databases to suppliers is what made Wal-Mart the powerhouse it is today,' Rena Granofsky, a senior partner at J. C. Williams Group Ltd., a Toronto-based retail consulting firm," said in the 2002 *Computerworld* article on Wal-Mart. " 'While its competition guarded sales information, Wal-Mart approached its suppliers as if they were partners, not adversaries,' " says Granofsky. By implementing a collaborative planning, forecasting, and replenishment (CPFR) program, Wal-Mart began a just-in-time inventory program that reduced carrying costs for both the retailer and its suppliers. 'There's a lot less excess inventory in the supply chain because of it,' Granofsky says." Thanks to the efficiency of its supply chain alone, Wal-Mart's cost of goods is estimated to be 5 to 10 percent less than that of most of its competitors.

Now Wal-Mart, in its latest supply-chain innovation, has introduced RFID—radio frequency identification microchips, attached to each pallet and merchandise box that comes into Wal-Mart, to replace bar codes, which have to be scanned individually and can get ripped or soiled. In June 2003, Wal-Mart informed its top one hundred suppliers that by January 1, 2005, all pallets and boxes that they ship to Wal-Mart distribution centers have to come equipped with RFID tags. (According to the *RFID Journal*, "RFID is a generic term for technologies that use radio waves to automatically identify people or objects. There are several methods of identification, but the most common is to store a serial number that identifies a person or object, and perhaps other information, on a microchip that is attached to an antenna—the chip and the antenna together are called an RFID transponder or an RFID tag. The antenna enables the chip to transmit the identification information to a reader. The reader converts the radio waves reflected back from the RFID tag into digital information that can then be passed on to computers that can make use of it.") RFID will allow Wal-Mart to track any pallet or box at each stage in its supply chain and know exactly what product from which manufacturer is inside, with what expiration date. If a grocery item has to be stored at a certain temperature, the RFID tag will tell Wal-Mart when the temperature is too high or too low. Because each of these tags costs around 20¢, Wal-Mart is reserving them now for big boxes and pallets, not individual items. This is clearly the wave of the future. RFID technology and sophisticated order analysis tools that monitor even the most minute market activity are rapidly leading us toward industry's holy grail—absolute balance in supply and demand.

"When you have RFID," said Rollin Ford, the Wal-Mart logistics vice president, "you have more insights." You can tell even faster which stores sell more of which shampoo on Fridays and which ones on Sundays, and whether Hispanics prefer to shop more on Saturday nights rather than Mondays in the stores in their neighborhoods. "When all this information is fed into our demand models, we can become more efficient on when we produce [a product] and when we ship it and then put it on the trucks in exactly the right place inside the trucks so it can flow more efficiently," added Ford. "We used to have to count each piece, and scanning it at [the receiving end] was a bottleneck. Now [with RFID], we just scan the whole pallet under a bubble, and it says you have all thirty items you ordered and each box tells you, 'This is what I am and this is how I am feeling, this is what color I am, and am I in good shape'—so it makes receiving hugely easier." Procter & Gamble spokesperson Jeannie Tharrington talked to Salon.com (September 20, 2004) about Wal-Mart's move to RFID: "We see this as beneficial to the entire supply chain. Right now our out-of-stock levels are higher than we'd like and certainly higher than the consumer would like, and we think this technology can help us to keep the products on the shelf more often." RFID will also allow for quicker remixing of the supply chain in response to events.

During hurricanes, Wal-Mart officials told me, Wal-Mart knows that people eat more things like Pop-Tarts—easy-to-store, nonperishable items—and that their stores also sell a lot of kids' games that don't require electricity and can substitute for TV. It also knows that when hurricanes are coming, people tend to drink more beer. So the minute Wal-Mart's meteorologists tell headquarters a hurricane is bearing down on Florida, its supply chain automatically adjusts to a hurricane mix in the Florida stores—more beer early, more Pop-Tarts later.

Wal-Mart is constantly looking for new ways to collaborate with its customers. Lately, it has gone into banking. It found that in areas with large Hispanic populations, many people had no affiliation with a bank and were getting ripped off by check-cashing outlets. So Wal-Mart offered them payroll check cashing, money orders, money transfers, and even bill payment services for standard items like electricity bills—all for very small fees. Wal-Mart had an internal capability to do that for its own employees and simply turned it into an external business.

TOO MUCH OF A GOOD THING

Unfortunately for Wal-Mart, the same factors that drove its instinct for constant innovation—its isolation from the world, its need to dig inside itself, and its need to connect remote locations to a global supply chain—

also got it in trouble. It is hard to exaggerate how isolated Bentonville, Arkansas, is from the currents of global debate on labor and human rights, and it is easy to see how this insular company, obsessed with lowering prices, could have gone over the edge in some of its practices.

Sam Walton bred not only a kind of ruthless quest for efficiency in improving Wal-Mart's supply chain but also a degree of ruthlessness period. I am talking about everything from Wal-Mart's recently exposed practice of locking overnight workers into its stores, to its allowing Wal-Mart's maintenance contractors to use illegal immigrants as janitors, to its role as defendant in the largest civil-rights class-action lawsuit in history, to its refusal to stock certain magazines—like *Playboy*—on its shelves, even in small towns where Wal-Mart is the only major store. This is all aside from the fact that some of Wal-Mart's biggest competitors complain that they have had to cut health-care benefits and create a lower wage tier to compete with Wal-Mart, which pays less and covers less than most big companies (more on this later). One can only hope that all the bad publicity Wal-Mart has received in the last few years will force it to understand that there is a fine line between a hyperefficient global supply chain that is helping people save money and improve their lives and one that has pursued cost cutting and profit margins to such a degree that whatever social benefits it is offering with one hand, it is taking away with the other.

Wal-Mart is the China of companies. It has so much leverage that it can grind down any supplier to the last halfpenny. And it is not at all hesitant about using its ability to play its foreign and domestic suppliers off against one another.

Some suppliers have found ways to flourish under the pressure and become better at what they do. If all of Wal-Mart's suppliers were being squeezed dry by Wal-Mart, Wal-Mart would have no suppliers. So obviously many of them are thriving as Wal-Mart's partners. But some no doubt have translated Wal-Mart's incessant price pressure into lower wages and benefits for their employees or watched as their business moved to China, whence Wal-Mart's supply chain pulled in $18 billion worth of goods in 2004 from five thousand Chinese suppliers. "If Wal-Mart were an individual economy, it would rank as China's eighth-biggest trading partner, ahead of Russia, Australia and Canada," Xu Jun, the spokesman for Wal-Mart China, told the *China Business Weekly* (November 29, 2004).

The successor generation to Sam Walton's leadership seems to recognize that it has both an image and a reality to fix. How far Wal-Mart will adjust remains to be seen. But when I asked Wal-Mart's CEO, H. Lee Scott Jr., directly about all these issues, he did not duck. In fact, he wanted to talk about it. "What I think I have to do is institutionalize this sense of obligation to society to the same extent that we have institutionalized the commitment to the customer," said Scott. "The world has changed and we have missed that. We believed that good intentions and good stores and good prices would cause people to forgive what we are not as good at, and we were wrong." In certain areas, he added, "we are not as good as we should be. We just have to get better."

One trend that Wal-Mart insists it is not responsible for is the offshoring of manufacturing. "We are much better off if we can buy merchandise made in the United States," said Glass. "I spent two years going around this country trying to talk people into manufacturing here. We would pay more to buy it here because the manufacturing facilities in those towns [would create jobs for] all those people who shopped in our stores. Sanyo had a plant here [in Arkansas] making television sets for Sears, and Sears cut them off, so they decided they were closing the plant and going to move part to Mexico and part to Asia. Our governor asked if we would help. We decided we would buy television sets from Sanyo [if they would keep the plant in Arkansas], and they didn't want to do it. They wanted to move it, and [the governor] even talked to the [Japanese owning] family to try to persuade them to stay. Between his efforts and ours, we persuaded them to do it. They are now the world's largest producer of televisions. We just bought our fifty millionth set from them. But for the most part people in this country have just abandoned the manufacturing process. They say, 'I want to sell to you, but I don't want the responsibility for the buildings and employees [and health care]. I want to source it somewhere else.' So we were forced to source merchandise in other places in the world." He added, "One of my concerns is that, with the manufacturing out of this country, one day we'll all be selling hamburgers to each other."

The best way to get a taste of Wal-Mart's power as a global flattener is to visit Japan. Commodore Matthew Calbraith Perry opened a largely closed Japanese society to the Western world on July 8, 1853, when he arrived in Edo (Tokyo) Bay with four big black steamships bristling with guns. According to the Naval Historical Center Web site, the Japanese, not knowing that steamships even existed, were shocked by the sight of them and thought they were "giant dragons puffing smoke." Commodore Perry returned a year later, and on March 31, 1854, concluded the Treaty of Kanagawa with the Japanese authorities, gaining U.S. vessels access to the ports of Shimoda and Hakodate and opening a U.S. consulate in Shimoda. This treaty led to an explosion of trade between Japan and the United States, helped open Japan to the Western world generally, and is widely credited with triggering the modernization of the Japanese state, as the Japanese realized how far behind they were and rushed to catch up. And catch up they did. In so many areas, from automobiles to consumer electronics to machine tools, from the Sony Walkman to the Lexus, the Japanese learned every lesson they could from Western nations and then proceeded to beat us at our own game—except one: retailing, especially discount retailing. Japan could make those Sonys like nobody else, but when it came to selling them at a discount, well, that was another matter.

So almost exactly 150 years after Commodore Perry signed that treaty, another lesser-known treaty was signed, actually a business partnership. Call it the Seiyu–Wal-Mart Treaty of 2003. Unlike Commodore Perry, Wal-Mart did not have to muscle its way into Japan with warships. Its reputation preceded it, which is why it was invited in by Seiyu, a struggling Japanese retail chain desperate to adapt the Wal-Mart formula in Japan, a country notorious for resisting big-box discount stores. As I traveled on the bullet train from Tokyo to Numazu, site of the first Seiyu store that was using the Wal-Mart methods, the *New York Times* translator pointed out that this store was located about one hundred miles from Shimoda and that first U.S. consulate. Commodore Perry probably would have loved shopping in the new Seiyu store, where all the music piped in consists of Western tunes designed to lull shoppers into filling their carts, and where you can buy a man's suit—made in China—for $65 and a white shirt to go with it for $5. Around Wal-Mart that's called

EDLP—Every Day Low Prices—and this was one of the first phrases Wal-Mart folks learned to say in Japanese.

Wal-Mart's flattening effects are fully on display in the Seiyu store in Numazu—not just the everyday low prices, but the wide aisles, the big pallets of household goods, the huge signs displaying the lowest prices in each category, and the Wal-Mart supply-chain computer system so that store managers can quickly adjust stock.

I asked Seiyu's CEO, Masao Kiuchi, why he had turned to Wal-Mart. "The first time I knew about Wal-Mart was about fifteen years ago," explained Kiuchi. "I went to Dallas to see the Wal-Mart stores, and I thought this was a very rational method. It was two things: One was the signage showing the prices. It was very easy for us to understand." The second, he said, was that the Japanese thought a discount store meant that you sold cheap products at cheap prices. What he realized from shopping at Wal-Mart, and seeing everything from plasma TVs to top-brand pet products, was that Wal-Mart sold quality products at low prices.

"At the store in Dallas, I took pictures, and I brought those pictures to my colleagues in Seiyu and said, 'Look, we have to see what Wal-Mart is doing on the other side of the planet.' But showing pictures was not good enough, because how can you understand by just looking at pictures?" recalled Kiuchi. Eventually, Kiuchi approached Wal-Mart, and they signed a partnership on December 31, 2003. Wal-Mart bought a piece of Seiyu; in return, Wal-Mart agreed to teach Seiyu its unique form of collaboration: global supply-chaining to bring consumers the best goods at the lowest prices.

There was one big thing, though, that Seiyu had to teach Wal-Mart, Kiuchi told me: how to sell raw fish. Japanese discounters and department stores all have grocery sections, and they all carry fish for very discriminating Japanese consumers. Seiyu will discount fish several times during each day, as the freshness declines.

"Wal-Mart doesn't understand raw fish," said Kiuchi. "We are expecting their help with general merchandising."

Give Wal-Mart time. I expect that in the not-too-distant future we will see Wal-Mart sushi.

Somebody had better warn the tuna.

INSOURCING
What the Guys in Funny Brown Shorts
Are Really Doing

One of the most enjoyable things about researching this book has been discovering all sorts of things happening in the world around me of which I had no clue. Nothing was more surprisingly interesting than pulling the curtain back on UPS, United Parcel Service. Yes, those folks, the ones who wear the homely brown shorts and drive those ugly brown trucks. Turns out that while I was sleeping, stodgy old UPS became a huge force flattening the world.

Once again, it was one of my Indian tutors, Nandan Nilekani, the Infosys CEO, who tipped me off to this. "FedEx and UPS should be one of your flatteners. They're not just delivering packages, they are doing logistics," he told me on the phone from Bangalore one day. Naturally, I filed the thought away, making a note to check it out, without having any clue what he was getting at. A few months later I went to China, and while there I was afflicted with jet lag one night and was watching CNN International to pass the wee hours of the morning. At one point, a commercial came on for UPS, and its tag line was UPS's new slogan: "Your World Synchronized."

The thought occurred to me: That must be what Nandan was talking about! UPS, I learned, was not just delivering packages anymore; it was synchronizing global supply chains for companies large and small. The next day I made an appointment to visit UPS headquarters in Atlanta. I later toured the UPS Worldport distribution hub adjacent to the Louisville International Airport, which at night is basically taken over by the UPS fleet of cargo jets, as packages are flown in from all over the world, sorted, and flown back out again a few hours later. (The UPS fleet of 270 aircraft is the eleventh largest airline in the world.) What I discovered on these visits was that this is not your father's UPS. Yes, UPS still pulls in most of its $36 billion in sales by shipping more than 13.5 million packages a day from point A to point B. But behind that innocuous façade, the company founded in Seattle in 1907 as a messenger service has reinvented itself as a dynamic supply-chain manager.

Consider this: If you own a Toshiba laptop computer that is under warranty and it breaks and you call Toshiba to have it repaired, Toshiba will tell you to drop it off at a UPS store and have it shipped to Toshiba, and it will get repaired and then be shipped back to you. But here's what they don't tell you: UPS doesn't just pick up and deliver your Toshiba laptop. UPS actually repairs the computer in its own UPS-run workshop dedicated to computer and printer repairs at its Louisville hub. I went to tour that hub expecting to see only packages moving around, and instead I found myself dressed in a blue smock, in a special clean room, watching UPS employees replacing motherboards in broken Toshiba laptops. Toshiba had developed an image problem several years ago, with some customers concluding that its repair process for broken machines took too long. So Toshiba came to UPS and asked it to design a better system. UPS said, "Look, instead of us picking up the machine from your customers, bringing it to our hub, then flying it from our hub to your repair facility and then flying it back to our hub and then from our hub to your customer's house, let's cut out all the middle steps. We, UPS, will pick it up, repair it ourselves, and send it right back to your customer." It is now possible to send your Toshiba laptop in one day, get it repaired the next, and have it back the third day. The UPS repairmen and -women are all certified by Toshiba, and its customer complaints have gone down dramatically.

But this is just a sliver of what UPS does today. Eaten a Papa John's pizza lately? If you see the branded Papa John's supply truck go by, ask who's dispatching the drivers and scheduling the pickups of supplies, like tomatoes, pizza sauce, and onions. Answer: UPS. UPS comes inside a lot of companies now and takes over their branded vehicles to assure on-time delivery, which in the case of Papa John's includes getting the pizza dough from bakeries to outlets at exactly the right times each day. Tired of shopping for tennis shoes at the mall? Go online and order a pair of Nikes from its Web site, Nike.com. The order, though, is actually routed to UPS, and a UPS employee picks, inspects, packs, and delivers your shoes for Nike online from a warehouse in Kentucky managed by UPS. Ditto if you order some underwear from Jockey.com. UPS employees, who manage Jockey products at a UPS warehouse, will actually fill the order, bag it, label it, and deliver it to you. Your HP printer breaks in Europe or Latin America? The field service repairman who comes to your door to fix it works for UPS, which manages the replacement parts and repairs divisions for HP in those markets. Order some tropical fish from Segrest Farms in Florida to be delivered to your door in Canada by UPS? UPS worked with the company to develop a special packaging for the fish so they would not be injured as they traveled through UPS's sorting systems. The fish are even mildly sedated for safe travel (like kids on Dramamine). "We wanted them to have a pleasant ride," said UPS spokesman Steve Holmes.

What is going on here? It's a process that has come to be called "insourcing"—a whole new form of collaboration and creating value horizontally, made possible by the flat world and flattening it even more. In the previous section I discussed why supply-chaining is so important in the flat world. But not every company, indeed very few companies, can afford to develop and support a complex global supply chain of the scale and scope that Wal-Mart has developed. That is what gave birth to insourcing. Insourcing came about because once the world went flat, the small could act big—small companies could suddenly see around the world. Once they did, they saw a lot of places where they could sell their goods, manufacture their goods, or buy their raw materials in a more efficient manner. But many of them either didn't know how to pull all this off or couldn't afford to manage a complex global supply chain on their own. Many big companies didn't want to manage this complexity, which they felt was not part of their core competency. Nike would rather spend its cash and energy designing better tennis shoes, not supply chains.

This created a whole new global business opportunity for traditional package delivery firms like UPS. In 1996, UPS went into the business of "synchronized commerce solutions." It has spent $1 billion since then to buy twenty-five different global logistics and freight-forwarding firms so that it can service virtually any supply chain from one corner of the flat earth to the other. The business took off right around 2000. I like the term "insourcing" because UPS engineers come right inside your company; analyze its manufacturing, packaging, and delivery processes; and then design, redesign, and manage your whole global supply chain. And, if necessary, they'll even finance parts of it, such as receivables and COD payments. There are companies today (many of them don't want their names mentioned) that never touch their own products anymore. UPS oversees the whole journey from factory to warehouse to customer to repair. It even collects the money from customers if need be. This form of deep collaboration, which involves a huge amount of trust and intimacy among UPS, its client, and its client's customers, is a uniquely new flattener.

"You know who the majority of our customers and partners are? Small businesses," said UPS chairman and CEO Mike Eskew. "That's right . . . They are asking us to take them global. We help these companies achieve parity with the bigger guys."

Indeed, when you are a small business or individual working at home, and you can plug into UPS and have it become your global supply-chain manager, you can pretend you are a lot bigger than you are. When the small can act big, it levels the competitive playing field even more. UPS bought Mail Boxes, Etc. (now "The UPS Store" in the United States) so that it could offer individuals and small businesses the power of its global supply-chain services. But UPS also helps the big to act small. When you are a huge conglomerate, like HP, and you can get packages delivered or goods repaired quickly anywhere in the world, you can act really small.

In addition, by making the delivery of goods and services around the world superefficient and superfast—and in huge volumes—UPS is helping to level customs barriers and harmonize trade by getting more and more people to adopt the same rules and labels and tracking systems for transporting goods. UPS has a smart label on all its packages so that packages can be tracked and traced anywhere in its network.

Working with the U.S. Customs Service, UPS designed a software program that allows customs to say to UPS, "I want to see any package moving through your Worldport hub that was sent from Cali, Colombia, to Miami by someone named Carlos." Or, "I want to see any package sent from Germany to the United States by someone named Osama." When the package arrives for sorting, the UPS computers will automatically route that package to a customs officer in the UPS hub. A computerized arm will literally slide it off the conveyor belt and dump it into a bin for a closer look. It makes the inspection process more efficient and does not interrupt the general flow of packages. These efficiencies of time and scale save UPS's clients money, enabling them to recycle their capital and fund more innovation. But the level of collaboration it requires between UPS and its clients is unusual.

Plow & Hearth is a large national catalog and Internet retailer specializing in "Products for Country Living." P&H came to UPS one day and said that too many of its furniture deliveries were coming to customers with a piece broken. Did UPS have any ideas? UPS sent its "package engineers" over and conducted a packaging seminar for the P&H procurement group. UPS also provided guidelines for them to use in the selection of their suppliers. The objective was to help P&H understand that its purchase decisions from its suppliers should be influenced not only by the quality of the products being offered but also by how those products were being packaged and delivered. UPS couldn't help its customer P&H without looking deep inside its business and then into its suppliers' businesses—what boxes and packing materials they were using. That is insourcing.

Consider the collaboration today among eBay sellers, UPS, PayPal, and eBay buyers. Say I offer to sell a golf club on eBay and you decide to buy it. I e-mail you a PayPal invoice, which has your name and mailing address on it. At the same time, eBay offers me an icon on its Web site to print out a UPS mailing label to you. When I print that mailing label on my own printer, it comes out with a UPS tracking bar code on it. At the same time, UPS, through its computer system, creates a tracking number that corresponds to that label, which automatically gets e-mailed to you—the person who bought my golf club—so you can track the package by yourself, online, on a regular basis and know exactly when it will reach you.

If UPS had not gone into this business, someone would have had to invent it. With so many more people working through horizontal global supply chains far from home, somebody had to fill in the inevitable holes and tighten the weak links. Said Kurt Kuehn, UPS's senior vice president for sales and marketing, "The Texas machine parts guy is worried that the customer in Malaysia is a credit risk. We step in as a trusted broker. If we have control of that package, we can collect funds subject to acceptance and eliminate letters of credit. Trust can be created through personal relations or through systems and controls. If you don't have trust, you can rely on a shipper who does not turn [your package] over until he is paid. We have more ability than a bank to manage this, because we have the package and the ongoing relationship with the customer as collateral, so we have two points of leverage."

More than sixty companies have moved operations closer to the UPS hub in Louisville since 1997, so they can make things and ship them straight from the hub, without having to warehouse them. But it is not just the little guys who benefit from the better logistics and more efficient supply chains that insourcing can provide. In 2001, Ford Motor Co. turned over its snarled and slow distribution network to UPS, allowing UPS to come deep inside Ford to figure out what its problems were and smooth out its supply chain.

"For years, the bane of most Ford dealers was the automaker's Rube Goldberg–like system for getting cars from factory to showroom," *BusinessWeek* reported in its July 19, 2004, issue. "Cars could take as long as a month to arrive—that is, when they weren't lost along the way. And Ford Motor Co. was not always able to tell its dealers exactly what was coming, or even what was in inventory at the nearest rail yards. 'We'd lose track of whole trainloads of cars,' recalls Jerry Reynolds, owner of Prestige Ford in Garland, Tex. 'It was crazy.'" But after UPS got under Ford's hood, "UPS engineers . . . redesigned Ford's entire North American delivery network, streamlining everything from the route cars take from the factory to how they're processed at regional sorting hubs"— including pasting bar codes on the windshields of the four million cars coming out of Ford's U.S. plants so they could be tracked just like packages. As a result, UPS cut the time it takes autos to arrive at dealer lots by 40 percent, to ten days on average. *BusinessWeek* reported: "That saves Ford millions in working capital each year and makes it easy for its 6,500 dealers to track down the models most in demand . . . 'It was the most amazing transformation I had ever seen,' marvels Reynolds. 'My last comment to UPS was: 'Can you get us spare parts like this?'"

UPS maintains a think tank, the Operations Research Division, in

Timonium, Maryland, which works on supply-chain algorithms. This "school" of mathematics is called "package flow technology," and it is designed to constantly match the deployment of UPS trucks, ships, airplanes, and sorting capabilities with that day's flow of packages around the world. "Now we can make changes in our network in hours to adjust to changes in volume," says UPS CEO Eskew. "How I optimize the total supply chain is the key to the math." The sixty-person UPS team in Timonium is made up largely of people with engineering and math degrees, including several Ph.D.'s.

UPS also employs its own meteorologists and strategic threat analysts to track which atmospheric or geopolitical thunderstorms it will have to work around on any given day. To further grease its supply chains, UPS is the largest private user of wireless technology in the world, as its drivers alone make over one million phone calls a day in the process of picking up and delivering packages through its eighty-eight thousand package cars, vans, tractors, and motorcycles. On any given day, according to UPS, 2 percent of the world's GDP can be found in UPS delivery trucks or package cars. Oh, and did I mention that UPS also has a financing arm—UPS Capital—that will put up the money for the transformation of your supply chain, particularly if you are a small business and don't have the capital?

For example, notes Eskew, UPS was doing business with a small biotech company in Canada that sold blood adhesives, a highly perishable alternative to stitches. The company had a growing market among the major hospital chains, but it had a problem keeping up with demand and could not get financing. It had distribution centers on the East and West coasts. UPS redesigned the company's system based around a refrigerator hub in Dallas and extended it financing through UPS Capital. The result, said Eskew, was less inventory, better cash flow, better customer service—and an embedded customer for UPS. A maker of bridal headpieces and veils in Montreal wanted to improve its flow of business with the United States. Eskew recalled, "We designed a system for consolidated [customs] clearances, so their veils and headpieces would not have to come over [the border] one by one. And then we put [the merchandise] in a warehouse in [Upstate] New York. We took the orders by Internet, we put the labels on, we delivered the packages and collected the money, and we put that money through UPS Capital into their banks electronically so they had the cash back. That allows them to enter new markets and minimize their inventory."

Eskew explained, "When our grandfathers owned shops, inventory was what was in the back room. Now it is a box two hours away on a package car, or it might be hundreds more crossing the country by rail or jet, and you have thousands more crossing the ocean. And because we all have visibility into that supply chain, we can coordinate all those modes of transportation."

Indeed, as consumers have become more empowered to pull their own products via the Internet and customize them for themselves, UPS has found itself in the interesting position of being not only the company actually taking the orders but also, as the delivery service, the one handing the goods to the buyer at the front door. As a result, companies said, "Let's try to push as many differentiating things to the end of the supply chain, rather than the beginning." And because UPS was the last link in the supply chain before these goods were loaded onto planes, trains, and trucks, it took over many of these functions, creating a whole new business called End of Runway Services. The day I visited Louisville, two young UPS women were putting together Nikon cameras, with special memory cards and leather cases, which some store had offered as a weekend special. They were even putting them in special boxes just for that store. By taking over this function, UPS gives companies more options to customize products at the last minute.

UPS has also taken full advantage of the Netscape and work flow flatteners. Before 1995, all tracking and tracing of UPS packages for customers was done through a call center. You called a UPS 800 number and asked an operator where your package was. During the week before Christmas, UPS operators were fielding six hundred thousand calls on the peak days. Each one of those calls cost UPS $2.10 to handle. Then, through the 1990s, as more and more UPS customers became empowered and comfortable with the Internet, and as its own tracking and tracing system improved with advances in wireless technology, UPS invited its customers to track packages themselves over the Internet, at a cost to UPS of 5¢ to 10¢ a query.

"So we dramatically reduced our service costs and increased service," said UPS vice president Ken Sternad, especially since UPS now pulls in seven million tracking requests on an average day and a staggering twelve million on peak days. At the same time, its drivers also became more empowered with their DIADs—driver delivery information acquisition devices. These are the brown electronic clipboards that you always see the UPS drivers carrying around. The latest generation of them tells each driver where in his truck to load each package—exactly what position on the shelf. It also tells him where his next stop is, and if he goes to the wrong address, the GPS system built into the DIAD won't allow him to deliver the package. It also allows Mom to go online and find out when the driver will be in her neighborhood dropping off her package.

Insourcing is distinct from supply-chaining because it goes well beyond supply-chain management. Because it is third-party-managed logistics, it requires a much more intimate and extensive kind of collaboration among UPS and its clients and its clients' clients. In many cases today, UPS and its employees are so deep inside their clients' infrastructure that it is almost impossible to determine where one stops and the other starts. The UPS people are not just synchronizing your packages—they are synchronizing your whole company and its interaction with both customers and suppliers.

"This is no longer a vendor-customer relationship," said Eskew. "We answer your phones, we talk to your customers, we house your inventory, and we tell you what sells and doesn't sell. We have access to your information and you have to trust us. We manage competitors, and the only way for this to work, as our founders told Gimbels and Macy's, is 'trust us.' I won't violate that. Because we are asking people to let go of part of their business, and that really requires trust."

UPS is creating enabling platforms for anyone to take his or her business global or to vastly improve the efficiency of his or her global supply chain. It is a totally new business, but UPS is convinced it has an almost limitless upside. Time will tell. Though margins are still thin in this kind of work, in 2003 alone insourcing pulled in $2.4 billion in revenues for UPS. My gut tells me the folks in the funny brown shorts and funny brown trucks are on to something big—something made possible only by the flattening of the world and something that is going to flatten it a lot more.

FLATTENER #9
IN-FORMING
Google, Yahoo!, MSN Web Search

My friend and I met a guy at a restaurant. My friend was very taken with him, but I was suspiciously curious about this guy. After a few minutes of Googling, I found out that he was arrested for felony assault. Although I was once again disappointed with the quality of the dating pool, I was at least able to warn my friend about this guy's violent past.

— Testimonial from Google user

I am completely delighted with the translation service. My partner arranged for two laborers to come and help with some demolition. There was a miscommunication: she asked for the workers to come at 11 a.m., and the labor service sent them at 8:30. They speak only Spanish, and I speak English and some French. Our Hispanic neighbors were out. With the help of the translation service, I was able to communicate with the workers, to apologize for the miscommunication, establish the expectation, and ask them to come back at 11. Thank you for providing this connection . . . Thank you Google.

— Testimonial from Google user

I just want to thank Google for teaching me how to find love. While looking for my estranged brother, I stumbled across a Mexican Web site for male strippers — and I was shocked. My brother was working as a male prostitute! The first chance I got, I flew to the city he was working in to liberate him from this degrading profession. I went to the club he was working at and found my brother. But more than that, I met one of his co-workers . . . We got married last weekend [in Mexico], and I am positive without Google's services, I never would have found my brother, my husband, or the surprisingly lucrative nature of the male stripping industry in Mexico!! Thank you, Google!

— Testimonial from Google user

Google headquarters in Mountain View, California, has a certain Epcot Center feel to it—so many fun space-age toys to play with, so little time. In one corner is a spinning globe that emits light beams based on the volume of people searching on Google. As you would expect, most of the shafts of light are shooting up from North America, Europe, Korea, Japan, and coastal China. The Middle East and Africa remain pretty dark. In another corner is a screen that shows a sample of what things people are searching for at that moment, all over the world. When I was there in 2001, I asked my hosts what had been the most frequent searches lately. One, of course, was "sex," a perennial favorite of Googlers. Another was "God." Lots of people searching for Him or Her. A third was "jobs"—you can't find enough of those. And the fourth most searched item around the time of my visit? I didn't know whether to laugh or cry: "professional wrestling." The weirdest one, though, is the Google recipe book, where people just open their refrigerators, see what ingredients are inside, type three of them into Google, and see what recipes come up!

Fortunately, no single word or subject accounts for more than 1 or 2 percent of all Google searches at any given time, so no one should get too worried about the fate of humanity on the basis of Google's top search items on any particular day. Indeed, it is the remarkable diversity of searches going on via Google, in so many different tongues, that makes the Google search engine (and search engines in general) such huge flatteners. Never before in the history of the planet have so many people—*on their own*—had the ability to find so much information about so many things and about so many other people.

Said Russian-born Google cofounder Sergey Brin, "If someone has broadband, dial-up, or access to an Internet café, whether a kid in Cambodia, the university professor, or me who runs this search engine, all have the same basic access to overall research information that any-one has. It is a total equalizer. This is very different than how I grew up. My best access was some library, and it did not have all that much stuff, and you either had to hope for a miracle or search for something very simple or something very recent." When Google came along, he added, suddenly that kid had "universal access" to the information in libraries all over the world.

That is certainly Google's goal—to make easily available all the world's knowledge in every language. And Google hopes that in time, with a PalmPilot or a cell phone, everyone everywhere will be able to carry around access to all the world's knowledge in their pockets. "Everything" and "everyone" are key words that you hear around Google all the time. Indeed, the official Google history carried on its home page notes that the name "Google" is a play on the word "'googol,' which is the number represented by the numeral 1 followed by 100 zeros. Google's use of the term reflects the company's mission to organize the immense, seemingly infinite amount of information available on the Web," just for you. What Google's success reflects is how much people are interested in having just that—all the world's knowledge at their fingertips. There is no bigger flattener than the idea of making all the world's knowledge, or even just a big chunk of it, available to anyone and everyone, anytime, anywhere.

"We do discriminate only to the degree that if you can't use a computer or don't have access to one, you can't use Google, but other than that, if you can type, you can use Google," said Google CEO Eric Schmidt. And surely if the flattening of the world means anything, he added, it means that "there is no discrimination in accessing knowledge. Google is now searchable in one hundred languages, and every time we find another we increase it. Let's imagine a group with a Google iPod one day and you can tell it to search by voice—that would take care of people who can't use a computer—and then [Google access] just becomes about the rate at which we can get cheap devices into people's hands."

How does searching fit into the concept of collaboration? I call it "in-forming." In-forming is the individual's personal analog to uploading, outsourcing, insourcing, supply-chaining, and offshoring. In-forming is the ability to build and deploy your own personal supply chain—a supply chain of information, knowledge, and entertainment. In-forming is about self-collaboration—becoming your own self-directed and self-empowered researcher, editor, and selector of entertainment, without having to go to the library or the movie theater or through network television. In-forming is searching for knowledge. It is about seeking like-minded people and communities. Google's phenomenal global popularity, which has spurred Yahoo! and Microsoft (through its MSN Search) also to make power searching and in-forming prominent features of their Web sites, shows how hungry people are for this form of collaboration. Google is now processing roughly one billion searches per day, up from 150 million just three years ago.

The easier and more accurate searching becomes, added Larry Page, Google's other cofounder, the more global Google's user base becomes, and the more powerful a flattener it becomes. Every day more and more people are able to in-form themselves in their own language. Today, said Page, "only a third of our searches are U.S.-based, and less than half are in English." Moreover, he added, "as people are searching for more obscure things, people are publishing more obscure things," which drives the flattening effect of in-forming even more. All the major search engines have also recently added the capability for users to search not only the Web for information but also their own computer's hard drive for words or data or e-mail they know is in there somewhere but have forgotten where. When you can search your own memory more efficiently, that is really in-forming. In late 2004, Google announced plans to scan the entire contents of both the University of Michigan and Stanford University libraries, making tens of thousands of books available and searchable online.

In the earliest days of search engines, people were amazed and delighted to stumble across the information they sought; eureka moments were unexpected surprises, said Yahoo!'s cofounder Jerry Yang. "Today their attitudes are much more presumptive. They presume that the information they're looking for is certainly available and that it's just a matter of technologists making it easier to get to, and in fewer keystrokes," he said. "The democratization of information is having a profound impact on society. Today's consumers are much more efficient—they can find information, products, services, faster [through search engines] than through traditional means. They are better informed about issues related to work, health, leisure, etc. Small towns are no longer disadvantaged relative to those with better access to information. And people have the ability to be better connected to things that interest them, to quickly and easily become experts in given subjects and to connect with others who share their interests."

Google's founders understood that by the late 1990s hundreds of thousands of Web pages were being added to the Internet each day, and that existing search engines, which tended to search for keywords, could not keep pace. Brin and Page, who met as Stanford University graduate students in computer science in 1995, developed a mathematical formula that ranked a Web page by how many other Web pages were linked to it, on the assumption that the more people linked to a certain page, the more important the page. The key breakthrough that enabled Google to become first among search engines was its ability to combine its PageRank technology with an analysis of page content, which determines which pages are most relevant to the specific search being conducted. Even though Google entered the market after other major search players, its answers were seen by people as more accurate and relevant to what they were looking for. The fact that one search engine was just a little better than the others led a tidal wave of people to switch to it. (Google now employs scores of mathematicians working on its search algorithms, in an effort to always keep them one step more relevant than the competition.)

For some reason, said Brin, "people underestimated the importance of finding information, as opposed to other things you would do online. If you are searching for something like a health issue, you really want to know; in some cases it is a life-and-death matter. We have people who search Google for heart-attack symptoms and then call nine-one-one." But sometimes you really want to in-form yourself about something much simpler.

When I was in Beijing in June 2004, I was riding the elevator down one morning with my wife, Ann, and sixteen-year-old daughter, Natalie, who was carrying a fistful of postcards written to her friends. Ann said to her, "Did you bring their addresses along?" Natalie looked at her as if she were positively nineteenth-century. "No," she said, with that you-are-so-out-of-it-Mom tone of voice. "I just Googled their phone numbers, and their home addresses came up."

Address book? You dummy, Mom.

All that Natalie was doing was in-forming, using Google in a way that I had no idea was possible. Thanks to Google, all that digitized information that we were creating with our PCs was suddenly searchable. It could suddenly be mined. What is staggering is how much information there is out there—information that was never searchable, but will be in the future, thanks to ever smarter search engines, which will be able to sift through larger and larger mountains of different kinds of data—from pictures to videos to home listings to traffic reports to high school newspapers and health cures. "People have thought about text as the one source of information," said Kai-Fu Lee, who originally set up the Microsoft research center in Beijing and now directs Google's operations in China. "But there are images, videos, books, even from ages ago, that now will be searchable. There is geographical information, maps, and there is local information and there is personal information. Information on your computer . . . Basically everything we see, hear, touch, read, and write is information—and right now Internet search covers only a tiny, tiny fraction of everything that could be browsed and searched and navigated." In time, individuals will have the power to find anything in the world at any time on all kinds of devices—and that will be enormously empowering. "What excites me is the empowerment," added Lee. "I will be able to focus my time and attention and brainpower on what I do best, which is not looking for stuff." It is building, designing, imagining, and creating stuff.

While we were traveling in China, Natalie also had her iPod with her, which empowered her to in-form herself in another way—with entertainment instead of knowledge. She had become her own music editor and loaded all her favorite songs onto her iPod and was carrying them all over China. Think about it: For decades the broadcast industry was built around the idea that you shoot out ads on network television or radio and hope that someone is watching or listening. But thanks to the flattening technologies in entertainment, that world is quickly fading away. Now with TiVo you can become your own TV editor. TiVo allows viewers to digitally record their favorite programs and skip the ads, except those they want to see. You watch what you want when you want. You don't have to make an appointment with a TV channel at the time and place someone else sets and watch the commercials foisted on you. With TiVo you can watch only your own shows and the commercials you want for only those products in which you might be interested.

But just as Google can track what you are searching for, so too can TiVo, which knows which shows and which ads you are freezing, storing, and rewinding on your own TV. So here's a news quiz: Guess what was the most rewound moment in TV history? Answer: Janet's Jackson breast exposure, or, as it was euphemistically called, her "wardrobe malfunction," at the 2004 Super Bowl. Just ask TiVo. In a press release it issued on February 2, 2004, TiVo said, "Justin Timberlake and Janet Jackson stole the show during Sunday's Super Bowl, attracting almost twice as many viewers as the most thrilling moments on the field, according to an annual measurement of second-by-second viewership in TiVo households. The Jackson-Timberlake moment drew the biggest spike in audience reaction TiVo has ever measured. TiVo said viewership spiked up to 180 percent as hundreds of thousands of households used TiVo's unique capabilities to pause and replay live television to view the incident again and again."

So if everyone can increasingly watch what he wants however many times he wants when he wants, the whole notion of broadcast TV— which is that we throw shows out there one time, along with their commercials, and then try to survey who is watching—will increasingly make less and less sense. The companies you want to bet on are those that, like Google or Yahoo! or TiVo, learn to collaborate with their users and offer them shows and advertisements tailored just for them. I can imagine a day soon when advertisers won't pay for anything other than that.

Companies like Google, Yahoo!, Amazon.com, and TiVo have learned to thrive not by pushing products and services on their customers so much as by building collaborative systems that enable customers to pull on their own, and then responding with lightning quickness to what they pull. It is so much more efficient.

"Search is so highly personal that searching is empowering for humans like nothing else," said Google CEO Eric Schmidt. "It is the antithesis of being told or taught. It is about self-empowerment; it is empowering individuals to do what they think best with the information they want. It is very different from anything else that preceded it. Radio was one-to-many. TV was one-to-many. The telephone was one-to-one. Search is the ultimate expression of the power of the individual, using a computer, looking at the world, and finding exactly what they want—and everyone is different when it comes to that."

Of course what made Google not just a search engine but a hugely profitable business was its founders' realization that they could build a targeted advertising model that would show you ads that are relevant to you when you searched for a specific topic and then could charge advertisers for the number of times Google users clicked on their ads. Whereas CBS broadcasts a movie and has only a rough idea who is watching it or the advertisements, Google knows exactly what you are interested in—after all, you are searching for it—and can link you up with advertisers directly or indirectly connected to your searches. In late 2004, Google began a service whereby if you are walking around Bethesda, Maryland, and are in the mood for sushi, you just send Google an SMS message on your cell phone that says "Sushi 20817"—the Bethesda zip code—and it will send you back a text message of choices. Lord only knows where this will go.

In-forming, though, also involves searching for friends, allies, and collaborators. It is empowering the formation of global communities, across all international and cultural boundaries, which is another critically important flattening function. People can now search out fellow collaborators on any subject, project, or theme—particularly through portals like Yahoo! Groups. Yahoo! has about 300 million users and 4 million active groups. Those groups have 13 million unique individuals accessing them each month from all over the world.

"The Internet is growing in the self-services area, and Yahoo! Groups exemplifies this trend," said Jerry Yang. "It provides a forum, a platform, a set of tools for people to have private, semiprivate, or public gatherings on the Internet regardless of geography or time. It enables consumers to gather around topics that are meaningful to them in ways that are either impractical or impossible offline. Groups can serve as support groups for complete strangers who are galvanized by a common issue (coping with rare diseases, first-time parents, spouses of active-duty personnel) or who seek others who share similar interests (hobbies as esoteric as dog-sledding, blackjack, and indoor tanning have large memberships). Existing communities can migrate online and flourish in an interactive environment (local kids' soccer league, church youth group, alumni organizations), providing a virtual home for groups interested in sharing, organizing, and communicating information valuable to cultivating vi-brant communities. Some groups exist only online and could never be as successful offline, while others mirror strong real-world communities. Groups can be created instantaneously and dissolved; topics can change or stay constant. This trend will only grow as consumers increasingly be-come publishers, and they can seek the affinity and community *they* choose—when, where, and how they choose it."

When individuals are empowered to inform themselves in all these new ways, it is enormously flattening—but also enormously frightening. Why? Because people will be able to drill down for information about you and me that used to be either impossible or very difficult to locate. Our lives and our pasts used to have rock-hard cement floors under them. It took a lot to drill through those floors and even then it was of-ten hard to find out what was really down there. Yes, those hard floors sometimes protected bad people—from con men to pedophiles—as they moved from town to town. But they also protected you and me and our basic privacy, making it difficult for prying strangers to dig too deeply into our past or present. But Google, Yahoo!, and MSN Search are getting rid of those hard floors, very quickly, so anyone can drill into anyone else's past with a few thumb clicks on a PalmPilot. You never know anymore what kind of electronic footprints you are leaving in databases that you assume are private and will now, or soon will be, searchable. And you may be shocked to discover all the things that people, or companies, can find out about you—from your salary to where you live to your favorite books—just by Googling you.

Everyone can now be Googled—but everyone now can also Google.

Google also equalizes access to information—it has no class boundaries, few education boundaries, few linguistic boundaries, and virtually no money boundaries. If you can get on Google, you have access to the world's greatest research tool, without having to go to MIT. "If I can operate Google, I can find anything," said Alan Cohen, then vice president of Airespace, which sells wireless technology. "Google is like God. God is wireless, God is everywhere, and God sees everything. Any questions in the world, you ask Google."

FLATTENER #10
THE STEROIDS
Digital, Mobile, Personal, and Virtual

But this iPaq's real distinction is its wirelessness. It's the first palmtop that can connect to the Internet and other gadgets in four wireless ways. For distances up to 30 inches, the iPaq can beam information, like your electronic business card, to another palmtop using an infrared transmitter. For distances up to 30 feet, it has built-in Bluetooth circuitry . . . For distances up to 150 feet, it has a Wi-Fi antenna. And for transmissions around the entire planet, the iPaq has one other trick up its sleeve: it's also a cell phone. If your office can't reach you on this, then you must be on the International Space Station.

—From a *New York Times* article about HP's new PocketPC,
July 29, 2004

I am on the bullet train speeding southwest from Tokyo to Mishima. The view is spectacular: fishing villages on my left and a snow-dusted Mt. Fuji on my right. My colleague Jim Brooke, a Tokyo-based reporter for *The New York Times*, is sitting across the aisle and paying no attention to the view. He is engrossed in his computer. So am I, actually, but he's online through a wireless connection, and I'm just typing away on a column on my unconnected laptop. Ever since we took a cab together the other day in downtown Tokyo and Jim whipped out his wireless-enabled laptop in the backseat and e-mailed me something through Yahoo!, I have been exclaiming at the amazing degree of wireless penetration and connectivity in Japan. Save for a few remote islands and mountain villages, if you have a wireless card in your computer, or any Japanese cell phone, you can get online anywhere—from deep inside the subway stations to the bullet trains speeding through the countryside. Jim knows I am slightly obsessed with the fact that Japan, not to mention most of the rest of the world, has so much better wireless connectivity than America. Anyway, Jim likes to rub it in.

"See, Tom, I am online right now," he says, as the Japanese countryside whizzes by. "A friend of mine who's the *Times's* stringer in Alma Ata just had a baby and I am congratulating him. He had a baby girl last night." Jim keeps giving me updates. "Now I'm reading the frontings!"—a summary of the day's *New York Times* headlines. Finally, I ask Jim, who speaks some Japanese, to ask the train conductor to come over. The conductor ambles by. I ask Jim to ask him how fast we are going. They rattle back and forth in Japanese for a few seconds before Jim translates: "240 kilometers per hour." I shake my head. We are on a bullet train going 240 km per hour—that's 150 mph—and my colleague is answering e-mail from Kazakhstan, and I can't drive from my home in suburban Washington to downtown D.C. without my cell phone service being interrupted at least twice. The day before, I was in Tokyo waiting for an appointment with Jim's colleague Todd Zaun, and he was preoccupied with his Japanese cell phone, which easily connects to the Internet from anywhere. "I am a surfer," Todd explained, as he used his thumb to manipulate the keypad. "For $3 a month I subscribe to this [Japanese] site that tells me each morning how high the waves are at the beaches near my house. I check it out, and I decide where the best place to surf is that day."

(The more I thought about this, the more I wanted to run for president on a one-issue ticket: "I promise, if elected, that within four years America will have as good cell phone coverage as Ghana, and in eight years as good as Japan—provided that the Japanese sign a standstill agreement and won't innovate for eight years so we can catch up." My campaign bumper sticker will be very simple: "Can You Hear Me Now?")

I know that America will catch up sooner or later with the rest of the world in wireless technology. It's already happening. But this section about the tenth flattener is not just about wireless. It is about what I call the "steroids." I call certain new technologies the steroids because they are amplifying and turbocharging all the other flatteners. They are taking all the forms of collaboration highlighted in this section—outsourcing, off-shoring, uploading, supply-chaining, insourcing, and in-forming—and making it possible to do each and every one of them in a way that is "dig-ital, mobile, virtual, and personal," as former HP CEO Carly Fiorina put it in her speeches, thereby enhancing each one and making the world flatter by the day.

By "digital," Fiorina means that thanks to the PC–Windows–Netscape–work flow revolutions, all analog content and processes—everything from photography to entertainment to communication to word processing to architectural design to the management of my home lawn sprinkler system—are being digitized and therefore can be shaped, manipulated, and transmitted over computers, the Internet, satellites, or fiber-optic cable. By "virtual," she means that the process of shaping, ma-nipulating, and transmitting this digitized content can be done at very high speeds, with total ease, so that you never have to think about it—thanks to all the underlying digital pipes, protocols, and standards that have now been installed. By "mobile," she means that thanks to wireless technology, all this can be done from anywhere, with anyone, through any device, and can be taken anywhere. And by "personal," she means that it can be done by you, just for you, on your own device.

What does the flat world look like when you take all these new forms of collaboration and turbocharge them in this way? Let me give just one example. Bill Brody, the president of Johns Hopkins, told me this story in the summer of 2004: "I am sitting in a medical meeting in Vail and the [doctor] giving a lecture quotes a study from Johns Hopkins University. And the guy speaking is touting a new approach to treating prostate can-cer that went against the grain of the current surgical method. It was a minimally invasive approach to prostate cancer. So he quotes a study by Dr. Patrick Walsh, who had developed the state-of-the-art standard of care for prostate surgery. This guy who is speaking proposes an alternate method—which was controversial—but he quotes from Walsh's Hopkins study in a way that supported his approach. When he said that, I said to myself, 'That doesn't sound like Dr. Walsh's study.' So I had a PDA [personal digital assistant], and I immediately went online [wirelessly] and got into the Johns Hopkins portal and into Medline and did a search right while I was sitting there. Up come all the Walsh abstracts. I toggled on one and read it, and it was not at all what the guy was saying it was. So I raised my hand during the Q and A and read two lines from the abstract, and the guy just turned beet red."

The digitization and storage of all the Johns Hopkins faculty research in recent years made it possible for Brody to search it instantly and virtually without giving it a second thought. The advances in wireless technology made it possible for him to do that search from anywhere with any device. And his handheld personal computer enabled him to do that search personally—by himself, just for himself.

What are the steroids that made all this possible?

The first steroid has to do with computing: One simple way to think about computing, at any scale, is that it is composed of three things: computational capability, storage capability, and input/output capability—the speed by which information is drawn in and out of the computer/storage complexes. And all of these have been steadily increasing since the days of the first bulky mainframes. This mutually reinforcing progress constitutes a significant steroid. As a result of it, year after year we have been able to digitize, shape, crunch, and transmit more words, music, data, and entertainment than ever before.

For instance, for several decades now chipmakers have been steadily "shrinking the transistors on chips so that electrons have less distance to travel, thereby speeding up the processing of data," noted *BusinessWeek* (June 20, 2005). MIPS stands for "millions of instructions per second," and it is one measure of the computational capability of a computer's microchips. In 1971, the Intel 4004 microprocessor produced .06 MIPS, or 60,000 instructions per second. Today's Intel Pentium Processor Extreme Edition (with two cores) approaches a theoretical maximum of over 20 billion instructions per second. In 1971, the Intel 4004 microprocessor contained 2,300 transistors. Intel's highest-end Itanium processor for 2006 packs 1.7 billion transistors.

One problem, though, is that these miniature circuits are getting crammed together so tightly that they are heating up and affecting the performance of chips. Not to worry. Chipmakers are continuing to juice up this steroid to make superfast and superfaster chips, by replacing the single powerful microprocessor at the heart of a PC with two or more "computing cores" that work together in one microprocessor, noted *BusinesssWeek*. These cores can share the load, so that neither one overheats or uses too much energy.

Meanwhile, inputting and outputting data have leaped ahead at a staggering rate. At the speeds that disk drives operated back in the early days of 286 and 386 chips, it would have taken about a minute to download a single photo from my latest digital camera. Today I can do that almost instantaneously on a USB 2.0 disk drive and the latest Intel processor. At the same time, the amount of stuff you can now store to input and output "is off the charts, thanks to the steady advances in storage devices," said Craig Mundie, Microsoft's chief technology officer. "Storage is growing exponentially, and this is really as much a factor in the revolution as anything else." It's what is allowing all forms of content to become digital and to some extent portable. It is also becoming cheap enough that you can put massive amounts on even the personal devices people carry around with them. Five years ago, no one would have believed that you would be able to sell iPods with forty gigabytes of storage, capable of holding thousands of songs, for prices that teenagers could afford. Now it's seen as ho-hum. And when it comes to moving all these bits around, the computing world has been turbocharged. Advances in fiber optics will soon allow a single fiber to carry one terabit per second. With forty-eight fibers in a cable, that's forty-eight terabits per second. Henry Schacht, the former CEO of Lucent, which specialized in this technology, pointed out that with that much capacity, you could "transmit all the printed material in the world in minutes in a single cable. This means unlimited transmitting capacity at zero incremental cost." Even though the speeds that Schacht was talking about apply only to the backbone of the fiber network, and not that last mile into your house and into your computer, we are still talking about a quantum leap forward.

In *The Lexus and the Olive Tree*, I wrote about a 1999 Qwest commercial showing a businessman, tired and dusty, checking in to a roadside motel in the middle of nowhere. He asks the bored-looking desk clerk whether they have room service and other amenities. She says yes. Then he asks her whether entertainment is available on his room television, and the clerk answers in a what-do-you-think-you-idiot monotone, "All rooms have every movie ever made in every language, anytime, day or night." I wrote about that back then as an example of what happens when you get connected to the Internet. Today it is an example of how much you can now get *disconnected* from the Internet, because in the next few years, as storage continues to advance and become more and more miniaturized, you will be able to buy enough storage to carry many of those movies around in your pocket.

The second steroid involves breakthroughs in instant messaging and file sharing. File sharing, the peer-to-peer model, allows computer users to share songs, video, and other kinds of files with one another online. Peer-to-peer networks emerged in the public eye with Napster, which enabled any two of us to share songs stored on each other's computers. "At its peak," according to Howstuffworks.com, "Napster was perhaps the most popular Web site ever created. In less than a year, it went from zero to 60 million visitors per month. Then it was shut down by a court order because of copyright violations, and wouldn't re-launch until 2003 as a legal music-download site. The original Napster became so popular so quickly because it offered a unique product—free music that you could obtain nearly effortlessly from a gigantic database." That database was actually a file-sharing architecture by which Napster facilitated a connection between my computer and yours so that we could swap music files. The original Napster is dead, but file-sharing technology is still around and is getting more sophisticated every day, greatly enhancing collaboration. Some 330 million tracks were purchased online in 2004 from online stores such as Apple's iTunes, the Associated Press reported on June 22, 2005, but around 5 billion were downloaded for free by people tapping open file-sharing networks using freely downloadable file-sharing programs such as eDonkey, BitTorrent, and Kazaa.

The third steroid involves breakthroughs in making phone calls over the Internet. Collaborating with all this digitized data is going to be made even easier and cheaper thanks to another burgeoning steroid—voice over Internet protocol service, known as VoIP. VoIP allows you to make phone calls over the Internet by turning voices into data packets that are sent down Internet networks and converted back into voices on the other end. VoIP allows anyone who subscribes to the service through his phone company or private operator to receive unlimited local and long-distance phone calls, via the Internet, over his personal computer, laptop, or PDA—with just a small microphone attachment. It is personal and it will be delivered virtually—the underlying pipes will make it happen without your having to think about it at all. It will make every business and personal phone call to anywhere in the world as cheap as a local call—i.e., almost free. If that won't amplify every form of collaboration, I don't know what will.

Consider this item from the November 1, 2004, *BusinessWeek*, about the pioneering VoIP company Skype: "Eriksen Translations Inc. is a small business with a big footprint. The Brooklyn (N.Y.) company relies on 5,000 freelancers scattered around the world to help translate business documents in 75 languages for U.S. clients. That means phone bills of about $1,000 a month. So when business development manager Claudia Waitman heard about a new company called Skype Technologies that offers free voice calls over the Internet to other Skype users anywhere in the world, she jumped. Six months after signing up, Eriksen's phone costs already have fallen 10 percent. Even better, its employees and freelancers confer more often, allowing them to work faster and more efficiently. 'It has changed the whole way we work,' Waitman says." In late 2005, Skype came out with a 2.0 beta version of its phone-calling software that some say will make this technology even more popular. It includes videoconferencing capability, a smoother, clearer interface, and a handset system so you can make Internet-based phone calls without being tied to a microphone attached to your computer. More and more I run into parents who tell me they have kids studying or stationed around the world whom they talk to regularly now, for virtually nothing, thanks to Skype and other VoIP systems.

VoIP is going to revolutionize the telecommunications industry, which, since its inception, has been based on the simple notion that companies charge you for how long you talk and over what distance. As consumers get more VoIP choices, the competition will be such that telecom companies won't be able to charge for time and distance much longer. Voice will become free. What phone companies will compete over, and charge for, will be the add-ons. The old voice platform did not lend itself well to innovation. But when you put voice on an Internet platform, all sorts of innovative options for collaboration become possible. You will have a buddy list of people and all you will have to do is double-click on a name and the call will go through. You want caller ID? The caller's picture will come up on your screen. Companies will compete over SoIP (services over the Internet protocol): who can offer you the best videoconferencing while you are talking over your computer, PDA, or laptop; who can enable you to talk to someone while easily inviting a third or fourth person into the conversation; who can enable you to talk and swap document files and send text messages at the same time, so you can actually speak and work on a document together while talking. You will be able to leave someone a voice message that can be converted to text, along with a document attachment that the two of you may be working on. Said Mike Volpi, Cisco's senior vice president for routing technology, "It won't be about distance and how long you talk, but how you create value around voice communication. The voice will be free; it's what you enable customers to do around it that will differentiate companies."

People who live in Bangalore or Beijing will be able to get themselves listed in the Yellow Pages in New York. Looking for an accountant? Just double-click Hang Zhou in Beijing or Vladimir Tolstoy in Moscow or Ernst & Young in New York. Take your choice for accounting: Tiananmen Square, Red Square, or Union Square. They'll be happy to collaborate with you in filling out your tax returns.

The fourth steroid is videoconferencing, which is going to a whole new level. HP and the film company DreamWorks SKG collaborated on the design of a videoconferencing suite—with DreamWorks bringing its movie and sound expertise and HP contributing its computing and compression technology—that is breathtaking. Each party to the video-conference sits at a long table facing a wall of flat-panel TV screens and cameras pointed at them. The flat-panel screens display the people at the other site, which could be anywhere in the world. It creates an effect of everyone sitting around a single conference table and is apparently a qual-itatively different experience from anything that has been on the market before. I had a chance to participate in a demonstration of it, and it was so realistic that you could practically feel the breath of the other parties to the videoconference, when in fact half of us were in Santa Barbara and half were five hundred miles away. Because DreamWorks is doing film and an-imation work all over the world, it felt that it had to have a videoconfer-encing solution where its creative people could really communicate all their thoughts, facial expressions, feelings, ire, enthusiasm, and raised eye-brows. HP's chief strategy and technology officer, Shane Robison, told me that HP plans to have these videoconferencing suites for sale by 2005 at a cost of roughly $250,000 each. That is nothing compared to the airline tickets and wear and tear on executives having to travel regularly to London or Tokyo for face-to-face meetings. Companies could easily make one of these suites pay for itself in a year. This level of videoconferencing, once it proliferates, will make remote development, outsourcing, and off-shoring that much easier and more efficient.

A fifth steroid involves recent advances in computer graphics—driven in part by the advances in computer games. These are greatly en-hancing video collaboration and computing generally by offering so much sharper images and so many more ways to illustrate and manipu-late those images on a screen. IBM's Irving Wladawsky-Berger intro-duced me to this steroid in his blog. "One of the most exciting areas of innovation is emerging around what I'd like to call 3rd Generation User Interfaces, inspired by game players," he wrote. "[These promise] to bring highly visual, interactive interfaces to all sorts of applications in health care, education, science and business." This is important, he added, "because every time a new paradigm emerges in the way people interact with computers, we've seen all kinds of new applications begin

to appear, qualitatively better than and different from anything before . . . Video games are particularly important in this regard, because
in addition to their very realistic visual images and great sound, they are
also highly interactive and increasingly collaborative, and thus a good
launch pad for thinking about how people should best interact with all
kinds of computer applications as well as with each other in the future."

The sixth, and maybe most important, steroid—really a group of
steroids—involves the new wireless technologies and devices. These are
the übersteroids that make us, and all the new forms of collaboration,
mobile, so that now we can manipulate, share, and shape our digital content from anywhere, with anyone, totally mobilely.

"The natural state of communications is wireless," argued Alan
Cohen, the senior vice president at Airespace. It started with voice, because people wanted to be able to make a phone call anytime, from any-
place, to anywhere. That is why for many people the cell phone is the
most important phone they own. By the early twenty-first century, people
began to develop that same expectation and with it the desire for data
communication—the ability to access the Internet, e-mail, or any business files anytime, anywhere, using a cell phone, PalmPilot, or some
other personal device. (And now a third element is entering the picture,
creating more demand for wireless technology and enhancing the flattening of the earth: machines talking to machines wirelessly, such as
Wal-Mart's RFID chips, the little wireless devices that automatically
transmit information to suppliers' computers, allowing them to track
inventory.)

In the early days of computing (Globalization 2.0), you worked in the
office. There was a big mainframe computer, and you literally had to
walk over and get the people running the mainframe to extract or input
information for you. It was like an oracle. Then, thanks to the PC and the
Internet, e-mail, the laptop, the browser, and the client server, I could access from my own screen all sorts of data and information being stored on
the network. In this era you were delinked from the office and could
work at home, at the beach house, or in a hotel. Now we are in Globalization 3.0, where, thanks to digitization, miniaturization, virtualization,
personalization, and wireless, I can be processing, collecting, or trans-

mitting voice or data from anywhere to anywhere — as an individual or as a machine.

"Your desk goes with you everywhere you are now," said Cohen. And the more people have the ability to push and pull information from anywhere to anywhere faster, the more barriers to competition and communication disappear. All of a sudden, my business has phenomenal distribution. I don't care whether you are in Bangalore or Bangor, I can get to you and you can get to me. More and more, people now want and expect wireless mobility to be there, just like electricity. We are rapidly moving into the age of the "mobile me," said Padmasree Warrior, the chief technology officer of Motorola. If consumers are paying for any form of content, whether it is information, entertainment, data, games, or stock quotes, they increasingly want to be able to access it anytime, anywhere.

Right now consumers are caught in a maze of wireless technology offerings and standards that are still not totally interoperable. As we all know, some wireless technology works in one neighborhood, state, or country and not in another.

The "mobile me" revolution will be complete when you can move seamlessly around the town, the country, or the world with whatever device you want. The technology is getting there. When this is fully diffused, the "mobile me" will have its full flattening effect, by freeing people to truly be able to work and communicate from anywhere to anywhere with anything.

I got a taste of what is coming by spending a morning at the Tokyo headquarters of NTT DoCoMo, the Japanese cellular giant that is at the cutting edge of this process and far ahead of America in offering total interoperability inside Japan. DoCoMo is an abbreviation for Do Communications Over the Mobile Network; it also means "anywhere" in Japanese. My day at DoCoMo's headquarters started with a tour conducted by a robot, which bowed in perfect Japanese fashion and then gave me a spin around DoCoMo's showroom, which now features handheld video cell phones so you can see the person you are speaking with.

"Young people are using our mobile phones today as two-way videophones," explained Tamon Mitsuishi, senior VP of the Ubiquitous Business Department at DoCoMo. "Everyone takes out their phones, they start dialing each other and have visual conversations. Of course there are some people who prefer not to see each other's faces." Thanks to DoCoMo technology, if you don't want to show your face you can substitute a cartoon character for yourself and manipulate the keyboard so that it not only will speak for you but also will get angry for you and get happy for you. "So this is a mobile phone, and video camera, but it has also evolved to the extent that it has functions similar to a PC," he added. "You need to move your buttons quickly [with your thumb]. We call ourselves 'the thumb people.' Young girls in high school can now move their thumbs faster than they can type on a PC."

By the way, I asked, what does the "Ubiquitous Department" do?

"Now that we have seen the spread of the Internet around the world," answered Mitsuishi, "what we believe we have to offer is the next step. Internet communication until today has been mostly between individuals—e-mail and other information. But what we are already starting to see is communication between individuals and machines and between machines. We are moving into that kind of phenomenon, because people want to lead a richer lifestyle, and businesses want more efficient practices . . . So young people in their business life use PCs in the offices, but in their private time they base their lifestyles on a mobile phone. There is now a growing movement to allow payment by mobile phone. [With] a smart card you will be able to make payments in virtual shops and smart shops. So next to the cash register there will be a reader of the card, and you just scan your phone and it becomes your credit card too . . .

"We believe that the mobile phone will become the essential controller of a person's life," added Mitsuishi, oblivious of the double meaning of the English word "control." "For example, in the medical field it will be your authentication system and you can examine your medical records, and to make payments you will have to hold a mobile phone. You will not be able to lead a life without a mobile phone, and it will control things at home too. We believe that we need to expand the range of machines that can be controlled by mobile phone."

There is plenty to worry about in this future, from kids being lured by online sexual predators through their cell phones, to employees spending too much time playing mindless phone games, to people using their phone cameras for all sorts of illicit activities. Some Japanese were going into bookstores, pulling down cookbooks, and taking pictures of the recipes and then walking out. Fortunately, camera phones are now being enabled to make a noise when they shoot a picture, so that a store owner, or the person standing next to you in the locker room, will know if he is on *Candid Camera*. Because your Internet-enabled camera phone is not just a camera; it is also a copy machine, with worldwide distribution potential.

DoCoMo is now working with other Japanese companies on an arrangement by which you may be walking down the street and see a poster of a concert by Madonna in Tokyo. The poster will have a bar code and you can buy your tickets by just scanning the bar code. Another poster might be for a new Madonna CD. Just scan the bar code with your cell phone and it will give you a sample of the songs. If you like them, scan it again and you can buy the whole album and have it home-delivered. No wonder my *New York Times* colleague in Japan, Todd Zaun, who is married to a Japanese woman, remarked to me that there is so much information the Japanese can now access from their Internet-enabled wireless phones that "when I am with my Japanese relatives and someone has a question, the first thing they do is reach for the phone."

I'm exhausted just writing about all this. But it is hard to exaggerate how much this tenth flattener—the steroids—is going to amplify and further empower all the other forms of collaboration. These steroids should make uploading that much more open, because they will enable more individuals to collaborate with one another in more ways and from more places than ever before. They will enhance outsourcing, because they will make it so much easier for a single department of any company to collaborate with another company. They will enhance supply-chaining, because headquarters will be able to be connected in real time with every individual employee stocking the shelves, every individual package, and every Chinese factory manufacturing the stuff inside those packages. They will enhance insourcing—having a company like UPS come deep inside a retailer and manage its whole supply chain, using drivers who can interact with its warehouses, and with every customer, carrying his own PDA. And most obviously, they will enhance in-forming— the ability to manage your own knowledge supply chain.

Sir John Rose, the chief executive of Rolls-Royce, gave me a wonderful example of how wireless and other steroids are enhancing Rolls-Royce's ability to do work flow and other new forms of collaboration with its customers. Let's say you are British Airways and you are flying a Boeing 777 across the Atlantic. Somewhere over Greenland, one of your Rolls-Royce engines gets hit with lightning. The passengers and pilots might be worried, but there is no need. Rolls-Royce is on the case. That Rolls-Royce engine is connected by transponder to a satellite and is beaming data about its condition and performance, at all times, down into a computer in Rolls-Royce's operations room. That is true of many Rolls-Royce airplane engines in operation. Thanks to the artificial intelligence in the Rolls-Royce computer, based on complex algorithms, it can track anomalies in its engines while they are in operation. That artificial intelligence system knows that this engine was probably hit by lightning, and it immediately feeds out a report to a Rolls-Royce engineer.

"With the real-time data we receive via satellites, we can identify an 'event' and our engineers can make remote diagnoses," said Rose. "Under normal circumstances, after an engine gets hit by lightning you would have to land the plane, call in an engineer, do a visual inspection, and make a decision about how much damage might have been done and whether the plane has to be delayed in order to do a repair.

"But remember, these airlines do not have much turnaround time. If this plane is delayed, you throw off the crews, you drop out of your position to fly back home. It gets very costly. We can monitor and analyze engine performance automatically in real time, with our engineers making decisions about exactly what is needed by the time the plane has landed. And if we can determine by all the information we have about the engine that no intervention or even inspection is needed, the airplane can return on schedule, and that saves our customers time and money."

As a result of these steroids, engines can now talk to computers, people can talk to people, computers can talk to computers, and people can talk to computers farther, faster, more cheaply, and more easily than ever before. And as that has happened, more people from more places have started asking one another the same two questions: Can you hear me now? Can we work together now?

THREE

The Triple Convergence

W hat is the triple convergence? In order to explain what I mean, let me tell a personal story and share one of my favorite television commercials.

The story took place in March 2004. I had made plans to fly from Baltimore to Hartford on Southwest Airlines to visit my daughter Orly, who was going to school in New Haven, Connecticut. Being a tech-savvy guy, I didn't bother with a paper ticket but ordered an e-ticket through American Express. As anyone who flies regularly on Southwest knows, the cheapo airline has no reserved seats. When you check in, your ticket says simply A, B, or C, with the As boarding first, the Bs boarding second, and the Cs boarding last. As veterans of Southwest also know, you do not want to be a C. In fact, you don't even want to be a B if you want to be sure that you will have room above the seat to stuff the spring clothes you are carrying for your daughter and not get stuck in a middle seat. If you want to sit in a window or aisle seat and be able to store your bags, you want to be an A on Southwest Airlines. So, even though I had ordered an e-ticket, I got up early to make sure I got to the Baltimore airport ninety-five minutes before my scheduled departure— because I was going to be an A. I walked up to the Southwest e-ticket machine, stuck in my credit card, and used the touch screen to get my ticket—a thoroughly modern man, right? Well, out came the ticket— and it said B.

I was fuming. "How in the world could I be a B?" I said to myself, looking at my watch. "There is no way that many people got here before me. This thing is rigged! This is fixed! This is nothing more than a slot machine!"

I stomped off, went through security, bought myself a Cinnabon, and glumly sat at the back of the B line, waiting to be herded on board, so I could hunt for space in the overhead bins. Forty minutes later, the flight was called. From the B line, I enviously watched all the As file on board ahead of me, with a certain barely detectable air of superiority.

And then I saw it.

Many of the people in the A line didn't have normal tickets like mine. They were carrying what looked to me like crumpled pieces of white home printer paper, but those pieces of paper weren't blank. They had boarding passes and bar codes printed on them, as if . . . as if . . . as if . . . all the As had downloaded their boarding passes off the Web at home and printed them out on their home printers. Which, I quickly learned, was exactly what they had done! I didn't know it, but Southwest had recently announced that beginning at 12:01 a.m. the day of a flight, you—the individual—could download your own ticket at home, print it out, and then just have the bar code scanned by the gate agent before you boarded.

"Friedman," I said to myself, looking at this scene, "you are so twentieth-century . . . You are so Globalization 2.0." Think about it: In Globalization 1.0, there was a ticket agent—a living, breathing person. I used to have to go to the airline office in downtown Washington, D.C., take a number, wait in line, and then come face-to-face with a ticket agent in order to negotiate my flight arrangements. In Globalization 2.0, the e-ticket machine replaced the ticket agent. We thought that was pretty cool. And that was just a couple of years ago. But while you were sleeping, we entered Globalization 3.0, and now you—the individual—became your own ticket agent. Or, to look at it another way, you, the individual, became an employee of Southwest Airlines. Or, to look at it still another way: If you happen to value your own time staying up past midnight the night before a flight to do your own ticketing, you, the individual, are *paying* Southwest Airlines to be their employee!

The television commercial is from Konica Minolta Business Technologies for a new multipurpose device it sells called bizhub, a piece of office machinery that allows you to do black-and-white or color printing, copy a document, fax it, scan it, scan it to e-mail, or Internet-fax it—all from the same machine. The commercial begins with a rapid cutting back and forth between two guys, one in his office and the other standing at the bizhub machine. They are close enough to talk by raising their voices. Dom is senior in authority but slow on the uptake—the kind of guy who hasn't kept up with changing technology (my kind of guy!). He can see Ted standing at the bizhub machine when he leans back in his chair and peers out his office doorway.

> Dom: *(At his desk)* Hey, I need that chart.
> Ted: *(At the bizhub)* I'm e-mailing it now.
> Dom: You're e-mailing from the copy machine?
> Ted: No, I'm e-mailing from bizhub.
> Dom: Bizhub? Wait, did you make my copies yet?
> Ted: Right after I scan this.
> Dom: You're scanning at an e-mail machine?
> Ted: E-mail machine? I'm at the bizhub machine.
> Dom: *(Bewildered)* Copying?
> Ted: *(Trying to be patient)* E-mailing, *then* scanning, *then* copying.
> Dom: *(Long pause)* Bizhub?
> VO: *(Over an animated graphic of bizhub illustrating its multiple functions)* Amazing versatility *and* affordable color. That's bizhub, from Konica Minolta.
> *(Cut to Dom alone at the bizhub machine, trying to see if it will also dispense coffee into his mug.)*

Southwest was able to offer its at-home ticketing, and Konica Minolta could offer bizhub, because of what I call the triple convergence. What are the components of this triple convergence? The short answer is this: First, right around the year 2000, all ten of the flatteners discussed in the previous chapter started to converge and work together in ways that created a new, flatter, global playing field. As this new playing field became established, both businesses and individuals began to adopt new habits, skills, and processes to get the most out of it. They moved from largely vertical means of creating value to more horizontal ones. The merger of this new playing field for doing business with the new ways of doing business was the second convergence, and it actually helped to flatten the world even further. Finally, just when all of this flattening was happening, a whole new group of people, several billion, in fact, walked out onto the playing field from China, India, and the former Soviet Empire. Thanks to the new flat world, and its new tools, some of them were quickly able to plug and play, compete, connect, and collaborate with your kids and mine, more directly, cheaply, and powerfully than ever. This was the third convergence. Now let's look at each in detail.

CONVERGENCE I

All ten flatteners discussed in the previous chapter have been around, we know, since the 1990s, if not earlier. But they had to spread and take root and connect with one another to work their magic on the world. For instance, at some point around 2003, Southwest Airlines realized that there were enough PCs around, enough bandwidth, enough computer storage, enough Internet-comfortable customers, and enough software know-how for Southwest to create a work flow system that empowered its customers to download and print out their own boarding passes at home, as easily as downloading a piece of e-mail. Southwest could collaborate with its customers and they with Southwest in a new way. And somewhere around the same time, the work flow software and hardware converged in a way that enabled Konica Minolta to offer scanning, e-mailing, printing, faxing, and copying *all from the same machine*. This is the first convergence.

As Stanford University economist Paul Romer pointed out, economists have known for a long time that "there are goods that are complementary—whereby good A is a lot more valuable if you also have good B. It was good to have paper and then it was good to have pencils, and soon as you got more of one you got more of the other, and as you got a better quality of one and better quality of the other, your productivity improved. This is known as the simultaneous improvement of complementary goods."

It is my contention that the fall of the Berlin Wall, the rise of the PC, Netscape, work flow, outsourcing, offshoring, uploading, insourcing, supply-chaining, in-forming, and the steroids reinforced one another, like complementary goods. These flattening forces needed time to start to work together in a mutually enhancing fashion. That tipping point was reached sometime around the year 2000, when the ten flatteners converged on such a scale and with such intensity that millions of people on different continents suddenly started to feel that something . . . something . . . was new. They couldn't always quite describe what was happening, but by 2000 they sensed that they were in touch with people they'd never been in touch with before, were being challenged by people who had never challenged them before, were competing with people with whom they had never competed before, were collaborating with people with whom they had never collaborated before, and were doing things *as individuals* they had never dreamt of doing before.

What they were feeling was the flattening of the world.

The convergence of the ten flatteners had created a whole new platform. It is a global, Web-enabled platform for multiple forms of collaboration. This platform enables individuals, groups, companies, and universities anywhere in the world to collaborate—for the purposes of innovation, production, education, research, entertainment, and, alas, war-making—like no creative platform ever before. This platform now operates without regard to geography, distance, time, and, in the near future, even language. Going forward, this platform is going to be at the center of everything. Wealth and power will increasingly accrue to those countries, companies, individuals, universities, and groups who get three basic things right: the infrastructure to connect with this flat-world platform, the education to get more of their people innovating on, working off of, and tapping into this platform, and, finally, the governance to get the best out of this platform and cushion its worst side effects.

No, not everyone has access yet to this new platform, this new playing field. No, when I say the world is being flattened, I don't mean we are all becoming equal. What I do mean is that more people in more places now have the power to access the flat-world platform—to connect, compete, collaborate, and, unfortunately, destroy—than ever before.

After this book came out, Kevin Kelly, one of the founders of Wired magazine, wrote an essay marking the tenth anniversary of the Netscape IPO, in which he too concluded, in his own way, that this platform (what he calls "The Machine") for multiple forms of collaboration was indeed the start of something very, very new and very, very big. As he put it in the August 2005 issue of Wired: "Three thousand years from now, when keen minds review the past, I believe that our ancient time, here at the cusp of the third millennium, will be seen as [the start of a major new historical epoch]. In the years roughly coincidental with the Netscape IPO, humans began animating inert objects with tiny slivers of intelligence, connecting them into a global field, and linking their own minds into a single thing. This will be recognized as the largest, most complex, and most surprising event on the planet. Weaving nerves out of glass and radio waves, our species began wiring up all regions, all processes, all facts and notions into a grand network. From this embryonic neural net was born a collaborative interface for our civilization."

CONVERGENCE II

Platforms—the basic underlying operating systems for innovation and production—do not change very often. And introducing a new technology, or platform like the flat world, alone is never enough to boost productivity. The big spurts in productivity come when a new technology, or a new platform of technologies, is combined with new *ways* of doing business, and this always takes time. It takes time for all the flanking technologies, and the business processes and habits needed to get the most out of them, to converge and create that next productivity breakthrough. Wal-Mart got big productivity boosts when it combined big-box stores—where people could buy soap supplies for six months—with new, horizontal supply-chain management systems that allowed Wal-Mart instantly to connect what a consumer took off the shelf from a Wal-Mart in Kansas City with what a Wal-Mart supplier in coastal China could produce. We are now just at the beginning of a massive, worldwide change in habits, as more people get access to this platform and learn how to use it. It is a process that I like to call "horizontalization," and it is the second big convergence that is taking place today to make the world flat. Here is what I mean.

When computers were first introduced into offices, everyone expected a big boost in productivity. But that did not happen right away, and it sparked both disappointment and a little confusion. The noted economist Robert Solow quipped that computers are everywhere — except "in the productivity statistics."

In a pathbreaking 1989 essay, "Computer and Dynamo: The Modern Productivity Paradox in a Not-Too Distant Mirror," the economic historian Paul A. David explained such a lag by pointing to a historical precedent. He noted that while the lightbulb was invented in 1879, it took several decades for electrification to kick in and have a big economic and productivity impact. Why? Because it was not enough just to install electric motors and scrap the old technology — steam engines. The whole way of doing manufacturing had to be reconfigured. In the case of electricity, David pointed out, the key breakthrough was in how buildings, and assembly lines, were redesigned and managed. Factories in the steam age tended to be heavy, costly multistory buildings designed to brace the weighty belts and other big transmission devices needed to drive steam-powered systems. Once small, powerful electric motors were introduced, everyone hoped for a quick productivity boost. It took time, though. To get all the savings, you needed to redesign enough buildings. You needed to have long, low, cheaper-to-build single-story factories, with small electric motors powering machines of all sizes. Only when there was a critical mass of experienced factory architects and electrical engineers and managers, who understood the complementarities among the electric motor, the redesign of the factory, and the redesign of the production line, did electrification really deliver the productivity breakthrough in manufacturing, David wrote.

The same thing is happening today with the flattening of the world.

Many of the ten flatteners have been around for years. But for the full flattening effects to be felt, we needed not only the ten flatteners to converge but also something else. We needed the emergence of a large cadre of managers, innovators, business consultants, business schools, designers, IT specialists, CEOs, and workers to get comfortable with, and develop, the sorts of horizontal collaboration and value-creation processes and habits that could take advantage of this new, flatter playing field. In short, the convergence of the ten flatteners begat the convergence of a set of business practices and skills that would get the most out of the flat world. And then the two began to mutually reinforce each other.

"When people asked, 'Why didn't the IT revolution lead to more productivity right away?' it was because you needed more than just new computers," said Romer. "You needed new business processes and new types of skills to go with them. The new way of doing things makes the information technologies more valuable, and the new and better information technologies make the new ways of doing things more possible."

Globalization 2.0 was really the era of mainframe computing, which was very vertical—command-and-control oriented, with companies and their individual departments tending to be organized in vertical silos. Globalization 3.0, which is built around the convergence of the ten flatteners, and particularly the combination of the PC, the microprocessor, the Internet, and fiber optics, flipped the playing field from largely top-down to more side to side. And this naturally fostered and demanded new business practices, which were less about command and control and more about connecting and collaborating horizontally.

"We have gone from a vertical chain of command for value creation to a much more horizontal chain of command for value creation," explained Carly Fiorina. Innovations in companies like HP, she said, now come more and more often from horizontal collaboration among different departments and teams spread all across the globe. For instance, HP, Cisco, and Nokia collaborated on the development of a camera/cell phone that beams its digitized pictures to an HP printer, which quickly prints them out. Each company had developed a very sophisticated technological specialty, but it could add value only when its specialty was horizontally combined with the specialties of the other two companies.

"How you collaborate horizontally and manage horizontally requires a totally different set of skills" from traditional top-down approaches, Fiorina added.

Let me offer just a few examples. In the past five years, HP has gone from a company that had eighty-seven different supply chains—each managed vertically and independently, with its own hierarchy of managers and back-office support—to a company with just five supply chains that manage $50 billion in business, and where functions like accounting, billing, and human resources are handled through a companywide system.

Southwest Airlines took advantage of the convergence of the ten flatteners to create a system where its customers could download their boarding passes at home. Or, to put it differently, Southwest Airlines understood that the world was flat and that it could interface differently with its customers, and vice versa, to improve its productivity and lower its costs. But until I personally altered my ticket-buying habits and reengineered myself to collaborate horizontally with Southwest, this technological breakthrough didn't produce a productivity breakthrough for me. So I did start to horizontalize myself. I realized I could download and print out my own boarding pass and bar code and arrive at the Baltimore airport sixty-five minutes before my flight, instead of ninety-five minutes. And when I did, I would capture thirty minutes of productivity for myself. That is a lot of work time. What the bizhub commercial is about is the difference between the employee who understands the convergent technologies in the new bizhub machine (and how to get the most out of them) and the employee in the very same office who does not. Not until the latter changes his work habits will productivity in that fictional office go up, even though the office has this amazing new machine.

Finally, consider the example of WPP—the second-largest advertising-marketing-communications consortium in the world. WPP, which is based in England, did not exist as we now know it twenty years ago. It is a product of the consolidation of some of the biggest names in the business—from Young & Rubicam to Ogilvy & Mather to Hill & Knowlton. The alliance was put together to capture more and more of big clients' marketing needs, such as advertising, direct mail, media buying, and branding.

"For years the big challenge for WPP was how to get its own companies to collaborate," said Allen Adamson, managing director of WPP's branding firm, Landor Associates. "Now, though, it is often no longer enough just to get the companies in WPP to work together per se. Increasingly, we find ourselves pulling together individuals from within each of these companies to form a customized collaborative team just for one client. The solution that will create value for that client did not exist in any one company or even in the traditional integration of the companies. It had to be much more specifically tailored. So we had to go down inside the whole group and pluck the individual who is the right ad person, to work with the right branding person, to work with the right media person for this particular client."

When GE decided in 2003 to spin off its insurance businesses into a separate company, WPP assembled a customized team to handle everything from the naming of the new company—Genworth—all the way down to its first advertising campaign and direct-marketing program. "As a leader within this organization," said Adamson, "what you have to do is figure out the value proposition that is needed for each client and then identify and assemble the individual talents within WPP's workforce that will in effect form a virtual company just for that client. In the case of GE, we even gave a name to the virtual collaborative team we formed: Klamath Communications."

When the world went flat, WPP adapted itself to get the most out of itself. It changed its office architecture and practices—basically tearing down its walls and silos—just like those companies that adjusted the architecture of their steam-run factories to the electric motor. By opening itself up this way, WPP actually unlocked so much more energy and intelligence. Suddenly, it could look at all its employees from all its companies as a vast pool of individual specialists, who could be assembled horizontally into any number of collaborative teams, depending on the unique demands of any given project. And that team would then become a de facto new company with its own name.

Thinking horizontally applies to everything from business to education to military planning. It takes an adjustment to move from vertical to horizontal thinking, as WPP did. Because vertical thinking often requires you to start by asking who controls what system, not what is the outcome or effect you want to create. Let's see, if I am a general in Iraq, the effect I want to create is to get better real-time battlefield intelligence. Okay, well, if that is the case, then my top priority is not whether I control the drone that flies over the battlefield space and takes the aerial photos. No, my top priority is finding a way to get the pictures that this drone is sending back analyzed as deeply and quickly as possible. When that is my priority, then I start thinking horizontally. I start thinking about how I can use the flat-world platform—that is, how I can use my own network or network of networks—to take the streaming video coming off that drone and feed it, live, to flat-screen TVs in the CIA, the DIA, the NSA, army intelligence, and air force intelligence, and then integrate each of those analysts into a single chat room, so they can type in their responses to what they are seeing and what sort of threat it poses, as the video is streaming, and that chat will come up alongside the screen, so we all can analyze it together. With that approach, I have gotten away from vertical thinking—that I, the air force, control the drone in my silo and therefore my analysts alone must analyze the video and then tell the army in its silo what we have found. Instead, I am saying that the effect I want to create is to get the smartest analysis in real time, and the way I get that is by horizontally connecting different nodes in my whole network. Because all of us are smarter than one of us, my priority is not who controls the video but how do I create a horizontal response system to extract the most intelligence, from all of us, to understand what the video is showing.

It will take time for this new playing field and the new business practices to be fully aligned. It's a work in progress. But here's a little warning: It is happening much faster than you think, and it is happening globally. *Remember, this was a triple convergence!*

CONVERGENCE III

How so? Just as we finished creating this new, more horizontal playing field, and companies and individuals primarily in the West started quickly adapting to it, three billion people who had been locked out of the field suddenly found themselves liberated to plug and play with everybody else.

Save for a tiny minority, these three billion people had never been allowed to compete and collaborate before, because they lived in largely closed economies with very vertical, hierarchical political and economic structures. I am talking about the people of China, India, Russia, Eastern Europe, Latin America, and Central Asia. Their economies and political systems all opened up during the course of the 1990s, so that their people were increasingly free to join the free-market game. And when did these three billion people converge with the new playing field and the new processes? Right when the field was being flattened, right when millions of them could compete and collaborate more equally, more horizontally, and with cheaper and more readily available work flow tools than ever before. Indeed, thanks to the flattening of the world, many of these new entrants didn't even have to leave home to participate. Thanks to the ten flatteners, the playing field came to them!

It is this triple convergence—of new players, on a new playing field, developing new processes and habits for horizontal collaboration—that I believe is the most important force shaping global economics and politics in the early twenty-first century. Giving so many people access to all these tools of collaboration, along with the ability through search engines and the Web to access billions of pages of raw information, ensures that the next generation of innovations will come from all over Planet Flat. The scale of the global community that is soon going to be able to participate in all sorts of discovery and innovation is something the world has simply never seen before.

Throughout the Cold War there were just three major trading blocs—North America, Western Europe, and Japan plus East Asia—and the competition among the three was relatively controlled, since they were all Cold War allies on the same side of the great global divide. There were also still a lot of walls around for labor and industries to hide behind. The wage rates in these three trading blocs were roughly the same, the workforces roughly the same size, and the education levels roughly equivalent. "You had a gentlemanly competition," noted Intel's Chairman Craig Barrett.

Then along came the triple convergence. The Berlin Wall came down, the Berlin mall opened up, and suddenly some three billion people who had been behind walls walked onto the flattened global piazza.

Here's how it looked in round numbers: According to a November 2004 study by Harvard University economist Richard B. Freeman, in 1985 "the global economic world" consisted of North America, Western Europe, Japan, as well as chunks of Latin America, Africa, and the countries of East Asia. The total population of this global economic world, taking part in international trade and commerce, said Freeman, was about 2.5 billion people.

By 2000, as a result of the collapse of communism in the Soviet Empire, India's turn from autarky, China's shift to market capitalism, and population growth all over, the global economic world expanded to encompass 6 billion people.

As a result of this widening, another roughly 1.5 billion new workers entered the global economic labor force, Freeman said, which is almost exactly double the number we would have had in 2000 had China, India, and the Soviet Empire not joined.

True, maybe only 10 percent of this new 1.5 billion–strong workforce entering the global economy have the education and connectivity to collaborate and compete at a meaningful level. But that is still 150 million people, roughly the size of the entire U.S. workforce. Said Barrett, "You don't bring three billion people into the world economy overnight without huge consequences, especially from three societies [like India, China, and Russia] with rich educational heritages."

That is exactly right. These societies that we are now melding with have a very high ethic of education. Consider this story from *Education Week*, the weekly paper for American schoolteachers. In its November 30, 2005, issue it ran a special report on the Indian middle class and its aspirations. The story, datelined Chennai, India, began like this: "In one of Chennai's ubiquitous academic-coaching classes, a hundred 12th graders are crammed into a purple room, about 30 feet long and 25 feet wide. The energy-sapping temperature is well over 100 degrees despite the constant whirr of overhead fans. On a wooden dais, Muthukrishnan Arulselvan draws a triangle on a blackboard, marks angles inside it, and explains a geometrical formula into a microphone. The students listen, rapt, although it is nearly 10:00 p.m. When Mr. Arulselvan asks a question, the students rush to reply in a chorus. When the tutor poses a problem, they bury their heads in notebooks, chewing on pencils, eager to finish before everyone else. This intensive, seven-days-a-week class represents life as usual for these Indian high schoolers, who are hoping to earn an engineering slot at one of the colleges here in Chennai . . . When they return home, most will gulp down a cup of strong, sweet coffee to keep them up studying several hours longer . . . In India, putting a child through engineering or medical college is, for many middle-class families, a life's mission in a way that is almost unknown in the United States. In the country that invented the decimal scale, such long-dead geniuses of mathematics and science as Srinivasa Ramanujam and Aryabhatta are still revered, and children who do well in those subjects are considered especially prized."

According to the Institute of International Education, India sent more students to college in the United States in 2004–05 than did any other country in the world. According to the IIE, 80,466 foreign students enrolled in the United States were from India, followed by 62,523 from China, and 53,358 from South Korea. Most of those students are studying business, engineering, math, or computer science. India is a long way away. It's a very different culture. It's not easy coming that far. You have to be hungry.

Indeed, a lot of those new players from India, China, and the former Soviet Empire are not just walking onto the flat-world field with their enormous hunger to get ahead by outlearning their competition. What we are witnessing is a mad dash—born of fifty years of pent-up aspirations in places like India, China, and the former Soviet Empire, where for five decades young people were educated, but not given an outlet at home to really fulfill their potential. Imagine shaking a champagne bottle for fifty years and then finally uncorking it. You get quite a pop when the cork comes off. That's the kind of explosion of aspirations coming out of India, China, and the former Soviet Empire today. You don't want to get in the way of that cork.

And that is why this is no slow-motion triple convergence. It's happening fast. Because once the world has been flattened and the new forms of collaboration made available to more and more people, the winners will be those who learn the habits, processes, and skills most quickly—and there is nothing that guarantees it will be Americans or Western Europeans permanently leading the way. And take note, these new players are often stepping onto the playing field legacy free, meaning that many of them were so far behind they can leap right into the new technologies without having to worry about all the sunken costs of old systems. It means that they can move very fast to adopt new, state-of-the-art technologies, which is why there are already more cell phones in use in China today than there are people in the United States. Many Chinese just skipped over the landline phase. To put it another way, many Chinese just went from no phones to cell phones in the space of a decade. I cotaught a course on globalization at Harvard in the spring of 2005. One day after class, one of my students came up to me and told me this story: He and his Harvard colleagues had formed a student organization with students in China. They help one another on everything from writing résumés to joint study projects. The interesting thing, he said, though, was how they communicate. They use Skype, with its free voice over the Internet technology. But the even more interesting thing he said to me was this: It was the Chinese students who introduced the American students in the group to Skype. And most of those Chinese students, he pointed out, didn't come from big cities but from smaller towns around China.

We tend to think of global trade and economics as something driven by the IMF, the G-8, the World Bank, the WTO, and the trade treaties forged by trade ministers. I don't want to suggest that these governmental agencies are irrelevant. They are not. But they are going to become less important. In the future, globalization is going to be increasingly driven by the *individuals* who understand the flat world, adapt themselves quickly to its processes and technologies, and start to march forward—without any treaties or advice from the IMF. They will be every color of the rainbow and from every corner of the world.

The global economy from here forward will be shaped less by the ponderous deliberations of finance ministers and more by the spontaneous explosion of energy from the zippies. Yes, Americans grew up with the hippies in the 1960s. Thanks to the high-tech revolution, many of us became yuppies in the 1980s. Well, now let me introduce the zippies.

"The Zippies Are Here," declared the Indian weekly magazine *Outlook*. Zippies are the huge cohort of Indian youth who are the first to come of age since India shifted away from socialism and dived headfirst into global trade and the information revolution by turning itself into the world's service center. *Outlook* called India's zippies "Liberalization's Children" and defined a zippie as a "young city or suburban resident, between 15 and 25 years of age, with a zip in the stride. Belongs to Generation Z. Can be male or female, studying or working. Oozes attitude, ambition and aspiration. Cool, confident and creative. Seeks challenges, loves risks and shuns fear." Indian zippies feel no guilt about making money or spending it. They are, says one Indian analyst quoted by *Outlook*, "destination driven, not destiny driven, outward looking, not inward, upwardly mobile, not stuck-in-my-station-in-life." With 54 percent of India under the age of twenty-five—that's 555 million people—six out of ten Indian households have at least one potential zippie. And the zippies don't just have a pent-up demand for good jobs; they want the good life.

It all happened so fast. P. V. Kannan, the CEO and cofounder of the Indian call-center company 24/7 Customer, told me that in the last decade, he went from sweating out whether he would ever get a chance to work in America to becoming one of the leading figures in the outsourcing of services from America to the rest of the world.

"I will never forget when I applied for a visa to come to the United States," Kannan recalled. "It was March 1991. I had gotten a B.A. in chartered accountancy from the [Indian] Institute of Chartered Accountants. I was twenty-three, and my girlfriend was twenty-five. She was also a chartered accountant. I had graduated at age twenty and had been working for the Tata Consultancy group. So was my girlfriend. And we both got job offers through a body shop [a recruiting firm specializing in importing Indian talent for companies in America] to work as programmers for IBM. So we went to the U.S. consulate in Bombay. The recruiting service was based in Bombay. In those days, there was always a very long line to get visas to the United States, and there were people who would actually sleep in the line and hold places and you could go buy their place for 20 rupees. But we went by ourselves and stood in line and we finally got in to see the man who did the interview. He was an American [consular official]. His job was to ask questions and try to figure out whether we were going to do the work and then come back to India or try to stay in America. They judge by some secret formula. We used to call it 'the lottery'—you went and stood in line and it was a life lottery, because everything was dependent on it."

There were actually books and seminars in India devoted entirely to the subject of how to prepare for a work visa interview at the U.S. embassy. It was the only way for skilled Indian engineers really to exploit their talent. "I remember one tip was to always go professionally dressed," said Kannan, "so [my girlfriend and I] were both in our best clothes. After the interview is over, the man doesn't tell you anything. You had to wait until the evening to know the results. But meanwhile, the whole day was hell. To distract our minds, we just walked the streets of Bombay and went shopping. We would go back and forth, 'What if I get in and you don't? What if you get in and I don't?' I can't tell you how anxious we were, because so much was riding on it. It was torture. So in the evening we go back and both of us got visas, but I got a five-year multiple entry and my girlfriend got a six-month visa. She was crying. She did not understand what it meant. 'I can only stay for six months?' I tried to explain to her that you just need to get in and then everything can be worked out."

While many Indians still want to come to America to work and study, thanks to the triple convergence many of them can now compete at the highest levels, and be decently paid, by staying at home. In a flat world, you can innovate without having to emigrate. Said Kannan, "My daughter will never have to sweat that out." In a flat world, he explained, "there is no one visa officer who can keep you out of the system . . . It's a plug-and-play world." Because you can now innovate without having to emigrate, more and more world-class innovation, particularly in software, is now starting from India—not just being worked on from India. This is both keeping Indians at home and attracting others. P. Anandan, an Indian-American computer engineer who worked for Microsoft in Redmond, returned to India in 2005 to open Microsoft's research center in Bangalore. "I have two non-Indians working for me here, one Japanese and one American, and they could work anywhere in the world," Anandan told me. He added that when he got his engineering degree in India twenty-eight years ago, all the competition was to get a job abroad. Now the fiercest competition is to get an IT job in India: "It is no longer, 'Well I have to stay here,' but, 'Do I get a chance to stay here?'"

One of the most dynamic young pluggers and players I met in India was Rajesh Rao, founder and CEO of Dhruva Interactive, a small game company based in Bangalore. If I could offer you one person who embodies the triple convergence, it is Rajesh. He and his firm show us what happens when an Indian zippie plugs into the ten flatteners.

Dhruva is located in a converted house on a quiet street in a residential neighborhood of Bangalore. When I stopped in for a visit, I found two floors of Indian game designers and artists, trained in computer graphics, working on PCs, drawing various games and animated characters for American and European clients. The artists and designers were listening to music on headphones as they worked. Occasionally, they took a break by playing a group computer game, in which all the designers could try to chase and kill one another at once on their computer screens. Dhruva has already produced some very innovative games—from a computer tennis game you can play on the screen of your cell phone to a computer pool game you can play on your PC or laptop. In 2004, it bought the rights to use Charlie Chaplin's image for mobile computer games. That's right—a start-up Indian game company today owns the Chaplin image for use in mobile computer games.

In Bangalore and in later e-mail conversations, I asked Rajesh, who is in his mid-thirties, to walk me through how he became a player in the global game business from Bangalore.

"The first defining moment for me dates back to the early nineties," said Rajesh, a smallish, mustachioed figure with the ambition of a heavyweight boxer. "Having lived and worked in Europe, as a student, I was clear in my choice that I would not leave India. I wanted to do my thing from India, do something that would be globally respected and something that would make a difference in India. I started my company in Bangalore as a one-man operation on March 15, 1995. My father gave me the seed money for the bank loan that bought me a computer and a

14.4 kbp modem. I set out to do multimedia applications aimed at the education and industry sectors. By 1997, we were a five-man team. We had done some pathbreaking work in our chosen field, but we realized that this was not challenging us enough. End of Dhruva 1.0.

"In March 1997, we partnered with Intel and began the process of reinventing ourselves into a gaming company. By mid-1998, we were showing global players what we were capable of by way of both designing games and developing the outsourced portions of games designed by others. On November 26, 1998, we signed our first major game development project with Infogrames Entertainment, a French gaming company. In hindsight, I think the deal we landed was due to the pragmatism of one man in Infogrames more than anything else. We did a great job on the game, but it was never published. It was a big blow for us, but the quality of our work spoke for itself, so we survived. The most important lesson we learned: We could do it, but we had to get smart. Going for all or nothing—that is, signing up to make only a full game or nothing at all—was not sustainable. We had to look at positioning ourselves differently. End of Dhruva 2.0."

This led to the start of Dhruva's 3.0 era—positioning Dhruva as a provider of game development services. The computer game business is already enormous, every year grossing more revenue than Hollywood, and it already had some tradition of outsourcing game characters to countries like Canada and Australia. "In March 2001, we sent out our new game demo, Saloon, to the world," said Rajesh. "The theme was the American Wild Wild West, and the setting was a saloon in a small town after business hours, with the barman cleaning up . . . None of us had ever seen a real saloon before, but we researched the look and feel [of a saloon] using the Internet and Google. The choice of the theme was deliberate. We wanted potential clients in the U.S.A. and Europe to be convinced that Indians can 'get it.' The demo was a hit, it landed us a bunch of outsourced business, and we have been a successful company ever since."

Could he have done this a decade earlier, before the world got so flat?

"Never," said Rajesh. Several things had to come together. The first was to have enough installed bandwidth so he could e-mail game con-

tent and instructions back and forth between his own company and his
American clients. The second factor, said Rajesh, was the spread of PCs
for use in both business and at home, with people getting very comfortable using them in a variety of tasks. "PCs are everywhere," he said. "The
penetration is relatively decent even in India today."

The third factor, though, was the emergence of the work flow software
and Internet applications that made it possible for a Dhruva to go into business as a minimultinational from day one: Word, Outlook, NetMeeting,
3D Studio MAX. But Google is the key. "It's fantastic," said Rajesh. "One
of the things that's always an issue for our clients from the West is, 'Will
you Indians be able to understand the subtle nuances of Western content?' Now, to a large extent, it was a very valid question. But the Internet
has helped us to be able to aggregate different kinds of content at the
touch of a button, and today if someone asks you to make something that
looks like Tom and Jerry, you just say 'Google Tom and Jerry' and you've
got tons and tons of pictures and information and reviews and write-ups
about Tom and Jerry, which you can read and simulate."

While people were focusing on the boom and bust of the dot-coms,
Rajesh explained, the real revolution was taking place more quietly. It was
the fact that all over the world, people, en masse, were starting to get comfortable with the new global infrastructure. "We are just at the beginning
of being efficient in using it," he said. "There is a lot more we can do with
this infrastructure, as more and more people shift to becoming paperless
in their offices and realize that distances really [do] not matter . . . It will
supercharge all of this. It's really going to be a different world."

Moreover, in the old days, these software programs would have been
priced beyond the means of a little Indian game start-up, but not anymore, thanks in part to the open-source free software movement. Said
Rajesh, "The cost of software tools would have remained where the interested parties wanted them to be if it was not for the deluge of rather efficient freeware and shareware products that sprung up in the early 2000s.
Microsoft Windows, Office, 3D Studio MAX, Adobe Photoshop—each
of these programs would have been priced higher than they are today if
not for the many freeware/shareware programs that were comparable
and compelling. The Internet brought to the table the element of choice

and instant comparison that did not exist before for a little company like ours . . . Already we have in our gaming industry artists and designers working from home, something unimaginable a few years back, given the fact that developing games is a highly interactive process. They connect into the company's internal system over the Internet, using a secure feature called VPN [virtual private network], making their presence no different from the guy in the next cubicle."

The Internet now makes this whole world "like one marketplace," added Rajesh. "This infrastructure is not only going to facilitate sourcing of work to the best price, best quality, from the best place, it is also going to enable a great amount of sharing of practices and knowledge, and it's going to be 'I can learn from you and you can learn from me' like never before. It's very good for the world. The economy is going to drive integration, and the integration is going to drive the economy."

There is no reason the United States should not benefit from this trend, Rajesh insisted. What Dhruva is doing is pioneering computer gaming within Indian society. When the Indian market starts to embrace gaming as a mainstream social activity, Dhruva will already be positioned to take advantage. But by then, he argued, the market "will be so huge that there will be a lot of opportunity for content to come from outside. And, hey, the Americans are way ahead in terms of the ability to know what games can work and what won't work and in terms of being at the cutting edge of design — so this is a bilateral thing . . . Every perceived dollar or opportunity that is lost today [from an American point of view because of outsourcing] is actually going to come back to you times ten, once the market here is unleashed . . . Just remember, we are a three-hundred-million middle class, larger than the size of your country or Europe."

Yes, he noted, India right now has a great advantage in having a pool of educated, low-wage English speakers with a strong service etiquette in their DNA and an enterprising spirit. "So, sure, for the moment, we are leading the so-called wave of service outsourcing of various kinds of new things," said Rajesh. "But I believe that there should be no doubt that this is just the beginning. If [Indians] think that they've got something going and there is something they can keep that's not going to go anywhere, that will be a big mistake, because we have got Eastern Europe, which is waking up, and we have got China, which is waiting to get on the services bandwagon to do various things. I mean, you can source the best product or service or capacity or competency from anywhere in the world today, because of this whole infrastructure that is being put into place. The only thing that inhibits you from doing that is your readiness to make use of this infrastructure. So as different businesses, and as different people, get more comfortable using this infrastructure, you are going to see a huge explosion. It is a matter of five to seven years and we will have a huge batch of excellent English-speaking Chinese graduates coming out of their universities. Poles and Hungarians are already very well connected, very close to Europe, and their cultures are very similar [to Western Europe's]. So today India is ahead, but it has to work very hard if it wants to keep this position. It has to never stop inventing and reinventing itself."

The raw ambition that Rajesh and so many of his generation possess is worthy of note by Americans—a point I elaborate on later.

"We can't relax," said Rajesh. "I think in the case of the United States that is what happened a bit. Please look at me: I am from India. We have been at a very different level before in terms of technology and business. But once we saw we had an infrastructure which made the world a small place, we promptly tried to make the best use of it. We saw there were so many things we could do. We went ahead, and today what we are seeing is a result of that . . . There is no time to rest. That is gone. There are dozens of people who are doing the same thing you are doing, and they are trying to do it better. It is like water in a tray, you shake it and it will find the path of least resistance. That is what is going to happen to so many jobs—they will go to that corner of the world where there is the least resistance and the most opportunity. If there is a skilled person in Timbuktu, he will get work if he knows how to access the rest of the world, which is quite easy today. You can make a Web site and have an e-mail address and you are up and running. And if you are able to demonstrate your work, using the same infrastructure, and if people are comfortable giving work to you, and if you are diligent and clean in your transactions, then you are in business."

Instead of complaining about outsourcing, said Rajesh, Americans and Western Europeans would "be better off thinking about how you can raise your bar and raise yourselves into doing something better. Americans have consistently led in innovation over the last century. Americans whining—we have never seen that before. People like me have learned a lot from Americans. We have learned to become a little more aggressive in the way we market ourselves, which is something we would not have done given our typical British background."

So what is your overall message? I asked Rajesh, before leaving with my head spinning.

"My message is that what's happening now is just the tip of the iceberg . . . What is really necessary is for everybody to wake up to the fact that there is a fundamental shift that is happening in the way people are going to do business. And everyone is going to have to improve themselves and be able to compete. It is just going to be one global market. Look, we just made [baseball] caps for Dhruva to give away. They came from Sri Lanka."

Not from a factory in South Bangalore? I asked.

"Not from South Bangalore," said Rajesh, "even though Bangalore is one of the export hubs for garments. Among the three or four caps we got quotations for, this [Sri Lankan one] was the best in terms of quality and the right price, and we thought the finish was great.

"This is the situation you are going to see moving forward," Rajesh concluded. "If you are seeing all this energy coming out of Indians, it's because we have been underdogs and we have that drive to kind of achieve and to get there . . . India is going to be a superpower and we are going to rule."

Rule whom? I asked.

Rajesh laughed at his own choice of words. "It's not about ruling anybody. That's the point. There is nobody to rule anymore. It's about how you can create a great opportunity for yourself and hold on to that or keep creating new opportunities where you can thrive. I think today that rule is about efficiency, it's about collaboration and it is about competitiveness and it is about being a player. It is about staying sharp and being in the game . . . The world is a football field now and you've got to be sharp to be on the team which plays on that field. If you're not good enough, you're going to be sitting and watching the game. That's all."

How Do You Say "Zippie" in Chinese?

As in Bangalore ten years ago, the best place to meet zippies in Beijing today is in the line at the consular section of the U.S. embassy. In Beijing in the summer of 2004, I discovered that the quest by Chinese students for visas to study or work in America was so intense that it had spawned dedicated Internet chat rooms, where Chinese students swapped stories about which arguments worked best with which U.S. embassy consular officials. They even gave the U.S. diplomats names like "Amazon Goddess," "Too Tall Baldy," and "Handsome Guy." Just how intensely Chinese students strategize over the Internet was revealed, U.S. embassy officials told me, when one day a rookie U.S. consular official had student after student come before him with the same line that some chat room had suggested would work for getting a visa: "I want to go to America to become a famous professor."

After hearing this all day, the U.S. official was suddenly surprised to get one student who came before him and pronounced, "My mother has an artificial limb and I want to go to America to learn how to build a better artificial limb for her." The official was so relieved to hear a new line that he told the young man, "You know, this is the best story I've heard all day. I really salute you. I'm going to give you a visa."

You guessed it.

The next day, a bunch of students showed up at the embassy saying they wanted a visa to go to America to learn how to build better artificial limbs for their mothers.

Talking to these U.S. embassy officials in Beijing, who are the gatekeepers for these visas, it quickly became apparent to me that they had mixed feelings about the process. On the one hand, they were pleased that so many Chinese wanted to come study and work in America. On the other hand, they wanted to warn American kids: Do you realize what is coming your way? As one U.S. embassy official in Beijing said to me, "What I see happening [in China] is what has been going on for the last several decades in the rest of Asia—the tech booms, the tremendous energy of the people. I saw it elsewhere, but now it is happening here."

I was visiting Yale in the spring of 2004. As I was strolling through the central quad, near the statue of Elihu Yale, two Chinese-speaking tours came through, with Chinese tourists of all ages. The Chinese have started to tour the world in large numbers, and as China continues to develop toward a more open society, it is quite likely that Chinese leisure tourists will alter the whole world-tourism industry.

But the Chinese are not visiting Yale just to admire the ivy. Consider these statistics from Yale's admissions office. The fall 1985 class had 71 graduate and undergraduate students from China and 1 from the Soviet Union. The fall 2003 class had 297 Chinese graduate and undergraduate students and 23 Russians. Yale's total international student contingent went from 836 in the fall of 1985 to 1,775 in the fall of 2003. Applications from Chinese and Russian high school students to attend Yale as undergraduates have gone from a total of 40 Chinese for the class of 2001 to 276 for the class of 2008, and from 18 Russians for the class of 2001 to 30 for the class of 2008. In 1999, Yiting Liu, a schoolgirl from Chengdu, China, got accepted to Harvard on a full scholarship. Her parents then wrote a build-your-own handbook about how they managed to prepare their daughter to get accepted to Harvard. The book, in Chinese, titled *Harvard Girl Yiting Liu*, offered "scientifically proven methods" to get your Chinese kid into Harvard. The book became a runaway bestseller in China. By 2003 it had sold some three million copies and spawned more than a dozen copycat books about how to get your kid into Columbia, Oxford, or Cambridge.

While many Chinese aspire to go to Harvard and Yale, they aren't just waiting around to get into an American university. They are also trying to build their own at home. In 2004, I was a speaker for the 150th anniversary of Washington University in St. Louis, a school noted for its strength in science and engineering. Mark Wrighton, the university's thoughtful chancellor, and I were chatting before the ceremony. He mentioned in passing that in the spring of 2001 he had been invited (along with many other foreign and American academic leaders) to Tsinghua University in Beijing, one of the finest in China, to participate in the celebration of its ninetieth anniversary. He said the invitation left him scratching his head at first: Why would any university celebrate its ninetieth anniversary—not its hundredth?

"Perhaps a Chinese tradition?" Wrighton asked himself. When he arrived at Tsinghua, though, he learned the answer. The Chinese had brought academics from all over the world to Tsinghua—more than ten thousand people attended the ceremony—in order to make the declaration "that at the one hundredth anniversary Tsinghua University would be among the world's premier universities," Wrighton later explained to me in an e-mail. "The event involved all of the leaders of the Chinese government, from the Mayor of Beijing to the head of state. Each expressed the conviction that an investment in the university to support its development as one of the world's great universities within ten years would be a rewarding one. With Tsinghua University already regarded as one of the leading universities in China, focused on science and technology, it was evident that there is a seriousness of purpose in striving for a world leadership position in [all the areas involved] in spawning technological innovation."

And as a result of China's drive to succeed, Microsoft chairman Bill Gates argued to me, the "ovarian lottery" has changed—as has the whole relationship between geography and talent. Thirty years ago, he said, if you had a choice between being born a genius on the outskirts of Bombay or Shanghai or being born an average person in Poughkeepsie, you would take Poughkeepsie, because your chances of thriving and living a decent life there, even with average talent, were much greater. But as the world has gone flat, Gates said, and so many people can now plug and play from anywhere, natural talent has started to trump geography.

"Now," he said, "I would rather be a genius born in China than an average guy born in Poughkeepsie."

That's what happens when the Berlin Wall turns into the Berlin mall and three billion people converge with all these new tools for collaboration. "We're going to tap into the energy and talent of five times as many people as we did before," said Gates.

From Russia with Love

I didn't get a chance to visit Russia and interview Russian zippies for this book, but I did the next best thing. I asked my friend Thomas R. Pickering, the former U.S. ambassador to Moscow and now a top international relations executive with Boeing, to explain a new development I had heard about: that Boeing was using Russian engineers and scientists, who once worked on MiGs, to help design its next generation of passenger planes.

Pickering unraveled the story for me. Beginning in 1991, Boeing started assigning out work to Russian scientists to take advantage of their expertise in aerodynamic problems and new aviation alloys. In 1998, Boeing decided to take this a step further and open an aeronautical engineering design office in Moscow. Boeing located the office in the twelve-story Moscow tower that McDonald's built with all the rubles it made from selling Big Macs in Moscow before the end of communism—money that McDonald's had pledged not to take out of the country.

Seven years later, said Pickering, "we now have eight hundred Russian engineers and scientists working for us and we're going up to at least one thousand and maybe, over time, to fifteen hundred." The way it works, he explained, is that Boeing contracts with different Russian aircraft companies—companies that were famous in the Cold War for making warplanes, companies with names like Ilyushin, Tupolev, and Sukhoi—and they provide the engineers-to-order for Boeing's different projects. Using French-made airplane design software, the Russian engineers collaborate with their colleagues at Boeing America—in both Seattle and Wichita, Kansas—in computer-aided airplane designs. Boeing has set up a twenty-four-hour workday. It consists of two shifts in Moscow and one shift in America. Using fiber-optic cables, advanced compression technologies, and aeronautical work flow software, "they just pass their designs back and forth from Moscow to America," Pickering said. There are videoconferencing facilities on every floor of Boeing's Moscow office, so the engineers don't have to rely on e-mail when they have a problem to solve with their American counterparts. They can have a face-to-face conversation.

Boeing started outsourcing airplane design work to Moscow as an experiment, a sideline; but today, with a shortage of aeronautical engineers in America, it is a necessity. Boeing's ability to blend these lower-cost Russian engineers with higher-cost, more advanced American design teams is enabling Boeing to compete head-to-head with its archrival, Airbus Industries, which is subsidized by a consortium of European governments and is using Russian talent as well. A U.S. aeronautical engineer costs $120 per design hour; a Russian costs about one-third of that.

But the outsourcees are also outsourcers. The Russian engineers have outsourced elements of their work for Boeing to Hindustan Aeronautics in Bangalore, which specializes in digitizing airplane designs to make them easier to manufacture. But this isn't the half of it. In the old days, explained Pickering, Boeing would say to its Japanese subcontractors, "We will send you the plans for the wings of the 777. We will let you make some of them and then we will count on you buying the whole airplanes from us. It's a win-win."

Today Boeing says to the giant Japanese industrial company Mitsubishi, "Here are the general parameters for the wings of the new 7E7. You design the finished product and build it." But Japanese engineers are very expensive. So what happens? Mitsubishi outsources elements of the outsourced 7E7 wing to the same Russian engineers Boeing is using for other parts of the plane. Meanwhile, some of these Russian engineers and scientists are leaving the big Russian airplane companies and setting up their own firms, and Boeing is considering buying shares in some of these start-ups to have reserve engineering capacity.

All of this global sourcing is for the purpose of designing and building planes faster and cheaper, so that Boeing can use its cash to keep innovating for the next generation and survive the withering competition from Airbus. Thanks to the triple convergence, it now takes Boeing eleven days to build a 737, down from twenty-eight days just a few years ago. Boeing will build its next generation of planes in three days, because all the parts are being computer-designed for assembly, and Boeing's global supply chain will enable it to move parts from one facility to another just in time.

To make sure that it is getting the best deals on its parts and other supplies, Boeing now runs regular "reverse auctions," in which companies bid down against each other rather than bid up against each other. They bid for contracts on everything from toilet paper for the Boeing factories to nuts and bolts—the off-the-shelf commodity parts—for Boeing's supply chain. Boeing will announce an auction for a stated time on a specially designed Internet site. It will begin the auction for each supply item at what it considers a fair price. Then it will just sit back and watch how far each supplier wants to undercut the others to win Boeing's business. Bidders are prequalified by Boeing, and everyone can see everyone else's bids as they are submitted.

"You can really see the pressures of the marketplace and how they work," said Pickering. "It's like watching a horse race."

THE OTHER TRIPLE CONVERGENCE

I once heard Bill Bradley tell a story about a high-society woman from Boston who goes to San Francisco for the first time. When she comes home and is asked by a friend how she liked it, she says, "Not very much—it's too far from the ocean."

The perspective and predispositions that you carry around in your head are very important in shaping what you see and what you don't see. That helps to explain why a lot of people missed the triple convergence. Their heads were completely somewhere else—even though it was happening right before their eyes. Three other things—another convergence—came together to create this smoke screen.

The first was the dot-com bust, which began in March 2001. As I said earlier, many people wrongly equated the dot-com boom with globalization. So when the dot-com boom went bust, and so many dot-coms (and the firms that supported them) imploded, these same people assumed that globalization was imploding as well. The sudden flameout of dogfood.com and ten other Web sites offering to deliver ten pounds of puppy chow to your door in thirty minutes was supposed to be proof that globalization and the IT revolution were all sizzle and no beef.

This was pure foolishness. Those who thought that globalization was the same thing as the dot-com boom and that the dot-com bust marked the end of globalization *could not have been more wrong*. To say it again, the dot-com bust actually drove globalization into hypermode by forcing companies to outsource and offshore more and more functions in order to save on scarce capital. This was a key factor in laying the groundwork for Globalization 3.0. Between the dot-com bust and today, Google went from processing roughly 150 million searches per day to more than one billion searches per day, with only a third coming from inside the United States. As its auction model caught on worldwide, eBay went from twelve hundred employees in early 2000 to sixty-three hundred by 2004, all in the period when globalization was supposed to be "over." Between 2000 and 2004, total global Internet usage grew 125 percent, including 186 percent in Africa, 209 percent in Latin America, 124 percent in Europe, and 105 percent in North America, according to Nielsen/NetRatings. Yes, globalization sure ended, all right.

It was not just the dot-com bust and all the hot air surrounding it that obscured all this from view. There were two other big clouds that moved in. The biggest, of course, was 9/11, which was a profound shock to the American body politic. Given 9/11, and the Afghanistan and Iraq invasions that followed, it's not surprising that the triple convergence was lost in the fog of war and the chatter of cable television. Finally, there was the Enron corporate governance scandal, quickly followed by blowups at Tyco and WorldCom—which all sent CEOs and the Bush administration running for cover. CEOs, with some justification, became guilty until proven innocent of boardroom shenanigans, and even the slavishly probusiness, pro-CEO Bush administration was wary of appearing—in public—to be overly solicitous of the concerns of big business. In the spring of 2004, I met with the head of one of America's biggest technology companies, who had come to Washington to lobby for more federal funding for the National Science Foundation to help nurture a stronger industrial base for American industry. I asked him why the administration wasn't convening a summit of CEOs to highlight this issue, and he just shook his head and said one word: "Enron."

The result: At the precise moment when the world was being flattened, and the triple convergence was reshaping the whole global

business environment—requiring some very important adjustments in
our own society and that of many other Western developed nations—
American politicians not only were not educating the American public,
they were actively working to make it stupid. During the 2004 election
campaign we saw the Democrats debating whether NAFTA was a good
idea and the Bush White House putting duct tape over the mouth of
N. Gregory Mankiw, the chairman of the White House Council of
Economic Advisers, and stashing him away in Dick Cheney's basement,
because Mankiw, author of a popular college economics textbook, had
dared to speak approvingly of outsourcing as just the "latest manifesta-
tion of the gains from trade that economists have talked about at least
since Adam Smith."

Mankiw's statement triggered a competition for who could say the
most ridiculous thing in response. The winner was speaker of the house
Dennis Hastert, who said that Mankiw's "theory fails a basic test of real
economics." And what test was that, Dennis? Poor Mankiw was barely
heard from again.

For all these reasons, most people missed the triple convergence.
Something really big was happening, and it was simply not part of public discourse in America or Europe. Until I visited India in early 2004, I
too was largely ignorant of it, although I was picking up a few hints that
something was brewing. One of the most thoughtful business leaders I
have come to know over the years is Nobuyuki Idei, the chairman of
Sony. Whenever he speaks, I pay close attention. We saw each other
twice during 2004, and both times he said something through his heavy
Japanese accent that stuck in my ear. Idei said that a change was under
way in the business-technology world that would be remembered, in
time, like "the meteor that hit the earth and killed all the dinosaurs."
Fortunately, the cutting-edge global companies knew what was going on
out there, and the best companies were quietly adapting to it so that they
would not be one of those dinosaurs.

As I started researching this book, I felt at times like I was in a *Twilight
Zone* segment. I would interview CEOs and technologists from major
companies, both American-based and foreign, and they would describe
in their own ways what I came to call the triple convergence. But, for all

the reasons I explained above, most of them weren't telling the public or the politicians. They were either too distracted, too focused on their own businesses, or too afraid. It was like they were all "pod people," living in a parallel universe, who were in on a big secret. Yes, they all knew the secret. They were already innovating off this flat-world platform. They had no choice. They had to if they wanted their companies just to survive, let alone thrive. In doing so they were also strengthening and spreading the platform worldwide. *But nobody wanted to tell the kids.*

Well, here's the truth that no one wanted to tell you: Thanks to the triple convergence, this new flat-world platform is, in effect, blowing away our walls, ceilings, and floors—all at the same time. That is, the wiring of the world with fiber-optic cable, the Internet, and work flow software has blown down many of the walls that prevented collaboration. Individuals who never dreamt they could work together, and jobs no one ever dreamt could be shifted from country to country, are suddenly on the move, now that many traditional high walls are gone. This same platform has also blown away our ceilings. Individuals who never dreamt they could upload—upload their opinions on blogs, or upload a new political vision, or upload an encyclopedia, or upload a new piece of software—suddenly found that they can have a global impact on the world, *as individuals.* With the traditional ceilings gone, they can push upward and outward in ways that were previously unimaginable. And then, finally, the floors went. Thanks to the new industry called "search," individuals can now drill down and search out facts, quotations, history, and the personal data of strangers as never before. The old rock-hard cement floors that limited how deeply we could dig into the past or present of any subject or any person are gone.

Yes, of course, these walls, ceilings, and floors had been eroding for a while. The flattening started in the late 1980s, but, with the triple convergence, it has now reached critical mass, and it involves so many more people and places.

So let me leave you with this thought: You know the "IT revolution" that the business press has been touting for the last twenty years? Sorry to tell you, but that was only the prologue. The last twenty years were just about forging, sharpening, and distributing all the new tools with which to collaborate and connect. Now the real IT revolution is about to begin, as all the complementarities between these tools start to really work together to level the playing field. One of those who pulled back the curtain and called this moment by its real name was HP's Carly Fiorina, who in 2004 began to declare in her public speeches that the dot-com boom and bust were just "the end of the beginning." The last twenty-five years in technology, said Fiorina, have been just "the warm-up act." Now we are going into the main event, she said, "and by the main event, I mean an era in which technology will literally transform every aspect of business, every aspect of life and every aspect of society."

FOUR

The Great Sorting Out

A s the world starts to move from a primarily vertical—*command and control*—system for creating value to a more horizontal—*connect and collaborate*—value-creation model, and as we blow away more walls, ceilings, and floors at the same time, societies are going to find themselves facing a lot of very profound changes all at once. But these changes won't just affect how business gets done. They will affect how individuals, communities, and companies organize themselves, where companies and communities stop and start, how individuals balance their different identities as consumers, employees, shareholders, and citizens, how people define themselves politically, and what role government plays in managing all of this flux. This won't all happen overnight, but over time many roles, habits, political identities, and management practices that we had grown used to in the round world are going to have to be profoundly adjusted for the age of flatness. To put it simply, following the great triple convergence that started right around the year 2000, we are going to experience what I would call "the great sorting out."

I first began thinking about the great sorting out after a conversation with Harvard University's noted political theorist Michael J. Sandel. Sandel startled me slightly by remarking that the sort of flattening process that I was describing was actually first identified by Karl Marx and Friedrich Engels in the *Communist Manifesto*, published in 1848. While the shrinking and flattening of the world that we are seeing today constitute a difference of degree from what Marx saw happening in his day, said Sandel, it is nevertheless part of the same historical trend Marx highlighted in his writings on capitalism—the inexorable march of technology and capital to remove all barriers, boundaries, frictions, and restraints to global commerce.

"Marx was one of the first to glimpse the possibility of the world as a global market, uncomplicated by national boundaries," Sandel explained. "Marx was capitalism's fiercest critic, and yet he stood in awe of its power to break down barriers and create a worldwide system of production and consumption. In the *Communist Manifesto*, he described capitalism as a force that would dissolve all feudal, national, and religious identities, giving rise to a universal civilization governed by market imperatives. Marx considered it inevitable that capital would have its way—inevitable and also desirable. Because once capitalism destroyed all national and religious allegiances, Marx thought, it would lay bare the stark struggle between capital and labor. Forced to compete in a global race to the bottom, the workers of the world would unite in a global revolution to end oppression. Deprived of consoling distractions such as patriotism and religion, they would see their exploitation clearly and rise up to end it."

Indeed, reading the *Communist Manifesto* today, I am in awe at how incisively Marx detailed the forces that were flattening the world during the rise of the Industrial Revolution, and how much he foreshadowed the way these same forces would keep flattening the world right up to the present. In what are probably the key paragraphs of the *Communist Manifesto*, Marx and Engels wrote:

All fixed, fast, frozen relations, with their train of ancient and venerable prejudices and opinions, are swept away, all new-formed ones become antiquated before they can ossify. All that is solid melts into air, all that is holy is profaned, and man is at last compelled to face with sober senses his real conditions of life and his relations with his kind. The need of a constantly expanding market for its products chases the bourgeoisie over the whole surface of the globe. It must nestle everywhere, settle everywhere, establish connections everywhere. The bourgeoisie has through its exploitation of the world market given a cosmopolitan character to production and consumption in every country. To the great chagrin of reactionaries, it has drawn from under the feet of industry the national ground on which it stood. All old-established national industries have been destroyed or are daily being destroyed. They are dislodged by new industries, whose introduction becomes a life and death question for all civilised nations, by industries that no longer work up indigenous raw material, but raw material drawn from the remotest zones; industries whose products are consumed, not only at home, but in every quarter of the globe. In place of the old wants, satisfied by the production of the country, we find new wants, requiring for their satisfaction the products of distant lands and climes. In place of the old local and national seclusion and self-sufficiency, we have intercourse in every direction, universal inter-dependence of nations. And as in material, so also in intellectual production. The intellectual creations of individual nations become common property. National one-sidedness and narrow-mindedness become more and more impossible, and from the numerous national and local literatures there arises a world literature.

The bourgeoisie, by the rapid improvement of all instruments of production, by the immensely facilitated means of communication, draws all, even the most barbarian nations into civilisation. The cheap prices of commodities are the heavy artillery with which it batters down all Chinese walls, with which it forces the barbarians' intensely obstinate hatred of foreigners to capitulate. It compels all nations, on pain of extinction, to adopt the bourgeois mode of production; it compels them to introduce what it calls civilisation into their midst, i.e., to become bourgeois themselves. In one word, it creates a world after its own image.

It is hard to believe that Marx published that in 1848. Referring to the *Communist Manifesto*, Sandel told me, "You are arguing something similar. What you are arguing is that developments in information technology are enabling companies to squeeze out all the inefficiencies and friction from their markets and business operations. That is what your notion of 'flattening' really means. But a flat, frictionless world is a mixed blessing. It may, as you suggest, be good for global business. Or it may, as Marx believed, augur well for a proletarian revolution. But it may also pose a threat to the distinctive places and communities that give us our bearings, that locate us in the world. From the first stirrings of capitalism, people have imagined the possibility of the world as a perfect market—unimpeded by protectionist pressures, disparate legal systems, cultural and linguistic differences, or ideological disagreement. But this vision has always bumped up against the world as it actually is—full of sources of friction and inefficiency. Some obstacles to a frictionless global market are truly sources of waste and lost opportunities. But some of these inefficiencies are institutions, habits, cultures, and traditions that people cherish precisely because they reflect nonmarket values like social cohesion, religious faith, and national pride. If global markets and new communications technologies flatten those differences, we may lose something important. That is why the debate about capitalism has been, from the very beginning, about which frictions, barriers, and boundaries are mere sources of waste and inefficiency, and which are sources of identity and belonging that we should try to protect. From the telegraph to the Internet, every new communications technology has promised to shrink the distance between people, to increase access to information, and to bring us ever closer to the dream of a perfectly efficient, frictionless global market. And each time, the question for society arises with renewed urgency: To what extent should we stand aside, 'get with the program,' and do all we can to squeeze out yet more inefficiencies, and to what extent should we lean against the current for the sake of values that global markets can't supply? Some sources of friction are worth protecting, even in the face of a global economy that threatens to flatten them."

The biggest source of friction, of course, has always been the nation-state, with its clearly defined boundaries and laws. Nation-states traditionally provided the walls, ceilings, and floors that organized so much of our lives. Are national boundaries a source of friction we should want to preserve, or even can preserve, in a flat world? What about legal barriers to the free flow of information, intellectual property, and capital—such as copyrights, worker protections, and minimum wages? In the wake of the triple convergence, the more the flattening forces reduce friction and barriers, the sharper the challenge they will pose to the nation-state and to the particular cultures, values, national identities, democratic traditions, and bonds of restraint that have historically provided some protection and cushioning for workers and communities. Which do we keep and which do we let melt away into air so we can all collaborate more easily?

To be sure, the walls, ceilings, and floors that structured our economic and political life are not disappearing swiftly everywhere. But they *are* disappearing, and it can be incredibly disruptive to those traditional institutions that have been doing business in the same way for decades and are slow to make the transition. Think about my business, the newspaper business, and how it has been disrupted by the flattening of the world. The flattening process simultaneously broke the traditional newspapers' monopoly on classified advertising (thanks to Google), its near monopoly on written news and commentary (thanks to bloggers), and its monopoly on distribution (thanks to the Internet). The business model for newspapers has been turned on its head, and the new—survivable—hybrid model for newspapers in a flat world still has not been sorted out.

Or think of the real estate business and the changes in how we buy and sell homes now. "Gone are the days when real estate agents could guard the information about homes for sale in their Multiple Listing Service," USA *Today* reported in a May 8, 2006, article. "Now, buyers and sellers can see all the homes for sale on 800 regional multiple listing services on the Web. They can see thousands of newly built homes for sale and apartments for rent nationwide. They can view aerial photos of homes and neighborhoods. They can get appraisals or see how much the house down the block fetched. They can shop for loans and compare mortgage rates. They can check out local schools and community features for towns across America. They can ask questions and get answers in online forums. And all of it's free. 'The Internet has done what no consumer advocate could ever do: It has reduced the distance between the consumer and the real estate expert to the point where the consumer is so much more informed, they don't need the expert as much as they used to,' says Art Raby, an agent for McColly Real Estate in Valparaiso, Ind. . . . In 1995, just 2% of home buyers used the Internet to look for a home. Last year, 77% of home shoppers went house-hunting online, and nearly one-fourth of buyers first found the property they bought on the Internet, according to the National Association of Realtors."

Are we all going to read newspapers online? No. Are we all going to buy homes on the Internet? No. But as more of us do so, the traditional walls, ceilings, and floors that held up the old newspaper or real estate business models are going to be taken apart and either reassembled in new ways that respond to and take advantage of the flat world—or done away with once and for all.

Monday Morning, one of Scandinavia's leading independent think tanks, found a compelling way to describe the disorienting sorting-out process that many institutions are now going through: "With accelerating speed, we have moved from the industrial society via the knowledge society to the present stage of a disintegrating society" on our way to "a new global collaborative society" in which "old power structures and lessons learned are challenged by new market forces and values."

Some people will respond to this disintegrating phase with a sense of exhilaration and freedom—seeing an opportunity to soar, expand, dig, or build in any direction with a whole new set of tools. Others will react with the anxiety of people in free fall, with nothing to hold them up or in place. Some will feel liberated, others totally disoriented. Anthropologists and historians tell us that rapid social change is highly destabilizing. What will happen to a society undergoing so much change from three directions is anybody's guess. It is becoming stressful already. The old boundaries— walls, ceilings, and floors—are going, and we do not yet know exactly what will replace them. But we do know that we are all still human beings and that human beings need walls, ceilings, and floors—we need agreed-upon norms of behavior and rules of commerce. We need agreed-upon ways of establishing authority and building communities, doing work, protecting copyrights, and determining whom to trust.

Where might these norms or standards come from? Devotees of the open-source movement will tell you that "the network" will establish new norms. This is true—up to a point. It is true that in the case, for instance, of the eBay community—a marketplace with virtually no walls, ceilings, or floors—the community adopted a system of norms by awarding one another stars for honest transactions and offering users the opportunity to provide feedback, making everyone's transactional history totally transparent to everyone in the community. The result was a framework encouraging good behavior that largely emerged from the community and is certainly maintained from the bottom up. But the open-source devotees are a little too glib when they say that the "network" always can be relied upon to establish these new norms. After all, al-Qaeda is a network, and the values that it promotes are hardly enhancing of peace, tranquility, and the global community. Networks can also transmit rumors and lies faster than ever, and they don't always cure them right away. Recall the poison that was spread on Wikipedia about John Seigenthaler Sr. The big lie that Jews were warned not to go to work at the World Trade Center on the morning of 9/11 began somewhere in the Muslim world and spread like a wildfire on the Internet, and no amount of news stories debunking it could eradicate that rumor. Much depends, I believe, on the diversity of a network community. The network that spread the lie that the Jews were warned not to go to work on 9/11 was a highly homogenous network made up entirely, I suspect, of like-minded people who wanted to believe the lie they were spreading and did not open or expose themselves to alternative points of view. This is true of many networks in the flat world.

For all of these reasons, the ceilings, walls, and floors that will define us in the future are likely to be blended, collaborative models, which combine the old and the new. Traditional nation-states, governments, corporations, and news organizations will have to work together with emergent networks, virtual communities, superempowered individuals, and companies to hammer out the new norms, new boundaries, new mechanisms for operating in the flat world. It will all be part of the great sorting out that is sure to be at the forefront of our political and economic debates. Here are a few more examples of what I mean.

India Versus Indiana:
Who Is Exploiting Whom?

Professor Sandel argued that what I call collaboration could be seen by others as just a nice name for the ability to hire cheap labor in India. You cannot deny that—when you look at it from an American perspective. But that is only if you look at it from one side. From the Indian worker's perspective, that same form of collaboration, outsourcing, could be seen as another name for empowering individuals in the developing world as never before, enabling them to nurture, exploit, and profit from their God-given intellectual talents—talents that before the flattening of the world often rotted on the docks of Mumbai and Calcutta. Looking at it from the American corner of the flat world, you might conclude that the frictions, barriers, and values that restrain outsourcing should be maintained, maybe even strengthened. But from the point of view of Indians, fairness, justice, and their own aspirations demand that those same barriers and sources of friction be removed. In the flat world, one person's economic liberation could be another's unemployment.

Consider this real-world case: In 2003, the state of Indiana put out to bid a contract to upgrade the state's computer systems that process unemployment claims. Guess who won? Tata America International, which is the U.S.-based subsidiary of India's Tata Consultancy Services Ltd. Tata's bid of $15.2 million came in $8.1 million lower than that of its closest rivals, the New York–based companies Deloitte Consulting and Accenture Ltd. No Indiana firms bid on the contract, because it was too big for them to handle.

In other words, an Indian consulting firm won the contract to upgrade the unemployment department of the state of Indiana! You couldn't make this up. Indiana was outsourcing the very department that would cushion the people of Indiana from the effects of outsourcing. Tata was planning to send some sixty-five contract employees to work in the Indiana Government Center, alongside eighteen state workers. Tata also said it would hire local subcontractors and do some local recruiting, but most workers would come from India to do the computer overhauls, which, once completed, were "supposed to speed the processing of unemployment claims, as well as save postage and reduce hassles for businesses that pay unemployment taxes," the *Indianapolis Star* reported on June 25, 2004. You can probably guess how the story ended: "Top aides to then-Gov. Frank O'Bannon had signed off on the politically sensitive, four-year contract before his death [on] September 13, [2003]." But when word of the contract was made public, Republicans made it a campaign issue. It became such a political hot potato that Governor Joe Kernan, a Democrat who had succeeded O'Bannon, ordered the state agency, which helps out-of-work Indiana residents, to cancel the contract—and also to put up some legal barriers and friction to prevent such a thing from happening again. He also ordered that the contract be broken up into smaller bites that Indiana firms could bid for—good for Indiana firms but very costly and inefficient for the state. The *Indianapolis Star* reported that a check for $993,587 was sent to pay off Tata for eight weeks of work, during which it had trained forty-five state programmers in the development and engineering of up-to-date software: "'The company was great to work with,' said Alan Degner, Indiana's commissioner of workforce development."

So now I have just one simple question: Who is the exploiter and who is the exploited in this India-Indiana story? The American arm of an Indian consulting firm proposes to save the taxpayers of Indiana $8.1 million by revamping their computers—using both its Indian employees and local hires from Indiana. The deal would greatly benefit the American arm of the Indian consultancy; it would benefit some Indiana tech workers; and it would save Indiana state residents precious tax dollars that could be deployed to hire more state workers somewhere else, or build new schools that would permanently shrink its roles of unemployed. And yet the whole contract, which was signed by pro-labor Democrats, got torn up under pressure from free-trade Republicans.

Sort that out.

In the old world, where value was largely being created vertically, usually within a single company and from the top down, it was very easy to see who was on the top and who was on the bottom, who was exploiting and who was being exploited. But when the world starts to flatten out and value increasingly gets created horizontally (through multiple forms of collaboration, in which individuals and little guys have much more power), who is on the top and who is on the bottom, who is exploiter and who is exploited, gets very complicated. Some of our old political reflexes no longer apply. Were the Indian engineers not being "exploited" when their government educated them in some of the best technical institutes in the world inside India, but then that same Indian government pursued a socialist economic policy that could not provide those engineers with work in India, so that those who could not get out of India had to drive taxis to eat? Are those same engineers now being exploited when they join the biggest consulting company in India, are paid a very comfortable wage in Indian terms, and, thanks to the flat world, can now apply their skills globally? Or are those Indian engineers now exploiting the people of Indiana by offering to revamp their state unemployment system for much less money than an American consulting firm? Or were the people of Indiana exploiting those cheaper Indian engineers? Someone please tell me: *Who is exploiting whom in this story?* With whom does the traditional Left stand in this story? With the knowledge workers from the developing world, being paid a decent wage, who are trying to use their hard-won talents in the developed world? Or with the politicians of Indiana, who wanted to deprive these Indian engineers of work so that it could be done, more expensively, by their constituents? And with whom does the traditional Right stand in this story? With those who want to hold down taxes and shrink the state budget of Indiana by outsourcing some work, or with those who say, "Let's raise taxes more in order to reserve the work here and reserve it just for people from Indiana"? With those who want to keep some friction in the system, even though that goes against every Republican instinct on free trade, just to help people from Indiana? If you are against globalization because you think it harms people in developing countries, whose side are you on in this story: India's or Indiana's?

The India versus Indiana dispute highlights the difficulties in drawing lines between the interests of two communities that never before imagined they were connected, much less collaborators. But suddenly they each woke up and discovered that in a flat world, where work increasingly becomes a horizontal collaboration, they were not only connected and collaborating but badly in need of a social contract to govern their relations.

The larger point here is this: Whether we are talking about management science or political science, manufacturing or research and development, many, many players and processes are going to have to come to grips with "horizontalization." And it is going to take a lot of sorting out.

WHERE DO COMPANIES STOP AND START?

Just as the relationship between different groups of workers will have to be sorted out in a flat world, so too will the relationship between companies and the communities in which they operate. Whose values will govern a particular company and whose interests will that company respect and promote? It is clear that in a flat world, global corporations will adapt to make the most of global opportunities and global resources—and that increasingly means adapting themselves to a flat world. In the past, though, a country benefited from and depended upon the success or hegemony of its leading companies to define its economic well-being and its standing in the world. What happens as businesses define their interests and labor opportunities more globally than domestically, and as the whole shareholding process demands more and more that these companies perform against global standards, opportunities, and resources? What happens is that the interests and needs of these companies align less and less perfectly with those of the national domains (the countries) in which they are headquartered. It used to be said that as General Motors goes, so goes America. But today it would be said, "As Dell goes, so goes Malaysia, Taiwan, China, Ireland, India . . ." HP today has well over 150,000 employees in at least 170 countries. It is not only the largest consumer technology company in the world; it is the largest IT company in Europe, the largest IT company in Russia, the largest IT company in the Middle East, and the largest IT company in South Africa. Is HP an American company if a majority of its employees and customers are outside of America, even though it is headquartered in Palo Alto? Corporations cannot survive today as entities bounded by any single nation-state, not even one as big as the United States. So the current keep-you-awake-at-night issue

for nation-states and their citizens is how to deal with these corporations. To whom are they loyal?

"Corporate America has done very well, and there is nothing wrong
with that, but it has done well by aligning itself with the flat world," said
Dinakar Singh, the hedge fund manager. "It has done that by outsourcing
as many components as possible to the cheapest, most efficient suppliers.
If Dell can build every component of its computers in coastal China and
sell them in coastal America, Dell benefits, and American consumers
benefit, but it is hard to make the case that American labor benefits." So
Dell wants as flat a world as possible, with as little friction and as few barriers as possible. So do most other corporations today, because this allows
them to build things in the most low-cost, efficient markets and sell in the
most lucrative markets. There is almost nothing about Globalization 3.0
that is not good for capital. Capitalists can sit back, buy up any innovation, and then hire the best, cheapest labor input from anywhere in the
world to research it, develop it, produce it, and distribute it. Dell stock
does well, Dell shareholders do well, Dell customers do well, and the
Nasdaq does well. All the things related to capital do fine. But only some
American workers will benefit, and only some communities. Others will
feel the pain that the flattening of the world brings about.

Since multinationals first started scouring the earth for labor and
markets, their interests have always gone beyond those of the nation-state
in which they were headquartered. But what is going on today, on the flat
earth, is such a difference of degree that it amounts to a difference in
kind. Companies have never had more freedom, and less friction, in the
way of assigning research, low-end manufacturing, and high-end manufacturing anywhere in the world. What this will mean for the long-term
relationship between companies and the country in which they are
headquartered is simply unclear.

Consider this vivid example: On December 7, 2004, IBM announced that it was selling its whole Personal Computing Division to
the Chinese computer company Lenovo to create a new worldwide PC
company—the globe's third largest—with approximately $12 billion in
annual revenue. Simultaneously, though, IBM said that it would be
taking an 18.9 percent equity stake in Lenovo, creating a strategic al-

liance between IBM and Lenovo in PC sales, financing, and service worldwide. The new combined company's worldwide headquarters, it was announced, would be in New York, but its principal manufacturing operations would be in Beijing and Raleigh, North Carolina; research centers would be in China, the United States, and Japan; and sales offices would be around the world. The new Lenovo will be the preferred supplier of PCs to IBM, and IBM will also be the new Lenovo's preferred supplier of services and financing.

Are you still with me? About ten thousand people will move from IBM to Lenovo, which was created in 1984 and was the first company to introduce the home computer concept in China. Since 1997, Lenovo has been the leading PC brand in China. My favorite part of the press release is the following, which identifies the new company's senior executives: "Yang Yuanqing—Chairman of the Board. [He's currently CEO of Lenovo.] Steve Ward—Chief Executive Officer. [He's currently IBM's senior vice president and general manager of IBM's Personal Systems Group.] Fran O'Sullivan—Chief Operating Officer. [She's currently general manager of IBM's PC division.] Mary Ma—Chief Financial Officer. [She's currently CFO of Lenovo.]"

Talk about horizontal value creation: This new Chinese-owned computer company headquartered in New York with factories in Raleigh and Beijing will have a Chinese chairman, an American CEO, an American CPO, and a Chinese CFO, and it will be listed on the Hong Kong stock exchange. Would you call this an American company? A Chinese company? To which country will Lenovo feel more attached? Or will it just see itself sort of floating above a flat earth?

This question was anticipated in the press release announcing the new company: "Where will Lenovo be headquartered?" it asked.

Answer: "As a global business, the new Lenovo will be geographically dispersed, with people and physical assets located worldwide."

Sort that out.

The cold, hard truth is that management, shareholders, and investors are largely indifferent to where their profits come from or even where the employment is created. But they do want sustainable companies. Politicians, though, are compelled to stimulate the creation of jobs in a certain place.

And residents—whether they are Americans, Europeans, or Indians—want to know that the good jobs are going to stay close to home.

The CEO of a major European multinational remarked to me, "We are a global research company now." That's great news for his shareholders and investors. He is accessing the best brains on the planet, wherever they are, and almost certainly saving money by not doing all the research in his backyard. "But ultimately," he confided to me, "this is going to have implications down the road on jobs in my own country— maybe not this year but in five or fifteen years." As a CEO and European Union citizen, "you might have a dialogue with your government about how we can retain capabilities in [our own country]—but day by day you have to make decisions with the shareholders in mind."

Translation: If I can buy five brilliant researchers in China and/or India for the price of one in Europe or America, I will buy the five; and if, in the long run, that means my own society loses part of its skills base, so be it. The only way to converge the interests of the two—the company and its country of origin—is to have a really smart population that can not only claim its slice of the bigger global pie but invent its own new slices as well. "We have grown addicted to our high salaries, and now we are really going to have to earn them," the CEO said.

But even identifying a company's country of origin today is getting harder and harder. Sir John Rose, the chief executive of Rolls-Royce, told me once, "We have a big business in Germany. We are the biggest high-tech employer in the state of Brandenburg. I was recently at a dinner with Chancellor [Gerhard] Schroeder. And he said to me, 'You are a German company, why don't you come along with me on my next visit to Russia'— to try to drum up business there for German companies." The German chancellor, said Rose, "was recognizing that although my headquarters were in London, my business was involved in creating value in Germany, and that could be constructive in his relationship with Russia."

Here you have the quintessential British company, Rolls-Royce, which, though still headquartered in England, now operates through a horizontal global supply chain, and its CEO, a British citizen knighted by the queen, is being courted by the chancellor of Germany to help him drum up business in Russia, because one link in the Rolls-Royce supply chain happens to run through Brandenburg.

My friend Glen Fukushima is an American of Japanese ancestry. His father, also a Japanese American, was based in Japan with the U.S. Army, so Glen was born in a U.S. military hospital there in 1949. He graduated from Stanford and Harvard and eventually moved in 1985 from law practice to become director for Japanese affairs at the Office of the U.S. Trade Representative (USTR) and then deputy assistant USTR for Japan and China, representing the United States in its tough trade disputes with these two Asian giants. In 1990 he moved to Tokyo, where he subsequently held a series of high-level executive jobs with AT&T and other multinational U.S. corporations. In 1997 he was elected by his American peers to be president of the American Chamber of Commerce in Japan, a volunteer job he held with great distinction. When I passed through Tokyo in September 2005, we had our usual breakfast at his corner table at the Hotel Okura. I asked Fukushima about his work, and he surprised me by announcing that he had a new job: He had just become the president of Japan operations for the European consortium Airbus. He was now running the Japan business of the crown jewel manufacturing company of Europe, helping it try to beat out the crown jewel manufacturing company of America, Boeing, in selling passenger aircraft to Japan, the country of his ancestors.

"When I joined Airbus, the U.S. embassy here told me that I was no longer allowed to attend the monthly meeting that the board of governors of the American Chamber of Commerce in Japan has with the U.S. ambassador," said Fukushima, who, when he was president of that Chamber, presided over its fiftieth anniversary. The embassy employees, reacting on ingrained instincts, didn't want a person they saw as representing Europe's leading industrial consortium to gain any assistance from the U.S. embassy that might help him compete against one of America's biggest industrial firms. Fukushima, however, argued that "I am doing something new and different that reflects the times and that defies neat national categories." There is no longer a correlation, he said, among the nationality of a global corporation's executives, the geographic location of the corporation's headquarters, and the market in which its top executives are doing their most important business. Quite a few ACCJ board members who attended the monthly meeting, for instance, were U.S. citizens who had started their own companies in Japan, with no U.S. operations or employees, or they were U.S. citizens working for non-U.S. companies, or they were Japanese citizens working for American companies. Moreover, roughly 35 percent of the new Boeing 787's airframe is being made in Japan by Mitsubishi Heavy Industries and other Japanese manufacturers. Another significant amount is being made or designed in Europe, Russia, China, and other places — even though Boeing (which is headquartered in Chicago) is usually touted as "America's biggest exporter."

Yes, sort that out.

FROM COMMAND AND CONTROL TO COLLABORATE AND CONNECT

Before Colin Powell stepped down as secretary of state, I went in for an interview, which was also attended by two of his press advisers, in his seventh-floor State Department suite. I could not resist asking him about where he was when he realized the world had gone flat. He answered with one word: "Google." Powell said that when he took over as secretary of state in 2001, and he needed some bit of information—say, the text of a UN resolution—he would call an aide and have to wait for minutes or even hours for someone to dig it up for him.

"Now I just type into Google 'UNSC Resolution 242' and up comes the text," he said. Powell explained that with each passing year, he found himself doing more and more of his own research, at which point one of his press advisers remarked, "Yes, now he no longer comes asking for information. He already has the information. He comes asking for action."

Powell, a former member of the AOL board, also regularly used e-mail to contact other foreign ministers and, according to one of his aides, kept up a constant instant-messaging relationship with Britain's foreign secretary, Jack Straw, at summit meetings, as if they were a couple of college students. Thanks to the cell phone and wireless technology, said Powell, no foreign minister can run and hide from him. He said he had been looking for Russia's foreign minister the previous week. First he tracked him down on his cell phone in Moscow, then on his cell phone in Iceland, and then on his cell phone in Vientiane, Laos. "We have everyone's cell phone number," said Powell of his fellow foreign ministers.

The point I take away from all this is that when the world goes flat, hierarchies are not being leveled just by little people being able to act big. They are also being leveled by big people being able to act really small—in the sense that they are enabled to do many more things on their own. It really hit me when Powell's junior media adviser, a young woman, walked me down from his office and remarked along the way that because of e-mail, Powell could get hold of her and her boss at any hour, via their BlackBerrys—and did.

"I can't get away from the guy," she said jokingly of his constant e-mail instructions. But in the next breath she added that on the previous weekend, she was shopping at the mall with some friends when she got an instant message from Powell asking her to do some public affairs task. "My friends were all impressed," she said. "Little me, and I'm talking to the secretary of state!"

This is what happens when you move from a vertical (command and control) world to a much more horizontal (connect and collaborate) flat world. Your boss can do his job *and your job*. He can be secretary of state and his own secretary. He can give you instructions day or night. So you are never out. You are always in. Therefore, you are always on. Bosses, if they are inclined, can collaborate more directly with more of their staff than ever before—no matter who they are or where they are in the hierarchy. But staffers will also have to work much harder to be better informed than their bosses. There are a lot more conversations between bosses and staffers today that start like this: "I know that already! I Googled it myself. Now what do I do about it?"

Multiple Identity Disorder

It is not only communities and companies that have multiple identities that will need sorting out in a flat world. So too will individuals. In a flat world, the tensions among our identities as consumers, employees, citizens, taxpayers, and shareholders are going to come into sharper and sharper conflict.

"In the nineteenth century," said business consultant Michael Hammer, "the great conflict was between labor and capital. Now it is between customer and worker, and the company is the guy in the middle. The consumer turns to the company and says, 'Give me more for less.' And then companies turn to employees and say, 'If we don't give them more for less, we are in trouble. I can't guarantee you a job and a union steward can't guarantee you a job, only a customer can.'"

The New York Times reported (November 1, 2004) that Wal-Mart spent about $1.3 billion of its $256 billion in revenue in 2003 on employee health care, to insure about 537,000 people, or about 45 percent of its workforce. Wal-Mart's biggest competitor, though, Costco Wholesale, insured 96 percent of its eligible full-time or part-time employees. Costco employees become eligible for health insurance after three months working full-time or six months working part-time. At Wal-Mart, most full-time employees have to wait six months to become eligible, while part-timers are not eligible for at least two years. According to the Times, full-time employees at Wal-Mart make about $1,200 per month, or $8 per hour. Wal-Mart requires employees to cover 33 percent of the cost of their benefits, and it plans to reduce that employee contribution to 30 percent. Wal-Mart-sponsored health plans have monthly premiums for family coverage ranging as high as $264 and out-of-pocket expenses as high as $13,000 in some cases, and such medical costs make health coverage unaffordable even for many Wal-Mart employees who are covered, the Times said.

But the same article went on to say this: "If there is any place where Wal-Mart's labor costs find support, it is Wall Street, where Costco has taken a drubbing from analysts who say its labor costs are too high." Wal-Mart has taken more fat and friction out than Costco, which has kept more in, because it feels a different obligation to its workers. Costco's pre-tax profit margin is only 2.7 percent of revenue, less than half Wal-Mart's margin of 5.5 percent.

But wait a minute, doesn't the Wal-Mart shopper in all of us want the lowest prices possible, with all the middlemen, fat, and friction removed? And don't the poorest Americans—those often also without health care—benefit most from that? That is a point Sebastian Mallaby made in an opinion essay in *The Washington Post* (November 28, 2005). Listen to his argument: "Wal-Mart's critics allege that the retailer is bad for poor Americans. This claim is backward: As Jason Furman of New York University puts it, Wal-Mart is 'a progressive success story.' Furman advised John 'Benedict Arnold' Kerry in the 2004 campaign and has never received any payment from Wal-Mart; he is no corporate apologist. But he points out that Wal-Mart's discounting on food alone boosts the welfare of American shoppers by at least $50 billion a year. The savings are possibly five times that much if you count all of Wal-Mart's products. These gains are especially important to poor and moderate-income families. The average Wal-Mart customer earns $35,000 a year, compared with $50,000 at Target and $74,000 at Costco. Moreover, Wal-Mart's 'every day low prices' make the biggest difference to the poor, since they spend a higher proportion of income on food and other basics. As a force for poverty relief, Wal-Mart's $200 billion–plus assistance to consumers may rival many federal programs."

So the Wal-Mart shareholder and shopper in us wants Wal-Mart to be relentless about removing the fat and friction in its supply chain and in its employee benefits packages in order to fatten the company's profits—and to keep its prices low. But the Wal-Mart worker in us hates the limited benefits and low pay packages that Wal-Mart offers its starting employees. And the Wal-Mart citizen in us knows that because Wal-Mart, the biggest company in America, doesn't cover all its employees with health care, some of them will just go to the emergency ward of the local hospital and the taxpayers will end up picking up the tab. The *Times* reported that a survey by Georgia officials found that "more than 10,000 children of Wal-Mart employees were in the state's health program for children at an annual cost of nearly $10 million to taxpayers."

Similarly, it said, a "North Carolina hospital found that 31 percent of 1,900 patients who described themselves as Wal-Mart employees were on Medicaid, while an additional 16 percent had no insurance at all."

In her 2004 book, *Selling Women Short: The Landmark Battle for Workers' Rights at Wal-Mart,* journalist Liza Featherstone followed the huge women's discrimination suit against Wal-Mart. In an interview about the book with Salon.com (November 22, 2004), she made the following important point: "American taxpayers chip in to pay for many full-time Wal-Mart employees because they usually require incremental health insurance, public housing, food stamps—there are so many ways in which Wal-Mart employees are not able to be self-sufficient. This is very ironic, because Sam Walton is embraced as the American symbol of self-sufficiency. It is really troubling and dishonest that Wal-Mart supports Republican candidates in the way that they do: 80 percent of their corporate campaign contributions go to Republicans. But Republicans tend not to support the types of public assistance programs that Wal-Mart depends on. If anything, Wal-Mart should be crusading for national health insurance. They should at least be acknowledging that because they are unable to provide these things for their employees, we should have a more general welfare state."

As you sort out and weigh your multiple identities—consumer, employee, citizen, taxpayer, shareholder—you have to decide: Do you prefer the Wal-Mart approach or the Costco approach? This is going to be an important political issue in a flat world: Just how flat do you want corporations to be when you factor in all your different identities? Because when you take the middleman out of business, when you totally flatten your supply chain, you also take a certain element of humanity out of life.

The same question applies to government. How flat do you want government to be? How much friction would you like to see government remove, through deregulation, to make it easier for companies to compete on Planet Flat?

Said Congressman Rahm Emanuel, an Illinois Democrat who was a senior adviser to President Clinton, "When I served in the White House, we streamlined the FDA's drug approval process in response to concerns about its cumbersome nature. We took those steps with one objective in mind: to move drugs to the marketplace more quickly. The result, however, has been an increasingly cozy relationship between the FDA and the pharmaceutical industry, which has put public health at risk. The Vioxx debacle [over an anti-inflammatory drug that was found to lead to an increased risk for heart attacks and strokes] shows the extent to which drug safety has taken a backseat to speedy approval. A recent Senate hearing on Vioxx's recall revealed major deficiencies in the FDA's ability to remove dangerous drugs from the market."

As consumers we want the cheapest drugs that the global supply chains can offer, but as citizens we want and need government to oversee and regulate that supply chain, even if it means preserving or adding friction.

Sort that out.

WHO OWNS WHAT?

Something else is absolutely going to have to be sorted out in a flat world: Who owns what? How do we build legal barriers to protect an innovator's intellectual property so he or she can reap its financial benefits and plow those profits into a new invention? And from the other side, how do we keep walls low enough so that we encourage the sharing of intellectual property, which is required more and more to do cutting-edge innovation?

"The world is decidedly not flat when it comes to uniform treatment of intellectual property," said Craig Mundie, Microsoft's chief technology officer. It is wonderful, he noted, to have a world where a single innovator can summon so many resources by himself or herself, assemble a team of partners from around the flat world, and make a real breakthrough with some product or service. But what does that wonderful innovative engineer do, asked Mundie, "when someone else uses the same flat-world platform and tools to clone and distribute his wonderful new product?" This happens in the world of software, music, and pharmaceuticals every day. And the technology is reaching a point now where "you should assume that there isn't anything that can't be counterfeited quickly"—from Microsoft Word to airplane parts, he added. The flatter the world gets, the more we are going to need a system of global governance that keeps up with all the new legal and illegal forms of collaboration.

We can also see this in the case of patent law as it has evolved in the United States. Companies can do one of three things with an innovation: They can patent the widget they invent and sell it themselves; they can patent it and license it to someone else to manufacture; or they can patent it and cross-license with several other companies so that they all have freedom of action to make a product—like a PC—that comes from melding many different patents. American patent law is technically neutral on this. But the way established case law has evolved, experts tell me, it is decidedly biased against cross-licensing and other arrangements that encourage collaboration or freedom of action for as many players as possible; it is more focused on protecting the rights of individual firms to manufacture their own patents. In a flat world, companies need a patent system that encourages both approaches. The more your legal structure fosters cross-licensing and standards, the more collaborative innovation you will get. The PC is the product of a lot of cross-licensing between the company that had the patent on the cursor and the company that had the patent on the mouse and the screen.

So, with more and more innovation emerging from open-source collaborations and communities, intellectual property law has to adjust—or else we as a society will not get the benefits or be protected from the drawbacks of a flat world. "For collaborative innovation to flourish, we must rethink our ideas about intellectual property," argues IBM's chairman Sam Palmisano. "Intellectual property laws were created to enable individuals and institutions to reap the rewards of their inventions, while at the same time making these intellectual assets available for society as a whole. Within this rather delicate framework, however, there are diverging opinions about whose interests should come first. Some believe the best way to provide incentives for innovation is by fiercely protecting the inventor's proprietary interest. Others argue that we should open the doors and give full access to intellectual assets. I believe we need a new path forward, an approach that offers a balance of those two extremes. We must protect the interests of individuals and companies that create truly new, novel, and useful inventions. But at the same time, we need to protect the interests of innovative communities, creative ecosystems—groups that are not incorporated or chartered but that nonetheless are engaged in genuine—and genuinely important—innovation. We need expanded notions of ownership, for a postindustrial world."

And while you are sorting out that ownership question, sort this one out as well. On November 13, 2004, Lance Corporal Justin M. Ellsworth, twenty, was killed by a roadside bomb during a foot patrol in Iraq. On December 21, 2004, the Associated Press reported that his family was demanding that Yahoo! give them the password for their deceased son's e-mail account so they could have access to all his e-mail, including notes to and from others. "I want to be able to remember him in his words. I know he thought he was doing what he needed to do. I want to have that for the future," John Ellsworth, Justin's father, told the AP. "It's the last thing I have of my son." We are moving into a world where more and more communication is in the form of bits traveling through cyberspace and stored on servers located all over the world. No government controls this cyberrealm. So the question is: Who owns your bits when you die? The AP reported that Yahoo! denied the Ellsworth family their son's password, citing the fact that Yahoo! policy calls for erasing all accounts that are inactive for ninety days and the fact that all Yahoo! users agree at sign-up that rights to a member's ID or account contents terminate upon death. "While we sympathize with any grieving family, Yahoo! accounts and any contents therein are nontransferable" even after death, Karen Mahon, a Yahoo! spokeswoman, told the AP. As we get rid of more and more paper and communicate through more and more digitized formats, you better sort out before you die, and include in your will, to whom, if anyone, you want to leave your bits. This is very real. I stored many chapters of this book in my AOL account, feeling it would be safest in cyberspace. If something had happened to me during my writing, my family and publisher would have had to sue AOL to try to get this text. Somebody, please, sort all this out.

DEATH OF THE SALESMEN

In the fall of 2004, I went out to Minneapolis to visit my mother and had three world-is-flat encounters right in a row. First, before I left home in Washington, I dialed 411—directory assistance—to try to get a friend's phone number in Minneapolis. A computer answered and a computerized voice asked me to pronounce the name of the person whose number I was requesting. For whatever reason, I could not get the computer to hear me correctly, and it kept saying back to me in a computerized voice, "Did you say . . . ?" I kept having to say the family name in a voice that masked my exasperation (otherwise the computer never would have understood me). "No, I didn't say that . . . I said . . ." Eventually, I was connected to an operator, but I did not enjoy this friction-free encounter with directory information. I craved the friction of another human being. It may be cheaper and more efficient to have a computer dispense phone numbers, but for me it brought only frustration.

When I arrived in Minneapolis, I had dinner with family friends, one of whom has spent his life working as a wholesaler in the Midwest, selling goods to the biggest retailers in the region. He is a natural salesman. When I asked him what was new, he sighed and said that business just wasn't what it used to be. Everything was now being sold at 1 percent margins, he explained. No problem. He was selling mostly commodity items so that, given his volumes, he could handle the slim profit margin. But what bothered him was the fact that he no longer had human contact with some of his biggest accounts. Even commodities and low-cost goods have certain differentiating elements that need to be sold and highlighted. "Everything is by e-mail now," he said. "I am dealing with a young kid at [one of the biggest retailers in the nation], and he says, 'Just e-mail me your bid.' I've never met him. Half the time he doesn't get back to me. I am not sure how to deal with him . . . In the old days, I used to stop by the office, give the buyers a few Vikings tickets. We were friends . . . Tommy, all anyone cares about today is price."

Fortunately, my friend is a successful businessman and has a range of enterprises. But as I reflected later on what he was saying, I was drawn back to that scene in *Death of a Salesman* in which Willy Loman says that, unlike his colleague Charley, he intends to be "well liked." He tells his sons that in business and in life, character, personality, and human connections are more important than smarts. Says Willy, "The man who makes an appearance in the business world, the man who creates personal interest, is the man who gets ahead. Be liked and you will never want."

Not when the world goes flat. It's hard to create a human bond with e-mail and streaming Internet. The next day, I had dinner with my friend Ken Greer, who runs a media company that I discuss in greater detail later. Ken had a similar lament: So many contracts were going these days to the advertising firms that were selling just numbers, not creative instinct. Then Ken said something that really hit home with me: "It is like they have cut all the fat out of the business" and turned everything into a numbers game. "But fat is what gives meat its taste," Ken added. "The leanest cuts of meat don't taste very good. You want it marbled with at least a little fat."

The flattening process relentlessly trims the fat out of business and life, but, as Ken noted, fat is what gives life taste and texture. Fat is also what keeps us warm.

Yes, the consumer in us wants Wal-Mart prices, with all the fat gone. But the employee in us wants a little fat left on the bone, the way Costco does it, so that it can offer health care to almost all its employees, rather than just less than half of them, as Wal-Mart does. But the shareholder in us wants Wal-Mart's profit margins, not Costco's. Yet the citizen in us wants Costco's benefits, rather than Wal-Mart's, because the difference ultimately may have to be paid for by society. The consumer in me wants lower phone bills, but the human being in me also wants to speak to an operator when I call 411. Yes, the reader in me loves to surf the Net and read the bloggers, but the citizen in me also wishes that some of those bloggers had an editor, a middleman, to tell them to check some of their facts one more time before they pressed the Send button and told the whole world that something was wrong or unfair.

Given these conflicting emotions and pressures, there is potential here for American politics to get completely reshuffled—with workers and corporate interests realigning themselves into different parties. Think about it: Social conservatives from the right wing of the Republican party, who do not like globalization or closer integration with the world because it brings too many foreigners and foreign cultural mores into America, might align themselves with unions from the left wing of the Democratic Party, who don't like globalization for the way it facilitates the outsourcing and offshoring of jobs. They might be called the Wall Party and militate for more friction and fat everywhere. Let's face it: Republican cultural conservatives have much more in common with the steelworkers of Youngstown, Ohio, the farmers of rural China, and the mullahs of central Saudi Arabia, who would also like more walls, than they do with investment bankers on Wall Street or service workers linked to the global economy in Palo Alto, who have been enriched by the flattening of the world.

Meanwhile, the business wing of the Republican Party, which believes in free trade, deregulation, more integration, and lower taxes—everything that would flatten the world even more—may end up aligning itself with the social liberals of the Democratic Party, many of whom are East Coast or West Coast global service industry workers. They might also be joined by Hollywood and other entertainment workers. All of them are huge beneficiaries of the flat world. They might be called the Web Party, whose main platform would be to promote more global integration. Many residents of Manhattan and Palo Alto have more interests in common with the people of Shanghai and Bangalore than they do with the residents of Youngstown or Topeka. In short, in a flat world, we are likely to see many social liberals, white-collar global service industry workers, and Wall Street types driven together, and many social conservatives, white-collar local service industry workers, and labor unions driven together.

The *Passion of the Christ* audience will be in the same trench with the Teamsters and the AFL-CIO, while the Hollywood and Wall Street liberals and the *You've Got Mail* crowd will be in the same trench with the high-tech workers of Silicon Valley and the global service providers of Manhattan and San Francisco. It will be Mel Gibson and Jimmy Hoffa Jr. versus Bill Gates and Meg Ryan.

More and more, politics in the flat world will consist of asking which values, frictions, and fats are worth preserving—which should, in Marx's language, be kept solid—and which must be left to melt away into the air. Countries, companies, and individuals will be able to give intelligent answers to these questions only if they understand the real nature and texture of the global playing field and how different it is from the one that existed in the Cold War era and before. And countries, companies, and individuals will be able to make sound political choices only if they fully appreciate the flattened playing field and understand all the new tools now available to them for collaborating and competing on it. I hope this book will provide a nuanced framework for this hugely important political debate and the great sorting out that is just around the corner.

To that end, the next three sections look at how the flattening of the world and the triple convergence will affect Americans, developing countries, and companies.

Brace yourself: You are about to enter the flat world.

America and the
Flat World

FIVE

America and Free Trade

Is Ricardo Still Right?

A s an American who has always believed in the merits of free trade, I had an important question to answer after my India trip: Should I still believe in free trade in a flat world? Here was an issue that needed sorting out immediately—not only because it was becoming a hot issue in national politics but also because my whole view of the flat world would depend on my view of free trade. I know that free trade won't necessarily benefit every American, and that our society will have to help those who are harmed by it. But for me the key question was: Will free trade benefit America *as a whole* when the world becomes so flat and so many more people can collaborate, and compete, with my kids? It seems that so many more jobs that we think of as "American" are going to be up for grabs. Wouldn't individual Americans be better off if our government erected some walls and banned some outsourcing and offshoring?

I first wrestled with this issue while filming the Discovery Times documentary in Bangalore. One day we went to the Infosys campus around five p.m.—just when the Infosys call-center workers were flooding into the grounds for the overnight shift on foot, minibus, and motor scooter, while many of the more advanced engineers were leaving at the end of the day shift. The crew and I were standing at the gate observing this river of educated young people flowing in and out, many in animated conversation. They all looked as if they had scored 1,600 on their SATs, and I felt a real mind-eye split overtaking me. My mind just kept telling me, "Ricardo is right, Ricardo is right, Ricardo is right." David Ricardo (1772–1823) was the English economist who developed the free-trade theory of comparative advantage, which stipulates that if each nation specializes in the production of goods in which it has a comparative cost advantage and then trades with other nations for the goods in which they specialize, there will be an overall gain in trade, and overall income levels should rise in each trading country. So if all these Indian techies were doing what was their comparative advantage and then turning around and using their income to buy all the products from America that are our comparative advantage—from Corning Glass to Microsoft Windows—both our countries would benefit, even if some individual Indians or Americans might have to shift jobs in the transition. And one can see evidence of this mutual benefit in the sharp increase in exports and imports between the United States and India in recent years.

But my eye kept looking at all these Indian zippies and telling me something else: "Oh, my God, there are so many of them, and they all look so serious, so eager for work. And they just keep coming, wave after wave. How in the world can it possibly be good for my daughters and millions of other young Americans that these Indians can do the same jobs as they can for a fraction of the wages?" When Ricardo was writing, goods were tradable, but for the most part knowledge work and services were not. There was no undersea fiber-optic cable to make knowledge jobs tradable between America and India back then. Just as I was getting worked up with worry, the Infosys spokeswoman accompanying me casually mentioned that last year Infosys India received "one million applications" from young Indians for nine thousand tech jobs.

Have a nice day.

I struggled over what to make of this scene. I don't want to see any American lose his or her job to foreign competition or to technological innovation. I sure wouldn't want to lose mine. When you lose your job, the unemployment rate is not 5.2 percent; it's 100 percent. No book about the flat world would be honest if it did not acknowledge such concerns, or acknowledge that there is some debate among economists about whether Ricardo *is* still right. Having listened to the arguments on both sides, though, I come down where the great majority of economists come down—that Ricardo is still right and that more American individuals will be better off if we don't erect barriers to outsourcing, supply-chaining, and offshoring than if we do.

That is the simple message of this chapter: Even as the world gets flat, America as a whole will benefit more by sticking to the general principles of free trade, as it always has, than by trying to erect walls, which will only provoke others to do the same and impoverish us all. But the broader argument of this whole section of the book—"America and the Flat World"—is that while protectionism would be counterproductive, a policy of free trade, while necessary, is not enough by itself. It must be accompanied by a focused domestic strategy aimed at upgrading the education of every American, so that he or she will be able to compete for the new jobs in a flat world. And it must be accompanied by a foreign strategy of opening restricted markets all over the world (including some of our own, like agriculture), thereby bringing more countries into the global free-trade system—which will increase demand for goods and services, spur innovation, and reduce both unemployment and job migration across the globe.

Of course, the protectionist/anti-outsourcing school disagrees. Neither of the above strategies will work anymore, this school insists. The anti-outsourcers argue that in a flat world not only are more goods tradable, but many services have become tradable as well—the very service jobs that support the American middle class but were never exposed to the forces of automation or outsourcing to the degree they are now. Because of this change, America and other developed countries could be headed for an absolute decline, not just a relative one, in their economic power and living standards unless they move to formally protect certain jobs, both blue-collar and white-collar, from foreign competition. There is no way that so many new players can enter the global economy, in services and high-end manufacturing—fields long dominated by Americans, Europeans, and Japanese—without wages settling in at a newer, lower equilibrium.

What are the main counterarguments from free-trade/outsourcing advocates, such as myself, who still believe that Ricardo is right? To begin with, while there may be a transition phase in certain fields, during which wages are dampened in developed countries, there is no reason to believe that this dip will be permanent or across the board, as long as the global pie keeps growing. To suggest that it will be permanent is to invoke the so-called lump of labor theory—the notion that there is a fixed lump of labor in the world and that once that lump is gobbled up, whether by Americans or Indians or Japanese, there won't be any more jobs to go around. If we have the biggest lump of labor now, and then Indians offer to do this same work for less, they will get a bigger piece of the lump, and we will have less, or so this argument goes.

The main reason the lump of labor theory is wrong is that it is based on the assumption that everything that is going to be invented has been invented, and that therefore economic competition is a zero-sum game, a fight over a fixed lump. This assumption misses the fact that although jobs are often lost in bulk—to outsourcing or to offshoring or to new technologies—by big individual companies, and this loss tends to make headlines, new jobs are also being created in fives, tens, and twenties by small companies that you can't see. It often takes a leap of faith to believe that it is happening. *But it is happening.* If it were not, America's unemployment rate would be much higher today than 4.5 percent. The reason it is happening is that as lower-end service and manufacturing jobs move out of Europe, America, and Japan to India, China, and the former Soviet Empire, the global pie not only grows larger—because more people have more income to spend—it also grows more complex, as more new jobs, and new specialties, are created.

Let me illustrate this with a simple example. Imagine that there are only two countries in the world—America and China. And imagine that the American economy has only 100 people. Of those 100 people, 80 are well-educated knowledge workers and 20 are less-educated low-skilled workers. Now imagine that the world goes flat and America enters into a free-trade agreement with China, which has 1,000 people but is a less developed country. So today China too has only 80 well-educated knowledge workers out of that 1,000, and it has 920 low-skilled workers. Before America entered into its free-trade agreement with China, there were only 80 knowledge workers in its world. Now there are 160 in our two-country world. The American knowledge workers feel like they have more competition, and they do. But if you look at the prize they are going after, it is now a much expanded and more complex market. It went from a market of 100 people to a market of 1,100 people, with many more needs and wants. So it should be win-win for both the American and Chinese knowledge workers.

Sure, some of the knowledge workers in America may have to move *horizontally* into new knowledge jobs, because of the competition from China. But with a market that big and complex, you can be sure that new knowledge jobs will open up at decent wages for anyone who keeps up his or her skills. So do not worry about our knowledge workers or the Chinese knowledge workers. They will both do fine with this bigger market.

"What do you mean, don't worry?" you ask. "How do we deal with the fact that those eighty knowledge workers from China will be willing to work for so much less than the eighty knowledge workers from America? How will this difference get resolved?"

It won't happen overnight, so some American knowledge workers may be affected in the transition, but the effects will not be permanent. Here, argues Stanford new economy specialist Paul Romer, is what you need to understand: The wages for the Chinese knowledge workers were so low because, although their skills were marketable globally like those of their American counterparts, they were trapped inside a stifled economy. Imagine how little a North Korean computer expert or brain surgeon is paid inside that huge prison of a nation! But as the Chinese economy opens up to the world and reforms, the wages of Chinese knowledge workers will rise up to American/world levels. Ours will not go down to the level of a stifled, walled-in economy. You can already see this happening in Bangalore, where competition for Indian software writers is rapidly pushing up their wages toward American/European levels—after decades of languishing salaries while the Indian economy was closed. This is why Americans should be doing all they can to promote the gradual but sustained opening and reform of the Indian and Chinese economies—because in the long term overall wages will rise in a more open and productive world economy.

Do worry, though, about the 20 low-skilled Americans, who now have to compete more directly with the 920 low-skilled Chinese. One reason the 20 low-skilled Americans were paid a decent wage before was that, relative to the 80 skilled Americans, there were not that many of them. Every economy needs some low-skilled manual labor. But now that China and America have signed their free-trade pact, there are a total of

940 low-skilled workers and 160 knowledge workers in our two-country world. Those American low-skilled workers doing fungible jobs—jobs that can easily be moved to China—will have a problem. There is no denying this. Their wages are certain to be depressed. In order to maintain or improve their living standards, they will have to move *vertically*, not horizontally. They will have to upgrade their education and upgrade their knowledge skills so that they can occupy one of the new jobs sure to be created in the much expanded United States–China market. (In the coming chapters I will discuss our society's need and obligation to ensure that everyone gets a chance to acquire those skills.)

As Romer notes, we know from the history of our own country that an increase in knowledge workers does not necessarily lead to a decrease in their pay the way it does with low-skilled workers. From the 1960s to the 1980s, the supply of college-educated workers grew dramatically, and yet their wages grew even faster. Because as the pie grew in size and complexity, so too did people's wants, and this increased the demand for people able to do complex work and specialized tasks. Romer explains this in part by the fact that "there is a difference between idea-based goods and physical goods." If you are a knowledge worker making and selling some kind of idea-based product—consulting or financial services or music or software or marketing or design or new drugs—the bigger the market is, the more people there are out there to whom you can sell your product. And the bigger the market, the more new specialties and niches it will create. If you come up with the next Windows or Viagra, you can potentially sell one to everyone in the world. So idea-based workers do well in globalization, and fortunately America as a whole has more idea-driven workers than any other country in the world.

But if you are selling manual labor—or a piece of lumber or a slab of steel—the value of what you have to sell does not necessarily increase when the market expands, and it may decrease, argues Romer. There are only so many factories that will buy your manual labor, and there are many more people selling it. What the carpenter or nanny has to sell can be bought by only one factory or one family at a time, explains Romer, while what the software writer or drug inventor has to sell—idea-based products—can be sold to everyone in the global market at once.

That is why America, as a whole, will do fine in a flat world with free trade—provided it continues to churn out knowledge workers who are able to produce idea-based goods that can be sold globally and who are able to fill the knowledge jobs that will be created as we not only expand the global economy but connect all the knowledge pools in the world together. There may be a limit to the number of good factory jobs in the world, *but there is no limit to the number of idea-generated jobs in the world.* If we go from a world in which there were fifteen drug companies and fifteen software companies in America (thirty in all) and two drug companies and two software companies in China (four in all) to a world in which there are thirty drug and software companies in America and thirty drug and software companies in China, it is going to mean more innovation, more cures, more niches to specialize in, more new products to customize to individuals or markets, and many more people with higher incomes to buy those products.

"The pie keeps growing because things that look like wants today are needs tomorrow," argued Marc Andreessen, the Netscape cofounder, who helped to ignite a whole new industry, e-commerce, that now employs millions of specialists around the world, specialists whose jobs weren't even imagined when Bill Clinton became president. I like going to coffee shops occasionally, but now that Starbucks is here, I *need* my coffee, and that new need has spawned a whole new industry. I always wanted to be able to search for things, but once Google was created, I *must* have my search engine. So a whole new industry has been built up around search, and Google is hiring math Ph.D.'s by the bushel—before Yahoo! or Microsoft hires them. People are always assuming that everything that is going to be invented must have been invented already. *But it hasn't.*

"If you believe human wants and needs are infinite," said Andreessen, "then there are infinite industries to be created, infinite businesses to be started, and infinite jobs to be done, and the only limiting factor is human imagination. The world is flattening and rising at the same time. And I think the evidence is overwhelmingly clear: If you look over the sweep of history, every time we had more trade, more communications, we had a big upswing in economic activity and standard of living."

America integrated a broken Europe and Japan into the global economy after World War II, with both Europe and Japan every year upgrading their manufacturing, knowledge, and service skills, often importing and sometimes stealing ideas and equipment from the United States, just as America did from Britain in the late 1770s. Yet in the sixty years since World War II, our standard of living has increased every decade, and our unemployment rate—even with all the outcry about outsourcing—stands at only a little above 5 percent, roughly half that of the most developed countries in Western Europe.

"We just started a company that created 180 new jobs in the middle of a recession," said Andreessen, whose company, Opsware, uses automation and software to replace human beings in the operation of huge server farms in remote locations. By automating these jobs, Opsware enables companies to save money and free up talented brainpower from relatively mundane tasks to start new businesses in other areas. You should be afraid of free markets, argued Andreessen, only if you believe that you will never need new medicines, new work flow software, new industries, new forms of entertainment, new coffeehouses, and only if you believe that your country's citizens will never be able to develop the knowledge skills to fill the jobs these new industries or business models will spin off.

"Yes," he concluded, "it takes a leap of faith, based on economics, to say there will be new things to do." But there always have been new jobs to do, and there is no fundamental reason to believe the future will be different.

Some 150 years ago, 90 percent of Americans worked in agriculture and related fields, driving plows pulled by horses and harvesting crops by hand. Today, due to the industrialization of agriculture, we need less than 3 percent of the population to grow all our food and more. What if long ago the government had decided to protect and subsidize all those manual agricultural jobs and refused to embrace mechanized and eventually computerized agriculture? Hey, if horses could have voted, there never would have been cars. Would America as a whole be better off today? Hardly. Of course, it is true that as Indians and Chinese move up the value chain and start producing more knowledge-intensive goods— the sorts of things Americans have specialized in—our comparative advantage in some of these areas will diminish, explains Jagdish Bhagwati, the Columbia University expert on free trade. There will be a downward pressure on wages in certain fields, and some of the jobs in those fields may permanently migrate abroad. That is why some knowledge workers will have to move horizontally. But the growing pie will surely create new specialties for them to fill, and new areas of comparative advantage, that are impossible to predict right now. It all depends on how many new services or products we can imagine. And, as I said, there is just no limit to that.

For instance, there was a time when America's semiconductor industry dominated the world, but then companies from other countries came along and gobbled up the low end of the market. Some even moved into the higher end. American companies were then forced to find newer, deeper specialties in the expanded market. If that weren't happening, Intel would be out of business today. Instead, it is thriving. Paul Otellini, Intel's president, told *The Economist* (May 8, 2003) that as chips become good enough for certain applications, new applications pop up that demand more powerful and more complex chips, which are Intel's specialty.

As Google, Yahoo!, and Microsoft start offering video searches, for instance, there will be demand for new devices and the chips that power them, things most of us couldn't have imagined possible ten years ago. This process takes time to unfold. But it will, argued Bhagwati, because what is happening in services today is the same thing that happened in manufacturing as trade barriers were lowered. In manufacturing, said Bhagwati, as the global market expanded and more and more players came onto the field, you saw greater and greater "intraindustry trade." So Mexico specialized in making tires and China specialized in making camshafts and America specialized in overall automobile design. As we move into the knowledge economy, you are now seeing more and more "intraservice trade," with more and more slices of specialization emerging within different service sectors as they grow more complex.

So Mom and Dad, don't be surprised if your kid comes home from college one day and announces that he or she wants to be a "search engine optimizer." Yes, you will be tempted to respond, "Wait one minute. I sent you to college to be a doctor or a lawyer! What the hell is a search engine optimizer? Why couldn't you be an ophthalmologist like your uncle Louie?" But don't succumb to such words. Search engine optimizer is just one of those new specialties emerging in the flat world. Here's how: Let's say there are two giant suitcase companies in the world—"Tom's Suitcases" and "Samsonite." It can mean millions of dollars in profits if, when someone searches for "suitcase" on Google, Tom's Suitcases comes up before Samsonite on Google or Microsoft's first page of search results. More people will likely click on Tom's Suitcases, and because the people who click through to a Web site are those most likely to buy, Tom's Suitcases will enjoy the majority of business. What search engine optimizers (SEOs as they are called in the trade) do is constantly study the algorithms being used by the major search engines to produce their search results, and then try to design marketing and Web strategies that will push your company up the rankings. The SEOs are such algorithm buffs that they are known as "algoholics." Their business involves a synthesis of math and marketing—a whole new specialty created entirely by the flattening of the world. Remember the days when you used to ask your friend who was majoring in math, "What are you going to do with that?" Well, don't ask anymore.

Search engine optimizing has become such a big business that Google now holds an annual dance party at its headquarters for all the SEOs trying to break its code. On August 20, 2005, the Associated Press ran a story describing the Google Dance: "Free-flowing beer, live music, karaoke and arcade games kept the party raging at the Googleplex the other night, but the real action was unfolding inside a sterile conference room at Google Inc. headquarters. That's where the cunning Internet entrepreneurs who constantly try to manipulate Google's search engine results for a competitive edge were trying to make the most of a rare opportunity to match wits face-to-face with the company's top engineers. Google's code-talking experts, despite putting on a show of being helpful, weren't about to reveal their 'secret sauce'—Google's tightly guarded formula for ranking Web sites . . . The efforts to outsmart Google gall some Webmasters such as Shari Thurow, who says the best way to increase a site's search engine ranking is to offer valuable content and products."

There is nothing about the flat world that makes obsolete Ricardo's basic insight about comparative advantage—nothing at all. What is new is how developed and developing countries will define their comparative advantage in a flat world—what new and old services and industries their companies and individuals will choose to specialize in at any given time. This is where the new challenge will arise. It would appear that in a flatter world a country can and will lose its comparative advantage in one field much more quickly than in the round world. It is obvious, for instance, that countries like India and China can now compete in many more fields—fields that were once seen as the exclusive preserve of developed Western nations. These developed Western countries will need to adapt, and move into still newer fields, much more quickly, if they want to maintain their standards of living. At the same time, as India and China develop, they will lose their comparative advantage in certain lower-rung fields, like basic manufacturing or textiles, to places like Vietnam or Madagascar. No country is immune to these economic laws of gravity. The good news for America, though, as I have tried to suggest, is that in the flat world there also will be an inexorable flow of new jobs, as whole new fields of endeavor are spun off faster and faster—jobs that educated Americans and Europeans should be able to specialize in, like search engine optimizing. And, at the same time, there will be an inexorable flow of jobs from the developed world to the developing world, as these new jobs regularly become commoditized and more easily tradable—and therefore advantageous to do in India or China.

And still at the same time, thanks to the ten flatteners, more and more jobs will be broken apart, with the more sophisticated tasks being done in the developed world and the less sophisticated tasks in the developing world—where each has its comparative advantage. And you will start to see more innovations emerging from China and India, with some of the production, design, and marketing being outsourced to the West, where, yes, we still may have some comparative advantage. You are going to see all of these things—all at once. But as long as the pie keeps growing and getting more complex, and as long as the individuals in your country keep adding to that pie by imagining new services and products in which to specialize, and as long as those individuals keep educating themselves and developing the skills needed to master these new jobs, workers in India, China, Europe, and America can all do well at the same time.

Always remember: *The Indians and Chinese are not racing us to the bottom. They are racing us to the top—and that is a good thing!* They want higher standards of living, not sweatshops; they want brand names, not junk; they want to trade in their motor scooters for cars, and their pens and pencils for computers. And the more they do that, the higher they climb, the more room is created at the top—because the more they have, the more they spend, the more diverse product markets become, and the more niches for specialization are created as well. Look at what is happening already: As American companies send knowledge work to India, Indian companies are turning around and using their earnings and insights to start inventing new products that poorer Indians can use to lift themselves out of poverty into the middle class, where they will surely become consumers of American products. Both China and India are rapidly developing from a focus on low-cost production and copying to a focus on low-cost innovation of their own. They need to find innovative and affordable ways to solve their own problems—and they are doing just that. And once they perfect some of these affordable solutions in their own markets—a medical insurance program in India that covers the poor for as little as $10 a year, cheap laptops, super-cheap cell phones, and even a low-fare Indian airline ($75 one-way for the three-hour Bangalore to Delhi flight) that sells tickets from Internet kiosks in gas stations—they will take them global. *BusinessWeek* (October 11, 2004) cited the Tata Motors factory, near Pune, south of Mumbai, "where a group of young designers, technicians, and marketers pore over drawings and examine samples of steel and composite plastics. By early next year, they plan to design a prototype for Tata Group's most ambitious project yet: a compact car that will sell for $2,200. The company hopes the car will beat out Suzuki's $5,000 Maruti compact to become India's cheapest car—and an export model for the rest of the developing world. 'This is the need of the day in India—a people's car,' says Ratan Tata, chairman of the $12.5 billion Tata Group. Indians are increasingly demanding better products and services at an affordable cost. Strong economic growth this year will only enlarge that demand.

The phrase 'Made in India' may come to represent innovation in the new global economy."

Raghuram Rajan, the director of research for the International Monetary Fund, sits on the board of HeyMath.com, a very innovative Indian education company that puts Indian students to work over the Internet tutoring students in Singapore and elsewhere, and also employs Indian, British, and Chinese experts to help HeyMath design the best ways to teach various math and science concepts to young people in grades K–12. In working with public schools in Singapore, and now even in the United States, HeyMath provides teachers with lesson plans, PowerPoint presentations, online homework packets, and other jazzy ways for them to teach math and science. This saves teachers time, which they can then use to customize certain lessons just for their class or spend more time with one-on-one interactions. HeyMath, headquartered in Chennai, India, is paid for by the schools in Singapore and elsewhere. But Cambridge University in England is also part of this equation, providing the overall quality controls and certifying the lesson plans and teaching methods.

"Everyone wins," says Rajan. "The company is run by two Indians who worked for Citibank and CSFB in London and came back to India to start this business . . . Cambridge University is making money from a company that has created a whole new niche. The Indian students are making pocket money. And the Singapore students are learning better." Meanwhile, the underlying software is probably being provided by Microsoft and the chips by Intel, and the enriched Indian students are probably buying cheap personal computers from Apple, Dell, or HP. *But you can't really see any of this.* "The pie grew, but no one saw it," said Rajan. No one anywhere lost a job because HeyMath went into business, but lots of people in all different places got jobs that did not exist five years ago.

An essay in the *McKinsey Quarterly*, "Beyond Cheap Labor: Lessons for Developing Economies" (January 2005), offers a nice example of companies and countries moving from one comparative advantage to another: "In northern Italy's textile and apparel industry . . . the majority of garment production has moved to lower-cost locations, but employment remains stable because companies have put more resources into tasks such as designing clothes and coordinating global production networks."

It is so easy to demonize free markets—and the freedom to outsource and offshore—because it is so much easier to see people being laid off in big bunches, which makes headlines, than to see them being hired in fives and tens by small and medium-size companies, which rarely makes news. But occasionally a newspaper tries to dig deep into the issue. My hometown paper, the Minneapolis *Star Tribune*, did just that. It looked at exactly how the Minnesota economy was being affected by the flattening of the world, actually daring to run an article on September 5, 2004, headlined, "Offshore Jobs Bring Gains at Home." The article, datelined Wuxi, China, began like this: "Outside the air is dank, dusty and hot as tropical fever. Inside, in an environment that's dry, spotless and cool, hundreds of former farm laborers covered head to toe in suits looking like something out of NASA are performing work for Bloomington-based Donaldson Co. Inc. . . . In Donaldson's case, the company has twice as many workers in China—2,500—as the 1,100 it has in Bloomington. The Chinese operation not only has allowed Donaldson to keep making a product it no longer could make at a profit in the United States, it also has helped boost the company's Minnesota employment, up by 400 people since 1990. Donaldson's highly paid engineers, chemists and designers in Minnesota spend their days designing updated filters that the Chinese plant will make for use in computers, MP3 players and digital video recorders. The falling disk-drive prices made possible by Chinese production are feeding demand for the gadgets. 'If we didn't follow [the trend], we'd be out of business,' said David Timm, general manager of Donaldson's disk-drive and microelectronics unit. In Minnesota, Global Insight estimates that 1,854 jobs were created as a result of foreign outsourcing in 2003. By 2008, the firm expects nearly 6,700 new jobs in Minnesota as a consequence of the trend."

Economists often compare China's and India's entry into the global economy to the moment when the railroad lines crossing America finally connected New Mexico to California, with its much larger population. "When the railroad comes to town," noted Vivek Paul, the Wipro president, "the first thing you see is extra capacity, and all the people in

New Mexico say those people—Californians—will wipe out all our factories along the line. That will happen in some areas, and some companies along the line will go out of business. But then capital will get reallocated. In the end, everyone along the line will benefit. Sure, there is fear, and that fear is good because that stimulates a willingness to change and explore and find more things to do better."

It happened when we connected New York, New Mexico, and California. It happened when we connected Western Europe, America, and Japan. And it will happen when we connect India and China with America, Europe, and Japan. The way to succeed is not by stopping the railroad line from connecting you, but by firing up your imagination, by upgrading your skills, and by adopting those practices, rules, policies, and educational institutions that will enable you and your society to claim a healthy slice of the bigger but more complex pie.

SIX

The Untouchables

Finding the New Middle

If the flattening of the world is largely (but not entirely) unstoppable, and if it holds out the potential to be as beneficial to American society in general as past market evolutions have been, how does an individual get the best out of it? What do we tell our kids?

My simple answer is this: There will be plenty of good jobs out there in the flat world for people with the right knowledge, skills, ideas, and self-motivation to seize them. But there is no sugar-coating the new challenge: Every young American today would be wise to think of himself or herself as competing against every young Chinese, Indian, and Brazilian. In Globalization 1.0, countries had to think globally to thrive, or at least survive. In Globalization 2.0, companies had to think globally to thrive, or at least survive. In Globalization 3.0, individuals have to think globally to thrive, or at least survive. This requires not only a new level of technical skills but also a certain mental flexibility, self-motivation, and psychological mobility. I am certain that we Americans can indeed thrive in this world. But I am also certain that it will not be as easy as it was in the last fifty years. Each of us, as an individual, will have to work a little harder and run a little faster to keep our standard of living rising.

"Globalization went from globalizing industries to globalizing individuals," said Vivek Paul, the Wipro president. "I think today that people working in most jobs can sense how what they are doing integrates globally: 'I am working with someone in India. I am buying from someone in China. I am selling to someone in England.' As a result of the ability to move work around, we have created an amazing awareness on the part of every individual that says: 'Not only does my work have to fit into somebody's global supply chain, but I myself have to understand how I need to compete and have the skill sets required to work at a pace that fits the supply chain. And I had better be able to do that as well or better than anyone else in the world.'" That sense of responsibility for one's own advancement runs deeper than ever today. In many global industries now, you have got to justify your job every day with the value you create and the unique skills you contribute. And if you don't, that job can fly away farther and faster than ever.

In sum, it was never good to be mediocre in your job, but in a world of walls, mediocrity could still earn you a decent wage. You could get by and then some. In a flatter world, you *really* do not want to be mediocre or lack any passion for what you do. You don't want to find yourself in the shoes of Willy Loman in *Death of a Salesman,* when his son Biff dispels his idea that the Loman family is special by declaring, "Pop! I'm a dime a dozen, and so are you!" An angry Willy retorts, "I am not a dime a dozen! I am Willy Loman, and you are Biff Loman!"

I don't care to have that conversation with my girls, so my advice to them in this flat world is very brief and very blunt: "Girls, when I was growing up, my parents used to say to me, 'Tom, finish your dinner— people in China and India are starving.' My advice to you is: Girls, finish your homework—people in China and India are starving for your jobs." And in a flat world, they can have them, because in a flat world there is no such thing as an American job. There is just a job, and in more cases than ever before it will go to the best, smartest, most productive, or cheapest worker—wherever he or she resides.

THE NEW MIDDLE

It is going to take more than just doing your homework to thrive in a flat world, though. You are going to have to do the *right kind* of homework as well. Because the companies that are adjusting best to the flat world are not just making minor changes, they are changing the whole model of the work they do and how they do it—in order to take advantage of the flat-world platform and to compete with others who are doing the same. What this means is that students also have to fundamentally reorient what they are learning and educators how they are teaching it. They can't just keep the same old model that worked for the past fifty years, when the world was round. This set of issues is what I will explore in this and the next chapter: What kind of good middle-class jobs are successful companies and entrepreneurs creating today? How do workers need to prepare them-selves for those jobs, and how can educators help them do just that?

Let's start at the beginning. The key to thriving, as an individual, in a flat world is figuring out how to make yourself an "untouchable." That's right. When the world goes flat, the caste system gets turned up-side down. In India, untouchables are the lowest social class, but in a flat world everyone should want to be an untouchable. "Untouch-ables," in my lexicon, are people whose jobs cannot be outsourced, dig-itized, or automated. And remember, as analyst David Rothkopf notes, most jobs are not lost to outsourcing to India or China—most lost jobs are "outsourced to the past." That is, they get digitized and automated. The *New York Times*'s Washington bureau used to have a telephone operator–receptionist. Now it has a recorded greeting and voice mail. That reception job didn't go to India; it went to the past or it went to a microchip. The flatter the world gets, the more anything that can be digitized, automated, or outsourced will be digitized, automated, or outsourced. As Infosys CEO Nandan Nilekani likes to say, in a flat world there is "fungible and nonfungible work." Work that can be eas-ily digitized, automated, or transferred abroad is fungible. One of the most distinguishing features of the flat world is how many jobs—not just blue-collar manufacturing jobs but now also *white-collar service jobs*—are becoming fungible. Since more of us work in those service jobs than ever before, more of us will be affected.

Have no illusions: We live in a world now where more and more things are becoming tradable, Alan Blinder, the noted Princeton econ-omist, argued in a very smart essay titled "Fear of Offshoring." He explained:

At any point in time, the available technology—especially transportation and communications technologies—largely determines
which goods and services are easy to trade internationally and which
are hard or impossible to trade. Simplifying this underlying reality,
economic theorists typically conceptualize the world's goods and
services as falling into one of two bins: "tradable" or "non-tradable"
[what Nilekani calls fungible and nonfungible]. Traditionally, any
item that can be put in a box and shipped (roughly, manufactured
goods) was considered tradable, while anything that cannot be put
in a box (like services) or was too heavy for shipping (like cement)
was thought of as non-tradable. But that is now vestigial thinking.

Because technology is constantly improving, and because
transportation seems to grow easier and cheaper over time, the
boundary between what is tradable and what is not tradable is
constantly shifting . . . *Over time, more and more things become
tradable.* In particular, boxes are simply not what they once were.
The old assumption that, if you can put it in a box, you can trade
it, is now hopelessly obsolete . . . Because packets of digitized information can now play the role that boxes used to play, *many services are now tradable and many more will surely become so.*

Indeed, let me make a bold prediction . . . In the future, and to
a great extent already in the present, the key distinction for international trade will no longer be between things that can be put in a
box and things that cannot. It will, instead, be between services that
can be delivered electronically over long distances with little or no
degradation of quality, and those that cannot. The tradability of a
vast array of services is, as they say, the New New Thing. And there
is little doubt that the fraction of services that can be delivered electronically will grow. (Princeton University Center for Economic
Policy Studies Working Paper No. 119, December 2005.)

So if that is the direction of the global economy, who will the untouchables be? What jobs are not likely to become fungible, easy to
automate, digitize, or outsource? I would argue that the untouchables in
a flat world will fall into three broad categories. First are people who are

really "special or specialized." This label would apply to Michael Jordan, Madonna, Elton John, J. K. Rowling, your brain surgeon, and the top cancer researcher at the National Institutes of Health. These people perform functions in ways that are so special or specialized that they can never be outsourced, automated, or made tradable by electronic transfer. They are untouchables. They have a global market for their goods and services and can command global wages.

Second are people who are really "localized" and "anchored." This category includes many, many people. They are untouchables because their jobs must be done in a specific location, either because they involve some specific local knowledge or because they require face-to-face, personalized contact or interaction with a customer, client, patient, colleague, or audience. All these people are untouchables because they are anchored: my barber, the waitress at lunch, the chefs in the kitchen, the plumber, nurses, my dentist, lounge singers, masseurs, retail sales clerks, repairmen, electricians, nannies, gardeners, cleaning ladies, and divorce lawyers. Note that these people can be working in high-end jobs (divorce lawyer, dentist), vocational jobs (plumber, carpenter), or low-end jobs (garbage collector, maid). Regardless of that worker's level of sophistication, their wages will be set by the local market forces of supply and demand.

That then brings me to the third broad category. This category includes people in many formerly middle-class jobs—from assembly line work to data entry to securities analysis to certain forms of accounting and radiology—that were once deemed nonfungible or nontradable and are now being made quite fungible and tradable thanks to the ten flatteners. Let's call these the "old middle" jobs. Many of them are now under pressure from the flattening of the world. As Nandan Nilekani puts it: "The problem [for America] is in the middle. Because the days when you could count on being an accounts-payable clerk are gone. And a lot of the middle class are where that [old] middle is . . . This middle has not yet grasped the competitive intensity of the future. Unless they [do], they will not make the investments in reskilling themselves and you will end up with a lot of people stranded on an island."

Some are noticing, though. They are noticing that the rising threats of a machine or a worker from India taking their jobs have left them with stagnating wages—even though they are more productive and their companies more profitable.

How does it all work in real life? *The Financial Times* (November 2, 2006) explained: "Jack Drake understands better than most Americans how strongly the U.S. economy has performed over recent years. His job with a media company in Atlanta involves transcribing conference calls hosted by public companies to deliver financial information to analysts and investors. 'Almost every day, I listen to chief executives explaining how well their companies are doing,' he says. But Mr. Drake, 42, complains that the soaring corporate profits and robust economic growth he helps document are not reflected in his own financial circumstances. His $47,000 annual salary has barely moved for five years. 'Healthcare costs are up. Energy is up. But my income is standing still.' Mr. Drake is among millions of educated middle-class Americans seeing their pay stagnate and blaming that on technology and globalization. 'It would be hard to outsource my job because there is so much specialist knowledge and business jargon involved,' he says. 'But it is used as an unspoken threat to keep wages down.'"

What to do? One thing is to make sure we take the full picture into account. Yes, it is true that median wages are stagnating for white-collar workers in developed countries. But it is also true that those workers can buy so many more things with those wages, because prices are falling thanks to the same globalization that is pinching their salaries. China's holding of about $1 trillion of U.S. Treasury securities and dollars, at very low interest rates, has kept American interest rates down, enabling many Americans to buy homes with extremely cheap mortgages. Thanks to globalization, they can also buy flat-screen TVs, cell phones, computers, shoes, clothing, and cars at ever lower prices. It is not only wages that are affected by globalization but prices as well.

That said, our ability to keep global integration advancing will depend on workers at all levels feeling that globalization and free trade have more positive than negative effects on their lives as a whole—that they enable them not just to buy cheap DVDs but also educate their kids and afford health care for their families the way that middle-class parents could in the past. Stagnating middle-class wages and rising job insecurity, coupled with soaring executive pay, are a bad combination. And a lecture on the wisdom of Ricardo will not satisfy people who are caught in this squeeze. Average Americans historically never resented the rich as long as they felt they too had a fair chance to get rich or advance. So if too many feel left out, it could shake America's vaunted political stability.

The U.S. economy used to look like a bell curve, with a big bulge in the middle. That bulge of middle-class jobs has been the foundation not only of our economic stability but of our political stability as well. Democracy cannot be stable without a broad and deep middle class. We cannot afford to move from a bell curve economy to a barbell economy— with a big high end and a bigger low end and nothing in the middle. It would be economically unfair and politically unstable. As former Clinton national economic adviser Gene Sperling rightly argues, "We either grow together or we will grow apart."

So I repeat: What to do? Obviously, we need to make sure our tax system is fair, but I will leave that for others to detail. Equally obvious to me is that putting up walls is not the answer. We don't want to choke off the very openness and flexibility of the American economy that make it so unique. We want to enable more American workers to be able to take part in that openness, to derive its benefits and remain part of a flourishing middle class or move up into it. The demand and payoff for skilled, educated workers who can adapt to rapid technological change, respond to international competition, and claim new middle jobs is greater than ever today. "In 1979, median compensation for college graduates was 38% higher than for high school graduates. Last year, that difference was 75%" (*BusinessWeek*, February 9, 2007).

Therefore, of the many things we need to do, in my view the most important is to identify the new middle jobs that will be less vulnerable to the downward wage pressures of outsourcing, automation, and technological change and to identify the particular skills and education they will demand—so that more weakers can reap the benefits. In the United States, new middle jobs are coming into being all the time; that is why we don't have large-scale unemployment, despite the flattening of the world. But to acquire and hold one of these new middle jobs you need certain skills that are suited to the flat world—skills that can make you (at least temporarily) special, specialized, or anchored, and therefore (at least temporarily) untouchable and more likely to reap rising wages.

THE NEW MIDDLERS

In order to identify those jobs and those skills, I worked backward. I went out to successful flat-world companies around America and asked a simple question: "Obviously you have a lot of good middle-class jobs here. Who works here and what sorts of things do they do?" What follows is a general list of categories that many new middle jobs will fall into, or grow out of, and the skill sets they require. To put it another way, here is what the "Help Wanted" ads look like in a flat world.

GREAT COLLABORATORS AND ORCHESTRATORS

Clearly, a lot of new middle jobs will involve collaborating with others or orchestrating collaboration within and between companies, especially those employing diverse workforces from around the world. So as more and more companies start out, from day one, as global companies with global supply chains, a key new middle job will be that of the manager who can work in and orchestrate 24/7/7 supply chains—which are supply chains that run twenty-four hours a day, seven days a week, across seven continents.

I first started to realize this in the summer of 2005 when I took my daughter Orly to Bangalore, where she volunteered as a teacher in a school outside of town. One day she joined me on a visit to my friends at Infosys. When we arrived at the Infosys headquarters, a spokeswoman gave us a tour of the building. As we walked through the halls, she said to me in passing, "Our interns heard that you were going to be here today and asked if you would come and speak to them."

Sure, I said, I'd love to speak to the interns. I always love interacting with these young Indians.

"No, no," she said. "It's our *American* interns."

"You have *American* interns at Infosys?!"

They sure did, she told me. For its one hundred internship positions that summer, Infosys received about 9,000 applications, primarily from North America, China, France, and Germany. I asked one of these interns, Vicki Chen, a Chinese-American business student from the Claremont Colleges in California, why she had sought out an internship in Bangalore. "All the business is coming to India, and I don't see why I shouldn't follow the business," she said. "If this is where the center of gravity is, you should go check it out, and then you become more valuable."

As Infosys CEO Nilekani pointed out to me, even though Infosys is one of the biggest outsourcing firms in the world headquartered in Bangalore, "30 percent of our employees are outside of India, around the world"—working at the front end, soliciting new business, implementing new software, and servicing existing accounts. "There will be a lot of good jobs that will involve being at the front end of this new global collaboration model," said Nilekani. "Suppose you are working for a big pharma company and it starts doing a lot more research in India. You will need people to talk to the FDA in Washington and deal with the local marketplace. There is always a local phase to this global process." These new middle collaboration jobs will be in sales, marketing, maintenance, and management, but what they will all demand is the ability to be a good horizontal collaborator, comfortable working for a global company (one whose headquarters may be in Beijing or Bangalore, not Boston), and translating its services for the local market, wherever that may be. It is about being able to operate in, mobilize, inspire, and manage a multidimensional and multicultural workforce.

Although good people skills were always an asset in the working world, they will be even more so in a flat world, because many more products will be made in global supply chains, many new middle jobs will involve making supply chains more efficient. "The more complex the globalized networks," says Carlota Perez, a Venezuelan-born expert on technology and socioeconomic development, who is best known for her detailed tracking of large technoeconomic paradigm shifts, "the more [companies] will need various forms of coordination and management [around] specifications, compatibility, research and design, global marketing, distribution chains, data sharing and storage, and security." There will be a lot of good new middle jobs along that chain.

Being a good collaborator or team leader will earn you a good new middle job for another reason. "We actually have no shortage of ideas," says John Doerr, the Silicon Valley venture capitalist. "What we are short is people who can execute them. Everyone has this image of the lone entrepreneur in a Silicon Valley garage. In reality, it takes teams of people to win, to translate a new idea into a product." And the more complex the product or service, the bigger the team. That means, added Doerr, "that you need people who can work well with others, and, even more importantly, you need team leaders who know how to speak to people, to explain, and inspire." People don't realize that the most important thing a venture capitalist does is not write a check to a start-up company. The most important thing a venture capitalist does, notes Doerr, is find the right managerial talent to lead and inspire the start-up company so that it can grow to the next level.

THE GREAT SYNTHESIZERS

The further we push out the boundaries of knowledge and innovation, the more the next great value breakthroughs—that is, the next new hotselling products and services—will come from putting together disparate things that you would not think of as going together. Search engine optimizing, for example, brings together mathematicians and marketing experts. The next great breakthrough in bioscience is going to result from computer engineers who can map the human genome working with pharma companies that can turn these insights into life-saving drugs. This synthesis is where the new jobs are going to emerge.

As I write this chapter, one of the hottest new businesses involves what is called "mash-ups," where you just mash together two different Webbased tools. So, for instance, some local realtors might mash together Craigslist with Google, which would mean matching up the local online directory of everyone selling a house or renting an apartment in a particular town with Google's maps—instantly producing a real estate map that pinpoints every one of those houses and rental properties—and is updated every second.

"Can you bring an artist and clinical engineer together?" Infosys chief operating officer S. "Kris" Gopalakrishnan asked me one day in Bangalore. "If the value comes from synthesizing, then you need synthesizers. Conventionally your approach to any problem or challenge was breaking it down to manageable bits and smaller parts, but today you are trying to create value by synthesizing disparate parts together. IBM used to make the chip, the computer, and the software, all vertically [all by itself]. But if you look at Dell, it does very little design and manufacturing. It brings all of the parts together from others and puts them in front of the customer. [Dell's] value is its ability to synthesize much better than everyone else. Synthesizing it all together around consumer demand is the key . . . So in an organization you need the dot people and the big-picture people [who can connect the dots]. And the change that is happening in India and at Infosys is that we are moving more into the capability of creating the synthesis for the client. We understand the trends in the industry and anticipate trends and come out with a synthesized solution."

Jeff Wacker, who works as the futurist for Electronic Data Systems Corporation (EDS), once wrote a company memo predicting which jobs would not be around in fifteen or twenty years. His first category was the CIO. "There will still be a CIO," he wrote, "but the chief information officer will be replaced with a chief *integration* officer. Information technology will be so fully embedded in every aspect of a business that the IT organization will move away from technology to the integration of business processes."

THE GREAT EXPLAINERS

The more we have good synthesizers, who can bring disparate things together, the more we will need managers, writers, teachers, producers, journalists, and editors who are also good explainers—who can see the complexity but explain it with simplicity. Marcia Loughry is an enterprise

architect who also works for EDS. She is a classic example of a new mid-
dler for reasons that I will explain shortly. One reason is that she learned
how to be a great explainer. It is more important to be able to explain
something to someone else than to sit down and do the work yourself,
she *explained* to me on a visit to EDS headquarters. "I have fields of
people who can distribute software," she said, "but someone has to go in
front of that customer and explain: 'Here is what this is going to do for
you, here is how it will tie into your existing systems, here is how it will
benefit you, and here is how much it will cost.'"

Think about it: If you can explain the complexity well, you can see the
opportunities better. For instance, you can see what parts to synthesize. At
the same time, the more content you can search and access, the more important the filters and explainers become. Amazon.com's value is in not
just selling you the book for 30 percent off the cover price, but actually
helping you sort through the ocean of books out there very quickly and
easily so you find the books you might be interested in reading.

Howard Freeman, fifty-three, owns a custom photography lab in
Aspen, Colorado, called SlideMaster Photo-Imaging. We met quite by accident. He was my ski instructor. Over lunch one day at the top of
Snowmass Mountain, he explained to me how his business was evolving,
and I explained to him, on the basis of what he explained to me, that he
had just entered the New Middle as a "Great Explainer." Let me explain:

When Freeman started his business in 1977, he specialized in processing, duplicating, and making enlargements of slides taken by professional photographers, such as those on assignment for *Architectural
Digest*, or by advanced amateurs. But thanks to the triple convergence,
and the rise of digital photography, the number of people shooting slide
film, or any film, dramatically diminished.

As that business tapered off, Freeman found himself spending more
time every day explaining to customers how to operate a digital camera
and how to process and touch up film digitally, using computers. Some
days, he told me, he would be exhausted by five p.m.—yet realize that he
had not really gotten anything done on his core business. He was spending all his time explaining to customers or his own employees the fine
points of digital photography and processing.

So, Freeman recalled, one day he finally said to himself: "Since I am spending half my time explaining digital photography, I might as well make it half my business." In early 2006, he ripped out of his shop the big print processors that he used to make enlargements of slides and replaced them with a dozen computers (mostly Apple Macs), and an array of digital printers. He and his staff started using the computers not only for processing customers' digital photography, but, more important, to start a new career as explainers. They invited potential clients to come in during office hours or after and learn—for a fee—how to do sophisticated digital photo processing, retouching, and manipulation, using the latest computer software. They also offered to go out and teach—at a client's home or office computing environment—so the information could be applied immediately on the client's own digital photo systems.

"We used to sell film and develop and print the pictures—and give away the advice for free," explained Freeman. "Now we are selling the advice and, while not giving away the products, they have become a smaller part of our business . . . We are going to make explaining the business."

In light of that, Freeman told me he has had to think about his staff in different ways. The pure backroom technical person, who does not have good people skills, might be less in demand. And the good people person, who might be just one chapter ahead of the clients in terms of understanding digital photography, becomes more valuable—because he or she is a really good explainer.

THE GREAT LEVERAGERS

The man who invented information technology outsourcing is Ross Perot, the fast-talkin' Texan who ran for president in 1992. After his discharge from the navy in 1957, Perot went to work as a salesman for IBM, where he identified what he thought was a unique business opportunity—using downtime on one company's computers (back when computers were uncommon and expensive) to do data processing for other companies. Perot left IBM in 1962 and founded EDS to do just that, winning contracts from large corporations and eventually the U.S. government. This came to be known as business process outsourcing, and it has spread from Texas to Bangalore, thanks to the flattening of the world. EDS, which Perot sold in 1984, still does business process outsourcing today—competing with companies in India and across the world.

In November 2005 I visited the EDS campus in Plano, Texas, a modern grass, glass, and steel compound with a massive structure called the SMC—Systems Management Center—at the heart of it. There is a viewing area for visitors, with seats like a home theater. When you come in the curtains are closed and then suddenly they part, and laid out before you is a huge control room that looks like the NASA headquarters monitoring a moon shot. There are seven massive wall-size screens, below them smaller TV screens, and below them about one hundred individual control pods with screens and dials in front of them. Today only about twenty of those pods have people sitting at their controls, because today twenty people do the work that one hundred people did a decade ago. The only way EDS can compete with low-wage India is by having one person work smarter and faster, rather than cheaper and harder. Those twenty people can really leverage every drop out of every new technology as soon as it appears.

Taking in this scene, I had one question: Who are those twenty people down there and how come they have not been automated or outsourced? Here's what I learned: When the SMC was built, those one hundred people worked in shifts with constant "eyes on glass," because when you are running other people's data you cannot afford your computer systems, or theirs, to be even 99.999 percent operational. They have to be working perfectly all the time, or else a whole company's business processes could crash. So the SMC operators had to sit in those pods and constantly watch the information being spewed out on different screens by the EDS computers processing the data for all sorts of customers. You might see one thousand informational messages and then one error message that you couldn't afford to miss.

Some of the people who worked in the SMC didn't have college degrees, let alone computing expertise. EDS simply trained them to keep their eyes on the glass and raise an alarm when an error message appeared. So if you suddenly got a message "service unavailable," and the phone started ringing from the customer's headquarters, as an operator your job was to swivel around among four different screens and try to correlate all the information on all the screens and figure out the root cause of the problem. Was it the router? Was it the server? And two different operators would respond differently and come up with very different answers.

Over time, EDS was able to leverage more and more computing power and identify the root cause of any problem automatically. "Now the swivel chair is gone," my EDS guide explained, "and the screen simply has a message that says, 'The router has a problem.'" That's great, you might be saying to yourself—now I need to be even less well-educated to get one of those twenty jobs. But the opposite is true. The really special or specialized jobs at EDS are held by those people who can leverage technology, who can design precisely these computer programs that enable others to work smarter and faster. Those people are untouchables. The new middle jobs at EDS, for now at least, are held by the people who learn to operate these new programs. What does that involve?

Today, the people sitting at the twenty pods are computer engineers, and smart ones at that. "The people we are looking for," explained the EDS futurist Jeff Wacker, "are people who can not only catch a problem, but quickly come up with a solution that will fix the problem for good, so it will never happen again . . . Not only do they catch the fish, they fillet it and they reseed the pond . . . They see the problem, stop the problem, and then redesign the system so that that particular problem never, ever happens again—and it can't be a cowboy solution." It has to follow a standard protocol so that once you have fixed the problem and designed a better way of doing something, it is in a best-practice format that can be applied throughout the EDS system or, better yet, sold to a customer.

"Now we need people who have a better understanding of how things tie together from end to end—but the end to end is not just from our computers to our customers' computers," said Wacker. "Now the end to end is our business and our customer's business and our customers' customers' businesses. We have clients who may have clients who may serve Dell's supply chain, so you have to have people who understand Dell and how it meets its business objectives for its customers." For instance, EDS works for a Canadian lumber company. To become more efficient, that company needs to implement technology systems so that even before a tree is cut down the company knows whether it will be used for pulp or lumber, which mill will process it, which retailer will stock it, even the precise size of each piece of lumber that will come from it and which building, home, or office it will be used to build. If EDS can help run the business processes of that Canadian company in a way that seamlessly integrates the buildings that architects are designing into the materials contractors are buying into how that timber company cuts each tree, it will save everyone money, eliminate waste, lower transport costs, and make everyone more profitable.

America's long-term economic growth and standard of living have long depended on leveraging technology as a way to compete with cheaper foreign labor. Our focus has always been on achieving such high levels of productivity that we can produce goods and services at competitive prices and still pay our workers decent wages. To pull that off, though, we have had to combine the best of what computers and telecommunications can offer with the best-trained workforce we can build, and then constantly reintegrate the best practices and new skills being honed by that workforce with the best new technologies to make the whole—the machines and the people—more and more productive. There are lots of new middle jobs in that loop if we can keep it going.

THE GREAT ADAPTERS

The Gartner Group, the technology consultants, coined a term to describe the trend in the information technology world away from specialization and toward employees who are more adaptable and versatile. It calls them "versatilists." Building employee versatility and finding employees who already are or are willing to become versatilists "will be the new watchword for career planning," according to a Gartner study quoted by TechRepublic.com. The Gartner study noted that "specialists generally have deep skills and narrow scope, giving them expertise that is recognized by peers but seldom valued outside their immediate domain. Generalists have broad scope and shallow skills, enabling them to respond or act reasonably quickly but often without gaining or demonstrating the confidence of their partners or customers. Versatilists, in contrast, apply depth of skill to a progressively widening scope of situations and experiences, gaining new competencies, building relationships, and assuming new roles." Versatilists are capable not only of constantly adapting but also of constantly learning and growing. TechRepublic quoted Joe Santana, director of training at Siemens Business Services: "With flat or even smaller budgets and fewer people, managers need to make the most of the people they have . . . They can no longer see people as specialty tools. And their people need to become less like specialty tools and more like Swiss Army knives. Those 'Swiss Army knives' are the versatilists."

Let's face it, my kids have very little chance of working for the same company for twenty-five years, as I have. They have got to be adaptable — Swiss Army knives. Gene Sperling, the former economic adviser to President Clinton and author of *The Pro-Growth Progressive*, also has a nice way of expressing this. He remarked to me that today's workers need to approach the workplace much like athletes preparing for the Olympics, with one difference. "They have to prepare like someone who is training for the Olympics but doesn't know what sport they are going to enter," said Sperling. "They have to be ready to do anything."

If all that is true, then Marcia Loughry, the enterprise architect I met at EDS headquarters, is a gold medal Olympic adapter. She epitomizes for me the person who has adapted her way into the new middle — always staying just one step ahead of the job-devouring forces of automation and outsourcing.

"Sometimes I feel like it has been muddling instead of middling," remarked the good-natured forty-eight-year-old adapter, as she told me the story of her remarkable career path at EDS. "I started out in 1978. I thought I wanted to be an accountant so I was in college at the University of North Texas, but I was impatient to get on with my life, so I [dropped out of college] and went to night school, learned how to type and take shorthand, and I got a job in the EDS word-processing center." This was the days before PCs, so Loughry worked on a simple word processor, typing sales reports. After a few years, though, the PC came along on everyone's desk, and the sales reps typed their own reports. Good-bye to that job.

"So then I moved into mainframe and desktop publishing," she explained. "That was slightly more specialized and that involved formatting text, to prepare documents for publication using computers. But then the software got more advanced and people could do that for themselves." Good-bye to that job.

After that Loughry made a living for a short time helping EDS colleagues learn how to do desktop publishing themselves. "I automated the formatting process for people so they could publish their own documents," she said. From there she took a job at the EDS call center and help desk. "I was there for only about a year, because while I was at the help desk I realized that I would be a lot more successful at helping if I knew more about the network that we were supporting," she recalled. "So I simply got up one day, put down my headset, and asked one of the top-tier people working in the SMC [Systems Management Center], Sam Billings, 'How can I learn what you do? Sam, teach me.' And he did. He would let me observe what he was doing. He'd reach under his desk and pull out a manual and say, 'You need to know this.' When he was troubleshooting a problem, he would take me over to a network diagram and say, 'Let's use some logic here: You are getting a bunch of calls from people who have this symptom. What does it mean? Connect the dots.'"

While she was going through this phase, Loughry realized that she needed to package and promote herself, and compete as an individual against other individuals, inside EDS. "There were a lot of people who knew about technology, so what was going to differentiate me or make me get that new job as opposed to someone else?" she asked. "I concluded that I needed to keep constantly learning because there was always something new coming around the corner. That's when I understood that I was 'Marcia, Incorporated.' I concluded that I was solely responsible to [keep learning] by myself, that the resources were available, and that it was just a matter of me taking the initiative. But I decided that I needed some credentials." At the time, EDS was using Novell Netware as its primary network operating system. Loughry, studying on her own, got herself certified on that system. On weekends, she would come in and just hang out with the engineers when they were rolling out a new server.

"They were so willing to help me, I guess because they recognized the curiosity factor, so I got some practical hands-on experience," she recalled. "One day one of the managers called me and said, 'This Systems Management Center is growing rapidly.' He said he had five openings and I should pick one. I picked Windows NT, Microsoft's Network Operating System, and I became one of the first NT server technicians in the SMC. So I helped to develop a team of people who did that support . . . Then I started tagging around with some of the systems architects. I was going to school the whole time and switched over to Web-based courses. I eventually moved into engineering." Along the way, she also wrote a guidebook, *Active Directory for Dummies*. That, said Loughry, "was a calculated move to try to raise my profile within EDS. I needed to prove that there was more to me than just the eyes on glass technician, and I wanted to prove that I could compete with the big guys and breathe some of their rare air. Because to get to the highest job codes you have to publish, initiate patents, and work on globally important projects." Today, Marcia Loughry has reached the second highest technology rung at EDS — enterprise architect.

Loughry, a single mom, said her son is a marine reservist who recently returned from a tour in Iraq. "I tell him a lot, but I don't know if he is really listening," she says, like a good mom. "The deep technical skills around math and science are going to get you in the door, but they are not what are going to keep you there or make you wildly successful. The core competencies are [just] the entry-level requirements. What will keep you there is developing a broader view. Corporations are flattening as the world is flattening, and you have got to be able to see things from the business', the customers', and the market's perspective. You can't just be head down, eyes on glass."

Looking down at each rung of the ladder that got her here, Loughry said, they're all gone: "Every job I have done has to some degree been automated or is being done [at least in part] by someone in India . . . Maybe what set me apart was sheer dogged determination. I love to learn and there is so much available here to learn with." But Loughry knows even enterprise architecture could easily be done from anywhere. "I am not done adapting — not by a long shot," she said. "Sam told me way back, 'Be an expert on three topics, but know that those three topics will always be changing.' So I try to have something that is my core bread and butter right now, another topic closely associated with it, and then what I'm going to do next."

Oh, I forgot to mention, Marcia still does not have her B.A.—she's been too busy adapting. "Right now I am taking a geography course," she said with a chuckle. "I am close to having enough hours to graduate, [but] so far all my finance and tech courses don't add up to a B.A."

THE GREEN PEOPLE

When three billion people from China, India, and the former Soviet Empire walk onto the flat-world platform in a very short period of time, and every one of them wants a house, a car, a microwave, and a refrigerator, if we don't learn how to do more things with less energy and lower emissions, we are going to create an environmental disaster and make our planet unlivable for our children. So there are going to be a lot of jobs involving the words "sustainable" and "renewable"—renewable energies and environmentally sustainable systems. This is going to be a huge industry in the twenty-first century. As Carlota Perez puts it, "The more China, India, and other developing or ex-Socialist countries industrialize, the bigger the environmental problems and the larger the market to prevent, moderate, or overcome them will be." Not only will the further development of these big countries generate the need for these industries, added Perez, "but also stringent global regulation will create the conditions for them to emerge."

Steve Jurvetson, the venture capitalist and innovator who has focused recently on the idea of clean tech investing, talks about what he hopes will be a "biological renaissance"—a new era in which college students, instead of becoming doctors, might instead focus on "bio-derived or bio-inspired" solutions to our looming energy and environmental problems. There are going to be a lot of jobs there, too.

THE PASSIONATE PERSONALIZERS

Ann and I share season tickets to the Baltimore Orioles with friends. As anyone who attends games at Camden Yards knows, there is a guy there who sells lemonade in the lower deck who has perfected a dance routine around how he shakes and prepares the lemonade. He does a little jig and then high-fives you before he hands you the drink. I love to watch him operate because all he is selling is water with sugar and a lemon in a plastic cup. It couldn't be more of a commodity. It couldn't be a more vanilla job. Yet I always notice that by the end of the game he is carrying around a wad of bills—and tips—that is thicker than that of any other vendor I see. Why? Because he took a simple vanilla task and gave it a personal touch—his own chocolate sauce, whipped cream, and cherry on top—that made him special. I could get lemonade from plenty of vendors. I could also drink Coke or water, and he knows it. But I and others often shell out $3.50 (plus a tip) for his sugar water with lemon because it both quenches my thirst and puts a smile on my face. His something extra gives me something extra.

Now, the lemonade man was already an untouchable in the sense that his job was anchored in Baltimore. He was providing a localized service that could not be done as well by a machine or a person in India—because he was delivering lemonade to my seat so I wouldn't miss a pitch. I would argue, however, that he made himself something more, he elevated himself into the better-paying new middle, by adding a personal, intangible dimension to his vanilla work. In April 2006, I went to the Orioles' opening-day game. I scanned the stadium for this lemonade man, wanting to tell him that I had written about him. When I told my hosts whom I was looking for, one of them said, "Haven't you heard? He now rents himself out for private parties." He had developed a whole new side business and even handed out advertising brochures at the game! Is this a great country, or what?

Sometimes this personal dimension is pure passion, sometimes it is pure entertainment, sometimes it is a creative touch that no one else thought of adding—but in every case it takes a routine task and upgrades it into a new middle job. There is an elderly African-American woman who serves coffee at the Caribou Coffee outlet near my office on K Street in Washington. Every time I am there, she goes out of her way to be helpful and ask me about myself—not in a phony, overtrained way, like the staff at a Ritz-Carlton, but in a sincere way that I find charming. So I go out of my way to get my coffee from her. One day, they're going to make her the manager—if she isn't the manager already.

Anyone who can take an old middle service job—from telephone operator to health-care provider to service workers of all types to office receptionist—and give it something personal, something special, some real passion, will have a good chance of turning it into a new middle job that cannot be outsourced, automated, or digitized. Obviously, some services have to be delivered personally, like those provided by a nurse. Others, however, will have to be delivered depending only on your ability to endow them with a personal, passionate touch. Interestingly, the Princeton economist Alan Blinder argues in his paper on outsourcing that because so many new middle jobs will require this kind of personal touch, it may actually produce a revival in human interactive skills, skills that have atrophied to some degree because of the industrial age and the Internet. The renewed stress on personally delivered services, by humans, as opposed to impersonally delivered services by computer-generated voices or voices from India, writes Blinder, "may lead to just the opposite of the phenomena that Charlie Chaplin parodied so effectively in *Modern Times*. Human beings are social animals who enjoy human contact. In many past decades, it looked as if modern economic life were conspiring to minimize the volume of natural human contact that takes place on the job. In future decades, as personal services come to be more predominant, that trend seems likely to reverse—possibly leading to less alienation and greater average job satisfaction."

Indeed, adds Blinder, "Perhaps, contrary to what we have come to believe in recent years, people skills will become more valuable than computer skills. The geeks may not inherit the earth after all."

MATH LOVERS

One by-product of the fact that the PC enables all of us to become authors of our own content in digital form—whether it is words, spreadsheets, data, photos, blogs, music, or video—is that more and more of what we design, what we write, what we buy, what we sell, and what we invent is built on a foundation of math. How so? When words were just shapes or letters or musical notes on paper, there was only so much you could do with them. But once words or pictures or data or music of any kind could be digitized—that is, formatted in combinations of 1s and 0s—math could be used to search all this content for patterns, and to mix, match, and manipulate it in wholly new ways. This creates so many more opportunities to apply math to more stuff. And in a flat world, where getting a jump on your competitors by just a few weeks can make an enormous financial difference, those who can come up with the right mathematical formulas, and apply them, to get that jump will be more valuable than ever.

"It is all about math now," said Infosys CEO Nandan Nilekani. "Whether it is the search engine guys, or the Goldman Sachs guys, everything is boiling down to who can make those complex computations to get that little edge, to be just two weeks ahead of everyone else."

The new ways mathematics is being used—at all levels of marketing, management, research, and operations—were set out by *BusinessWeek*'s Stephen Baker in a cover story (January 23, 2006) titled, "Why Math Will Rock Your World." Every parent, and every aspirant to the new middle class, should read this story.

"The world is moving into a new age of numbers. Partnerships between mathematicians and computer scientists are bulling into whole new domains of business and imposing the efficiencies of math. This has happened before. In past decades, the marriage of higher math and computer modeling transformed science and engineering. Quants turned finance upside down a generation ago. And data miners plucked useful nuggets from vast consumer and business databases. But just look at where the mathematicians are now. They're helping to map out advertising campaigns, they're changing the nature of research in newsrooms and in biology labs, and they're enabling marketers to forge new one-on-one relationships with customers. As this occurs, more of the economy falls into the realm of numbers. Says James R. Schatz, chief of the mathematics research group at the National Security Agency: 'There has never been a better time to be a mathematician . . .' In the past decade, a sizable chunk of humanity has moved its work, play, chat, and shopping online. We feed networks gobs of digital data that once would have languished on scraps of paper—or vanished as forgotten conversations. These slices of our lives now sit in databases, many of them in the public domain. From a business point of view, they're just begging to be analyzed. But even with the most powerful computers and abundant, cheap storage, companies can't sort out their swelling oceans of data, much less build businesses on them, without enlisting skilled mathematicians and computer scientists. The rise of mathematics is heating up the job market for luminary quants, especially at the Internet powerhouses where new math grads land with six-figure salaries and rich stock deals. Tom Leighton, an entrepreneur and applied math professor at Massachusetts Institute of Technology, says: 'All of my students have standing offers at Yahoo! and Google.' Top mathematicians are becoming a new global elite. It's a force of barely 5,000, by some guesstimates, but every bit as powerful as the armies of Harvard University MBAs who shook up corner suites a generation ago . . . In a world teeming with data, we ourselves become the math nerds' most prized specimens. Researchers at Aetna Health Care, Amazon.com, and many other companies are piecing together mathematical models of customers and employees. Some models predict what music we'll buy, others figure out which worker is best equipped for a particular job. For now, these models are crude, the digital equivalent of stick figures. But over the coming decade, each of us will give birth to far more fleshed out simulations of ourselves. We'll be modeled as workers, shoppers, voters, and patients."

While society will clearly need and demand more high-end, genius mathematicians who can design and execute the sorts of algorithms that drive search engines and Wall Street derivative strategies, we also need more people trained in basic calculus, because more and more math and quantitative skills will be needed to do more and more standard new middle jobs. I had not been in a hospital for a long time before my mother fell ill in the spring of 2006. As I sat in the hall outside her room, I was amazed at how many computers were being used by the nursing staff—to track patients or administer dosages. You did not have to be a math genius to operate them. But you could not be a math illiterate either. Even the UPS delivery person has to be able to manage the simple math on that handheld tracking device now and be able to load the truck in a pattern that is determined by an algorithm designed by UPS headquarters—so packages are easily retrieved in order of delivery.

In an essay in *Ubiquity*, an IT magazine (March 21, 2006), Espen Andersen, associate professor at the Norwegian School of Management, listed all the reasons a young person should want to study math today, but one in particular stood out to me. "Choose math," he wrote, "because you will meet it more and more in the future. Math becomes more and more important in all areas of work and scholarship. Future journalists and politicians will talk less and analyze more. Future police officers and military personnel will use more and more complicated technology. Future nurses and teachers will have to relate to numbers and technology every day. Future car mechanics and carpenters will use chip-optimization and stress analysis as much as monkey wrenches and hammers. There will be more math at work, so you will need more math at school."

Fortunately, people are catching on. Thinkport.org is a Web site that provides advice for Maryland educators and families. In November 2006 it carried the following item: "How many times do we adults say to one another, 'I'm just not good at math!'? That may be true for some of us. But it won't be a good enough answer for our children. In fact, you may be shocked at the central role of math in the new generation of jobs. Consider: In 62 percent of American jobs over the next 10 years, entry-level workers will need to be proficient in algebra, geometry, data interpretation, probability, and statistics, according to a study by the American Diploma Project . . . If you are the parent of a high schooler: Make sure your child takes and passes Algebra I, Geometry, and Algebra II. Even if your child fulfills the math requirements by junior year, insist that he or she take a math class, such as calculus, senior year."

THE GREAT LOCALIZERS

While big business is certainly important for creating middle-class jobs, the fact is that small and medium-size businesses really do the majority of hiring and firing. When those small and medium-size businesses are growing and hiring people, the economy is robust, and when they are not, it is in recession. So, if there is to be a new middle, small and medium-size businesses must play key roles. What is exciting and encouraging about the flattening of the world—and innovations like the Business Web—is the degree to which they give small business so much more power and so many more cost savings to innovate and compete globally. Joel Cawley, the IBM strategist, calls this "localizing the global." As he puts it: "There is going to be a huge amount of business for those small and medium-size firms that learn how to take all the global capabilities that are now out there and tailor them to the needs of a local community . . . It's the localization of the global and we're just at the beginning of it. It has enormous potential to be very job-creating."

Those who are successful at this will understand the emerging global infrastructure, and then adapt all the new tools it offers to local needs and demands. This is going to create a lot of new middle jobs. The localization of the global will be the freelancer who finds a way to use a satellite dish, a DSL line, a BlackBerry, a PC, or some new software to become a book editor or a film editor or an eBay entrepreneur from his or her bedroom. It will be the sports bar owner who learns to use multiple satellite feeds on multiple flat-screen TVs to bring twelve NFL games at once, plus a golf tournament in Europe, a basketball game in China, and a soccer match in Australia to his bar patrons on Sunday afternoons. It will be the coffee bar that is able to keep customers in their seats much longer by offering free wireless connectivity. It will be the small-time entrepreneur who understands that he can now hire Amazon.com to provide a global logistics infrastructure to manage his sale of customized bookplates, and who understands he can go online and find a company in China that will make those bookplates, and who, therefore, overnight becomes an importer of bookplates for bookstores, all sold online. It will be the person who opens a UPS store and becomes overnight a global supply chain manager for other small businesses. It will be the local auto repair shop that suddenly discovers that it can get cheaper BMW hubcaps and Mercedes windshield wipers from a supplier in Romania than one in Rochester.

Finally, it will be people in all sorts of businesses and industries who understand the power of "modeling"—and I am not talking about Cindy Crawford. Using computer simulation and graphics, you can now bring all sorts of data together to create models that will show you how all kinds of complex things work together—before you actually go through the expensive process of building them. As a realtor who learns how to model, you can show prospective buyers the floor plan of a house or an apartment and let them move the walls around wherever they like. As an engineer who learns how to model, you can do the same with bridges and roads. So those landscape architects, financial planners, home designers, and real estate brokers who get it, who become skilled at working with clients to build, customize, and interpret models, will also find themselves with a pathway to the new middle.

These are broad categories, and new ones will surely be constantly emerging. And there are certainly no hard-and-fast boundaries between these different strategies, either. Often people will mix and match them. So let me leave you here with one last example—my childhood friend, Bill Greer, whom I think of now as a great adapter, localizer, and personalizer. He has drawn on all three strategies to secure a place in the new middle. Greer is fifty years old and has made his living as a freelance artist and graphic designer for twenty-eight years. From the late 1970s until right around 2000, the way Bill did his job and served his clients was pretty much the same.

"Clients, like The New York Times, would want a finished piece of artwork," Bill explained to me. So if he was doing an illustration for a newspaper or a magazine, or proposing a new logo for a product, he would actually create a piece of art—sketch it, color it, mount it on an illustration board, cover it with tissue, put it in a package that was opened with two flaps, and have it delivered by messenger or FedEx. He called it "flap art." In the industry it was known as "camera-ready art," because it needed to be shot, printed on four different layers of color film, or "separations," and prepared for publication. "It was a finished product, and it had a certain preciousness to it," said Bill. "It was a real piece of art, and sometimes people would hang them on their walls. In fact, *The New York Times* would have shows of works that were created by illustrators for its publications."

But in the last few years "that started to change," Bill told me, as publications and ad agencies moved to digital preparation, relying on the new software—namely, Quark, Photoshop, and Illustrator, which graphic artists refer to as "the trinity"—which made digital computer design so much easier. Everyone who went through art school got trained on these programs. Indeed, Bill explained, graphic design got so much easier that it became a commodity. It got turned into vanilla ice cream. "In terms of design," he said, "the technology gave everyone the same tools, so everyone could do straight lines and everyone could do work that was halfway decent. You used to need an eye to see if something was in balance and had the right typeface, but all of a sudden anyone could hammer out something that was acceptable."

So Greer pushed himself up the knowledge ladder. As publications demanded that all final products be presented as digital files that could be uploaded, and there was no longer any more demand for that precious flap art, he transformed himself into an ideas consultant. "Ideation" was what his clients, including McDonald's and Unilever, wanted. He stopped using pens and ink and would just do pencil sketches, scan them into his computer, color them by using the computer's mouse, and then e-mail them to the client, which would have some less skilled artists finish them.

"It was unconscious," said Greer. "I had to look for work that not everyone else could do, and that young artists couldn't do with technology for a fraction of what I was being paid. So I started getting offers where people would say to me, 'Can you do this and just give us the big idea?' They would give me a concept, and they would just want sketches, ideas, and not a finished piece of art. I still use the basic skill of drawing, but just to convey an idea—quick sketches, not finished artwork. And for these ideas they will still pay pretty good money. It has actually taken me to a different level. It is more like being a consultant rather than a JAFA (Just Another Fucking Artist). There are a lot of JAFAs out there. So now I am an idea man, and I have played off that. My clients just buy concepts." The JAFAs then do the art in-house or it gets outsourced. "They can take my raw sketches and finish them and illustrate them using computer programs, and it is not like I would do it, but it is good enough," Greer said.

But then another thing happened. While the evolving technology turned the lower end of Greer's business into a commodity, it opened up a whole new market at the upper end: Greer's magazine clients. One day, one of his regular clients approached him and asked if he could do morphs. Morphs are cartoon strips in which one character evolves into another. So Martha Stewart is in the opening frame and morphs into Courtney Love by the closing frame. Drew Barrymore morphs into Drew Carey. Mariah Carey morphs into Jim Carrey. Cher morphs into Britney Spears. When he was first approached to do these, Greer had no idea where to begin. So he went onto Amazon.com and located some specialized software that would empower him to create morphs, bought it, tried it out for a few days, and produced his first morph drawings. Since then he has developed a specialty in the process, and the market for them has expanded to include *Maxim* magazine, *More,* and *Nickelodeon*—one a men's magazine, one a middle-aged women's magazine, and one a kids' magazine.

In other words, someone invented a whole new kind of sauce to go on the vanilla, and Greer jumped on it. This is exactly what happens in the global economy as a whole. "I was experienced enough to pick these [morphs] up pretty quickly," said Greer. "Now I do them on my Mac laptop, anywhere I am, from Santa Barbara to Minneapolis to my apartment in New York. Sometimes clients give me a subject, and sometimes I just come up with them. Morphing used to be one of those really high-end things you saw on TV, and then they came out with this consumer [software] program and people could do it themselves, and I shaped them so magazines could use them. I just upload them as a series of JPEG files . . . Morphs have been a good business for different magazines. I even get fan mail from kids!"

Greer had never done morphs until the technology evolved and created a new, specialized niche, just when a changing market for his work made him eager to learn new skills. "I wish I could say it was all intentional," he confessed. "I was just available for work and just lucky they gave me a chance to do these things. I know so many artists who got washed out. One guy who was an illustrator has become a package designer, some have gotten out of the field altogether; one of the best designers I know became a landscape architect. She is still a designer but changed her medium altogether. Visual people can adapt, but I am still nervous about the future."

I told Greer his story fit well into some of the terms I was using in this book. He began as a chocolate sauce (a classic illustrator), was turned into a vanilla commodity (a classic illustrator in the computer age), upgraded his skills to become a special chocolate sauce again (a design consultant), then learned how to become a cherry on top (a morphs artist) by using the new tools of the flat world to fill a new market niche.

Greer contemplated my compliment for a moment and then said, "And here all I was trying to do was survive—and I still am." As he got up to leave, though, he told me that he was going out to meet a friend "to juggle together." They have been juggling partners for years, just a little side business they sometimes do on a street corner or for private parties. Greer has very good hand-eye coordination. "But even juggling is being commoditized," he complained. "It used to be if you could juggle five balls, you were really special. Now juggling five balls is like just anteing up. My partner and I used to perform together, and he was the seven-ball champ when I met him. Now fourteen-year-old kids can juggle seven balls, no problem. Now they have these books, like *Juggling for Dummies*, and kits that will teach you how to juggle. So they've just upped the standard."

SEVEN

The Right Stuff

Tubas and Test Tubes

A friend once asked Isidor I. Rabi, a Nobel Prize winner in physics, how he became a scientist. Rabi replied that every day after school his mother would talk to him about his school day. She wasn't so much interested in what he had learned that day, but she always inquired, "Did you ask a good question today?" "Asking good questions," Rabi said, "made me become a scientist."

—Source unknown

In the past two years I have had a chance to travel around America and speak about globalization and the flat world to many different audiences, from retirees in Palm Springs to high school principals in Bethesda to parents in suburban book clubs. What struck me most was the undertow of concern I found in the country around the issues of education and competition. If I had to summarize that anxiety, I would put it like this: Our parents were sure that they were going to live better than their parents and that we, their children, were going to live better than them. We, alas, are growing quite concerned that we are not going to retire as well-off as our parents did, and our kids probably are not going to be as well-off as we were. Everyone seemed to me to be looking for the magic formula that would spare their kids from a future of downward mobility. Twice I had parents ask me a question that went roughly like this: "My daughter is studying Chinese. She's going to be okay, right?"

"Well," I would answer, "not exactly."

Why not exactly? Because there is no magic formula. At a moment like this one, I feel it would be useful to step back, take a deep breath, and ask: If the strategies detailed in the previous chapter really are going to be the best way for individuals to obtain and retain jobs in the new middle, then, generally speaking, what is the right kind of education to prepare our young people for those jobs? As Princeton economist Alan Blinder perceptively notes, "It is clear that the U.S. and other rich nations will have to transform their educational systems so as to produce workers for the jobs that will actually exist in their societies . . . Simply providing *more* education is probably a good thing on balance, especially if a more educated labor force is a more flexible labor force that can cope more readily with non-routine tasks and occupational change. But it is far from a panacea . . . In the future, *how* we educate our children may prove to be more important than *how much* we educate them."

So what is the right stuff? I am not an educator, but I am a reporter, and in this chapter I want to share what I have learned from asking employers and educators precisely that question. It would be utterly presumptuous of me to suggest that I have the magic formula or the complete list. But what follows are five skill sets or attitudes toward learning that my own reporting suggests would be helpful in preparing young people for the new middle jobs in a flat world.

WHICH CLASS DO I TAKE
TO LEARN HOW TO LEARN?

The first, and most important, ability you can develop in a flat world is the ability to "learn how to learn"—to constantly absorb, and teach yourself, new ways of doing old things or new ways of doing new things. That is an ability every worker should cultivate in an age when parts or all of many jobs are constantly going to be exposed to digitization, automation, and outsourcing, and where new jobs, and whole new industries, will be churned up faster and faster. In such a world, it is not only what you know but how you learn that will set you apart. Because what you know today will be out-of-date sooner than you think.

In a talk I gave in St. Paul, Minnesota, I made this point, and during the question-and-answer period afterward a young man in the balcony raised his hand, identified himself as a ninth grader, and asked: "Mr. Friedman, if it is that important to learn how to learn, how do you learn how to learn? What course should I take?"

From the mouths of babes . . .

It's a logical question. At the time I had not thought it through in detail. So I ad-libbed an answer, which I think is in the right direction: "Go around to your friends and ask them just one question: 'Who are your favorite teachers?' Then make a list of those teachers and go out and take their courses—no matter what they are teaching, no matter what the subject." It doesn't matter whether they are teaching Greek mythology, calculus, art history, or American literature—take their courses. Because when I think back on my favorite teachers, I don't remember the specifics of what they taught me, but I sure remember being excited about learning it. What has stayed with me are not the facts they imparted but the excitement about learning they inspired. To learn how to learn, you have to love learning—or you have to at least enjoy it—because so much learning is about being motivated to teach yourself. And while it seems that some people are just born with that motivation, many others can develop it or have it implanted with the right teacher (or parent).

NAVIGATION

Second, we need to think more about how we teach "navigation" skills. As the world flattens out, more and more knowledge, information, news, software, commerce, and communities will reside on the World Wide Web. Our children will interact with each other, with the wider world, and with all that resides on that Web without many filters. Therefore, teaching them how to navigate that virtual world, and how to sift through it and separate the noise, the filth, and the lies from the facts, the wisdom, and the real sources of knowledge becomes more important than ever. When the Web first emerged, I used to joke that if I had one fervent wish it would be that every modem sold would come with a warning label from the surgeon general that would say: "Judgment Not Included."

In May 2002, I sat with twenty thoughtful young Indonesians in the garden of the Pondok Pesantren Darunnajah, one of Jakarta's finest Islamic boarding schools, to ask them for their views of America. I wanted to understand how the world's largest Muslim nation was reacting to September 11 and the Middle East crisis. I could tell you in my own words, but let me instead run the tape of my chat with the most articulate student—an eighteen-year-old girl.

"Most Muslims are afraid of America because they think America is against Islam," she began. "You can see that America is backing the Israelians, and the enmity between Islam and Israel, the Jews [and] Judaism, is obvious. It is not that Americans are afraid of Muslims, but that Muslims are afraid of Americans. As for the [September 11] tragedy, we can't prove that Muslims did it. Because up to now they have not found evidence to prove that [bin Laden] is the one who did it. Also I read in some newspaper that the real people who did that tragedy are Americans . . . I don't know [what] percent of the Congress are Jewish, [but] America is backing Israel, and I think therein lies the feeling of enmity toward America."

What do you think of President George W. Bush? I asked her. "At the beginning, when George Bush became president, some people thought he is only going to be like his father and he's not going to make anything new—and also people did not want Al Gore to win because he was Jewish. So people said, 'Okay, George Bush is better . . .' He promised a lot of really good things but [has] not realized them up to now."

She was absolutely certain Al Gore was Jewish.

Where do you get your news? I asked her. "I get most information from the TV, from the Internet, too . . . I really like to read the [online] Arabic magazines because they give a different point of view. If I read Indonesian magazines, they don't have a lot of information about Muslims and Islam."

I always think of that young woman as someone who lacked, among other things, navigation skills—the ability to sort out truth from fiction in

this open sewer of information, facts, insights, lies, and half-truths called
the World Wide Web. How many times have you heard someone say, "But
I read it on the Internet . . ." as if that should settle the matter? Because the
Internet comes with a patina of technology, things that are read there, particularly by those without navigation skills, seem more believable. There is
a great line in the Robin Williams movie *Man of the Year*, which is about
politics, television, and a comedian—Williams—who runs for president.
At one point, one of candidate Williams's aides remarks to him that the
problem with television is that it makes everything and everyone "seem
credible"—and when everyone is credible, no one is credible. A comedian
debating an expert: both seem equal. The same could be said of the
Internet. It makes everything seem equally credible to the uninitiated. So
BBCNews.com says Al Gore is Christian on its Web site and Jihad.com
says Al Gore is Jewish on its Web site. On a flat screen, they both seem
equal.

In the Indian newspaper *Daily News and Analysis* (November 5,
2005), Sachin Kalbag, the paper's Washington correspondent, wrote the
following, which caught my eye: "The Web is undeniably the ultimate
storehouse of information, a sort of *Encyclopaedia Britannica's Encyclopaedia Britannica*. So, you can be as sure to find the real reason for pigeons
bobbing their heads as you can be 100 per cent pukka about finding what
'colitas' actually means in the hit Eagles' song 'Hotel California.' A whole
new generation is now waking up with the Web as its constant companion
just as the previous one went to sleep with a security blanket. If you need
stuff for your Ph.D. research, go to the Web . . . If you need to plagiarize
something for your academic thesis or an office report, the Web is there for
you. It is, as if, we are giving rise to an army of instant masterminds just like
the 50-odd news channels on television have given rise to rent-a-minute experts on any topic. The result is that the same generation is in danger of
growing up with 170 terabytes of knowledge and information, but not
more than a few bits of wisdom. The challenge for the next generation of
parents, educationists and thinkers will, therefore, not be the dissemination
of information, but to change the way people differentiate between information and wisdom. Indeed the lines that divide the two have been
blurred so much that information is often confused as wisdom."

To be sure, navigation skills, judgment, and the ability to find wisdom and knowledge in the fire hose flow of information were always important. But they are more important than ever as the world flattens out and more people are getting their information from news sites that are not edited with the rigor of *The New York Times* or the BBC, as more people are asked to learn on their own in nonclassroom settings, particularly online, as more people are generating their own content—blogs and podcasts—without conventional standards, and as more people interact with more other people whom they do not know and may never meet.

We cannot stick our heads in the sand on this. Joel Cawley of IBM told me that at his daughter's high school they forbid students to cite Wikipedia entries in footnotes of their papers. Cawley rightly disagreed with this policy. "They meant well—they thought they were teaching kids to be careful," said Cawley. "But what they were actually doing is missing an opportunity to teach them how to navigate"—how to go about sorting and cross-checking facts wherever they might find them. We can't tell our kids to ignore the resources on the Web. But we can and must teach them better how to navigate them.

CQ + PQ > IQ

My third broad theme would be passion and curiosity. It was and always will be a great advantage to have passion and curiosity for anything. But again, when the world is flat, curiosity and passion for a job, for success, for a subject area or even a hobby are so much more important than they once were. Because in the flat world you have so many more tools to take you and your curiosity so much farther and so much deeper.

Doc Searls, senior editor of the *Linux Journal* and one of the most respected technology writers in America, spoke to this point in a review of the first edition of this book (April 28, 2005). He said: "In the flat new world, educational opportunities are limitless, even without help from school, government, churches or business. Much of what you need to

know about pretty much everything is out there on the Web somewhere—
especially if you're a technologist. Yes, the Web isn't everywhere. But it's
in all the flat places, and the flatness is spreading, fast . . . Of course, the
average and the dumb are still plentiful, no doubt about it. But try this
concept on for size: Most of them were made that way. They were shaped
in large measure by school systems that have had, from the dawn of the industrial age, a main purpose: to produce employees for boxed positions in
corporate org charts that take the shape of pyramids, wide at the bottom
and narrow at the top . . . There were few alternatives in the industrial
age, aside from farming and other relatively solitary occupations. But
there are plenty of alternatives now, as many as there are individuals with
access to broadband."

For all these reasons, I have concluded that in a flat world, IQ—
intelligence quotient—still matters, but CQ and PQ—curiosity quotient
and passion quotient—matter even more. I live by the equation $CQ + PQ$
$> IQ$. Give me a kid with a passion to learn and a curiosity to discover and
I will take him or her over a less passionate kid with a high IQ every day of
the week. Curious, passionate kids are self-educators and self-motivators.
They will always be able to learn how to learn, especially on the flat-world
platform, where you can both download and upload. "Work matters," said
Searls, "but curiosity matters more. Nobody works harder at learning than
a curious kid."

For my money, they could engrave that onto the doorway of every
school in America: *Nobody works harder at learning than a curious kid.*

Some kids are just born that way, but for the many who are not, the
best way to make kids love learning is either to instill in them a sense of
curiosity, by great teaching, or to stimulate their own innate curiosity by
making available to them all the technologies of the flat-world platform so
they can educate themselves in an enormously rich way. Consider this
story from *The New York Times*'s Education Life supplement (April 24,
2005). It was about Britney Schmidt, a student at the University of
Arizona, who was utterly bored with her courses, mostly because her professors seemed interested only in giving lectures and leaving.

"I was getting A's in all my classes, but I wasn't being challenged, and
I wasn't thinking about new things," she told a *Times* reporter. One se-

mester, though, Ms. Schmidt had to take a natural-science course, and it turned out to have a great professor and teaching assistants, who stoked her curiosity and lit a fire in her. "I was lucky," she said. "I took a class from somebody who really cared." The result: A scientist was born. Many more science courses later, Ms. Schmidt was accepted to graduate school at UCLA in planetary physics and the University of Chicago in cosmochemistry.

You can't light the fire of passion in someone else if it doesn't burn in you to begin with. Hilarie Rooney, the principal of Laytonsville Elementary School in Maryland's Montgomery County, came up to me after a lecture one day and told me that what she looked for in hiring teachers was one simple thing: "whether they loved kids." Because if you don't connect with the kids, you will never be able to convey the material, she said. If you can't feel the music, you'll never be able to play the music.

"But if you love kids," she said, "and you convey that, even if you don't really know that much about the subject you're teaching, they will be inspired by you and they will go out and learn it themselves. I can teach anyone a strategy, but I can't teach a person to love kids. And you can feel it in a classroom as soon as you walk in [whether that teacher loves kids]. Kids at the elementary level all love their teachers, but boy, you can see the teachers who love those kids back. They motivate those kids to keep trying to do their best for that teacher. The [kids] are really doing it for themselves, but if they see that teacher really cares, is invested in their learning, that child will never be turned off. That is what real learning is."

Is it possible to generate your own high PQ—a high passion quotient for a subject—without a teacher or parent stimulating you? Of course. Just think back to when you were a kid and you got your first fire truck or doll or doctor's kit or astronaut's helmet, and you told everyone you wanted to be a fireman or a fashion model or a doctor or an astronaut when you grew up. That innocent passion for a certain job, without knowing the salary or the working hours or the preparation required, is what you need to get back in touch with. It's that childlike feeling of "I want to do that because I want to do that—and I don't have to explain why" that we all need to rediscover. To put it simply: You need to rediscover your inner fire truck. We all have one, and when you find it, you'll know it.

STRESSING LIBERAL ARTS

Fourth, since one of the new middle jobs is great synthesizers, encouraging young people early to think horizontally and to connect disparate dots has to be a priority. Because this is where and how so much innovation happens. But first you need dots to connect. And to me that means a liberal arts education. Liberal arts is a very horizontal form of education (which is to say, a flat form of education). It is all about making connections among history, art, politics, and science. Yes, we need to be more rigorous in training our young people in math and science, which are the building blocks of so much knowledge. But we also need to be vigilant in upholding the teaching of art and music and literature, because they too are essential for innovation. I like how Marc Tucker, who heads the National Center on Education and the Economy, puts it: "One thing we know about creativity is that it typically occurs when people who have mastered two or more quite different fields use the framework in one to think afresh about the other. Intuitively, you know this is true. Leonardo da Vinci was a great artist, scientist, and inventor, and each specialty nourished the other. He was a great lateral thinker. But if you spend your whole life in one silo, you will never have either the knowledge or mental agility to do the synthesis, connect the dots, which is usually where the next great breakthrough is found."

One of the best examples of that I can think of is the story that Steve Jobs, the cofounder of Apple Computer, told about himself in a commencement speech at Stanford University (June 12, 2005):

I am honored to be with you today at your commencement from one of the finest universities in the world. I never graduated from college. Truth be told, this is the closest I've ever gotten to a college graduation. Today I want to tell you three stories from my life . . .

The first story is about connecting the dots.

I dropped out of Reed College after the first 6 months, but then stayed around as a drop-in for another 18 months or so before I really quit. So why did I drop out?

It started before I was born. My biological mother was a young, unwed college graduate student, and she decided to put me up for adoption. She felt very strongly that I should be adopted by college graduates, so everything was all set for me to be adopted at birth by a lawyer and his wife. Except that when I popped out they decided at the last minute that they really wanted a girl. So my parents, who were on a waiting list, got a call in the middle of the night asking: "We have an unexpected baby boy; do you want him?" They said: "Of course." My biological mother later found out that my mother had never graduated from college and that my father had never graduated from high school. She refused to sign the final adoption papers. She only relented a few months later when my parents promised that I would someday go to college.

And 17 years later I did go to college. But I naively chose a college that was almost as expensive as Stanford, and all of my working-class parents' savings were being spent on my college tuition. After six months, I couldn't see the value in it. I had no idea what I wanted to do with my life and no idea how college was going to help me figure it out. And here I was spending all of the money my parents had saved their entire life. So I decided to drop out and trust that it would all work out OK. It was pretty scary at the time, but looking back it was one of the best decisions I ever made. The minute I dropped out I could stop taking the required classes that didn't interest me, and begin dropping in on the ones that looked interesting.

It wasn't all romantic. I didn't have a dorm room, so I slept on the floor in friends' rooms, I returned coke bottles for the 5¢ deposits to buy food with, and I would walk the 7 miles across town every Sunday night to get one good meal a week at the Hare Krishna temple. I loved it. And much of what I stumbled into by following my curiosity and intuition turned out to be priceless later on. Let me give you one example:

Reed College at that time offered perhaps the best calligraphy instruction in the country. Throughout the campus every poster, every label on every drawer, was beautifully hand calligraphed. Because I had dropped out and didn't have to take the normal classes, I decided to take a calligraphy class to learn how to do this. I learned about serif and sans serif typefaces, about varying the amount of space between different letter combinations, about what makes great typography great. It was beautiful, historical, artistically subtle in a way that science can't capture, and I found it fascinating.

None of this had even a hope of any practical application in my life. But ten years later, when we were designing the first Macintosh computer, it all came back to me. And we designed it all into the Mac. It was the first computer with beautiful typography. If I had never dropped in on that single course in college, the Mac would have never had multiple typefaces or proportionally spaced fonts. And since Windows just copied the Mac, it's likely that no personal computer would have them . . . Of course it was impossible to connect the dots looking forward when I was in college. But it was very, very clear looking backwards ten years later.

Again, you can't connect the dots looking forward; you can only connect them looking backwards. So you have to trust that the dots will somehow connect in your future. You have to trust in something—your gut, destiny, life, karma, whatever. This approach has never let me down, and it has made all the difference in my life.

Steve Jobs's story underscores that the inspiration for technological breakthroughs is not always rooted in technological knowledge alone. Math and science are necessary—critically necessary—but they are not sufficient. I think one reason America has always been a leader in innovation of new products and services—from IBMs to iPods—is that our society has always valued both technology and liberal arts. In our justifiable desire to leave no child behind, we need to make sure that we don't leave art and music and theater and literature classes behind as well. It would undermine a critical source of our economic strength and our ability to generate good new middle jobs and the workers to fill them.

As Marc Tucker notes:

Those countries that produce the most important new products
and services can capture a premium in world markets that will enable them to pay high wages to their citizens . . . But that kind of
leadership does not depend on technology alone. It depends on a
deep vein of creativity that is constantly renewing itself, and on a
myriad of people who can imagine how people can use things
that have never been available before, create ingenious marketing
and sales campaigns, write books, build furniture, make movies,
imagine new kinds of software that will capture people's imagination and become indispensable to millions.

This is a world in which a very high level of preparation in
reading, writing, speaking, mathematics, science, literature, history and the arts will be an indispensable foundation for everything that comes after for most members of the workforce. It is a
world in which comfort with ideas and abstractions is the passport
to a good job, in which creativity and innovation are the key to a
good life, in which high levels of education—a very different kind
of education than most of us have had—are going to be the only
security there is.

A world in which routine work is largely done by machines is a
world in which mathematical reasoning will be no less important
than math facts, in which line workers who cannot contribute to
the design of the products they are fabricating may be as obsolete
as the last model of that product, . . . in which software engineers
who are also musicians and artists will have an edge over those who
are not, as the entertainment industry evolves, [a world] in which
it will pay architects to know something about nano-technology
and small businessmen who build custom yachts and fishing boats
will be able to survive only if they quickly learn a lot about the scientific foundations of carbon fiber composites.

As I have said, India and China have provided large numbers of their
young people with solid foundations in math and science, and it has been

extremely important in their rise out of poverty. But it is no accident that when you talk to Indian and Chinese businesspeople and even educators, some now openly express their concerns that if math and science are not leavened by art, literature, music, and the humanities, their countries will be at a competitive disadvantage as they try to get to the next level of global competition.

Jerry Rao, the cofounder of MphasiS, the big Indian outsourcing firm, put it to me this way: "We have no one going into the liberal arts and everyone going into engineering and MBAs. We're becoming a nation of aspiring programmers and salespeople."

Fifty years ago, the Sanskrit scholar was respected in India, Mr. Rao noted, but today it is all about becoming an engineer, a programmer, an MBA, or a doctor. "More people will get Ph.D.'s [in the study of] Sanskrit in America this year than in India," Mr. Rao asserted, "and Sanskrit is the root of our culture!

"If we don't have enough people with the humanities, we will lose the [next generation of] V. S. Naipauls and Amartya Sens," he added, referring to the Indian-Trinidadian author and the Indian economist, both Nobel laureates. "That is sad and dangerous."

RIGHT BRAIN

Finally, if creativity depends on connecting disparate dots, then we need to be educating our young people not only in more dots, à la the liberal arts, but also in the ability to think horizontally—to mesh together different perspectives and disciplines to produce a third thing. That skill is something that happens on the right side of our brains—and educators need to think about how we nurture that. Daniel Pink, author of *A Whole New Mind: Moving from the Information Age to the Conceptual Age*, explains:

Scientists have long known that a neurological Mason-Dixon line cleaves our brains into two regions—the left and right hemispheres. But in the last 10 years, thanks in part to advances in functional magnetic resonance imaging, researchers have begun to identify more precisely how the two sides divide responsibilities. The left hemisphere handles sequence, literalness, and analysis. The right hemisphere, meanwhile, takes care of context, emotional expression, and synthesis. Of course, the human brain, with its 100 billion cells forging 1 quadrillion connections, is breathtakingly complex. The two hemispheres work in concert, and we enlist both sides for nearly everything we do. But the structure of our brains can help explain the contours of our times.

Until recently, the abilities that led to success in school, work, and business were characteristic of the left hemisphere. They were the sorts of linear, logical, analytical talents measured by SATs and deployed by CPAs. Today, those capabilities are still necessary. But they're no longer sufficient. In a world upended by outsourcing, deluged with data, and choked with choices, the abilities that matter most are now closer in spirit to the specialties of the right hemisphere—artistry, empathy, seeing the big picture, and pursuing the transcendent.

If we want more of our young people to be untouchables—that is, people with jobs that "a computer or robot cannot do faster or some talented foreigner cannot do cheaper and just as well," we need to focus education on constantly developing our students' right-brain skills—"such as forging relationships rather than executing transactions, tackling novel challenges instead of solving routine problems, and synthesizing the big picture rather than analyzing a single component," argues Pink.

We're not all going to lose our jobs tomorrow . . . But as the cost of communicating with the other side of the globe falls essentially to zero, as India becomes (by 2010) the country with the most English speakers in the world, and as developing nations continue to mint millions of extremely capable knowledge workers, the professional lives of people in the West will change dramatically. If number crunching, chart reading, and code writing can be done for a lot less overseas and delivered to clients instantly via fiber-optic cable, that's where the work will go.

But these gusts of comparative advantage are blowing away only certain kinds of white-collar jobs—those that can be reduced to a set of rules, routines, and instructions. That's why narrow left-brain work such as basic computer coding, accounting, legal re-search, and financial analysis is migrating across the oceans. But that's also why plenty of opportunities remain for people and com-panies doing less routine work—programmers who can design en-tire systems, accountants who serve as life planners, and bankers expert less in the intricacies of Excel than in the art of the deal.

"Now that foreigners can do left-brain work cheaper," Pink argues, "we in the U.S. must do right-brain work better." You cannot stress that enough: *Now that foreigners can do left-brain work cheaper, we in the U.S. must do right-brain work better.*
He elaborates:

Last century, machines proved they could replace human muscle. This century, technologies are proving they can outperform hu-man left brains—they can execute sequential, reductive, compu-tational work better, faster, and more accurately than even those with the highest IQs. (Just ask chess grandmaster Garry Kasparov [who lost a match to a chess-playing computer].) . . .

To flourish in this age, we'll need to supplement our well-developed high-tech abilities with aptitudes that are "high con-cept" and "high touch." High concept involves the ability to create artistic and emotional beauty, to detect patterns and opportunities, to craft a satisfying narrative, and to come up with inventions the world didn't know it was missing. High touch involves the capacity to empathize, to understand the subtleties of human interaction, to find joy in one's self and to elicit it in others, and to stretch be-yond the quotidian in pursuit of purpose and meaning.

Developing these high concept, high touch abilities won't be easy for everyone. For some, the prospect seems unattainable. Fear not (or at least fear less). The sorts of abilities that now matter most are fundamentally human attributes. After all, back on the savannah, our caveperson ancestors weren't plugging numbers into spreadsheets or debugging code. But they were telling stories, demonstrating empathy, and designing innovations. These abilities have always been part of what it means to be human. It's just that after a few generations in the Information Age, many of our high concept, high touch muscles have atrophied. The challenge is to work them back into shape.

But how exactly do you go about nurturing your right-brain skills? I have to leave the details to education experts. But I would guess that one way you nurture your right brain is by doing something you love to do—or at least like to do—because you will bring something intangible to it, something out of your right brain, which cannot be easily repeated, automated, or outsourced. As Pink put it: "The sorts of abilities that matter most now it turns out are also the sorts of things that people do out of intrinsic motivation. Relatively few people become accountants out of a sense of intrinsic motivation. But intrinsic motivation is what propels people to become creators and empathizers, to become designers and storytellers and counselors and consultants. This weekend there will be accountants painting watercolors in their garages. There will be lawyers writing screenplays. But I guarantee you that you won't find any sculptors who on weekends will be doing other people's taxes for fun. In other words, there is a growing congruence between the sorts of things that people do because they love doing them and the sorts of things that confer economic advantage."

And so, concludes Pink, when you hear your parents or your college graduation speaker telling you to "do what you love," they are not giving you some syrupy pabulum. They are giving you a survival strategy.

Tubas and Test Tubes

So let's work backward now just one more step. If the jobs of the new middle require you to be a good collaborator, leverager, adapter, explainer, synthesizer, model builder, localizer, or personalizer, and these approaches require you, among other things, to be able to learn how to learn, to bring curiosity and passion to your work, to play well with others, and to nurture your right-brain skills, what does that mean specifically for education?

Again, I am not an educator, so I come to this question with great humility. I am a reporter, though, and I can report that there are some real educators out there who have tried to address this question head-on. I am impressed by the amount of experimentation I have seen on college campuses as they try to design the "right education" for the new middle. I am going to focus on one school—Georgia Institute of Technology, based in Atlanta—to illustrate one thoughtful approach.

G. Wayne Clough, Georgia Tech's president, had to rethink education in a flattening world out of sheer necessity. Clough took over as president in 1994. "When I came to Tech as an awestruck freshman back in the sixties," Clough told me, "they had this drill for the incoming students. They would tell us: 'Look to your left. Look to your right. Only one of you will graduate.'"

Georgia Tech was not as selective in admissions back then as it is today, and it relied instead on a sort of Darwinian weeding-out process, focused entirely on grades. As Clough tells it, it was a very cold social and academic environment—not a lot of fun. Even by the early 1990s, Georgia Tech was graduating only 65 percent of its incoming students. Students were not finishing because they found both the curriculum and the atmosphere rather gray—and the school a place that did not celebrate student success.

Clough's view as he assumed the presidency was that our country desperately needed more good scientists, engineers, and entrepreneurs, so his school couldn't afford to be losing one-third of its prospective grads by graduation day. Clough realized that only by offering the right education, not just more education, "would we get more students applying and more students graduating."

Clough began rethinking Georgia Tech's approach by reflecting on his own experiences as a working engineer. Some of the best engineers he had collaborated with over the years had not been the best engineering students. "They knew how to think creatively," he said. "They might not be the ones who could solve the calculus equation better than anyone else, but they were the ones who could define the problem that the calculus had to solve better than anyone else . . . They were often people with character and that something intangible."

The more time he spent on campus, the more Clough also noticed that an "awful lot of the talented students were interested in creative outlets other than what they were experiencing in the classroom"—filmmaking, or music making, or some other offbeat hobby. "These students were interesting people when you talked to them. I began to think, 'Boy, wouldn't it be nice to have more of these sorts of interesting people around campus. It makes the place more enjoyable and it helps make the student who is more one-dimensional more multidimensional [by having him or her] bump shoulders with these other kinds of kids."

So beginning in the late 1990s, Clough gradually altered the admissions policies at Georgia Tech, having his admissions office focus specifically on recruiting and admitting good engineering students who also played musical instruments, sang in a chorus, or played on a team.

"The idea was that people who have other interests tend to be able to communicate, tend to be more social, tend to ask for help more readily when they need help, tend to help others more who need help, tend to think horizontally, . . . tend to be able to tie things together from different disciplines and fields."

The result, said Clough: Today more than 50 percent of Georgia Tech's entering freshmen have played musical instruments or participated in some kind of musical group—so many that Clough's biggest challenge now is building more recital rooms and concert areas on campus. "I created a monster," he joked. He also created more graduates. Graduation rates rose from 65 percent when he arrived to 76 percent by 2005. And they are different kinds of graduates.

"The student response has been great," said Clough. "We have seen a large increase in students taking music courses. We had little in the way of chamber ensembles, and now [we have] over a dozen. We never had a chamber orchestra group on this campus. Now we have five. We have computer music synthesizing groups, jazz groups, and virtual and robotic drummers all over the place." Virtual and robotic drummers—only at tech school!

At the same time, Clough told me, Georgia Tech's large music ensembles, like the marching band and the symphony orchestra, have increased significantly in numbers of participants and sophistication, and smaller groups like its glee clubs and a capella groups also have grown dramatically. We're talking Georgia Tech, folks, not Juilliard. "So many students are seeking these kinds of opportunities," Clough added, that "we had an old high school on campus that we renovated into our music building and an old church with a big main hall that worked for some of our singing groups. We also created more casual places for students to exercise their talents, like a stage in the new student center."

Clough's effort to make Georgia Tech sing was helped in 1996, when the school served as the Olympic village, housing athletes for the Atlanta Olympics. Georgia Tech's band director was selected as director of the Atlanta Olympics Band. When the Games were over, Georgia Tech was offered the chance to buy many of the instruments the musicians had used for half price. "So we doubled the size of our band overnight," said Clough. "That was one of the triggers that got us started. It was great stuff. Because of that we have twenty-four tubas in our marching band. Very few schools have twenty-four tubas. You check it out next time you watch a bowl game."

And very few presidents of premier technology universities boast about their tubas as much as their test tubes. But Clough has reason to boast, because my guess is that by making Georgia Tech sing—and by making other user-friendly additions to the undergraduate teaching system, and by making education overseas easily available for Georgia Tech students—he is producing not just more engineers but more of the right kind of engineers.

"People who play instruments or are part of a band have more social skills—they are not just burrowed down in their work," said Clough. And that kind of person, he added, has a better chance of synthesizing and orchestrating insights from many different fields. For instance, said Clough, there is going to be a big demand for engineering around photonics—turning sunlight into electricity. That requires students who are trained in basic engineering, chemical engineering, and electrical engineering. Clough quoted the head of a big engineering firm, who told him recently, "Don't send me engineers who can be duplicated by a computer. I am sending that work to India. Send me engineers who are adaptable—who can think across disciplines."

As above, so below. Georgia Tech's College of Computing has picked up on these broad themes and has translated them into specific courses. After the dot-com bubble burst, computer science enrollment at Georgia Tech started to drop precipitously. "Everyone was reading the articles about all the jobs going to India and China," said Rich DeMillo, the former HP chief technology officer, who is now dean of the College of Computing. "The number one question from parents was, 'What will my kid do if all the programming jobs go offshore?'" So DeMillo and Merrick Furst, the associate dean, who was brought in from the International Computer Science Institute at Berkeley, went out into the business world and asked employers two simple questions: Who were they looking to hire and how were computer geeks being used to add value at their companies? They visited CNN's headquarters in Atlanta, for instance, and were exposed to the massive amounts of digital and analog content the network had piled up. It became obvious that managing all of this content via computing, and finding ways to deploy it, from televisions to cell phones to video iPods to Web sites, was going to be a huge growth industry for the right computer science grads—ones who could help tell stories with technology.

After thinking all this through, in 2004 DeMillo and Furst redesigned the computer science major at Georgia Tech around nine "threads," as they refer to them. Each thread is a combination of computing with another field, producing a synthesis of knowledge—where the real value is going to be created.

"Threads represent a departure from a vertically oriented curriculum whose goal is the creation of students with a fixed set of skills and knowledge," explained Furst in his course description. "A thread is a fundamentally horizontal idea whose goal is to give students the broad collection of skills and learning experiences they need to thrive in the globally competitive Conceptual Age. A thread provides an intuitive, flexible and mutually strengthening set of courses that allows a student to craft his or her own distinctive future."

The nine threads are Computing and Intelligence, Computing and Embodiment, Computing and Internetworking, Computing and Platforms, Computing and Information, Computing and People, Computing and Media, Computing and Modeling, and Computing Foundations. You need to take two threads to get a degree in computer science today from Georgia Tech.

The Computing and Media thread, for instance, requires students to take courses in computer science, communications, writing, and liberal arts. The idea behind this thread, said Furst, is to teach students "what they need to know to tell stories and create experiences for humans through technology." Here you'll see courses on topics ranging from computational graphics to *Hamlet*, from human perception to interactive fiction engines, Furst added. So, for instance, if you want to be a top-notch game designer, this is where to start.

The Computing and People thread prepares students by helping them to understand the theoretical and computational foundations for designing, building, and evaluating systems that treat the human being as a central component. The student who pursues Computing and People might want to combine it with Computing and Embodiment to study human-robot interaction. There are almost as many mix-and-match permutations with these threads as there are coffee options at Starbucks.

"Imagine," wrote DeMillo in an essay describing his program, "a Georgia Tech undergraduate computer-science student in her sophomore year interested in computer security. She might combine the Computing and Information thread—to learn how data is stored, retrieved, encoded, and transmitted—with the Computing and People thread—to learn how people use technology and how to run experiments with human subjects . . . She will craft a valuable computing identity and become someone able to design, invent, and build secure computing systems enabling people to securely manage their information." The point about each of these threads, individually and in combination, said

DeMillo, is that they provide a skill set and credential basis that allows graduates to create value in ways beyond what would be possible with only a narrowly focused tool set—and that skill set is certain to have value in the emerging flat-world marketplace.

Twenty-five years ago, computer science was easy, added DeMillo. "There was a clear stack—hardware, software, and algorithms—and if you could fit in anywhere in that stack, you had a job. You just picked one of those sweet spots to specialize in and you were off and running. You could work on hardware, you could program system software, or you could work on application algorithms. Now fast-forward twenty-five years. There is no clear-cut hardware, software, algorithm stack. Instead there is business process, change management, and ERP. Now it is all horizontal and in constant motion. So if you are an educator, what do you do? What remains unchanged is the need to be able to tell stories, to be able to build things that have intelligence in them, and to be able to create networks. All that remains constant. But now the way you do that is by aggregating pieces horizontally. The threads are aimed at putting things together that make sense. That is why you need to run a whole university this way. The whole notion of separate departments is crazy. You really need to change the whole approach. This is not about small tinkering."

What the Georgia Tech model recognizes is that the world is increasingly going to be operating off the flat-world platform, with its tools for all kinds of horizontal collaboration. So schools had better make sure they are embedding these tools and concepts of collaboration into the education process. "It has to run through the whole curriculum," said Furst. "It can't just be a single course; otherwise we will never nurture a high enough percentage of the population to be competitive."

THE RIGHT COUNTRY

So if these are the jobs and the pathways to the new middle, how well suited is America generally, in this flattening world, to creating these jobs and paving these pathways? The short answer is that we have—in theory—all it takes to produce the jobs and educate the sorts of people who will thrive in a flat world. Yes, we really do.

Let's go down the list. To begin with, we have a relatively flexible, deregulated free-market economy, with lots of experimentation and competition between states and universities—like Georgia Tech. The general flexibility of the American economy is a huge asset, at a time when constant change is required to stay competitive. So far America has not succumbed either to economic protectionists, who want to put up walls to keep jobs in, or national security protectionists, who want to keep workers out. As Senator Jim DeMint of South Carolina once remarked to me, the one thing we can't do is try to "protect our way to prosperity."

It is essential that we stay as open and flexible as possible. America's cultural willingness to tear things down and rebuild them anew gives us an enormous advantage in the age of flatness, when you are required to tear down and build up more often to achieve innovation and growth. We made the transition from agriculture to industry, and then from industry to services. Now we need to go to the next phase, which is services delivered globally. Each of these transitions was wrenching in its own way, but we were able to accomplish each faster and more efficiently than any other major economy because we were open and flexible and let the market do its work—which it did, though not without pain for plenty of people. The transition to the flat world will be particularly wrenching because it is likely to touch many more white-collar workers. Nevertheless, this is no time to freeze up.

"You [Americans] have all the things you need to get your people from the old middle to the new middle," said Nandan Nilekani of Infosys. "If you get through this transition first, you will be kings of the hill . . . [But] if people lose their nerve and protectionists come along and start building walls, you will [fail]. It is an act of faith—you have to believe that it will happen."

Underneath this umbrella of flexibility, America has a myriad of institutional strengths. It starts with a network of research universities, which spin off a steady stream of competitive experiments, innovations, and scientific breakthroughs—from mathematics to biology to physics to chemistry. "Our university system is the best," said Bill Gates. "We fund our universities to do a lot of research and that is an amazing thing. High-IQ people come here, and we allow them to innovate and turn [their innovations] into products. We reward risk taking. Our university system is competitive and experimental. They can try out different approaches. There are one hundred universities making contributions to robotics. And each one is saying that the other is doing it all wrong, or my piece actually fits together with theirs. It is a chaotic system, but it is a great engine of innovation in the world, and with federal tax money, with some philanthropy on top of that, [it will continue to flourish] . . . We will really have to screw things up for our absolute wealth not to increase. If we are smart, we can increase it faster by embracing this stuff."

The Web browser, magnetic resonance imaging (MRI), superfast computers, global position technology, space exploration devices, and fiber optics are just a few of the many inventions that got started through basic university research projects. The BankBoston Economics Department did a study titled "MIT: The Impact of Innovation." Among its conclusions was that MIT graduates have founded 4,000 companies, creating at least 1.1 million jobs worldwide and generating sales of $232 billion.

What makes America unique is not that it built MIT, or that its grads are generating economic growth and innovation, but that every state in the country has universities trying to do the same. "America has 4,000 colleges and universities," said Allan E. Goodman, president of the Institute of International Education. "The rest of the world combined has 7,768 institutions of higher education. In the state of California alone, there are about 130 colleges and universities. There are only 14 countries in the world that have more than that number."

Take a state you normally wouldn't think of in this regard: Oklahoma. It has its own Oklahoma Center for the Advancement of Science and Technology (OCAST), which, on its Web site, describes its mission as follows: "In order to compete effectively in the new economy, Oklahoma must continue to develop a well-educated population; a collaborative, focused university research and technology base; and a nurturing environment for cutting-edge businesses, from the smallest start-up to the largest international headquarters . . . [OCAST promotes] University-Business technology centers, which may span several schools and businesses, resulting in new businesses being spawned, new products being manufactured, and new manufacturing technologies employed." No wonder that in 2003, American universities reaped $1.3 billion from patents, according to the Association of University Technology Managers.

Coupled with America's unique innovation-generating machines— universities, public and private research labs, and retailers—we have the best-regulated and most efficient capital markets in the world for taking new ideas and turning them into products and services. Dick Foster, director of McKinsey & Co. and the author of two books on innovation, remarked to me, "We have an 'industrial policy' in the U.S.—it is called the stock exchange, whether it is the NYSE or the Nasdaq." That is where risk capital is collected and assigned to emerging ideas or growing companies, Foster said, and no capital market in the world does that better and more efficiently than the American one. The easy availability of venture capital to fund new products and innovations is a hugely important factor in enabling America to get the most of the flat-world platform. Why? Because old traditional companies are rarely early adopters or innovators of the next great breakthrough technology. The people who invented radio didn't invent television. CBS didn't invent CNN. Lexis/Nexis didn't invent Google. Having lots of venture capital and capitalists around, though, to take a risk and underwrite the next Google, CNN, or other untested innovation means that those individuals who want to get the most out of the flat-world platform, who really understand its power to create new products, forms of entertainment, and communities, can do so.

What makes capital provision work so well in America is the security and regulation of our capital markets, where minority shareholders are protected. Lord knows, there are scams, excesses, and corruption in our capital markets. That always happens when a lot of money is at stake. What distinguishes our capital markets is not that Enrons don't happen in America—they sure do. It is that when they happen, they usually get exposed, either by the Securities and Exchange Commission or by the business press, and get corrected. What makes America unique is not Enron but Eliot Spitzer, the attorney general of New York State, who has doggedly sought to clean up the securities industry and corporate boardrooms. This sort of capital market has proved very, very difficult to duplicate outside of New York, London, Frankfurt, and Tokyo. Said Foster, "China and India and other Asian countries will not be successful at innovation until they have successful capital markets, and they will not have successful capital markets until they have rule of law which protects minority interests under conditions of risk . . . We in the U.S. are the lucky beneficiaries of centuries of economic experimentation, and we are the experiment that has worked."

While these are the core secrets of America's sauce, there are others that need to be preserved and nurtured. Sometimes you have to talk to outsiders to appreciate them, such as Indian-born Vivek Paul of Wipro. "I would add three to your list," he said to me. "One is the sheer openness of American society." We Americans often forget what an incredibly open, say-anything-do-anything-start-anything-go-bankrupt-and-start-anything-again society the United States is. There is no other place like it in the world, and our openness is a huge asset and attraction to foreigners, many of whom come from countries where the sky is not the limit.

Another, said Paul, is the "quality of American intellectual property protection," which further enhances and encourages people to come up with new ideas. In a flat world, there is a great incentive to develop a new product or process, because it can achieve global scale in a flash. But if you are the person who comes up with that new idea, you want your intellectual property protected. "No country respects and protects intellectual property better than America," said Paul, and as a result, a lot of innovators want to come here to work and lodge their intellectual property.

The United States also has among the most flexible labor laws in the world. The easier it is to fire someone in a dying industry, the easier it is to hire someone in a rising industry that no one knew would exist five years earlier. This is a great asset, especially when you compare the situation in the United States to inflexible, rigidly regulated labor markets like Germany's, full of government restrictions on hiring and firing. Flexibility to quickly deploy labor and capital where the greatest opportunity exists, and the ability to quickly redeploy it if the earlier deployment is no longer profitable, is essential in a flattening world.

Still another secret to America's sauce is the fact that it has the world's largest domestic consumer market, with the most first adopters, which means that if you are introducing a new product, technology, or service, you have to have a presence in America. All this means a steady flow of jobs for Americans.

There is also the little-discussed American attribute of political stability. Yes, China has had a good run for the past twenty-five years, and it may make the transition from communism to a more pluralistic system without the wheels coming off. But it may not. Who would want all his or her eggs in that basket?

If you wanted to summarize the net effect of all these institutions, cultural norms, business practices, and legal systems, it can be reduced to one word: trust. They create and inspire a high level of trust—and a high level of trust is the most important feature any open society can possess. Trust, in many ways, is the product of all the ingredients in America's secret sauce.

"We are a high-trust country, because we agree that we are going to be governed by a set of values and principles reflected in our institutions and laws—which are higher and more enduring than any individual," said Dov Seidman, the founder of LRN, the company that provides ethics and governance advice for global corporations, which I will discuss in detail in Chapter 11. Together, these norms and institutions create predictability and confidence and that creates trust—a trust that my innovations will be protected, a trust in my currency, and a trust in my justice system. And all of that, argued Seidman, propels innovation.

Why? Because in a high-trust society, such as America, people know what ground they are standing on all the time and can count on a certain framework of rules and principles to govern their personal and business lives. "If you jump off sand and another person jumps off a hard floor," asked Seidman, "who jumps higher? The person who jumps off a hard floor, of course. Well, trust is that hard floor. It is what gives you the predictability that allows you to take a big leap . . . Without trust there is no risk-taking and without risk-taking there is no innovation . . . If you want to get more people to take the necessary risk to innovate, just put more trust in the room." No low-trust society will ever produce sustained innovation.

In a flat world, where value is increasingly created, and complex problems increasingly solved, by whom you connect with horizontally, having a high-trust society is even more of an advantage.

"Having an abundance of trust is essential in a world of collaboration," added Seidman, "because the more people trust each other, or their leaders, the more likely they are going to work well together."

Indeed, the United States has become one of the great meeting points in the world, a place where lots of different people bond, learn to trust one another, and build myriad horizontal friendships and alliances. An Indian student who is educated at the University of Oklahoma and then gets his first job with a software firm in Oklahoma City forges bonds of trust and understanding that are really important for future collaboration, even if he winds up returning to India. Nothing illustrates this point better than Yale University's outsourcing of research to China. Yale president Richard C. Levin explained to me that Yale has two big research operations running in China today, one at Peking University in Beijing and the other at Fudan University in Shanghai. "Most of these institutional collaborations arise not from top-down directives of university administrators, but rather from long-standing personal relationships among scholars and scientists," said Levin.

How did the Yale-Fudan collaboration arise? To begin with, said Levin, Yale professor Tian Xu, its director, had a deep affiliation with both institutions. He did his undergraduate work at Fudan and received his Ph.D. from Yale. "Five of Professor Xu's collaborators, who are now professors at Fudan, were also trained at Yale," explained Levin. One was Professor Xu's friend when both were Yale graduate students; another was a visiting scholar in the laboratory of a Yale colleague; one was an exchange student who came to Yale from Fudan and returned to earn his Ph.D. in China; and the other two were postdoctoral fellows in Professor Xu's Yale lab. A similar story underlies the formation of the Peking-Yale Joint Center for Plant Molecular Genetics and Agrobiotechnology.

Professor Xu is a leading expert on genetics and has won grants from the National Institutes of Health and the Howard Hughes Foundation to study the connection between genetics and cancer and certain neurodegenerative diseases. This kind of research requires the study of large numbers of genetic mutations in lab animals. "When you want to test many genes and trace for a given gene that may be responsible for certain diseases, you need to run a lot of tests. Having a bigger staff is a huge advantage," explained Levin. So what Yale did was essentially outsource the lab work to Fudan by creating the Fudan-Yale Biomedical Research Center. Each university pays for its own staff and research, so no money changes hands, but the Chinese side does the basic technical work using large numbers of technicians and lab animals, which cost so much less in China, and Yale does the high-end analysis of the data. The Fudan staff, students, and technicians get great exposure to high-end research, and Yale gets a large-scale testing facility that would have been prohibitively expensive if Yale had tried to duplicate it in New Haven. A support lab in America for a project like this one might have 30 technicians, but the one in Fudan has 150.

"The gains are very much two-way," said Levin. "Our investigators get substantially enhanced productivity, and the Chinese get their graduate students trained, and their young faculty become collaborators with our professors, who are the leaders in their fields. It builds human capital for China and innovation for Yale." Graduate students from both universities go back and forth, forging relationships that will no doubt produce more collaborations in the future. At the same time, he added, a lot of legal preparation went into this collaboration to make sure that Yale would be able to harvest the intellectual property that is created.

"There is one world of science out there," said Levin, "and this kind of international division of labor makes a lot of sense." Yale, he said, also insisted that the working conditions at the Chinese labs be world-class, and, as a result, it has also helped to lift the quality of the Chinese facilities. "The living conditions of the lab animals are right up to U.S. standards," remarked Levin. "These are not mouse sweatshops."

Put all the above together and you have America's secret sauce—a mix of institutions, laws, and cultural norms that produce a level of trust, innovation, and collaboration that has enabled us to constantly renew our economy and raise our standard of living. There is nothing about the flat world—nothing—that Americans cannot handle, as long as we roll up our sleeves, educate our young people the right way for these times, and tend to and enrich the secrets of our sauce. So are we doing that? That's what the next two chapters are about. But let me give you a hint: The answer is no.

EIGHT

The Quiet Crisis

Close games for the Americans were rare in previous Olympics, but now it appears to be something the Americans should get used to.

— From an August 17, 2004, AP article from the Athens Olympics titled
"U.S. Men's Basketball Team Narrowly Beats Greece"

Chinese pity comes from their belief that we are a country in decline. More than a few Chinese friends have quoted to me the proverb *fu bu guo san dai* (wealth doesn't make it past three generations) as they wonder how we became so ill-disciplined, distracted and dissolute. The fury surrounding Monica-gate seemed an incomprehensible waste of time to a nation whose emperors were supplied with thousands of concubines. Chinese are equally astonished that Americans are allowing themselves to drown in debt and under-fund public schools while the media focus on fights over feeding tubes, displays of the Ten Commandments and how to eat as much as we can without getting fat.

— James McGregor, a journalist-turned-businessman based in China, and a
former chairman of the American Chamber of Commerce in China,
writing in *The Washington Post*, July 31, 2005

You could find no better metaphor for the way the rest of the world can now compete head-to-head more effectively than ever with America than the struggles of the U.S. Olympic basketball team in 2004. The American team, made up of NBA stars, limped home to a bronze medal after losing to Puerto Rico, Lithuania, and Argentina. Previously, the United States Olympic basketball team had lost only one game in the history of the modern Olympics. Remember when America sent only NCAA stars to the Olympic basketball events? For a long time these teams totally dominated all comers. Then they started getting challenged. So we sent our pros. And they started getting challenged. Because the world keeps learning, the diffusion of knowledge happens faster; coaches in other countries now download American coaching methods off the Internet and watch NBA games in their own living rooms on satellite TV. Many of them can even get ESPN and watch the highlight reels. And thanks to the triple convergence, there is a lot of new raw talent walking onto the NBA courts from all over the world—including many new stars from China, Latin America, and Eastern Europe. They go back and play for their national teams in the Olympics, using the skills they honed in America. So the automatic American superiority of twenty years ago is now gone in Olympic basketball. The NBA standard is increasingly becoming a global commodity—pure vanilla. If the United States wants to continue to dominate in Olympic basketball, we must, in that great sports cliché, step it up a notch. The old standard won't do anymore. As Joel Cawley of IBM remarked to me, "Star for star, the basketball teams from places like Lithuania or Puerto Rico still don't rank well versus the Americans, but when they play as a team—when they *collaborate* better than we do—they are extremely competitive."

Sportswriter John Feinstein could have been referring to either American engineering skills or American basketball skills when he wrote in an August 26, 2004, AOL essay on Olympic basketball that the performance of the U.S. basketball team is a result of "the rise of the international player" and "the decline and fall of the U.S. game." And the decline and fall of the U.S. game, argued Feinstein, is a result of two long-term trends. The first is a steady decline "in basketball skills," with American kids just wanting either to shoot three-point shots or to dunk—the sort of stuff that gets you on the highlight reel on ESPN's *SportsCenter*—instead of learning how to make precise passes, or go into the lane and shoot a pull-up jumper, or snake through big men to get to the basket. Those skills take a lot of hard work and coaching to learn.

Today, said Feinstein, you have an American generation that relies almost completely on athleticism and almost not at all on basketball skills. And there is also that ugly little problem of ambition. While the rest of the world was getting better in basketball, "more and more NBA players were yawning at the notion of playing in the Olympics," noted Feinstein. "We have come a long way from 1984, when Bob Knight told Charles Barkley to show up to the second Olympic training camp at 265 pounds or else. Barkley showed up weighing 280. Knight cut him that day. In today's world, the Olympic coach wouldn't even have checked Barkley's weight in the first place. He would have sent a limousine to the airport to get him and stopped at Dunkin' Donuts on the way to the hotel if the player requested it . . . The world changes. In the case of American basketball, it hasn't changed for the better."

There is something about post–World War II America that reminds me of the classic wealthy family that by the third generation starts to squander its wealth. The members of the first generation are nose-to-the-grindstone innovators or entrepreneurs; the second generation holds it all together; then their kids come along and get fat, dumb, and lazy and slowly squander it all. I know that is both overly harsh and a gross generalization, but there is nevertheless some truth in it. American society started to coast in the 1990s, when our third postwar generation came of age. The dot-com boom left too many people with the impression that they could get rich without investing in hard work. All it took was an MBA and a quick IPO, or one NBA contract, and you were set for life. Who needed an education? Who needed to sweat over an engineering degree? But while we were admiring the flat world we had created, a lot of people in India, China, and Eastern Europe were busy figuring out how to take advantage of it. Lucky for us, we were the only economy standing after World War II, and we had no serious competition for forty years. That gave us a huge head of steam but also gradually bred a sense of entitlement and a culture of complacency. That is, a pronounced tendency in recent years to extol consumption over hard work and investment, immediate gratification over long-term thinking and sacrifice. When we got hit with 9/11, it was a once-in-a-generation opportunity to summon the nation to sacrifice, to address some of its pressing fiscal, energy, science, and education shortfalls—all the things that we had let slide. But our president did not summon us to sacrifice. He summoned us to go shopping.

In the previous chapters, I tried to explain why both classic economic theory and the inherent strengths of the American economy leave me convinced that Americans can thrive and claim the jobs of the new middle—provided we get ready to compete, get every individual to think about how he or she can upgrade his or her educational skills, and keep investing in the secrets of America's sauce. This chapter is about why we are not doing those things and what will happen if we don't change course.

The truth is, we're in a crisis now, but it is a crisis that is unfolding very quietly. We're a bit like a person who is sleeping on an air mattress, and the air is slowly coming out—so slowly you barely feel it, until your head hits the cement. By then, it's really hard to reinflate the mattress. It is "a quiet crisis," explained Shirley Ann Jackson, the 2004 president of the American Association for the Advancement of Science and president of Rensselaer Polytechnic Institute since 1999. (Rensselaer is America's oldest technological college, founded in 1824.) And this quiet crisis involves the steady erosion of America's scientific and engineering base, which has long been the source of American innovation and our rising standard of living.

"The sky is not falling, nothing horrible is going to happen today," said Jackson, a physicist by training who chooses her words carefully. "The U.S. is still the leading engine for innovation in the world. It has the best graduate programs, the best scientific infrastructure, and the capital markets to exploit it. But there is a quiet crisis in U.S. science and technology that we have to wake up to. The U.S. today is in a truly global environment, and those competitor countries are not only wide awake, they are running a marathon while we are running sprints. If left unchecked, this could challenge our preeminence and capacity to innovate."

Shirley Ann Jackson knows of what she speaks, because her career exemplifies as well as anyone's both why America thrived so much in the past fifty years and why it won't automatically do the same in the next fifty. An African-American woman, Jackson was born in Washington, D.C., in 1946. She started kindergarten in a segregated public school but was one of the first public school students to benefit from desegregation, as a result of the Supreme Court ruling in *Brown v. Board of Education.* Just when she was getting a chance to go to a better school, the Russians launched Sputnik in 1957, and the U.S. government became obsessed with educating young people to become scientists and engineers, a trend that was intensified by John F. Kennedy's commitment to a manned space program. When Kennedy spoke about putting a man on the moon, Shirley Ann Jackson was one of the millions of American young people who were listening. His words, she recalled, "inspired, assisted, and launched many of my generation into science, engineering, and mathematics," and the breakthroughs and inventions they spawned went well beyond the space program. "The space race was really a science race," she said.

Thanks in part to desegregation, both Jackson's inspiration and intellect were recognized early, and she ultimately became the first African-American woman to earn a Ph.D. in physics from MIT (her degree was in theoretical elementary particle physics). From there, she spent many years working for AT&T Bell Laboratories, and in 1995 was appointed by President Clinton to chair the U.S. Nuclear Regulatory Commission.

As the years went by, though, Jackson began to notice that fewer and fewer young Americans were captivated by national challenges like the race to the moon, or felt the allure of math, science, and engineering. In universities, she noted, graduate enrollment in science and engineering programs, having grown for decades, peaked in 1993, and despite some recent progress, it remains today below the level of a decade ago. So the science and engineering generations that followed Jackson's got smaller and smaller relative to our needs. By the time Jackson took the job as Rensselaer Polytechnic's president to put her heart and soul into reinvigorating American science and engineering, she realized that a "perfect storm" was brewing—one that posed a real long-term danger to America's economic health—and she started speaking out about it.

"The phrase 'the perfect storm' is associated with meteorological events in October 1991," said Jackson in a speech in May 2004, when "a powerful weather system gathered force, ravaging the Atlantic Ocean over the course of several days, [and] caused the deaths of several Massachusetts-based fishermen and billions of dollars of damage. [Meteorologists emphasized] the unlikely confluence of conditions [which] converged to bring about an event of devastating magnitude. [A] similar worst-case scenario could arrest the progress of our national scientific and technological capacity. The forces at work are multiple and complex. They are demographic, political, economic, cultural, even social." At heart, this perfect storm involves the collision of an older generation of American engineers and scientists who are retiring at the same time that a younger generation is not stepping into their shoes in sufficient numbers—and at the same time that the foreigners who used to make up the difference are either staying home or being kept out of America for security reasons. Individually, each of these forces would be problematic, added Jackson. In combination, they could be devastating. "For the first time in more than a century, the United States could well find itself falling behind other countries in the capacity for scientific discovery, innovation, and economic development."

Although knowledge has always mattered, it matters more than ever today. As economist Jeffrey Sachs has pointed out, until the scientific revolution began in the seventeenth century, virtually everyone everywhere was living on the edge of subsistence. But after three centuries of technological and scientific advances, subsistence is no longer the norm. Steam power, machine tools, electricity, and ultimately computers and the Internet have enabled individuals to become vastly more productive. So now the Industrial Age and the Information Age are giving way to the Talent Age. The flattening of the world has brought the tools of the Industrial Age and the Information Age to more people and places than ever. As these tools have become commodities, widely dispersed to everyone, business strategist John Hagel III noted, the "only sustainable edge" for companies and countries is the distinctive talents and entrepreneurship of their workforce. Economics can always be win-win. But those who will win the most today, added Hagel, will be those who are best and fastest at attracting talent.

That is why I insist that wealth in the age of flatness will increasingly gravitate to those countries who get three basic things right: the infrastructure to connect as efficiently and speedily as possible with the flat world platform, the right education programs and knowledge skills to empower more of their people to innovate and do value-added work on that platform, and, finally, the right governance—that is, the right tax policies, the right investment and trade laws, the right support for research, the right intellectual property laws, and, most of all, the right inspirational leadership—to enhance and manage the flow with the flat world.

Unfortunately, the United States has serious gaps developing in all of these areas. In the Cold War, one of the deepest concerns of American society was the putative missile gap between us and the Soviet Union, which threatened America from outside. Today we should be concerned about the gaps in our education, infrastructure, and ambitions that threaten to weaken us from within. These gaps are our dirty little secrets. If we continue to ignore them, then this won't be a quiet crisis anymore, said Rensselaer's Jackson, "it will be the real McCoy."

DIRTY LITTLE SECRET #1: THE NUMBERS GAP

Dirty little secret number one is that the generation of scientists and engineers who were motivated to go into science by the threat of Sputnik in 1957 and the inspiration of JFK are reaching their retirement years and are not being replaced in the numbers that they must be if an advanced economy like that of the United States is to remain at the head of the pack. According to the National Science Foundation, half of America's scientists and engineers are forty years or older, and the average age is steadily rising.

Just take one example—NASA. An analysis of NASA records conducted by the newspaper *Florida Today* (March 7, 2004), which covers the Kennedy Space Center, showed the following: Nearly 40 percent of the 18,146 people at NASA are age fifty or older. Those with twenty years of government service are eligible for early retirement. Twenty-two percent of NASA workers are fifty-five or older. NASA employees over sixty outnumber those under thirty by a ratio of about three to one. Only 4 percent of NASA workers are under thirty. A 2003 Government Accounting Office study concluded that NASA was having difficulty hiring people with the sufficient science, engineering, and information-technology skills that are critical to its operations. Many of these jobs are reserved for American citizens, because of national security concerns. Then–NASA administrator Sean O'Keefe testified before Congress in 2002: "Our mission of understanding and protecting our home planet and exploring the universe and searching for life will not be carried out if we don't have the people to do it." The National Commission on Mathematics and Science Teaching for the Twenty-first Century, chaired by the former astronaut and senator John Glenn, found that two-thirds of the nation's mathematics and science teaching force will retire by 2010.

Traditionally we made up for any shortages of engineers and science faculty by educating more at home and importing more from abroad. But both of those remedies have been stalled of late.

Every two years the National Science Board supervises the collection of a very broad set of data trends in science and technology in the United States, which it publishes as *Science and Engineering Indicators*. In preparing *Indicators* 2004, the NSB said, "We have observed a troubling decline in the number of U.S. citizens who are training to become scientists and engineers, whereas the number of jobs requiring science and engineering (S&E) training continues to grow." These trends threaten the economic welfare and security of our country, it said, adding that if the trends identified in *Indicators* 2004 continue undeterred, three things will happen: "The number of jobs in the U.S. economy that require science and engineering training will grow; the number of U.S. citizens prepared for those jobs will, at best, be level; and the availability of people from other countries who have science and engineering training will decline, either because of limits to entry imposed by U.S. national security restrictions or because of intense global competition for people with these skills."

The NSB report found that the number of American eighteen- to twenty-four-year-olds who receive science degrees has fallen to seventeenth in the world, whereas we ranked third three decades ago. It said that of the 2.8 million first university degrees (what we call bachelor's degrees) in science and engineering granted worldwide in 2003, 1.2 million were earned by Asian students in Asian universities, 830,000 were granted in Europe, and 400,000 in the United States. In engineering specifically, universities in Asian countries now produce eight times as many bachelor's degrees as the United States.

Moreover, "the proportional emphasis on science and engineering is greater in other nations," noted Shirley Ann Jackson. Science and engineering degrees now represent 60 percent of all bachelor's degrees earned in China, 33 percent in South Korea, 41 percent in Taiwan — and roughly 31 percent in the United States. The United States has always depended on the inventiveness of its people in order to compete in the world marketplace, said the NSB. "Preparation of the S&E workforce is a vital arena for national competitiveness. [But] even if action is taken today to change these trends, the reversal is 10 to 20 years away." The students entering the science and engineering workforce with advanced degrees in 2004 decided to take the necessary math courses to enable this career path when they were in middle school, up to fourteen years ago, the NSB noted. The students making that same decision in middle school today won't complete advanced training for science and engineering occupations until 2018 or 2020. "If action is not taken now to change these trends, we could reach 2020 and find that the ability of U.S. research and education institutions to regenerate has been damaged and that their preeminence has been lost to other areas of the world," the science board said.

These shortages could not be happening at a worse time — just when the world is going flat. "The number of jobs requiring science and engineering skills in the U.S. labor force," the NSB said, "is growing almost 5 percent per year. In comparison, the rest of the labor force is growing at just over 1 percent. Before September 11, 2001, the Bureau of Labor Statistics (BLS) projected that science and engineering occupations would increase at three times the rate of all occupations." Unfortunately, the NSB reported, the average age of the science and engineering workforce is rising.

"Many of those who entered the expanding S&E workforce in the

1960s and 1970s (the baby boom generation) are expected to retire in the next twenty years, and their children are not choosing science and engineering careers in the same numbers as their parents," the NSB report said. "The percentage of women, for example, choosing math and computer science careers fell 4 percentage points between 1993 and 1999." The 2002 NSB indicators showed that the number of science and engineering Ph.D.'s awarded in the United States dropped from twenty-nine thousand in 1998 to twenty-seven thousand in 1999. The total number of engineering undergraduates in America fell about 12 percent between the mid-1980s and 1998.

Nevertheless, America's science and engineering labor force grew at a rate well above that of America's production of science and engineering degrees, because a large number of foreign-born S&E graduates migrated to the United States. The proportion of foreign-born students in S&E fields and workers in S&E occupations continued to rise steadily in the 1990s. The NSB said that persons born outside the United States accounted for 14 percent of all S&E occupations in 1990. Between 1990 and 2000, the proportion of foreign-born people with bachelor's degrees in S&E occupations rose from 11 to 17 percent, the proportion of foreign-born with master's degrees rose from 19 to 29 percent, and the proportion of foreign-born with Ph.D.'s in the S&E labor force rose from 24 to 38 percent. By attracting scientists and engineers born and trained in other countries, we have maintained the growth of the S&E labor force without a commensurate increase in support for the long-term costs of training and attracting native U.S citizens to these fields, the NSB said.

But now, the simultaneous flattening and wiring of the world have made it much easier for foreigners to innovate without having to emigrate. They can now do world-class work for world-class companies at very decent wages at home. As Allan E. Goodman, president of the Institute of International Education, put it, "When the world was round, they could not go back home, because there was no lab to go back to and no Internet to connect to. But now all those things are there, so they are going back. Now they are saying, 'I feel more comfortable back home. I can live more comfortably back home than in New York City and I can do good work, so why not go back?'" This trend started even before the visa hassles brought on by 9/11, said Goodman. "The brain gain started to go to brain drain around the year 2000."

As the NSB study noted, "Since the 1980s other countries have increased investment in S&E education and the S&E workforce at higher rates than the United States has. Between 1993 and 1997, the OECD countries [Organization for Economic Co-operation and Development, a group of forty nations with highly developed market economies] increased their number of S&E research jobs 23 percent, more than twice the 11 percent increase in S&E research jobs in the United States."

In addition, it said, visas for students and S&E workers have been issued more slowly since the events of September 11, owing to both increased security restrictions and a drop in applications. The U.S. State Department issued 20 percent fewer visas for foreign students in 2001 than in 2000, and the rate fell further in subsequent years. While university presidents told me in 2004 that the situation was getting better, and that the Department of Homeland Security was trying to both speed up and simplify its visa procedures for foreign students and scientists, a lot of damage has been done, and the situation for foreign students or scientists wanting to work in any areas deemed to have national security implications is becoming a real problem. No wonder *New York Times* education writer Sam Dillon reported on December 21, 2004, that "foreign applications to American graduate schools declined 28 percent this year. Actual foreign graduate student enrollments dropped 6 percent. Enrollments of all foreign students, in undergraduate, graduate and postdoctoral programs, fell for the first time in three decades in an annual census released this fall. Meanwhile, university enrollments have been surging in England, Germany and other countries . . . Chinese applications to American graduate schools fell 45 percent this year, while several European countries announced surges in Chinese enrollment."

Some analysts have argued that it can be very misleading to quote the gross number of engineers graduating every year in India, China, and the United States—and therefore conclude that America must be falling behind—because accurate statistics are not only hard to come by, they often ignore the different quality of engineering degrees in the respective countries. For instance, a December 2005 study by Duke University's

Master of Engineering Management Program, entitled "Framing the Engineering Outsourcing Debate: Placing the United States on a Level Playing Field with China and India," concluded that the Indian and Chinese numbers often include graduates from less rigorous two- or three-year training programs—while the U.S. numbers usually capture only accredited four-year bachelor degree programs. The Duke study also differentiates between two groups of engineering graduates, what it calls "dynamic engineers" and "transactional engineers." Dynamic engineers, it says, "are individuals capable of abstract thinking and high-level problem solving using scientific knowledge." These dynamic engineers usually come out of at least four-year, accredited engineering programs, and their jobs are not easily outsourced. Transactional engineers, who often receive associate, technician, or diploma awards rather than bachelor's degrees, may possess engineering fundamentals, but not the experience or expertise to apply this knowledge to larger problems, the Duke study said. These jobs can be easily outsourced. America, the Duke study concluded, is still producing a relatively high proportion of dynamic engineers and computer scientists compared to India and China, and therefore remains very competitive.

I would add the following caveat to this caveat, though. First, I would bet that many of the engineering degrees being granted by American universities are going not to American citizens but to foreign students, who will return to their home countries. Second, yes, the average engineering degree in India or China today may not be the same quality as at the average accredited four-year American university. But let me put this in very simple language: There are many more Indians and Chinese than there are Americans and a much, much higher percentage of them are studying science, computer science, and engineering—in their home countries and in American universities. In a flat world, best practices travel fast. So I have no doubt that within the next twenty years the average quality of undergraduate engineering degrees in China and India will start to mirror the American average. Look at the trend lines, not today's snapshot.

DIRTY LITTLE SECRET #2:
THE EDUCATION GAP AT THE TOP

The most important reason for the numbers gap, of course, is our education gap. We simply are not educating, or even interesting, enough of our own young people in advanced math, science, and engineering. Consider the annual worldwide Intel International Science and Engineering Fair. About forty countries participate by nominating talent through local affiliate affairs. In 2004, the Intel Fair attracted around sixty-five thousand American kids, according to Intel. How about in China? I asked Wee Theng Tan, the president of Intel China, during a visit to Beijing. In China, he told me, there is a national affiliate science fair, which acts as a feeder system to select kids for the global Intel fair. "Almost every single province has students going to one of these affiliate fairs," said Tan. "We have as many as six million kids competing, although not all are competing for the top levels . . . [But] you know how seriously they take it. Those selected to go to the international [Intel] fair are immediately exempted from college entrance exams," and basically get their choice of any top university in China. In the 2004 Intel Science Fair, China came home with thirty-five awards, more than any other country in Asia, including one of the top three global awards.

No wonder that *Education Week*, which is read by teachers all over America, ran an article (July 28, 2004) with the headline "Immigrants' Children Inhabit the Top Ranks of Math, Science Meets." It said: "Research conducted by the National Foundation for American Policy shows that 60 percent of the nation's top science students and 65 percent of the top mathematics students are children of recent immigrants, according to an analysis of award winners in three scholastic competitions . . . the Intel Science Talent Search, the U.S. team for the International Mathematical Olympiad, and the U.S. Physics Team." The study's author, Stuart Anderson, attributed the immigrant students' success "partly to their parents' insistence that they manage study time wisely," *Education Week* said. "Many immigrant parents also encouraged their children to pursue mathematics and science interests, believing those skills would lead to strong career opportunities and insulate them

from bias and lack of connections in the workplace . . . A strong percentage of the students surveyed had parents who arrived in the United States
on H-1B visas, reserved for professional workers. U.S. policymakers who
back overly restrictive immigration policies do so at the risk of cutting off
a steady infusion of technological and scientific skill," said Anderson, the
executive director of the foundation. The article quoted Andrei Munteanu, eighteen, a finalist for the 2004 Intel competition, whose parents
had moved from Romania to the United States five years earlier.
Munteanu started American public school in the seventh grade and found
it a breeze compared to his Romanian school. "The math and science
classes [covered the same subject matter] I was taking in Romania . . .
when I was in fourth grade," he said.

Help does not appear to be on the way. Every four years the United
States takes part in the Trends in International Mathematics and Science
Study, which assesses students after fourth grade and eighth grade.
Altogether, the most recent study involved roughly a half million students from forty-one countries and the use of thirty languages, making it
the largest and most comprehensive international study of education
that has ever been undertaken.

The 2004 results (for tests taken in 2003) showed American students
making only marginal improvements over the 2000 results, which revealed the American labor force to be weaker in science than those of its
peer countries. The Associated Press reported (December 4, 2004) that
American eighth graders had improved their scores in science and math
since 1995, when the test first was given, but their math improvement
came mainly between 1995 and 1999, and not in recent years. The rising
scores of American eighth graders in science were an improvement over
1999 and lifted the United States to a higher ranking relative to other
countries. The worrying news, though, was that the scores of American
fourth graders were stagnant, neither improving nor declining in science
or math since 1995. As a result, the United States slipped in the international rankings as other countries made gains. "Asian countries are setting
the pace in advanced science and math," Ina Mullis, codirector of the
International Study Center at Boston College, which manages the study,
told the AP. "As one example, 44 percent of eighth-graders in Singapore

scored at the most advanced level in math, as did 38 percent in Taiwan. Only 7 percent in the United States did." Results from another international education test also came out in December 2004, from the Program for International Student Assessment. It showed that American fifteen-year-olds are below the international average when it comes to applying math skills to real-life tasks.

That may be partly explained by a 2005 study by the National Academy of Sciences, the National Academy of Engineering, and the Institute of Medicine titled "Rising Above the Gathering Storm." It found that in 1999, only 41 percent of American eighth-grade students received instruction from a mathematics teacher who specialized in mathematics, considerably lower than the international average of 71 percent. The education in American junior high schools, in particular, seems to be a black hole that is sapping the interest of young people, particularly young women, when it comes to the sciences.

In October 2005, my wife and I went up to New Haven to attend parents' weekend at Yale. We went out for a pizza lunch with our daughter and her roommates, and one roommate's boyfriend. I sat across from the boyfriend, Eric Stern, twenty-four, who was getting a Ph.D. from Yale in biomedical engineering, with an expertise in nanotechnology. Eric is precisely the sort of young person we want the American education system to keep churning out. His grandfather was a watchmaker, his father a medical doctor and science professor at Columbia, and so he got interested in science at a very young age—in part from hanging around in his father's lab and in part by building things with his grandfather. He was a Westinghouse science finalist in high school, got his undergraduate degree at Yale, and was speeding his way through graduate school, working on a government-funded project using nanotechnology to detect various toxins in the air, which could have wide application in the war on terrorism. Stern and I immediately fell into conversation about the state of science education in America today.

For starters, he said, "Look around at this table," motioning to the five Yale undergraduate women. "I am sitting at a table eating pizza with all

these smart women, and it never occurred to them to do science." They
were all in the humanities. Why? I asked Stern. There were a variety of
reasons, and they applied to both young women and men in America today, he said. To begin with, "People want to do stuff that is fun. But there
is no fun in algebra or memorizing the multiplication tables. But [those
fundamentals] eventually become freshman chemistry. And that's bor-
ing too. You can't say anything good about it. So it's not until you get to
the senior level of advanced classes that you can start to have fun. But
you need to have acquired all these fundamentals beforehand . . . and
getting those fundamentals is not fun . . . The culture now is geared
toward having fun."

Speaking of Yale, Stern told me, "I love it here, but none of my
friends were really interested in what I did and, if I wanted to communicate what I did, man, I really had to make it interesting. [Yale's] business
is making presidents, and they are great at it. It is not making scientists.
But the presidents they make don't value the sciences, because they
don't hang out with those kids—and who epitomizes that more than
Bush?" Stern added, "I was at a wedding recently, and all my college
buddies were there who are now [investment] bankers, and they were
talking about how much they made. And I started figuring out how
much I make, and it came to about $3 an hour for working eighty hours
a week. But I never really think about it that way."

It appears that young Americans wanting to be lawyers started to
swamp those wanting to be engineers and scientists in the 1970s and
early 1980s. Then, with the dot-com boom, those wanting to go to business school and earn MBAs swamped engineering students and lawyers
in the 1990s.

Stern said he believed that American culture is still producing some
of the most creative scientists and engineers, though other societies are
closing the gap due to their dedication to teaching fundamentals and
their newfound interest in instilling more creative approaches to education in their systems. Which is why, added Stern, as important as it is for
American kids to upgrade their foundational skills in math and science,
we have to do it without giving up those things in our culture that also inspire and instill creativity. In that vein, he argued, it is crazy to see public

schools getting rid of art and music programs. "One very formative part of my life that led to creative thinking as well as a work ethic was music," he said. "I was a serious classical musician, which definitely teaches hard work—and, for that matter, hard work all on your own, not like practicing with a sports team. But it also teaches you to interpret themes and ideas in new ways to make them your own."

Thank goodness American society still produces young men like Eric Stern, but we should have no illusions: He and his scientific colleagues are a minority that is getting smaller. In American society today, added Stern, "the highest thing you can be is a doctor or lawyer or investment banker—not an engineer or scientist." What worries him, he added, is where is the innovation going to happen?

"Are we going to be trading our stuff, or China's stuff?" he asked. "I want to make sure we are trading our stuff." But that gets back to the need for our people to have sound fundamentals. So much of science and engineering is about work ethic—the willingness not only to slog through all the fundamentals but also to stick with an experiment even when it fails the first twenty times, said Stern. The thing that impresses him most about the Asian students, and the best American ones, he concluded, is their work ethic. "When a Chinese graduate student comes up to me in the lab and says, 'How do you work so hard?' that is the best compliment I can get."

I wish more young Americans felt that way, but the statistics say otherwise—and the problem is not just with math and science. It's now infecting plain old reading and writing. On December 16, 2005, *The New York Times* carried a story reporting that the average American college graduate's literacy in English had declined significantly over the past decade, according to a widely respected nationwide test. This is college grads—not dropouts! "The National Assessment of Adult Literacy, given in 2003 by the Department of Education, is the nation's most important test of how well adult Americans can read," the *Times* said. "The test also found steep declines in the English literacy of Hispanics in the United States, and significant increases among blacks and Asians. When the test was last administered, in 1992, 40 percent of the nation's college graduates scored at the proficient level, meaning that they were able to read lengthy, complex English texts and draw complicated inferences. But on the 2003 test, only 31 percent of the graduates demonstrated those high-level skills. There were 26.4 million college graduates . . . Grover J. Whitehurst, director of an institute within the Department of Education that helped to oversee the test, said he believed that the literacy of college graduates had dropped because a rising number of young Americans in recent years had spent their free time watching television and surfing the Internet. 'We're seeing substantial declines in reading for pleasure, and it's showing up in our literacy levels,' he said."

DIRTY LITTLE SECRET #3: THE AMBITION GAP

Our love of television and video and online games helps to explain our third dirty little secret, one that several prominent American CEOs would tell me only in a whisper. It goes like this: When they send jobs abroad, they not only save 75 percent on wages, they get a 100 percent increase in productivity. In a sense, that's understandable. When you take a low-wage, low-prestige job in America, like a call center operator, and bring it over to India, where it becomes a high-wage, high-prestige job, you end up with workers who are paid less but motivated more. "The dirty little secret is that not only is [outsourcing] cheaper and efficient," the American CEO of a London-headquartered multinational told me, "but the quality and productivity [boost] is huge." In addition to the wage compression, he said, one Bangalore Indian employee will do the work of two or three Europeans, and the Bangalore employees don't take six weeks of holidays. "When you think it's only about wages," he added, "you can still hold your dignity, but the fact that they work better is awful."

A short time after returning from India, I was approached in an airport by a young man who wanted to talk about some columns I had written from there. We had a nice chat, I asked him for his card, and we struck up an e-mail friendship. His name is Mike Arguello, and he is an IT systems architect living in San Antonio. He does high-end IT systems design and does not feel threatened by foreign competition. He also teaches computer science. When I asked him what we needed to do in America to get our edge back, he sent me this e-mail:

> I taught at a local university. It was disheartening to see the poor work ethic of many of my students. Of the students I taught over six semesters, I'd only consider hiring two of them. The rest lacked the creativity, problem-solving abilities and passion for learning. As you well know, India's biggest advantage over the Chinese and Russians is that they speak English. But it would be wrong to assume the top Indian developers are better than their American counterparts. The advantage they have is the number of bodies they can throw at a problem. The Indians that I work with are the cream of the crop. They are educated by the equivalents of MIT back in India and there are plenty of them. If you were to follow me in my daily meetings it would become very obvious that a great deal of my time is spent working with Indians. Most managers are probably still under the impression that all Indians are doing is lower-end software development—"software assembly." But technologies, such as Linux, are allowing them to start taking higher-paying system design jobs that had previously been the exclusive domain of American workers. It has provided them with the means to move up the technology food chain, putting them on par with domestic workers. It's brain power against brain power, and in this area they are formidable. From a technology perspective, the world is flat and getting flatter (if that is possible). The only two areas that I have not seen Indian labor in are networking architects and system architects, but it is only a matter of time. Indians are very bright and they are quickly learning from their interaction with system architects just how all of the pieces of the IT puzzle fit together . . . Were Congress to pass legislation to stop the flow of Indian labor, you would have major software systems that would have nobody who knew what was going on. It is unfortunate that many management positions in IT are filled with non-technical managers who may not be fully

aware of their exposure . . . I'm an expert in information systems, not economics, but I know a high-paying job requires one be able to produce something of high value. The economy is producing the jobs both at the high end and low end, but increasingly the high-end jobs are out of reach of many. Low education means low-paying jobs, plain and simple, and this is where more and more Americans are finding themselves. Many Americans can't believe they aren't qualified for high-paying jobs. I call this the "American Idol problem." If you've ever seen the reaction of contestants when Simon Cowell tells them they have no talent, they look at him in total disbelief. I'm just hoping someday I'm not given such a rude awakening.

But the trouble starts in high school, if not sooner. In the summer of 2005, I received the following letter from Malcolm Davidson, a high school teacher in Washington State:

Dear Mr. Friedman, I teach fifth grade reading and social studies at the Annie Wright School, a private school in Tacoma, Washington. While many of the families I teach are ethnically diverse and well educated, most are white, upper middle class American families. I recently finished your new book "The World Is Flat." Two of the chapters, "The Triple Convergence" and "The Quiet Crisis," I experienced years ago, long before you wrote them. Reading them made me realize that the world was flat. I wish that I could have shared these thoughts with you before you wrote these two chapters. Parent conferences are one of the more interesting aspects of my job; I never realized that they were such a cultural study, though. Two parent conferences two years ago were my flat earth moment. One conference was with Deven and Swati Vora. (Guess where the Vora family immigrated from?) As we chatted about their daughter Sonia, they told me not only did our school not give enough homework but also that it wasn't challenging enough. Later that day in another conference, Irena Mikeladze, an immigrant from Eastern Europe, wanted to know why her son Timothy had no science book and such a flimsy science curriculum. How could we be a competitive school when we didn't have a science book? Representing two different national characters, the three parents made me think. Sadly, many . . . white, American, middle class parents [told me] that the 5th grade work was too hard on their kids. They couldn't possibly complete it and have time to "be a kid." Soccer, gymnastics, [music] lessons and dinner out squeezed their education time. Some parents would ask for my colleagues and me to lighten the load. These worrisome parents merely set low expectations for children by running interference; the scary parents . . . think everything is great and never demand more. If their kids do OK and have fun, then they must be getting a great education. Our schools tend to live back in an 11/9 mindset. I know as a school, my school compares itself with schools down the road or in the next town. If my students' parents believe that we are better than the local public, parochial and private schools, then they are content. As you wrote, and I realized in the two conferences, the real competition is not from the next town or the neighboring state any more. You're right—in many ways we are fooling ourselves. In an academic sense we lost our hunger (except for cheerleading and football and failing bond measures). We're complacent and headed for trouble. Sadly, national leadership is worried about not leaving kids behind, and states like Kansas and Georgia seem more concerned with eliminating Darwin and adding intelligent design. If one puts his ear to the flat Earth, one can hear the competition from overseas. My goal as an educator is to stop being the best local school, or regional school, and start being the best on the planet.

Essentially, before the world started getting flattened, the United States was an island—an island of innovation and safety and growing incomes. And therefore it became a magnet for the world's capital and the world's talent. When your currency is the world's currency and every brain wants to come over and work in your backyard, you start to take things for granted.

Asian countries have not had that luxury. In the winter of 2004 I had tea in Tokyo with Richard C. Koo, chief economist for the Nomura Research Institute. I tested out on Richard my "coefficient of flatness," the notion that the flatter one's country is—that is, the fewer natural resources it has—the better off it will be in a flat world. The ideal country in a flat world is the one with *no natural resources*, because countries with no natural resources tend to dig inside themselves. They try to tap the energy, entrepreneurship, creativity, and intelligence of their own people—men and women—rather than drill an oil well. Taiwan is a barren rock in a typhoon-laden sea, with virtually no natural resources—nothing but the energy, ambition, and talent of its own people—and today it has the third-largest financial reserves in the world. The success of Hong Kong, Japan, South Korea, and coastal China can all be traced to a similar flatness.

"I am a Taiwanese American with a father from Taiwan and with a Japanese mother," Koo told me. "I was born in Japan and went to Japanese elementary school and then moved to the States. There is a saying in China that whatever you put in your head and your stomach, no one can take away from you. In this whole region, that is in the DNA. You just have to study hard and move forward. I was told relatively early by my teachers, 'We can never live like Americans and Canadians. We have no resources. We have to study hard, work hard, and export hard.'"

A short time later I read a column by Steven Pearlstein, *The Washington Post's* business columnist/reporter, under the headline "Europe's Capitalism Curtain." From Wroclaw, Poland (July 23, 2004), Pearlstein wrote: "A curtain has descended across Europe. On one side are hope, optimism, freedom and prospects for a better life. On the other side, fear, pessimism, suffocating government regulations and a sense that the best times are in the past." This new curtain, Pearlstein argued, demarks Eastern Europe, which is embracing capitalism, and Western Europe, which is wishing desperately that it would go away.

"This time, however, it is the East that is likely to prevail," he continued. "The energy and sense of possibility are almost palpable here . . . Money and companies are pouring in—not just the prestige nameplates like Bombardier, Siemens, Whirlpool, Toyota and Volvo, but also the network of suppliers that inevitably follows them. At first, most of the new jobs were of the semi-skilled variety. Now they have been followed by de-sign and engineering work that aims to tap into the largest concentration of university students in Eastern Europe . . . The secret isn't just lower wages. It's also the attitude of workers who take pride and are willing to do what is necessary to succeed, even if it means outsourcing parts produc-tion or working on weekends or altering vacation schedules—things that would almost certainly trigger months of acrimony and negotiation in Western Europe. 'The people back home, they haven't got any idea how much they need to change if they want to preserve what they have,' said José Ugarte [a Basque who heads the appliance manufacturing opera-tions of Mondragon, the giant Spanish industrial cooperative]. 'The dan-ger to them is enormous. They don't realize how fast this is happening . . .' It's not the dream of riches that animates the people of Wroclaw so much as the determination to work hard, sacrifice what needs to be sacrificed and change what needs to be changed to close the gap with the West. It is that pride and determination, says Wroclaw's mayor, Rafal Dutkiewicz, that explain why they are such a threat to the 'leisure-time society' on the other side of the curtain."

Dirty Little Secret #4:
The Education Gap at the Bottom

If you look back to America in the first third of the last century, you will find the roots of the public education system we have today—a system that is now outmoded for a flat world. Back in the early twentieth century, America decided to organize its education system by delegating the power and responsibility for education to local school boards. We basically al-lowed each community to organize its own school system, with its own ap-proach to teaching and textbooks, and its own salary structures—as opposed to doing it either on a national level, as most countries do, or on a state level as, say, Germany does. The net effect of this approach, argues Marc Tucker, president of the National Center on Education and the Economy, was a patchwork system in which we delegated education power to local school boards "organized by wealth." That is, "these school board districts were essentially organized around patterns of residents," explained Tucker. "So it made it possible for relatively wealthy people to organize into self-taxing districts. And that meant that wealthy people, by associating with each other, could tax themselves at relatively low rates and still produce very high per capita per student school budgets" because of their bigger homes and higher property tax assessments. If you went to the other end of the spectrum, you found relatively poor people associated with each other in school districts, paying a much larger portion of their income in school taxes but nevertheless winding up with very low per-pupil expenditures. And in those communities you also had very high social noise and low expectations.

This was greatly reinforced by the advent of home mortgage subsidies and the highway construction subsidies after World War II, noted Tucker, which combined to create the suburbs as we know them. As a result, despite the gains of the civil rights movement, the 1960s witnessed growing de facto racial segregation in the schools, as white families with children largely abandoned the cities, leaving behind what we now know is an even more segregated (by race and class) city. All these postwar developments combined to create large metropolitan areas in the United States surrounded by suburbs that can be arrayed along a finely graded scale of race and class, in most cases with matching school districts.

Without any question the wealthiest school districts attracted the best teachers, principals, and curriculum planners, along with the most demanding parents and PTAs, while the poorest districts attracted the weakest teachers and principals and parents who had to work three jobs just to survive (leaving them with less time to help their kids with their homework). By contrast, other industrialized countries fund their schools according to what it will take to deliver a standard curriculum, and then they take the money out of the state's general budget.

Americans have always wanted and expected their public schools to be the agent of social mobility, the principal means by which poor people can lift themselves up by their bootstraps to grab the American brass ring. But that is no longer the reality in too many parts of the country today, because of the disparities in funding.

The reason America has managed to get by with this system for so long, added Tucker, was that beginning in the 1930s, when the mass-production economy became dominant, "we were actually doing something very efficient. We were educating a group of mass production workers at the level they needed and we poured money into the elite who could innovate." So if you went to an elite private school or a public school in a wealthy neighborhood, you got an education that reinforced innovation and creativity, while the worst public high schools focused on just getting kids through with the bread-and-butter basics. That was all fine as long as there were a lot of basic bread-and-butter mass-production jobs, paying decent wages, waiting on the other side of the high school gates.

Unfortunately, as the world has flattened out, those mass-production jobs are increasingly being automated or outsourced. There are fewer and fewer decent jobs for those without a lot of knowledge. There are several American cities, for instance, where thirty years ago the biggest employer was a manufacturing plant and today it is a medical center or a technology hub. So a poorly funded and staffed high school today is a pathway to a dead end. "There is no future down there anymore," said Tucker. "Therefore, we have to find a way to educate all of our young people to a very high standard. Otherwise, if you don't upgrade their skills, the only way the low-skilled can compete is by driving down their wages."

DIRTY LITTLE SECRET #5: THE FUNDING GAP

For now, the United States still excels at teaching science and engineering at the graduate level, and also in university-based research. But as the Chinese get more feeder stock coming up through their improving high schools and universities, "they will get to the same level as us after a decade," said Intel chairman Craig Barrett. "We are not graduating the volume, we do not have a lock on the infrastructure, we do not have a lock on the new ideas, and we are either flat-lining, or in real dollars cutting back, our investments in physical science."

Continued American technological leadership in building the jobs of

tomorrow, added Barrett, requires "a commitment to basic research funding today." Unfortunately, the 2004 Task Force on the Future of American
Innovation found that federal funding for research in physical and mathematical sciences and engineering, as a share of GDP, actually declined by
37 percent between 1970 and 2004. In the fiscal year 2005 budget passed
by the Republican-led Congress in November 2004, the budget for the
National Science Foundation, which is the federal body most responsible
for promoting research and funding more and better science education,
was actually cut by 1.9 percent, or $105 million. History will show that
when America should have been doubling the NSF funding, its Congress
passed a pork-laden budget that actually cut assistance for science and engineering. There was tiny improvement in the fiscal 2006 budget—an increase of 2.4 percent. The Department of Energy's Office of Science, the
most important funder of physics research in America, got only a 2.9 percent increase in fiscal 2005 and a 0.9 percent boost in 2006, which
amounts to a budget cut after inflation. This is outrageous.

In his January 2006 State of the Union address, President Bush vowed
to reverse this decline in a big way. We'll see. What should we be doing?
The October 2005 National Academy of Sciences, National Academy of
Engineering, and Institute of Medicine report, "Rising Above the
Gathering Storm," which was put together by a blue-ribbon panel of scientists and entrepreneurs, concluded that for America to be prepared for
the twenty-first century, it must increase federal investment in such research *by 10 percent a year over the next seven years.* It also recom-
mended new research grants, each of $500,000 a year for five years, to be
given to two hundred of the most outstanding early-career researchers.
Republican congressman Vern Ehlers of Michigan, a voice in the wilderness, said the following, after Congress cut the NSF's 2005 budget:
"While I understand the need to make hard choices in the face of fiscal
constraint, I do not see the wisdom in putting science funding behind
other priorities . . . Not only are we not keeping pace with inflationary
growth, we are actually cutting the portion basic research receives in the
overall budget. This decision shows dangerous disregard for our nation's
future, and I am both concerned and astonished that we would make this

decision at a time when other nations continue to surpass our students in math and science and consistently increase their funding of basic research. We cannot hope to fight jobs lost to international competition without a well-trained and educated workforce."

The effects are starting to show. According to the National Science Board, the percentage of scientific papers written by Americans has fallen 10 percent since 1992. The percentage of American papers published in the top physics journal, *Physical Review*, has fallen from 61 percent to 29 percent since 1983. And now we are starting to see a surge in patents awarded to Asian countries. From 1980 to 2003, Japan's share of world industrial patents rose from 12 percent to 21 percent, and Taiwan's from 0 percent to 3 percent. By contrast, the U.S. share of patents has fallen from 60 percent to 52 percent since 1980.

Congress has a long history of wasting money on pork barrel highway projects. From now on, let's waste our money on test tube projects instead—just in case.

Dirty Little Secret #6:
The Infrastructure Gap

Thomas Bleha, a former U.S. foreign service officer who was based in Japan, wrote a telling article for *Foreign Affairs* (May–June 2005) that began like this: "In the first three years of the Bush Administration, the United States dropped from 4th to 13th place in the global rankings of broadband Internet usage. Today, most U.S. homes can access only 'basic' broadband, among the slowest, most expensive, and least reliable in the developed world, and the United States has fallen even further behind in mobile-phone-based Internet access. The lag is arguably the result of the Bush Administration's failure to make a priority of developing these networks. In fact, the United States is the only industrialized state without an explicit national policy for promoting broadband."

Since it took over in 2001, the Bush team has made clear that its priorities are tax cuts, missile defense, and the war on terrorism—not keeping the United States at the forefront of Internet innovation. Things have actually gotten worse since Bleha wrote his article, based on 2004 statistics. According to the data released in April 2005 by the International Telecommunication Union (ITU), America's global broadband penetration dropped from thirteenth place to sixteenth. The ITU ranked the United States at 11.4 broadband subscribers per 100 inhabitants as of December 31, 2004, which is less than half that of South Korea—the most wired country in the world—with 24.9 broadband subscribers per 100 inhabitants. "Norway, Israel and Finland each surpassed the United States in broadband penetration for the first time," the *National Journal* reported on April 25, 2005. "And an aggressive rollout in France almost pushed the U.S. even lower. High-speed Internet use in France doubled from 5.61 subscribers per 100 inhabitants at the end of 2003 to 11.2 per 100 last year, putting the nation at 17th, just one notch below the United States."

In the current administration's first three years, noted Bleha, President George W. Bush mentioned broadband just twice and only in passing. Not only that, but what the United States measures as broadband service—200 Kbps—"wouldn't cut the mustard in much of the rest of the world," noted Mark Lloyd, writing in the daily Progress Report for the Center for American Progress (October 7, 2004). In Japan, for instance, consumers pay the equivalent of $10 a month for service forty times as fast as 200 Kbps. The smartest countries, and cities, in the world are offering their residents not just the fastest broadband, but at the lowest prices to the widest areas.

Why should Americans care?

Broadband and information technologies are important not only because they are big global businesses in and of themselves, but also because they are critical to advancing productivity and innovation in every sector in the economy. The more you connect an educated population to the flat-world platform in an easy and affordable way, the more things they can automate, and therefore the more time and energy they have to innovate. The more they innovate, the more they produce things that improve the platform. It is a virtuous cycle, one that you always want to encourage to the greatest degree possible.

If the flat-world platform makes innovation and production so much more efficient, "but your people can't take advantage of it, because they don't have the infrastructure or the education to do so," remarked Craig Mundie of Microsoft, "then sooner or later you are going to get hosed."

THE BOTTOM LINE

When I asked Bill Gates about the supposed American education advantage—an education that stresses creativity, not rote learning—he was utterly dismissive. In his view, the people who think that the more rote-oriented learning systems of China and Japan can't turn out innovators who can compete with Americans are sadly mistaken. Said Gates, "I have never met the guy who doesn't know how to multiply who created software . . . Who has the most creative video games in the world? Japan! I never met these 'rote people' . . . Some of my best software developers are Japanese. You need to understand things in order to invent beyond them."

One cannot stress enough: Young Chinese, Indians, and Poles are not racing us to the bottom. They are racing us to the top. They do not want to work for us; they don't even want to be us. They want to dominate us—in the sense that they want to be creating the companies of the future, ones that people all over the world will admire and clamor to work for. They are in no way content with where they have come so far. I was talking to a Chinese American who worked for Microsoft and had accompanied Bill Gates on visits to China. He said Gates is recognized everywhere he goes in China. Young people there hang from the rafters and scalp tickets just to hear him speak. Same with Jerry Yang, the cofounder of Yahoo!

In China today, Bill Gates is Britney Spears. In America today, Britney Spears is Britney Spears—and that is our problem.

And no wonder. Johns Hopkins University president Bill Brody remarked to me, "Over 60 percent of our graduate students in the sciences [at Hopkins] are foreign students, and mostly from Asia. At one point four years ago all of our graduate students in mathematics were from the PRC [Communist China]. I only found out about it because we use them as

[teaching assistants] and some of them don't speak English all that well."
A Johns Hopkins parent wrote Brody to complain that his son could not
understand his calculus professor because of his heavy Chinese accent
and poor English.

There is an old techie adage that in places like China and Japan the
nail that stands up gets hammered, while in Silicon Valley the nail that
stands up drives a Ferrari and has stock options. Underlying that adage has
always been a certain American self-confidence that whatever America
lacks in preparing its kids with strong fundamentals in math and science,
it makes up by encouraging its best students to be independent, creative
thinkers. There is a lot of truth to that. Even the Chinese will tell you that
up to now they have been good at making the next new thing, and copying
the next new thing, but not *imagining* the next new thing. That may be
about to change, though. Confident that their best K–12 students will
usually outperform America's on the fundamentals of math and science,
China is now focusing on how to unleash more creative, innovative
juices among its youth.

In October 2005, on a visit to Beijing, I interviewed Wu Qidi, China's
vice minister of education. Here's what she told me over tea in her office
in the Ministry of Education—the newest and nicest government building in Beijing today: "Although we are enjoying a very fast growth of our
economy, we own very little intellectual property. We are so proud of
China's four great inventions [in the past]: the compass, papermaking,
printing, and gunpowder. But in the following centuries we did not keep
up that pace of invention. Those inventions fully prove what the
Chinese people are capable of doing—so why not now? We need to get
back to that nature."

Nurturing more "creative thinking and entrepreneurship are the exact issues we are putting attention to today," added Vice Minister Wu.
Yes, this is easier said than done. It bumps head-on into a Chinese culture and politics that still emphasize conformity. But do not kid yourself:
Cultures can change. And China is changing, particularly as more and
more young Chinese are educated in America and Europe.

"Ever since the policy of reform and opening up, we are seeing a
large number of scholars and teachers and professors going abroad," said

Vice Minister Wu, "and they are in the process of evolving and changing and they have imparted these changes to their students in classrooms. And now we are seeing that the world is changing and the Internet is changing our world so fast . . . I believe that arts will play an important role. It is even more important to have an integration in arts and science so people will have the creative and independent thinking . . . Among the teachers, some of them are not well trained to get the integration of arts and science."

She sounded to me just like Wayne Clough of Georgia Tech. And that is the point. *China is focused on overcoming its weaknesses—beginning with creative thinking—to match our strengths.*

It will take time, probably longer than China thinks. But when one looks at what China has been doing at the very top, I have no doubt that it will get where it wants to go. Let me take you for a little tour of Microsoft Research Asia, the research center that Bill Gates set up in Beijing to draw on Chinese brainpower. Microsoft has four major research centers in the world: in Cambridge, England; in Redmond, Washington, its headquarters; in Beijing; and most recently in Bangalore, India. Bill Gates told me that within just a couple of years of its opening in 1998, Microsoft Research Asia had become the most productive research arm in the Microsoft system "in terms of the quality of the ideas that they are turning out. It is mind-blowing."

In China, where there are 1.3 billion people and the universities are just starting to crack the top ranks, the competition for top spots is ferocious. The math/science salmon that swims upstream in China and gets itself admitted to a top Chinese university or hired by a foreign company is one smart fish. The folks at Microsoft have a saying about their research center in Beijing, which, for scientists and engineers, is one of the most desirable places to work in all of China. "Remember, in China when you are one in a million—there are thirteen hundred other people just like you."

In other words, the brainpower that rises to the Microsoft research center in Beijing is already one in a million.

Kai-Fu Lee, who has since left Microsoft, was originally assigned to build the Microsoft research center in Beijing. My first question to him was, "How did you go about recruiting the staff?" Lee said his team went to universities all over China and simply administered math, IQ, and programming tests to Ph.D.-level students or scientists.

"In the first year, we gave about 2,000 tests all around," he said. From the 2,000, they winnowed the group down to 400 with more tests, then 150, "and then we hired 20." They were given two-year contracts and told that at the end of two years, depending on the quality of their work, they would either be given a longer-term contract or granted a postdoctoral degree by Microsoft Research Asia. Yes, you read that right. The Chinese government gave Microsoft the right to grant postdocs. Of the original twenty who were hired, twelve survived the cut. The next year, nearly four thousand people were tested. After that, said Lee, "we stopped doing the test. By that time we became known as the number one place to work, where all the smart computer and math people wanted to work . . . We got to know all the students and professors. The professors would send their best people there, knowing that if the people did not work out, it would be their credibility [on the line]. Now we have the top professors at the top schools recommending their top students. A lot of students want to go to Stanford or MIT, but they want to spend two years at Microsoft first, as interns, so they can get a nice recommendation letter that says these are MIT quality."

They view this as "a once-in-a-lifetime income opportunity," said Lee of the team at Microsoft Research Asia. "They saw their parents going through the Cultural Revolution. The best they could do was become a professor, do a little project on the side because a professor's pay is horrible, and maybe get one paper published. Now they have this place where all they do is research, with great computers and lots of resources. They have administrators—we hire people to do the dirty work. They just could not believe it. They voluntarily work fifteen to eighteen hours a day and come in on weekends. They work through holidays, because their dream is to get to Microsoft." Lee, who had worked for other American high-tech firms before coming to Microsoft, said that until starting Microsoft Research Asia, he had never seen a research lab with the enthusiasm of a start-up company.

Today it has two hundred full-time researchers. Harry Shum, the

Carnegie Mellon–trained engineer who now runs Microsoft Research Asia, has a very clear view of what Chinese innovators can do when given the right environment. ACM Siggraph is the premier global conference for computer graphics and interactive technologies. At Siggraph 2005, a total of ninety-eight papers were published from universities and research institutes all over the world. Nine of them—almost 10 percent—came from Microsoft's Beijing office alone, beating out MIT and Stanford. Said Shum: "In 1999, we had one paper published. In 2000, we had one. In 2001, we had two. In 2002, we had four. In 2003 we had three. In 2004, we had five, and this year we are very lucky to have nine." Do you see a pattern developing?

In addition, Microsoft Research Asia has already contributed more than one hundred new technologies for current Microsoft products—from Xbox to Windows. It's a huge leap in seven years, but, outside of hothouses like Microsoft, China still has a way to go.

"A Chinese journalist once asked me, 'Harry, tell me honestly, what is the difference between China and the U.S.? How far is China behind?' I joked, 'Well, you know, the difference between China high tech and American high tech is only three months—if you don't count creativity.' When I was a student in China twenty years ago we didn't even know what was happening in the U.S. Now, any time an MIT guy puts up something on the Internet, students in China can absorb it in three months. But could someone here create it? That is a whole other issue. I learned mostly about how to do research right at Carnegie Mellon . . . Before you create anything new you need to understand what is already there. Once you have this foundation, being creative can be trainable. China is building that foundation. So very soon, in ten or twenty years, you will see a flood of top-quality research papers from China."

Once more original ideas start emerging here, though, China will still need more venture capital and the rule of law to get them to market. "Some aspects of Chinese culture did not encourage independent thinking," said Shum. (Obviously, I would add, the Communist political structure also doesn't promote free thinking in every direction, either.)

"But with venture capital coming into this country, it will definitely inspire a new generation of Chinese entrepreneurs. I will be teaching a

class at Tsinghua University next year on how to do technology-based
ventures . . . You have technology in [Chinese] universities, but people
don't know what to do with it—how to marketize it."

Some of his young Chinese researchers demonstrated their new research prototypes for me. I noticed that several of them had little granite
blocks lined up on their shelves. I asked one of them, who had seven or
eight on her shelf, "What are those?" She said the researchers get them
from Microsoft every time they invent "something that gets patented."

How do you say Ferrari in Chinese?

On December 15, 2004, the Council on Competitiveness hosted a
National Innovation Initiative Summit at the Ronald Reagan
Building in Washington, D.C., to release its long-term study "Innovate
America: Thriving in a World of Challenge and Change"—a detailed
bipartisan analysis by America's leading technologists and industrialists
about how to re-energize American competitiveness through more research, education, and innovation. Several months after the report came
out, the Council on Competitiveness was contacted by the Chinese embassy in Washington and told that China's vice minister of science and
technology would be visiting and would like to invite council members for
a lunch. Deborah Wince-Smith, the energetic president of the Council on
Competitiveness, told me that her colleagues were happy to share their
report with the Chinese visitor, as they had with other foreign delega-
tions. But it wasn't necessary.

"He said that they had already translated the report and were planning to integrate it into their twenty-year strategic plan," said Wince-
Smith, adding that while the council had taken the initiative to share
their report with other countries, "the Chinese came to us—we didn't
come to them." They had clearly been following the council's work,
which is published on its Web site, very closely. Wince-Smith said these
days she is wondering "whether we are going to implement [the Innovate
America report] or China is going to beat us to our own plan."

Don't laugh. The day the Innovate America report was released to the public in Washington, the authors, who, as I said, were a very high-powered group of American educators and business leaders, begged the White House to have President Bush attend the ceremony, in the hope that he would use his bully pulpit to highlight their report and draw national attention to it. The president's aides refused the request, apparently because they thought it would dilute his message of the day.

And where was President Bush speaking that day? He was literally down the hall, in the very same Reagan Building, at the exact same time the Innovate America report was being issued. And what was the president doing that was more important? He was holding his own economic summit, speaking to a carefully selected audience that included many Republican campaign donors, to push his ultimately failed plan to partially privatize Social Security. The president spoke against a backdrop that was printed with the words "Securing Our Economic Future." So there was the president trying to take apart the old New Deal—just when he should have been using his office to promote a New New Deal for the twenty-first century. And down the hall, a bipartisan group headed by Sam Palmisano, CEO of IBM, and G. Wayne Clough, president of Georgia Tech, was offering up just such a New New Deal agenda at a National Innovation Summit and the president could not devote five minutes to it. But the Chinese immediately translated it. I am not making this up.

A short while later I spoke with Craig Barrett, the Intel chairman, who seemed exasperated that Washington, including both political parties, didn't seem to really grasp this quiet crisis—or at least not with the urgency that was required.

"We will hire the talent wherever it resides," said Barrett. "We still have some good students coming out of our schools." But if you look at where Intel is making a lot of its new engineering-level investments, he added, it's in four or five countries—Russia, China, and India and to a lesser extent Malaysia and Israel. These and other emerging markets are also where Intel is selling more and more of its chips.

Then Barrett added something about Intel that is so true in a flat world, but nevertheless shocking to many Americans. Intel, he said, can thrive as a company "even if we never hire another American." He was quick to add that this is not Intel's intent or desire. "And we still do hire lots of Americans," said Barrett. "But today we can hire the best talent around the world and be very successful."

Intel has to seek IQ (and CQ and PQ) wherever it can, because that is what its competitors are doing. Remember, said Tracy Koon, Intel's director of corporate affairs, Intel's chips are made from just two things— sand and brains (silicon comes from sand)—"and right now the brains are the problem . . . We will need a stronger and more supportive immigration system if we want to hire the people who want to stay here. Otherwise, we will go where they are. What are the alternatives? I am not talking about data programmers or [people with] B.S. degrees in computer science. We are talking about high-end specialized engineering. We have just started a whole engineering function in Russia, where engineers have wonderful training—and talk about underemployed! We are beefing that up. Why wouldn't you?"

That is Shirley Ann Jackson's perfect storm—we don't let the talent in from abroad as much as we used to, the growing opportunities for our best companies shift more and more to foreign markets, and we don't do a better job educating our own kids to fill the gaps. If that storm comes to pass, American companies, like Intel, will just lift off American soil like rocket ships. They will hover over America. We will think of them as American companies, because they will be listed on the New York Stock Exchange and have post office boxes here, but they really will be flat-world companies. Where innovation happens really does matter, because that is where the best jobs are going to be located, and those best jobs spin off more good jobs and decent jobs in every community. It matters that Microsoft is headquartered in Redmond, Washington. It matters that Google is headquartered in Mountain View, California. And one day it will matter if they aren't.

"Standard of living is related to the average value add of your workforce," said Barrett, "and that is related to average educational level of your workforce. If you downgrade the average educational level of your workforce, relative to your competition, your standard of living will decline."

Look at the high-profile attention Congress has devoted to steroids in major-league baseball, Barrett said, and compare that with the attention it has focused on the crisis in science education in major-league American cities. How long did it take us to have congressional hearings on steroids in major-league baseball? Almost immediately after the scandal broke. The science crisis? That can wait. Congress has pork to distribute. The president has other priorities.

"As my wife likes to tell me," said Barrett, "when you study history and look at every civilization that has grown up and died off, they all leave one remnant—a major sports coliseum at the heart of their capital."

Our fate can be different, but only if we start doing things differently. It takes fifteen years to train a scientist or advanced engineer, starting from when that young man or woman first gets hooked on science and math in elementary school. Therefore, we should be embarking immediately on an all-hands-on-deck, no-holds-barred, no-budget-too-large crash program for science and engineering education. Scientists and engineers don't grow on trees. They have to be educated through a long process, because, ladies and gentlemen, this really *is* rocket science.

The fact that we have not been doing this is a crisis. It may be a creeping and quiet crisis, but it is here and it is real. And as Paul Romer, the Stanford economist, has so perceptively warned:

"A crisis is a terrible thing to waste."

NINE

This Is Not a Test

We have the power to shape the civilization that we want. But we need your will, your labor, your hearts, if we are to build that kind of society. Those who came to this land sought to build more than just a new country. They sought a new world. So I have come here today to your campus to say that you can make their vision our reality. So let us from this moment begin our work so that in the future men will look back and say: It was then, after a long and weary way, that man turned the exploits of his genius to the full enrichment of his life.

—Lyndon B. Johnson, "Great Society" speech, 1964

Most politicians here don't know the difference between a server and a waiter. That's why kids in South Korea have better Internet access than kids in the south Bronx.

—Andrew Rasiej, candidate in 2005 for New York City's office of public advocate, trying to run on a platform focused on upgrading New York City's IT infrastructure (he was not elected)

As a person who grew up during the Cold War, I'll always remember driving along down the highway and listening to the radio, when suddenly the music would stop and a grim-voiced announcer would come on the air and say, "This is a test of the Emergency Broadcast System," and then there would be a thirty-second high-pitched siren sound. Fortunately, we never had to live through a moment in the

Cold War where the announcer came on and said, "This is not a test." That, however, is exactly what I want to say here: *This is not a test.*

The long-term opportunities and challenges that the flattening of the world puts before the United States are profound. Therefore, our ability to get by doing things the way we've been doing them—which is to say, not always tending to our secret sauce and enriching it—will not suffice anymore. "For a country as wealthy as we are, it is amazing how little we are doing to enhance our natural competitiveness," said Dinakar Singh, the Indian-American hedge fund manager. "We are in a world that has a system that now allows convergence among many billions of people, and we had better step back and figure out what it means. It would be a nice coincidence if all the things that were true before are still true now—but there are quite a few things you actually need to do differently . . . You need to have a much more thoughtful national discussion."

If this moment has any parallel in American history, it is the height of the Cold War, around 1957, when the Soviet Union leaped ahead of America in the space race by putting up the Sputnik satellite. Yes, there are many differences between that age and our own. The main challenge then came from those who wanted to put up walls; the main challenge to America today comes from the fact that all the walls are being taken down, and other countries can now compete with us much more directly. The main challenge in that world was from those practicing extreme communism—namely, Russia, China, and North Korea. The main challenge to America today is from those practicing extreme capitalism—namely, China, India, and South Korea. The main objective in that era was building a strong state; the main objective in this era is building strong individuals.

What this era has in common with the Cold War era, though, is that meeting the challenges of flatism requires as comprehensive, energetic, and focused a response as did meeting the challenge of communism. It requires our own version of the New Frontier and Great Society adapted to the age of flatness. It requires a president who can summon the nation to get smarter and study harder in science, math, and engineering in order to reach the new frontiers of knowledge that the flat world is rapidly opening up and pushing out. And it requires a Great Society that commits our government to building the infrastructure, safety nets, and institutions that will help every American become more employable in an age when no one can be guaranteed lifetime employment. I call my own version of this approach "compassionate flatism."

Getting Americans to rally around compassionate flatism is much more difficult than getting them to rally around anticommunism. "National peril is a lot easier to convey than individual peril," noted Johns Hopkins University foreign policy expert Michael Mandelbaum. Economics, as noted, is not like war, because economics can always be a win-win game. But sometimes I wish economics were more like war. In the Cold War, we actually got to see the Soviets parade their missiles in Red Square. We all got to be scared together, from one end of the country to the other, and all our politicians had to be focused and serious about marshaling the resources and educational programs to make sure Americans could keep pace with the Soviet Union.

But today, alas, there is no missile threat coming from India. The "hotline," which used to connect the Kremlin with the White House, has been replaced by the "help line," which connects everyone in America to call centers in Bangalore. While the other end of the hotline might have had Leonid Brezhnev threatening nuclear war, the other end of the help line just has a soft voice eager to help you sort out your AOL bill or collaborate with you on a new piece of software. No, that voice has none of the menace of Nikita Khrushchev pounding a shoe on the table at the UN, and it has none of the sinister snarl of the bad guys in *From Russia with Love*. There is no Boris or Natasha saying, "We will bury you" in a thick Russian accent. No, that voice on the help line just has a friendly Indian lilt that masks any sense of threat or challenge. It simply says, "Hello, my name is Rajiv. Can I help you?"

No, Rajiv, actually, you can't.

When it comes to responding to the challenges of the flat world, there is no help line we can call. We have to dig into ourselves. We in America have all the tools to do that, as I argued in Chapter 7. But, as I argued in Chapter 8, we have not been tending to those tools as we should. Hence, our quiet crisis. The assumption that because America's economy has dominated the world for more than a century, it will and must always be that way is as dangerous an illusion today as the illusion that America would always dominate in science and technology was back in 1950. But this is not going to be easy. Getting our society up to speed for a flat world is going to involve a lot of pain. We are going to have to start doing a lot of things differently. It is going to take the sort of focus and national will that President John F. Kennedy called for in his famous May 25, 1961, speech to Congress on "urgent national needs." At that time, America was recovering from the twin shocks of Sputnik and the Soviet space launch of a cosmonaut, Yuri Gagarin, less than two months before Kennedy's speech. Kennedy knew that while America had enormous human and institutional assets—far more than the Soviet Union—they were not being fully utilized.

"I believe we possess all the resources and talents necessary," said President Kennedy. "But the facts of the matter are that we have never made the national decisions or marshaled the national resources required for such leadership. We have never specified long-range goals on an urgent time schedule, or managed our resources and our time so as to ensure their fulfillment." After then laying out his whole program for putting a man on the moon within ten years, President Kennedy added, "Let it be clear that I am asking the Congress and the country to accept a firm commitment to a new course of action, a course which will last for many years and carry very heavy costs . . . This decision demands a major national commitment of scientific and technical manpower, materiel and facilities, and the possibility of their diversion from other important activities where they are already thinly spread. It means a degree of dedication, organization and discipline which have not always characterized our research and development efforts."

In that speech, Kennedy made a vow that has amazing resonance today: "I am therefore transmitting to the Congress a new Manpower Development and Training program, to train or retrain several hundred thousand workers, particularly in those areas where we have seen chronic unemployment as a result of technological factors, in new occupational skills over a four-year period—in order to replace those skills made obsolete by automation and industrial change with the new skills which the new processes demand."

Amen. We too have to do things differently. We are going to have to sort out what to keep, what to discard, what to adapt, what to adopt, where to redouble our efforts, and where to intensify our focus. That is what this chapter is about. This is just an intuition, but the flattening of the world is going to be hugely disruptive to both traditional and developed societies. The weak will fall further behind faster. The traditional will feel the force of modernization much more profoundly. The new will get turned into old quicker. The developed will be challenged by the underdeveloped much more profoundly. I worry, because so much political stability is built on economic stability, and economic stability is not going to be a feature of the flat world. Add it all up and you can see that the disruptions are going to come faster and harder. No one is immune—not me, not you, not Microsoft. We are entering an era of creative destruction on steroids. Dealing with flatism is going to be a challenge of a whole new dimension, even if your country has a strategy. But if you don't have a strategy at all . . . well, again, you've been warned.

This is not a test.

Being an American, I am especially concerned about my own country. How do we go about maximizing the benefits and opportunities of the flat world, and providing protection for those who have difficulty with the transition? Some will offer traditional conservative responses; some will offer traditional liberal ones. I offer compassionate flatism. Compassionate flatism is my definition of what it means to be a progressive in a flat world. I start with the assumption that, barring some geopolitical explosion, the world is going to get more and more globalized and flattened, as surely as dawn will follow dusk. The job of government and politicians in such a flattening world is more important than ever. It is to embrace globalization and understand that a fairer, more compassionate, and more egalitarian society lies in a web of policies aimed not at strengthening the old welfare state—or in abolishing it and just letting the market rip—but at reconfiguring it to give more Americans the outlook, education, skills, and safety nets they will need to compete against other individuals in the flat world. In short, the one thing government can't do is promise to insulate American workers against the volatility of the global labor market in a flat world. But the one thing it must do is equip American workers with more tools and social supports to reduce the new pressures of global competition. That is what compassionate flatism stands for, and it is built around five action areas: leadership, muscle building, cushioning, social activism, and parenting.

LEADERSHIP

The job of the politician in America, whether at the local, state, or national level, should be, in good part, to help educate and explain to people what world they are living in and what they need to do if they want to thrive within it. One problem we have today, though, is that so many American politicians don't seem to have a clue about the flat world. As venture capitalist John Doerr once remarked to me, "You talk to the leadership in China, and they are all the engineers, and they get what is going on immediately. The Americans don't, because they're all lawyers." Added Bill Gates, "The Chinese have risk-taking down, hard work down, education, and when you meet with Chinese politicians, they are all scientists and engineers. You can have a numeric discussion with them — you are never discussing 'give me a one-liner to embarrass [my political rivals] with.' You are meeting with an intelligent bureaucracy."

When China's prime minister, Wen Jiabao, visited India for the first time in April 2005, he didn't fly into the capital, New Delhi—as foreign leaders usually do. He flew directly from Beijing to Bangalore—for a tech-tour—and then went on to New Delhi. No U.S. president or vice president has ever visited Bangalore. I am not saying we should require all politicians to hold engineering degrees, but it would be helpful if they had a basic understanding of the forces that are flattening the world, were able to educate constituents about them and galvanize a response. We have way too many politicians in America today who seem to do the opposite. They seem to go out of their way actually to make their constituents stupid—encouraging them to believe that certain jobs are "American jobs" and can be protected from foreign competition, or that because America has always dominated economically in our lifetimes it always will, or that compassion should be equated with protectionism. It is hard to have an American national strategy for dealing with flatism if people won't even acknowledge that there is an education gap emerging and that there is an ambition gap emerging and that we are in a quiet crisis. For instance, of all the policy choices that the Republican-led Congress could have made in forging the FY 2005 budget, how in the world could it have decided to cut the funding of the National Science Foundation by more than $100 million?

We need politicians who are able and willing to both explain and inspire. And what they most need to explain to Americans is pretty much what Lou Gerstner explained to the workforce of IBM when he took over as chairman in 1993, when the company was losing billions of dollars. At the time, IBM was facing a near-death experience owing to its failure to adapt to and capitalize on the business computing market that it invented. IBM got arrogant. It had built its whole franchise around helping customers solve problems. But after a while it stopped listening to its customers. It thought it didn't have to. And when IBM stopped listening to its customers, it stopped creating value that mattered for its customers, and that had been the whole strength of its business. A friend of mine who worked at IBM back then told me that when he was in his first year at the company and was taking an internal course, his IBM instructor boasted to him that IBM was such a great company, it could do "extraordinary things with just average people." As the world started to flatten, though, IBM found that it could not continue thriving with an overabundance of average people working for a company that had stopped being a good listener.

But when a company is the pioneer, the vanguard, the top dog, the crown jewel, it is hard to look in the mirror and tell itself it is in a not-so-quiet crisis and better start to make a new history or become history. Gerstner decided that he would be that mirror. He told IBM it was ugly and that a strategy built largely around designing and selling computers— rather than the services and strategies to get the most out of those computers for each customer—didn't make sense. Needless to say, this was a shock for IBMers.

"Transformation of an enterprise begins with a sense of crisis or urgency," Gerstner told students at Harvard Business School, in a December 9, 2002, talk. "No institution will go through fundamental change unless it believes it is in deep trouble and needs to do something different to survive." It is impossible to ignore the parallel with America as a whole in the early twenty-first century.

When Lou Gerstner came in, one of the first things he did was replace the notion of lifetime employment with the notion of lifetime employability. A friend of mine, Alex Attal, a French-born software engineer who was working for IBM at the time, described the shift this way: "Instead of IBM giving you a guarantee that you will be employed, you had to guarantee that you could stay employable. The company would give you the framework, but you had to build it yourself. It's all about adapting. I was head of sales for IBM France at the time. It was the mid-nineties. I told my people that in the old days [the concept of] lifetime employment was only a company's responsibility, not a personal responsibility. But once we move to a model of employability, that becomes a shared responsibility. The company will give you access to knowledge, but you have to take advantage of it . . . You have to build the skills because it will be you against a lot of other people."

When Gerstner started to change the paradigm at IBM, he kept stressing the issue of individual empowerment. Said Attal, "He understood that an extraordinary company could only be built on a critical mass of extraordinary people."

As at IBM, so in America. Average Joe has to become special, specialized, synthesizing, or adaptable Joe. The job of government and business is not to guarantee anyone a lifetime job—those days are over. That social contract has been ripped up with the flattening of the world. What government can and must guarantee people is the chance to make themselves more employable. We don't want America to be to the world what IBM was becoming to the computer industry in the 1980s: the people who opened the field and then became too timid, arrogant, and ordinary to play on it. We want America to be the born-again IBM.

Explaining a new challenge, though, is not just diagnosing the problem for people and telling them the truth about how we are falling behind. It is also opening their minds to the power of new technologies to solve old problems. There is more to political leadership than a competition for who can offer the most lavish safety nets. Yes, we must address people's fears, but we must also nurse their imaginations. Politicians can make us more fearful and thereby be disablers, or they can inspire us and thereby be enablers.

To be sure, it is not easy to get people passionate about the flat world. It takes some imagination. President Kennedy understood that the competition with the Soviet Union was not a space race but a science race, which was really an education race. Yet the way he chose to get Americans excited about sacrificing and buckling down to do what it took to win the Cold War—which required a large-scale push in science and engineering—was by laying out the vision of putting a man on the moon, not a missile into Moscow. If President Bush is looking for a similar legacy project, there is one just crying out—a national science initiative that would be our generation's moon shot: a crash program for alternative energy and conservation to make America energy-independent in ten years. If President Bush made energy independence his moon shot, in one fell swoop he would dry up revenue for terrorism, force Iran, Russia, Venezuela, and Saudi Arabia onto the path of reform—which they will never do with $60-a-barrel oil—strengthen the dollar, and improve his own standing in Europe by doing something huge to reduce global warming. He would also create a real magnet to inspire young people to contribute to both the war on terrorism and America's future by again becoming scientists, engineers, and mathematicians. "This is not just a win-win," said Michael Mandelbaum. "This is a win-win-win-win-win."

I have consistently been struck that my newspaper columns that have gotten the most positive feedback, especially from young people, have been those that urged the president to call the nation to this task. Summoning all our strengths and skills to produce a twenty-first-century renewable energy source is George W. Bush's opportunity to be both Nixon going to China and JFK going to the moon in one move. Mr. Bush tautly acknowledged this with his 2006 State of the Union address, but he did not go nearly far enough.

MUSCLES

Since lifetime employment is a form of fat that a flat world simply cannot sustain any longer, compassionate flatism seeks to focus its energy on how government and business can enhance every worker's lifetime employability. Lifetime employability requires replacing that fat with muscle. The social contract that progressives should try to enforce between government and workers, and companies and workers, is one in which government and companies say, "We cannot guarantee you any lifetime employment. But we can guarantee you that we will concentrate on giving you the tools to make yourself more lifetime employable—more able to acquire the knowledge or the experience needed to be a good adapter, synthesizer, collaborator etc." In the flat world, the individual worker is going to become more and more responsible for managing his or her own career, risks, and economic security, and the role of government and business is to help workers build all the muscles they need to do just that.

The "muscles" workers need most are portable benefits and opportunities for lifelong learning. Why those two? Because they are the most important assets in making a worker mobile and adaptable. As Harvard University economist Robert Lawrence notes, the greatest single asset that the American economy has always had is the flexibility and mobility of its labor force and labor laws.

Given that reality, argues Lawrence, it becomes increasingly important for society, to the extent possible, to make benefits and education—the two key ingredients of employability—as flexible as possible. You don't want people to feel that they have to stay with a company forever simply to keep their pension and health benefits. The more the workforce feels mobile—in terms of health care, pension benefits, and lifelong learning possibilities—the more it will be willing and able to jump into the new industries and new job niches spawned by the flat world and to move from dying companies to thriving companies.

Creating legal and institutional frameworks for universal portability of pensions and health care—in addition to Social Security, Medicare, and Medicaid—will help people build up such muscles. Today roughly 50 percent of Americans don't have a job-based pension plan, other than Social Security. Those who are fortunate enough to have one cannot easily take it with them from job to job. What is needed is one simple universal portable pension scheme, along the lines proposed by the Progressive Policy Institute, that would get rid of the confusing welter of sixteen different tax-deferred options now offered by the government and consolidate them all into a single vehicle. This universal plan, which you would open with your first job, would encourage workers to establish 401(k) tax-deferred savings programs. Each worker and his or her employer could make contributions of cash, bonuses, profit sharing, or stock, depending on what sorts of benefits the specific employer offered. These assets would be allowed to build up tax-free in whatever savings or investment portfolio options the worker chose. But if and when it came time to change jobs, the worker could take the whole portfolio with him or her and not have to either cash it out or leave it under the umbrella of the previous employer. Rollover provisions do exist today, but they are complicated and many workers don't take advantage of them because of that.

The universal pension format would make rollover simple, easy, and expected, so pension lockup per se would never keep someone from moving from one job to another. Each employer could still offer his or her own specific 401(k) benefit plan, as an incentive to attract employees. But once a worker moved to another job, the investments in that particular 401(k) would just automatically dump into his or her universal pension account. With each new job, a new 401(k) could be started, and with each move, the benefits deposited in that same universal pension account.

In addition to this simple, portable, and universal pension program, Will Marshall, president of the Progressive Policy Institute, proposes legislation that would make it much easier and more likely for workers to obtain stock options in the companies for which they work. Such legislation would give tax incentives to companies to give more workers more options earlier and penalize companies that do not. Part of making workers more mobile is creating more ways to make more workers owners of financial assets, not just their own labor. "We want a public that sees itself as stakeholders, sharing in the capital-creating side of the flat world, not just competing in global labor markets," argued Marshall. "We all have to be owners as well as wage earners. That is where public policy has to be focused—to make sure that people have wealth-producing assets as they enter the twenty-first century, the way homeownership accomplished that in the twentieth century."

Why? Because there is an increasing body of literature that says people who are stakeholders, people who have a slice of the pie, "are more deeply invested in our system of democratic capitalism and the policies that keep it dynamic," said Marshall. It is another way, besides homeownership, to underpin the legitimacy of democratic capitalism. It is also another way to energize it, because workers who are also owners are more productive on the job. Moreover, in a flat world where every worker is going to face stiffer competition, the more opportunities everyone has to build wealth through the power of markets and compounding interest, the more he or she will be able to be self-reliant. We need to give workers every stabilizer we can and make it as easy for them to get stock options as it is for the plutocrats. Instead of just being focused on protecting those with existing capital, as conservatives so often seem to be, let's focus instead on widening the circle of capital owners.

On the health-care side, which I won't delve into in great detail, since that would be a book unto itself, it is essential that we develop a scheme for portable health insurance that reduces some of the burden on employers for providing and managing coverage. Virtually every entrepreneur I talked to for this book cited soaring and uncontrolled health-care costs in America as a reason to move factories abroad to countries where benefits were more limited, or nonexistent, or where there was national health insurance. Again, I favor the type of portable health-care program proposed by PPI. The idea is to set up state-by-state collective purchasing pools, the way Congress and federal employees now cover themselves. These pools would set the rules and create the marketplace in which insurance companies could offer a menu of options. Each employer would then be responsible for offering this menu of options to each new employee. Workers could choose high, medium, or low coverage. Everyone, though, would have to be covered. Depending on the employer, it would cover part or all of the premiums and the employee the rest. But employers would not be responsible for negotiating plans with insurance companies, where they have little individual clout.

The state or federal pools would do that. This way employees would be totally mobile and could take their health-care coverage wherever they went. This type of plan has worked like a charm for members of Congress, so why not offer it to the wider public? Needy and low-income workers who could not afford to join a plan would get some government subsidy to do so. But the main idea is to establish a government-supervised, -regulated, and -subsidized private insurance market in which government sets the broad rules so that there is no cherry-picking of healthy workers or arbitrary denial of treatment. The health care itself is administered privately, and the job of employers is to facilitate their workers' entry into one of these state pools and, ideally, help them pay for some or all of the premiums, but not be responsible for the health care themselves. In the transition, though, employers could continue to offer health-care plans as an incentive, and workers would have the option of going with either the plan offered by their employers or the menu of options available through the state purchasing pools. (For details, go to ppionline.org.)

One can quibble about the details of any of these proposals, but I think the basic inspiration behind them is exactly right: In a flattening world, where worker security can no longer be guaranteed by Fortune 500 corporations with top-down pension and health plans, we need more collaborative solutions—among government, labor, and business—that will promote self-reliant workers but not just leave them to fend for themselves.

When it comes to building muscles of lifetime employability, government has another critical role to play: upgrading the educational level of the entire American workforce. In Chapter 7, I discussed the right kind of education for the jobs of the new middle. But for people to be able to learn how to learn, to nurture their right brains, to be adaptable, and to become synthesizers, they have to start by learning sound fundamentals. The right education can be built only on top of a sound education in the fundamentals—reading comprehension, writing, arithmetic, and basic science. Without more Americans with this solid grounding, we can't possibly build a new middle of the size we need to keep our standard of living rising.

We've been here before. Each century, as we push out the frontiers of human knowledge, work at every level becomes more complex, requiring more pattern recognition and problem solving. Somehow we got through this transition from an agriculture-based society 150 years ago to an industrial-based one—and still ended up with a higher standard of living for the vast majority of Americans. How did we do it? We began by making high school mandatory.

"We said everyone is going to have to have a secondary education," said Stanford University economist Paul Romer. "That was what the high school movement in the early part of the twentieth century was all about." As economic historians have demonstrated in a variety of research (see particularly the work of Harvard economists Claudia Goldin and Larry Katz), both technology and trade are making the pie bigger, but they are also shifting the shares of that pie away from low-skilled labor to high-skilled labor. As American society produced more higher-skilled people by making high school mandatory, it empowered more people to get a bigger slice of the bigger, more complex economic pie. As that century progressed, we added, on top of the high school movement, the GI Bill and the modern university system.

"These were big ideas," noted Romer, "and what is missing at the moment is a political imagination of how do we do something just as big and just as important for the transition into the twenty-first century as we did for the nineteenth and twentieth." The obvious challenge, Romer added, is to make tertiary education, if not compulsory, then government-subsidized for at least two years, whether it is at a state university, a community college, or a technical school. Tertiary education is more critical the flatter the world gets, because technology will be churning old jobs, and spawning new, more complex ones, much faster than during the transition from the agricultural economy to the industrial one.

Educating more people at the tertiary level has two effects. First, it produces more people with the skills to claim higher-value-added work in the new niches that require more pattern recognition, synthesizing,

and complex problem solving. Second, it shrinks the pool of people looking for lower-skilled work, from road maintenance to home repair to
Starbucks baristas. By shrinking the pool of lower-skilled workers, we
help to stabilize their wages (provided we also control low-skilled immigration), because there are fewer people available to do those jobs. It is
not an accident that plumbers can charge $75 an hour in major urban
areas or that quality housekeepers or cooks are hard to find. That's good.
We want them to be more in demand and to make a decent wage.

America's ability from the mid-nineteenth century on into the mid-
twentieth century to train people, limit immigration, and make low-skilled
work scarce enough to win decent wages was the key to creating a middle
class without too disparate an income gap. "Indeed," noted Romer, "from
the end of the nineteenth century to the middle of the twentieth, we had a
narrowing of the income gap. Now we have seen an increase of that gap
over the last twenty or thirty years. That is telling us that you have to run
faster in order to stay in the same place." With each advance in technology
and increase in the complexity of services, you need an even higher level
of skills to do the new jobs. Moving from being a farmhand to a phone operator who spoke proper English and could be polite was one thing. But
moving from being a phone operator after the job got outsourced to India
to being able to install or repair phone-mail systems—or write their software—requires a whole new leap upward.

While expanding research universities on the high end of the spectrum is important, so is expanding the availability of technical schools
and community colleges. Everyone should have a chance to be educated
beyond high school. Otherwise upper-income kids will get those skills
and their slice, and the lower-income kids will never get a chance. We
have to increase the government subsidies that make it possible for more
and more kids to attend community colleges and more and more low-
skilled workers to get retrained.

JFK wanted to put a man on the moon. My vision is to put every
American man or woman on a campus.

Employers have a critical contribution to make to their workers' lifetime employability, and it starts by helping them become more adaptable

through lifetime learning. Take, for instance, CapitalOne, the global credit card company, which began outsourcing elements of its backroom operations to Wipro and Infosys in India over the past few years. Competing in the global financial services market, the company felt it had to take advantage of all the cost-saving opportunities that its competitors were using. CapitalOne began, though, by trying to educate its employees through workshops about the company's competitive predicament. It made clear that there is no safe haven where lifetime employment is possible anymore—inside CapitalOne or outside. Then it developed a program for the cross training of computer programmers, those most affected by outsourcing. The company would take a programmer who specialized in mainframes and teach him or her to be a distributed systems programmer as well. CapitalOne did similar cross training on its business side, in everything from auto loans to risk management. As a result, the workers who were eventually let go in an outsourcing move were much better synthesizers, much more versatile, and therefore in a much better position to get new jobs, because they were cross trained. And those who were cross trained but retained by CapitalOne were more versatile and therefore more valuable to CapitalOne, because they could do multiple tasks.

That is why our whole society benefits when government provides subsidies or tax incentives to companies to offer as wide an array as possible of in-house learning opportunities. The menu of Internet-based worker-training programs today is enormous—from online degree programs to in-house guided training for different specializations. (And every week brings a technological breakthrough that makes this easier and richer. For instance, we have not even begun to tap the potential of putting the lectures of great teachers on video. Why suffer through bad teachers when a great teacher is just a flat screen away?) Not only is the menu enormous and growing, but the cost to the company for offering these educational options is very low. The more lifetime learning opportunities that companies provide, the more they are both widening the skill base of their own workforce and fulfilling a moral obligation to workers whose jobs are outsourced to see to it that they leave more employable than they came. If there is a new social contract implicit between employers and employees today, it should be this: *You give me your labor, and I will guarantee that as long as you work here, I will give you every opportunity—through either career advancement or training—to become more employable, more versatile.*

George Miller, a wise longtime Democratic congressman from the East Bay district in San Francisco, who is deeply involved with public schools there, once remarked to me, "Education is a process, not a place." Education can and must go on everywhere all the time—in schools, offices, at home, online, in the classroom, over your iPod—with conventional teachers, self-teaching methods, online games, whatever works. You cannot let up, because somewhere out there there's a competitor who isn't letting up.

While we need to redouble our efforts to build the muscles of each individual American, we have to continue to import muscles from abroad as well to make up for what we cannot educate here. Most of the Indian, Chinese, Russian, Japanese, Korean, Iranian, Arab, and Israeli engineers, physicists, and scientists who come to work or study in the United States make great citizens. They are family-oriented, educated, and hardworking, and most would jump at the chance to become an American. They are exactly the type of people this country needs, and we cannot let the FBI, CIA, and Homeland Security, in their zeal to keep out the next Mohammed Atta, also keep out the next Sergey Brin, one of the cofounders of Google, who was born in Russia. As a computer architect friend of mine says, "If a foreign-born person is one day going to take my job, I'd prefer they be American citizens helping pay for my retirement benefits."

I would favor an immigration policy that gives a five-year work visa to any foreign student who completes a Ph.D. at an accredited American university in any subject. I don't care if it is Greek mythology or mathematics. If we can cream off the first-round intellectual draft choices from around the world, it will always end up a net plus for America. If the flat world is about connecting all the knowledge pools together, we want our knowledge pool to be the biggest. Said Bill Brody, the president of Johns Hopkins, "We are in a global talent search, so anything we can do in America to get those top draft choices we should do, because one of them is going to be Babe Ruth, and why should we let him or her go somewhere else?"

GOOD FAT
Cushions Worth Keeping

W hile many of the old corporate and government safety nets will
vanish under global competition in the flat world, some fat still
needs to be maintained, and even added. As everyone who worries about
his or her health knows, there is "good fat" and "bad fat"—but everybody
needs some fat. That is also true of every country in the flat world. Social
Security is good fat. We need to keep it. A welfare system that discourages
people from working is bad fat. The sort of good fat that actually needs to
be added for a flat world is wage insurance.

According to a study by Lori Kletzer, an economist at the University
of California, Santa Cruz, in the 1980s and '90s, two-thirds of workers
who lost jobs in manufacturing industries hit by overseas competition
earned less on their next job. A quarter of workers who lost their jobs and
were reemployed saw their income fall 30 percent or more. Losing a job
for any reason is a trauma—for the worker and his or her family—but
particularly for older workers who are less able to adapt to new production techniques or lack the education to move up into more skilled service jobs.

This idea of wage insurance was first proposed in 1986 by Harvard's
Robert Lawrence and Robert E. Litan of the Brookings Institution, in a
book called *Saving Free Trade*. The idea languished for a while until it
started to catch fire again with an updated analysis by Kletzer and Litan in
2001. It got further political clout from the bipartisan U.S. Trade Deficit
Commission in 2001. This commission couldn't agree on anything—
including the causes of or what to do about the trade deficit—other than
the wisdom of wage insurance.

"Trade creates winners and losers, and what we were thinking about
were mechanisms by which the winners could compensate the losers,
and particularly losers who were enjoying high wages in a particular job
and suddenly found their new employment at much lower wages," said
Lawrence. The way to think about this, he explained, is that every worker
has "general skills and specific skills" for which he or she is paid, and
when you switch jobs you quickly discover which is which. So you might

have a college and CPA degree, or you might have a high school degree and the ability to operate a lathe. Both skills were reflected in your wages. But suppose one day your lathe job gets moved to China or your basic accounting work is outsourced to India and you have to go out and find a new job. Your new employer will not likely compensate you much for your specific skills, because your knowledge as a machine tool operator or a general accountant is probably of less use to him or her. You will be paid largely for your general skills, your high school education or college degree. Wage insurance would compensate you for your old specific skills, for a set period of time, while you take a new job and learn new specific skills.

The standard state-run unemployment insurance program eases some of this pain for workers, but it does not address their bigger concerns of declining wages in a new job and the inability to pay for health insurance while they are unemployed and searching. To qualify for wage insurance, workers seeking compensation for job loss would have to meet three criteria. First, they would have to have lost their job through some form of displacement—offshoring, outsourcing, downsizing, or factory closure. Second, they would have to have held the job for at least two years. And third, the wage insurance would not be paid until the workers found new jobs, which would provide a strong incentive to look for work quickly and increase the chances that they would get on-the-job retraining. On-the-job training is always the best way to learn new skills—instead of having to sign up for some general government training program, with no promise of a job at the other end, and go through that while remaining unemployed.

Workers who met those three conditions would then receive payments for two years, covering half the drop in their income from their previous job (capped at $10,000 a year). Kletzer and Litan also proposed that the government pay half the health insurance premiums for all "displaced" workers for up to six months. Wage insurance seems to me a much better idea than relying only on the traditional unemployment insurance offered by states, which usually covers only about 50 percent of most workers' previous wages, is limited to six months, and does not help workers who suffer a loss of earnings after they take a new job.

Moreover, as Kletzer and Litan noted, although all laid-off workers now have the right to purchase unsubsidized health insurance from their former employer if health coverage was offered when they were employed, many jobless workers do not have the money to take advantage of this guarantee. Also, while unemployed workers can earn an additional fifty-two weeks of unemployment insurance if they enroll in an approved retraining program, workers have no guarantee that when they finish such a program they will have a job.

For all these reasons, the Kletzer-Litan proposal makes a lot of sense to me as the right benefit for cushioning workers in a flat world. Moreover, such a program would be eminently affordable. Litan estimated that at an unemployment rate of 5 percent, the wage insurance and health-care subsidy today would cost around $8 billion a year, which is peanuts compared to the positive impact it could have on workers. This program would not replace classic state-run unemployment insurance for workers who opt for that, but if it worked as projected, it could actually reduce the cost of such programs by moving people back to work quicker.

Some might ask, Why be compassionate at all? Why keep any fat, friction, or barriers? Let me put it as bluntly as I can: If you are not a compassionate flatist—if you are just a let 'er rip free-market flatist—you are not only cruel, you are a fool. You are courting a political backlash by those who can and will get churned up by this flattening process, and that backlash could become ferocious if we hit any kind of prolonged recession.

The transition to a flat world is going to stress many people. As Joshua S. Levine, E*Trade's chief technology officer, put it to me, "You know how sometimes you go through a harrowing experience and you need a respite, but the respite never seems to come. Look at the airline workers. They go through this [terrible] event like 9/11, and management and the airline unions all negotiate for four months and management says, 'If the unions don't cut $2 billion in salary and benefits they will have to shut the airline down.' And after these wrenching negotiations the unions agree. I just have to laugh, because you know that in a few months management is going to come right back . . . There is no end. No one has to ask me to cut my budget each year. We all just know that each year we will be expected to do more with less. If you are a revenue producer, you are expected to come up with more revenue every year, and if you are an expense saver, you are expected to come up with more savings every year. You never get a break from it."

If societies are unable to manage the strains that are produced by this flattening, there will be a backlash, and political forces will attempt to reinsert some of the frictions and protectionist barriers that the flattening forces have eliminated, but they will do it in a crude way that will, in the name of protecting the weak, end up lowering everyone's standard of living. Former Mexican president Ernesto Zedillo is very sensitive to this problem, having had to manage Mexico's transition into NAFTA, with all of the strains that put on Mexican society. Speaking of the flattening process, he said to me, "It would be very hard to stop, but it can be stopped for a time. Maybe you can't stop it totally, but you can slow it down. And it makes a difference whether you get there in twenty-five years or fifty years. In between, two or three generations—who could have benefited a lot from more trade and globalization—will end up with crumbs."

Always remember, said Zedillo, that behind all this technology is a political infrastructure that enables it to play out. "There have been a series of concrete political decisions, taken over the last fifty years, that put the world where it is right now," he said. "Therefore, there are political decisions that could screw up the whole process too."

As the saying goes: If you want to live like a Republican, vote like a Democrat—take good care of the losers and left-behinds. The only way to be a flatist is to be a compassionate flatist.

PARENTING

No discussion of compassionate flatism would be complete without also discussing the need for improved parenting. Helping individuals adapt to a flat world is not only the job of governments and companies. It is also the job of parents. They too need to know in what world their kids are growing up and what it will take for them to thrive. In short, we need a new generation of parents ready to administer tough love:

There comes a time when you've got to put away the Game Boys, turn off the television, shut off the iPod, and get your kids down to work.

The sense of entitlement, the sense that because we once dominated global commerce and geopolitics—and Olympic basketball—we always will, the sense that delayed gratification is a punishment worse than a spanking, the sense that our kids have to be swaddled in cotton wool so that nothing bad or disappointing or stressful ever happens to them at school is, quite simply, a growing cancer on American society. And if we don't start to reverse it, our kids are going to be in for a huge and socially disruptive shock from the flat world. While a different approach by politicians is necessary, it is not sufficient.

Shortly after this book first came out my wife (a schoolteacher) pointed out to me a letter to the editor in *The New York Times* (September 1, 2005) in response to a column on faltering American education by my colleague Bob Herbert. The letter summed up my feelings exactly: "To the Editor: Regarding the state of education in the United States, Bob Herbert writes, 'I respectfully suggest that we may be looking at a crisis here' . . . As a highly qualified teacher of English at the high school level, I agree. But this crisis we see in our schools has its roots in American homes increasingly devoid of books and printed material, where children turn exclusively to television, computers and electronic games for entertainment—and see the adults around them doing the same. Instant-gratification technology has, for many students, replaced the task—and the thrill—of reading. One cannot develop solid writing skills without first being a decent reader; underdevelopment of these skills translates to low scores in standardized testing across racial and economic lines, and in all subject areas. Education begins in a home where reading is intrinsically valuable and necessary; where recognition of the hard work associated with education and doing well in school are top priorities; and where parents join schools in having high expectations for their children's success. Without this initial foundation and continued support at home, a teacher's hands are tied at school. Jo Ann Price, Freehold, N.J."

David Baltimore, the Nobel Prize–winning president of Caltech, knows what it takes to get your child ready to compete against the cream of the global crop. He told me that he is struck by the fact that almost all the students who make it to Caltech, one of the best scientific universities in the world, come from public schools, not from private schools that sometimes nurture a sense that just because you are there, you are special and entitled. "I look at the kids who come to Caltech, and they grew up in families that encouraged them to work hard and to put off a little bit of gratification for the future and to understand that they need to hone their skills to play an important role in the world," Baltimore said. "I give parents enormous credit for this, because these kids are all coming from public schools that people are calling failures. Public education is producing these remarkable students—so it *can* be done. Their parents have nurtured them to make sure that they realize their potential. I think we need a revolution in this country when it comes to parenting around education."

Foreign-born parents, particularly from Asia and Eastern Europe, often seem to do this better. "About one-third of our students have an Asian background or are recent immigrants," said Baltimore. A significant majority of the students coming to Caltech in the engineering disciplines are foreign-born, and a large fraction of its current faculty is foreign-born. "In biology, at the postdoc level, the dominance of Chinese students is overwhelming," he added. No wonder that at the big scientific conferences today, a majority of the research papers dealing with cutting-edge bioscience have at least one Chinese name on them. By the way, nearly 90 percent of the kids who go to MIT, a school just like Caltech, also come from two-parent homes, where both parents can help guide a child down the straight and narrow.

In July 2004, comedian Bill Cosby used an appearance at Jesse Jackson's Rainbow/PUSH Coalition & Citizenship Education Fund's annual conference to upbraid African Americans for not teaching their children proper grammar and for black kids not striving to learn more themselves. Cosby had already declared, "Everybody knows it's important to speak English except these knuckleheads. You can't be a doctor with that kind of crap coming out of your mouth." Referring to African Americans who squandered their chances for a better life, Cosby told the Rainbow Coalition, "You've got to stop beating up your women because you can't find a job, because you didn't want to get an education and now you're [earning] minimum wage. You should have thought more of your-self when you were in high school, when you had an opportunity." When Cosby's remarks attracted a lot of criticism, Reverend Jackson defended him, arguing, "Bill is saying, let's fight the right fight. Let's level the play-ing field. Drunk people can't do that. Illiterate people can't do that."

That is right. Americans are the ones who increasingly need to level the playing field—not by pulling others down, not by feeling sorry for our-selves, but by lifting ourselves up. But when it comes to how to do that, Cosby was saying something that is important for black and white Ameri-cans, rich and poor. Education, whether it comes from parents or schools, has to be about more than just cognitive skills. It also has to include char-acter building. The fact is, parents and schools and cultures can and do shape people. The most important influence in my life, outside of my fam-ily, was my high school journalism teacher, Hattie M. Steinberg. She pounded the fundamentals of journalism into her students—not simply how to write a lead or accurately transcribe a quote but, more important, how to comport yourself in a professional way. She was nearing sixty at the time I had her as my teacher and high school newspaper adviser in the late 1960s. She was the polar opposite of "cool," but we hung around her classroom like it was the malt shop and she was Wolfman Jack. None of us could have articulated it then, but it was because we enjoyed being harangued by her, disciplined by her, and taught by her. She was a woman of clarity and principles in an age of uncertainty. I sit up straight just thinking about her! Our children will increasingly be competing head-to-head with Chinese, Indian, and Asian kids, whose parents have a lot more of Hattie's character-building approach than their own American parents. I am not suggesting that we militarize education, but I am suggesting that we do more to push our young people to go beyond their comfort zones, to do things right, and to be ready to suffer some short-run pain for longer gain.

Unfortunately, it has been too long since America had a leader ready and willing to call on our nation to do something hard—to give some-thing up, not just to get something more, and to sacrifice for a great na-tional cause in the future, rather than live for today. But maybe we also have the leaders we deserve—a perfect reflection of who we are and how we raise our own children. Paul A. Samuelson, the Nobel Prize–winning economist from MIT whose textbooks have shaped economics students around the world for nearly five decades, gave a rare interview with the German weekly *Der Spiegel*, for a special issue titled *Globalization: The New World* (December 2005). Asked what he saw as the future of the American economy, Samuelson answered, "We may still be the lead cyclist breaking the wind for the riders behind us, but the others are closing in. America's status as a leading nation is growing increasingly tenuous because we have become such a low-savings society. We are a society of me, me, me, and now—not thinking about others and tomorrow. I suppose the problem is the electorate, not its leaders . . . In the past, bright kids who later became mathematicians were doing challenging puzzles. Today they watch TV. There are too many distractions, which is another reason why we have this attitude of me, me, me, and now."

If this is a test, and I think it is, our leaders and our parents have not done as good a job as they could to prepare our young people for the world ahead. "We are like a glass beaker that is filled three-quarters of the way to the top, and the liquid is our wealth," said Steve Jobs, the founder of Apple Computer and one of America's greatest innovators. "There is this much bigger beaker next to it, but it is filled to a much lower level. What we are doing today is we're connecting a hose between these two beakers, which have never been connected before." As a result, he said, our standard of living is almost certain to go down unless we can continue to be "incredibly innovative."

But, added Jobs, "I am afraid we are getting close to it being too late. Because you can't change the school system in the short term, we might be just beginning to pay the price for the neglect of the last twenty years." Jobs noted that his company recently decided to build a major plant in China, and he was amazed at how quickly the Chinese government made the decision to locate the factory, provide capital to subsidize its building, and help assemble a workforce. "Boom, it was done just like that," he said. "Fifteen years ago, ten years ago, that would have happened in Texas or somewhere else [in America]. Now it is happening in China. So the liquid is already flowing from one beaker to the other. And it will flow even more when they start designing the products. I am an optimist [about America's future], but if we are sitting around watching Rome burn, it's hard to be an optimist."

Steve Jobs's rallying call is a good place to end this chapter, a chapter that began with President Kennedy rallying the country to rise to the challenge of putting a man on the moon. Because, in some way, they were both engaged in the same endeavor—calling on Americans to do what they do best, which is invent the future.

On October 24, 2005, *Time* magazine ran a cover story about Apple's latest invention. The cover showed Jobs holding up the newest Apple iPod, the one that plays videos as well as music. And the headline said, "The Man Who Always Seems to Know . . . WHAT'S NEXT." That is the only way America is going to thrive in a flat world—if we keep inventing the next new thing. My friend Jerry Rao, the Indian entrepreneur who founded MphasiS, made an offhand comment to me one day that still rings in my ear. For India and China the future is very clear, he said. They know exactly what they are going to do in the future. "We are going to do in the future what Americans are doing today," he said. "Your job is to invent the future." That is so right—America's job is not to fight with India and China over the old middle but to invent the new middle, and more. "That is always hard," added Jerry, "because you don't know what the future looks like," and because it always takes a leap of faith to believe that you will always be able to invent that next new thing.

But that is our mission—and our best hope. That is what President Kennedy understood. It is what Steve Jobs, Marc Andreessen, Shirley Ann Jackson, Michael Dell, Craig Barrett, and Bill Gates understand. The *only* way we are going to keep our standard of living rising is to build a society that produces people who can keep inventing the future. But as knowledge hurtles forward, inventing the future becomes a harder and harder task—one that takes more of the right education, the right infrastructure, the right ambition, the right leadership, the right parenting. We need to get our whole country focused around meeting this challenge.

The future won't wait for us, and if we don't invent it, someone else will. Because, as Jerry Rao will also tell you, India and China will be doing tomorrow what America does today, but, thanks to the flat-world platform, the day after tomorrow, India, China, and many others will also be inventing the future. As I have tried to stress, Globalization 3.0, which brought us to this flattening world, is not just Globalization 2.0 intensified. It is a whole different model. It is not just about the ability of developed countries to tap into more markets or access more cheap labor. It is a difference in degree so great—the degree of low-cost interconnectivity, the degree of individual empowerment, the degree of global networks for collaboration—that it is a *difference in kind*. It changes everything about who can compete and how they compete. An essay in the November 2005 *Mercer Management Journal*, "Are You Enjoying Globalization Yet?" summed up those differences well, noting that the flat world gives more people in more places the ability to pull together low-cost labor and high-power technology. We have never seen that combination before—and it alone is already a challenge to developed countries. But the Indias and Chinas are increasingly adding one more thing to low-cost labor and high-power technology: unfettered imagination—that is, high innovative and creative capacities. They will focus first on solving their own problems with cheap labor, high technology, and high creativity— re-imagining their own futures. Then they will focus on ours. We must have people, lots of people, who can do the same. So, for the last time, you have been warned. This is not a test.

Developing Countries and the Flat World

TEN

The Virgin of Guadalupe

It's not that we are becoming more Anglo-Saxon. It's that we are having an encounter with reality.

— Frank Schirrmacher, publisher of the German newspaper *Frankfurter*
Allgemeine Zeitung, commenting to *The New York Times* about the need
for German workers to retool and work longer hours

Seek knowledge even unto China.

— saying of the Prophet Muhammad

The more I worked on this book, the more I found myself asking
people I met around the world where they were when they first
discovered that the world was flat.

In the space of two weeks, I got two revealing answers, one from
Mexico, one from Egypt. I was in Mexico City in the spring of 2004, and
I put the question on the table during lunch with a few Mexican journalist colleagues. One of them said he realized that he was living in a
new world when he started seeing reports appearing in the Mexican media and on the Internet that some statuettes of Mexico's patron saint, the
Virgin of Guadalupe, were being imported into Mexico from China,
probably via ports in California. When you are Mexico and your claim
to fame is that you are a low-wage manufacturing country, and some of
your people are importing statuettes of your own patron saint from

China, because China can make them and ship them all the way across the Pacific more cheaply than you can produce them, you are living in a flat world.

You've also got a problem. Over at the Central Bank of Mexico, I asked its governor, Guillermo Ortiz, whether he was aware of this issue. He rolled his eyes and told me that for some time now just by staring at the numbers on his computer screen he could feel the competitive playing field being leveled—and see that Mexico was losing some of its natural geographic advantages with the U.S. market. "We started looking at the numbers in 2001—it was the first year in two decades that [Mexico's] exports to the U.S. declined," said Ortiz. "That was a real shock. We started reducing our gains in market share and then started losing them. We said that there is a real change here . . . And it was about China."

China is such a powerhouse of low-cost manufacturing that even though the NAFTA accord has given Mexico a leg up with the United States, and even though Mexico is right next door to us, China in 2003 replaced Mexico as the number two exporter to the United States. (Canada remains number one.) Though Mexico still has a strong position in big-ticket exports that are costly to ship, such as cars, auto parts, and refrigerators, China is coming on strong and has already displaced Mexico in areas such as computer parts, electrical components, toys, textiles, sporting goods, and tennis shoes. But what's even worse for Mexico is that China is displacing some Mexican companies in Mexico, where Chinese-made clothing and toys are now showing up on store shelves everywhere. No wonder a Mexican journalist told me about the day he interviewed a Chinese central bank official, who told him something about China's relationship with America that really rattled him: "First we were afraid of the wolf, then we wanted to dance with the wolf, and now we want to be the wolf."

A few days after returning from Mexico, I had breakfast in Washington with a friend from Egypt, Lamees El-Hadidy, a longtime business reporter in Cairo. Naturally I asked her where she was when she discovered the world was flat. She answered that it was just a few weeks earlier, during the Muslim holy month of Ramadan. She had done a story for CNBC Arabiya Television about the colorful lanterns called *fawanis*, each with a burning candle inside, that Egyptian schoolchildren traditionally carried around during Ramadan, a tradition dating back centuries to the Fatimid period in Egypt. Kids swing the lanterns and sing songs, and people give them candy or gifts, as in America on Halloween. For centuries, small, low-wage workshops in Cairo's older neighborhoods have manufactured these lanterns—until the last few years.

That was when plastic Chinese-made Ramadan lanterns, each with a battery-powered light instead of a candle, began flooding the market, crippling the traditional Egyptian workshops. Said Lamees, "They are invading our tradition—in an innovative way—and we are doing nothing about it . . . These lanterns come out of our tradition, our soul, but [the Chinese versions] are more creative and advanced than the Egyptian ones." Lamees said that when she asked Egyptians, "Do you know where these are made?" they would all answer no. Then they would turn the lamps over and see that they came from China.

Many mothers, like Lamees, though, appreciated the fact that the Chinese versions are safer than the traditional Egyptian ones, which are made with sharp metal edges and glass, and usually still use candles. The Chinese versions are made of plastic and feature flashing lights and have an embedded microchip that plays traditional Egyptian Ramadan tunes and even the theme song to the popular Ramadan TV cartoon series *Bakkar*. As *Business Monthly*, published by the American Chamber of Commerce in Egypt, reported in its December 2001 issue, Chinese importers "are pitted not only against each other, but also against the several-hundred-year-old Egyptian industry. But the Chinese models are destined to prevail, according to [a] famous importer, Taha Zayat. 'Imports have definitely cut down on sales of traditional fawanis,' he said. 'Of all fawanis on the market, I don't think that more than 5 percent are now made in Egypt.' People with ties to the Egyptian [fawanis] industry believe China has a clear advantage over Egypt. With its superior technology, they said, China can make mass quantities, which helps to keep prices relatively low. Egypt's traditional [fawanis] industry, by contrast, is characterized by a series of workshops specialized in different stages of the production process. Glassmakers, painters, welders and metal craftsmen all have their role to play. 'There will always be fawanis in Ramadan, but in the future I think Egyptian-made ones could become extinct,' Zayat said. 'There is no way they can ever compete with things made in China.'"

Think how crazy that statement is: Egypt has masses of low-wage workers, like China. It sits right next to Europe, on the Suez Canal. It could be and should be the Taiwan of the eastern Mediterranean, but instead it is throwing in the towel to atheistic China on the manufacture of one of Muslim Egypt's most cherished cultural artifacts. Ibrahim El Esway, one of the main importers from China of fawanis, gave *Business Monthly* a tour of his warehouse in the Egyptian town of Muski: He had imported sixteen different models of Ramadan lanterns from China in 2004. "Amid the crowds at Muski, [El Esway] gestured to one of his employees, who promptly opened a dust-covered box and pulled out a plastic fawanis shaped like the head of Simba, from *The Lion King.* 'This is the first model we imported back in 1994,' he said. He switched it on. As the blue-colored lion's head lit up, the song 'It's a Small World' rang out."

INTROSPECTION

The previous section of this book looked at how individuals, particularly Americans, should think about meeting the challenge posed by the flattening of the world. This chapter focuses on what sort of policies developing countries need to undertake in order to create the right environment for their companies and entrepreneurs to thrive in a flat world, although many of the things I am about to say apply to many developed countries as well.

When developing countries start thinking about the challenge of flatism, the first thing they need to do is engage in some brutally honest introspection. A country, its people and leaders alike, has to be honest with itself and look clearly at exactly where it stands in relation to other countries and in relation to the ten flatteners. It has to ask itself, "To what extent is my country advancing or being left behind by the flattening of the world, and to what extent is it adapting to and taking advantage of all the new platforms for collaboration and competition?" As that Chinese banking official boasted to my Mexican colleague, China is the wolf. Of all the ten flatteners, the entry of China into the world market is the most important for developing countries, and for many developed countries. China can do high-quality low-cost manufacturing better than any other country, and increasingly, it also can do high-quality higher-cost manufacturing. With China and the other nine flatteners coming on so strong, no country today can afford to be anything less than brutally honest with itself.

To that end, I believe that what the world needs today is a club that would be modeled after Alcoholics Anonymous (A.A.). It would be called Developing Countries Anonymous (D.C.A.). And just as at the first A.A. meeting you attend you have to stand up and say, "My name is Thomas Friedman and I'm an alcoholic," so at Developing Countries Anonymous, countries would have to stand up at their first meeting and say, "My name is Syria and I'm underdeveloped." Or "My name is Argentina and I'm underachieving. I have not lived up to my potential."

Every country needs "the ability to make [its] own introspection," since "no country develops without going through an X-ray of where you are and where your limits are," said Luis de la Calle, one of Mexico's chief NAFTA crafters and negotiators. Countries that fall off the development wagon are a bit like drunks; to get back on they have to learn to see themselves as they really are. Development is a voluntary process. You need a positive decision to make the right steps, but it starts with introspection—looking brutally honestly at your strengths and your weaknesses, and exactly what both will mean in a flattening world.

"When you and I were born," de la Calle said to me, "our competition [was] our next-door neighbors. Today our competition is a Japanese or a Frenchman or a Chinese. You know where you rank very quickly in a flat world . . . You are now competing with everyone else." The best talent in a flat world will earn more, he added, "and if you don't measure up, someone will replace you—and it will not be the guy across the street."

I Can Get It for You Wholesale

As I have tried to argue throughout this book, a country's decision to develop when the world becomes flat is really a decision to focus on getting four basic things right. The first is the right infrastructure to connect more of your people with the flat-world platform—from cheap Internet bandwidth and mobile phones to modern airports and roads. The second is the right educational system to get more of your people innovating and collaborating on the flat-world platform. The third is the right governance—from fiscal policy to the rule of law to the quality of the bureaucracy—to manage the flow between your people and the flat-world platform in the most productive way possible. This point is often lost. With all the discussion about the economics of globalization, people lose sight of the fact that *globalization is also a competition between one country's public sector and another's.* That is, you need a quality bureaucracy to channel, govern, and enhance the creative energies of a country so your people, as individuals, can not only imagine new products and services but also bring them to life and take them to the marketplace. Fourth, you need the right environment. You can get along as a country for a number of years while despoiling your environment. But at the end of the day, countries that preserve their green spaces are much more likely to preserve and attract the knowledge workers—who are mobile, have choices, and can make the decisive difference in turning a developing economy into a developed one.

During the late 1970s, but particularly after the fall of the Berlin Wall, as the world really started to flatten out, a lot of countries began trying to reform themselves accordingly. They focused on improving education and infrastructure and, in particular, adopting better governance. But most of the focus in the area of governance was really about adopting more market-friendly macroeconomic policies. I call this "reform wholesale." The era of Globalization 2.0, when the world shrank from a size medium to a size small, was the era of reform wholesale, an era of broad macroeconomic reform. These wholesale reforms were initiated by a small handful of leaders in countries such as China, Russia, Mexico,

Brazil, and India. These small groups of reformers often relied on the leverage of authoritarian political systems to unleash the state-smothered market forces in their societies. They pushed their countries into more export-oriented, free-market strategies—based on privatization of state companies, deregulation of financial markets, currency adjustments, foreign direct investment, shrinking subsidies, lowering of protectionist tariff barriers, and introduction of more flexible labor laws—from the top down without ever really asking the people. Ernesto Zedillo, who served as president of Mexico from 1994 to 2000 and was minister of planning and budget before that, once remarked to me that all the decisions to open the Mexican economy were taken by three people. How many people do you suppose Deng Xiaoping consulted before he declared, "To get rich is glorious," and uncorked the Chinese economy, or when he dismissed those who questioned China's move from communism to free markets by saying that what mattered was jobs and incomes, not ideology? Deng tossed over decades of Communist ideology with one sentence: "Black cat, white cat, all that matters is that it catches mice." In 1991, when India's finance minister, Manmohan Singh, took the first tentative steps to open India's economy to more foreign trade, investment, and competition, it was a result not of some considered national debate and dialogue, but of the fact that India's economy at that moment was so sclerotic, so unappealing to foreign investors, that it had almost run out of foreign currency. When Mikhail Gorbachev started dabbling with perestroika, it was with his back up against the Kremlin wall and with few allies in the Soviet leadership. The same was true of Margaret Thatcher when she took on the striking coal miners' union in 1984 and forced reform wholesale onto the sagging British economy.

What all these leaders confronted was the irrefutable fact that more open and competitive markets are the only sustainable vehicle for growing a nation out of poverty, because they are the only guarantee that new ideas, technologies, and best practices will easily flow into your country and that private enterprises, and even government, will have the competitive incentive and flexibility to adopt those new ideas and turn them into jobs and products. This is why the nonglobalizing countries, those

that refused to do any reform wholesale—North Korea, for instance—
actually saw their per capita GDP growth shrink in the 1990s, while
countries that moved from a more socialist model to a globalizing model
saw their per capita GDP grow in the 1990s. As David Dollar and Art
Kray conclude in their book *Trade, Growth, and Poverty*, economic
growth and trade remain the best antipoverty program in the world.

The World Bank reported that in 1990 there were roughly 375 million
people in China living in extreme poverty, on less than $1 per day. By 2001,
there were 212 million Chinese living in extreme poverty, and by 2015, if
current trends hold, there will be only 16 million living on less than $1 a
day. In South Asia—primarily India, Pakistan, and Bangladesh—the numbers go from 462 million in 1990 living on less than $1 a day down to
431 million by 2001 and down to 216 million in 2015. In sub-Saharan
Africa, by contrast, where globalization has been slow to take hold, there
were 227 million people living on less than $1 a day in 1990, 313 million
in 2001, and an expected 340 million by 2015.

The problem for any globalizing country lies in thinking that it can
stop with reform wholesale. In the 1990s, some countries thought that if
they got their ten commandments of economic reform wholesale right—
thou shall privatize state-owned industries, thou shall deregulate utilities,
thou shall lower tariffs and encourage export industries, etc.—they had a
successful development strategy. But as the world started to get smaller
and flatter—enabling China to compete everywhere with everyone on a
broad range of manufactured products, enabling India to export its
brainpower everywhere, enabling corporations to outsource any task anywhere, and enabling individuals to compete globally as never before—
reform wholesale, confined largely to macroeconomics, was no longer
sufficient to keep countries on a sustainable growth path. A deeper
process of reform was required—one that would transform education, infrastructure, and governance in a much more profound manner.

I Can Only Get It for You Retail

What if regions of the world were like the neighborhoods of a city? What would the world look like? I'd describe it like this: Western Europe would be an assisted-living facility, with an aging population lavishly attended to by Turkish nurses. The United States would be a gated community, with a metal detector at the front gate and a lot of people sitting in their front yards complaining about how lazy everyone else was, even though out back there was a small opening in the fence for Mexican labor and other energetic immigrants who helped to make the gated community function. Latin America would be the fun part of town, the club district, where the workday doesn't begin until ten p.m. and everyone sleeps until midmorning. It's definitely the place to hang out, but in between the clubs, you don't see a lot of new businesses opening up, except on the street where the Chileans live. The landlords in this neighborhood almost never reinvest their profits here, but keep them in a bank across town. The Arab street would be a dark alley where outsiders fear to tread, except for a few side streets called Dubai, Jordan, Bahrain, Qatar, and Morocco. The only new businesses are gas stations, whose owners, like the elites in the Latin neighborhood, rarely reinvest their funds in the neighborhood. Many people on the Arab street have their curtains closed, their shutters drawn, and signs on their front lawn that say, "No Trespassing. Beware of Dog." India, China, and East Asia would be "the other side of the tracks." Their neighborhood is a big teeming market, made up of small shops and one-room factories, interspersed with Stanley Kaplan SAT prep schools and engineering colleges. Nobody ever sleeps in this neighborhood, everyone lives in extended families, and everyone is working and saving to get to "the right side of the tracks." On the Chinese streets, there's no rule of law, but the roads are all well paved; there are no potholes, and the streetlights all work. On the Indian streets, by contrast, no one ever repairs the streetlights, the roads are full of ruts, but the police are sticklers for the rules. You need a license to open a lemonade stand on the Indian streets. Luckily, the local cops can be bribed, and the successful entrepreneurs all have their own generators to run their factories and the latest cell phones to get around the fact that the local telephone poles are all down. Africa, sadly, is that part of town where the businesses are boarded up, life expectancy is declining, and the only new buildings are health-care clinics.

My point here is that every region of the world has its strengths and weaknesses, and all are in need of reform retail to some degree. What is reform retail? In the simplest terms, it is more than just opening your country to more foreign trade and investment and making a few macroeconomic policy changes from the top. Reform retail presumes you have already done reform wholesale. It involves looking at infrastructure, education, and governance and upgrading each one, so more of your people have the tools and legal framework to innovate and collaborate at the highest levels.

Many of the key elements of reform retail were best defined by the research done by the World Bank's International Finance Corporation (IFC) and its economic analysis team led by its chief economist, Michael Klein. What do we learn from their work? To begin with, you don't grow your country out of poverty by guaranteeing everyone a job. Egypt guarantees all college graduates a job each year, and it has been mired in poverty with a slow-growing economy for fifty years.

"If it were just a matter of the number of jobs, solutions would be easy," note Klein and Bita Hadjimichael in their World Bank Study, *The Private Sector in Development*. "For example, state-owned enterprises could absorb all those in need of employment. The real issue is not just employment, but increasingly productive employment that allows living standards to rise." State-owned enterprises and state-subsidized private firms usually have not delivered sustainable productivity growth, and neither have a lot of other approaches that people assume are elixirs of growth, they add. Just attracting more foreign investment into a country also doesn't automatically do it. And even massive investments in education won't guarantee it.

"Productivity growth and, hence, the way out of poverty, is not simply a matter of throwing resources at the problem," say Klein and Hadjimichael. "More important, it is a matter of using resources well." In other words, countries grow out of poverty not only when they manage their fiscal and monetary policies responsibly from above, i.e., reform wholesale. In recent years, a lot of attention and moral concern has been devoted to the problem of persistent poverty, particularly in Africa. That is a good thing. But persistent poverty is a practical problem as well as a moral one, and we do ourselves no good to focus on our moral failings and not the practical shortcomings of the countries and governments involved. Poor people grow out of poverty when their governments create an environment in which educated workers and capitalists have the physical and legal infrastructure that makes it easy to start businesses, raise capital, and become entrepreneurs, and when they subject their people to at least some competition from beyond—because companies and countries with competitors always innovate more, better, and faster.

The IFC drove home this point with a comprehensive study of more than 130 countries, called *Doing Business in 2004.* The IFC asked five basic questions about doing business in each of these countries, questions about how easy or difficult it is to (1) start a business in terms of local rules, regulations, and license fees, (2) hire and fire workers, (3) enforce a contract, (4) get credit, and (5) close a business that goes bankrupt or is failing. To translate it into my own lexicon, those countries that make all these things relatively simple and friction-free have undertaken reform retail, and those that have not are stalled in reform wholesale and are not likely to thrive in a flat world. The IFC's criteria were inspired by the brilliant and innovative work of Hernando de Soto, who has demonstrated in Peru and other developing nations that if you change the regulatory and business environment for the poor, and give them the tools to collaborate, they will do the rest.

Doing Business in 2004 tries to explain each of its points with a few colorful examples:

Teuku, an entrepreneur in Jakarta, wants to open a textile factory. He has customers lined up, imported machinery, and a promising business plan. Teuku's first encounter with the government is when registering his business. He gets the standard forms from the Ministry of Justice, and completes and notarizes them. Teuku proves that he is a local resident and does not have a criminal record. He obtains a tax number, applies for a business license, and deposits the minimum capital (three times national income per capita) in the bank. He then publishes the articles of association in the official gazette, pays a stamp fee, registers at the Ministry of Justice, and waits 90 days before filing for social security. One hundred sixty-eight days after he commences the process, Teuku can legally start operations. In the meantime, his customers have contracted with another business.

In Panama, another entrepreneur, Ina, registers her construction company in only 19 days. Business is booming and Ina wants to hire someone for a two-year appointment. But the employment law only allows fixed-term appointments for specific tasks, and even then requires a maximum term of one year. At the same time, one of her current workers often leaves early, with no excuse, and makes costly mistakes. To replace him, Ina needs to notify and get approval from the union, and pay five months' severance pay. Ina rejects the more qualified applicant she would like to hire and keeps the underperforming worker on staff.

Ali, a trader in the United Arab Emirates, can hire and fire with ease. But one of his customers refuses to pay for equipment delivered three months earlier. It takes 27 procedures and more than 550 days to resolve the payment dispute in court. Almost all procedures must be made in writing, and require extensive legal justification and the use of lawyers. After this experience, Ali decides to deal only with customers he knows well.

Timnit, a young entrepreneur in Ethiopia, wants to expand her successful consulting business by taking a loan. But she has no proof of good credit history because there are no credit information registries. Although her business has substantial assets in accounts receivable, laws restrict her bank from using these as collateral. The bank knows it cannot recover the debt if Timnit defaults, because courts are inefficient and laws give creditors few powers. Credit is denied. The business stays small.

Having registered, hired workers, enforced contracts, and obtained credit, Avik, a businessman in India, cannot make a profit and goes out of business. Faced with a 10-year-long process of going through bankruptcy, Avik absconds, leaving his workers, the bank, and the tax agency with nothing.

If you want to know why two decades of macroeconomic reform wholesale at the top have not slowed the spread of poverty and produced enough new jobs in key countries of Latin America, Africa, the Arab world, and the former Soviet Empire, it is because there has been too little reform retail. According to the IFC report, if you want to create productive jobs (the kind that lead to rising standards of living), and if you want to stimulate the growth of new businesses (the kind that innovate, compete, and create wealth), you need a regulatory environment that makes it easy to start a business, easy to adjust a business to changing market circumstances and opportunities, and easy to close a business that goes bankrupt, so that the capital can be freed up for more productive uses.

"It takes two days to start a business in Australia, but 203 days in Haiti and 215 days in the Democratic Republic of Congo," the IFC study found. "There are no monetary costs to start a new business in Denmark, but it costs more than five times income per capita in Cambodia and over thirteen times in Sierra Leone. Hong Kong, Singapore, Thailand and more than three dozen other economies require no minimum capital from start-ups. In contrast, in Syria the capital requirement is equivalent to fifty-six times income per capita . . . Businesses in the Czech Republic and Denmark can hire workers on part-time or fixed-term contracts for any job, without specifying maximum duration of the contract. In contrast, employment laws in El Salvador allow fixed-term contracts only for specific jobs, and set their duration to be at most one year . . . A simple commercial contract is enforced in seven days in Tunisia and thirty-nine days in the Netherlands, but takes almost 1,500 days in Guatemala. The cost of enforcement is less than 1 percent of the disputed amount in Austria, Canada and the United Kingdom, but more than 100 percent in Burkina Faso, the Dominican Republic, Indonesia . . . and the Philippines. Credit bureaus contain credit histories on almost every adult in New Zealand, Norway and the United States. But the credit registries in Cameroon, Ghana, Pakistan, Nigeria and Serbia and Montenegro have credit histories for less than 1 percent of adults. In the United Kingdom, laws on collateral and bankruptcy give creditors strong powers to recover their money if a debtor defaults. In Colombia, the Republic of Congo, Mexico, Oman and Tunisia, a creditor has no such rights. It takes less than six months to go through bankruptcy proceedings in Ireland and Japan, but more than ten years in Brazil and India. It costs less than 1 percent of the value of the estate to resolve insolvency in Finland, the Netherlands, Norway and Singapore—and nearly half the estate value in Chad, Panama, Macedonia, Venezuela, Serbia and Montenegro, and Sierra Leone."

As the IFC report notes, excessive regulation also tends to hurt most the very people it is supposed to protect. The rich and the well connected just buy or hustle their way around onerous regulations. In countries that have very regulated labor markets where it is difficult to hire and fire people, women, especially, have a hard time finding employment.

"Good regulation does not mean zero regulation," concludes the IFC study. "The optimal level of regulation is not none, but may be less than what is currently found in most countries, and especially poor ones." The study offers what I call a five-step checklist for reform retail. One, simplify and deregulate wherever possible in competitive markets, because competition for consumers and workers can be the best source of pressure for best practices, and overregulation just opens the door for corrupt bureaucrats to demand bribes. "There is no reason for Angola to have one of the most rigid employment laws if Portugal, whose laws Angola adapted, has already revised them twice to make the labor market more flexible," says the IFC study. Two, focus on enhancing property rights. Under de Soto's initiative, the Peruvian government in the last decade has issued property titles to 1.2 million urban squatter households. "Secure property rights have enabled parents to leave their homes and find jobs instead of staying in to protect the property," says the IFC study. "The main beneficiaries are their children, who can now go to school." Three, expand the use of the Internet for regulation fulfillment. It makes it faster, more transparent, and far less open to bribery. Four, reduce court involvement in business matters. And last but certainly not least, advises the IFC study, "Make reform a continuous process . . . Countries that consistently perform well across the *Doing Business* indicators do so because of continuous reform."

What is striking about the IFC's criteria is that many people think they are relevant only for Peru and Argentina, but in fact some of the countries that score worst are places like Germany and Italy. (Indeed, the German government protested some of the findings.)

FOLLOW THE LEAPIN' LEPRECHAUNS

One of the best examples of a country that has made a huge leap forward by choosing development and reform retail of its governance, infrastructure, and education is Ireland. Here's something you probably didn't know: Ireland today is the richest country in the European Union after Luxembourg. Yes, the country that for hundreds of years was best known for emigration, tragic poets, famines, civil wars, and leprechauns today has a per capita GDP higher than that of Germany, France, and Britain. How Ireland went from the sick man of Europe to the rich man in less than a generation is an amazing story. Ireland's turnaround actually began in the late 1960s, when the government eliminated the fee for secondary education, enabling a lot more working-class kids to get a high school or technical degree. As a result, in the years after Ireland joined the European Community in 1973, it was able to draw on a much more educated workforce than it had had in the previous generation. By the mid-1980s, though, Ireland had reaped the initial benefits of EC membership—subsidies to build better infrastructure and a bigger market to sell its products into. But it did not have enough competitive products to sell, because of the legacy of years of protectionism and fiscal mismanagement. The country was going broke, and most college grads were emigrating. It hadn't gotten its governance right.

"We went on a borrowing, spending, and taxing spree, and that nearly drove us under," Deputy Prime Minister Mary Harney told me while I was on a visit to Dublin in June 2005. "It was because we nearly went under that we got the courage to change." And change Ireland did. In a quite unusual development, the government, the main trade unions, farmers, and industrialists came together and agreed on a program of fiscal austerity, slashing corporate taxes to 12.5 percent (far below the rest

of Europe), moderating wages and prices, and aggressively courting foreign investment. In 1996, Ireland made public college education basically free, creating an even more educated workforce. The results have
been striking. Today, nine of the world's ten top pharmaceutical companies have operations in Ireland, as do sixteen of the top twenty medical
device companies and seven of the top ten software firms. In 2004,
Ireland got more foreign direct investment from America than China got
from America. And overall government tax receipts have risen steadily.

"We set up in Ireland in 1990," Michael Dell, founder of Dell
Computer, explained to me in an e-mail. "What attracted us? [A] well-
educated workforce—and good universities close by. [Also,] Ireland has
an industrial and tax policy which is consistently very supportive of businesses, independent of which political party is in power. I believe this is
because there are enough people who remember the very bad times to
de-politicize economic development. [Ireland also has] very good transportation and logistics and a good location—easy to move products to
major markets in Europe quickly." Finally, added Dell, "they're competitive, want to succeed, hungry and know how to win. Our factory is in
Limerick, but we also have several thousand sales and technical people
outside of Dublin. The talent in Ireland has proven to be a wonderful resource for us. Fun fact: We are Ireland's largest exporter."

Intel opened its first chip factory in Ireland in 1993. James Jarrett, an
Intel vice president, said Intel was attracted by Ireland's large pool of educated young men and women, low corporate taxes, and other incentives
that saved Intel roughly $1 billion over ten years. Ireland's national health
care—which certainly lightens Intel's health coverage obligations—didn't
hurt, either. "We have forty-seven hundred employees there now in four
factories, and we are even doing some high-end chip designing in
Shannon with Irish engineers," he said.

Harry Kraemer Jr., the former CEO of Baxter International, a medical
equipment maker that has made several investments in Ireland, explained
that "the energy level, the work ethic, the tax optimization, and the flexibility of the labor supply" all made Ireland infinitely more attractive to invest in than France or Germany, where it is enormously costly to fire even
one worker. The Irish, he added, had the self-confidence that if they kept

their labor laws flexible, some jobs would go, but new jobs would keep coming—and that is exactly what has happened. Ireland is "playing offense," Kraemer said, while Germany and France are "playing defense," and the more they try to protect every old job, the fewer new ones they attract. Look at the results: In 1990, Ireland's total workforce was 1.1 million. By the end of 2005, it was roughly 2 million, with no real unemployment.

But Ireland has started to play offense in a lot of other ways as well. It initially focused on attracting investments from U.S. high-tech companies by offering them quality infrastructure, a flexible, educated workforce, and low corporate taxes. But now, explained Ireland's minister of education, Mary Hanafin, the country wants to take reform retail in education to a new level. It has started a campaign to double the number of Ph.D.'s it graduates in science and engineering by 2010, and it has set up various funds to get global companies, and brainy people of all kinds, to come to Ireland to do research. Ireland is now actively recruiting Chinese scientists in particular. "It is good for our own quality students to be mixing with quality students from abroad," Hanafin said. "Industry will go where the major research goes." Ireland set up a science foundation to give grants to any researcher from anywhere in the world who had an idea that he or she would pursue in Ireland and that might one day produce a company or a product. Between 2001 and 2005, Science Foundation Ireland established more than 160 new research groups, 34 of them led by leading scientists who have come to Ireland from laboratories abroad, according to an independent report commissioned by the Irish government. Incidentally, the first head of Science Foundation Ireland was an American who had worked at the National Science Foundation.

Ireland's story underscores the fact that capital does not just move around the world looking for the cheapest labor. If it did, all the jobs would be in Haiti and Bangladesh. It is looking for the most productive labor at the lowest price, which means that in order to attract the capital, your country has to get those four basics—infrastructure, education, governance, and environment—right. John Chambers, the CEO of Cisco Systems, which uses a global supply chain to build the routers that run the Internet and is constantly being wooed to invest in one country or another, said it best: "The jobs are going to go where the best-educated workforce is with the most competitive infrastructure and environment for creativity and supportive government. It is inevitable. And by definition those people will have the best standard of living. This may or may not be the countries who led the Industrial Revolution."

Indeed, Sir John Rose, the chief executive of Rolls-Royce, once remarked to me that in what I call the flat world we will speak less and less about "developed, developing, and underdeveloped countries" and more and more about "smart, smarter, and smartest countries."

At least some countries are paying attention. Ireland's prime minister, Bertie Ahern, told me in June 2005, "I've met the premier of China five times in the last two years."

CULTURE MATTERS: GLOCALIZATION

While the stakes in reform retail today are higher than ever, and most countries know it, one need only look around the world to notice that not every country can pull it off. Unlike reform wholesale, which could be done by a handful of people using administrative orders or just authoritarian dictates, reform retail requires a much wider base of public and parliamentary buy-in if it is going to overcome vested economic and political interests. So why do some countries get over this reform retail hump, with leaders able to mobilize their people to really improve their infrastructure, education, and governance, and other countries stall?

One answer is culture.

To reduce a country's economic performance to culture alone is ridiculous, but to analyze a country's economic performance without reference to culture is equally ridiculous, although that is what many economists and political scientists want to do. This subject is highly controversial and is viewed as politically incorrect to introduce. So it is often the elephant in the room that no one wants to speak about. But I am going to speak about it here, for a very simple reason: As the world goes flat, and more and more of the tools of collaboration get distributed and commoditized, the gap between cultures that have the will, the way, and the focus to quickly adopt these new tools and apply them and those that do not will matter more. The differences between the two will become amplified.

Two books strongly influenced my thinking in this regard. One is *The Wealth and Poverty of Nations*, by the economist David Landes. He argues that although climate, natural resources, and geography all help to explain why some countries are able to make the leap to industrialization and others are not, the key factor is actually a country's cultural endowments, particularly the degree to which it has internalized the values of hard work, thrift, honesty, patience, and tenacity, as well as the degree to which it is open to change, new technology, and equality for women. The other book is *The Central Liberal Truth: How Politics Can Change a Culture and Save It from Itself* by Lawrence E. Harrison, a retired USAID diplomat who is now a professor at Tufts. Harrison argues that a society maintains cultural continuity through a variety of instruments and institutions "that transmit its values and attitudes from generation to generation [through] child-rearing, education, the media, and leadership," as well as religion, which may be the most salient of all. Indeed, Harrison argues that "when it comes to the relationship between religion and human progress, I find compelling evidence that some religions do better than others in promoting the goals of democratic politics, social justice and prosperity." Some religions and cultures are "progress prone," argues Harrison, and some are "progress resistant," but history is full of examples of cultures changing from one to the other under different political and economic circumstances or leaders.

In my own travels, two aspects of culture have struck me as particularly relevant in the flat world. One is how outward your culture is: To what degree is it open to foreign influences and ideas? How well does it "glocalize"? The other, more intangible, is how inward your culture is. By that I mean, to what degree is there a sense of national solidarity and a focus on development, to what degree is there trust within the society for strangers to collaborate together, and to what degree are the elites in the country concerned with the masses and ready to invest at home, or are they indifferent to their own poor and more interested in investing abroad?

The more you have a culture that naturally glocalizes—that is, the more your culture easily absorbs foreign ideas and global best practices and melds those with its own traditions—the greater advantage you will have in a flat world. The natural ability to glocalize has been one of the strengths of Indian culture, American culture, Japanese culture, and, lately, Chinese culture. The Indians, for instance, take the view that the Moguls come, the Moguls go, the British come, the British go, we take the best and leave the rest—but we still eat curry, our women still wear saris, and we still live in tightly bound extended family units. That's glocalizing at its best.

"Cultures that are open and willing to change have a huge advantage in this world," said Jerry Rao, the MphasiS CEO who heads the Indian high-tech trade association. "My great-grandmother was illiterate. My grandmother went to grade two. My mother did not go to college. My sister has a master's degree in economics, and my daughter is at the University of Chicago. We have done all this in living memory, but we have been willing to change . . . You have to have a strong culture, but also the openness to adapt and adopt from others. The cultural exclusivists have a real disadvantage. Think about it, think about the time when the emperor in China threw out the British ambassador. Who did it hurt? It hurt the Chinese. Exclusivity is a dangerous thing."

Openness is critical, added Rao, "because you start tending to respect people for their talent and abilities. When you are chatting with another developer in another part of the world, you don't know what his or her color is. You are dealing with people on the basis of talent—not race or ethnicity—and that changes, subtly, over time your whole view of human beings, if you are in this talent-based and performance-based world rather than the background-based world."

This helps explain why so many Muslim countries have been struggling as the world goes flat. For complicated cultural and historical reasons, many of them do not glocalize well, although there are plenty of exceptions—namely, Turkey, Lebanon, Bahrain, Dubai, Indonesia, and Malaysia. All of these latter countries, though, tend to be the more secu-

lar Muslim nations. In a world where the single greatest advantage a culture can have is the ability to foster adaptability and adoptability, the
Muslim world today is dominated by a religious clergy that literally bans
ijtihad, reinterpretation of the principles of Islam in light of current
circumstances.

Think about the whole mind-set of bin Ladenism. It is to "purge"
Saudi Arabia of all foreigners and foreign influences. That is exactly the
opposite of glocalizing and collaborating. Tribal culture and thinking
still dominate in many Arab countries, and the tribal mind-set is also
anathema to collaboration. What is the motto of the tribalist? "Me and
my brother against my cousin; me, my brother, and my cousin against
the outsider." And what is the motto of the globalists, those who build
collaborative supply chains? "Me and my brother and my cousin, three
friends from childhood, four people in Australia, two in Beijing, six in
Bangalore, three from Germany, and four people we've met only over
the Internet all make up a single global supply chain." In the flat world,
the division of labor is steadily becoming more and more complex, with
a lot more people interacting with a lot of other people they don't know
and may never meet. If you want to have a modern complex division of
labor, you have to be able to put more trust in strangers.

In the Arab-Muslim world, argues David Landes, certain cultural attitudes have in many ways become a barrier to development, particularly
the tendency to still treat women as a source of danger or pollution to be
cut off from the public space and denied entry into economic activities.
When a culture believes that, it loses a large portion of potential productivity of the society. A system that privileges the men from birth on,
Landes also argues, simply because they are male, and gives them power
over their sisters and other female members of society, is bad for the men.
It builds in them a sense of entitlement that discourages what it takes to
improve, to advance, and to achieve. This sort of discrimination, he
notes, is not something limited to the Arab Middle East, of course.
Indeed, strains of it are found in different degrees all around the world,
even in so-called advanced industrial societies.

The Arab-Muslim world's resistance to glocalization is something that
some liberal Arab commentators are now focusing on. Consider a May 5,

2004, article in the Saudi English-language daily *Arab News* by liberal
Saudi journalist Raid Qusti, titled "How Long Before the First Step?"

"Terrorist incidents in Saudi Arabia are more or less becoming everyday news. Every time I hope and pray that it ends, it only seems to get
worse," Qusti wrote. "One explanation to why all of this is happening was
brought up by the editor in chief of *Al-Riyadh* newspaper, Turki Al-Sudairi,
on a program about determining the roots of the terrorist acts. He said that
the people carrying out these attacks shared the ideology of the Juhaiman
movement that seized the Grand Mosque in the seventies. They had an
ideology of accusing others of being infidels and giving themselves a free
hand to kill them, be it Westerners—who, according to them, ought to be
kicked out of the Arabian Peninsula—or the Muslim believer who does
not follow their path. They disappeared in the eighties and nineties from
the public eye and have again emerged with their destructive ideology.
The question Al-Sudairi forgot to bring up was: What are we Saudis going
to do about it? If we as a nation decline to look at the root causes, as we
have for the past two decades, it will only be a matter of time before another group of people with the same ideology springs up. Have we helped
create these monsters? Our education system, which does not stress tolerance of other faiths—let alone tolerance of followers of other Islamic
schools of thought—is one thing that needs to be re-evaluated from top to
bottom. Saudi culture itself and the fact that the majority of us do not accept other lifestyles and impose our own on other people is another. And
the fact that from fourth to 12th grade we do not teach our children that
there are other civilizations in the world and that we are part of the global
community and only stress the Islamic empires over and over is also
worth re-evaluating."

It is simply too easily forgotten that when it comes to economic activities, one of the greatest virtues a country or community can have is a culture
of tolerance. When tolerance is the norm, everyone flourishes—because
tolerance breeds trust, and trust is the foundation of innovation and entrepreneurship. Increase the level of trust in any group, company, or
society, and only good things happen. "China began its astounding commercial and industrial takeoff only when Mao Zedong's odiously intolerant form of communism was scrapped in favor of what might be called

totalitarian laissez-faire," wrote the British historian Paul Johnson in a June 21, 2004, essay in *Forbes*. "India is another example. It is the nature of the Hindu religion to be tolerant and, in its own curious way, permissive . . . When left to themselves, Indians (like the Chinese) always prosper as a community. Take the case of Uganda's Indian population, which was expelled by the horrific dictator Idi Amin and received into the tolerant society of Britain. There are now more millionaires in this group than in any other recent immigrant community in Britain. They are a striking example of how far hard work, strong family bonds and devotion to education can carry a people who have been stripped of all their worldly assets." Islam, down through the years, has thrived when it fostered a culture of tolerance, as in Moorish Spain. But in its modern form, in too many cases Islam has been captured and interpreted by spiritual leaders who do not embrace a culture of tolerance, change, or innovation, and that, Johnson noted, surely has contributed to lagging economic growth in many Muslim lands.

Here we come again to the coefficient of flatness. Countries without natural resources are much more likely, through human evolution, to develop the habits of openness to new ideas, because it is the only way they can survive and advance.

The good news, though, is that not only does culture matter, but culture can change. Cultures are not wired into our human DNA. They are a product of the context—geography, education level, leadership, and historical experience—of any society. As those change, so too can culture. Japan and Germany went from highly militarized societies to highly pacifist and staunchly democratic societies in the last fifty years. Bahrain was one of the first Arab countries to discover oil. It was the first Arab country to run out of oil. And it was the first Arab country in the Arab Gulf to hold an election for parliament where women could run and vote. China during the Cultural Revolution seemed like a nation in the grip of a culture of ideological madness. China today is a synonym for pragmatism. Muslim Spain was one of the most tolerant societies in the history of the world. Muslim Saudi Arabia today is one of the most intolerant. Muslim Spain was a trading and merchant culture where people had to live by their wits and therefore learned to live well with others;

Saudi Arabia today can get by just selling oil. Yet right next to Saudi Arabia sits Dubai, an Arab city-state that has used its petrodollars to build *the* trading, tourist, service, and computing center of the Arab Gulf. Dubai is one of the most tolerant, cosmopolitan places in the world, with, it often seems, more sushi bars and golf courses than mosques—and tourists don't even need a visa. So yes, culture matters, but culture is nested in contexts, not genes, and as those contexts, and local leaders, change and adapt, so too can culture.

THE INTANGIBLE THINGS

You can tell a lot by just comparing skylines. Like many Indian Americans, Dinakar Singh, the hedge fund manager, regularly goes back to India to visit family. In the winter of 2004, he went back to New Delhi for a visit. When I saw him a few months later, he told me about the moment when he realized why India's economy as a whole still had not taken off as much as it should have—outside of the high-tech sector.

"I was on the sixth floor of a hotel in New Delhi," he recalled, "and when I looked out the window I could see for miles. How come? Because you do not have assured power in Delhi for elevators, so there are not many tall buildings." No sensible investor would want to build a tall building in a city where the power could go out at any moment and you might have to walk up twenty flights of stairs. The result is more urban sprawl and an inefficient use of space. I told Singh that his story reminded me of a trip I had just taken to Dalian, China. I had been to Dalian in 1998, and when I went back in 2004, I did not recognize the city. There were so many new buildings, including modern glass-and-steel towers, that I began to question whether I had actually visited there in 1998. Then I added another recollection. I went to school in Cairo in the summer of 1974. The three most prominent buildings in the city then were the Nile Hilton, the Cairo Tower, and the Egyptian TV building. Thirty years later, in 2004, they are still the most prominent buildings there; the Cairo skyline has barely changed. Whenever I go back to Cairo, I know exactly where I am. I visited Mexico City shortly before Dalian, where I had not visited in five years. I found it much cleaner than I had remembered, thanks to a citywide campaign by the mayor. There were also a few new buildings up, but not as many as I expected after a decade of NAFTA. Inside the buildings, though, I found my Mexican friends a little depressed. They told me that Mexico had lost its groove—it just wasn't growing like it had been, and people's self-confidence was waning.

So in Delhi, you can see forever. In Cairo, the skyline seems forever the same. In China, if you miss visiting a city for a year, it's like you haven't been there in forever. And in Mexico City, just when Mexicans thought they had turned the corner forever, they ran smack into China, coming the other way and running much faster.

What explains these differences? We know the basic formula for economic success—reform wholesale, followed by reform retail, plus good governance, education, infrastructure, and the ability to glocalize. What we don't know, though, and what I would bottle and sell if I did, is the answer to the question of why one country gets its act together to do all these things in a sustained manner and why another one doesn't. Why does one country's skyline change overnight and another's doesn't change over half a century? The only answer I have been able to find is something that cannot be defined: I call it "the intangible things." These are primarily two qualities: a society's ability and willingness to pull together and sacrifice for the sake of economic development and the presence in a society of leaders with the vision to see what needs to be done in terms of development and the willingness to use power to push for change rather than to enrich themselves and preserve the status quo. Some countries (such as South Korea and Taiwan) seem to be able to focus their energies on the priority of economic development, and others (such as Egypt and Syria) get distracted by ideology or local feuds. Some countries have leaders who use their time in office to try to drive modernization rather than to personally enrich themselves. And some countries simply have venal elites, who use their time in office to line their pockets and then invest those riches in Swiss real estate. Why India had leaders who built institutes of technology and Pakistan had leaders who did not is a product of history, geography, and culture that I can only summarize as one of those intangible things. But even though these intangibles are not easily measured, they really do matter.

The best way I know to illustrate this is by comparing Mexico and China. Mexico, on paper, seemed perfectly positioned to thrive in a flat world. It was right next door to the biggest, most powerful economy in the world. It signed a free-trade agreement with the United States and Canada in the 1990s and was poised to be a springboard to Latin America for both these huge economies. And it had a valuable natural resource in oil, which accounted for more than a third of government income. China, by contrast, was thousands of miles away, burdened by overpopulation, with few natural resources, with its best labor crowded onto a coastal plain, and with a burdensome debt legacy from fifty years of Communist rule. Ten years ago, if you took the names off these two countries and just gave someone their profiles, he surely would have bet on Mexico. And yet China has replaced Mexico as the second-largest exporter of goods into the United States. And there is a general sense, even among Mexicans, that even though China is thousands of miles away from America, it is growing closer to America economically, while Mexico, right on America's border, is becoming thousands of miles away.

I am by no means writing Mexico off. Mexico, in the fullness of time, may turn out to be the slow-but-sure tortoise to China's hare. China still has a huge political transition to get through, which could derail it at any moment. Moreover, Mexico has many entrepreneurs who are as Chinese as the most entrepreneurial Chinese. Mexico would not have exported $138 billion worth of goods to the United States in 2003 if that were not the case. And you have many rural Chinese who are no more advanced or productive than rural Mexicans. But on balance, when you add it all up, the fact is that China has become the hare and Mexico has not, even though Mexico seemed to start with so many more natural advantages when the world went flat. Why?

This is a question Mexicans themselves are asking. When you go to Mexico City these days, Mexicans will tell you that they are hearing that "giant sucking sound" in stereo. "We are caught between India and China," Jorge Castaneda, Mexico's former foreign minister, told me in

2004. "It is very difficult for us to compete with the Chinese, except with high-value-added industries. Where we should be competing, the services area, we are hit by the Indians with their back offices and call centers."

No doubt China is benefiting to some degree from the fact that it still has an authoritarian system that can steamroll vested interests and archaic practices. Beijing's leadership can order many reforms from the top down, whether it is a new road or accession to the World Trade Organization.

But China today also has better intangibles—an ability to summon and focus local energies on reform retail. China may be an authoritarian state, but it nevertheless has strong state institutions and a bureaucracy that manages to promote a lot of people on merit to key decision-making positions, and it has a certain public-spiritedness. The Mandarin tradition of promoting bureaucrats who see their role as promoting and protecting the interests of the state is still alive and well in China. "China has a tradition of meritocracy—a tradition that is also carried on in Korea and Japan," said Francis Fukuyama, author of the classic *The End of History and the Last Man*. "All of them also have a basic sense of 'stateness' where [public servants] are expected to look to the long-term interests of the state" and are rewarded by the system for doing so.

Mexico, by contrast, moved during the 1990s from a basically one-party authoritarian state to a multiparty democracy. So just when Mexico needs to summon all its will and energy for reform retail on the micro level, it has to go through the much slower, albeit more legitimate, democratic process of constituency building. In Mexico, "we did the first stages of structural reform from the top down," said Guillermo Ortiz, the Central Bank governor. "The next stage is much more difficult. You have to work from the bottom up. You have to create the wider consensus to push the reforms in a democratic context." In other words, any Mexican president who wants to make changes has to aggregate so many more interest groups—like herding cats—to implement a reform than his autocratic predecessors, who could have done it by fiat. A lot of these interest groups, whether unions or oligarchs, have powerful vested interests in the status quo and the power to strangle reforms. And Mexico's state system, like that of so many of its Latin American neighbors, has a long history of simply being an instrument of patronage for the ruling party or local interests, not the national interest.

Another of these intangible things is how much your culture prizes education. India and China both have a long tradition of parents telling their children that the greatest thing they can be in life is an engineer or a doctor. But building the schools to make that happen in Mexico simply has not been done. India and China each have more than fifty thousand students studying in the United States today. They come from about twelve time zones away. Mexico, which is smaller but right next door, has only about ten thousand. Mexico is also right next door to the world's biggest economy, which speaks English. But Mexico has not launched any crash program in English education or invested in scholarships to send large numbers of Mexican students to the United States to study. There is a "disconnect," said President Zedillo, among Mexico's political establishment, the challenges of globalization, and the degree to which anyone is educating and harnessing the Mexican public to this task. You would have to look a long time for a graduate science or math program at an American university that is dominated by Mexican students the way most are dominated by Chinese and Indian students.

It would be easy to conclude from just looking at Mexico and China that democracy may be a hindrance to reform retail. I think it is premature to conclude that. I think the real issue is leadership. There are democracies that are blessed with leaders who are able to make the sale and get their people focused on reform retail—Margaret Thatcher in England comes to mind—and there are democracies that drift for a long time without biting the bullet—modern Germany, for example. There are autocracies that really get focused—modern China—and there are others that just drift aimlessly, unwilling to summon their people because the leaders are so illegitimate they are afraid of inflicting any pain—Zimbabwe.

Mexico and Latin America generally have "fantastic potential," says President Zedillo. "Latin America was ahead of everyone thirty years ago, but for twenty-five years we have been basically stagnant and the others are moving closer and well ahead. Our political systems are not capable of processing and adopting and executing those [reform retail] ideas. We are still discussing prehistory. Things that are taken for granted everywhere we are still discussing as if we are living in the 1960s. To this day you cannot speak openly about a market economy in Latin America." China is moving every month, added Zedillo, "and we are taking years and years to decide on elementary reforms whose needs should be strikingly urgent for any human being. We are not competitive because we don't have infrastructure; you need people to pay taxes. How many new highways have been built connecting Mexico with the U.S. since NAFTA? [Virtually none.] Many people who would benefit from government expenditure don't pay taxes. The only way for government to serve is to get people to pay higher taxes, [but] then the populism comes up and kills it."

A Mexican newspaper recently ran a story about how the Converse shoe company was making tennis shoes in China using Mexican glue. "The whole article was about why are we giving them our glue," said Zedillo, "when the right attitude would be, How much more glue can we sell them? We still need to break some mental barriers."

It is not that Mexico has failed to modernize its export industries. It is losing ground to China primarily because China has changed even faster and more broadly, particularly in educating knowledge workers. As business consultant Daniel H. Rosen pointed out in an essay in The International Economy (Spring 2003), Mexico and China both saw their share of global exports grow in many of the same areas during the booming 1990s—from auto parts to electronics to toys and sporting goods— but China's share was growing faster. This was not just because of what China was doing right but also because of what Mexico was doing wrong, which was not steadily honing its competitiveness with microreforms. What Mexico succeeded in doing was to create islands of competitiveness, like Monterrey, where it got things right and could take advantage of proximity to the United States, but the Mexican government never had a strategy for melting those islands into the rest of the country. This helps explain why from 1996 to 2002, Mexico's ranking in the Global Competitiveness Report actually fell while China's rose. And this was not just about cheap wages, said Rosen. It was about China's advantages in education, privatization, infrastructure, quality control, midlevel management, and the introduction of new technology.

"So China is eating Mexico's lunch," concluded Rosen, "but more due to the Mexican inability to capitalize on successes and induce broader reform than to China's lower wage workers per se." In other words, it's reform retail, stupid. According to the *Doing Business in 2005* report, it takes an average of fifty-eight days to start a business in Mexico, compared with eight in Singapore and nine in Turkey. It takes seventy-four days to register a property in Mexico, but only twelve in the United States. Mexico's corporate income tax rate of 34 percent is twice as high as China's.

The *McKinsey Quarterly* report "Beyond Cheap Labor" noted that since 2000, as China joined the WTO and started to take advantage of the flattening of the world, Mexico lost 270,000 assembly jobs, and hundreds of factories closed. But the main advice the report had for Mexico and other middle-income countries feeling squeezed by China was this: "Rather than fixating on jobs lost to China, these countries should remember a fact of economic life: no place can remain the world's low-cost producer forever—even China will lose that title one day. Instead of trying to defend low-wage assembly jobs, Mexico and other middle-income countries should focus on creating jobs that add higher value. Only if more productive companies with higher-value-added activities replace less productive ones can middle-income economies continue down the development path."

In short, the only way for Mexico to thrive is with a strategy of reform retail that will enable it to beat China to the top, not the bottom, because China is not focused on beating Mexico as much as it is on beating America. But winning that kind of race to the top takes intangible focus and will.

You cannot maintain rising standards of living in a flattening world when you are up against competitors who are getting not only their fundamentals right but also their intangibles. China does not just want to get rich. It wants to get powerful. China doesn't just want to learn how to make GM cars. It wants to be GM and put GM out of business. Anyone who doubts that should spend time with young Chinese.

Said Luis Rubio, president of Mexico's Center of Research for Development, "The more self-confidence you have, the more it diminishes your mythologies and complexes. One of the great things about Mexico in the early 1990s was that Mexicans saw that they could do it, they could make it." A lot of that self-confidence, though, has been lost in Mexico in recent years, because the government stopped reforming. "A lack of self-confidence leads a country to keep chewing on the past," added Rubio. "A lack of self-confidence [in Mexico] means that everyone in the country thinks the U.S. is going to take Mexico to the cleaners." That is why NAFTA was so important for Mexico's self-confidence. "What NAFTA accomplished was to get Mexicans to think forward and outward instead of inward and backward. [But] NAFTA was seen [by its architects] as an end more than a beginning. It was seen as the conclusion of a process of political and economic reforms." Unfortunately, he added, "Mexico did not have a strategy for going forward."

Will Rogers said it a long time ago: "Even if you're on the right track, you'll get run over if you just sit there." The flatter the world gets, the faster that will happen. Mexico got itself on the right track with reform wholesale, but then, for a lot of tangible and intangible reasons, it just sat there and reform retail stalled. The more Mexico just sits there, the more it is going to get run over.

MANY SPEEDS, ONE DIRECTION

I am often criticized as being a starry-eyed advocate of globalization. Well, anyone reading this book knows that globalization has its upsides and downsides. But I will plead guilty to one thing: I do get a little lump in my throat when I see countries like China, India, or Ireland adopting a basically proglobalization strategy, adapting it to their own political, social, and economic conditions, and reaping the benefits. Of course, there are costs to this growth as well—in terms of environment, social cohesion, and economic equality, which governments need to monitor and mitigate—but let's stop downplaying the economic benefits, and let's stop pretending that the antiglobalization advocates have any realistic strategy for bringing as many people out of poverty as quickly—if at all. There are many speeds that a country can go at down this globalization path—and each country has to choose the right speed for its particular social and political circumstances. But there is only one right direction.

No one said this better than Baldev Raj Nayar, emeritus professor of political science at McGill University, in his monograph *India's Globalization: Evaluating the Economic Impact*, which was excerpted by YaleGlobal Online, February 1, 2007. While Nayar uses the language of economics, what he is saying in essence is that thanks to adopting a globalization strategy India has experienced an economic revolution:

> As the driving force of the world economy since the mid-1970s, globalization has become a lodestone for a wide-ranging attack across a large expanse of the developing world for its alleged malign consequences. Reduced to its essentials, the attack posits the impact of globalization to be economic stagnation, deindustrialization, economic destabilization and growing inequality.
>
> Marked by vigor, the critique lacks in empirical rigor . . . Put simply, India has been a significant beneficiary of globalization despite its rather modest integration into the world economy.
>
> After a stringent regime of "autarky and command and control economy," from 1956 to 1975, India started on a slow path of reintegration into the world economy, albeit in nascent form. Interestingly, India's reintegration coincides with the onset of the larger process of globalization. However, carried out in stealth, economic liberalization, the national policy counterpart of globalization, remained tentative and minimal in India. Not until 1991 did India, amidst enormous economic crisis, make a paradigm shift to liberalization, though still limited.
>
> Empirical comparison of the period before and after liberalization demonstrates that, instead of economic stagnation, India achieved a marked acceleration in economic growth after liberal-

ization. Indeed, India broke the barrier of stagnation that had been the lot of the country before globalization. India's rate of growth from 1975 to 2007 has been over 5.5 percent, compared to the derisively termed "Hindu" rate of growth of 3.4 percent over the period 1956 to 1975, and especially to the pathetic 2.6 percent over the decade prior to the nascent liberalization in 1975. In the dozen years from 1995 to 2007 the growth rate has been over 6.5 percent; during the last four years India has sustained an unprecedented average growth rate of over 8 percent.

It is difficult to exaggerate this accomplishment in growth acceleration. It has provided additional resources not only for investment in human capital but also for expenditures on the social sectors and poverty alleviation. Besides, the economic dynamism associated with this growth has imparted a self-confidence for successfully building a consolidated nation-state. It has indeed transformed a country that had been mocked as "the sick man of Asia"—an inveterate supplicant for foreign aid—into a credible contender for a major role in the balance of power in Asia.

Similarly, far from the specter of deindustrialization held out by the critics, foreign imports have not swamped Indian industry after tariffs were lowered as part of India's reintegration into the world economy. Rather, Indian industry has grown at a higher rate than it had prior to liberalization of the economy. The growth rate of manufacturing has been around 6.5 percent since 1975 and close to 7 percent during the dozen years up to 2006. At the latter rate, the value of manufacturing doubles about every 10 years—not exactly deindustrialization. The advance in manufacturing has been broad-based and not limited to consumption goods . . .

As for economic destabilization, the autarkic period prior to the initial and nascent opening to globalization in 1975 was ridden with grave economic crises. Indeed, throughout that entire period, India labored under an enormous and debilitating foreign-exchange constraint, which both retarded and distorted its development . . . After the paradigm shift to economic liberalization in the early 1990s, India has not yet seen another economic crisis and no longer faces a foreign-exchange constraint because of its accumulating reserves, currently at some $170 billion. The absence of a foreign-exchange crisis has boosted the self-confidence of the nation. The reserves had sunk to $1.2 billion during the 1991 crisis.

As for impoverishment, the globalization period has seen welfare enhancement through a long-term decline in poverty. The proportion of population below the poverty line was 55 percent in 1973, after which there has occurred a secular decline. By 2000 it stood at 26 percent. Although the last figure is disputed because of changes in survey design, there can be no doubt about the long-term decline. The line of causality here clearly runs from globalization and liberalization to acceleration in the growth rate and then to poverty reduction—a remarkable testimony to the robustness of the much-maligned "trickle down theory."

Still, it would be heartless, indeed cruel, to make the performance on poverty reduction an occasion to celebrate liberalization, as much poverty still remains, even when defined minimally in caloric-intake terms. Indeed, the persistence of poverty for massive numbers, inherited from the past, underscores the passion that goes into critiques of globalization. However, the conclusion that flows from a comparative analysis of the trends since the beginning of liberalization in 1975—when set against the condition prior to it, of staggeringly high poverty and economic stagnation—is different. Higher rates of economic growth, facilitated by periodic doses of liberalization, pushed forward poverty reduction. The policy implication therefore is that more, not less, liberalization fosters and sustains rapid economic growth . . .

[C]ontrary to the position of the critics, globalization has served as the agent of deliverance for India from economic stagnation and perpetual economic crises even as it has reduced poverty. However, India continues to be dogged by deep-seated societal problems that persisted throughout the autarkic period.

But it is precisely the accelerated growth generated by globalization that has provided the additional resources to alleviate, if not yet to remove, them.

Let's cut the nonsense: When done right and in a sustained manner, globalization has a huge potential to lift large numbers of people out of poverty. And when I see large numbers of people escaping poverty, in places like India, China, or Ireland, well, yes, I get a little emotional. No apologies.

Companies and
the Flat World

ELEVEN

How Companies Cope

Out of clutter, find simplicity.
From discord, find harmony.
In the middle of difficulty, lies opportunity.

—Albert Einstein

As I conducted interviews for this book, I kept hearing the same phrase from different business executives. It was strange; they all used it, as if they had all been talking to one another. The phrase was, "Just in the last couple of years . . ." Time and again, entrepreneurs and innovators from all different types of businesses, large and small, told me that "just in the last couple of years" they had been able to do things they had never dreamed possible before, or that they were being forced to do things they had never dreamed necessary before.

I am convinced that these entrepreneurs and CEOs were responding to the flattening of the world. Each was figuring out a strategy for his or her company to thrive or at least survive in this new environment. Just as individuals need a strategy for coping with the flattening of the world, so too do companies. Economist Paul Romer is fond of saying, "Everyone wants economic growth, but nobody wants change." Unfortunately, you cannot have one without the other, especially when the playing field shifts as dramatically as it has since the year 2000.

This is not a how-to-succeed-in-business book. What I have learned in researching this book, though, is that the companies that have managed to survive and grow today are those that are most prepared to change. They are the ones that recognize—faster than their competitors—everything new that the flattening of the world enables and everything new that it enjoins and are the first to develop strategies to exploit the new possibilities and to cope with the new requirements.

This chapter highlights some of the rules that these companies live by in a flat world.

Rule #1: When the world is flat, whatever can be done will be done. The only question is whether it will be done by you or to you.

This rule should come as no surprise: When, as a result of the flattening of the world, so many people have so much connectivity, and so many people have access to low-cost tools of innovation, and so many people are able to tap into each other's markets, workforces, brainpower, and ideas to discover and invent new things—and then quickly disseminate them around the globe—well, then, whatever can be done will be done. So if you have an idea, pursue it. Because someone else will have a similar idea, and pursue it, faster than you think.

I see evidence of this everywhere I go today—individuals, entrepreneurs, and big companies mixing and mashing together all sorts of technologies, markets, and innovations to start new businesses out of nowhere or give old businesses some totally new dimension. I can't prove it, but I think this trend, which is not always easy to see, is becoming one of the most powerful drivers of the global economy today, fostering more small and medium-size businesses with a global reach than anyone realizes or economists can fully measure. Let me give you just a few examples:

In May 2006, I was invited to a conference at the Central European University in Budapest. While I was there, the conference organizers arranged a car to pick me up, drive me to appointments, and return me to the airport at the close of the meeting. On my way from downtown Budapest to the airport, early on a Sunday morning, the driver, József Bakó, said to me that if I had any friends who were planning to come to Hungary, would I please have them contact him through his Web site?

He explained that on the site, they could see the different cars he has to offer and could choose which one they'd like to ride in and what sort of service they would need—diplomatic, business, or tourism. I was half awake at the time, but the notion that my Hungarian driver had his own Web site piqued my interest.

"How much business do you get online?" I asked him. "About 20 to 25 percent," the Communist-era-engineer-turned-limo-proprietor answered. So as soon as I got home I checked out his site: www.felimo.hu. It was very elaborate, describing Bakó's services in English, Magyar, and German, with pictures of all the different cars. It even had music! Suddenly a thought popped into my head. It was something former secretary of state James A. Baker III used to say after he retired from government: In Washington, you know you're out of office "when your limousine is yellow and your driver speaks Farsi." I would say, "You know that in the flat world, whatever can be done is being done when your Hungarian driver has his own Web site in Magyar, German, and English—with music!"

I visited Peru in June 2006 on a tour sponsored by Conservation International. One day our tour guide, Alfredo Ferreyros, mentioned a Peruvian friend of his who was selling traditional handcrafted Peruvian dishware from his village near Cuzco "on the Internet." I thought to myself, "Well, that's nice. I am glad e-commerce is getting down to Peruvian villages." But then Alfredo added this kicker: His friend was looking into whether he could get his traditional Peruvian ceramics made more cheaply in China and have them shipped directly to the United States from there! Whatever can be done will be done—and better to do it with China yourself before the villager next door does.

The New Yorker ran a cartoon by Peter Steiner of two dogs, one sitting at a computer keyboard saying to the other, "On the Internet, nobody knows you're a dog." When the world is flat, nobody knows you're Uruguay.

A tiny country of 3.4 million people, wedged between Brazil and Argentina, Uruguay has come from nowhere to partner with India's biggest software company, Tata Consultancy Services, to create in just five years one of the largest outsourcing operations in Latin America. Yes, when Tata's Indian employees in Mumbai are asleep, its 650 Uruguayan engineers and programmers now pick up the work and help run the computers and backroom operations for the likes of American Express, Procter & Gamble, and some major U.S. banks—all from Montevideo. How did this happen? Simple. Today, with the right imagination, Internet bandwidth, and a modest amount of capital, anyone can assemble a global company by matching workers and customers from anywhere to do anything for anyone.

So Gabriel Rozman decided it was going to be done by him, not to him. A retired partner from Ernst & Young in America who was raised in Uruguay, he hatched the idea of partnering with Tata to make Montevideo a global outsourcing hub. He did not have a single client or employee when he approached Tata. He had just two things: a gut instinct that Uruguay's quality educational system had produced plenty of good, low-cost engineers and a gut desire to do something good for Uruguay—the country that gave his Hungarian parents sanctuary from Hitler. Five years later, TCS Iberoamerica can't hire workers fast enough. When I visited its head office, people were working on computers in hallways and stairwells. (Rozman also oversees thirteen hundred employees in Brazil and twelve hundred in Chile.) It turns out that many multinationals like the idea of spreading out their risks and not having all their outsourcing done from India—especially after one big U.S. bank nearly had to shut down last year when a flood in Mumbai paralyzed its India data center the same day a hurricane paralyzed its Florida operation. And there is no risk of nuclear war with Pakistan in Uruguay, either.

"When I first approached this big U.S. bank to outsource some of its services to Montevideo, instead of India," recalled Rozman, "the guy I was speaking with said, 'I don't even know where Montevideo is.' So I said to him, 'That's the point!'" Another factor, added Rozman, was that multinationals that were depending on Indian firms alone to run their back rooms twenty-four hours a day were getting the third team for eight hours, since the best Indian engineers didn't want to work the late-night shift—the heart of America's day. By creating an outsourcing center in Montevideo, which is just one hour ahead of New York, Tata could offer its clients its best Indian engineers during India's day (America's night) and its best Uruguayan engineers during America's day (India's night).

Most employees here are Uruguayans, but there are also lots of Indians sent over by Tata. It produces both a culture shock—Montevideo doesn't have one Indian restaurant—and a cultural cacophony. The firm runs on strict Tata principles, as if it were in Mumbai, so to see Uruguayans pretending to be Indians serving Americans is quite a scene. Rosina Marmion, twenty-seven, an Uruguayan manager, explained, "Our customers expect us to behave like Indians, to react the same way."

Whatever can be done . . . In today's world, having an Indian company led by a Hungarian-Uruguayan CEO, servicing American banks with Montevidean engineers managed by Indian technologists who have learned to eat Uruguayan veggie is just the new normal.

One day in the spring of 2006 I was interviewing B. Ramalinga Raju, chairman of Satyam Computer Services, one of India's top firms doing outsourced work from America, and he mentioned in passing how Satyam had just started outsourcing some of its American work to Indian villages. The outsourcee has become the outsourcer! Why not? Raju explained: "We told ourselves: If business process outsourcing can be done from cities in India to support cities in the developed world, why can't it be done by villages in India to support cities in India? Things like processing employee records can be done from anywhere, so there is no reason they can't be done from a village." Satyam began with two villages a year ago and plans to scale up to 150. There is enough bandwidth now, even reaching big Indian villages, to parcel out this work, and the villagers are very eager. "The attrition level is low, and the commitment levels high," Raju said. "It is a way of breathing economic life into villages."

In the fall of 2006, I visited South Sioux City, Nebraska, where I met Doug Palmer. He and his partner, Pat Boeshart, make insulated concrete forms for buildings. The traditional way to insulate concrete with foam is to make the foam and then truck it around the country to building sites to be attached to concrete. Their company, Lite-Form, found a South Korean machine that, when combined with devices added by his firm, can make the foam and concrete together on site, saving big dollars in trucking. Today, the South Sioux City company imports these machines from South Korea, attaches its devices, and exports them to Kuwait. His company has an Arabic brochure that tells Kuwaitis how to use the device. The brochure was produced by a local ad agency owned by the Winnebago Indian tribe of Nebraska. The agency was started by the tribe's economic development corporation, in an effort to diversify from its gambling casino called "WinnaVegas." You read this right: Plains Indians publishing Arabic brochures for Nebraskans who are importing machinery from Koreans to be customized by a South Sioux City company for customers in Kuwait.

The old left thinks free trade is something that benefits only multinationals. In fact, free trade is critical for small businesses and individuals, who can now act multinationally. "Protectionism scares us," said Palmer, whose company has twenty-eight employees. "If we put up a moat and keep doing what we're doing, thinking we're the smartest in the world, we're going to die. We have to have that flexibility to barter and trade."

A few weeks later, in Silicon Valley, I met Arijit Sengupta, a young Indian American educated at Stanford and Harvard Business School, whose company, BeyondCore, developed a software algorithm to be able to detect and reduce errors in outsourced back-office work. When I met Mr. Sengupta, he handed me a card with his logo, which, he explained, was designed by a graphic artist he found online in Romania through a Web site that brings together freelancers from all over the world. He put his need for a design out for bid on the site, got a bunch of proposals from Argentina, India, Italy, Malaysia, New Zealand, Romania, Ukraine, Uruguay, and the United States, chose the best one, and a few hundred dollars and a few days later had his own corporate logo for his business card. His database and Web server were drawn from free software, his blog and part of his Web site were hosted for free by Google, and he had outsourced his marketing, sales support, and patent filings to Indian firms. When I asked, "Where's your office?" he held up his BlackBerry, which took calls forwarded from phone numbers he set up in India, Boston, and Palo Alto. At the time, he and his seven workers already had one Fortune 500 client. "When I started this company I never had to think about geography," he said. "All I had to think about was: Where was the best resource to get something done? What you need are the big ideas. That is the tough thing to come up with." Sengupta had a great sense of everything that could be done, and he was doing it to create his own global small business from scratch.

Remember: Small business is the engine of employment, and this flatter world is clearly igniting a new era for small businesses to dream, create, and sell—no matter how small they are. Joel Cawley of IBM told me about a young man he knew who thought it would be a great idea to have colored iPod earphones, instead of just the all-white ones. He went online to Alibaba.com, an English-language Web site that helps small and medium-size businesses contract with traders, sellers, and manufacturers globally. On Alibaba, he found someone in China to design the earphones and someone else to produce them. He then contracted with Amazon.com to serve as his logistics, merchandising, and fulfillment platform. "With very little capital," said Cawley, "he started a global supply chain with global fulfillment."

What all these stories tell me is that, thanks to the flat-world platform, we are seeing the emergence of collaborative, build-your-own business models that are unprecedented in history—and that whatever can be done is being done.

Rule #2: This is an outgrowth of rule #1. Because we are in a world where whatever can be done will be done, the most important competition today is between you and your own imagination.

Yes, of course, countries still compete with one another and always will. Yes, of course, companies still compete with one another and always will. But what is unique about the flat world is the degree to which individuals, or small groups, can now act and compete globally. When individuals can upload and globalize their own ideas, products, or services—as individuals—then what they imagine matters more than ever. And that is why the biggest competition going forward is between you and your own imagination, because you can now do so much more on your own. I got this idea from B. Ramalinga Raju, who told me, "Getting the most out of your own imagination, or your employees'," is going to be the defining feature of our age. The countries and companies that will thrive will be those which create an environment where their people can stretch their imaginations to the horizon and beyond, and turn their visions into new products and services. What the above stories

have in common is that the products and services provided by these individuals—or by the companies they started—did not previously exist.
These entrepreneurs didn't simply adapt or improve someone else's idea
and make it cheaper or better. No. Most of them were just competing
with themselves, with their own imagination, about what could be done.
And they acted on their own imagination before someone else imagined
the same thing and acted before them.

That is one reason we need to ignore those in America who would advocate putting up higher walls of protectionism today or restricting free
trade. It would be exactly the wrong thing at the wrong time for the
wrong country. I tell people now: "I've rethought my position on trade.
I am no longer a free-trader. No, sir. I am now a *radical free-trader.*"
Because if whatever can be done will be done, then the society that is
most open to what is being done anywhere in the world, most open to the
competition, while also being most inviting of its own people and immigrants to imagine and do whatever can be done, is the society that will
thrive the most.

And this also explains why I am still optimistic about America's potential in a flat world. I am optimistic because we still have more of the
above attributes than any other country, and we must never tamper with
them. Washington, D.C., may be brain-dead. The Democratic and
Republican parties may be brain-dead. Congress may be brain-dead—
but America's free, open, imagine-anything-you-want, flexible economy
and society are still very much alive out there. I see this every day when I
travel the country outside Washington. That free, open, and competitive
environment is not only what makes us unique; it is what saves us from
our brain-dead politicians.

"The society which has the least resistance to the uninterrupted flow
of ideas, diversity, concepts, and competitive signals wins," said Nandan
Nilekani. "And the society that has the efficiencies to translate whatever
can be done quickly—from idea to market—also wins."

That still sounds like America to me. So pardon me if I resist those
who want to put up walls. And pardon me also when I hear people say,
"Britain dominated the nineteenth century, America dominated the
twentieth century, and China will dominate the twenty-first century,"

and I respond, "Not so fast." Maybe China will become the dominant economic power in the twenty-first century, but maybe not. I am not ready to cede the twenty-first century to China just yet. We Americans certainly are not going to dominate the twenty-first century by default or by resting on our laurels. We have to work harder and smarter. But we are not automatically going to be roadkill for China, either. In China they censor Google, and censoring Google is a proxy for a lot of impediments and restrictions to imagining and doing whatever can be done.

That is why I like to joke that my grandmother in Minnesota used to sit in her rocking chair by the fire during those cold Minnesota winters and impart to me this bit of wisdom that guides me to this day:

"Tommy," she would say, "never cede a century to a country that censors Google."

Rule #3: And the small shall act big . . . One way small companies flourish in the flat world is by learning to act really big. Imagination is necessary, but not sufficient. You have to be able to implement what you imagine. And the key to being small and acting big is being quick to take advantage of all the new tools for collaboration to reach farther, faster, wider, and deeper.

I can think of no better way to illustrate this rule than to tell the story of another friend, Fadi Ghandour, the cofounder and CEO of Aramex, the first home-grown package delivery service in the Arab world and the first and only Arab company to be listed on the Nasdaq. Originally from Lebanon, Ghandour's family moved to Jordan in the 1960s, where his father, Ali, founded Royal Jordanian Airlines. So Ghandour always had the airline business in his genes. Shortly after graduating from George Washington University in Washington, D.C., Ghandour returned home and saw a niche business he thought he could develop: He and an American cofounder, William Kingson, raised some money and in 1982 started a mini–Federal Express to do parcel delivery for the Middle East. At the time, there was only one global parcel delivery service operating in the Arab world: DHL, today owned by the German postal service. Ghandour's and Kingson's brainstorm was to approach

American companies, like Federal Express and Airborne Express, that did not have a Middle East presence and offer to become their local delivery service, playing on the fact that an Arab company would know the region and how to get around unpleasantries like Arab-Israeli clashes, the Iran-Iraq war, and the American invasion of Iraq.

"We said to them, 'Look, we don't compete with you locally in your home market, but we understand the Middle East market, so why not give your packages to us to deliver out here?'" said Ghandour, in laying out for me the whole Aramex story. "We will be your Middle East delivery arm. Why give them to your global competitor, like DHL?" Airborne responded positively, and Ghandour used that to build his own business and then buy up or partner with small delivery firms from Egypt to Turkey to Saudi Arabia and later all the way over to India, Pakistan, and Iran—creating his own regional network. Airborne did not have the money that Federal Express was investing in setting up its own operations in every region of the globe, so it created an alliance, bringing together some forty regional delivery companies, like Aramex, into a virtual global network. What Airborne's partners got was something none of them could individually afford to build at the time—a global geographic presence and a computerized package tracking and tracing system to compete with that of a FedEx or DHL.

Airborne "made their online computerized tracking and tracing system available to all its partners, so there was a unified language and set of quality standards for how everyone in the Airborne alliance would deliver and track and trace packages," explained Ghandour. With his company headquartered in Amman, Jordan, Ghandour tapped into the Airborne system by leasing a data line that was connected from Amman all the way to Airborne's big mainframe computer in its headquarters in Seattle. Through dumb terminals back in the Middle East, Aramex tracked and traced its packages using Airborne's back room. Aramex, in fact, was the earliest adopter of the Airborne system. Once Ghandour's Jordanian employees got up to speed on it, Airborne hired them to go around the world to install systems and train the other alliance partners. So these Jordanians, all of whom spoke English, went off to places like Sweden and the Far East and taught the Airborne methods of tracking and tracing. Eventually, Airborne bought 9 percent of Aramex to cement the relationship.

The arrangement worked well for everyone, and Aramex came to dominate the parcel delivery market in the Arab world, so well that in 1997, Ghandour decided to take the company public on Broadway, also known as the Nasdaq. Aramex continued to grow into a nearly $200-million-a-year company, with thirty-two hundred employees—and without any big government contracts. Its business was built for and with the private sector, highly unusual in the Arab world. Because of the dot-com boom, which deflected interest from brick-and-mortar companies like Aramex, and then the dot-com bust, which knocked out the Nasdaq, Aramex's stock price never really took off. Thinking that the market simply did not appreciate its value, Ghandour, along with a private equity firm from Dubai, bought the company back from its shareholders in early 2002.

Unbeknownst to Ghandour, this move coincided with the flattening of the world. He suddenly discovered that not only could he do new things, but he had to do new things he had never imagined doing before. He first felt the world going flat in 2003, when Airborne got bought out by DHL. Airborne announced that as of January 1, 2004, its tracking and tracing system would no longer be available to its former alliance partners. See you later. Good luck on your own.

While the flattening of the world enabled Airborne, the big guy, to get flatter, it allowed Ghandour, the little guy, to step up and replace it. "The minute Airborne announced that it was being bought and dissolving the alliance," said Ghandour, "I called a meeting in London of all the major partners in the group, and the first thing we did was found a new alliance." But Ghandour also came with a proposal: "I told them that Aramex was developing the software in Jordan to replace the Airborne tracking and tracing system, and I promised everyone there that our system would be up and running before Airborne switched theirs off."

Ghandour in effect told them that the mouse would replace the elephant. Not only would his relatively small company provide the same backroom support out of Amman that Airborne had provided out of Seattle with its big mainframe, but he would also find more global partners to fill in the holes in the alliance left by Airborne's departure. To do this, he told the prospective partners that he would hire Jordanian professionals to manage all the alliance's back-office needs at a fraction of the cost they were paying to have it all done from Europe or America. "I am not the largest company in the group," said Ghandour, who is now in his midforties and still full of energy, "but I took leadership. My German partners were a $1.2 billion company, but they could not react as fast."

How could he move so quickly? The triple convergence.

First of all, a young generation of Jordanian software and industrial engineers had just come of age and walked out onto the level playing field. They found that all the collaborative tools they needed to act big were as available to them as to Airborne's employees in Seattle. It was just a question of having the energy and imagination to adopt these tools and put them to good use.

"The key for us," said Ghandour, "was to come up with the technology and immediately replace the Airborne technology, because without online, real-time tracking and tracing, you can't compete with the big boys. With our own software engineers, we produced a Web-based tracking and tracing and shipment management system."

Managing the back room for all the alliance partners through the Internet was actually much more efficient than plugging everyone into Airborne's mainframe back in Seattle, which was very centralized and had already been struggling to adapt to the new Web architecture. With the Web, said Ghandour, every employee in every alliance company could access the Aramex tracking and tracing system through smart PC terminals or handheld devices, using the Internet and wireless. A couple of months after making his proposal in London, Ghandour brought all the would-be partners together in Amman to show them the proprietary system that Aramex was developing and to meet some of his Jordanian software professionals and industrial engineers. (Some of the programming was being done in-house at Aramex and some was outsourced. Outsourcing meant Aramex too could tap the best brains.) The partners liked it, and thus the Global Distribution Alliance was born—with Aramex providing the back room from the backwater of Amman, where

Lawrence of Arabia once prowled, replacing Airborne, which was located just down the highway from Microsoft and Bill Gates.

Another reason Ghandour could replace Airborne so quickly, he explained, was that he was not stuck with any "legacy" system that he had to adapt. "I could go right to the Internet and use the latest technologies," he said. "The Web enabled me to act big and replicate a massive technology that the big guys had invested millions in, at a fraction of the cost . . . From a cost perspective, for me as a small guy, it was ideal . . . I knew the world was flat. All my preaching to our employees as the CEO was that we can compete, we can have a niche, the rules of the game are changing, you don't need to be a giant, you can find a niche, and technology will enable us to compete with the big boys."

When January 2004 rolled around and Airborne began switching off its system, Aramex was up and running for a seamless handoff. And because Aramex was able to run its new system off an Internet platform, with software designed primarily by lower-cost Jordanian programmers, installation of the new system took place virtually, without Aramex having to send its engineers to train any of the alliance partners. Each partner company could build its own client base over the Internet through the Aramex system, do its own tracking and tracing, and be part of the new virtual global air freight network.

"So now we are managing this global network, with forty alliance partners, and we cover every geographic area in the world," said Ghandour. "We saved so much money . . . With our Web-based system all you needed was a browser and a password to get into the Aramex network, and suddenly you're inside a global shipment management system." Aramex trained many of the employees of the other alliance companies how to use its system by using various online channels, including voice over the Internet, online chatting, and other virtual training tools available on Aramex's intranet—making the training incredibly cheap.

Like UPS, Aramex has quickly moved into insourcing. Arab and foreign banks in the Middle East have outsourced the delivery of their credit cards to Aramex; mobile phone companies are using Aramex deliverymen to collect bills on their behalf, with the deliverymen just scanning the customer's credit card and then issuing a receipt. (Aramex may be high-tech, but it has not shrunk from using donkeys to cross military roadblocks to deliver packages in the West Bank when Israeli-Palestinian clashes have closed roads.)

"We are a very flat organization," Ghandour explained. "This is not traditional, because Arab institutions in the private sector tend to look like the governments—very hierarchal and patriarchal. That is not how Aramex works. There are no more than two to three layers between me and anyone in the company. Every single knowledge worker in this organization has a computer with e-mail and Internet access. Right here from your computer I can access my intranet and see exactly what is happening in the organization without my senior people having to report to me."

In sum, Fadi Ghandour took advantage of several new forms of collaboration—supply-chaining, outsourcing, insourcing, and all the steroids—to make his little $200-million-a-year company very big. Or, as he put it with a smile, "I was big locally and small internationally—and I reversed that."

Rule #4: And the big shall act small . . . One way that big companies learn to flourish in the flat world is by learning how to act really small by enabling their customers to act really big.

Howard Schultz, the founder and chairman of Starbucks, says that Starbucks estimates that it is possible to make nineteen thousand variations of coffee on the basis of the menus posted at any Starbucks outlet. What Starbucks did, in other words, was make its customers its drink designers and allow them to customize their drinks to their exact specifications. Starbucks never thought of offering soy milk, Schultz told me, until store managers started to get bombarded with demands for it from customers, to the point where they were going to the grocery store across the street in the middle of the day to buy cartons of soy milk. Starbucks learned from its customers, and today some 8 percent of all the drinks that Starbucks sells include soy milk. "We didn't dream up the different concoctions with soy milk," said Schultz, "the customers did." Starbucks just collaborated with them. The smartest big companies clearly understand that the triple convergence allows them to collaborate with their customers in a totally new fashion—and, by doing so, to act really small. The way that big companies act small is not by targeting each individual consumer and trying to serve that customer individually. That would be impossible and impossibly expensive. They do it by making their business, as much as possible, into a buffet. These companies create a platform that allows individual customers *to serve themselves* in their own way, at their own pace, in their own time, according to their own tastes. They are actually making their customers their employees and having them pay the company for that pleasure at the same time!

One of those big companies that have learned to act small in this way is E*Trade, the online bank and brokerage house. It did so, explained Mitchell H. Caplan, the CEO of E*Trade as well as a friend and neighbor, by recognizing that behind all the hoopla around the dot-com boom and bust, something very important was happening. "Some people thought the Internet was going to revolutionize everything in the world with no limits—it was going to cure the common cold," said Caplan. Sure, it was hype, and it led to crazy valuations and expectations, which eventually came crashing down. But meanwhile, with much less fanfare, the Internet was creating "a whole new distribution platform for companies to reach consumers in a whole new way and for consumers to reach your company in a whole new way," Caplan said. "While we were sleeping, my mom figured out how to use e-mail and connect with the kids. My kids were instant-messaging all their friends. My mom figured out how to go online and check her E*Trade balances."

Companies that were paying attention understood they were witnessing the birth of the "self-directed consumer," because the Internet and all the other tools of the flat world had created a means for every consumer to customize exactly the price, experience, and service he or she wanted. Big companies that could adapt their technology and business processes to empower this self-directed consumer could act very small *by enabling their customers to act very big.* They could make the consumer feel that every product or service was being tailored for his or her specific needs and desires, when in fact all that the company was doing was creating a digital buffet for them to serve themselves.

In the financial services industry, this constituted a profound change in approach. Historically, financial services were dominated by large banks, large brokerage houses, and large insurance companies that told you what you were getting, how you were getting it, when and where you were getting it, and the price you had to pay for it. Customers reacted to these big companies with emotions ranging from apathy to distaste. But if I didn't like the way my bank was treating me, I didn't have any real choice. Then the world was flattened and the Internet came along. Consumers started to feel that they could have more control, and the more they adapted their buying habits to the Internet, the more companies—from booksellers to financial services—had to adapt and offer them the tools to be in control.

"Sure, the Internet stocks blew up when the bubble burst," said Caplan, whose own company's stock price took a big dip in that market storm, "but underneath, consumers were getting a taste of power, and once they tasted it, things went from companies being in control of consumers' behavior to consumers being in control of companies' behavior. The rules of engagement changed, and if you did not respond and offer customers what they wanted, someone else would, and you would be dead." Where once the financial services companies acted big, now they strove to act small and to enable the consumer to act big. "Companies who prosper today," argued Caplan, "are the ones who understand the self-directed consumer." For E*Trade, that meant thinking of the company not as a collection of individual financial services—a bank, a brokerage, and a lending business—but as an integrated financial experience that could serve the most self-directed financial consumers. "The self-directed consumer wanted one-stop financial shopping," said Caplan. "When they came to our site they wanted everything integrated, with them in control. Only recently, though, did we have the technology to really integrate all our three businesses—banking, lending, and brokerage—and pull them together in a way that didn't just deliver the price, not just the service, but the total experience they wanted."

If you came to the E*Trade site just three or four years ago, you would see your brokerage account on one screen page and your lending on another. Today, said Caplan, "On one page you can now see exactly where you stand in terms of your brokerage in real time, including your buying

power, and you see your bank account and the scheduled payments for
your loans—what is pending, what is the balance on your home mortgage, and [what is your] line of credit—and you have the ability to move
seamlessly between all three to maximize the benefit of your cash."

While Fadi Ghandour coped with the triple convergence by taking a
small company and devising a strategy to make it act very big, Mitchell
Caplan survived by taking a big company and making it act very small so
that his customers could act very big.

*Rule #5: The best companies are the best collaborators. In the flat world,
more and more business will be done through collaborations within and
between companies, for a very simple reason: The next layers of value creation—whether in technology, marketing, biomedicine, or manufacturing—are becoming so complex that no single firm or department is going
to be able to master them alone.*

"What we are seeing in so many different fields," said Joel Cawley, the
head of IBM's strategic planning unit, "is that the next layers of innovation involve the intersection of very advanced specialties. The cutting
edge of technical innovation in every field is increasingly specialized." In
most cases, your own company's or your own department's specialization
is going to be applicable to only a very small piece of any meaningful
business or social challenge. "Therefore, to come up with any valuable
new breakthrough, you have to be able to combine more and more of
these increasingly granular specialties. That is why collaboration is so important," Cawley said. So you might find that a pharmaceutical company
has invented a new stent that allows it to dispense a whole new class of
drugs that a biomedical company has been working on, and the real
breakthrough—where the real profit is created for both—is in their collaboration in getting the breakthrough drugs from one firm together with
the breakthrough delivery system from another.

Or take a more colorful example: video games. Game makers have
long been commissioning special music to go with games. They eventually discovered that when they combined the right music with the right
game they not only sold many, many more copies of that game, but they

could spin off the music for sale on CD or download as well. So some big game companies have recently started their own music divisions, and some artists have decided that they have a better chance of getting their music heard by launching it with a new digital game than on the radio.

As I noted earlier, many of the new middle jobs will go to people who are great synthesizers—because the more the flattening of the world connects all the knowledge pools together, the more new specialties will be spawned, and the more innovation will come from putting these specialties together in new and different combinations. And the more that is true, the more good management, too, will be about nurturing synthesis and collaboration within your company—at a much deeper level. In the *Time* magazine cover story (October 24, 2005) on Steve Jobs and the Apple video iPod, one paragraph jumped out at me. It said: "Apple employees talk incessantly about what they call 'deep collaboration' or 'cross-pollination' or 'concurrent engineering.' Essentially it means that products don't pass from team to team. There aren't discrete, sequential development stages. Instead, it's simultaneous and organic. Products get worked on in parallel by all departments at once—design, hardware, software—in endless rounds of interdisciplinary design reviews. Managers elsewhere boast about what little time they waste in meetings; Apple is big on them and proud of it. 'The historical way of developing products just doesn't work when you're as ambitious as we are,' says [Jonathan] Ive, [head of design], an affable, bear-like Brit. 'When the challenges are that complex, you have to develop a product in a more collaborative, integrated way.'"

Perhaps the best way to illustrate this paradigm shift is to show how a very traditional manufacturer—Rolls-Royce—has adapted to it. When you hear the word "Rolls-Royce," what immediately comes to mind is a shiny handmade car, with a uniformed chauffeur sitting in the driver's seat and a perfectly tailored couple in the back on their way to Ascot or Wimbledon. Rolls-Royce, the quintessential stodgy British company, right? What if I told you, though, that Rolls-Royce doesn't even make cars anymore (that business was sold in 1972 and the brand was licensed to BMW in 1998), that 50 percent of its income comes from services, and that in 1990 all of its employees were in Great Britain and today 40 percent are based outside of the United Kingdom, integrated into a global operation that stretches from China to Singapore to India to Italy to Spain to Germany to Japan and up to Scandinavia?

No, this is not your father's Rolls-Royce.

"Quite a long time ago we said, 'We cannot be just a U.K. company,'" Sir John Rose, chief executive of Rolls-Royce PLC, told me in an interview while we were both visiting China. "The U.K. is a tiny market. In the late 1980s, 60 percent of our business was defense [particularly jet engines] and our primary customer was Her Majesty's government. But we needed to become a world player, and if we were going to do that we had to recognize that the biggest customer in everything we could do was the U.S., and we had to be successful in nondefense markets. So we became a technology company [specializing in] power systems." Today Rolls-Royce's core competency is making gas turbines for civilian and military airplanes, for helicopters, for ships, and for the oil and gas and power-generation industries.

Rolls-Royce has customers now in 120 countries and employs around thirty-five thousand people, but only twenty-one thousand are located in the United Kingdom, with the rest part of a global network of research, service, and manufacturing workers. Half of Rolls-Royce's revenue is now generated by businesses outside the United Kingdom. "In the U.K. we are thought of as a British company," said Rose, "but in Germany we are a German company. In America we are an American company, in Singapore we are a Singaporean company—you have to be in order to be close to the customer but also to the suppliers, employees, and communities in which we operate." Today Rolls-Royce employs people of about fifty nationalities in fifty countries speaking about fifty languages. It outsources and offshores about 75 percent of its components to its global supply chain. "The 25 percent that we make are the differentiating elements," said Rose. "These are the hot end of the engine, the turbines, the compressors and fans and the alloys, and the aerodynamics of how they are made. A turbine blade is grown from a single crystal in a vacuum furnace from a proprietary alloy, with a very complex cooling system. This very-high-value-added manufacturing is one of our core competencies." In short, said Rose, "We still own the key technologies, we own the ability to identify and define what product is required by our customers, we own the ability to integrate the latest science into making these products, we own the route to the market for these products, and we own the ability to collect and understand the data generated by those customers using our products, enabling us to support that product while in service and constantly add value."

But outside of these core areas, Rolls-Royce has adopted a much more horizontal approach to outsourcing noncore components to suppliers anywhere in the world, and to seeking out IQ far beyond the British Isles. The sun may have set on the British Empire, and it used to set on the old Rolls-Royce. But it never sets on the new Rolls-Royce. To produce breakthroughs in the power-generation business today, the company has to meld together the insights of many more specialists from around the world, explained Rose. And to be able to commercialize the next energy frontier—fuel cell technology—will require that even more.

"One of the core competencies of the business today is partnering," said Rose. "We partner on products and on service provisions, we partner with universities and with other participants in our industry. You have to be disciplined about what they can provide and what we can sensibly undertake . . . There is a market in R & D and a market in suppliers and a market in products, and you need to have a structure that responds to all of them."

A decade ago, he added, "We did 98 percent of our research and technology in the U.K. and now we do less than 40 percent in the U.K. Now we do it as well in the U.S., Germany, India, Scandinavia, Japan, Singapore, Spain, and Italy. We now recruit from a much more international group of universities to anticipate the mix of skills and nationalities we will want in ten or fifteen years."

When Rolls-Royce was a U.K.-centric company, he added, it was very vertically organized. "But we had to flatten ourselves," said Rose, as more and more markets opened worldwide that Rolls-Royce could sell into and from which it could extract knowledge.

And what does the future hold?

This approach to change that Rolls-Royce has perfected in response to the flattening of the world is going to become the standard for more and more new start-up companies. If you were to approach venture capital firms in Silicon Valley today and tell them that you wanted to start a new company but refused to outsource or offshore anything, they would show you the door immediately. Venture capitalists today want to know from day one that your start-up is going to take advantage of the triple convergence to collaborate with the smartest, most efficient people you can find anywhere in the world. Which is why in the flat world, more and more companies are now being born global.

"In the old days," said Vivek Paul, the Wipro president, "when you started a company, you might say to yourself, 'Boy, in twenty years, I hope we will be a multinational company.' Today, you say to yourself that on day two I will be a multinational. Today, there are thirty-person companies starting out with twenty employees in Silicon Valley and ten in India . . . And if you are a multiproduct company, you are probably going to have some manufacturing relationships in Malaysia and China, some design in Taiwan, some customer support in India and the Philippines, and possibly some engineering in Russia and the U.S." These are the so-called micromultinationals, and they are the wave of the future.

Today, your first management job out of business school could be melding the specialties of a knowledge team that is one-third in India, one-third in China, and a sixth each in Palo Alto and Boston. That takes a very special kind of skill, and it is going to be much in demand in the flat world.

Rule #6: In a flat world, the best companies stay healthy by getting regular chest X-rays and then selling the results to their clients.

Because niche businesses can get turned into vanilla commodity businesses faster than ever in a flat world, the best companies today really do get chest X-rays regularly—to constantly identify and strengthen their niches and outsource the stuff that is not very differentiating. What do I mean by chest X-rays? Let me introduce Laurie Tropiano, IBM's vice president for business consulting services, who is what I would call a corporate radiologist. What Tropiano and her team at IBM do is basically X-ray your company and break down every component of your business and then put it up on a wall-size screen so you can study your corporate skeleton. Every department, every function, is broken out and put in a box and identified as to whether it is a cost for the company or a source of income, or a little of both, and whether it is a unique core competency of the company or some vanilla function that anyone else could do— possibly cheaper and better.

"A typical company has forty to fifty components," Tropiano explained to me one day at IBM, as she displayed a corporate skeleton up on her screen, "so what we do is identify and isolate these forty to fifty components and then sit down and ask [the company], 'How much money are you spending in each component? Where are you best in class? Where are you differentiated? What are the totally nondifferentiated components of your business? Where do you think you have capabilities but are not sure you are ever going to be great there because you'd have to put more money in than you want?'"

When you are done, said Tropiano, you basically have an X-ray of the company, identifying four or five "hot spots." One or two might be core competencies; others might be skills that the company wasn't fully aware that it even had and that should be built up. Other hot spots on the X-ray, though, might be components where five different departments are duplicating the same functions or services that others outside the company could do better and more cheaply and so should be outsourced—provided there is still a savings to be made once all the costs and disruptions of outsourcing are taken into account.

"So you go look at this [X-ray] and say, 'I have these areas here that are going to be really hot and core,'" says Tropiano, "and then let go of the things that you can outsource, and free up those funds and focus on the projects that could one day be part of your core competency. For the average company, you are doing well if 25 percent is core competency and strategic and really differentiating, and the rest you may continue to do and try to improve or you may outsource."

I first got interested in this phenomenon when an Internet business news headline caught my eye: "HP bags $150 million India bank contract." The story on Computerworld.com (February 25, 2004) quoted a statement by HP saying that it had inked a ten-year outsourcing contract with the Bank of India in Mumbai. The $150 million contract was the largest ever won by HP Services in the Asia-Pacific region, according to Natarajan Sundaram, head of marketing for HP Services India. The deal called for HP to implement and manage a core banking system across 750 Bank of India branches. "This is the first time we at HP are looking at the outsourcing of the core banking function in the Asia-Pacific region," said Sundaram. Several multinational companies competed for the contract, including IBM. Under the contract, HP would take charge of data warehousing and document-imaging technology, telebanking, Internet banking, and automated teller machines for the whole bank chain.

Other stories explained that the Bank of India had been facing increasing competition from both public- and private-sector banks and multinational corporations. It realized that it needed to adopt Web-based banking, standardize and upgrade its computer systems, lower its transaction costs, and generally become more customer-friendly. So it did what any other multinational would do—it gave itself a chest X-ray and decided to outsource all the functions it did not believe were part of its core competency or that it simply did not have the internal skills to do at the highest level.

Still, when the Bank of India decides to outsource its back room to an American-owned computer company, well, that just seemed too weird for words. "Run that by me again," I said, rubbing my eyes. "HP, the folks I call when my printer breaks, won the outsourcing contract for managing the back room of India's 750-branch state-owned bank? What in the world does Hewlett-Packard know about running the backroom systems of an Indian bank?"

Out of curiosity, I decided to visit the HP headquarters in Palo Alto to find out. There, I met Maureen Conway, HP's vice president for emerging market solutions, and put the above question directly to her.

"How did we think we could take our internal capabilities and make them good for other people?" she answered rhetorically. In brief, she explained, HP is constantly hosting customer visits, where its corporate clients come to its headquarters and see the innovations that HP has brought to managing its own information systems. Many of those customers go away intrigued at how this big company has adapted itself to the flat world. How, they ask, did HP, which once had eighty-seven different supply chains—each managed vertically and independently, with its own hierarchy of managers and back-office support—compress them into just five supply chains that manage $50 billion in business, and in which functions like accounting, billing, and human resources are handled through a companywide system? What computers and business processes did HP install to consolidate all this efficiently? HP, which does business in 178 countries, used to handle all its accounts payable and receivable for each individual country in that country. It was totally chopped up. Just in the last couple of years, HP created three transaction-processing hubs—in Bangalore, Barcelona, and Guadalajara—with uniform standards and special work flow software that allowed HP offices in all 178 countries to process all billing functions through these three hubs.

Seeing the reaction of its customers to its own internal operations, HP said one day, "Hey, why don't we commercialize this?" Said Conway, "That became the nucleus of our business process outsourcing service . . . We were doing our own chest X-rays and discovered we had assets that other people cared about, and that is a business."

In other words, the flattening of the world was both the disease and the cure for the Bank of India. It clearly could not keep up with its competitors in the flattening banking environment of India, and, at the same time, it was able to get a chest X-ray and then outsource to HP all those things that it no longer made sense to do itself. And HP, having done its own chest X-ray, discovered that it was carrying a whole new consulting business inside its breast. Sure, most of the work for the Bank of India will be done by HP employees in India or Bank of India employees who will actually join HP. But some of the profits will find their way back to the mother ship in Palo Alto, which will be supporting the whole operation through its global knowledge supply chain.

Most of HP's revenues today come from outside the United States. But the core HP knowledge and infrastructure teams who can put together the processes that win those contracts—like running the back room of the Bank of India—are still in the United States.

"The ability to dream is here, more than in other parts of the world," said Conway. "The nucleus of creativity is here, not because people are smarter—it is the environment, the freedom of thought. The dream machine is still here."

Rule #7: The best companies outsource to win, not to shrink. They out-source to innovate faster and more cheaply in order to grow larger, gain market share, and hire more and different specialists—not to save money by firing more people.

As noted earlier, Dov Seidman runs LRN, a business that provides on-line legal, compliance, and ethics education to employees of global companies and helps executives and board members manage corporate governance responsibilities. We were having lunch in the fall of 2004 when Seidman casually mentioned that he had recently signed an out-sourcing contract with the Indian consulting firm MindTree.

"Why are you cutting costs?" I asked him.

"I am outsourcing to win, not to save money," Seidman answered. "Go to our Web site. I currently have over thirty job openings, and these are knowledge jobs. We're expanding. We're hiring. I am adding people and creating new processes."

Seidman's experience is what most outsourcing is actually about—companies outsourcing to acquire knowledge talent to grow their busi-ness faster, not simply to cut costs and cut back. Seidman's company is a leader in one of those completely new industries that just appeared in the flat world—helping multinationals foster an ethical corporate cul-ture around an employee base spread all over the world. Although LRN is a BE company—founded ten years before Enron exploded—demand for its services surged in the PE era—post-Enron. In the wake of the col-lapse of Enron and other corporate governance scandals, a lot more companies became interested in what LRN was offering—online pro-grams for companies to forge common expectations and understandings of their legal and ethical responsibilities, from the boardroom to the fac-tory floor. When companies sign up with LRN, their employees are given an online education, including tests that cover everything from your company's code of conduct to when you are allowed to accept a gift to what you need to think about before hitting Send on an e-mail to what constitutes a bribe of a foreign official.

As the corporate governance issue began to mushroom in the early 2000s, Seidman realized that his customers, much like E*Trade's customers, would need a more integrated platform. While it was great that he was educating their employees with one online curriculum and advising boards on ethics issues with another, he knew that company executives would want a one-stop Web-based interface where they could get a handle on all the governance and ethics issues facing their organizations—whether it was employee education, the reporting of any anomalous behavior, stewardship of a hard-earned corporate reputation, or government compliance—and where they could get immediate visibility into where their company stood.

So Seidman faced a double challenge. He needed to do two things at once: keep growing his market share in the online compliance education industry, and design a whole new integrated platform for the companies he was already working with, one that would require a real technological leap. It was when faced with this challenge that he decided to enlist MindTree, the Indian consulting firm, in an outsourced relationship that offered him about five well-qualified software engineers for the price of one in America.

"Look," said Seidman, "when things are on sale, you tend to buy more. MindTree offered a sale not on last season's closeout, but on top-notch software engineering talent that I would have been hard-pressed to find elsewhere. I needed to spend a lot of money defending and extending my core business and continue to take care of my customers, who were working off my current programs. And at the same time, I had to make a giant leap to offer my customers what they were asking for next, which was a much more robust and total online solution to all their ethics, governance, and compliance questions. If I don't meet their needs, someone else will. Partnering with MindTree allows me to basically have two teams—one team [mostly Americans] that is focused on defending and extending our core business, and the other team, including our Indian consultants, focused on making our next strategic leap to grow our business."

Since ethics is at the core of Seidman's Los Angeles–headquartered business, *how* he went about outsourcing was as important as the ultimate results of the relationship. Rather than announcing the MindTree partnership as a done deal, Seidman conducted an all-hands town-hall meeting of his 170 or so employees to discuss the outsourcing he had in mind. He laid out all the economic arguments, let his staff weigh in, and gave everyone a picture of which jobs would be needed in the future and how people could prepare themselves to fit in. "I needed to show my company that this is what it would take to win," he said.

Have no doubt, there are firms that do and will outsource good jobs just to save money and disperse it to shareholders or management. To think that this is not happening or will not happen is beyond naïve. But firms that are using outsourcing primarily as a tool to cut costs, not enhance innovation and speed growth, are the minority, not the majority— and I would not want to own stock in any of them. The best companies are finding ways to leverage the best of what is in India with the best of what is in North Dakota with the best of what is in Los Angeles. In that sense, the word "outsourcing" should really be retired. The applicable word is really "sourcing." That is what the flat world both enables and demands, and the companies that do sourcing right end up with bigger market shares and more employees everywhere—not smaller and fewer.

"This is about trying to get bigger faster, about how we make our next leap in less time with greater assurance of success," said Seidman of his decision to source critical areas of development of his new platform to MindTree. "It is not about cutting corners. We have over two hundred clients all over the world now. If I can grow this company the way that I want to, I will be able to hire even more people in all our current offices, promote even more people, and give our current employees even more opportunities and more rewarding career paths—because LRN's agenda is going to be broader, more complex, and more global . . . We are in a very competitive space. This [decision to use outsourcing] is all about playing offense, not defense. I am trying to run up the score before it's run up on me."

Rule #8: HOW you do things as a company matters more today than ever.

I draw this concept from Dov Seidman's book *How.* Seidman's essential argument is twofold: One reason that how you do business today is so much more important is that most aspects of business in a flat world will

468 THE WORLD IS FLAT

be easily commoditized and copied. To differentiate yourself from your competition, you can no longer rely on price and service, or even on best practices. Everyone will have those sooner or later—everyone who stays in business. You will differentiate your company from the others by *how* you do business. After all, how much difference is there today among Target, Kmart, Wal-Mart, and Costco, or Nordstrom, Saks, and Nieman Marcus? In price, or basic store design and operations, not much.

The difference among them lies in "how they treat their colleagues, customers, suppliers, and investors," says Seidman. "If your interactions with others deliver a more meaningful customer experience, if you deal more consistently, openly, and honestly with your suppliers and investors, and more decently with your employees, you engender loyalty that brings them all back and trust that enables greater collaboration. When it comes to conduct—*the hows*—there is still tremendous variation in the marketplace. And where variation exists, opportunity exists. The tapestry of human behavior is so varied, so rich, so global that it presents a rare opportunity—the opportunity to not only outperform the competition but to outbehave the competition."

The other reason is that companies today are more transparent—and their customers more powerful. When the world was round and full of walls, a boss would say to an employee, "Just get it done. I don't care how, just don't break the law." And that boss could do that because it was very difficult for anyone else to see inside his business. Plausible deniability and "don't ask/don't tell" ruled the day. Companies were fortresses and one-way communicators, and they had the power to define themselves through proxies—marketers, advertisements, spokespeople, official statements—without consumers being able to compare notes. Companies could differentiate themselves by simply hiring the best ad agency or crafting the best "message." Not anymore. Little guys and gals can now talk back in ways the whole world can hear—by blogging or podcasting about your company or by mocking your product on YouTube with a video that can be downloaded all over the world.

"Companies used to be monologists," says Seidman. "Now we are in a world of two-way dialogue. When I want to go to a resort, or buy an appliance, or read a book, I check the reader reviews, where consumers compare notes. And I will put more trust in those than anything a company says about itself. Customers can not only talk back, they can look into the very workings of your business and decide if you conduct yourself in a way they approve of. In this world, your reputation will be the sum total of all your conduct and interactions, which will now be so much more measurable by outsiders."

Consumers' insights into the how of your business will affect not only who comes in your door to shop but also who wants to collaborate with you. And in the flat world, your company's ability to inspire trust is everything. If your business partners are on the other side of the world, and from a different culture, and if you and they have never met, the fact that you've developed a reputation for behaving ethically is critical. They will give you the benefit of the doubt. But you will have to earn that trust "one interaction at a time," says Seidman. You can't buy it from Hill & Knowlton anymore. "Before, you just needed to do the right things," Seidman concludes. "Now you need to do them the right way."

Rule #9: When the world goes flat—and you are feeling flattened—reach for a shovel and dig inside yourself. Don't try to build walls.

Going to India gave me an inkling that the world was flat, but only when I went back to my roots and spoke to my friends from Minnesota did I realize just how flat. Some twenty-five years ago Jill and Ken Greer (whose brother Bill I profiled earlier) started their own multimedia company, Greer & Associates, which specialized in developing commercials for TV and doing commercial photography for retail catalogs. They have built up a nice business in Minneapolis, with more than forty employees, including graphic artists and Web designers, their own studio, and a small stable of local and national clients. As a midsize firm, Greer always had to hustle for work, but over the years Ken always found a way to make a good living.

In early April 2004, Ken and Jill came to Washington to spend a weekend for my wife's fiftieth birthday. I could tell that Ken had a lot on his mind regarding his business. We took a long walk one morning in rural Virginia. I told him about the book I was writing, and he told me about how his business was doing. After a while, we realized that we were both talking about the same thing: The world had grown flat, and it had happened so fast, and had affected his business so profoundly, that he was still wrestling with how to adjust. It was clear to him that he was facing competition and pricing pressure of a type and degree that he had never faced before.

"Freelancers," said Greer, speaking about these independent contractors as if they were a plague of locusts that suddenly had descended on his business, eating everything in sight. "We are now competing against freelancers! We never really competed against freelancers before. Our competition used to be firms of similar size and capability. We used to do similar things in somewhat different ways, and each firm was able to find a niche and make a living." Today the dynamic is totally different, he said. "Our competition is not only those firms we always used to compete against. Now we have to deal with giant firms, who have the capability to handle small, medium, and large jobs, and also with the solo practitioners working out of their home offices, who [by making use of today's technology and software] can theoretically do the same thing that a person sitting in our office can do. What's the difference in output, from our clients' point of view, between the giant company who hires a kid designer and puts him in front of a computer, and our company that hires a kid designer and puts him in front of a computer, and the kid designer with a computer in his own basement? . . . The technology and software are so empowering that it makes us all look the same. In the last month we have lost three jobs to freelance solo practitioners who used to work for good companies and have experience and then just went out on their own. Our clients all said the same thing to us: 'Your firm was really qualified. John was very qualified. John was cheaper.' We used to feel bad losing to another firm, but now we are losing to another *person!*"

How did this change happen so fast? I asked.

A big part of their business is photography—shooting both products and models for catalogs, Greer explained. For twenty-five years, the way the business worked was that Greer & Associates would get an assignment. The client would tell Greer exactly what sort of shot he was looking for and would "trust" the Greer team to come up with the right image. Like all commercial photographers, Greer would use a Polaroid camera to take a picture of the model or product he was shooting, to see if his creative instinct was right, and then shoot with real film. Once the pictures were taken, Greer would send the film out to a photo lab to be developed and color-separated. If a picture needed to be touched up, it would be sent to another lab that specialized in retouching.

"Twenty years ago, we decided we would not process the film we shot," Greer explained. "We would leave that technical aspect to other professionals who had the exact technology, training, and expertise — and a desire to make money that way. We wanted to make money by taking the pictures. It was a good plan then, and may be a good plan today, but it is no longer possible."

Why? The world went flat, and every analog process went digital, virtual, mobile, and personal. In the last three years, digital cameras for professional photographers achieved a whole new technical level that made them equal, if not superior, to traditional film cameras.

"So we experimented with several different cameras and chose the current state-of-the-art camera that was most like our [analog] film cameras," Greer said. "It's called a Canon D1, and it's the same exact camera as our film camera, except there's a computer inside with a little TV-screen display on the back that shows us what picture we're taking. But it uses all the same lenses, you set things the same way, shutter speed and aperture, it has the same ergonomics. It was the first professional digital camera that worked exactly like a film camera. This was a defining moment.

"After we got this digital camera, it was incredibly liberating at first," said Greer. "All of the thrill and excitement of photography were there — except that the film was free. Because it was digital, we didn't have to buy film and we didn't have to go to the lab to have it processed and wait to get it back. If we were on location and shooting something, we could see if we got the shot right away. There was instant gratification. We referred to it as an 'electronic Polaroid.' We used to have an art director who would oversee everything to make sure that we were capturing the image we were trying to create, but we would never really know until we got it developed. Everyone had to go on faith, on trust. Our clients paid us a professional fee because they felt they needed an expert who could not only click a button, but knew exactly how to shape and frame the image. And they *trusted* us to do that."

For a year or so there was this new sense of empowerment, freedom, creativity, and control. But then Ken and his team discovered that this new liberating technology could also be enslaving. "We discovered that not only did we now have the responsibility of shooting the picture and defining the desired artistic expression, we had to get involved in the technology of the photograph. We had to become the lab. We woke up one morning and said, 'We are the lab.'"

How so? Because digital cameras gave Greer the ability to download those digital images into a PC or laptop and, with a little magic software and hardware, perform all sorts of new functions. "So in addition to being the photographer, we had to become the processing lab and the color separator," said Greer. Once the technology made that possible, Greer's customers demanded it. Because Greer *could* control the image farther down the supply chain, they said he *should* control it, he *must* control it. And then they also said because it was all digital now, and all under his control, it should be included among the services his team provided as the photographic creators of the image. "The clients said, 'We will not pay you extra for it,'" said Greer. "We used to go to an outside service to touch up the pictures—to remove red-eye or blemishes—but now we have to be the retouchers ourselves also. They expect [red-eye] to be removed by us, digitally, even before they see it. For twenty years we only practiced the art of photography—color and composition and texture and how to make people comfortable in front of a camera. This is what we were good at. Now we had to learn to be good at all these other things. It is not what we signed up for, but the competitive marketplace and the technology forced us into it."

Greer said every aspect of his company went through a similar flattening. Film production went digital, so the marketplace and the technology forced them to become their own film editors, graphics studio, sound production facility, and everything else, including producers of their own DVDs. Each of those functions used to be farmed out to a separate company. The whole supply chain got flattened and shrunk into one box that sat on someone's desktop. The same thing happened in the graphics part of their business: Greer & Associates became their own typesetters, illustrators, and sometimes even printers, because they owned digital color printers. "Things were supposed to get easier," he said. "Now I feel like I'm going to McDonald's, but instead of getting fast food, I'm being asked to bus my own table and wash the dishes too."

He continued: "It is as if the manufacturers of technology got together with our clients and outsourced all of these different tasks to us. If we put our foot down and say you have to pay for each of these services, there is someone right behind us saying, 'I will do it all.' So the services required go up significantly and the fees you can charge stay the same or go down."

It's called commoditization, and in the wake of the triple convergence, it is happening faster and faster across a whole range of industries. As more and more analog processes become digital, virtual, mobile, and personal, more and more jobs and functions are being standardized, digitized, and made both easy to manipulate and available to more players.

When everything is the same and supply is plentiful, said Greer, clients have too many choices and no basis on which to make the right choice. And when that happens, you're a commodity. You are vanilla.

Fortunately, Greer responded to commoditization by opting for the only survival strategy that works: a shovel, not a wall. He and his associates dug inside themselves to locate the company's real core competency, and this has become the primary energy source propelling their business forward in the flat world. "What we sell now," said Greer, "is strategic insight, creative instinct, and artistic flair. We sell inspired, creative solutions, we sell personality. Our core competence and focus is now on all those things that cannot be digitized. I know our clients today and our clients in the future will only come to us and stick with us for those things . . . So we hired more thinkers and outsourced more technology pieces."

In the old days, said Greer, many companies "hid behind technology. You could be very good, but you didn't have to be the world's best, because you never thought you were competing with the world. There was a horizon out there and no one could see beyond that horizon. But just in the space of a few years we went from competing with firms down the street to competing with firms across the globe. Three years ago it was in-

conceivable that Greer & Associates would lose a contract to a company
in England, and now we have. Everyone can see what everyone else is
doing now, and everyone has the same tools, so you have to be the very
best, the most creative thinker."

Vanilla just won't put food on the table anymore. "You have to offer
something totally unique," said Greer. "You need be able to make
Chocolate Chip Cookie Dough, or Cherry Garcia, or Chunky Monkey"—
three of the more exotic brands of Ben & Jerry's ice cream that are very
nonvanilla. "It used to be about what you were able to do," said Greer.
"Clients would say, 'Can you do this? Can you do that?' Now it's much
more about the creative flair and personality you can bring to [the as-
signment] . . . It's all about imagination."

You and the
Flat World

TWELVE

Globalization of the Local

The Cultural Revolution Is About to Begin

My 1999 book *The Lexus and the Olive Tree* attempted to describe the forces that were globalizing the world at the end of the twentieth century and their effects on economics, politics, geopolitics, environment, and culture. After the first edition of *The World Is Flat* first came out, several readers complained to me that I had not followed up on the cultural part of my argument in *The Lexus and the Olive Tree*—I had made no mention of how this new flattening era of globalization, at the dawn of the twenty-first century, was affecting culture around the world. I acknowledged this and explained that it was simply a matter of not having had enough time to think through that issue. This updated edition of the book has given me a chance to do just that, and I am glad it has, because the flattening of the world is having surprising, important, and paradoxical effects on culture around the world.

As the flattening phase of globalization began to gain momentum following the fall of the Berlin Wall, there was a considerable and justifiable worry around the world that "globalization means Americanization." This worry was not unreasonable, because it was primarily American-based manufacturers and service providers, American brands and American moviemakers, American singers and American entertainers, American clothing designers and American fast-food chains that were in the best position to take advantage of the falling of the walls and flattening of the world. They were the first out of the gates, and it seemed inevitable and unstoppable that they would take advantage of the flat world to homogenize culture. If you were from another culture, no matter how robust and vibrant your distinctive dress, language, food, or music, you had to worry that you could be easily steamrolled. In the constant struggle between the homogenizing and particularizing forces of globalization, it seemed like the homogenizing-Americanizing forces were destined to triumph. Globalization would have an American face, an American look, and an American taste.

This naturally triggered a backlash against globalization as a form of "American cultural imperialism." Many people around the world argued that unless we took serious steps to strengthen cultures—and protect the environment—the juggernaut of globalization as Americanization could, in just a few decades, wipe out the cultural, ecological, and zoological diversity that took millions of years of human, plant, and animal evolution to produce.

There is no minimizing the dangers posed to the environment by the flattening of the world, as I explained in the previous chapter. However, as far as culture is concerned, there is reason to hope that the flattening of the world will not necessarily pave the way for a red, white, and blue cultural homogenization. Indeed, it is becoming clear that the flat-world platform, while it has the potential to homogenize cultures, also has, I would argue, an even greater potential to nourish diversity to a degree that the world has never seen before.

Why? Primarily because of uploading. Uploading makes possible "the globalization of the local." The fact that so many people worldwide now have the tools to create and upload their own content—their own news reports, their own opinions, their own music, their own videos, their own photos, their own software, their own encyclopedias, their own dictionaries— is a very powerful force for the preservation and enhancement of cultural autonomy and particularity. The flat-world platform enables you to take your own local culture and upload it to the world. It means you aren't stuck downloading Mickey Mouse and McDonald's. No, no, no. You can now write your own song, create a podcast version in any language you like, and share it with the world on some podcast site, and if people like it, it will spread. You can now make your own home video with a cheap Webcam and Microsoft Movie Maker that comes bundled with your software and upload that as well. The most popular food in the world is not the Big Mac. It's pizza. And what is pizza? It is just a flat piece of dough on which every culture puts its own distinctive foods and flavors. So Japan has sushi pizza and Bangkok has Thai pizza and Lebanon has mezze pizza. The flat-world platform is just like that pizza dough. It allows different cultures to season and flavor it as they like—and you are going to see that more now than ever.

At the same time, the fact that people in rising nations like India and China will be able to innovate without having to emigrate means that local cultures have a much better chance of being preserved. A young Indian engineer no longer has to stand in line outside the U.S. embassy in New Delhi and pray to win the lottery and secure a visa to America so that he or she can move to frigid Minnesota and give up his or her native dress, native cuisine, native music, and extended family—all the things that make up a native culture—just to get a decent engineering job at 3M. That is a very good thing for the preservation of Indian local culture. Cultures are nested in environments, and the fact that more people can now not only survive but even thrive by staying home in their native region, in their own environment, has got to be a net plus for the forces of cultural diversity versus the forces of homogeneity.

Moreover, even those individuals who have had to uproot themselves from developing countries to go west—to Europe or America in particular—have been able to take advantage of the flattening of the world to hold on to many aspects of their local culture, even if they are living in the midst of a different one thousands of miles away. Thanks to their ability to read their local newspapers online, to communicate with family and friends by phone for almost nothing using voice over the Internet technology, to watch daily news from Cairo or Calcutta (in Arabic and Hindi) thanks to Internet or satellite TV, the forces of particularization now seem to be as strong as the forces of homogenization.

Of course, Americanization via globalization is still a very powerful force. One should never underestimate it. But somehow, more than a decade after the fall of the Berlin Wall, it no longer seems inevitable that everyone is going to look, speak, sing, dance, and think like an American because of globalization.

As it happens, "globalization of the local" is an expression I first saw used by an Indian-born expert on globalization and cultural identity, Indrajit Banerjee, the secretary general of the Asian Media Information

and Communication Centre (AMIC). In an interview with Felix Soh of
The Straits Times of Singapore (September 11, 2005), Banerjee explained that he coined the term to describe the phenomenon that allows
diaspora communities around the world to use today's global media networks to cling to their local mores, news, traditions, and friends—no
matter where they are living. As Soh put it in the introduction to his interview with Banerjee, globalization of the local "is globalization in reverse. Instead of global media enveloping Asia, the region's 'local' media
are going global. This phenomenon of the globalization of the local is
being driven by the demand for local news and information from Asia's
diasporas, notably the millions of Chinese and Indian emigres now living
in all parts of the world."

Banerjee, who has a Ph.D. in communications from the Sorbonne, in
Paris, sees this from his perch in Singapore, where he teaches at a university:
"One would think that globalization in Asia would mean going English, but
that's not the case," he said in the interview with *The Straits Times*. "The di-
asporic market means you can have international newspapers, international
TV and radio channels which are completely based on local languages. This
is what I call the globalization of the local. It is not the global which comes
and envelops us. It is the local which goes global."

Today Britain and the United States have television channels where the
programming is all in Chinese, Spanish, Arabic, or Japanese. "If you have
populations spread all over the world, then you can use effectively the satellite platforms to broadcast to pockets all over the world," added Banerjee.
"If you put these pockets together, they become a huge global market."

Soh pointed out that Zee TV, the biggest Indian entertainment network, had blazed a trail for other Indian TV channels to go regional in
Asia. Said Banerjee: "Zee TV has a very clear Indian market—it is the
Indian diaspora. Its programming is in Hindi. For Zee TV, competition
is really not an issue. It doesn't want to capture the other language audiences." He added, "Also, in the near future, Asia will be a major producer of media content, which is a very positive development. For a long
time, Asia was a receiver of content from the West. Now because we're
coming of age and becoming mature, our media experiences are substantial. This, together with the rich culture and heritage of Asia, pre-

sents the region with tremendous potential to be a content-trading hub. India has one of the world's biggest film industries. It is producing a lot of television content. South Korea and Japan are very strong in animation . . . My belief is that the global is going to be interesting only if it is a range of the local. The whole diversity of local experiences and local content is present, rather than one content producer, one language, one cultural perspective and one ideology dominating the world."

India, for instance, has exploded recently as a platform for the outsourcing of game designs and cartoon animation. I was struck by something the head of one of these companies said to me when I visited. Ashish Kulkarni, COO of JadooWorks in Bangalore, explained that India had an abundance of traditional artists, who were able to make the transition easily to computerized digital painting. Many of these artists are the children of Hindu temple sculptors and painters. "We train them to transform their traditional skills to animation in a digital format," said Kulkarni. But to keep up their traditional Indian painting skills, JadooWorks also had set aside a room where artists could retreat to indulge in their native artistry—because the two skills reinforce each other. Companies like JadooWorks come and go with the demands of the global market and who can offer the best, cheapest artists at any given time. But before the world got flat, India had virtually no companies doing this business at all. Now, a new generation of Indian artists at least has a chance to maintain or advance their skills rather than drive taxis to earn a living. "We now tell the parents: 'If your kids are doing well in drawing in seventh grade, you must think of making a career in animation,'" said Kulkarni. "That was difficult five years back, but today, because of more exposure, we can get people to think they can transform their skills that their fathers had" and thereby hold on to them. I interviewed Deepak Ganguly, a slender twenty-eight-year-old computer artist who was then working at JadooWorks. "My parents are artists, my mother is a sculptor at home," he explained. "My father was a carpet designer, he made designs for Indian carpets. I had a knack for drawing, because I was brought up in this kind of climate, so I came into this field. When I started this animation career, at the time 3-D [computers for drawing] were not here in India . . . So I did a course in 2-D classical animation and I was a 2-D animator. When this 3-D boom happened in India [in the past couple years], I decided to jump. I was working at a small studio in Delhi. We used to watch movies and *Star Wars* and their computer-generated things. Then I got the chance to learn that skill." Globalization, said Ganguly, was enabling him to take his skills and now sell them all over the world. "With all the easy sharing in the electronic media," he said, "we can get the work here easier, we can send our skills over there easier."

To listen to some of the critics, though, you would think that global-ization was only about the spread of crass capitalism, global brands, fast food, and consumer values all crowding out warm, cozy, thriving local communities, industries, and cultures. There is no question that the forces of globalization do some or all of these things in many places on many days. But globalization is not simply about the spread of capitalism or markets or enhanced trade. It is not an exclusively economic phe-nomenon and its impact is not exclusively economic. It is a much broader, deeper, and more complex phenomenon, involving new forms of communication and innovation. The flattening of the world is about the creation of a global platform for multiple forms of sharing work, knowledge, and entertainment. Worrying about the pulverizing effects of globalization is very legitimate, indeed very important, but ignoring its ability also to empower individuals and enrich our cultural cornucopia misses its potentially positive effects on human freedom and diversity. My point here is not that the flattening of the world will always enrich and preserve culture. My point is that it doesn't always destroy culture, which is the message you hear if you listen only to the globalization crit-ics. The iron law of globalization is very simple: If you think it is all good or all bad, you don't get it. Globalization has empowering and disem-powering, homogenizing and particularizing, democratizing and au-thoritarian tendencies all built into it. It is about the global market, but it is also about the Internet and Google.

One should have no doubt—I certainly don't—that the flat world empowers the forces of darkness as well as the forces of light. You can up-load homemade pornography, homegrown racism, lies, conspiracy theo-ries, and just plain hokum, and spread them easier, faster, and farther on the flat-world platform as well. *The New York Times*, on December 19, 2005, ran a chilling front-page story about a teenage boy, Justin Berry, "who was drawn into performing in front of [a] Webcam—undressing, showering, masturbating and even having sex—for an audience of more than 1,500 people, who paid him, over the years, hundreds of thousands of dollars." What is really ironic is that they often paid him by using PayPal.com—the online payment system owned by eBay to make it easy for individuals to buy and sell on its auction site.

For all these reasons, our job is not to trash this platform but to get the best out of it and to prevent the worst.

The kind of globalization we are talking about now—with the Internet and the flattening of the world—"is a different kind of globalization than the one that is in the minds of the people who have been criticizing globalization," remarked Israeli political theorist Yaron Ezrahi. "It has different opportunities and dangers." In cultural terms, the globalization of the local "is allowing a local group of human rights supporters to become part of an international community and feel that solidarity, and the same with environmentalists. And the same, unfortunately, is true with neo-Nazis and al-Qaeda sympathizers. Wherever human beings have the freedom to create communities, they can create progressive or criminal ones . . . But the fact is that the Internet has magnified the capacity of individuals to generate their own stories and inscribe themselves on the world, both as individuals and as part of communities. Should we be against that? Of course not."

As of the printing of this book, Google was available in 116 different languages, from Arabic to Zulu to several versions of Chinese. The more people can easily inform themselves in their own languages, the more likely those languages and texts are to survive and the more likely others will write in them and not feel compelled to switch to English. Search is one of the ten flatteners, and the globalization of the local will be steadily enhanced as search engines gradually spread to every corner of the flat world.

But the flattening of the world is bringing diversity to different corners of the world, even without the Internet. There is more radio today, more TV, more phone, more travel, more trade. The Ghana-born Princeton professor and philosopher Kwame Anthony Appiah expressed this well in an essay for *The New York Times Magazine* (January 1, 2006) titled "The

Case for Contamination." Using a visit to his mother in Kumasi, Ghana—the town he grew up in—he adduced a variety of examples to make the point that people in Africa today, even villagers, are not just objects that the West or the modern world inscribes itself upon. They are also subjects—subjects who are in a much more dynamic give-and-take—adopt, adapt, import, re-export, and innovate—relationship with the world, thanks to globalization. "Yes, globalization can produce homogeneity," he wrote. "But globalization is also a threat to homogeneity . . . When people talk of the homogeneity produced by globalization, what they are talking about is this: Even here, the villagers will have radios (though the language will be local); you will be able to get a discussion going about Ronaldo, Mike Tyson, or Tupac; and you will probably be able to find a bottle of Guinness or Coca-Cola (as well as of Star or Club, Ghana's own fine lagers). But has access to these things made the place more homogeneous or less? And what can you tell about people's souls from the fact that they drink Coca-Cola? It's true that the enclaves of homogeneity you find these days—in Asante as in Pennsylvania—are less distinctive than they were a century ago, but mostly in good ways. More of them have access to effective medicines. More of them have access to clean drinking water, and more of them have schools. Where, as is still too common, they don't have these things, it's something not to celebrate but to deplore. And whatever loss of difference there has been, they are constantly inventing new forms of difference: new hairstyles, new slang, even, from time to time, new religions. No one could say that the world's villages are becoming anything like the same."

The newest anti-homogenizing force is podcasting—a whole new tool for globalizing the local. I got a glimpse into this phenomenon in October 2005 when I visited a small apartment in suburban Shanghai that is home to China's leading podcasting Web site, Toodou.com. "We already have thirteen thousand channels on our site, and about five thousand of them are updated regularly," explained Gary Wang, thirty-two, the Fuzhou-born and U.S.- and French-educated Chinese engineer who founded Toodou, which means "potato" in Chinese. Any Chinese can create his or her own channel of video or audio content on Toodou, and other individuals sign up to get the content on that channel each time new material is uploaded. For now, the service is free; eventually Toodou will charge a monthly subscription.

"I want to create hundreds of thousands of different channels, maintained by just average people, where other people can access them and download the material," added Wang. And he will, because the ease of uploading and podcasting means there are almost no barriers to entry, as long as you have a computer, a camera, and a microphone. (There are still political limits on what you can say from China, but who knows how long those limits will be sustainable. Toodou.com censors porn and anything that violates Chinese law or directly threatens the Communist government.)

Toodou's most popular podcast when I visited was a video of two twenty-year-old Chinese women lip-synching a popular Cantonese rock tune. "They got bored," explained Wang, so they went out and bought their own Webcam (which can be found in Shanghai for the equivalent of $6), used Microsoft Movie Maker (software that comes bundled with Windows XP), made their own three-minute MTV-like podcast, and uploaded it onto Toodou.com. It was viewed seventy-five thousand times in the first three months. "It took them one hour to make and fifteen minutes to edit," said Wang. The girls, who call themselves "The Beans," now have their own online fan club.

Another favorite is a podcast by two Chinese architecture students wearing Houston Rockets jerseys (the team of Chinese-born NBA star Yao Ming) and lip-synching a Backstreet Boys tune. A slide show on life in Shenzhen had been viewed sixteen thousand times, prompting all sorts of accompanying commentary from viewers around China. The second-highest-viewed podcast when I visited was a concert by an underground rock band at a Shanghai bar. Toodou's goal, said Wang, "will be to connect [Chinese] people to their tastes and to their potential collaborators. We will have a huge content database and we will share the revenue with content providers." Wang added: "We created this platform for free participation, and people [just] come in. With all kinds of tools becoming cheaper and cheaper, the creative part of people will naturally grow."

Yes, I know, I am a little ahead of myself. Very few Chinese have ever even seen an iPod, so most of the podcasting that does exist here is created and viewed or heard on PCs. Once the price of an iPod (music or video) comes down, though, there will be a huge podcast market here. Many of the current podcasts are junk, but the quality, too, will surely improve. The ease of podcasting will force competition and experimentation. Wang first heard of podcasting only in 2004. Some thirteen months later he had the most popular podcasting site in China, with one hundred thousand registered users, eight employees, forty volunteers, and a U.S. venture capital backer. News of his site was spread for free by Chinese bloggers. The office/apartment he was using when I visited rents for $500 a month, and some of his employees also slept there. Almost all the software that runs Toodou.com is from free, open-source material on the Web—an Apache Webserver; FreeBSD, a free Unix operating system; MySQL, a free database system; and PHP, free programming language. Wang wrote the algorithms that run Toodou.com himself. Comparing China to America and Europe, where he studied, Wang said, "With the same amount of money, I can do ten times more here . . . I can live on $1,000 a month in Shanghai and have the latest technology and all these servers—anything you can find in the U.S. is here."

In China, the combination of low costs and lowered barriers is making the process of creating cultural content cheaper and as a result more popular. That's why I am confident that this flattening phase of globalization is not going to mean more Americanization, but more globalization of local cultures, art forms, styles, recipes, literature, videos, and opinions—more and more local content made global.

"We have different songs [than Americans] and we want to express different things, but the desire is the same," said Wang. "We all want to be seen and heard and be able to create stuff we like and share it . . . People from all over the world will draw knowledge and inspiration from the same technology platform, but different cultures will flourish on it. It is the same soil, but different trees will grow."

And you thought the Cultural Revolution was over. Sorry, it's just beginning. Only China's newest Cultural Revolution is going to be driven this time from the bottom up—thanks to the flat-world platform—by podcasters with Apple's little white iPods, not from the top down by Maoists with Little Red Books.

The globalization of the local is not only happening culturally but also commercially. Just as the flattening of the world is starting to equalize and diversify the flow of culture, it is also starting to equalize and diversify the flow of investment—so globalization is no longer driven primarily by American or Western multinationals. More and more Chinese, Indian, Brazilian, Russian, Asian, and even African companies are doing business globally.

The Davos World Economic Forum is always a useful barometer of global trends, and at Davos 2007, for the first time, I began to really feel the globalization of the local happening in business to a significant degree. First, I had breakfast with Mohammed Shafik Gabr, a leading Egyptian entrepreneur. Shafik's company, the Artoc Group for Investment and Development, was involved in building two new cities in Egypt from the ground up, but that's not what struck me most. I was struck by the managers Shafik was recruiting to Cairo to run his rapidly expanding company. He explained to me that he had just hired as his new group COO an American of Egyptian origin who had worked for Coca-Cola in Atlanta, London, and Africa; he had hired an American Asia expert based in Hong Kong as his vice chairman for policy and business development; and he had hired a Frenchman as group general manager for his real estate subsidiary. It was clear that Shafik was preparing to go aggressively into new markets—the "new markets" of America, Asia, and France! A week later (January 31, 2007), the *Financial Times* carried the following lead story: "Tata Steel of India won the battle to control Anglo-Dutch steelmaker Corus on Wednesday, after more than eight hours of head-to-head bidding against Companhia Siderúrgica Nacional of Brazil." This was the first large foreign acquisition by an Indian company, and it was a doozy — £6.2 billion to take over Corus, which owns almost the entire steel industries of Britain and the Netherlands. So an Indian company outbid a Brazilian company to take over the biggest steel companies in Britain and the Netherlands!

In the middle of the Davos forum, Nathan Gardels, editor of *Global Viewpoint* magazine, wrote an essay for the *International Herald Tribune*

(January 24, 2007) that summarized these trends: "Globalization now belongs to everyone who can figure out how to take advantage of its opportunities and minimize its dislocations. American-bred technology may be its midwife, but Americans are no longer solely the parents. That's a big power shift indeed."

Indeed, if these trends continue, it is inevitable that globalization will finally become, well, *global*—both culturally and commercially—a process no longer driven from America and Europe but from all four corners of the flat world.

THIRTEEN

If It's Not Happening,
It's Because You're Not Doing It

"So I came into the office in the morning and I turned on my computer and suddenly I found five thousand e-mails waiting for me, all with the same basic complaint, all stirred up by the same organization that I'd never heard of before—some little group with a Web site in Canada run by two people, a dog, and $10,000. So I turned to my secretary and asked, 'Who are these people? Where did they come from?' She had no clue. 'Never heard of them, boss,' she said to me. 'Let me check with my kids.' 'Oh, that's great—check with your kids,' I thought. 'My secretary's kids are now my strategic advisers!' So I called our corporate PR folks and asked, 'Somebody tell me, what do I have to do to make these people go away?'"

I've just made up this story, but not from whole cloth. I heard many different variations on this theme from CEOs while working on the updated version of the book. It is all about the moment when the CEO had his or her first encounter with "these people." "These people" are this generation's social activists and social entrepreneurs, who have been superempowered by the flattening of the world. The Internet today gives even the smallest groups the ability to upload and globalize their activism—by building global coalitions that expose or embarrass the biggest multinationals. If these guys or gals use the Internet and the flat world to mount a campaign that is bogus or dishonest, it won't have any lasting impact. But if it has merit, they can get the biggest multinational to change its behavior, or beg for mercy, overnight. And if and when companies do the right things, the praise they win from the activist community can have real value to them.

I realized just how much social entrepreneurs can affect business decisions when I picked up *The New York Times* (March 8, 2007) and read that the NGO Environmental Defense had just hired the boutique Wall Street firm Perella Weinberg Partners to advise it on a megadeal it had become involved in negotiating. The story started in 2006 when the giant Texas power company, TXU Corp., announced plans to build eleven new coal-fired, CO_2-belching power plants, raising the ire of environmentalists worried about climate change. Fred Krupp, the president of Environmental Defense, which has an office in Texas, wrote C. John Wilder, the CEO of TXU, and asked for a meeting, but he was brushed off. TXU made clear that it was on a fast track to build its plants and had the governor of Texas on its side. Message to environmentalists: GET LOST.

Talk about not knowing what world you're living in.

So Environmental Defense turned to the Web and created StopTXU .com, a site that put out regular electronic newsletters on the TXU plans and built a national constituency opposed to the deal.

"TXU's plans to build eleven power plants made it a Goliath, given the scale of carbon emissions that would have resulted—seventy-eight million tons of CO_2 a year—and the scale of its disdain for the public interest," said Krupp. "We had to establish just how far out of the mainstream TXU was in terms of carbon emissions and keep them in a very public bull's-eye, which we did via a dedicated Web site and a regular e-newsletter to Texas media, political players, opinion leaders, and activists."

All of those efforts paid off when the big buyout firms Kohlberg Kravis Roberts and Texas Pacific Group teamed up to offer $45 billion to buy TXU in early 2007. It was going to be the largest leveraged buyout in history, but there was a catch: "The buyers did not want to take over a company enmeshed in a war with environmentalists," said Krupp, "so they came to us and said, 'We only want to go forward if you and NRDC [Natural Resources Defense Council, an environmental advocacy group] will praise what we are trying to do here.'" Environmental Defense and NRDC were ready to engage, but only if the deal would make the new company more climate friendly.

"The negotiations involved talks over ten days," said Krupp, "and the key session was compressed into seventeen hours in the Mandarin Oriental hotel in San Francisco—from eight a.m. to one a.m. the next morning." Eventually, the buyout group agreed to cut the number of new TXU coal plants from eleven to three, to support a federal cap on carbon emissions, and to commit TXU to plowing $400 million into energy-efficiency programs and doubling its purchase of wind power. In return, the environmentalists blessed the deal, but Krupp also hired Perella Weinberg to help negotiate the fine print as the contracts closed.

That is a pretty good day's work for people who had no money on the table.

What are the lessons? Krupp answered with a question: "What is the message when the largest buyout in history is made contingent [by the buyers] on winning praise for its greenhouse-gas plan? It tells us that the markets are ahead of the politicians. The world has changed and these guys see it."

TXU had not. Talking to itself in Texas, it didn't understand that it could not manage its reputation simply by putting out press releases, because, thanks to the Internet, ordinary people could shape TXU's image on a global basis through the Web—for almost no money.

"The reputations of companies are going to be less determined by the quality of their PR people and more by their actual actions, and that empowers more of an honest debate on the merits," said Krupp. "Going online, we shifted this from a local debate over generating electricity to a national debate over capping and reducing carbon emissions. So what TXU hoped would be just a local skirmish instead was watched on computer screens in every global market." The TXU example shows that truth plus passion plus the Internet, said Krupp, "can create an irresistible tide for change."

Referring to these sudden outbreaks of citizen activism, the Washington lobbyist of a major global biochemical company put it to me this way: "We were operating under the old rules and then the old rules changed, but nobody put up a sign." The old paradigm, she explained, was simple: Your company develops a product, government approves the product, people buy the product, and everyone is happy. New paradigm: You develop the product, you test the product, government approves the product, farmers buy the product, farmers use the product, consumers say, "Hey, wait a second, we don't like this product!" and suddenly there is a vast Internet campaign against bioengineering directed at your company, with people all over the world demanding: "Who are you to play with my food?"

Let me introduce the people who changed the rules overnight. They come in many forms. Some are business school grads with the soul of Peace Corps volunteers, some are political activists with a knack for using the Web to raise money or raise an army, some are environmentalists who hope to save the planet by tutoring the biggest corporations on how to increase their profits by getting green, and some are philanthropists who see in the proliferation of low-cost communication devices a whole new tool kit to help the poor help themselves.

What they all have in common, though, is a burning desire to make an impact and a firm belief that the flattening of the world makes being an activist-entrepreneur easier and cheaper than ever before. In fact, this kind of activism is now so easy, so cheap, so readily available to even the smallest player that I would throw down this gauntlet to today's young generation: If it's not happening, it's because you're not doing it.

You want to raise money for African poverty relief, for Darfur refugees, or to save the elephants of Sri Lanka? The Web provides you a global platform and a global audience. You want to highlight environmental degradation in the Amazon or potholes in your own neighborhood? You can post the pictures on www.flickr.com or upload your own documentary on YouTube or record your own podcast. You can blog about injustice and you can blog to raise money for your favorite candidate. If your arguments or video or photos or voice are compelling, you'll eventually find an audience or it will find you.

But you can also be effective without the Web. If you have an entrepreneurial bent, a passport, a little cash, and a lot of gumption, you can go off and start a small business just about anywhere—and create better jobs for people who are making only $1 a day rather than just protesting on their behalf at the next World Bank meeting. Because the flattening of the world extends free markets farther into different corners of the world, now social entrepreneurs can leverage those markets to deliver jobs, services, and profits for all kinds of people—not just for the rich but also for the poor and the aspiring middle class.

Here's a quick survey of some of the types of social entrepreneurship and activism being enabled by the flattening of the world.

P ossibly the best-known social entrepreneur-activist in the world to-day is Muhammad Yunus, a Bangladeshi who was awarded the 2006 Nobel Peace Prize. In 1976, Yunus founded the Grameen Bank, which granted small loans, without collateral, to the very poorest members of his society. In the quarter century that followed, by proving that the poor could make good use of this money and pay back the loans, he helped to inspire a whole new banking industry—"microfinance." When I inter-viewed Yunus in the fall of 2005, the thing that struck me most about him was his unbounded energy and obvious inner drive. His work had already gained much international attention, and he was about to win a Nobel Prize, but all he wanted to do was grab me by the lapels to tell me about his current project and solicit ideas for his next one.

I have never met a man who had more respect for the entrepreneur-ial talents of the poor and a better grasp of how much self-respect comes from starting a business of your own, no matter how small. For a poor person, Yunus explained to me, "microcredit is the key to unlocking yourself, and once you do that you see yourself differently. Instead of al-ways petitioning, you go through self-discovery. You explore your own limitless potential." That was why he had recently begun a program to give small loans, as small as the equivalent of $10, to beggars—yes, beg-gars! Yunus said his bank has employees who approach beggars on the streets of Dhaka, Bangladesh, and asks them, "'As you go from house to house, would you like to carry some sweets and toys, so you do both beg-ging and selling—and whichever works out best, you go with that.' And what a change that makes! Because then you [as a beggar] start to think, 'What will sell well? Oh, you like this? I can bring you more tomorrow.' We have more than eighty thousand beggars in that program and many already quit begging, because they're already successful sellers. Many have become part-time beggars and full-time salespeople."

At Grameen Bank, 97 percent of the borrowers are women, and the payback rate is 98 percent. As Yunus said to me, "Not having collateral is one thing, but not being creditworthy is another." The poor are very creditworthy when given the chance.

Who knew—until Yunus tried? He was teaching "elegant theories" of economics at Chittagong University in 1976 but wanted to find a way to help the poor and starving people he saw all around him on campus. "I saw the moneylenders squeezing the last drop of blood from people before they went down," he said, referring to the way scoundrels in the developing world prey on the poor by lending them money at exorbitant rates and then breaking their bones if they don't pay it back. So, on a hunch, he lent $27 to a group of poor local craftsmen and then, to leverage that amount, offered himself as guarantor of a larger loan they took from a traditional bank. The loan worked out well, and that little spark grew into the Grameen Bank Project.

"Yunus' innovation has broad appeal," *BusinessWeek* reported in its December 26, 2005, issue. "In 1997 only about 7.6 million families had been served by microcredit worldwide, according to the 2005 State of the Microcredit Summit Campaign Report. As of Dec. 31, 2004, some 3,200 microcredit institutions reported reaching more than 92 million clients, according to the report. Almost 73% of them were living in dire poverty at the time of their first loan . . . 'If banks made large loans, he made small loans. If banks required paperwork, his loans were for the illiterate. Whatever banks did, he did the opposite,' marvels Sam Daley-Harris, director of the Microcredit Summit Campaign."

I see social entrepreneurs like Yunus popping up everywhere, and not all of them are focused on just the bottom rung of society. As important as it is to help make poor people into small business people, it is just as important to make small business people in a developing country into big business people who can employ lots of their neighbors. As the saying goes: *Feed* a person a fish and you have fed that person only for a day. *Teach* a person to fish and you have fed that person for a lifetime. But I would add: Help that person *grow* a fishing business and you will have fed not only his family but also half the village.

Consider, for instance, Endeavor, founded in 1997 by Linda Rottenberg and Peter Kellner, who are what I would call "mentor capitalists." Endeavor (www.endeavor.org) was formed for the purpose of promoting entrepreneurship in emerging markets, beginning in Latin America. Its basic model is to link up small and midsize businesses with seasoned entrepreneurs so that the little guys and gals can get the advice and contacts they need to grow their companies into bigger businesses that can employ more people—the best antipoverty program of all. This form of social entrepreneurship is critically important but is not always appreciated. As *The Wall Street Journal* reported in a story about Endeavor (April 15, 2003), "Latin America has long been viewed as a wasteland of business start-ups, with neither the financing nor the social mobility needed to nourish entrepreneurial dreams . . . Many development agencies in the region were focused on microcredits . . . Endeavor's chosen beneficiaries—people with small to midsize businesses hoping to strike it rich—didn't always elicit sympathy from donors. Ms. Rottenberg remembers one foundation rejecting her on the grounds that she was 'just helping the middle class.'"

But it is precisely these sorts of middle-class start-ups and small businesses that create the most jobs and the greatest innovation in a society. As Rottenberg, Endeavor's cofounder and CEO, explained to me in an e-mail, "The important work done by Grameen, Acción, BancoSol and other terrific micro-finance institutions has drawn attention to the need for small-scale loans to assist women and men at the bottom of the pyramid. But what we've found consistently in emerging markets is a gap: there is little support for entrepreneurs beyond the micro-credit stage. At the other extreme, access to world-class consulting and investment is limited to companies with $50 million to $100 million in revenues."

By contrast, she explained, "Endeavor enters the picture when entrepreneurs have a proven business model that's yielded $500,000 to $20 million in revenues—with significant future growth potential. We occasionally take on pure start-ups, but we've found that the true inflection point comes after the entrepreneur has taken the company to a certain point but needs mentoring and strategic assistance to go to scale. Most companies in emerging markets fail at this inflection point."

Endeavor's results are impressive: Rottenberg says that 96 percent of the entrepreneurs supported by the program are still operating and generating sustainable, well-paying jobs—an average of 214 jobs per Endeavor company at ten times the minimum wage, and with significantly better benefits, too. "For us, the leverage in supporting these 'high-impact' entrepreneurs comes not only through the direct jobs but also through a multiplier effect: one high-impact entrepreneur creates hundreds of jobs, inspires thousands of future entrepreneurs, and the cycle continues. This point rarely enters the debate on philanthropy or even economic development.

"A decade ago when Endeavor was starting, there were neither Spanish nor Portuguese words for entrepreneur(ship). In small part due to our efforts and in larger part due to the global economy, the words 'emprendedor/empreendedor' and 'emprendedorismo/empreende-dorismo' have entered into the lexicon."

There is huge untapped potential in this form of social entrepreneurship. Too often, we have antipoverty debates but not proentrepreneurship debates. The inspirational power of a local business success story is incalculable: There is no greater motivator for the poor than looking at one of their own who makes it big and saying: "If she can do it, I can do it."

Yet another form of social entrepreneurship is the if-I-build-it-they-will-benefit model. My favorite example is Jeremy Hockenstein, a young man who first followed a time-honored path of studying at Harvard and going to work for the McKinsey & Company consulting firm, but then, with a colleague from McKinsey, veered totally off course and started a not-for-profit firm that does outsourced data entry for American-based companies in one of the least hospitable business environments in the world—post–Pol Pot Cambodia. Only in a flat world!

Here's the story: In February 2001, Hockenstein and some colleagues from McKinsey decided to go to Phnom Penh, half on vacation and half on a scouting mission for some social entrepreneurship. They were surprised to find a city salted with Internet cafés and schools for learning English—but with no jobs, or at best limited jobs, for those who graduated.

"We decided we would leverage our connections in North America to try to bridge the gap and create some income-generating opportunities for people," Hockenstein said. That summer, after another trip funded by themselves, Hockenstein and his colleagues opened Digital Divide Data, with a plan to start a small operation in Phnom Penh that would do data entry—hiring locals to type into computers printed materials that companies in the United States wanted in digitized form, so that the data could be stored on databases and retrieved and searched on computers. The material would be scanned in the United States and the files transmitted over the Internet. Their first move was to hire two local Cambodian managers. Hockenstein's partner from McKinsey, Jaeson Rosenfeld, went to New Delhi and knocked on the doors of Indian data-entry companies to see if he could find one—just one—that would take on his two Cambodian managers as trainees. Nine of the Indian companies slammed their doors. The last thing they wanted was even lower-cost competition emerging in Cambodia. But a generous Hindu soul, Lalit Gupta, agreed, and Hockenstein got his managers trained.

They then hired their first twenty data-entry operators, many of whom were Cambodian war refugees, and bought twenty computers and an Internet line that cost them $100 a month. The project was financed with $25,000 of their own money and a $25,000 grant from the Global Catalyst Foundation, started by Silicon Valley venture capitalists. They opened for business in July 2001, and their first work assignment was for the *Harvard Crimson*, Harvard's undergraduate daily newspaper.

"The *Crimson* was digitizing their archives to make them available online, and because we were Harvard grads they threw some business our way," said Hockenstein, recalling the company's start-up. "So our first project was having Cambodians typing news articles from the *Harvard Crimson* from 1873 to 1899, which reported on Harvard-Yale crew races. Later, actually, when we got to the years 1969 to 1971, when the turmoil in Cambodia was all happening, they were typing [*Crimson* stories] about their own story . . . We would convert the old *Crimsons*, which were on microfilm, to digital images in the United States through a company in Oklahoma that specialized in that sort of thing, and then we would just transfer the digital images to Cambodia by FTP [file transfer protocol]. Now you can go to thecrimson.com and download these stories." The Cambodian typists did not have to know English, only how to type English characters; they worked in pairs, each typing the same article, and then the computer program compared their work to make sure that there were no errors.

Hockenstein said that each of the typists works six hours a day, six days a week, and is paid $75 a month, twice the minimum wage in Cambodia, where the average annual income is less than $400. In addition, each typist receives a matching scholarship for the rest of the workday to go to school, which for most means completing high school but for some has meant going to college. "Our goal was to break the vicious cycle there of [young people] having to drop out of school to support families," said Hockenstein. "We have tried to pioneer socially responsible outsourcing. The U.S. companies working with us are not just saving money that they can invest somewhere else. They are actually creating better lives for some of the poor citizens of the world."

Four years after starting up, Digital Divide Data now has 400 employees in three offices: Phnom Penh; Battambang, the second-largest city in Cambodia; and a new office in Vientiane, Laos. "We recruited our first two managers in Phnom Penh and sent them to India to get trained in data entry, and then, when we opened the Laos office, we recruited two managers who were trained by our staff in the Phnom Penh office," Hockenstein said.

This tree has scattered all kinds of seeds. In 2005, when Google announced a controversial project to scan libraries full of books, DDD was concerned that this would cut into its business. However, in the flat world, this project announced in Silicon Valley has ended up creating more jobs in Laos. Here's how: Another major search portal decided also to scan tens of thousands of books in the United States. So the books from an Ivy League university are physically scanned in America, but

DDD employees in Laos get paid to log on to the computers in the United States and review each image. "Our team checks to make sure the images are not crooked or the scanner did not skip a page," explained Hockenstein. "Because of the flat world, it is now affordable to scan many more books with higher quality, whereas before all the steps had to be done by hand in the library."

Besides book digitizing and the *Harvard Crimson*, one of the biggest sources of data-entry work came from NGOs, which wanted the results of their field surveys about health or families or labor conditions digitized. So—and this is my favorite part—some of the first wave of Digital Divide Data's Cambodian workers left the company shortly after it started and spun off their own firm to design databases for NGOs that want to do surveys! Why? Because while they were working for Digital Divide Data, said Hockenstein, they kept getting survey work from NGOs that needed to be digitized. But because the NGOs had not done enough work in advance to standardize all the data they were collecting, it was very hard to digitize it in any efficient manner. So these Cambodian workers realized that there was value earlier in the supply chain and that they could get paid more for it—not for typing but for designing standardized formats for NGOs to collect survey data, which would make the surveys easier and cheaper to digitize, collate, and manipulate. So they started their own company to do just that—in Cambodia.

Hockenstein argued that none of the jobs being done in Cambodia came from the United States. This sort of basic data-entry work got outsourced to India and the Caribbean a long time ago, and, if anywhere, that is where the jobs were taken from. But none of this would have been possible to set up in Cambodia a decade ago. It all came together in just the last few years.

Hockenstein told me about his Cambodian partner, Sophary. "Until 1992 he was living in a refugee camp on the Cambodia-Thai border, while I was living in Harvard Square as an undergrad. We were worlds apart. After the UN peace treaty [in Cambodia], he walked home ten days to his village, and now today he lives in Phnom Penh running Digital Divide Data's office." They now instant-message each other each night to collaborate on the delivery of services to people and companies around the world. The type of collaboration that is possible today "allows us to be partners and equals," said Hockenstein.

By early 2007, 200 people had graduated from Digital Divide Data's program, and they were working in jobs averaging $153 a month. Almost all of them had dropped out of high school and before joining the company never thought they would earn more than a dollar a day. As important as the money is for them, the confidence and the new sense of what is possible that it gives them are equally valuable. "It is not one of us dominating the other," said Hockenstein. "It is real collaboration that is creating better futures for the people at the bottom and the top."

Not surprisingly, as news of the program spread, Hockenstein and his partners began getting calls from people in Mongolia, Pakistan, Iran, and Jordan who wanted to provide IT services to the world. In mid-2004, a client approached Digital Divide Data to digitize an English-Arabic dictionary. Around the same time, Hockenstein's office received an unsolicited e-mail from a company in Iran that was running a data-entry firm there. "They found us through a Google search," said Hockenstein. He asked the Iranians whether they could do an English-Arabic dictionary, even though the language of Iran is Farsi, which uses some but not all of the same letters as Arabic. "He said they could," said Hockenstein, "so we partnered on a joint project for this client to digitize an Arabic dictionary."

What I like most about the story, and why it is so telling of the flat world, is Hockenstein's kicker: "I still have never met the guy [in Iran]. We did the whole deal over Yahoo! instant messenger and e-mail. We wired him the money through Cambodia . . . I invited him to my wedding, but he wasn't able to come."

Today, Hockenstein pointed out, "you're just one degree from anyone or anything." Reflecting on his and his partner's experience in starting Digital Divide Data, he added: "Two people and a computer were able to create better lives for three hundred people . . . Two people and a Web site can now do anything."

No one assigned Hockenstein to go to Cambodia. No one paid him to go, either. He just went. "We showed up in Phnom Penh not knowing a person, rented an apartment, and knocked on doors," said Hockenstein. "And twenty-four hours later we were in the office of the person who had brought the Internet to Cambodia and was searching for a way to create jobs." So I asked him: "If you were counseling young people today, what would you tell them? Go to work for an NGO? The World Bank? A charity? Or business school?"

"True sustainability depends on market solutions," Hockenstein replied. "There are hundreds of NGOs training people to use computers and subsidizing the [enterprise]. But when the money runs out, only a very small fraction of these people are able to create any kind of livelihood for themselves on their own. Most in Cambodia had to go back to their family farms or sex trafficking." When you are trying to root out something like sex trafficking or drug harvesting, "you need alternative economic opportunities to solve it permanently, if you are talking about large numbers of people. We have rescued twenty women in Cambodia who now work at our place and have not had to go back to their previous lives. Many others have had to go back [to sex work] to earn a living."

Of course, the vast majority of people in Cambodia remain poor and disadvantaged. That is old. What is new is the emergence of home-grown Cambodian and Laotian engines to make Cambodia and Laos less poor. There are still miles to go, but you have to start somewhere.

Hockenstein's advice to college grads: "Young people find it hard to get involved with meaningful work even when they want to do something which matters. One reason is they are waiting for the corporate recruiters who come on campus to sit down and offer them a job which changes the world. Instead, consulting firms and investment banks show up. Don't wait for the recruiter from HR to come on campus to interview you. Get together the money for a plane ticket yourself."

Two teachers from opposite sides of the globe decided that they could take advantage of the flat world to teach about collaboration in a totally different way—and they did so without waiting for any administrator to change their curricula or direct them from above. I happened to come across the work of Julie Lindsay, from the International School Dhaka, in Bangladesh, and Vicki Davis, from Westwood Schools in Camilla, Georgia, while surfing the Web. They were using this book in their courses, and their goal was to teach their respective high school students about the flat world by allowing them to experience its various aspects on their own.

"When Vicki posted on her blog comments about her students' views of the book [The World Is Flat], I knew we had a match," Lindsay recalled. "By reading the blogs of other teachers, I realized that I could flatten the world by going directly to other teachers with common curricular purposes, and this is just what we did."

Added Davis: "When Julie contacted me, I knew that our project-based learning environment would mesh well with Julie's, and we immediately created a wiki and began planning" an educational joint venture.

The Flat Classroom Project (http://flatclassroomproject.wikispaces .com) took six weeks to plan and lasted for two weeks. Students from the class in Bangladesh and the class in Georgia were partnered and given the task to create a wiki page (a common Web page whose "members" can upload and edit content) based on one of the ten flatteners. To do this effectively, the students communicated regularly over the Internet, shared resources (photographs, music, and the like), and planned their project as if they were literally face-to-face in one classroom. They experienced the flatteners firsthand. Some students, for example, "outsourced" portions of their video presentation to their international partner, their teachers explained to me. The time difference was a challenge, with the two teachers often instant-messaging each other in the early morning or late at night. The students were never in the same classroom, on the same continent, or in the same time zone at the same time.

The students moved seamlessly among many types of software, hardware, and Web applications to create an effective Web presentation on their topic, the teachers said in a joint e-mail they sent me. These included "a central wiki, wiki discussion areas for conversation and teacher feedback, and RSS feeds to monitor changes. Students and teachers also used VoIP (Skype), IM chat, MySpace (to connect), Evoca (to share audio), YouTube, Google Video, Dropload (to transfer files), and many other resources to collaborate." In one instance, the teachers said, two students who called themselves "The C Team" (their names were Casey and Cannelle), tackled the topic of "virtual communications."

Lindsay and Davis agreed that social networking has great potential for learning and inspiring global collaboration. "This project also created friendships across the world and promoted a cultural understanding that is needed in our world today," they said. "We may be from opposite sides of the world, but our students became one class tethered by invisible strings of bits and bytes."

When I asked Lindsay and Davis what *they* learned from doing this, I got an earful: "Students are hungering for meaningful connections with one another. They want to understand if the stereotypes portrayed by much of the mass media are true and they want to connect and decide for themselves—thus the explosive growth of sites like MySpace and YouTube. This ability to connect has largely been ignored and blocked by many in the educational community who would rather maintain the entrenched style of a classroom that has been around for over a hundred years. But there are some educators creating safe, meaningful, engaging 'flat' online projects and collaboratives who are experiencing incredible results in their classrooms and sharing it with one another."

Not only did the projects give the students "intentional knowledge"— knowledge the teacher intends for them to learn—they also gain the "unintentional" knowledge that comes with the experience of collaborating with people halfway across the world. "We build relational bridges that the students of tomorrow can walk across," the two teachers explained. "We've connected the technology; now it is truly time to connect the people."

It is heartening to see educators now bypassing traditional intermediaries to share resources, best practices, and information. Teachers interested in learning how to do more can contact flatclassroomproject@gmail.com.

S ome other social entrepreneurs are now using the flat-world platform to try to improve government in the United States, because they understand that this new platform gives a whole new power to grassroots activists in a democracy—as opposed to party machines or big media. Consider my friend Andrew Rasiej, a former music promoter who founded MOUSE.org to bring more technology to New York City schools and who, in 2005, was a Democratic candidate for New York City's Office of Public Advocate—a city ombudsman who is supposed to hold the mayor accountable on community relations and investigates complaints about everything from potholes to city services. I met Rasiej during his campaign, when he was trying to get attention for his proposal that New York City provide universal Wi-Fi infrastructure, so anyone anywhere could get access to high-speed Internet and cell phone coverage. His candidacy ultimately failed. He was ahead of his time. But eventually, time will catch up to him.

The old industrial approach to politics, argued Rasiej, "is one to many." That is, we elect someone who will solve our problems for us. The new model in business is that you involve your community and customers in an ongoing conversation about every aspect of your business, from the moment you conceive a product, to how you design it, to the supply chain that builds it and delivers it, to the way you collect and absorb customer feedback and respond more quickly to changing tastes.

"Well, the time is here to apply the same principle—the power of many—to reinventing civic life and reinvigorating our democracy," insisted Rasiej. "Not only are you improving city services and the quality of life, but you are giving people a way to participate in the decisions that affect their lives in a way that is easy and where they see the results."

Rasiej proposed the creation of a Web site where any citizen using his or her cell phone could take a picture of a pothole, any dangerous broken railing, or even a suspected crime and immediately e-mail it to City Hall or post it on the official Web site, so every citizen, in effect, becomes a potential ombudsman. Two years later, New York City started implementing just such a program.

Rasiej believes that 2004 Democratic presidential candidate Howard Dean accidentally discovered the power of the network when he started online fund-raising in his failed bid for the White House, but never had a chance to follow it up. "Dean did not realize that the money that was flowing into his campaign, via the Internet, was actually the by-product of the vibrant community of Democratic and angry anti-Bush and anti-war voters who were talking to each other and propelling his candidacy," said Rasiej. Neither did any other candidate; no one tried to run a flat campaign in 2004. But trust me, in the near future candidates will figure this out. There is an iron law in American politics: The party that most quickly absorbs and adopts the latest technology dominates politics. FDR dominated the radio through the fireside chat; JFK triumphed over Nixon in televised debates; Republicans rose to power on talk radio; and Karl Rove mastered the use of direct mail and computerized databases. The next technological political model will revolve around the power of community and individual uploading. In this model, the public officeholder will no longer be the one who promises to solve the problems of the many. Rather, he or she will become a hub of connectivity for the many to work with the many, creating networks of public advocates to identify problems, solve them, and get behind candidates who are ready to mobilize the government and the people in the right direction.

"One elected official [alone] cannot solve the problems of eight million people," said Rasiej, "but eight million people networked together can solve one city's problems. They can spot and offer solutions better and faster than any bureaucrat.

"The party that stakes out this new frontier is the party that will be the majority party in the twenty-first century," Rasiej argues. "And the Democrats had better understand something: Their base right now is the most disconnected from the network."

Democracy in America is changing, and it was with this change in mind that Rasiej joined with former *Nation* editor Micah Sifry to form www.personaldemocracy.com. They write: "A new force, rooted in new tools and practices built on and around the Internet, is rising alongside the old system of capital-intensive broadcast politics . . . Networked voices are reviving the civic conversation. More people, every day, are discovering this new power. After years of being treated like passive subjects of marketing and manipulation, they want to be heard. Members expect a say in the decision-making process of the organizations they join. Readers want to talk back to the news-makers. Citizens are insisting

on more openness and transparency from government. All the old institutions and players—big money, top-down parties, big-foot journalism,
cloistered organizations—must adapt or face losing status and power.
Personal democracy, where everyone is a full participant, is coming."

Just look at how Virginia's Senator George Allen was caught on video
using the term "macaca" to dismiss a young critic—an insult that was uploaded to the Internet, where it fatally wounded his reelection campaign.
Future elections, note Rasiej and Sifry, are sure to be even further affected
by the scope and reach of the Internet, "with all kinds of voter-generated
content, citizen activism, social networks, and the power of the technology to force transparency in the electoral process and in government."

W alls simply aren't what they used to be—even for kings and
queens—and this change is opening new opportunities for political activism where it was previously unimaginable. A vivid example of this
was described by William Wallis in the *Financial Times* (November 24,
2006). Writing from Manama, Bahrain, Wallis reported that "[s]ince
Bahrain's government blocked the Google Earth Web site earlier this year
for its intrusion into private homes and royal palaces, Googling their island kingdom has become a national pastime for many Bahrainis."

Bahrain is a tiny island state off the east coast of Saudi Arabia. About
60 per cent of Bahrain's population are Shiite Muslims, but the ruling al-
Khalifa family are Sunnis. The Bahraini Shiites have long insisted on a
greater share of wealth and power. "Opposition activists claim that 80 per
cent of the island has been carved up between royals and other private
landlords, while much of the rest of the population faces an acute housing shortage," added Wallis.

"The site allows Internet users to view satellite images of the world in
varying degrees of detail. When Google updated its images of Bahrain to
higher definition, cyber-activists seized on the view it gave of estates and
private islands belonging to the ruling al-Khalifa family to highlight the
inequity of land distribution in the tiny Gulf kingdom," Wallis explained.
A senior government official told Wallis that Google Earth "had allowed
the public to pry into private homes and ogle people's motor yachts and

swimming pools. But he acknowledged that the government's three-day attempt to block the site had proved counterproductive. It gave instant publicity to Google Earth and contributed to growing sophistication among Bahrainis in circumventing web censorship. It also provided more ammunition to democracy activists ahead of [the 2006] parliamentary elections . . . the second since King Hamad bin Issa al-Khalifa began introducing limited political reforms in 2001."

Wallis explained: "Mahmood al-Yousif, a businessman whose political chat and blog site Mahmood's Den is among Bahrain's most popular, says that in the tense run-up to the polls, few Bahrainis have not surfed over the contours of their kingdom, comparing vast royal palaces, marinas and golf courses with crowded Shia villages nearby, where unemployment is rife and services meagre. For those with insufficient bandwidth to access Google Earth, a PDF file with dozens of downloaded images of royal estates has been circulated anonymously by e-mail. Mr Yousif, among others, initially encouraged web users to post images on photo-sharing websites. 'Some of the palaces take up more space than three or four villages nearby and block access to the sea for fishermen. People knew this already. But they never saw it. All they saw were the surrounding walls,' said Mr Yousif, who is seen in Bahrain as the grandfather of its blogging community.

"He and other activists believe creative use of the Internet—connectivity in Bahrain is among the highest in the Arab world—is forcing the country to confront awkward realities and will speed the march towards a more egalitarian society. But loyalists find irreverent discussion of the royal family on the Web offensive and dangerous. While some younger members of the royal family apparently saw the futility of blocking Google Earth and reversed it quickly, others in government have waged a virtual battle with the nation's proliferating cyber-activists using technology as well as an arsenal of press censorship laws . . . 'There are some in the government who are still living in the age of the telex, when you could very easily put controls on communications. But these Orwellian policing methods do not have a place in this modern age,' says Mr Yousif."

As they have been for generations, all of these Bahraini royal palaces are surrounded by high walls, keeping people from looking inside. And then along came Google Earth. It flattened all the walls, and suddenly *everyone* could look inside—and act on what they saw.

While covering the Arab-Israeli conflict, I learned that the way you get big change is by getting the big players to do the right thing for the wrong reasons. That is, if you wait for everyone to do the right things for the right reasons, you can wait forever. This approach really underpins another kind of social entrepreneurship being made possible by the flat world—activists partnering with the world's largest multinational corporations to get them to change their business practices, with far-reaching effects.

In the flat world, the balance of power between global companies and the individual communities in which they operate is tilting more and more in favor of the companies, many of them American-based. These companies command as much if not more power than many governments, not only to create value but also to transmit values. The desire of corporations to avoid being the target of global protest in a flat world has made them much more open to working with social and environmental activists, who are collaborating with progressive companies in ways that can make the companies more profitable and the flat earth more livable.

Let me illustrate this notion with a couple of examples. If you think about the forces that are gobbling up biodiversity around the planet, no force is more powerful than farming. So how and where the big food producers farm and fish really matters as to whether we manage to preserve natural habitats and species. Conservation International, one of the biggest environmental NGOs in the world, has as its main mission preserving biodiversity. It is also a big believer in trying, when possible, to collaborate with big business, because when you bring a major global player around, it can have a huge impact on the environment. In 2002, McDonald's and Conservation International forged a partnership to use the McDonald's global supply chain—a behemoth that sucks beef, fish, chicken, pork, bread, lettuce, pickles, tomatoes, and potatoes from all four corners of the flat world—to produce not just monetary value but also different values about the environment. "We and McDonald's looked at a set of environmental issues and said, 'Here are the things the food suppliers could do to reduce the environmental impact at little or no cost,'" explained Glenn Prickett, senior vice president of Conservation International.

McDonald's then met with its key suppliers and worked out, with them and with CI, a set of guidelines for what McDonald's calls "socially responsible food supply." "For conservationists, the challenge is how do you get your arms around hundreds of millions of decisions and decision makers involved in agriculture and fisheries, who are not coordinated in any way except by the market," said Prickett. "So what we look for are partners who can put their purchasing power behind a set of environmentally friendly practices in a way that is good for them, works for the producers, and is good for biodiversity. In that way, you can start to capture so many more decision makers . . . There is no global government authority to protect biodiversity. You have to collaborate with the players who can make a difference, and one of them is McDonald's."

Conservation International is already seeing improvements in conservation of water, energy, and waste, as well as steps to encourage better management of fisheries, among McDonald's suppliers. But it is still early, and one will have to assess over a period of years, with comprehensive data collection, whether this is really having a positive impact on the environment. This form of collaboration cannot and should never be a substitute for government rules and oversight. But if it works, it can be a vehicle for actually getting government rules implemented. Environmentalists who prefer government regulation to these more collaborative efforts often ignore the fact that strong rules imposed against the will of farmers end up being weakly enforced—or not enforced at all.

What is in this for McDonald's? It is a huge opportunity to improve its global brand by acting as a good global citizen. Conservation International has struck similar supply-chain collaborations with Starbucks, setting rules for its supply chain of coffee farmers, and Office Depot, with its supply chain of paper-product providers.

What these collaborations do is start to "break down the walls between different interest groups," said Prickett. Normally you would have
the environmentalists on one side and the farmers on the other and each
side trying to get the government to write the regulations in the way that
would serve it. Government would end up writing the rules largely to
benefit business. "Now, instead, we have a private entity saying, 'We want
to use our global supply chain to do some good, but we understand that
to be effective it has to be a collaboration with the farmers and the environmentalists if it is going to have any impact,'" Prickett said.

Following his work with McDonald's, Prickett turned his attention to
Wal-Mart, the world's biggest retailer. Conservation International is working with Wal-Mart's executives to think about their environmental footprint and create a strategy to turn that from a negative to a positive—from
how they use energy to the packaging of the products they sell to how
those products are produced around the world.

"What is exciting about working with Wal-Mart is that it is the world's
largest retailer," said Prickett, "and when you start to impact its supply
chain in terms of the standards it expects its suppliers to adopt, you are
talking about more than sixty thousand suppliers across every merchandise supply chain and around the world. What is also exciting about Wal-
Mart is the signal it sends to the business community at large. It tells
other CEOs that if the world's largest retailer has taken this seriously,
there must be something to it. And suddenly 'green' becomes an acceptable business strategy. We have already seen that begin to empower individuals in big companies who have had great green ideas for their supply
chains but have never had the executive-level mandate to act on them.
Now they do—either because they are a Wal-Mart supplier and have to
go green, or because they have experienced the Wal-Mart effect and
their bosses are saying, 'Hey, there is something to this.' Suddenly with
Wal-Mart going green, you are putting the green movement on Main
Street. Ultimately that will have a political impact. It is the democratization of sustainability. It is not just an elite cause for people on the
coasts anymore."

A similar movement has been under way for a while in the consumer
electronics world, with an HP-Dell-IBM alliance. In October 2004,

these three giants joined forces, in a collaborative effort with key members of their computer and printer supply chains, to promote a unified code of socially responsible manufacturing practices across the world. The new Electronics Industry Code of Conduct includes bans on bribes, child labor, embezzlement and extortion, and violations of intellectual property; rules governing usage of wastewater, hazardous materials, pollutants; and regulations on the reporting of occupational injuries. Several major electronics manufacturers who serve the IBM, Dell, and HP supply chains collaborated on writing the code, including Celestica, Flextronics, Jabil, Sanmina-SCI, and Solectron.

Compliance is everything, and so, again, it remains to be seen just how vigilant the corporations will be with their suppliers. Nevertheless, this use of supply chains to create values—not just value—could be a wave of the future.

"As we have begun to look to other [offshore] suppliers to do most of our manufacturing, it has become clear to us that we have to assume some responsibility for how they do that work," explained Debra Dunn, HP's senior vice president of corporate affairs and global citizenship. First and foremost, that is what many of HP's customers want. "Customers care," said Dunn, "and European customers lead the way in caring. And human rights groups and NGOs, who are gaining increasing global influence as trust in corporations declines, are basically saying, 'You guys have the power here. You are global companies, you can set expectations that will influence environmental practices and human rights practices in emerging markets.'"

Those voices are right, and what is more, they can use the Internet to drive the point home to companies that don't get it.

"When you have the procurement dollars that HP and McDonald's have," said Dunn, "people really want to do business with you, so you have leverage and are in a position to set standards, and [therefore] you have a responsibility to set standards . . . We used to say that as long as we complied with the local law, that was all we could be expected to do. But now the imbalance of power is so huge it is not practical to say that Wal-Mart or HP can do whatever they want as long as a state government or country does not stop them. The leverage HP would leave on the table would be immoral given its superior power . . . We have the power to transmit global governance to our universe of suppliers and employees and consumers, which is a pretty broad universe."

I have no doubt that plenty of abuse remains in electronics factories in the developing world—particularly in China—even in those producing for the likes of HP, Dell, and IBM. But I also have no doubt that programs like the Electronics Industry Code of Conduct create a baseline that give labor activists a much more powerful club to wield in pressing for improved working conditions. The key is enforcement. And the key to enforcement is for social entrepreneurs to educate consumers to the fact that they have power, that their buying decisions and buying power are political tools and they need to use them.

But is it a sell-out for social entrepreneurs to try to change the world through markets rather than marches? I posed that question to Rob Watson, chairman and CEO of EcoTech International. Watson grew up in the environmental movement, was one of the most respected environmentalists working on China, but eventually decided to go to business school and start a company. When I asked him why, he sent me the following e-mail, titled "What I Learned in Business School." It is an important message:

> What would possess a 43-year-old father to abandon an extremely successful 20-plus-year career in the non-profit world for a two-year slog through business school and the trauma of starting a new business halfway around the world? My life has always been about doing the greatest good for the greatest number. I have chosen to focus my efforts on protecting the environment, which is the underpinning of human existence on the Earth. For me it has always been about the mission, with organizations being the means to that end. For over twenty years that organization was the non-profit Natural Resources Defense Council (NRDC), one of the world's most effective environmental advocacy groups. At NRDC I had the good fortune to have worked on four continents helping

governments and businesses create policies, programs and projects that help the environment. As a founding member and volunteer for the U.S. Green Building Council, I founded the LEED (Leadership in Energy and Environmental Design) green building rating system, which—due to the dedication of hundreds of volunteers like myself and tireless efforts of the USGBC staff—has become the premier green building certification system in the world. Without a doubt I had made a difference.

Yet, my experience in the field made me realize that I needed to chart a different course. For many years when people came to me at NRDC for advice about how to get involved and make a difference with the environment, invariably they would ask me to which law program or environmental science program they should apply. Instead, I would recommend that people go to business school. My advice was based on my belief that the legal and regulatory frameworks for environmental protection largely have been established. Given our current situation, I realized that now it was about diffusion and implementation—and implementation is where business excels. This belief coupled with the simple fact that there were far more environmental lawyers and scientists floating around than environmental businessmen and that green business was needed to put environmental protection on the ground.

I felt that the main reason mainstream business continues to be a cause of environmental problems instead of its solution is that business-as-usual continues to use 19th-century economics and 20th-century engineering when trying to solve 21st-century problems. I saw the need for new green frameworks for business—where the clean path is the most profitable. Economics, finance and accounting are human laws and can be changed unlike, say, gravity, which is a natural law—one that applies to all species, not just one. We need to realign these human laws with natural law unless we want to be a bad biological experiment on the planet. I felt that as a (hopefully to be successful) businessperson I could make the case for this paradigm shift more effectively than as a non-profit environmental advocate. But to be an effective change agent, I felt I needed to know something about the system I was trying to change. So I finally took my own advice and went to Columbia Business School. Over the course of my MBA program I learned or reaffirmed three main things:

1. Doing business well is very, very hard.
2. Few people do business well.
3. The conceptual frameworks and tools underlying the conduct of today's business are hopelessly outdated—as noted above.

I think the process of establishing a new business framework will be one of learning by doing—where theory and observation play off each other to create a truly sustainable way of providing people with what they want. As a first step, we need to get the market and regulatory polemicists off each other's back. Both are right and both are wrong: markets and regulations each are necessary, but not sufficient. Good regulation makes markets work properly and removes the worst actors, while markets stimulate innovation and efficient delivery of goods and services. My goal in going to business school and switching hats from the non-profit to the business sector is to be a model for a new paradigm where business can effectively and efficiently operate on a large scale for the betterment of humankind. Wish me luck.

Good luck, Rob. As for the rest of you, well, like I said, if it's not happening, it's because you're not doing it.

FOURTEEN

What Happens When We
All Have Dog's Hearing?

In the fall of 2006 I took a reporting/book-promotion trip to Germany and France. The night I arrived at Paris's Charles de Gaulle International Airport I was met by a driver sent by my French publisher. A young man of African descent, the driver was carrying a sign with my name on it, and as I approached him I noticed that he was talking to himself, in French, very animatedly. As I got closer, I realized he had a Bluetooth wireless phone clipped to his ear and was deep in conversation with someone else. I pointed at myself as the person he was supposed to meet. He nodded and went on talking to whoever was on the other end of his phone. When my luggage arrived, I grabbed it off the belt; he pointed toward the exit and I followed while he kept talking. When we got into the car, I said, "Do you know my hotel?" He said, "*Non*." I showed him the address on a piece of paper, and he went back to talking on the phone. After the car started to roll, I saw that he had a movie playing on the little flat screen in the dashboard, the one that usually displays the GPS road map. I noticed this because I was in the backseat trying to finish writing a column on my laptop, and between the sound of his talking on the phone and the soundtrack of the movie, I could barely concentrate. When I had written all that I could, I got out my iPod, put in the earphones, and zoned out on a Stevie Nicks album—while the driver went on talking, steering, and watching the movie. As we arrived at my hotel, I reflected on our trip: He and I had been together for an hour, and between the two of us we had been doing six different things. He was driving, talking on his phone, and watching a movie. I was riding, working on my laptop, and listening to my iPod.

There was only one thing we never did: talk to each other.

It's a pity. He probably had a lot to tell me. When I related all this to my friend Alain Frachon, a senior editor at *Le Monde*, he quipped, "I guess the era of foreign correspondents quoting taxi drivers is over!" Alain meant the old-school opinion pieces that invariably began, "As my Paris taxi driver said to me about the French elections . . ." Well, you can forget about reading columns starting that way anymore. My Paris taxi driver was too busy to say hello, let alone opine on politics; and I was too busy finishing a column I'd started on the plane to pay full attention to my new surroundings.

Yes, technology can make the far feel very near. But it can also make the near feel very far. For all I know, the driver was talking to his parents somewhere in Africa. How wonderful! But that meant the two of us wouldn't talk at all. And we were sitting two feet away from each other. When I shared this story with Linda Stone, the technologist who labeled the disease of the Internet age "continuous partial attention"—two people doing six things, devoting only partial attention to each one—she remarked to me, "We're so accessible, we're inaccessible. We can't find the off switch on our devices or on ourselves. We want to wear an iPod as much to listen to our own playlists as to block out the rest of the world and protect ourselves from all that noise. We are everywhere—except where we actually are physically."

A month before my visit to Paris, I was in San Francisco. I was standing at an intersection waiting to cross the street when a man jogging and wearing an iPod came up next to me. As soon as the light turned green he sprinted into the crosswalk. But a woman driving a car—running a yellow light—almost hit him before she hit the brakes. She was holding a cell phone to her right ear and driving with her left hand. I thought to myself, "I've just witnessed the first postmodern local news story," and I immediately crafted the lead in my head: "A woman driving her car while speaking on her cell phone ran over a man jogging across the street while listening to his iPod. See page 6."

These encounters illustrate a few of the many social downsides of all the connectivity that has helped to flatten the world—and those downsides are what I want to explore in this chapter. By social downsides, I do not mean things like Osama bin Laden using a cell phone or terrorist networks setting up Web sites. I mean the social downsides for you and me, our children and neighbors, strangers and friends, and the effects all this new connectivity is having on our interactions and public life.

The very technologies that are uniting us are also clearly dividing us. The same technologies that allow us to connect with each other as never before also allow us to interrupt each other as never before. The technologies that are empowering individuals to upload their own content—through blogs, podcasts, and instant messaging—and to inscribe themselves on the world also contribute to a coarsening of our language and the dumbing down of our discourse. And most troubling, but still not yet fully understood, is what happens when we can all not only author our own content and upload it globally, but, thanks to improved connectivity and search engines, read all the content people are authoring about us. What happens when the Internet becomes so ubiquitous and search engines so refined that we can all suddenly hear everything whispered about us? What happens when we all have dog's hearing?

Let's look at each of these issues. The real meaning of what happened with my Paris driver is that every new technology or toy that connects us more easily divides us more easily—and you can now see and feel that everywhere. Our family has gone skiing in Colorado over Christmas for twenty-five years. Riding on the lift or in the big gondola car with strangers was always fun, because you never knew whom you might be paired with on a long ride up the mountain. Often the person was a foreigner and you could actually learn something from a chance encounter on the chairlift. Now it is almost standard that the minute you get into the gondola someone in the cabin will whip out a cell phone and your chances of having a conversation with him or her, or with anyone else in the car, for that matter, are zero. Who hasn't sat on a train behind a person who is talking on the phone and been forced to listen to the conversation, which is often so personal—about money, family or a relationship—that you can't believe this person is broadcasting it to a bunch of strangers? I am amazed at the personal things people will say loudly into a cell phone that they would never even whisper to a stranger if they were just sitting next to him or her.

No wonder people have to do online dating: Your chances of a chance encounter now on a ski lift or on a train or a bus are so much lower today than they used to be, because the chances that the person sitting next to you will be absorbed in a handheld device, rather than being open to engaging the person next to him or her, are so much higher. Meetings, too, are not what they used to be, not when half the people in the room are checking their PalmPilots and BlackBerrys under the table, while they occasionally nod their head at you or glance your way. Whenever I am in a group meeting around a conference table, I want to start by saying: "All right everybody, both hands on the table. I want to see all ten of your fingers at all times. No BlackBerrys allowed." It is the only hope you have of them listening to you.

I love having lots of contacts and easy connectivity, but in an age when so many people you know—and even more you don't know—can contact you, I'm finding this more and more disconcerting. I call it "the Age of Interruption," because it really is an age of constant interruptions—unless you totally unplug. We have gone from the Iron Age to the Industrial Age to the Information Age to the Age of Interruption. All we do now is interrupt each other (and ourselves) with these instant messages, e-mail, or cell phone calls. And when someone isn't deliberately interrupting you, someone else is accidentally doing it with a ringing cell phone, jangling you with Tchaikovsky's 1812 Overture, while you are trying to nap or write on the train. Who can think or innovate under such conditions? I know that connectivity means productivity. But it is possible to overdose, to reach a point where connectivity leads to so many interruptions that it stifles our creativity. Indeed, one wonders whether the Age of Interruption will lead to a decline in civilization as ideas and attention spans shrink and we all get diagnosed with some version of attention deficit disorder.

After writing a column about this, I was inundated with reader comments. One of my favorites was a letter from Elizabeth Winthrop of

Williamstown, Mass., who wrote: "Friends laugh when I tell them that as a novelist I am looking for a shack in the woods where I can completely unplug. Otherwise, how will I ever be able to get still enough to hear the next character talking to me when cell phones are ringing and e-mail is calling and the Web, that ever-present temptress, is wooing me?"

I know how she feels. I often feel that I was much smarter when I could do only one thing at a time, and I know that I am not alone in that feeling. One day in the fall of 2006, I was trying to track down my friend Yaron Ezrahi in Jerusalem to ask him a question. I kept calling his cell phone and getting no answer. I eventually reached him at home. "Yaron, what's wrong with your cell phone?" I asked.

"It was stolen a few months ago," he answered, adding that he decided not to replace it because its ringing was constantly breaking his concentration. "Since then, the first thing I do every morning is thank the thief and wish him a long life."

While the cell phone had made Yaron more mobile, it also had made him more distracted. Suddenly, his office was tethered to him wherever he went, like a ball and chain. That level of connectivity may be very useful if you are a stockbroker, but not if you're a thinker, a professor, or an author. When you're always connected, you're always "in." You're never "out." Out is over. The only way really to get out of your office now is both to walk out the door and turn off every mobile device you own.

The fact that technology allows us to access, create, and receive more and more information doesn't mean that our minds can absorb it all. Moore's Law applies to microchips, but not to the human brain. Our capacity to process and analyze information doesn't double every twenty-four months. Some days I look at all the e-mail waiting in my computer and I just want to delete it all—without reading a word. I feel like the proverbial glass that is already full but that someone is still constantly pouring water into. There is so much information coming at us now, we find it harder and harder to set priorities—to separate the merely insistent from the truly important. There is no clerk down the hall to sort it all out for you. Now everyone is their own mailroom—which is fine, except that I have another job.

You don't appreciate just how liberating getting away can be until you really go cold turkey. In June 2006, after touring the Peruvian rain forest, I was left with two especially strong impressions. First, I was struck by what an incredibly violent place the rain forest is, with trees, plants, and vines all struggling with each other for sunlight, and animals, insects, and birds doing the same for food. But I was also struck by how disconnected it is. Yes, I had to go to the Tambopata Research Center, deep in the Peruvian rain forest, to find it, but I can report there is still a place with no Internet or cell phone service. Of course, there are many such places, but the fact that I had seen people using their cell phones from atop the sacred Inca ruin of Machu Picchu two days earlier reminded me that there are fewer and fewer each day, even in the Andes. There was something cleansing about spending four days totally disconnected. It was the best possible antidote to Linda Stone's "continuous partial attention."

Maybe soon we'll have to artificially re-create the experience of being "out." Maybe soon we'll see ads for a Four Seasons resort that promises not only beautiful beaches and beautiful rooms—but also *no connectivity*. The ad might read: "We guarantee that every room comes WITHOUT Internet service." Or, "Our entire hotel is a cold zone. We have no hot zones here, no wireless service available whatsoever." You would surely return home better rested.

Our Peruvian rain forest guide, Gilbert, carried no handheld devices and no cell phone and did not suffer from continuous partial attention. Just the opposite. He heard every chirp, whistle, howl, and crackle in the rain forest and would stop us in our tracks and immediately identify the bird, insect, or animal we were hearing. He also had incredible vision and never missed a spider's web, or a butterfly, or a toucan, or a column of marching termites. He was totally disconnected from the Web but totally in touch with the incredible web of life around him.

There's a lesson there.

Too much connectivity may be bad not only for your peace of mind—it may not be healthy for society as a whole. When so many people can upload and globalize their voice, their video, their blog, their instant message—when it is so easy to do—it's also much more addictive for them and for us. I am not sure it is good to have millions of people addicted to a form of communication that, by its nature, is unedited, spontaneous, unfiltered, and uncensored. There are some great bloggers and podcasters, who could be working anywhere, and the flat world has opened up wonderful new opportunities for them to emerge—and even take down a TXU. I enjoy and respect their work. But there are plenty of others who either could really use an editor or should be keeping their thoughts to themselves—or reading a book or taking a class, rather than blogging and podcasting in their spare time.

When *Time* magazine celebrated "You" (as in YouTube) as its Person of the Year for 2006, the magazine's cover package included a skeptical piece by *NBC Nightly News* anchor Brian Williams, a piece that raised this issue. With all this emerging connectivity that is allowing everyone to blog, or podcast, or instant-message his or her opinions or ideas whenever the urge strikes, Williams wrote, "The danger just might be that we miss the next great book or the next great idea, or that we fail to meet the next great challenge . . . because we are too busy celebrating ourselves." In *The Washington Post* (December 21, 2006), columnist George F. Will also poured a dose of skepticism on this celebration of the power of "You" to author your own content. Will wrote: "Richard Stengel, *Time*'s managing editor, says, 'Thomas Paine was in effect the first blogger' and 'Ben Franklin was essentially loading his persona into the MySpace of the 18th century, "Poor Richard's Almanack."' Not exactly. Franklin's extraordinary persona informed what he wrote but was not the subject of what he wrote. Paine was perhaps history's most consequential pamphleteer. There are expected to be 100 million bloggers worldwide by the middle of 2007, which is why none will be like Franklin or Paine. Both were geniuses; genius is scarce."

Another effect of the Age of Interruption is the sheer corruption of the language that it brings about. Now that we all are connected to each other all the time, many people have too little time to spend on writing properly. No one ever wrote a great book with his thumbs, which is how many young people type SMS—short message service—text messages on their cell phones. *The Washington Post*'s Lori Aratani, in a December

25, 2006, article, described how instant-messaging shorthand was creeping into the essays of high school and college students. Imagine what English prose is going to look like in ten years:

> Zoe Bambery, a senior at Walter Johnson High School in Bethesda, might send more than 100 instant messages — IMs — during a typical evening. So during the SAT exam, the 18-year-old found herself inadvertently lapsing into IM-speak, using "b/c" instead of "because" as she scrambled to finish her essay.
>
> She caught herself and now is careful to proofread before hitting print. But she is hardly the only student to find IM phrases creeping into schoolwork.
>
> "They are using it absolutely everywhere," said Sara Goodman, an English teacher at Clarksburg High School in Montgomery County, who has worn out many purple and red markers circling the offending phrases in papers and tests.
>
> Wendy Borelli, a seasoned English teacher at Springbrook High in Silver Spring, finds photo captions for the school yearbook sprinkled with shorthand such as "B4" and "nite." A student who left on a brief errand to the office announced he would "BRB." . . .
>
> It's not just teenagers. Some college professors say the lingo is popping up at their level as well.
>
> Jeff Stanton, an associate professor in the school of information sciences at Syracuse University, said sometimes he is taken aback at how informal students have become in the way they communicate.
>
> Stanton shared one of his favorite pieces of correspondence: "hi prof how are u culd u tell me my xm grade — tim." . . .
>
> After several weeks of grading papers filled with IM-speak and other jargon, Goodman took matters into her own hands.
>
> When the students showed up for class the following day, she asked them to read a paragraph she had written using many of the same phrases they used in their papers. "chaucer's the canterbury tales r a scathing attack on the catholic church of the late

1300s . . . he uses the descriptions of many pilgrims (including several very sketchy religious dawgs) 2 deliver a veiled message about the mad corruption he like saw in the church the greed that some of his characters have 4 money, represents like the use of church scratch 2 build some pretty tight cathedrals."

She said they laughed but understood her point.

There is one other social downside I worry about in this Age of Interruption: What happens when we can all not only rant or whisper anything we want in our MySpace blog or podcast, but also hear everything ranted or whispered about us?

What do I mean? Millions of people today are blogging, podcasting, and creating video content for YouTube or their own MySpace or Facebook or Yahoo! Groups or Friendster or Flickr or Second Life sites, or just writing for online newspapers or magazines. Beyond the sheer amateur-hour quality of a lot of this content, it is bringing some troubling social and legal issues our way much faster than we—or our legal systems—are ready to handle.

If you are any kind of public figure today—in politics, sports, entertainment, education, media, business, or government—chances are that someone out there somewhere is blogging about you right now. And if you want to find out what people are saying, all you have to do is type your name into Google or Technorati.com and hit Search. As I write these words, in April 2007, Google's search engine brings up 60,100,000 references to the phrase "The World Is Flat." I confess, there was a time when I would use Google to see what was being written about this book. I don't anymore. While many references are neutral or full of praise, others are vitriolic or flat-out nuts.

As someone who works in the public eye and is used to criticism, I have developed a thick skin. You have to if you are going to be a columnist. But here's my question for you, dear reader: What happens when all your neighbors, or all your students, have blogs of their own? Are you ready? How thick is your skin? Because when we are all publishers with our own blogs, and when we are all broadcasters through YouTube, and when we are all paparazzi thanks to our cell phone cameras, we are all public figures. Everybody is fair game. Everybody is news.

What happens when one of your neighbors makes a nasty comment or uploads some embarrassing pictures of you into his or her MySpace— so that now the whole world can see them, along with you? What happens if your neighbor hears shouting and crashing dishes from your house one evening and writes in her MySpace blog, "The Johnsons had a wild fight last night. I heard dishes breaking!"? What if the truth is that you have Greek ancestry and you and your husband like to celebrate birthdays by throwing dishes into the fireplace? How do you get the misperception corrected after it has been sent all over the neighborhood and all over the world?

We are already seeing some court cases arising around just such issues. Consider this October 11, 2006, article from the technology news site arstechnica.com: The headline read, "Principal Sues Students, Parents over MySpace Page." The article, by Nate Anderson, began: "MySpace will eventually be used to save the life of a cute puppy trapped in a well, and the company will bask in the glow of some unusual good press. But until that happens, we'll all have to settle for the more traditional stories of sexual predators, online harassment, and school officials who see MySpace as little more than a filthy cancer . . . That's the case in Texas, where an assistant principal is suing two students and their parents over a MySpace page that depicted the administrator as a lesbian and contained 'obscene comments, pictures and graphics,' according to the court filing."

Anderson went on to explain how the assistant principal at a San Antonio high school "had been forced to discipline [the two students] several times, and was aware of their animosity to her, but apparently did not suspect the lengths to which they would go to get a bit of revenge." The two students, Anderson explained, set up a MySpace page in the principal's name that suggested she was a lesbian, which she was not. Furthermore, the page featured comments from other MySpace users who knew the assistant principal. These messages were also abusive.

According to the court filing, Anderson reported, a school official brought the page to the attention of the assistant principal, upsetting her.

"The situation rattled the school administration enough that [the assistant principal]'s picture was removed from the school Web site and a brief video about the dangers of MySpace was posted instead. What sets this case apart from many other lawsuits filed over the content of blogs is that it doesn't target only the teenagers who created the site," wrote Anderson. "It also argues that the parents were guilty of negligence by failing to supervise their children, and that they bear some of the responsibility for the defaming site. The police were able to determine that the computers used to create the site were located in the students' homes, and [the] lawsuit says that the parents have a duty to know what their children are up to."

This is just the beginning. What Dov Seidman called "the dishonorable accuser," or the malicious gossip, always had power to ruin someone's life, but now that power has been magnified. In the old days, you pretty much had to be a movie star like Tom Cruise or a well-known politician to worry about what strangers might say about you in print, and usually the worst that these celebrities had to worry about was a false or exaggerated story in a supermarket tabloid like the *National Enquirer*. But as the world has gotten flat, and we all have started to become public figures to some degree—even an assistant principal in Texas—we all need to be worried about bad press. After all, what was the *National Enquirer*? It was a tabloid newspaper, sold largely in supermarkets. It had editors, reporters, and libel lawyers, all of whom knew something about journalism and its limits, even if they often went right up to the line—and over it once in a while. And as outrageous as the *National Enquirer* might be, it was always accountable for what it wrote—and could be held accountable in court, because it was published by a company whose address could be found inside. And while its reach was wide, it was only as wide as those who bought it or quoted it. You could not easily buy a copy outside of the United States. As a tabloid, it was not archived by libraries and the like. Once it was gone, it was gone, and the story often went with it.

Now fast-forward to today. Thanks to the flattening of the world, we are all potential pornographers, yellow journalists, and paparazzi. Almost no one has an editor or libel lawyer, and few people can be held accountable for the language or accuracy of the content they upload to the

Web. Most important of all, there are no longer any walls to contain what you write or what is written about you. Once it hits the Web, it goes worldwide.

Moreover, the buyers of the *National Enquirer* had no easy way to connect with one another, or, for that matter, with the tabloid's editors. The information flow was basically one way—from the *National Enquirer* to its readers. Not anymore. Now, not only can you broadcast by yourself globally without limits and without libel lawyers, but you can link to other people who come to your Web site. The dialogue is now two-way and multidimensional.

When people of like mind can connect this way easily, they can mobilize each other and create an enormous echo effect—for things that are true and untrue, constructive and destructive. If you visit extreme or narrowly defined Web sites or blogs—whether they are racist or liberal, atheist or environmentalist, radical Islamist or antiabortion Christian— you will notice that many have a real virulence to their tone or language. That virulence is the sound of a self-selecting community talking to itself and positively reinforcing itself, with no obligation to answer to anyone or look anyone in the eye. Skinheads or violent Islamic radicals had to expend a lot of energy to find each other in significant numbers twenty years ago. Now they can reinforce each other through the network and never have to show up together at a public convention. And just as Hurricane Katrina gained in virulence when it passed over the warm waters of the Gulf of Mexico before striking New Orleans, so these communities gain in virulence from the warmth they draw by connecting with one another.

The flat-world platform, alas, is a cheap, easy command-and-control system and network for any kind of organization or movement. People in democracies do not like to think about this, but we have put this system out into the world and made it available to every good-hearted social entrepreneur *and* every nut, no matter how small. We gave them all a free, private, global channel on which to mobilize, reinforce each other, and get psychic rewards by seeing their threats, challenges, or good deeds broadcast worldwide—with virtually no checks. Yes, the best bloggers

will correct themselves and one another, as any newspaper's ombudsman does, but it is not systematic or uniform. There are real penalties for
newspaper reporters who get caught fabricating or lying. They are often
suspended or lose their jobs. There is no such system for the blogosphere. You may lose readers—or you may not. But no one cuts off your
bandwidth for a month.

I don't think we are ready for the boundaries between the public and
private spheres to be erased so quickly. The loss of privacy is going to be
profound. I suspect it won't be long before people sit down at a dinner
party and the first thing the hostess declares is that "this evening will be
blog free—no one is allowed to blog about what is said here tonight." Are
we on the verge of parents telling their kids, "This conversation is off the
record. I don't want to read about this in your MySpace!"?

No, it won't be long. The fact is that the world has gotten flat and more
interconnected much faster than people have developed the norms and
ethics to have their words go everywhere unedited and uncensored, and
much faster than people have adapted to hearing everything whispered
about them. Democracy is great, but democracy without responsibility is
truly frightening.

What to do? The first rule is to develop a thicker skin. This is the
world we live in now: Those who court the public eye with their achievements or their antics, and even many who don't court it at all, will have
to learn to put up with more "digital stuff" being thrown at them by more
people from more places with fewer restraints and greater ease than ever
before.

Another rule: Try not to waste too much of your time reading this
stuff. "Internet addiction" afflicts adults and teenagers alike.

A third rule might be: Keep it all in perspective. Not all, but most of
this "stuff" just becomes more noise in the massive global echo chamber. And when there is so much noise out there, it eventually turns into
white noise. And white noise, as anyone who goes to sleep with the air
conditioner on knows, is its own kind of silence.

Oh, one more rule—maybe the most important one: Let your kids
know what world they are living in. As individuals are able to create more

of their own content in digital form, and as search engines and computers get better and better at sifting and storing all that digital content and delivering it back to us, the Internet will become a kind of permanent record, an always open book. Every e-mail you send, every entry you make in Facebook, in MySpace, or on YouTube is a digital footprint that will never be washed away by the sea. Every sound you make will soon be recorded somewhere. And that means that young people not only have to be smart about how they navigate around the Web—they have to be smart about what they leave behind there as well. In time, Google, MSN Search, and Yahoo! will be able to turn over smaller and smaller rocks to find out smaller and smaller details about movie stars, scientific breakthroughs, crazy conspiracies and, yes, about you and your kids. This is a new phenomenon. But it will only intensify. Therefore, parents and teachers need to help young people understand that their reputations will start to be cast in cement at a much earlier age than previous generations.

Dov Seidman, the business ethicist, uses the simple example of the personal résumé, which college grads have used for years to apply for their first job and for other jobs after that. The résumé was a very efficient device that society created to enable people to judge other people. Most important, though, you got to write your own résumé, tell your own life story the way you wanted it told, and it was generally accepted on faith (unless or until proved otherwise) that what you said was honest and true.

Those days are over. "Résumés are proxies—they are documents where you tell others about your life," notes Seidman. "Proxies like that were very efficient in a nontransparent world." For someone else to check every factoid in your résumé was very difficult and expensive in a world with walls—but not in a flat world, not in the age of Google. Now people can conduct their own X-ray of your life. And if it is easy today, imagine how much easier it will be in ten years. "Now we can blow right past proxies, like a résumé, and get a direct insight into you," said Seidman. "Employers no longer need a proxy to see into your life. They can go to your MySpace page and see how you write and get to know your friends, search the Web and see what you've done, right and wrong, or evaluate what you said about yourself in your online yearbook. They can reconstruct these artifacts of your life, even after you have tried to delete them."

Therefore, Seidman adds, "If character is destiny, and if strangers have so many more tools to look inside your character now, then you better start building a solid character early," and that is a lesson educators need to convey to young people.

The Washington Post reported (March 7, 2006) that many employers, including law firms, were now doing Google searches as part of due diligence checks on prospective employees. "According to a December survey by the Ponemon Institute, a privacy research organization, roughly half of U.S. hiring officials use the Internet in vetting job applications," the Post reported. "About one-third of the searches yielded content used to deny a job, the survey said. The legal hiring market is very competitive. What could tip the balance is the appearance that a candidate is a lightning rod for controversy, said Mark Rasch, a Washington lawyer and consultant who specializes in Internet issues." This trend, the paper noted, has spawned a new service, ReputationDefender, "whose mission is to search for damaging content online and destroy it on behalf of clients. Generally, the law exempts site operators from liability for the content posted by others, though it does not prevent them from removing offensive items. 'For many people the Internet has become a scarlet letter, an albatross,' said Michael Fertik, ReputationDefender's chief executive."

So momma, tell your kids: You will get fewer second chances in a flat world. "In this world you better do it right the first time—you don't get to pick up and move to the next town to reinvent yourself so easily," said Seidman. If George W. Bush had been born and raised in this era, he never would have been elected governor, let alone president. Can you imagine the digital footprints—the cell phone camera photos—he would have left behind at Yale, a period of his life that he once summed up in the phrase, "When I was young and irresponsible, I was young and irresponsible"?

In the world where your history lives online forever, accessible to all, noted Seidman, "your reputation will follow you and precede you on your next stop. It gets there before you do. You don't get to spend four years of college getting drunk. Your reputation is getting set much earlier in life. 'Always tell the truth,' said Mark Twain, 'that way you won't have to remember what you said.'" In a connected world, "how we conduct ourselves matters more than ever," added Seidman. "Not just avoiding impeachable behaviors, but developing those that foster strong connections with others. How we communicate, how we write letters, how we say 'I'm sorry' or don't say 'I'm sorry,' how we engender trust or don't, how well we collaborate, and what percentage of our promises do we keep— all matter now more than ever."

To be sure, there are some upsides to all these social downsides. "People who get their hows right will see that it becomes a source of power and strength," argues Seidman. "They will be the ones getting ahead and enlisting others in their visions. They will be the ones collaborating most with others to accomplish things that are difficult to do by themselves . . . This is a strategy for thriving that is available to everyone." Living your life the right way, earning your reputation one achievement at a time, and building a solid foundation for your reputation is a winning strategy—even when we all have dog's hearing.

And yet when I add it all up, I do come out "net worried." At its best, cyberspace adds to the richness of the public debate and brings forward new and valuable voices who might never have been heard from before. But at its worst, it brings forward more extreme and irresponsible voices with fewer restraints and enables them to throw more spitballs farther and bigger than ever before. I worry that because of the latter, more and more people will shun the public eye or public service for fear of falling into this echo chamber, like a tumble dryer, and never escaping it—or escaping so bruised and battered they never want to go near it again. At a time when democracies desperately need their best men and women leading public institutions, we want to make sure that our young people are running to the public sphere—not away from it.

Geopolitics and the Flat World

FIFTEEN

The Unflat World

No Guns or Cell Phones Allowed

To build may have to be the slow and laborious task of years. To destroy can be the thoughtless act of a single day.

—Sir Winston Churchill

On a trip back home to Minnesota in the winter of 2004, I was having lunch with my friends Ken and Jill Greer at Perkins pancake house when Jill mentioned that the state had recently passed a new gun law. The conceal and carry law, passed on May 28, 2003, established that local sheriffs had to issue permits for anyone—other than those with felony records or declared mentally ill—who requested to carry concealed firearms to work (unless the person's employer explicitly restricted that right). This law is supposed to deter criminals, because if they try to hold you up, they can't be sure that you too are not packing a weapon. The law, though, contained a provision to allow business owners to prevent nonemployees from bringing concealed weapons into a place of business, like a restaurant or health club. It said that any business could ban concealed handguns on its premises if it posted a sign at each entrance indicating that guns were not allowed there. (This reportedly led to some very creative signage, with one church suing the state for the right to use a biblical quote as its gun-banning sign and a restaurant using a picture of a woman in a cooking apron toting a machine gun.) The reason this all came up at our lunch was that Jill mentioned that at health clubs around the city, where she played tennis, she noticed two signs now popping up regularly, one right after the other. At their tennis club in Bloomington, for example, there is a sign right by the front door that says, "No Guns Allowed." And then nearby, outside the locker rooms, is another sign: "No Cell Phones Allowed."

Hmmm. No guns or cell phones allowed? Guns I understand, I said, but why cell phones?

Silly me. It was because some people were bringing cell phones with cameras into locker rooms, covertly taking pictures of naked men and women and then e-mailing them around the world. What will they think of next? Whatever the innovation, people will find a way to use it and abuse it.

While interviewing Promod Haque at Norwest Venture Partners in Palo Alto, I was helped by the firm's public relations director, Katie Belding, who later sent me this e-mail: "I was chatting with my husband about your meeting with Promod the other day . . . He is a history teacher at a high school in San Mateo. I asked him, 'Where were you when the world went flat?' He said it just happened the other day at school when he was in a faculty meeting. A student was suspended for helping another student cheat on a test—we're not talking the traditional writing answers on the bottom of your shoe or passing a note, though . . ." Intrigued, I called her husband, Brian, and he picked up the story: "At the end of the period, when all of the tests were being passed up to the front of the classroom, this student very quickly and slyly pulled out his cell phone and somehow snapped a picture of some test questions, and instantly e-mailed it to his friend who was taking the same test the next period. His friend also had a cell phone with a digital camera and e-mail capabilities, and was apparently able to view the questions before the next period. The student was caught by another teacher when he pulled out the cell phone between periods. It is against the rules to have a cell phone on campus—even though we know that all the kids do—so the teacher confiscated it and saw that the kid had a test on it. So the dean of discipline, at our regular faculty meeting, opened by saying, 'We have something new to worry about.' Essentially he said, 'Beware, keep your eyes open, because the kids are so far ahead of us in terms of the technology.'"

But things aren't all bad with this new technology, noted Brian: "I went to a Jimmy Buffett concert earlier this year. Cameras were not allowed, but cell phones were. So then the concert starts and everyone suddenly starts holding up their cell phones and taking pictures of Jimmy Buffett. I've got one right on my wall. We were sitting in the second row and the guy next to us held up his cell phone, and I said, 'Hey, would you mind e-mailing me some of those? No one will believe we sat this close.' He said 'Sure,' and we gave him a card with our e-mail [address]. We didn't really expect to see any, but the next day he e-mailed us a bunch."

My trip to Beijing described earlier fell right after the fifteenth anniversary of the Tiananmen Square massacre, which happened on June 4, 1989, that is, 6/4/89. My colleagues at the *Times* bureau informed me that on that day the Chinese government censors were blocking SMS messages on cell phones that contained any reference to Tiananmen Square or even the numbers 6 and 4. So if you happened to be dialing the phone number 664-6464, or sending a message in which you told someone you would meet at 6 p.m. on the 4th floor, the Chinese censors blocked it using their jamming technology.

Mark Steyn, writing in the *National Review* (October 25, 2004), related a story from the London Arabic newspaper *Al-Quds al-Arabi* about a panic that broke out in Khartoum, Sudan, after a crazy rumor swept the city, claiming that if an infidel shook a man's hand, that man could lose his manhood. "What struck me about the story," wrote Steyn, "was a detail: The hysteria was spread by cell phones and text messaging. Think about that: You can own a cell phone yet still believe a foreigner's handshake can melt away your penis. What happens when that kind of technologically advanced primitivism advances beyond text messaging?"

This is not a chapter about cell phones, so why do I raise these stories? Because ever since I began writing about globalization, I've been challenged by critics along one particular line: "Isn't there a certain technological determinism to your argument? To listen to you, Friedman, there are these ten flatteners, they are converging and flattening the earth, and there is nothing that people can do but bow to them and join the parade. And after a transition, everyone will get richer and smarter and it will all be fine. But you're wrong, because the history of the world suggests that ideological alternatives, and power alternatives, have always arisen to any system, and globalization will be no different."

This is a legitimate question, so let me try to answer it directly: *I am a technological determinist! Guilty as charged.*

I believe that capabilities create intentions. If we create an Internet where people can open an online store and have global suppliers, global customers, and global competitors, they will open that online store or bank or bookshop. If we create work flow platforms that allow companies to disaggregate any job and source it to the knowledge center anywhere in the world that can perform that task most efficiently at the lowest cost, companies will do that sort of outsourcing. If we create cell phones with cameras in them, people will use them for all sorts of tasks, from cheating on tests to calling Grandma in her nursing home on her ninetieth birthday from the top of a mountain in New Zealand. The history of economic development teaches this over and over: If you can do it, you must do it, otherwise your competitors will—and as this book has tried to demonstrate, there is a whole new universe of things that companies, countries, and individuals can and must do to thrive in a flat world.

But while I am a technological determinist, *I am not a historical determinist.* There is absolutely no guarantee that everyone will use these new technologies, or the triple convergence, for the benefit of themselves, their countries, or humanity. These are just technologies. Using them does not make you modern, smart, moral, wise, fair, or decent. It just makes you able to communicate, compete, and collaborate farther and faster. In the absence of a world-destabilizing war, every one of these technologies will become cheaper, lighter, smaller and more personal, mobile, digital, and virtual. Therefore, more and more people will find more and more ways to use them. We can only hope that more people in more places will use them to create, collaborate, and grow their living standards, not the opposite. But it doesn't have to happen.

To put it bluntly, I don't know how the flattening of the world will come out. Indeed, let me go even further and make a deeper confession: I know that the world is not flat.

Yes, you read me right: *I know that the world is not flat.* Don't worry. I know.

I am certain, though, that the world has been shrinking and flattening for some time now, and that process has quickened dramatically in recent years. Half the world today is directly or indirectly participating in the flattening process or feeling its effects. I have engaged in literary license in titling this book *The World Is Flat* to draw attention to this flattening and its quickening pace because I think it is the single most important trend in the world today.

But I am equally certain that it is not historically inevitable that the rest of the world will become flat or that the already flat parts of the world won't get unflattened by war, economic disruption, or politics. There are hundreds of millions of people on this planet who have been left behind by the flattening process or feel overwhelmed by it, and some of them have enough access to the flattening tools to use them against the system, not on its behalf. How the flattening could go wrong is the subject of this chapter, and I approach it by trying to answer the following questions: What are the biggest constituencies, forces, or problems impeding this flattening process, and how might we collaborate better to overcome them?

Too Sick

I once heard Jerry Yang, the cofounder of Yahoo!, quote a senior Chinese government official as saying, "Where people have hope, you have a middle class." I think this is a very useful insight. The existence of large, stable middle classes around the world is crucial to geopolitical stability, but middle class is a state of mind, not a state of income. That's why a majority of Americans always describe themselves as "middle class," even though by income statistics some of them wouldn't be considered as such. "Middle class" is another way of describing people who believe that they have a pathway out of poverty or lower-income status toward a higher standard of living and a better future for their kids. You can be in the middle class in your head whether you make $2 a day or $200, if you believe in social mobility—that your kids have a chance to live better than you do—and that hard work and playing by the rules of your society will get you where you want to go.

In many ways, the line between those who are in the flat world and those who are not is this line of hope. The good news in India and China and the countries of the former Soviet Empire today is that, with all their flaws and internal contradictions, these countries are now home to hundreds of millions of people who are hopeful enough to be middle class. The bad news in Africa today, as well as rural India, China, Latin America, and plenty of dark corners of the developed world, is that there are hundreds of millions of people who have no hope and therefore no chance of making it into the middle class. They have no hope for two reasons: Either they are too sick, or their local governments are too broken for them to believe they have a pathway forward.

The first group, those who are too sick, are those whose lives are stalked every day by HIV-AIDS, malaria, TB, and polio, and who do not even enjoy steady electricity or potable water. Many of these people live in shockingly close proximity with the flat world. While in Bangalore I visited an experimental school, Shanti Bhavan, or "Haven of Peace." It is located near the village of Baliganapalli, in Tamil Nadu Province, about an hour's drive from downtown Bangalore's glass-and-steel high-tech centers—one of which is aptly called "The Golden Enclave." On the drive there, the school's principal, Lalita Law, an intense, razor-sharp Indian Christian, explained to me, with barely controlled rage in her voice, that the school has 160 children, whose parents are all untouchables from the nearby village.

"These kids, their parents are ragpickers, coolies, and quarry laborers," she said as we bounced along in a jeep on the potholed roads to the school. "They come from homes below the poverty line, and from the lowest caste, the untouchables, who are supposed to be fulfilling their destiny and left where they are. We get these children at ages four and five. They don't know what it is to have a drink of clean water. They are used to drinking filthy gutter water, if they are lucky enough to have a gutter near where they live. They have never seen a toilet, they don't have baths . . . They don't even have proper scraps of clothing. We have to start by socializing them. When we first get them they run out and urinate and defecate wherever they want. [At first] we don't make them sleep on beds, because it is a culture shock."

I was typing frantically in the back of the jeep on my laptop to keep up with her scalding monologue about village life.

"This 'India Shining' thing [the slogan of the ruling Bharatiya Janata Party, BJP, in the 2004 election] irritates people like us," she added. "You have to come to the rural villages and see whether India is shining, and you look into a child's face and see whether India is shining. India is shining okay for the glossy magazines, but if you just go outside Bangalore you will see that everything about India shining is refuted . . . [In the villages] alcoholism is rife and female infanticide and crime are rising. You have to bribe to get electricity, water; you have to bribe the tax assessor to assess your home correctly. Yes, the middle and upper classes are taking off, but the seven hundred million who are left behind, all they see is gloom and darkness and despair. They are born to fulfill their destiny and have to live this way and die this way. The only thing that shines for them is the sun, and it is hot and unbearable and too many of them die of heatstroke." The only "mouse" these kids have ever encountered, she added, is not one that rests next to a computer but the real thing.

There are thousands of such villages in rural India, China, Africa, and Latin America. And that is why it is no wonder that children in the developing world—the unflat world—are ten times more likely to die of vaccine-preventable diseases than are children in the developed flat world. In the worst-affected regions of rural southern Africa, a full one-third of pregnant women are reportedly HIV-positive. The AIDS epidemic alone is enough to put a whole society into a tailspin: Many teachers in these African countries are now afflicted with AIDS, so they cannot teach, and young children, especially girls, have to drop out either because they must tend to sick and dying parents or because they have been orphaned by AIDS and cannot afford the school fees. And without education, young people cannot learn how to protect themselves from HIV-AIDS or other diseases, let alone acquire the life-advancing skills that enable women to gain greater control over their own bodies and sexual partners. The prospect of a full-blown AIDS epidemic in India and China, of the sort that has already debilitated southern Africa, remains very real, largely because only one-fifth of the people at risk for HIV worldwide have access to prevention services. Tens of millions of women who want and would benefit from family-planning resources don't have them for lack of local funding. You cannot drive economic growth in a place where 50 percent of the people are infected with malaria or half of the kids are malnourished or a third of the mothers are dying of AIDS.

There is no question that China and India are better off for having at least part of their population in the flat world. When societies begin to prosper, you get a virtuous cycle going: They begin to produce enough food for people to leave the land, the excess labor gets trained and educated, it begins working in services and industry; that leads to innovation and better education and universities, freer markets, economic growth and development, better infrastructure, fewer diseases, and slower population growth. It is that dynamic that is going on in parts of urban India and urban China today, enabling people to compete on a level playing field and attracting investment dollars by the billions.

But there are many, many others living outside this cycle. They live in villages or rural areas that only criminals would want to invest in, regions where violence, civil war, and disease compete with one another to see which can ravage the civilian population most. The world will be entirely flat only when all these people are brought into it. One of the few people with enough dollars to make a difference who has stepped up to this challenge is Microsoft chairman Bill Gates, whose $27 billion Bill and Melinda Gates Foundation has focused on this huge, disease-ravaged, opportunity-deprived population. I have been a critic of some of Microsoft's business practices over the years, and I do not regret one word I have written about some of its anticompetitive tactics. But I have been impressed by Gates's personal commitment of money and energy to address the unflat world. Both times I spoke to Gates, this is the subject he wanted to talk about most and addressed with the most passion.

"No one funds things for that other three billion," said Gates. "Someone estimated that the cost of saving a life in the U.S. is $5 or $6 million—that is how much our society is willing to spend. You can save a life outside of the U.S. for less than $100. But how many people want to make *that* investment?

"If it was just a matter of time," Gates continued, "you know, give it twenty or thirty years and the others will be there, then it would be great to declare that the whole world is flat. But the fact is, there is a trap that these three billion are caught in, and they may never get into the virtuous cycle of more education, more health, more capitalism, more rule of law, more wealth . . . I am worried that it could just be half the world that is flat and it stays that way."

Take malaria, a disease caused by a parasite carried by mosquitoes. It is the greatest killer of mothers on the planet right now. While virtually no one dies of malaria today in the flat world, more than one million people die from this disease each year in the unflat world, about seven hundred thousand of them children, most of them in Africa. Deaths from malaria have actually doubled in the last twenty years because the malaria parasite carried by mosquitoes has become resistant to many antimalarial drugs, and commercial drug companies have not invested much in new antimalarial vaccines because they believe there is no profitable market for them. If this crisis were happening in a flat country, noted Gates, the system would work: Government would do what it needed to do to contain the disease, pharmaceutical companies would do what they needed to do to get the drugs to market, schools would educate young people about preventive measures, and the problem would be licked. "But this nice response works only when the people who have the problem also have some money," said Gates. When the Gates Foundation issued a $50 million grant to combat malaria, he added, "people said we just doubled the amount of money [worldwide] going to fight malaria . . . When the people who have the need don't have the money, it takes outside groups and charities to get them to the point where the system can kick in for them."

Up to now, though, argued Gates, "we have not given these people a chance [to be in the flat world]. The kid who is connected to the Internet today, if he has the curiosity [he] is as [empowered] as me. But if he does not get the right nutrition, he will never play that game. Yes, the world is smaller, but do we really see the conditions that people live in? Isn't the world still really big enough that we don't see the real conditions that people live in, the kid whose life can be saved for $80?"

Let's stop here for a moment and imagine how beneficial it would be for the world, and for America, if rural China, India, and Africa were to grow into little Americas or European Unions in economic and opportunity terms. But the chances of their getting into such a virtuous cycle is tiny without a real humanitarian push by flat-world businesses, philanthropies, and governments to devote more resources to their problems. The only way out is through new ways of collaboration between the flat and unflat parts of the world.

In 2003, the Gates Foundation launched a project called Grand Challenges in Global Health. What I like about it is the way the Gates Foundation approached solving this problem. They didn't say, "We, the rich Western foundation, will now deliver you the solution," and then issue instructions and write some checks. They said, "Let's collaborate horizontally on defining both the problem and the solutions—let's create value that way—and then [the foundation] will invest our money in the solutions we both define." So the Gates Foundation placed ads on the Web and in more conventional channels across both the developed and the developing worlds, asking scientists to respond to one big question: What are the biggest problems that, if science attended to them and solved them, could most dramatically change the fate of the several billion people trapped in the vicious cycle of infant mortality, low life expectancy, and disease? The foundation got about eight thousand pages of ideas from hundreds of scientists from around the world, including Nobel laureates. A special board of scientists and doctors from around the world then culled through them and distilled them down to a list of fourteen Grand Challenges—challenges where a technological innovation could remove a critical barrier to the solving of an important health problem in the developing world. In the fall of 2003, it announced these fourteen Grand Challenges worldwide. They include the following: How to create effective single-dose vaccines that can be used soon after birth, how to prepare vaccines that do not require refrigeration, how to develop needle-free delivery systems for vaccines, how to better understand which immunological responses provide protective immunity, how to better control insects that transmit agents of disease, how to develop a genetic or chemical strategy to incapacitate a disease-transmitting insect population, how to create a full range of optimal bioavailable nutrients in a single staple plant species, and how to create immunological methods that can cure chronic infections. Within a year, the foundation received fifteen hundred proposals for ways to meet these challenges from scientists in seventy-five countries. The foundation then awarded forty-three grants worth $436 million in cash.

"We're trying to accomplish two things with this program," explained Rick Klausner, a former head of the National Cancer Institute who directed the global health programs for the Gates Foundation before stepping down in the fall of 2005. "The first is [to make] a moral appeal to the scientific imagination, [pointing out] that there are great problems to be solved that we, the scientific community, have ignored, even though we pride ourselves in how international we are. We have not taken our responsibilities as global problem solvers as seriously as our self-identity as an international community. We wanted the Grand Challenges to say these are the most exciting, sexy, scientific things that anyone in the world could work on right now . . . The idea was to fire the imagination. The second thing is to actually direct some of the foundation's resources to see if we could do it."

What was interesting, said Klausner, was how quickly the different grant winners assembled themselves into collaborative communities— because it really does take a village to solve such complex problems, and the scientists quickly realized that they were not competing with one another. "People said if you are really going to solve a big problem today, you need to do it with much more horizontal collaboration," he noted. "And this [flat] world enables it. You can do a project on your own, but you can't solve a big problem on your own. But we did not expect this. Because while we talk about collaboration, competition is so ingrained in the creative steroid of science, it just was not clear that people would put down the competition in order to be part of a larger community solving a problem. It is not the natural tendency. We were surprised by this."

Given the phenomenal advances in technology in the last twenty years, it is easy to assume that we already have all the tools to address some of these challenges and that the only thing lacking is money. I wish that were the case, but it is not. In the instance of malaria, for example, it isn't just the drugs that are missing. As anyone who has visited Africa or rural India knows, the health-care systems in these areas are often broken or functioning at a very low level. So the Gates Foundation is trying to stimulate the development of drugs and delivery systems that presume a broken health-care system and therefore can be safely self-administered by ordinary people in the field. That may be the grandest challenge of all: to use the tools of the flat world to design tools that work in an unflat world. "The most important health-care system in the world is a mother," said Klausner. "How do you get things in her hands that she understands and can afford and can use? When we think about health problems in the developing world, the men are almost invisible, except as a source of part of the problem. It is all about the women."

The tragedy of all these people is really a dual tragedy, added Klausner. There is the individual tragedy of facing a death sentence from disease or a life sentence of broken families and limited expectations. And there is the tragedy for the world because of the incredible lost contribution that all these people still outside the flat world could be making. In a flat world, where we are connecting all the knowledge pools together, imagine what knowledge those people could bring to science or education. In a flat world, where innovation can come from anywhere, we are letting a huge pool of potential contributors and collaborators slip under the waves. There is no question that poverty causes ill health, but ill health also traps people in poverty, which in turn weakens them and keeps them from grasping the first rung of the ladder to middle-class hope. Until and unless we can meet some of these grand challenges, much of that 50 percent of the world that is still not flat will stay that way—no matter how flat the other 50 percent gets.

There is another aspect of "too sick" that we need to consider, though: What happens if the too sick meet the really flat? Let me put it another way. The world has long witnessed pandemics that have wiped out millions of people in a very short period of time. And the world has recently witnessed the rise of Wal-Mart and its remarkable high-speed supply chain, which is able to transmit products from one corner of the world to another in a very short period of time. What the world has never witnessed is an old-style pandemic in a Wal-Mart world.

A flu pandemic in a Wal-Mart world would be a hugely unflattening nightmare from two directions at once: From one side, the flat world would enable any pandemic to spread much faster and much wider, probably killing many more people. And, from the other side, it would make the economic devastation from such a pandemic so much greater and more sudden, because our natural response to pandemics is to put up walls and to sever connectivity and face-to-face contact—since the movement and interaction of both people and goods is precisely what spreads something like the influenza virus. Even when the world was round, this was devastating, as we saw with the 1918 flu pandemic. But when the world is flattening—when some 80 percent of the raw materials that go into pharmaceutical drugs sold in America come from overseas suppliers, and when the rubber that keeps surgical masks tight on your face comes through a just-in-time supply chain that starts in Indonesia or Africa, stretches through Europe, and then skips over to America—our ability to cope with any pandemic would be sharply reduced. Everyone would be putting up roadblocks and "stay out" signs, disrupting every supply chain in the world. In short, a pandemic in a flattening world would make acquiring the lifesaving vaccines and other medical supplies just in time more important than ever. But our ability to acquire them just in time would be curtailed more than ever. And we wouldn't have the inventories to put to use—because in a flat world inventories have come to be viewed as waste. You want just-in-time delivery of everything.

Michael T. Osterholm, director of the Center for Infectious Disease Research and Policy and professor at the University of Minnesota's School of Public Health, notes that the spread of the SARS (Severe Acute Respiratory Syndrome) virus in 2003 demonstrated just how quickly such an infectious disease can move in a flattening world, given the speed and density of international air travel. Once SARS emerged in rural China, he noted, it spread to five countries within twenty-four hours, and to thirty countries on six continents within several months—causing billions of dollars in economic loss, because, for instance, longshoremen on the West Coast of the United States did not want to off-load cargo ships that had come from infected regions.

But the transmission rate of SARS is like a turtle compared to an influenza pandemic.

"We have set ourselves up for a much more rapid transmission of any virus," said Osterholm, "but the implications of a killer influenza pandemic will be so much more devastating in today's world."

It could undermine so many of the features, business practices, and conveniences we have come to take for granted in the modern age—as well as stop the flattening process dead in its tracks.

Too Disempowered

There's not just the flat world and the unflat world. Many people live in the twilight zone between the two. Among these are the people I call the too disempowered. They are a large group of people who have not been fully encompassed by the flattening of the world. Unlike the too sick, who have yet even to get a chance to step onto the flat world, the too disempowered are people who you might say are half flat. They are healthy people who live in countries with significant areas that have been flattened but who don't have the tools or the skills or the infrastructure to participate in any meaningful or sustained way. They have just enough information to know that the world is flattening around them and that they aren't really getting any of the benefits. Being flat is good but full of pressure, being unflat is awful and full of pain, but being half flat has its own special anxiety. As exciting and as visible as the flat Indian high-tech sector is, have no illusions: It accounts for 0.2 percent of employment in India. Add those Indians involved in manufacturing for export, and you get a total of 2 percent of employment in India.

The half flat are all those other hundreds of millions of people, particularly in rural India, rural China, and rural Eastern Europe, who are close enough to see, touch, and occasionally benefit from the flat world but who are not really living inside it themselves. We saw how big and how angry this group can be in the spring of 2004 Indian national elections, in which the ruling BJP was surprisingly tossed out of office—despite having overseen a surge in India's growth rate—largely because of the discontent of rural Indian voters with the slow pace of globalization outside the giant cities. These voters were not saying, "Stop the globalization train, we want to get off." They were saying, "Stop the globalization train, we want to get on, but someone needs to help us by building a better stepstool."

These rural voters—peasants and farmers, who form the bulk of India's population—just had to spend a day in any nearby big city to see the benefits of the flat world: the cars, the houses, the educational opportunities. "Every time a villager watches the community TV and sees an ad for soap or shampoo, what they notice are not the soap and shampoo but the lifestyle of the people using them—the kind of motorbikes they ride, their dress, and their homes," explained Indian-born Nayan Chanda, editor of YaleGlobal Online. "They see a world they want access to. This election was about envy and anger. It was a classic case of revolutions happening when things are getting better but not fast enough for many people."

At the same time, these rural Indians understood, at gut level, exactly why it was not happening for them: because local governments have become so eaten away by corruption and mismanagement that they cannot deliver to the poor the schools and infrastructure they need to get a fair share of the pie. As some of these millions of Indians on the outside of the gated communities looking in lose hope, "they become more religious, more tied to their caste/subcaste, more radical in their thinking, more willing to snatch than create, [and] view dirty politics as being the only way to get mobility, since economic mobility is stalled," said Vivek Paul of Wipro. India can have the smartest high-tech vanguard in the world, but if it does not find a way to bring along more of those who are unable, disabled, undereducated, and underserved, it will be like a rocket that takes off but quickly falls back to earth for lack of sustained thrust.

The Congress Party got the message, which was why as soon as it took office it chose as its prime minister not some antiglobalizer but Manmohan Singh, the former Indian finance minister, who in 1991 first opened the Indian economy to globalization, placing an emphasis on exports and trade and reform wholesale. And Singh, in turn, pledged himself to vastly increase government investments in rural infrastructure and to bring more reform retail to rural government.

How can outsiders collaborate in this process? I think, first and foremost, they can redefine the meaning of global populism. If populists

really want to help the rural poor, the way to do it is not by burning down
McDonald's and shutting down the IMF and trying to put up protectionist barriers that will unflatten the world. That will help the rural poor
not one iota. It has to be by refocusing the energies of the global populist
movement on how to improve local government, infrastructure, and education in places like rural India and China, so the populations there
can acquire the tools to collaborate and participate in the flat world. The
global populist movement, better known as the antiglobalization movement, has a great deal of energy, but up to now it has been too divided
and confused to effectively help the poor in any meaningful or sustained
manner. It needs a policy lobotomy. The world's poor do not resent the
rich anywhere nearly as much as the left-wing parties in the developed
world imagine. What they resent is not having any pathway to get rich
and to join the flat world and cross that line into the middle class that
Jerry Yang spoke about.

Let's pause for a minute here and trace how the antiglobalization
movement lost touch with the true aspirations of the world's poor. The
antiglobalization movement emerged at the World Trade Organization
conference in Seattle in 1999 and then spread around the world in subsequent years, usually gathering to attack meetings of the World Bank, the
IMF, and the G-8 industrialized nations. From its origins, the movement
that emerged in Seattle was a primarily Western-driven phenomenon,
which was why you saw so few people of color in the crowds. It was driven
by five disparate forces. One was upper-middle-class American liberal
guilt at the incredible wealth and power that America had amassed in the
wake of the fall of the Berlin Wall and the dot-com boom. At the peak of
the stock market boom, lots of pampered American college kids, wearing
their branded clothing, began to get interested in sweatshops as a way of
expiating their guilt. The second force driving it was a rear-guard push by
the Old Left—socialists, anarchists, and Trotskyites—in alliance with protectionist trade unions. Their strategy was to piggyback on rising concerns
about globalization to bring back some form of socialism, even though
these ideas had been rejected as bankrupt by the very people in the former
Soviet Empire and China who had lived under them longest. (Now you
know why there was no antiglobalization movement to speak of in Russia,

China, or Eastern Europe.) These Old Left forces wanted to spark a debate about *whether we globalize*. They claimed to speak in the name of the Third World poor, but the bankrupt economic policies they advocated made them, in my view, the Coalition to Keep Poor People Poor. The third force was a more amorphous group. It was made up of many people who gave passive support to the antiglobalization movement from many countries, because they saw in it some kind of protest against the speed at which the old world was disappearing and becoming flat.

The fourth force driving the movement, which was particularly strong in Europe and in the Islamic world, was anti-Americanism. The disparity between American economic and political power and everybody else's had grown so wide after the fall of the Soviet Empire that America began to — or was perceived to — touch people's lives around the planet, directly or indirectly, more than their own governments did. As people around the world began to intuit this, a movement emerged, which Seattle both reflected and helped to catalyze, whereby people said, in effect, "If America is now touching my life directly or indirectly more than my own government, then I want to have a vote in America's power." At the time of Seattle, the "touching" that people were most concerned with was from American economic and cultural power, and therefore the demand for a vote tended to focus on economic rule-making institutions like the World Trade Organization. America in the 1990s, under President Clinton, was perceived as a big dumb dragon, pushing people around in the economic and cultural spheres, knowingly and unknowingly. We were Puff the Magic Dragon, and people wanted a vote in what we were puffing.

Then came 9/11. And America transformed itself from Puff the Magic Dragon, touching people around the world economically and culturally, into Godzilla with an arrow in his shoulder, spitting fire and tossing around his tail wildly, touching people's lives in military and security terms, not just economic and cultural ones. As that happened, people in the world began to say, "Now we *really* want a vote in how America wields its power" — and in many ways the whole Iraq war debate was a surrogate debate about that.

Finally, the fifth force in this movement was a coalition of very serious, well-meaning, and constructive groups — from environmentalists to trade activists to NGOs concerned with governance—who became part of the populist antiglobalization movement in the 1990s in the hopes that they could catalyze a global discussion about *how we globalize*. I had a lot of respect and sympathy for this latter group. But in the end they got drowned out by the whether-we-globalize crowd, which began to turn the movement more violent at the July 2001 Genoa G-8 summit, when an antiglobalization protester was killed while attacking an Italian police jeep with a fire extinguisher.

The combination of the triple convergence, the violence at Genoa, 9/11, and tighter security measures fractured the antiglobalization movement. The more serious how-we-globalize groups did not want to be in the same trench with anarchists out to provoke a public clash with police, and after 9/11, many American labor groups did not want to be associated with a movement that appeared to be taken over by anti-American elements. This became even more pronounced when in late September 2001, just weeks after 9/11, antiglobalization leaders attempted a rerun of Genoa in the streets of Washington, to protest the IMF and World Bank meetings there. After 9/11, though, the IMF and World Bank canceled their meetings, and many American protesters shied away. Those who did turn up in the streets of Washington turned the event into a march against the imminent American invasion of Afghanistan to remove Osama bin Laden and al-Qaeda. At the same time, with the triple convergence making the Chinese, Indians, and Eastern Europeans some of the biggest beneficiaries of globalization, it was no longer possible to claim that this phenomenon was devastating the world's poor. Just the opposite: Millions of Chinese and Indians were entering the world's middle class thanks to the flattening of the world and globalization.

So as the how-we-globalize forces drifted away, and as the number of Third World people benefiting from globalization began to grow, and as America under the Bush administration began to exercise more unilateral military power, the anti-American element in the antiglobalization movement began to assume a much louder voice and role. As a result, the movement itself became both more anti-American and more unable and unwilling to play any constructive role in shaping the global debate on how we globalize, precisely when such a role has become even more important as the world has gotten flatter. As Hebrew University political theorist Yaron Ezrahi so aptly noted, "The important task of enlisting the people's power to influence globalism—making it more compassionate, fair, and compatible with human dignity—is way too important to be wasted on crass anti-Americanism or left in the hands of only anti-Americans."

There is a huge political vacuum now waiting to be filled. There is a real role today for a movement that could advance the agenda of how we globalize—not whether we globalize. The best place such a movement could start is rural India.

"Both the Congress [Party] and its left allies would be risking India's future if they draw the wrong conclusion from this [2004] election," Pratap Bhanu Mehta, who heads the Center for Policy Research in Delhi, wrote in *The Hindu* newspaper. "This is not a revolt against the market, it is a protest against the state; this is not resentment against the gains of liberalization, but a call for the state to put its house in order through even more reform . . . The revolt against holders of power is not a revolt of the poor against the rich: ordinary people are far less prone to resent other people's success than intellectuals suppose. It is rather an expression of the fact that the reform of the state has not gone far enough."

This is why the most important forces fighting poverty in India today, in my view, are those NGOs fighting for better local governance, using the Internet and other modern tools of the flat world to put a spotlight on corruption, mismanagement, and tax avoidance. The most important, effective, and meaningful populists in the world today are not those handing out money. They are those with an agenda to drive reform retail at the local level in their countries—to make it easier for the little men and women to register their land, even if they are squatters; to start a business, no matter how small; and to get minimal justice from the legal system. Modern populism, to be effective and meaningful, should be about reform retail—making globalization workable, sustainable, and fair for more people by improving their local governance, so that the money earmarked for the poor actually gets to them and so that their natural entrepreneurship can get unlocked. It is through local government that people plug into the system and get to enjoy the benefits of the flattening world rather than just observe them. The average Indian villagers cannot be like the Indian high-tech companies and just circumvent the government by supplying their own electricity, their own water resources, their own security, their own bus system, and their own satellite dishes. *They need the state for that.* The market cannot be counted on to make up for the failure of the state to deliver decent governance. The state has to get better. Precisely because the Indian state opted for a globalization strategy in 1991 and abandoned fifty years of socialism—which had brought its foreign reserves to near zero—New Delhi had reserves in 2004 of $100 billion, giving it the resources to help more of its people into the flat arena.

Ramesh Ramanathan, an Indian-born former Citibank executive who returned to India to lead an NGO called Janaagraha, dedicated to improving local governance, is precisely the kind of new populist I have in mind. "In India," he said, "clients of public education are sending a signal about the quality of service delivery: Whoever can afford to opt out does so. The same goes for health care. Given the escalating costs of health care, if we had a solid public health-care system, most citizens would opt to use it, not just the poor. Ditto for roads, highways, water supply, sanitation, registration of births and deaths, crematoria, driver's licenses, and so on. Wherever the government provides these services, it [should be] for the benefit of all citizens. [But] in fact, in some of these, like water supply and sanitation, the poor are actually not even getting the same basic services as the middle class and the rich. The challenge here is therefore universal access." Getting NGOs that can collaborate on the local level to ensure that the poor get the infrastructure and budgets to which they are entitled could have a major impact on poverty alleviation.

So although this may sound odd coming from me, it is totally consistent with this whole book: What the world doesn't need now is for the antiglobalization movement to go away. We just need it to grow up. This movement had a lot of energy and a lot of mobilizing capacity. What it lacked was a coherent agenda for assisting the poor by collaborating with them in a way that could actually help them. The activist groups that are helping alleviate poverty the most are those working at the local village level in places like rural India, Africa, and China to spotlight and fight corruption and to promote accountability, transparency, education, and property rights. You don't help the world's poor by dressing up in a turtle outfit and throwing a stone through McDonald's window. You help them by getting them the tools and institutions to help themselves. It may not be as sexy as protesting against world leaders in the streets of Washington and Genoa, and getting lots of attention on CNN, but it is a lot more important. Just ask any Indian villager.

Collaboration in poverty alleviation is not just for NGOs. It is also for multinational corporations. The rural poor in India, Africa, and China represent a huge market, and it is possible to make money there and serve them—if companies are ready to collaborate horizontally with the poor. One of the most interesting examples I have come across of this form of collaboration is a program run by Hewlett-Packard. HP is not an NGO. HP began with a simple question: What do poor people need most that we could sell to them? You cannot design this stuff in Palo Alto; you have to cocreate with the user-customer beneficiary. In order to answer that question, HP created a public-private partnership with the national government in India and the local government in Andhra Pradesh. Then a group of HP technologists convened a series of dialogues in the farming village of Kuppam. It asked residents two things: What are your hopes for the next three to five years? and What changes would really make your lives better? To help the villagers (many of them illiterate) express themselves, HP used a concept called graphic facilitation, whereby when people voiced their dreams and aspirations, a visual artist whom HP brought over from the United States drew images of those aspirations on craft paper put up on the walls around the room.

"When people, particularly people who are illiterate, say something and it gets immediately represented on the wall, they feel really validated, and therefore they get more animated and more engaged," said Maureen Conway, HP's vice president for emerging market solutions, who headed the project. "It raises self-esteem." Once these poor farmers living in a remote village got loose, they really started aspiring. "One of them said, 'What we really need here is an airport,'" said Conway.

After the visioning sessions were complete, HP employees spent more time in the village just observing how people lived. One technological thing missing in their lives was photography. Conway explained: "We noticed that there was a big demand for having pictures taken for identification purposes, for licenses, for applications and government permits, and we said to ourselves, 'Maybe there is an entrepreneurial opportunity here if we can turn people into village photographers.' There was one photo studio in downtown Kuppam. Everyone around [is a] farmer. We noticed that people would come back in from villages on a bus, spend two hours, get their pictures taken, come back a week later for the pictures, and find out that they were not done or done wrong. Time is as important for them as for us. So we said, 'Wait a minute, we make digital cameras and portable printers. So what is the problem?' Why doesn't HP sell them a bunch of digital cameras and printers? The villagers came back with a very short answer: 'Electricity.' They had no assured supply of electricity and little money to pay for it.

"So we said, 'We are technologists. Let's get a solar panel and put it on a backpack on wheels and see if there is a business for people here, and for HP, if we make a mobile photo studio.' That is the approach we took. The solar panel can charge both the camera and the printer. Then we went to a self-help women's group. We picked five women and said, 'We will train you how to use this equipment.' We gave them two weeks of training. And we said, 'We will provide you with the camera and supplies, and we will share revenue with you on every picture.'" This was not charity. Even after buying all their supplies from HP and sharing some of the revenue with HP, the women in the photography group doubled their family incomes. "And to be honest, what we found out was that less than 50 percent of the pictures they took were for identification pictures and the rest were people just wanting pictures of their kids, weddings, and themselves," said Conway. The poor like family photo albums as much as the rich and are ready to pay for them. The local government also made this women's group its official photographers for public works projects, which added to their income.

End of story? Not quite. As I said, HP is not an NGO. "After four months we said, 'Okay, the experiment is over, we're taking the camera back,'" said Conway. "And they said, 'You're crazy.'" So HP told the women that if they wanted to keep the camera, printer, and solar panel, they had to come up with a plan to pay for them. They eventually proposed renting them for $9 a month, and HP agreed. And now they are branching out into other villages. HP, meanwhile, has started working with an NGO to train multiple women's groups with the same mobile photography studio, and there is a potential here for HP to sell the studios to NGOs all over India, with all of them using HP ink and other supplies. And from India, who knows where?

"They are giving us feedback on the cameras and ease of use," said Conway. "What it has done to change the confidence of the women is absolutely amazing."

Too Frustrated

One of the unintended consequences of the flat world is that it puts different societies and cultures in much greater direct contact with one another. It connects people to people much faster than people and cultures can often prepare themselves. Some cultures thrive on the sudden opportunities for collaboration that this global intimacy makes possible. Others are threatened, frustrated, and even humiliated by this close contact, which, among other things, makes it very easy for people to see where they stand in the world vis-à-vis everyone else. All of this helps to explain the emergence of one of the most dangerous unflattening forces today—the suicide bombers of al-Qaeda and the other Islamist terror organizations, who are coming out of the Muslim world and Muslim communities in Europe.

The Arab-Muslim world is a vast, diverse civilization, encompassing over one billion people and stretching from Morocco to Indonesia and from Nigeria all the way to the suburbs of London. It is very dangerous to generalize about such a complex religious community, made up of so many different ethnicities and nationalities. But one need only look at the headlines in any day's newspaper to appreciate that a lot of anger and frustration seems to be boiling over from the Muslim world in general and from the Arab-Muslim world in particular, where many young people seem to be agitated by a combination of issues. One of the most obvious is the festering Arab-Israeli conflict, and the Israeli occupation of Palestinian land and East Jerusalem—a grievance that has a powerful emotional hold on the Arab-Muslim imagination and has long soured relations with America and the West.

But this is not the only reason for the brewing anger in these communities. This anger also has to do with the frustration of Arabs and Muslims at having to live, in many, many cases, under authoritarian governments, which not only deprive their people of a voice in their own future, but have deprived tens of millions of young people in particular of opportunities to achieve their full potential through good jobs and modern schools. The fact that the flat world enables people so easily to compare their circumstances with others only sharpens their frustrations.

Some of these Arab-Muslim young men and women have chosen to emigrate in order to find opportunities in the West; others have chosen to suffer in silence at home, hoping for some kind of change. The most powerful journalistic experiences I have had since 9/11 have been my encounters in the Arab world with some of these young people. Because my column with my picture runs in Arabic in the leading pan-Arab newspaper, the London-based *Al-Sharq Al-Awsat*, and because I often appear on Arab satellite-television news programs, many people in that part of the world know what I look like. I have been amazed by the number of young Arabs and Muslims—men and women—who have come up to me on the streets of Cairo or in the Arabian Gulf since 9/11 and said to me what one young man in Al-Azhar mosque did one Friday, after noon prayer: "You're Friedman, aren't you?"

I nodded yes.

"Keep writing what you're writing," he said. What he meant was writing about the importance of bringing more freedom of thought, expression, and opportunity to the Arab-Muslim world so its young people can realize their potential.

Unfortunately, though, these progressive young people are not the ones defining the relationship between the Arab-Muslim community and the world at large today. Increasingly, that relationship is being dominated by, and defined by, religious militants and extremists, who give vent to the frustrations in that part of the world by simply lashing out. The question that I want to explore in this section is: What produced this violent Islamist fringe, and why has it found so much passive support in the Arab-Muslim world today—even though, I am convinced, the vast majority there do not share the violent agenda of these groups or their apocalyptic visions?

The question is relevant to a book about the flat world for a very simple reason: Should there be another attack on the United States of the magnitude of 9/11, or worse, walls would go up everywhere and the flattening of the world would be set back for a long, long time.

That, of course, is precisely what the Islamists want.

When Muslim radicals and fundamentalists look at the West, they see only the openness that makes us, in their eyes, decadent and promiscuous. They see only the openness that has produced Britney Spears and Paris Hilton. They do not see, and do not want to see, the openness—the freedom of thought and inquiry—that has made us powerful, the openness that has produced Bill Gates and Sally Ride. They deliberately define it all as decadence. Because if openness, women's empowerment, and freedom of thought and inquiry are the real sources of the West's economic strength, then the Arab-Muslim world would have to change. And the fundamentalists and extremists do not want to change.

To beat back the threat of openness, the Muslim extremists have, quite deliberately, chosen to attack the very thing that keeps open societies open, innovating, and flattening, and that is *trust*. When terrorists take instruments from our daily lives—the car, the airplane, the tennis shoe, the cell phone—and turn them into weapons of indiscriminate violence, they reduce trust. We trust when we park our car downtown in the morning that the car next to it is not going to blow up; we trust when we go to Disney World that the man in the Mickey Mouse outfit is not wearing a bomb-laden vest underneath; we trust when we get on the shuttle flight from Boston to New York that the foreign student seated next to us isn't going to blow up his tennis shoes. Without trust, there is no open society, because there are not enough police to patrol every opening in an open society. Without trust, there can also be no flat world, because it is trust that allows us to take down walls, remove barriers, and eliminate friction at borders. Trust is essential for a flat world, where you have supply chains involving ten, a hundred, or a thousand people, most of whom have never met face-to-face. The more open societies are exposed to indiscriminate terrorism, the more trust is removed, and the more open societies will erect walls and dig moats instead.

The founders of al-Qaeda are not religious fundamentalists per se. That is, they are not focused simply on the relationship between themselves and God, and on the values and cultural norms of the religious community. They are a political phenomenon more than a religious one. I like to call them Islamo-Leninists. I use the term "Leninists" to convey the utopian-totalitarian vision of al-Qaeda as well as its self-image. As al-Qaeda's chief ideologist, Ayman al-Zawahiri, has put it, al-Qaeda is the ideological vanguard, whose attacks on the United States and other Western targets are designed to mobilize and energize the Muslim masses to rise up against their own corrupt rulers, who are propped up by America. Like all good Leninists, the Islamo-Leninists are certain that the Muslim masses are deeply dissatisfied with their lot and that one or two spectacular acts of jihad against the "pillars of tyranny" in the West will spark them to overthrow the secularizing, immoral, and unjust Arab-Muslim regimes that have defiled Islam. In their place, the Islamo-Leninists, however, do not want to establish a workers' paradise but rather a religious paradise. They vow to establish an Islamic state across the same territory that Islam ruled over at its height, led by a caliph, a supreme religious-political leader, who would unite all the Muslim peoples into a single community.

Islamo-Leninism in many ways emerged from the same historical context as the radical European ideologies of the nineteenth and twentieth centuries. Fascism and Marxism-Leninism grew out of the rapid industrialization and modernization of Germany and Central Europe, where communities living in tightly bonded villages and extended families suddenly got shattered and the sons and fathers went off to the urban areas to work for big industrial companies. In this age of transitions, young men in particular lost a sense of identity, rootedness, and personal dignity that had been provided by traditional social structures. In that vacuum, along came Hitler, Lenin, and Mussolini, who told these young

men that they had an answer for their feelings of dislocation and humiliation: You may not be in the village or small town anymore, but you are
still proud, dignified members of a larger community—the working
class, or the Aryan nation.

Bin Laden offered the same sort of ideological response for young
Arabs and Muslims. The first person to recognize the Islamo-Leninist
character of these 9/11 hijackers—that they were not fundamentalists but
adherents of an extreme, violent political cult—was Adrian Karatnycky,
the president of Freedom House. In a November 5, 2001, article in the
National Review, titled "Under Our Very Noses," Karatnycky makes the
following argument: "The key hijackers . . . were well-educated children
of privilege. None of them suffered first-hand economic privation or political oppression." And none of them seems to have been raised in a particularly fundamentalist household. Indeed, the top 9/11 operatives and
pilots, like Mohammed Atta and Marwan al-Shehhi, who shared an
apartment in Hamburg, where they both attended the Technical University of Hamburg-Harburg, all seem to have been recruited to al-Qaeda
through cells and prayer groups—after they moved to Europe.

None of these plotters was recruited in the Middle East and then
planted in Europe years in advance by bin Laden, notes Karatnycky. To
the contrary, virtually all of them seem to have lived in Europe on their
own, grown alienated from the European society around them, gravitated
to a local prayer group or mosque to find warmth and solidarity, undergone
a "born-again" conversion, gotten radicalized by Islamist elements, gone
off for training in Afghanistan, and presto, a terrorist was born. Their discovery of religion was not just part of a personal search for meaning. It went
far beyond fundamentalism. They converted Islam into a political ideology,
a religious totalitarianism. Had the 9/11 hijackers been students at
Berkeley in the early 1970s, they would have been Trotskyite radicals. "To
understand the September 11 terrorists, we should have in mind the profile
of the classic revolutionary: deracinated, middle class, shaped in part by ex-
ile. In other words, the image of Lenin in Zurich; or of Pol Pot or Ho Chi
Minh in Paris . . . For them Islamism is the new universal revolutionary
creed, and bin Laden is Sheikh Guevara," writes Karatnycky. "Like the
leaders of America's Weather Underground, Germany's Baader-Meinhof

Gang, Italy's Red Brigades, and Japan's Red Army Faction, the Islamic terrorists were university-educated converts to an all-encompassing neo-totalitarian ideology."

My friend Abdallah Schleifer, a journalism professor in Cairo, actually knew Ayman al-Zawahiri, bin Laden's number two and chief ideologue, when al-Zawahiri was a young doctor on his way to becoming a young neo-Leninist Muslim revolutionary. "Ayman was attracted from the time he was a teenager into a utopian vision of an Islamic state," Schleifer told me on a visit to Cairo. But instead of being drawn to the traditional concern of religion—the relationship between oneself and God—al-Zawahiri became drawn to religion as a political ideology. Like a good Marxist or Leninist, al-Zawahiri was interested in "building the Kingdom of God on earth," said Schleifer, and Islamism became his Marxism—his "utopian ideology." And where Mohammed Atta meets al-Zawahiri is the intersection where rage and humiliation meet the ideology that is going to make it all right. "Ayman is saying to someone like Mohammed Atta, 'You see injustice? We have a system—*a system, mind you, a system*—that will give you [justice], not a religion, because religion gives you inner peace.' It doesn't necessarily solve any social problem. But [al-Zawahiri] is saying we have a system that will give you justice. You feel frustration? We have a system that will enable you to flower. The system is what we call Islamism—an ideological, highly politicized Islam, in which the spiritual content—the personal relationship [with God]—is taken out of Islam and instead it is transformed into a religious ideology like fascism or communism." But unlike the Leninists, who wanted to install the reign of the perfect class, the working class, and unlike Nazis, who wanted to install the reign of the perfect race, the Aryan race, bin Laden and al-Zawahiri wanted to install the reign of the perfect religion.

Unfortunately, bin Laden and his colleagues have found it all too easy to enlist recruits in the Arab-Muslim world. I think this has to do, in part, with the state of half-flatness that many Arab-Muslim young people are living in, particularly those in Europe. They have been raised to believe that Islam is the most perfect and complete expression of God's monotheistic message and that the Prophet Muhammad is God's last and most perfect messenger. This is not a criticism. This is Islam's self-identity. Yet, in a flat world, these youth, particularly those living in Europe, can and do look around and see that the Arab-Muslim world, in too many cases, has fallen behind the rest of the planet. It is not living as prosperously or democratically as other civilizations. How can that be? these young Arabs and Muslims must ask themselves. If we have the superior faith, and if our faith is all encompassing of religion, politics, and economics, why are others living so much better?

This is a source of real cognitive dissonance for many Arab-Muslim youth—the sort of dissonance, and loss of self-esteem, that sparks rage and leads some of them to join violent groups and lash out at the world. It is also the sort of dissonance that leads many others, average folks, to give radical groups like al-Qaeda passive support. Again, the flattening of the world only sharpens that dissonance by making the backwardness of the Arab-Muslim region, compared to others, impossible to ignore. It has become so impossible to ignore that some Arab-Muslim intellectuals have started to point out this backwardness with brutal honesty and to demand solutions. They do this in defiance of their authoritarian governments, which prefer to use their media not to encourage honest debate but rather to blame all their problems on others—on America, on Israel, or on a legacy of Western colonialism, on anything and anyone but the dead hand of these authoritarian regimes.

According to the second Arab Human Development Report, which was written in 2003 for the United Nations Development Program by a group of courageous Arab social scientists, between 1980 and 1999, Arab countries produced 171 international patents. South Korea alone during that same period registered 16,328 patents. Hewlett-Packard registers, on average, 11 new patents a day. The average number of scientists and engineers working in research and development in the Arab countries is 371 per million people, while the world average, including countries in Africa, Asia, and Latin America, is 979, the report said. This helps to explain why although massive amounts of foreign technology are imported to the Arab regions, very little of it is internalized or supplanted by Arab innovations. Between 1995 and 1996, as many as 25 percent of the university graduates produced in the Arab world immigrated to some Western country. There are just eighteen computers per one thousand people in the Arab region today, compared with the global average of seventy-eight per one thousand, and only 1.6 percent of the Arab population has Internet access. While Arabs represent almost 5 percent of the world population, the report said, they produce only 1 percent of the books published, and an unusually high percentage of those are religious books—over triple the world average. Of the eighty-eight million unemployed males between fifteen and twenty-four worldwide, almost 26 percent are in the Middle East and North Africa, according to an International Labor Organization study (Associated Press, December 26, 2004).

The same study said the total population of Arab countries quadrupled in the past fifty years, to almost three hundred million, with 37.5 percent under fifteen, and three million coming onto the job market every year. But the good jobs are not being produced at home, because the environment of openness required to attract international investment and stimulate local innovation is all too rare in the Arab-Muslim world today. That virtuous cycle of universities spinning off people and ideas, and then those people and ideas getting funded and creating new jobs, simply does not exist there. Theodore Dalrymple is a physician and psychiatrist who practices in England and writes a column for the *London Spectator*. He wrote an essay in the urban policy magazine *City Journal* (Spring 2004) about what he learned from his contacts with Muslim youth in British prisons. Dalrymple noted that most schools of Islam today treat the Qur'an as a divinely inspired text that is not open to any literary criticism or creative reinterpretation. It is a sacred book to be memorized, not adapted to the demands and opportunities of modern life. But without a culture that encourages, and creates space for, such creative reinterpretation, critical thought and original thinking tend to wither. This may explain why so few world-class scientific papers cited by other scholars come out of the Arab-Muslim universities.

If the West had made Shakespeare "the sole object of our study and the sole guide of our lives," said Dalrymple, "we would soon enough fall into backwardness and stagnation. And the problem is that so many Muslims want both stagnation and power: they want a return to the perfection of the seventh century and to dominate the twenty-first, as they believe is the birthright of their doctrine, the last testament of God to man. If they were content to exist in a seventh-century backwater, secure in a quietist philosophy, there would be no problem for them or us; their problem, and ours, is that they want the power that free inquiry confers, without either the free inquiry or the philosophy and institutions that guarantee that free inquiry. They are faced with a dilemma: either they abandon their cherished religion, or they remain forever in the rear of human technical advance. Neither alternative is very appealing, and the tension between their desire for power and success in the modern world on the one hand, and their desire not to abandon their religion on the other, is resolvable for some only by exploding themselves as bombs. People grow angry when faced with an intractable dilemma; they lash out."

Indeed, talk to young Arabs and Muslims anywhere, and this cognitive dissonance and the word "humiliation" always come up very quickly in conversation. It was revealing that when Mahathir Mohammed made his October 16, 2003, farewell speech as prime minister of Malaysia at an Islamic summit he was hosting in his own country, he built his remarks to his fellow Muslim leaders around the question of why their civilization had become so humiliated—a term he used five times. "I will not enumerate the instances of our humiliation," said Mahathir. "Our only reaction is to become more and more angry. Angry people cannot think properly. There is a feeling of hopelessness among the Muslim countries and their people. They feel they can do nothing right . . ."

This humiliation is the key. It has always been my view that terrorism is not spawned by the poverty of money. It is spawned by *the poverty of dignity*. Humiliation is the most underestimated force in international relations and in human relations. It is when people or nations are humiliated that they really lash out and engage in extreme violence. When you take the economic and political backwardness of much of the Arab-Muslim world today, add its past grandeur and self-image of religious superiority, and combine it with the discrimination and alienation these Arab-Muslim males face when they leave home and move to Europe, or when they grow up in Europe, you have one powerful cocktail of rage.

As my friend the Egyptian playwright Ali Salem said of the 9/11 hijack-ers, they "are walking the streets of life, searching for tall buildings—for towers to bring down, because they are not able to be tall like them."

I fear that this sense of frustration that feeds recruits to bin Laden may get worse before it gets better. In the old days, leaders could count on walls and mountains and valleys to obstruct their people's view and keep them ignorant and passive about where they stood in comparison to oth-ers. You could see only to the next village. But as the world gets flatter, people can see for miles and miles.

In the flat world you get your humiliation dished up to you fiber-optically. I stumbled across a fascinating example of this involving bin Laden himself. On January 4, 2004, bin Laden issued one of his taped messages through al-Jazeera, the satellite television network based in Qatar. On March 7, the Web site of the Islamic Studies and Research Center published the entire text. One paragraph jumped out at me. It is in the middle of a section in which bin Laden is discussing the various evils of Arab rulers, particularly the Saudi ruling family.

"Thus, the situation of all Arab countries suffers from great deteriora-tion in all walks of life, in religious and worldly matters," says bin Laden. "It is enough to know that the economy of all Arab countries is weaker than the economy of one country that had once been part of our [Islamic] world when we used to truly adhere to Islam. That country is the lost Andalusia. Spain is an infidel country, but its economy is stronger than our economy because the ruler there is accountable. In our countries, there is no accountability or punishment, but there is only obedience to the rulers and prayers of long life for them."

The hair on my arms stood up when I read that. Why? Because what bin Laden was referring to was the first Arab Human Development Report, which came out in July 2002, well after he had been evicted from Afghanistan and was probably hiding out in a cave somewhere. The Arab authors of the report wanted to grab the attention of the Arab world as to how far behind it had fallen. So they looked for a country that had a GDP slightly more than that of all twenty-two Arab states combined. When they ran down the tables, the country that fit that bill perfectly was Spain. It could have been Norway or Italy, but Spain happened to have a GDP just slightly larger than all the Arab states together. Somehow, bin Laden heard or read about this first Arab Human Development Report from his cave. For all I know, he may have read my own column about it, which was the first to highlight the report and stressed the comparison with Spain. Or maybe he got it off the Internet. The report was downloaded from the Internet some one million times. So even though he was off in a cave somewhere, he could still get this report, and its humiliating conclusion, shoved right in his face—negatively comparing the Arab states to Spain, no less! And when he heard that comparison, wherever he was hiding, bin Laden took it as an insult, as a humiliation—the notion that Christian Spain, a country that was once controlled by Muslims, had a greater GDP today than all the Arab states combined. The authors of this report were themselves Arabs and Muslims; they were not trying to humiliate anyone—but that was how bin Laden interpreted it. And I am certain he got this dose of humiliation over a modem at 56K. They may even have broadband now in Tora Bora.

And having gotten his dose of humiliation this way, bin Laden and his emulators have learned to give it right back in the same coin. Want to understand why the Islamo-Leninists behead Americans in Iraq and Saudi Arabia and then distribute pictures on the Internet with the bloody head of the body resting on the headless corpse? It is because there is no more humiliating form of execution than chopping off someone's head. It is a way of showing utter contempt for that person and his or her physical being. It is no accident that the groups in Iraq who beheaded Americans dressed them first in the same orange jumpsuits that al-Qaeda prisoners in Guantánamo Bay are forced to wear. They had to learn about those jumpsuits either over the Internet or satellite TV. But it amazes me that in the middle of the Iraq war they were able to have the exact same jumpsuits made in Iraq to dress their prisoners in. You humiliate me, I humiliate you. And what do you suppose terrorist leader Abu Musab al-Zarqawi said in his audiotape released on September 11, 2004, the third anniversary of 9/11? He said, "The holy warriors made the international coalition taste humiliation . . . lessons from which they are still burning." The tape was titled "Where Is the Honor?"

As I said, however, this frustration and humiliation are not confined to the Islamist fringes. The reason the Islamo-Leninists have become the most energized and pronounced opponents of globalization/Americanization and the biggest threat to the flattening of the world today is not simply their extraordinary violence, but also that they enjoy some passive support around the Arab-Muslim world.

In part, this is because most governments in the Arab-Muslim world have refused to take on these radicals in a war of ideas. While Arab regimes have been very active in jailing their Islamo-Leninists when they can find and arrest them, they have been very passive in countering them with a modern, progressive interpretation of Islam. This is because almost all of these Arab-Muslim leaders are illegitimate themselves. Having come to power by force, they have no credibility as carriers of a moderate, progressive Islam, and they always feel vulnerable to hard-line Muslim preachers, who denounce them for not being good Muslims. So instead of taking on the Muslim radicals, the Arab regimes either throw them in jail or try to buy them off. This leaves a terrible spiritual and political void.

But the other reason for the passive support that the Islamo-Leninists enjoy—and the fact that they are able to raise so much money through charities and mosques in the Arab-Muslim world—is that too many good, decent people there feel the same frustration and tinge of humiliation that many of their most enraged youth do. And there is a certain respect for the way these violent youth have been ready to stand up to the world and to their own leaders and defend the honor of their civilization. When I visited Qatar a few months after 9/11, a friend of mine there—a sweet, thoughtful, liberal person who works for the Qatari government—confided to me something in a whisper that was deeply troubling to him: "My eleven-year-old son thinks bin Laden is a good man."

Most middle-class Arabs and Muslims, I am convinced, were not celebrating the death of three thousand innocent Americans on 9/11. I know my Arab and Muslim friends were not. But many Arabs and Muslims were celebrating the idea of putting a fist in America's face—and they were quietly applauding the men who did it. They were happy to see someone humiliating the people and the country that they felt was humiliating them and supporting what they saw as injustice in their world—whether it is America's backing of Arab kings and dictators who export oil to it or America's backing of Israel whether it does the right things or the wrong things.

Most American blacks, I am sure, had little doubt that O. J. Simpson murdered his ex-wife, but they applauded his acquittal as a stick in the eye of the Los Angeles Police Department and a justice system that they saw as consistently humiliating and unfair to them. Humiliation does that to people. Bin Laden is to the Arab masses what O.J. was to many American blacks—the stick they poke in the eye of an "unfair" America and their own leaders. I once interviewed Dyab Abou Jahjah, often called the Malcolm X of Belgium's alienated Moroccan youth. I asked him what he and his friends thought when they saw the World Trade Center being smashed. He said, "I think if we are honest with ourselves, most of the Muslims all over the world felt that . . . America got hit in the face and that cannot be bad. I don't want to make an intellectual answer for that. I'll give it very simply. America was kicking our butts for fifty years. And really badly. Supporting the bullies in the region, whether it is Israel or our own regimes, [America] is giving us not only a bleeding nose, but breaking a lot of our necks."

Just as America's economic depression in the 1920s and 1930s made many normal, intelligent, thinking Americans passive or active supporters of communism, so the humiliating economic, military, and emotional depression of the Arab-Muslim world has made too many normal, intelligent, and thinking Arabs and Muslims passive supporters of bin Ladenism.

Former Kuwaiti minister of information Dr. Sa'd Bin Tefla, a journalist, wrote an essay in the London Arabic daily *Al-Sharq Al-Awsat* on the third anniversary of September 11 titled "We Are All Bin Laden," which went right to this point. He asked why it is that Muslim scholars and clerics eagerly supported fatwas condemning Salman Rushdie to death for writing an allegedly blasphemous novel, *The Satanic Verses*, that wove in themes about the Prophet Muhammad, but to this day no Muslim cleric has issued a fatwa condemning Osama bin Laden for murdering three thousand innocent civilians. After the fatwa was declared against Salman Rushdie, Muslims staged protests against the book at British embassies all over the Islamic world and burned Salman Rushdie dolls along with copies of his book. Nine people were killed in an anti-Rushdie protest in Pakistan.

"Religious legal rulings were disseminated one after another banning Salman Rushdie's book and calling for him to be killed," Bin Tefla wrote. "Iran earmarked a reward of $1 million for whoever would implement Imam Khomeini's fatwa and kill Salman Rushdie." And bin Laden? Nothing—no condemnation. "Despite the fact that bin Laden murdered thousands of innocents in the name of our religion and despite the damage that he has caused to Muslims everywhere, and especially to innocent Muslims in the West, whose life is much better than the life of Muslims in Islamic lands, to this date not a single fatwa has been issued calling for the killing of bin Laden, on the pretext that bin Laden still proclaims 'there is no God other than Allah,'" Tefla wrote. Worse, he added, Arab and Muslim satellite television channels have "competed amongst themselves in broadcasting [bin Laden's] sermons and fatwas, instead of preventing their dissemination as they did in the case of Rushdie's book . . . With our equivocal stance on bin Laden, we from the very start left the world with the impression that we are all bin Laden."

Germany was humiliated after World War I, but it had the modern economic foundations to produce a state response to that humiliation—in the form of the Third Reich. The Arab world, by contrast, could not produce a state response to its humiliation. Instead, it has rattled the world stage in the last fifty years with two larger-than-life figures, rather than states, noted political theorist Yaron Ezrahi: One was the Saudi oil minister Ahmed Zaki Yamani, and the other was Osama bin Laden. Each achieved global notoriety, each briefly held the world in his palm—one by using oil as a weapon and the other by using the most unconventional suicide violence imaginable. Each gave a temporary "high" to the Arab-Muslim world, a feeling that it was exercising power on the world stage. But bin Laden and Yamani were only the illusions of power, noted Ezrahi: The Saudi oil weapon is economic power without productivity, and bin Laden's terrorism weapon is military force without a real army, state, economy, and engine of innovation to support it.

What makes Yamanism and bin Ladenism so unfortunate as strategies for Arab influence in the world is that they ignore the examples within

Arab culture and civilization—when it was at its height—of discipline, hard work, knowledge, achievement, scientific inquiry, and pluralism. As Nayan Chanda, the editor of YaleGlobal Online, pointed out to me, it was the Arab-Muslim world that gave birth to algebra and algorithms, both terms derived from Arabic words. In other words, noted Chanda, "The entire modern information revolution, which is built to a large degree on algorithms, can trace its roots all the way back to Arab-Muslim civilization and the great learning centers of Baghdad and Alexandria," which first introduced these concepts, then transferred them to Europe through Muslim Spain. The Arab-Muslim peoples have an incredibly rich cultural tradition and civilization, with long periods of success and innovation to draw on for inspiration and example for their young people. They have all the resources necessary for modernization in their own cultural terms, if they want to summon them.

Unfortunately, there is huge resistance to such modernization from the authoritarian and religiously obscurantist forces within the Arab-Muslim world. That is why this part of the world will be liberated, and feel truly empowered, only if it goes through its own war of ideas—and the moderates there win. We had a civil war in America some 150 years ago over ideas—the ideas of tolerance, pluralism, human dignity, and equality. The best thing outsiders can do for the Arab-Muslim world today is try to collaborate with its progressive forces in every way possible—from trying to solve the Arab-Israeli conflict, to stabilizing Iraq, to signing free-trade agreements with as many Arab countries as possible—so as to foster a similar war of ideas within their civilization. There is no other way. Otherwise this part of the world has the potential to be a huge unflattening force. We have to wish the good people there well. But the battle will be one for them to fight and to win. No one can do it for them.

No one has expressed what is needed better than Abdel Rahman al-Rashed, the general manager of the London-based al-Arabiya news channel. One of the best-known and most respected Arab journalists working today, he wrote the following, in *Al-Sharq Al-Awsat* (September 6, 2004), after a series of violent incidents involving Muslim extremist groups from Chechnya to Saudi Arabia to Iraq: "Self-cure starts with self-realization and confession. We should then run after our terrorist sons, in the full knowledge that they are the sour grapes of a deformed culture . . . The mosque used to be a haven, and the voice of religion used to be that of peace and reconciliation. Religious sermons were warm behests for a moral order and an ethical life. Then came the neo-Muslims. An innocent and benevolent religion, whose verses prohibit the felling of trees in the absence of urgent necessity, that calls murder the most heinous of crimes, that says explicitly that if you kill one person you have killed humanity as a whole, has been turned into a global message of hate and a universal war cry . . . We cannot clear our names unless we own up to the shameful fact that terrorism has become an Islamic enterprise; an almost exclusive monopoly, implemented by Muslim men and women. We cannot redeem our extremist youth, who commit all these heinous crimes, without confronting the Sheikhs who thought it ennobling to reinvent themselves as revolutionary ideologues, sending other people's sons and daughters to certain death, while sending their own children to European and American schools and colleges."

Too Many Toyotas

The problems of the too sick, the too disempowered, and the too humiliated are all in their own ways keeping the world from becoming entirely flat. They may do so even more in the future, if they are not properly addressed. But another enormously powerful threat to the flattening of the world is on the horizon. It is not a human resources constraint or a disease, but a natural resources constraint. If millions of people from India, China, Latin America, and the former Soviet Empire, who for years had been living largely outside the flat world, all start to walk onto the new flat-world platform—each with his or her own version of the American dream of owning a car, a house, a refrigerator, a microwave, and a toaster—we are, at best, going to experience a serious energy shortage. At worst, we are going to set off a global struggle for natural resources and junk up, heat up, garbage up, smoke up, and devour up our little planet faster than at any time in the history of the world. Be afraid. I certainly am.

In his classic work *Collapse,* Jared Diamond points out that when thinking about the issue of sustainability, what counts is not just the number of people inhabiting the planet Earth but the impact that their particular lifestyle is having on the environment. If most of the world's six billion people today were in cold storage, neither eating, breathing, nor metabolizing, he argues, their impact on the environment would be minimal. The problem we now face derives from the fact that we are not in a deep freeze. We are consuming resources and generating waste— and how! "That per capita impact—the resources consumed and the waste put out, by each person—varies greatly around the world, being highest in the first world and lowest in the third world," Diamond writes. "On the average, each citizen of the U.S., Western Europe and Japan consumes 32 times more resources, such as fossil fuels, and puts out 32 times more waste, than do inhabitants of the Third World. But low impact people are becoming high impact people."

Indeed. The flattening of the world is making low-impact people into high-impact people faster, in greater numbers, and with greater impacts than at any other time in the history of the world. "There are many 'optimists,'" notes Diamond, "who argue that the world could support double its human population . . . But I have not met anyone who seriously argues that the world could support 12 times its current impact, although an increase of that factor would result from all Third World inhabitants adopting first world living standards." And that is where we are heading.

As I mentioned earlier, I visited Beijing in the summer of 2004 with my wife and teenage daughter, Natalie. Before we left, I said to Natalie, "You're really going to like this city. They have these big bicycle lanes on all the main roads. Maybe when we get there we can rent bikes and just ride around Beijing. I did that last time I was there, and it was a lot of fun."

Silly Tom. I hadn't been to Beijing since 2001, and in just three years the explosive growth there had erased without a trace many of those charming bicycle lanes. They had been either shrunken or eliminated to add another lane for automobiles and buses. The only biking I did there was on the stationary exercise bike in our hotel, which was a good antidote to all the time spent sitting in cars stuck in Beijing traffic jams. I was in Beijing to attend an international business conference, and while there I discovered why all the bikes had disappeared. According to one speaker at the conference, some thirty thousand new cars were being added to the roads in Beijing *every month*—one thousand more new cars a day! I found that statistic so unbelievable that I asked Michael Zhao, a young researcher in the *Times*'s Beijing bureau, to double-check it, and he wrote me back the following e-mail:

> Hi Tom, Hope this email finds you well. On your question about how many cars are added each day in Beijing, I did some research on the Internet and found that . . . car sales in [Beijing] for April 2004 were 43,000—24.1% more than same period last year. So that is 1,433 cars added [daily] to Beijing, but including second-hand car sales. New car sales this month were 30,000, or 1,000 cars each day added to the city. The total car sales from Jan. to April 2004 were 165,000, that is about 1,375 cars added each day to Beijing over this period. This data is from the Beijing Municipal Bureau of Commerce. The city's bureau of statistics has it that the total car sales in 2003 were 407,649, or 1,117 cars each day added. The new car sales last year were 292,858, or 802 new cars each day . . . The total number of cars in Beijing is 2.1 million . . . But the recent months seem to have witnessed surging sales. Also noteworthy is last year's SARS outbreak, during which period a lot of families bought cars, due to panic about public contact and a sort of doomsday-stimulated enjoy-life mentality. And many new car owners did enjoy their time driving, as the traffic in the city so much improved with a lot of people voluntarily caged at home, without daring to go out. Since then, coupled with dropping car prices due to China's commitment to reduce tariffs after joining the WTO, a large number of families have advanced their timetable of buying a car, although some others decided to wait for further drops of prices. All the best, Michael

The thirty thousand new cars a month in Beijing, and the cloud of haze that envelops the city on so many days, and the fact that the city's official Web site actually keeps track of "blue sky" days all testify to the environmental destruction that could arise from the triple convergence—if clean alternative renewable energies are not developed soon. Already, according to the World Bank, sixteen of the twenty most polluted cities in the world are in China, and that pollution and environmental degradation together cost China $170 billion a year (*The Economist*, August 21, 2004).

And we have not seen anything yet. China, with its own oil and gas reserves, was once a net exporter. Not anymore. In 2003, China surged ahead of Japan as the second largest importer of oil in the world, after the United States. China's overall energy consumption is up 65 percent just from 2002 to 2005, and it has not even begun to reach its capacity for industrialization.

There is a Wal-Mart in Shenzhen, China, that sold 1,100 air conditioners in just one hot weekend in the summer of 2005. One store! Think of the environmental impact when there is a Wal-Mart in every major Chinese city.

Right now, about 700 to 800 million of China's 1.3 billion people still live in the countryside, but they are heading for the flat world, and roughly half are expected to try to migrate to the cities over the next two decades. If they can find work, this great migration will spur a huge surge in demand for cars, houses, steel beams, power plants, school buildings, sewage plants, electricity grids. No wonder then that a report in the *Financial Times* (August 16, 2005) noted that global energy demand has been growing since 2003 at about 2.5 times the rate of the prior decade, with China and India accounting for about 35 percent of the world's incremental increase in oil consumption, even though they account for just 15 percent of world output.

At the business conference I was attending in Beijing, I kept hearing references to the Strait of Malacca—the narrow passage between Malaysia and Indonesia that is patrolled by the U.S. Navy and controls all the oil tanker traffic from the Middle East to China and Japan. I hadn't heard anyone talking about the Strait of Malacca since the 1970s oil crises. But evidently Chinese strategic planners have begun to grow increasingly concerned that the United States could choke off China's economy at any time by just closing the Strait of Malacca, and this threat is now being increasingly and openly discussed in Chinese military circles. It is just a small hint of the potential struggle for power—energy power—that could ensue if the Great American Dream and the Great Chinese Dream and the Great Indian Dream and the Great Russian Dream come to be seen as mutually exclusive in energy terms.

Don't kid yourself: China's foreign policy today consists of just two things—preventing Taiwan from becoming independent and searching for oil and other natural resources. "It is not a conspiracy on our part," a Chinese foreign ministry official said to me of China's global quest for oil. "We're not trying to dominate anyone. We were just latecomers to the game and when we looked around we saw all the chairs were taken." China is particularly obsessed with acquiring secure oil supplies from countries that would not retaliate against China if it invaded Taiwan, and this is driving Beijing to get cozy with some of the most despotic regimes in the world. And the more desperate China becomes for oil, the more vigorously it will use its veto at the UN Security Council to prevent sanctions against its newfound providers of crude—no matter what horrible things they are doing on the world stage. The Islamic fundamentalist government in Sudan now supplies China with 7 percent of its oil supplies, and China has invested $3 billion in oil-drilling infrastructure there. In September 2004, China threatened to veto a move by the United Nations to impose sanctions on Sudan for the genocide that it is perpetrating in its Darfur province. China has only reluctantly joined international efforts to prevent Iran from developing a nuclear weapon. Iran supplies 13 percent of China's oil supplies. Meanwhile, as *The Daily Telegraph* reported (November 19, 2004), China has begun drilling for gas in the East China Sea, just west of the line that Japan regards as its border: "Japan protested, to no avail, that the project should be a joint one. The two are also set to clash over Russia's oil wealth. China is furious that Japan has outbid it in their battle to determine the route of the pipeline that Russia intends to build to the Far East." At the same time it was reported that a Chinese nuclear submarine had accidentally strayed into Japanese territorial waters. The Chinese government apologized for the "technical error." If you believe that, I have an oil well in Hawaii I would like to sell you . . .

In 2004, China began competing with the United States for oil exploration opportunities in Canada and Venezuela. If China has its way, it will stick a straw into Canada and Venezuela and suck out every drop of oil, which will have the side effect of making America more dependent on Saudi Arabia.

I interviewed the Japanese manager of a major U.S. multinational that is headquartered in northeastern China. "China is following the path of Japan and Korea," said the executive, on the condition that he and his company not be quoted by name, "and the big question is, Can the world afford to have 1.3 billion people following that path and driving the same cars and using the same amount of energy? So I see the flattening, but the challenge of the twenty-first century is, Are we going to hit another oil crisis? The oil crisis in the 1970s coincided with Japan and Europe rising. [There was a time] when the U.S. was the only big consumer of oil, but when Japan and Europe came in, OPEC got the power. But when China and India come into being the consumers, it will be a huge challenge that is an order of magnitude different. It is megapolitics. The limits of growth in the 1970s were overcome with technology. We got smarter than before, equipment became more efficient, and energy consumption per head was lower. But now [with China, India, and Russia all coming on strong] it is multiplied by a factor of ten. There is something we really need to be serious about. We cannot restrict China, [Russia,] and India. They will grow and they must grow."

One thing we will not be able to do is tell young Indians, Russians, Poles, or Chinese that just when they are arriving on the leveled playing field, they have to hold back and consume less for the greater global good. While giving a talk to students at the Beijing College of Foreign Affairs, I spoke about the most important issues that could threaten global stability, including the competition for oil and other energy resources that would naturally occur as China, India, and the former Soviet Union began to consume more oil. No sooner did I finish than a young Chinese woman student shot up her hand and basically asked: "Why should China have to restrain its energy consumption and worry about the environment, when America and Europe got to consume all the energy they wanted when they were developing?" I did not have a good answer. China is a high-pride country. Telling China, India, and Russia to consume less could have the same geopolitical impact that the world's inability to accommodate a rising Japan and Germany had after World War I.

If current trends hold, China will go from importing seven million barrels of oil today to fourteen million a day by 2012. For the world to accommodate that increase, it would have to find another Saudi Arabia. That is not likely, which doesn't leave many good options. "For geopolitical reasons, we cannot tell them no, we cannot tell China and India, it is not your turn," said Philip K. Verleger Jr., a leading oil economist. "And for moral reasons, we have lost the ability to lecture anyone." But if we do nothing, several things will likely result. First, gasoline prices will continue to go higher and higher. Second, we will be strengthening some of the worst political systems in the world—like Sudan, Iran, and Saudi Arabia. And third, the environment will be damaged more and more. Already, the newspaper headlines in China every day are about energy shortages, blackouts, and brownouts. U.S. officials estimate that twenty-four out of China's thirty-one provinces are now experiencing power shortages.

We are all stewards of this planet, and the test for our generation is whether we will pass on this planet in as good or better shape than we found it. The flattening process is going to challenge that responsibility. "Aldo Leopold, the father of wildlife ecology, once said: 'The first rule of intelligent tinkering is save all the pieces,'" remarked Glenn Prickett, senior vice president of Conservation International. "What if we don't? What if the three billion new entrants start gobbling up all the resources? Species and ecosystems can't adapt that fast, and we will lose a major portion of the earth's remaining biological diversity." Already, noted Prickett, if you look at what is happening in the Congo Basin, the Amazon, the rain forest of Indonesia—the last great wilderness areas—you find that they are being devoured by China's growing appetite. More and more palm oil is being extracted from Indonesia and Malaysia, soybeans out of Brazil, timber out of central Africa, and natural gas out of all of the above to serve China—and, as a result, all sorts of natural habitats are threatened. If these trends go on unchecked, with the natural habitats being converted to farmland and urban areas, and the globe getting warmer, many of the currently threatened species will be condemned to extinction.

The move to sharply reduce energy consumption has to come from within China, as the Chinese confront what the need for fossil fuel is doing to their own environment and growth aspirations. Fortunately, that is starting to happen. Listen to China's deputy minister of the environment, Pan Yue, in a stunning interview with *Der Spiegel* (March 7, 2005): "Our raw materials are scarce, we don't have enough land, and our population is constantly growing. Currently, there are 1.3 billion people living in China, that's twice as many as 50 years ago. In 2020, there will be 1.5 billion people in China. Cities are growing but desert areas are expanding at the same time; habitable and usable land has been halved over the past 50 years . . . [China's GDP miracle] will end soon because the environment can no longer keep pace . . . Half of the water in our seven largest rivers is completely useless . . . One third of the urban population is breathing polluted air . . . We are convinced that a prospering economy automatically goes hand in hand with political stability. And I think that's a major blunder . . . If the gap between the poor and the rich widens, then regions within China and the society as a whole will become unstable."

The best thing we in the United States can do to nudge China toward greater conservation is to set an example by changing our own consumption patterns. That would give us some credibility to lecture others. "Restoring our moral standing on energy is now a vital national security and environmental issue," said Verleger. The second best thing we can do is put America's best brainpower and biggest economic muscles behind developing emissions-free energy technologies and getting down the innovation and costs curves quickly so they hit the "China price" — the price at which China and other developing countries could afford to buy and deploy them at scale.

America could do this today, but it would require an energy strategy that is not simply the "sum of all lobbies," says Gal Luft, founding member of the Set America Free Coalition, a bipartisan alliance of national security, labor, environmental, and religious groups that believe reducing our oil consumption is a national priority. Rather, we would need a new strategic approach to both conservation and the development of clean and renewable energies supported by a new coalition. It is a philosophy that I like to call "geo-greenism." We geo-greens seek to combine into a single political movement environmentalists who want to reduce fossil fuels that cause climate change, evangelicals who want to protect God's green earth and all His creation, and geostrategists who want to reduce our dependence on crude oil because it fuels some of the worst regimes in the world.

The reluctance of the Bush team to develop such a comprehensive geo-green strategy—which would strengthen the dollar, reduce our trade deficit, make America the world leader in combating climate change, and stimulate U.S. companies to take the lead in producing the green technologies that the world will desperately need as China and India industrialize—has been so irresponsible that it takes your breath away. This is especially true when you realize that the solutions to many of our problems are already here. We don't need to reinvent the wheel or wait for sci-fi hydrogen fuel cells or dramatically cut back our standard of living in order to get green. All we need is some leadership. The worst energy deficit we have right now is among our leaders—who lack the energy to imagine alternatives to the path we are on and lack the will to push us in a new, geo-green direction.

If you have put a windmill in your yard or some solar panels on your roof, bless your heart. But we will green the world only when we change the very nature of the electricity grid—moving it away from dirty coal, gas, and oil to clean coal, nuclear, wind, and solar. And that will be a huge industrial project, bigger than any politician has ever explained to the American people. It will require a president and a Congress with the guts to undertake a "Green New Deal"—where government's role is not funding vast projects, like the original New Deal, but seeding basic research, providing loan guarantees where needed, and setting standards, regulations, taxes, and incentives that will shape the market and spawn one thousand new clean-tech companies, focused on everything from power generation to biofuels to more efficient transportation to green buildings.

A Green New Deal today requires getting two things right: government regulations and prices. Look at California. By setting steadily higher standards for the energy efficiency of buildings and appliances—and creating incentives for utilities to work with consumers to use less power—California has held its per capita electricity use roughly constant for thirty years, while the rest of the nation has seen per capita electricity use increase by nearly 50 percent, according to the Natural Resources Defense Council. This kind of energy conservation has saved California from building twenty-four giant power plants. High standards force innovation, and innovation leads to conservation at scale.

But prices also matter. I don't care whether it is a higher federal gasoline tax, a carbon tax, a BTU tax, or a cap-and-trade system, power utilities, factories, and car owners have to be required to pay the real and full cost to society of the carbon we put into the atmosphere. And higher costs for fossil fuels make more costly clean alternatives more competitive. "The regulated utilities are the most important consumers from the perspective of long-term investment, and if they are not required to value carbon reduction, then they will underinvest in energy efficiency and renewable energy," said Peter Darbee, chairman of Pacific Gas & Electric. Any energy policy that does not have increasingly high efficiency standards and higher prices for fossil fuels is not an energy policy at all.

The public is ready to be led on this issue. The business community is already moving, because more and more companies are finding that operating clean and green saves money and is a competitive advantage. So enough of this nonsense that conservation, energy efficiency, and environmentalism are hobbies we can't afford. I can't think of anything more cowardly or un-American or less realistic than that view. Real patriots, real advocates of spreading democracy around the world, real entrepreneurs, live, invest, build, and think green.

Green is the new red, white, and blue.

SIXTEEN

The Dell Theory of Conflict Prevention

Old-Time Versus Just-in-Time

Free Trade is God's diplomacy. There is no other certain way of uniting people in the bonds of peace.

—British politician Richard Cobden, 1857

B efore I share with you the subject of this chapter, I have to tell you a little bit about the computer that I wrote this book on. It's related to the theme I am about to discuss. This book was largely written on a Dell Inspiron 600m notebook, service tag number 9ZRJP41. As part of the research for this book, I visited with the management team at Dell near Austin, Texas. I shared with them the ideas in this book and in return I asked for one favor: I asked them to trace for me the entire global supply chain that assembled the pieces that built the laptop that wrote the book. Yes, I wanted to know every part that went into my Dell notebook, what country it came from, and, if possible, the names of the people who put it together along the way. Here is what I found out.

My computer was conceived when I phoned Dell's 800 number on April 2, 2004, and was connected to sales representative Mujteba Naqvi, who immediately entered my order into Dell's order management system. He typed in both the type of notebook I ordered as well as the special features I wanted, along with my personal information, shipping address, billing address, and credit card information. My credit card was verified by Dell through its work flow connection with Visa, and my order was then released to Dell's production system. Dell has six factories around the world—in Limerick, Ireland; Xiamen, China; Eldorado do Sul, Brazil; Nashville, Tennessee; Austin, Texas; and Penang, Malaysia. My order went out by e-mail to the Dell notebook factory in Malaysia, where the parts for the computer were immediately ordered from the supplier logistics centers (SLCs) next to the Penang factory. Surrounding every Dell factory in the world are these supplier logistics centers, owned by the different suppliers of Dell parts. These SLCs are like staging areas. If you are a Dell supplier anywhere in the world, your job is to keep your SLC full of your specific parts so they can constantly be trucked over to the Dell factory for just-in-time manufacturing.

"In an average day, we sell 140,000 to 150,000 computers," explained Dick Hunter, one of Dell's three global production managers. "Those orders come in over Dell.com or over the telephone. As soon as these orders come in, our suppliers know about it. They get a signal based on every component in the machine you ordered, so the supplier knows just what he has to deliver. If you are supplying power cords for desktops, you can see minute by minute how many power cords you are going to have to deliver." Every two hours, the Dell factory in Penang sends an e-mail to the various SLCs nearby, telling each one what parts and what quantities of those parts it wants delivered within the next ninety minutes—and not one minute later. Within ninety minutes, trucks from the various SLCs around Penang pull up to the Dell manufacturing plant and unload the parts needed for all those notebooks ordered in the last two hours. This goes on all day, every two hours. As soon as those parts arrive at the factory, it takes thirty minutes for Dell employees to unload the parts, register their bar codes, and put them into the bins for assembly. "We know where every part in every SLC is in the Dell system at all times," said Hunter.

So where did the parts for my notebook come from? I asked Hunter. To begin with, he said, the notebook was codesigned in Austin, Texas, and in Taiwan by a team of Dell engineers and a team of Taiwanese notebook designers. "The customer's needs, required technologies, and Dell's design innovations were all determined by Dell through our direct relationship with customers," he explained. "The basic design of the motherboard and case—the basic functionality of your machine—was designed to those specifications by an ODM [original design manufacturer] in Taiwan. We put our engineers in their facilities and they come to Austin and we actually codesign these systems. This global teamwork brings an added benefit—a globally distributed virtually twenty-four-hour-per-day development cycle. Our partners do the basic electronics and we help them design customer and reliability features that we know our customers want. We know the customers better than our suppliers and our competition, because we are dealing directly with them every day." Dell notebooks are completely redesigned roughly every twelve months, but new features are constantly added during the year—through the supply chain—as the hardware and software components advance.

It happened that when my notebook order hit the Dell factory in Penang, one part was not available—the wireless card—due to a quality control issue, so the assembly of the notebook was delayed for a few days. Then the truck full of good wireless cards arrived. On April 13, at 10:15 a.m., a Dell Malaysia worker pulled the order slip that automatically popped up once all my parts had arrived from the SLCs to the Penang factory. Another Dell Malaysia employee then took out a "traveler"—a special carrying tote designed to hold and protect parts—and started plucking all the parts that went into my notebook.

Where did those parts come from? Dell uses multiple suppliers for most of the thirty key components that go into its notebooks. That way if one supplier breaks down or cannot meet a surge in demand, Dell is not left in the lurch. So here are the key suppliers for my Inspiron 600m notebook: The Intel microprocessor came from an Intel factory either in the Philippines, Costa Rica, Malaysia, or China. The memory came from a Korean-owned factory in Korea (Samsung), a Taiwanese-owned factory in Taiwan (Nanya), a German-owned factory in Germany (Infineon), or a Japanese-owned factory in Japan (Elpida). My graphics card was shipped from either a Taiwanese-owned factory in China (MSI) or a Chinese-run factory in China (Foxconn). The cooling fan came from a Taiwanese-owned factory in Taiwan (CCI or Auras). The motherboard came from either a Korean-owned factory in Shanghai (Samsung), a Taiwanese-owned factory in Shanghai (Quanta), or a Taiwanese-owned factory in Taiwan (Compal or Wistron). The keyboard came from either a Japanese-owned company in Tianjin, China (Alps), a Taiwanese-owned factory in Shenzhen, China (Sunrex), or a Taiwanese-owned factory in Suzhou, China (Darfon). The LCD was made in either South Korea (Samsung or LG.Philips LCD), Japan (Toshiba or Sharp), or Taiwan (Chi Mei Optoelectronics, Hannstar Display, or AU Optronics). The wireless card came from either an American-owned factory in China (Agere) or Malaysia (Arrow), or a Taiwanese-owned factory in Taiwan (Askey or Gemtek) or China (USI). The modem was made by either a Taiwanese-owned company in China (Asustek or Liteon) or a Chinese-run company in China (Foxconn). The battery came from an American-owned factory in Malaysia (Motorola), a Japanese-owned factory in Mexico or Malaysia or China (Sanyo), or a South Korean or Taiwanese factory in either of those two countries (SDI or Simplo). The hard disk drive was made by an American-owned factory in Singapore (Seagate), a Japanese-owned company in Thailand (Hitachi or Fujitsu), or a Japanese-owned factory in the Philippines (Toshiba). The CD/DVD drive came from a South Korean–owned company with factories in Indonesia and the Philippines (Samsung); a Japanese-owned factory in China or Malaysia (NEC); a Japanese-owned factory in Indonesia, China, or Malaysia (Teac); or a Japanese-owned factory in China (Sony). The notebook carrying bag was made by either an Irish-owned company in China (Tenba) or an American-owned company in China (Targus, Samsonite, or Pacific Design). The power adapter was made by either a Thai-owned factory in Thailand (Delta) or a Taiwanese-, Korean-, or American-owned factory in China (Liteon, Samsung, or Mobility). The power cord was made by a British-owned company with factories in China, Malaysia, and India (Volex). The removable memory stick was made by either an Israeli-owned company in Israel (M-System) or an American-owned company with a factory in Malaysia (Smart Modular).

This supply chain symphony—from my order over the phone to production to delivery to my house—is one of the wonders of the flat world.

"We have to do a lot of collaborating," said Hunter. "Michael [Dell] personally knows the CEOs of these companies, and we are constantly working with them on process improvements and real-time demand/supply balancing." Demand shaping goes on constantly, said Hunter.

What is "demand shaping"? It works like this: At 10 a.m. Austin time, Dell discovers that so many customers have ordered notebooks with 40-gigabyte hard drives since the morning that its supply chain will run short in two hours. That signal is automatically relayed to Dell's marketing department and to Dell.com and to all the Dell phone operators taking orders. If I happen to call to place my Dell order at 10:30 a.m., the Dell representative will say to me, "Tom, it's your lucky day! For the next hour we are offering 60-gigabyte hard drives with the notebook you want—for only $10 more than the 40-gig drive. And if you act now, Dell will throw in a carrying case along with your purchase, because we so value you as a customer." In an hour or two, using such promotions, Dell can reshape the demand for any part of any notebook or desktop to correspond with the projected supply in its global supply chain. Today memory might be on sale, tomorrow it might be CD-ROMs.

Picking up the story of my notebook, on April 13, at 11:29 a.m., all the parts had been plucked from the just-in-time inventory bins in Penang, and the computer was assembled there by A. Sathini, a team member "who manually screwed together all of the parts from kitting as well as the labels needed for Tom's system," said Dell in their production report to me. "The system was then sent down the conveyor to go to burn, where Tom's specified software was downloaded." Dell has huge server banks stocked with the latest in Microsoft, Norton Utilities, and other popular software applications, which are downloaded into each new computer according to the specific tastes of the customer.

"By 2:45 p.m., Tom's software had been successfully downloaded, and [the system was] manually moved to the boxing line. By 4:05 p.m., Tom's system [was] placed in protective foam and a shuttle box, with a label, which contains his order number, tracking code, system type, and shipping code. By 6:04 p.m., Tom's system had been loaded on a pallet with a specified manifest, which gives the Merge facility visibility to when the system will arrive, what pallet it will be on (out of 75+ pallets with 152 systems per pallet), and to what address Tom's system will ship. By 6:26 p.m., Tom's system left [the Dell factory] to head to the Penang, Malaysia, airport."

Six days a week Dell charters a China Airlines 747 out of Taiwan and flies it from Penang to Nashville via Taipei. Each 747 leaves with twenty-five thousand Dell notebooks that weigh altogether 110,000 kilograms, or 242,506 pounds. It is the only 747 that ever lands in Nashville, except Air Force One, when the president visits. "By April 15, 2004, at 7:41 a.m., Tom's system arrived at [Nashville] with other Dell systems from Penang and Limerick. By 11:58 a.m., Tom's system [was] inserted into a larger box, which went down the boxing line to the specific external parts that Tom had ordered."

That was thirteen days after I'd ordered it. Had there not been a parts delay in Malaysia when my order first arrived, the time between when I phoned in my purchase, when the notebook was assembled in Penang, and its arrival in Nashville would have been only four days. Hunter said the total supply chain for my computer, including suppliers of suppliers, involved about four hundred companies in North America, Europe, and primarily Asia, but with thirty key players. Somehow, though, it all came together. As Dell reported: On April 15, 2004, at 12:59 p.m., "Tom's system had been shipped from [Nashville] and was tenured by UPS shipping LTL (3–5-day ground, specified by Tom), with UPS tracking number 1Z13WA374253514697. By April 19, 2004, at 6:41 p.m., Tom's system arrived in Bethesda, MD, and was signed for."

I am telling you the story of my notebook to tell a larger story of geopolitics in the flat world. To all the forces mentioned in the previous chapter that are still holding back the flattening of the world, or could actually reverse the process, one has to add a more traditional threat, and that is an outbreak of a good, old-fashioned, world-shaking, economy-destroying war. It could be China deciding once and for all to eliminate Taiwan as an independent state; or North Korea, out of fear or insanity, using one of its nuclear weapons against South Korea or Japan; or Israel and a soon-to-be-nuclear Iran going at each other; or India and Pakistan finally nuking it out. These and other classic geopolitical conflicts could erupt at any time and either slow the flattening of the world or seriously unflatten it.

The real subject of this chapter is how these classic geopolitical threats might be moderated or influenced by the new forms of collaboration fostered and demanded by the flat world—particularly supply-chaining. The flattening of the world is too young for us to draw any definitive conclusions. What is certain, though, is that as the world flattens, one of the most interesting dramas to watch in international relations will be the interplay between the traditional global threats and the newly emergent global supply chains. The interaction between old-time threats (like China *versus* Taiwan) and just-in-time supply chains (like China *plus* Taiwan) will be a rich source of study for the field of international relations in the early twenty-first century.

In *The Lexus and the Olive Tree* I argued that to the extent that countries tied their economies and futures to global integration and trade, it would act as a restraint on going to war with their neighbors. I first started thinking about this in the late 1990s, when, during my travels, I noticed that no two countries that both had McDonald's had ever fought a war against each other since each got its McDonald's. (Border skirmishes and civil wars don't count, because McDonald's usually served both sides.) After confirming this with McDonald's, I offered what I called the Golden Arches Theory of Conflict Prevention. The Golden Arches Theory stipulated that when a country reached the level of economic development where it had a middle class big enough to support a network of McDonald's, it became a McDonald's country. And people in McDonald's countries didn't like to fight wars anymore. They preferred to wait in line for burgers. While this was offered slightly tongue in cheek, the serious point I was trying to make was that as countries got woven into the fabric of global trade and rising living standards, which having a network of McDonald's franchises had come to symbolize, the cost of war for victor and vanquished became prohibitively high.

This McDonald's theory has held up pretty well, but now that almost every country has acquired a McDonald's, except the worst rogues like North Korea and Iran, it seemed to me that this theory needed updating for the flat world. In that spirit, and again with tongue slightly in cheek, I offer the Dell Theory of Conflict Prevention, the essence of which is that the advent and spread of just-in-time global supply chains in the flat world are an even greater restraint on geopolitical adventurism than the more general rising standard of living that McDonald's symbolized.

The Dell Theory stipulates: No two countries that are both part of a major global supply chain, like Dell's, will ever fight a war against each other as long as they are both part of the same global supply chain. Because people embedded in major global supply chains don't want to fight old-time wars anymore. They want to make just-in-time deliveries of goods and services—and enjoy the rising standards of living that come with that. One of the people with the best feel for the logic behind this theory is Michael Dell, the founder and chairman of Dell.

"These countries understand the risk premium that they have," said Dell of the countries in his Asian supply chain. "They are pretty careful to protect the equity that they have built up or tell us why we should not worry [about their doing anything adventurous]. My belief after visiting China is that the change that has occurred there is in the best interest of the world and China. Once people get a taste for whatever you want to call it—economic independence, a better lifestyle, and a better life for their child or children—they grab on to that and don't want to give it up."

Any sort of war or prolonged political upheaval in East Asia or China "would have a massive chilling effect on the investment there and on all the progress that has been made there," said Dell, who added that he believes the governments in that part of the world understand this very clearly. "We certainly make clear to them that stability is important to us. [Right now] it is not a day-to-day worry for us . . . I believe that as time and progress go on there, the chance for a really disruptive event goes down exponentially. I don't think our industry gets enough credit for the good we are doing in these areas. If you are making money and being productive and raising your standard of living, you're not sitting around thinking, Who did this to us? or Why is our life so bad?"

There is a lot of truth to this. Countries whose workers and industries are woven into a major global supply chain know that they cannot take an hour, a week, or a month off for war without disrupting industries and economies around the world and thereby risking the loss of their place in that supply chain for a long time, which could be extremely costly. For a country with no natural resources, being part of a global supply chain is like striking oil—oil that never runs out. And therefore, getting dropped from such a chain because you start a war is like having your oil wells go dry or having someone pour cement down them. They will not come back anytime soon.

"You are going to pay for it really dearly," said Glenn E. Neland, senior vice president for worldwide procurement at Dell, when I asked him what would happen to a major supply-chain member in Asia that decided to start fighting with its neighbor and disrupt the supply chain. "It will not only bring you to your knees [today], but you will pay for a long time— because you just won't have any credibility if you demonstrate you are going to go [off] the political deep end. And China is just now starting to develop a level of credibility in the business community that it is creating a business environment you can prosper in—with transparent and consistent rules." Neland said that suppliers regularly ask him whether he is worried about China and Taiwan, which have threatened to go to war at several points in the past half century, but his standard response is that he cannot imagine them "doing anything more than flexing muscles with each other." Neland said he can tell in his conversations and dealings with companies and governments in the Dell supply chain, particularly the Chinese, that "they recognize the opportunity and are really hungry to participate in the same things they have seen other countries in Asia do. They know there is a big economic pot at the end of the rainbow and they are really after it. We will spend about $35 billion producing parts this year, and 30 percent of that is [in] China."

If you follow the evolution of supply chains, added Neland, you see the prosperity and stability they promoted first in Japan, and then in Korea and Taiwan, and now in Malaysia, Singapore, the Philippines, Thailand, and Indonesia. Once countries get embedded in these global supply chains, "they feel part of something much bigger than their own businesses," he said. Osamu Watanabe, the CEO of the Japan External Trade Organization, was explaining to me one afternoon in Tokyo how Japanese companies were moving vast amounts of low- and middle-range technical work and manufacturing to China, doing the basic fabrication there, and then bringing it back to Japan for final assembly. Japan was doing this despite a bitter legacy of mistrust between the two countries, which was intensified by the Japanese invasion of China in the last century. Historically, he noted, a strong Japan and a strong China have had a hard time coexisting. But not today, at least not for the moment. Why not? I asked. The reason you can have a strong Japan and a strong China at the same time, he said, "is because of the supply chain." It is a win-win for both.

Obviously, since Iraq, Syria, south Lebanon, North Korea, Pakistan, Afghanistan, and Iran are not part of any major global supply chains, all of them remain hot spots that could explode at any time and slow or reverse the flattening of the world. As my own notebook story attests, the most important test case of the Dell Theory of Conflict Prevention is the situation between China and Taiwan—since both are deeply embedded in several of the world's most important computer, consumer electronics, and, increasingly, software supply chains. The vast majority of computer components for every major company come from coastal China, Taiwan, and East Asia. In addition, Taiwan alone has more than $100 billion in investments in mainland China today, and Taiwanese experts run many of the cutting-edge Chinese high-tech manufacturing companies.

It is no wonder that Craig Addison, the former editor of *Electronic Business Asia* magazine, wrote an essay for the *International Herald Tribune* (September 29, 2000) headlined "A 'Silicon Shield' Protects Taiwan from China." He argued that "Silicon-based products, such as computers and networking systems, form the basis of the digital economies in the United States, Japan and other developed nations. In the past decade, Taiwan has become the third-largest information technology hardware producer after the United States and Japan. Military aggression by China against Taiwan would cut off a large portion of the world's supply of these products . . . Such a development would wipe trillions of dollars off the market value of technology companies listed in the United States, Japan and Europe." Even if China's leaders, like former president Jiang Zemin, who was once minister of electronics, lose sight of how integrated China and Taiwan are in the world's computer supply chain, they need only ask their kids for an update. Jiang Zemin's son, Jiang Mianheng, wrote Addison, "is a partner in a wafer fabrication project in Shanghai with Winston Wang of Taiwan's Grace T.H.W. Group." And it is not just Taiwanese. Hundreds of big American tech companies now have R & D operations in China; a war that disrupted them could lead not only to the

companies moving their plants elsewhere but also to a significant loss of
R & D investment in China, which the Beijing government has been betting on to advance its development. Such a war could also, depending on
how it started, trigger a widespread American boycott of Chinese goods—
if China were to snuff out the Taiwanese democracy—which would lead
to serious economic turmoil inside China.

The Dell Theory had its first real test in December 2004, when
Taiwan held parliamentary elections. President Chen Shui-bian's pro-
independence Democratic Progressive Party was expected to win the
legislative runoff over the main opposition Nationalist Party, which favored closer ties with Beijing. Chen framed the election as a popular ref-
erendum on his proposal to write a new constitution that would formally
enshrine Taiwan's independence, ending the purposely ambiguous status quo. Had Chen won and moved ahead on his agenda to make
Taiwan its own motherland, as opposed to maintaining the status quo fiction that it is a province of the mainland, it could have led to a Chinese
military assault on Taiwan. Everyone in the region was holding his or her
breath. And what happened? *Motherboards won over motherland.* A majority of Taiwanese voted against the pro-independence governing party
legislative candidates, ensuring that the DPP would not have a majority
in parliament. I believe the message Taiwanese voters were sending was
not that they never want Taiwan to be independent. It was that they do
not want to upset the status quo right now, which has been so beneficial
to so many Taiwanese. The voters seemed to understand clearly how in-
terwoven they had become with the mainland, and they wisely opted to
maintain their de facto independence rather than force de jure independence, which might have triggered a Chinese invasion and a very
uncertain future.

Warning: What I said when I put forth the McDonald's theory, I
would repeat even more strenuously with the Dell Theory: It does not
make wars obsolete. And it does not guarantee that governments will not
engage in wars of choice, even governments that are part of major supply
chains. To suggest so would be naïve. It guarantees only that governments whose countries are enmeshed in global supply chains will have
to think three times, not just twice, about engaging in anything but a war

of self-defense. And if they choose to go to war anyway, the price they will pay will be ten times higher than it was a decade ago and probably ten times higher than whatever the leaders of that country think. It is one thing to lose your McDonald's. It's quite another to fight a war that costs you your place in a twenty-first-century supply chain that may not come back around for a long time.

While the biggest test case of the Dell Theory is China versus Taiwan, the fact is that the Dell Theory has already proved itself to some degree in the case of India and Pakistan, the context in which I first started to think about it. I happened to be in India in 2002, when its just-in-time services supply chains ran into some very old-time geopolitics—and the supply chain won. In the case of India and Pakistan, the Dell Theory was working on only one party—India—but it still had a major impact. India is to the world's knowledge and service supply chain what China and Taiwan are to the manufacturing ones. By now readers of this book know all the highlights: General Electric's biggest research center outside the United States is in Bangalore, with seventeen hundred Indian engineers, designers, and scientists. The brain chips for many brand-name cell phones are designed in Bangalore. Renting a car from Avis online? It's managed in Bangalore. Tracing your lost luggage on Delta or British Airways is done from Bangalore, and the backroom accounting and computer maintenance for scores of global firms are done from Bangalore, Mumbai, Chennai, and other major Indian cities.

Here's what happened: On May 31, 2002, State Department spokesman Richard Boucher issued a travel advisory saying, "We urge American citizens currently in India to depart the country," because the prospect of a nuclear exchange with Pakistan was becoming very real. Both nations were massing troops on their borders, intelligence reports were suggesting that they both might be dusting off their nuclear warheads, and CNN was flashing images of people flooding out of India. The global American firms that had moved their back rooms and R & D operations to Bangalore were deeply unnerved.

"I was actually surfing on the Web, and I saw a travel advisory come up on India on a Friday evening," said Vivek Paul, president of Wipro, which manages backroom operations from India of many American multinationals. "As soon as I saw that, I said, 'Oh my gosh, every customer that we have is going to have a million questions on this.' It was the Friday before a long weekend, so over the weekend we at Wipro developed a fail-safe business continuity plan for all of our customers." While Wipro's customers were pleased to see how on top of things the company was, many of them were nevertheless rattled. This was not in the plan when they decided to outsource mission-critical research and operations to India. Said Paul, "I had a CIO from one of our big American clients send me an e-mail saying, 'I am now spending a lot of time looking for alternative sources to India. I don't think you want me doing that, and I don't want to be doing it.' I immediately forwarded his message to the Indian ambassador in Washington and told him to get it to the right person." Paul would not tell me what company it was, but I have confirmed through diplomatic sources that it was United Technologies. And plenty of others, like American Express and General Electric, with back rooms in Bangalore, had to have been equally worried.

For many global companies, "the main heart of their business is now supported here," said N. Krishnakumar, president of MindTree, another leading Indian knowledge outsourcing firm based in Bangalore. "It can cause chaos if there is a disruption." While not trying to meddle in foreign affairs, he added, "What we explained to our government, through the Confederation of Indian Industry, is that providing a stable, predictable operating environment is now the key to India's development." This was a real education for India's elderly leaders in New Delhi, who had not fully absorbed how critical India had become to the world's knowledge supply chain. When you are managing vital backroom operations for American Express or General Electric or Avis, or are responsible for tracing all the lost luggage on British Airways or Delta, you cannot take a month, a week, or even a day off for war without causing major disruptions for those companies. Once those companies have made a commitment to outsource business operations or research to India, they expect it to stay there. That is a major commitment. And if geopolitics causes a serious disruption, they will leave, and they will not come back very easily. When you lose this kind of service trade, you can lose it for good.

"What ends up happening in the flat world you described," explained Paul, "is that you have only one opportunity to make it right if something [goes] wrong. Because the disadvantage of being in a flat world is that despite all the nice engagements and stuff and the exit barriers that you have, every customer has multiple options, and so the sense of responsibility you have is not just out of a desire to do good by your customers, but also a desire for self-preservation."

The Indian government got the message. Was India's central place in the world's services supply chain the only factor in getting Prime Minister Vajpayee to tone down his rhetoric and step back from the brink? Of course not. There were other factors, to be sure—most notably the deterrent effect of Pakistan's own nuclear arsenal. But clearly, India's role in global services was an important additional source of restraint on its behavior, and it was taken into account by New Delhi. "I think it sobered a lot of people," said Jerry Rao, who heads the Indian high-tech trade association. "We engaged very seriously, and we tried to make the point that this was very bad for Indian business. It was very bad for the Indian economy . . . [Many people] didn't realize till then how suddenly we had become integrated into the rest of the world. We are now partners in a twenty-four by seven by three-sixty-five supply chain."

Vivek Kulkarni, then information technology secretary for Bangalore's regional government, told me back in 2002, "We don't get involved in politics, but we did bring to the government's attention the problems the Indian IT industry might face if there were a war." And this was an altogether new factor for New Delhi to take into consideration. "Ten years ago, [a lobby of IT ministers from different Indian states] never existed," said Kulkarni. Now it is one of the most important business lobbies in India and a coalition that no Indian government can ignore.

"With all due respect, the McDonald's [shutting] down doesn't hurt anything," said Vivek Paul, "but if Wipro had to shut down we would affect the day-to-day operations of many, many companies." No one would answer the phones in call centers. Many e-commerce sites that are supported from Bangalore would shut down. Many major companies that rely on India to maintain their key computer applications or handle their human resources departments or billings would seize up. And these companies did not want to find alternatives, said Paul. Switching is very difficult, because taking over mission-critical day-to-day backroom operations of a global company takes a great deal of training and experience. It's not like opening a fast-food restaurant. That was why, said Paul, Wipro's clients were telling him, "'I have made an investment in you. I need you to be very responsible with the trust I have reposed in you.' And I think that created an enormous amount of back pressure on us that said we have to act in a responsible fashion . . . All of a sudden it became even clearer that there's more to gain by economic gains than by geopolitical gains. [We had more to gain from building] a vibrant, richer middle class able to create an export industry than we possibly could by having an ego-satisfying war with Pakistan." The Indian government also looked around and realized that the vast majority of India's billion people were saying, "I want a better future, not more territory." Over and over again, when I asked young Indians working at call centers how they felt about Kashmir or a war with Pakistan, they waved me off with the same answer: "We have better things to do." And they do. America needs to keep this in mind as it weighs its overall approach to outsourcing. I would never advocate shipping some American's job overseas just so it will keep Indians and Pakistanis at peace with one another. But I would say that to the extent that this process happens, driven by its own internal economic logic, it will have a net positive geopolitical effect. It will absolutely make the world safer for American kids.

Each of the Indian business leaders I interviewed noted that in the event of some outrageous act of terrorism or aggression from Pakistan, India would do whatever it takes to defend itself, and they would be the first to support that—the Dell Theory be damned. Sometimes war is unavoidable. It is imposed on you by the reckless behavior of others, and you have to just pay the price. But the more India and, one hopes, soon Pakistan get enmeshed in global service supply chains, the greater disincentive they have to fight anything but a border skirmish or a war of words.

The example of the 2002 India-Pakistan nuclear crisis at least gives us some hope. That cease-fire was brought to us not by General Powell but by General Electric.

We bring good things to life.

INFOSYS VERSUS AL-QAEDA

Unfortunately, even GE can do only so much. Because, alas, a new source for geopolitical instability has emerged only in recent years, for which even the updated Dell Theory can provide no restraint. It is the emergence of mutant global supply chains—that is, nonstate actors, be they criminals or terrorists, who learn to use all the elements of the flat world to advance a highly destabilizing, even nihilistic agenda. I first started thinking about this when Nandan Nilekani, the Infosys CEO, was giving me that tour I referred to in Chapter 1 of his company's global videoconferencing center at its Bangalore headquarters. As Nandan explained to me how Infosys could get its global supply chain together at once for a virtual conference in that room, a thought popped into my head: Who else uses uploading and supply-chaining so imaginatively? The answer, of course, is al-Qaeda.

Al-Qaeda has learned to use many of the same instruments for global collaboration that Infosys uses, but instead of producing products and profits with them, it has produced mayhem and murder. This is a particularly difficult problem. In fact, it may be the most vexing geopolitical problem for flat-world countries that want to focus on the future. The flat world—unfortunately—is a friend of both Infosys and al-Qaeda. The Dell Theory will not work at all against these informal Islamo-Leninist terror networks, because they are not a state with a population that will hold its leaders accountable or with a domestic business lobby that might restrain them. These mutant global supply chains are formed for the purpose of destruction, not profit. They don't need investors, only recruits, donors, and victims. Yet these mobile, self-financing mutant supply chains use all the tools of collaboration offered by the flat world—uploading to raise money, to recruit followers, and to stimulate and disseminate ideas; outsourcing to train recruits; and supply-chaining to distribute the tools and the suicide bombers to undertake operations. The U.S. Central Command has a name for this whole underground network: the Virtual Caliphate. And its leaders and innovators understand the flat world almost as well as Wal-Mart, Dell, and Infosys do.

In Chapter 15, I tried to explain that you cannot understand the rise of al-Qaeda emotionally and politically without reference to the flattening of the world. What I am arguing here is that you cannot understand the rise of al-Qaeda technically without reference to the flattening of the world, either. Globalization in general has been al-Qaeda's friend in that it has helped to solidify a revival of Muslim identity and solidarity, with Muslims in one country much better able to see and sympathize with the struggles of their brethren in another country—thanks to the Internet and satellite television. At the same time, as I pointed out, this flattening process has intensified the feelings of humiliation in some quarters of the Muslim world over the fact that civilizations to which the Muslim world once felt superior—Hindus, Jews, Christians, Chinese—are now all doing better than many Muslim countries, and everyone can see it. The flattening of the world has also led to more urbanization and large-scale immigration to the West of many of these young, unemployed, frustrated Arab-Muslim males, while simultaneously making it much easier for informal networks of these young men to form, operate, and interconnect. This certainly has been a boon for underground extremist Muslim political groups. There has been a proliferation of these informal mutual supply chains throughout the Arab-Muslim world today—small networks of people who move money through *hawalas* (hand-to-hand financing networks), who recruit through alternative education systems like the madrassas, and who communicate through the Internet and other tools of the global information revolution. Think about it: A century ago, anarchists were limited in their ability to communicate and collaborate with one another, to find sympathizers, and to band together for an operation. Today, with the Internet, that is not a problem. Today even the Unabomber could find friends to join a consortium where his "strengths" could be magnified and reinforced by others who had just as warped a worldview as he did.

What we have witnessed in Iraq is an even more perverse mutation of this mutant supply chain—the suicide supply chain. Since the start of the U.S. invasion in March 2003, hundreds of suicide bombers have been recruited from within Iraq and from across the Muslim world, brought to the Iraqi front by some underground railroad, connected with the bomb makers there, and then dispatched against U.S. and Iraqi targets according to whatever suits the daily tactical needs of the insurgent Islamist forces in Iraq. I can understand, but not accept, the notion that more than thirty-seven years of Israeli occupation of the West Bank might have driven some Palestinians into a suicidal rage. But the American occupation of Iraq was only a few months old before it started to get hit by this suicide supply chain. How do you recruit so many young men "off the shelf" who are ready to commit suicide in the cause of jihad, many of them apparently not even Iraqis? And they don't even identify themselves by name or want to get credit—at least in this world. The fact is that Western intelligence agencies seem to have little clue how this underground suicide supply chain works, and it has basically stymied the U.S. armed forces in Iraq. From what we do know, though, this Virtual Caliphate works just like the supply chains I described earlier. Just as you take an item off the shelf in a discount store in Birmingham and another one is immediately made in Beijing, so the retailers of suicide deploy a human bomber in Baghdad and another one is immediately recruited and indoctrinated in Beirut. To the extent that this tactic spreads, it will require a major rethinking of U.S. military doctrine.

The flat world has also been such a huge boon for al-Qaeda and its ilk because of the way it enables the small to act big, and the way it enables small acts—the killing of just a few people—to have big effects. The horrific video of the beheading of *Wall Street Journal* reporter Danny Pearl by Islamist militants in Pakistan was transmitted by the Internet all over the world. There is not a journalist anywhere who saw or even just read about that who was not terrified. But those same beheading videos are also used as tools of recruitment. The flat world makes it much easier for terrorists to transmit their terror. With the Internet they don't even have to go through Western or Arab news organizations but can broadcast right into your computer. It takes much less dynamite to transmit so much more anxiety. Just as the U.S. Army had embedded journalists, so the suicide supply chain has embedded terrorists, in their own way, to tell us their side of the story. How many times have I gotten up in the morning, fired up the Internet, and been confronted by the video image of some masked gunman threatening to behead an American—all brought to me courtesy of AOL's home page? The Internet is an enormously useful tool for the dissemination of propaganda, conspiracy theories, and plain old untruths, because it combines a huge reach with a patina of technology that makes anything on the Internet somehow more believable.

"The new system of diffusion—the Internet—is more likely to transmit irrationality than rationality," said political theorist Yaron Ezrahi, who specializes in the interaction between media and politics. "Because irrationality is more emotionally loaded, it requires less knowledge, it explains more to more people, it goes down easier." That is why conspiracy theories are so rife in the Arab-Muslim world today—and unfortunately are becoming so in many quarters of the Western world, for that matter. Conspiracy theories are like a drug that goes right into your bloodstream, enabling you to see "the Light." And the Internet is the needle. Young people used to have to take LSD to escape. Now they just go online. Now you don't shoot up, you download. You download the precise point of view that speaks to all your own biases. And the flat world makes it all so much easier.

In many cases, networks like al-Qaeda use the Internet—not only for easy, cheap, global command and control but, even more important, as a global megaphone to radiate ideas. Indeed, some Islamist radical movements have no real command and control and don't even pretend that they do. They simply disseminate their ideas globally, using the flat-world platform, and inspire and exhort people to use their own local capacity to take initiatives—to blow up a train in Spain or a subway in London. There are no orders going from a single headquarters to the field, just inspiration and maybe some training. The locals do the rest on their own.

Gabriel Weimann, a professor of communications at Haifa University, Israel, did an incisive study of terrorists' use of the Internet, which was published in March 2004 by the United States Institute of Peace and excerpted on YaleGlobal Online on April 26, 2004. He made the following points:

> While the danger that cyber-terrorism poses to the Internet is frequently debated, surprisingly little is known about the threat posed by terrorists' use of the Internet. A recent six-year-long study shows that terrorist organizations and their supporters have been using all of the tools that the Internet offers to recruit supporters, raise funds, and launch a worldwide campaign of fear. It is also clear that to combat terrorism effectively, mere suppression of their Internet tools is not enough. Our scan of the Internet in 2003–04 revealed the existence of hundreds of websites serving terrorists in different, albeit sometimes overlapping, ways . . . There are countless examples of how [terrorists] use this uncensored medium to spread disinformation, to deliver threats intended to instill fear and helplessness, and to disseminate horrific images of recent actions. Since September 11, 2001, al-Qaeda has festooned its websites with a string of announcements of an impending "large attack" on US targets. These warnings have received considerable media coverage, which has helped to generate a widespread sense of dread and insecurity among audiences throughout the world and especially within the United States . . .
>
> The Internet has significantly expanded the opportunities for terrorists to secure publicity. Until the advent of the Internet, terrorists' hopes of winning publicity for their causes and activities depended on attracting the attention of television, radio, or the print media. The fact that terrorists themselves have direct control over the content of their websites offers further opportunities to shape how they are perceived by different target audiences and to manipulate their image and the images of their enemies. Most terrorist sites do not celebrate their violent activities. Instead—regardless of their nature, motives, or location—most terrorist sites emphasize two issues: the restrictions placed on freedom of expression; and the plight of their comrades who are now political prisoners.

These issues resonate powerfully with their own supporters and are also calculated to elicit sympathy from Western audiences that cherish freedom of expression and frown on measures to silence political opposition . . .

Terrorists have proven not only skillful at online marketing but also adept at mining the data offered by the billion-some pages of the World Wide Web. They can learn from the Internet about the schedules and locations of targets such as transportation facilities, nuclear power plants, public buildings, airports and ports, and even counterterrorism measures. According to Secretary of Defense Donald Rumsfeld, an al-Qaeda training manual recovered in Afghanistan tells its readers, "Using public sources openly and without resorting to illegal means, it is possible to gather at least 80 percent of all information required about the enemy." One captured al-Qaeda computer contained engineering and structural architecture features of a dam, which had been downloaded from the Internet and which would enable al-Qaeda engineers and planners to simulate catastrophic failures. In other captured computers, U.S. investigators found evidence that al-Qaeda operators spent time on sites that offer software and programming instructions for the digital switches that run power, water, transportation, and communications grids.

Like many other political organizations, terrorist groups use the Internet to raise funds. Al-Qaeda, for instance, has always depended heavily on donations, and its global fundraising network is built upon a foundation of charities, nongovernmental organizations, and other financial institutions that use websites and Internet-based chat rooms and forums. The fighters in the Russian breakaway republic of Chechnya have likewise used the Internet to publicize the numbers of bank accounts to which sympathizers can contribute. And in December 2001, the U.S. government seized the assets of a Texas-based charity because of its ties to Hamas.

In addition to soliciting financial aid online, terrorists recruit converts by using the full panoply of website technologies (audio, digital video, etc.) to enhance the presentation of their message. And like commercial sites that track visitors to develop consumer profiles, terrorist organizations capture information about the users who browse their websites. Visitors who seem most interested in the organization's cause or well suited to carrying out its work are then contacted. Recruiters may also use more interactive Internet technology to roam online chat rooms and cyber cafes, looking for receptive members of the public, particularly young people. The SITE Institute, a Washington, D.C.–based terrorism research group that monitors al-Qaeda's Internet communications, has provided chilling details of a high-tech recruitment drive launched in 2003 to recruit fighters to travel to Iraq and attack U.S. and coalition forces there. The Internet also grants terrorists a cheap and efficient means of networking. Many terrorist groups, among them Hamas and al-Qaeda, have undergone a transformation from strictly hierarchical organizations with designated leaders to affiliations of semi-independent cells that have no single commanding hierarchy. Through the Internet, these loosely interconnected groups are able to maintain contact with one another—and with members of other terrorist groups. The Internet connects not only members of the same terrorist organizations but also members of different groups. For instance, dozens of sites supporting terrorism in the name of jihad permit terrorists in places as far removed from one another as Chechnya and Malaysia to exchange ideas and practical information about how to build bombs, establish terror cells, and carry out attacks . . . Al-Qaeda operatives relied heavily on the Internet in planning and coordinating the September 11 attacks.

For all of these reasons we are just at the beginning of understanding the geopolitical impact of the flattening of the world. On the one hand, failed states and failed regions are places we have every incentive to avoid today. They offer no economic opportunity and there is no Soviet Union out there competing with us for influence over such countries. On the other hand, there may be nothing more dangerous today than a failed state with broadband capability. That is, even failed states tend to have telecommunications systems and satellite links, and therefore if a terrorist group infiltrates a failed state, as al-Qaeda did with Afghanistan, it can amplify its power enormously. As much as big powers want to stay away from such states, they may feel compelled to get even more deeply embroiled in them. Think of America in Afghanistan and Iraq, Russia in Chechnya, Australia in East Timor.

In the flat world it is much more difficult to hide, but much easier to get connected. "Think of Mao at the beginning of the Chinese Communist revolution," remarked Michael Mandelbaum, the Johns Hopkins foreign policy specialist. "The Chinese Communists had to hide in caves in northwest China, but they could move around in whatever territory they were able to control. Bin Laden, by contrast, can't show his face, but he can reach every household in the world, thanks to the Internet." Bin Laden cannot capture any territory, but he can capture the imagination of millions of people. And he has, broadcasting right into American living rooms on the eve of the 2004 presidential election.

Hell hath no fury like a terrorist with a satellite dish and an interactive Web site.

Too Personally Insecure

In the fall of 2004, I was invited to speak at a synagogue in Woodstock, New York, not far from Yasgur's farm, home of the famous Woodstock music festival. I asked my hosts how was it that they were able to get a synagogue in Woodstock, of all places, big enough to support a lecture series. Very simple, they said. Since 9/11, Jews, and others, have been moving from New York City to places like Woodstock, to get away from what they fear will be the next ground zero. Right now this trend is a trickle, but it would become a torrent if a nuclear device were detonated in any European or American city.

Since this threat is the mother of all unflatteners, this book would not be complete without a discussion of it. We can live with a lot. We lived through 9/11. But we cannot live with nuclear terrorism. That would un-flatten the world permanently.

The only reason that Osama bin Laden did not use a nuclear device on 9/11 was not that he did not have the intention but that he did not have the capability. And since the Dell Theory offers no hope of re-straining the suicide supply chains, the only strategy we have is to limit their worst capabilities. That means a much more serious global effort to stanch nuclear proliferation by limiting the supply—to buy up the fissile material that is already out there, particularly in the former Soviet Union, and prevent more states from going nuclear. Harvard University international affairs expert Graham Allison, in his book *Nuclear Terrorism: The Ultimate Preventable Catastrophe,* outlines just such a strategy for denying terrorists access to nuclear weapons and nuclear materials. It can be done, he insists. It is a challenge to our will and convictions, but *not to our capabilities.* Allison proposes a new American-led interna-tional security order to deal with this problem based on what he calls "a doctrine of the Three No's: No loose nukes, No new nascent nukes, and No new nuclear states." No loose nukes, says Allison, means locking down all nuclear weapons and all nuclear material from which bombs could be made—in a much more serious way than we have done up till now. "We don't lose gold from Fort Knox," says Allison. "Russia doesn't lose treasures from the Kremlin armory. So we both know how to prevent theft of those things that are super valuable to us if we are determined to do it." No new nascent nukes means recognizing that there is a group of actors out there who can and do produce highly enriched uranium or plutonium, which is nothing more than nuclear bombs just about to hatch. We need a much more credible, multilateral nonproliferation regime that soaks up this fissile material. Finally, no new nuclear states means "drawing a line under the current eight nuclear powers and de-termining that, however unfair and unreasonable it may be, that club will have no more members than those eight," says Allison, adding that these three steps might then buy us time to develop a more formal, sus-tainable, internationally approved regime.

It would be nice also to be able to deny the Internet to al-Qaeda and its ilk, but that, alas, is impossible—without undermining ourselves.

That is why limiting their capabilities is necessary but not sufficient. We also have to find a way to get at their worst intentions. If we are not going to shut down the Internet and all the other creative and collaborative tools that have flattened the world, and if we can't restrict access to them, the only thing we can do is try to influence the imagination and intentions that people bring to them and draw from them. When I raised this issue, and the broad themes of this book, with my religious teacher, Rabbi Tzvi Marx from Holland, he surprised me by saying that the flat world I was describing reminded him of the story of the Tower of Babel.

How so? I asked. "The reason God banished all the people from the Tower of Babel and made them all speak different languages was not because he did not want them to collaborate per se," answered Rabbi Marx. "It was because he was enraged at what they were collaborating on—an effort to build a tower to the heavens so they could become God." This was a distortion of the human capacity, so God broke their union and their ability to communicate with one another. Now, all these years later, humankind has again created a new platform for more people from more places to communicate and collaborate with less friction and more ease than ever: the Internet. Would God see the Internet as heresy?

"Absolutely not," said Marx. "The heresy is not that mankind works together—it is to what ends. It is essential that we use this new ability to communicate and collaborate for the right ends—for constructive human aims and not megalomaniacal ends. Building a tower was megalomaniacal. Bin Laden's insistence that he has the truth and can flatten anyone else's tower who doesn't heed him is megalomaniacal. Collaborating so mankind can achieve its full potential is God's hope."

How we promote more of that kind of collaboration is what the final chapter is all about.

Conclusion: Imagination

SEVENTEEN

11/9 Versus 9/11

Imagination is more important than knowledge.

—Albert Einstein

Reflecting on this past decade and a half, during which the world went flat, it strikes me that our lives have been powerfully shaped by two dates: 11/9 and 9/11. These two dates represent the two competing forms of imagination at work in the world today: the creative imagination of 11/9 and the destructive imagination of 9/11. One brought down a wall and opened the windows of the world—both the operating system and the kind we look through. It unlocked half the planet and made the citizens there our collaborators and competitors. Another brought down the World Trade Center, closing its Windows on the World restaurant forever and putting up new invisible and concrete walls among people at a time when we thought 11/9 had erased them for good.

The dismantling of the Berlin Wall on 11/9 was brought about by people who dared to imagine a different, more open world—one where every human being would be free to realize his or her full potential—and who then summoned the courage to act on that imagination. Do you remember how it happened? It was so simple, really: In July 1989, hundreds of East Germans sought refuge at the West German embassy in Hungary. In September 1989, Hungary decided to remove its border restrictions with Austria. That meant that any East German who got into Hungary could pass through to Austria and the free world. Sure enough, more than thirteen thousand East Germans escaped through Hungary's back door. Pressure built up on the East German government. When in November it announced plans to ease travel restrictions, tens of thousands of East Germans converged on the Berlin Wall, where, on 11/9/89, border guards just opened the gates.

Someone there in Hungary, maybe it was the prime minister, maybe it was just a bureaucrat, must have said to himself or herself, "Imagine — imagine what might happen if we opened the border with Austria." Imagine if the Soviet Union were frozen in place. Imagine if East German citizens, young and old, men and women, were so emboldened by seeing their neighbors flee to the West that one day they just swarmed that Berlin Wall and started to tear it down. Some people must have had a conversation just like that, and because they did, millions of Eastern Europeans were able to walk out from behind the Iron Curtain and engage with a flattening world. It was a great era in which to be an American. We were the only superpower, and the world was our oyster. There were no walls. Young Americans could think about traveling, for a semester or a summer, to more countries than any American generation before them. Indeed, they could travel as far as their imaginations and wallets could take them. They could also look around at their classmates and see people from more different countries and cultures than any other class before them.

Nine-eleven, of course, changed all that. It showed us the power of a very different kind of imagination. It showed us the power of a group of hateful men who spent several years imagining how to kill as many innocent people as they could. At some point bin Laden and his gang literally must have looked at one another and said, "Imagine if we actually could hit both towers of the World Trade Center at the exact right spot, between the ninety-fourth and ninety-eighth floors. And imagine if each tower were to come crashing down like a house of cards." Yes, I am sorry to say, some people had that conversation, too. And, as a result, the world that was our oyster seemed to close up like a shell.

There has never been a time in history when human imagination wasn't important, but writing this book tells me that it has never been more important than now, because in a flat world so many of the tools of collaboration are becoming commodities available to everyone. So many more individuals now have the power to create their own content and globalize it. There is one thing, though, that has not and can never be commoditized, and that is imagination—what content we dream of creating.

When we lived in a more centralized, and more vertically organized, world—where states had a near total monopoly of power—individual imagination was a big problem when the leader of a superpower state—a Stalin, a Mao, or a Hitler—became warped. But today, when individuals can easily access all the tools of collaboration and superempower themselves, or their small cells, individuals do not need to control a country to threaten large numbers of other people. The small can act very big today and pose a serious danger to world order—without the instruments of a state.

Therefore, thinking about how we stimulate positive imaginations is of the utmost importance. As Irving Wladawsky-Berger, the IBM computer scientist, put it to me: We need to think more seriously than ever about how we encourage people to focus on productive outcomes that advance and unite civilization—peaceful imaginations that seek to "minimize alienation and celebrate interdependence rather than self-sufficiency, inclusion rather than exclusion," openness, opportunity, and hope rather than limits, suspicion, and grievance.

Let me try to illustrate this by example. In early 1999, two men started airlines from scratch, just a few weeks apart. Both men had a dream involving airplanes and the savvy to do something about it. One was David Neeleman. In February 1999, he started JetBlue. He assembled $130 million in venture capital, bought a fleet of Airbus A-320 passenger jets, recruited pilots and signed them to seven-year contracts, and outsourced his reservation system to stay-at-home moms and retirees living around Salt Lake City, Utah, who booked passengers on their home computers.

The other person who started an airline was, as we now know from the 9/11 Commission Report, Osama bin Laden. At a meeting in Kandahar, Afghanistan, in March or April 1999, he accepted a proposal initially drawn up by Khalid Sheikh Mohammed, the Pakistan-born mechanical engineer who was the architect of the 9/11 plot. JetBlue's motto was "Same Altitude. Different Attitude." Al-Qaeda's motto was "Allahu

Akbar," God is great. Both airlines were designed to fly into New York City—Neeleman's into JFK and bin Laden's into lower Manhattan.

Maybe it was because I read the 9/11 report while on a trip to Silicon Valley that I could not help but notice how much Khalid Sheikh Mohammed spoke and presented himself as just another eager engineer-entrepreneur, with his degree from North Carolina Agricultural and Technical State University, pitching his ideas to Osama bin Laden, who comes off as just another wealthy venture capitalist. But Mohammed, alas, was looking for *adventure capital.* As the 9/11 Commission Report put it, "No one exemplifies the model of the terrorist entrepreneur more clearly than Khalid Sheikh Mohammed (KSM), the principal architect of the 9/11 attacks . . . Highly educated and equally comfortable in a government office or a terrorist safe house, KSM applied his imagination, technical aptitude and managerial skills to hatching and planning an extraordinary array of terrorist schemes. These ideas included conventional car bombing, political assassination, aircraft bombing, hijacking, reservoir poisoning, and, ultimately, the use of aircraft as missiles guided by suicide operatives . . . KSM presents himself as an entrepreneur seeking venture capital and people . . . Bin Laden summoned KSM to Kandahar in March or April 1999 to tell him that al-Qaeda would support his proposal. The plot was now referred to within al-Qaeda as the 'planes operation.'"

From his corporate headquarters in Afghanistan, bin Laden proved to be a very deft supply chain manager. He assembled a virtual company just for this project—exactly like any global conglomerate would do in the flat world—finding just the right specialist for each task. He outsourced the overall design and blueprint for 9/11 to KSM and overall financial management to KSM's nephew, Ali Abdul Aziz Ali, who coordinated the dispersal of funds to the hijackers through wire transfers, cash, traveler's checks, and credit and debit cards from overseas bank accounts. Bin Laden recruited from the al-Qaeda roster just the right muscle guys from Asir Province, in Saudi Arabia, just the right pilots from Europe, just the right team leader from Hamburg, and just the right support staff from Pakistan. He outsourced the pilot training to flight schools in America. Bin Laden, who knew he needed only to "lease" the Boeing

757s, 767s, A320s, and possibly 747s for his operation, raised the necessary capital for training pilots on all these different aircraft from a syndi-
cate of pro-al-Qaeda Islamic charities and other Muslim adventure
capitalists ready to fund anti-American operations. In the case of 9/11,
the total budget was around $400,000. Once the team was assembled,
bin Laden focused on his own core competency—overall leadership and
ideological inspiration of his suicide supply chain, with assistance from
his deputies Mohammed Atef and Ayman al-Zawahiri.

You can get the full flavor of the bin Laden supply chain, and what an
aggressive adopter of new technology al-Qaeda was, by reading just one
entry from the December 2001 U.S. District Court for the Eastern
District of Virginia's official indictment of Zacarias Moussaoui, the so-
called nineteenth hijacker from 9/11. It reported the following: "In or
about June 1999, in an interview with an Arabic-language television station, Osama bin Laden issued a . . . threat indicating that all American
males should be killed." It then points out that throughout the year 2000,
all of the hijackers, including Moussaoui, began either attending or in-
quiring about flight school courses in America: "On or about September
29, 2000, Zacarias Moussaoui contacted Airman Flight School in
Norman, Oklahoma, using an e-mail account he set up on September 6
with an Internet service provider in Malaysia. In or about October 2000,
Zacarias Moussaoui received letters from Infocus Tech, a Malaysian company, stating that Moussaoui was appointed Infocus Tech's marketing
consultant in the United States, the United Kingdom and Europe, and
that he would receive, among other things, an allowance of $2,500 per
month . . . On or about December 11, 2000, Mohammed Atta purchased
flight deck videos for the Boeing 767 Model 300ER and the Airbus A320
Model 200 from the Ohio Pilot Store . . . In or about June 2001, in
Norman, Oklahoma, Zacarias Moussaoui made inquiries about starting a
cropdusting company . . . On or about August 16, 2001, Zacarias
Moussaoui possessed, among other things: two knives; a pair of binocu-
lars; flight manuals for the Boeing 747 Model 400; a flight simulator computer program; fighting gloves and shin guards; a piece of paper referring
to a handheld Global Positioning System receiver and a camcorder; software that could be used to review pilot procedures for the Boeing 747

Model 400; letters indicating that Moussaoui is a marketing consultant in the United States for Infocus Tech; a computer disk containing information related to the aerial application of pesticides; and a hand-held aviation radio."

A devout Mormon who grew up in Latin America where his father was a UPI correspondent, David Neeleman, by contrast, is one of those classic American entrepreneurs and a man of enormous integrity. He never went to college, but he has started two successful airlines, Morris Air and JetBlue, and played an important role in shaping a third, Southwest. He is the godfather of ticketless air travel, now known as e-ticketing. "I am a total optimist. I think my father is an optimist," he said to me, trying to explain where his innovative genes came from. "I grew up in a very happy home . . . JetBlue was created in my own mind before it was created on paper." Using his optimistic imagination and his ability also to quickly adopt all the latest technology because he had no legacy system to worry about, Neeleman started a highly profitable airline, creating jobs, low-cost travel, a unique onboard, satellite-supported entertainment system, and one of the most people-friendly places to work you can imagine. He also started a catastrophe relief fund in his company to help employee families who are faced with a sudden death or catastrophic illness of a loved one. Neeleman (who is now chairman of the board) donates $1 of his salary for every $1 any employee puts in the fund. "I think it is important that people give a little," said Neeleman. "I believe that there are irrevocable laws of heaven that when you serve others you get this little buzz." In 2003, Neeleman, already a wealthy man from his JetBlue stock, donated about $120,000 of his $200,000 salary to the JetBlue employee catastrophe fund.

In the waiting room outside his New York City office, there is a color photo of a JetBlue Airbus flying over the World Trade Center. Neeleman was in his office on 9/11 and watched the Twin Towers burn, while his own JetBlue airliners were circling JFK in a holding pattern. When I explained to him the comparison/contrast I was going to make between him and bin Laden, he was both uncomfortable and curious. As I closed up my computer and prepared to leave following our interview, he said he had one question for me: "Do you think Osama actually believes there is a God up there who is happy with what he is doing?"

I told him I just didn't know. What I do know is this: There are two ways to flatten the world. One is to use your imagination to bring everyone up to the same level, and the other is to use your imagination to bring everyone down to the same level. David Neeleman used his optimistic imagination and the easily available technologies of the flat world to lift people up. He launched a surprising and successful new airline, some profits of which he turns over to a catastrophe relief fund for his employees. Osama bin Laden and his disciples used their twisted imagination, and many of the same tools, to launch a surprise attack, which brought two enormous symbols of American power down to their level. Worse, they raised their money and created this massive human catastrophe under the guise of religion.

"From the primordial swamps of globalization have emerged two genetic variants," observed Infosys CEO Nandan Nilekani—one is al-Qaeda and the other are companies like Infosys or JetBlue. "Our focus therefore has to be how we can encourage more of the good mutations and keep out the bad."

I could not agree more. Indeed, that effort may be the most important thing we learn to do in order to keep this planet in one piece.

I have no doubt that advances in technology—from iris scans to X-ray machines—will help us to identify, expose, and capture those who are trying to use the easily available tools of the flat world to destroy it. But in the end, technology alone cannot keep us safe. We really do have to find ways to affect the imagination of those who would use the tools of collaboration to destroy the world that has invented those tools. But how does one go about nurturing a more hopeful, life-affirming, and tolerant imagination in others? Everyone has to ask himself or herself this question. I ask it as an American. I stress this last point because I think it starts first and foremost by America's setting an example. Those of us who are fortunate to live in free and progressive societies have to set an example.

We have to be the best global citizens we can be. We cannot retreat from the world. We have to make sure that we get the best of our own imaginations—and never let our imaginations get the best of us.

It is always hard to know when we have crossed the line between justified safety measures and letting our imaginations get the best of us and thereby paralyzing ourselves with precautions. I argued right after 9/11 that the reason our intelligence did not pick up the 9/11 plotters was "a failure of imagination." We just did not have enough people within our intelligence community with a sick enough imagination to match that of bin Laden and Khalid Sheikh Mohammed. We do need some people like that within our intelligence services. But we *all* don't need to go down that route. We all don't need to become so gripped by imagining the worst in everyone around us that we shrink into ourselves.

In 2003, my older daughter, Orly, was in her high school's symphonic orchestra. They spent all year practicing to take part in the national high school orchestra competition in New Orleans that March. When March rolled around, it appeared that we were heading for war in Iraq, so the Montgomery County School Board canceled all out-of-town trips by school groups—including the orchestra's attendance at New Orleans—fearing an outbreak of terrorism. I thought this was absolutely nuts. Even the evil imagination of 9/11 has its limits. At some point you do have to ask yourself whether Osama bin Laden and Ayman al-Zawahiri were really sitting around a cave in Afghanistan, with Ayman saying to Osama, "Say, Osama, d'you remember that annual high school orchestra competition in New Orleans? Well, it's coming up again next week. Let's really make a splash and go after it."

No, I don't think so. Let's leave the cave dwelling to bin Laden. We have to be the masters of our imaginations, not the prisoners. I had a friend in Beirut who used to joke that every time she flew on an airplane she packed a bomb in her suitcase, because the odds of two people carrying a bomb on the same plane were so much higher. Do whatever it takes, but get out the door.

Apropos of that, let me share the 9/11 story that touched me most from *The New York Times* series "Portraits of Grief," the little biographies of those who were killed. It was the story of Candace Lee Williams, the twenty-year-old business student at Northeastern University, who had worked from January to June of 2001 as a work-study intern at the Merrill Lynch office on the fourteenth floor of 1 World Trade Center. Both Candace's mother and colleagues described her to *The New York Times* as a young woman full of energy and ambition, who loved her internship. Indeed, Candace's colleagues at Merrill Lynch liked her so much they took her to dinner on her last day of work, sent her home in a limousine, and later wrote Northeastern to say, "Send us five more like Candace." A few weeks after finishing midterm exams—she was on a June–December academic schedule—Candace Lee Williams decided to meet her roommate at her home in California. Candace had recently made the dean's list. "They'd rented a convertible preparing for the occasion, and Candace wanted her picture taken with that Hollywood sign," her mother, Sherri, told the *Times*.

Unfortunately, Candace took the American Airlines Flight 11 that departed from Boston's Logan Airport on the morning of September 11, 2001, at 8:02 a.m. The plane was hijacked at 8:14 a.m. by five men, including Mohammed Atta, who was in seat 8D. With Atta at the controls, the Boeing 767-223ER was diverted to Manhattan and slammed Candace Lee Williams right back into the very same World Trade Center tower— between floors 94 and 98—where she had worked as an intern.

Airline records show that she was seated next to an eighty-year-old grandmother—two people at opposites ends of life: one full of memories, one full of dreams.

What does this story say to me? It says this: When Candace Lee Williams boarded Flight 11 she could not have imagined how it would end. But in the wake of 9/11, none of us can now board an airplane *without* imagining how it could end—that what happened to Candace Lee Williams could also happen to us. We all are now so much more conscious that a person's life can be wiped out by the arbitrary will of a madman in a cave in Afghanistan. But the fact is, the chances of our plane being hijacked by terrorists today are still infinitesimal. We are more likely to be killed hitting a deer with our car or being struck by lightning. So even though we *can* now imagine what could happen when we get on an airplane, we have to get on the plane anyway. Because the alternative to not getting on that plane is putting ourselves in our own cave. Imagination can't just be about reruns. It also has to be about writing our own new script. From what I read about Candace Lee Williams, she was an optimist. I'd bet anything she'd still be getting on planes today if she had the chance. And so must we all.

America's role in the world, from its inception, has been to be the country that looks forward, not back. One of the most dangerous things that has happened to America since 9/11, under the Bush administration, is that we have gone from exporting hope to exporting fear. We have gone from trying to coax the best out of the world to snarling at it way too often. And when you export fear, you end up importing everyone else's fears. Yes, we need people who can imagine the worst, because the worst did happen on 9/11 and it could happen again. But, as I said, there is a fine line between precaution and paranoia, and at times we have crossed it. Europeans and others often love to make fun of American optimism and naïveté—our crazy notion that every problem has a solution, that tomorrow can be better than yesterday, that the future can always bury the past. But I have always believed that deep down the rest of the world envies that American optimism and naïveté. It needs American optimism. It is one of the things that help keep the world spinning on its axis. If we go dark as a society, if we stop being the world's "dream factory," we will make the world not only a darker place but also a poorer place.

A nalysts have always tended to measure a society by classical economic and social statistics: its deficit-to-GDP ratio, or its unemployment rate, or the rate of literacy among its adult women. Such statistics are important and revealing. But there is another statistic, much harder to measure, that I think is even more important and revealing: Does your society have more memories than dreams or more dreams than memories?

By dreams I mean the positive, life-affirming variety. The business organization consultant Michael Hammer once remarked, "One thing that tells me a company is in trouble is when they tell me how good they were in the past. Same with countries. You don't want to forget your identity. I am glad you were great in the fourteenth century, but that was then and this is now. When memories exceed dreams, the end is near. The hallmark of a truly successful organization is the willingness to abandon what made it successful and start fresh."

In societies that have more memories than dreams, too many people are spending too many days looking backward. They see dignity, affirmation, and self-worth not by mining the present but by chewing on the past. And even that is usually not a real past but an imagined and adorned past. Indeed, such societies focus all their imagination on making that imagined past even more beautiful than it ever was, and then they cling to it like a rosary or a strand of worry beads, rather than imagining a better future and acting on that. It is dangerous enough when other countries go down that route; it would be disastrous for America to lose its bearings and move in that direction. I think my friend David Rothkopf, a former Commerce Department official and now a fellow at the Carnegie Endowment for International Peace, said it best: "The answer for us lies not in what has changed, but in recognizing what has not changed. Because only through this recognition will we begin to focus on the truly critical issues—an effective multilateral response to weapons of mass destruction proliferation, the creation of real stakeholders in globalization among the world's poor, the need for reform in the Arab world, and a style of U.S. leadership that seeks to build our base of support worldwide by getting more people to voluntarily sign onto our values. We need to remember that those values are the real foundation for our security and the real source of our strength. And we need to recognize that our enemies can never defeat us. Only we can defeat ourselves, by throwing out the rule book that has worked for us for a long, long time."

I believe that history will make very clear that President Bush shamelessly exploited the emotions around 9/11 for political purposes. He used those 9/11 emotions to take a far-right Republican domestic agenda on taxes, the environment, and social issues from 9/10—an agenda for which he had no popular mandate—and drive it into a 9/12 world. In doing so, Mr. Bush not only drove a wedge between Americans, and between Americans and the world, he drove a wedge between America and its own history and identity. His administration transformed the United

States into "the United States of Fighting Terrorism." This is the real reason, in my view, that so many people in the world dislike President Bush
so intensely. They feel that he has taken away something very dear to
them—an America that exports hope, not fear.

We need our president to restore September 11 to its rightful place on
the calendar—as the day after September 10 and before September 12.
We must never let it become a day that defines us. Because ultimately
September 11 is about *them*—the bad guys—not about us.

We're about the Fourth of July. We're about 11/9.

Beyond trying to retain the best of our own imaginations, what else
can we do as Americans and as a global society to try to nurture the
same in others? One has to approach this question with great humility.
What leads one person to the joy of destruction and what leads another
to the joy of creation, what leads one to imagine 11/9 and another to
imagine 9/11, is surely one of the great mysteries of contemporary life.
Moreover, while most of us might have some clue about how to nurture
a more positive imagination for our own kids, and maybe—maybe—for
our fellow citizens, it is presumptuous to think that we can do it for others, particularly those of a different culture, speaking different languages,
and living half a world away. Yet 9/11, the flattening of the world, and the
continuing threat of world-disrupting terrorism suggest that not thinking
about this is its own kind of dangerous naïveté. So I insist on trying to do
so, but I approach this issue with a keen awareness of the limits of what
any outsider can know or do.

Generally speaking, imagination is the product of two shaping forces.
One is the narratives that people are nurtured on—the stories and myths
they and their religious and national leaders tell themselves—and how
those narratives feed their imaginations one way or another. The other is
the context in which people grow up, which has a huge impact on shaping how they see the world and others. Outsiders cannot get inside and
adjust the Mexican or Arab or Chinese narrative any more than they can
get inside the American one. Only they can reinterpret their narrative,
make it more tolerant or forward looking, and adapt it to modernity. No

one can do that for them or even with them. But one can think about
how to collaborate with others to change their context—the context
within which people grow up and live their daily lives—to help nurture
more people with the imagination of 11/9 than 9/11.

Let me offer a few examples.

eBay

Meg Whitman, the CEO of eBay, once told me a wonderful story
that went like this: "We took eBay public in September 1998, in
the middle of the dot-com boom. And in September and October our
stock would go up eighty points and down fifty in a single day. I thought,
'This is insane.' Anyway, one day I am minding my own business, sitting
in my own cubicle, and my secretary runs over and says to me, 'Meg, it's
Arthur Levitt [chairman] of the SEC on the phone.'" The Securities and
Exchange Commission oversees the stock market and is always concerned about issues of volatility in a stock and whether there is manipulation behind it. In those days, for a CEO to hear that "Arthur Levitt is on
the line" was not a good way to start the day.

"So I called my general counsel," said Whitman, "who came over from
his cubicle, and he was white like a sheet. We called Levitt back together
and we put him on the speakerphone, and I said, 'Hi, it's Meg Whitman of
eBay.' And he said, 'Hi, it's Arthur Levitt of the SEC. I don't know you and
have never met you but I know that you just went public and I want to
know: How did it go? Were we [the SEC] customer-friendly?' And so we
breathed a sigh of relief, and we talked about that a little bit. And then
[Levitt] said, 'Well, actually, another reason that I am calling is that I just
got my tenth positive feedback on eBay and have earned my yellow star.
And I am so proud.' And then he said, 'I am actually a collector of
Depression-era glass, post-1929, and so I have bought and sold on eBay
and you get feedback as a buyer and seller. And I thought you would just
like to know.'"

Every eBay user has a feedback profile made up of comments from other eBay users who have done transactions with him or her, relating to whether the goods bought or sold were as expected and the transaction went off smoothly. This constitutes your official "eBay reputation." You get +1 point for each positive comment, 0 points for each neutral comment, and -1 for each negative comment. A colored star icon is attached to your user ID on eBay for ten or more feedback points. My user ID on eBay might be TOMF (50) and a blue star, which means that I have received positive feedback comments from fifty other eBay users. Next to that is a box that will tell you whether the seller has had 100 percent positive feedback comments or less, and also give you the chance to click and read all the buyers' comments about that seller.

The point, said Whitman, is that "I think every human being, Arthur Levitt or the janitor or the waitress or the doctor or the professor, needs and craves validation and positive feedback." And the big misconception is to think that it has to be money. "It can be really small things," said Whitman, "telling someone, 'You did a really great job, you were recognized as doing a great history paper.' Our users say to us [about eBay's star system], 'Where else can you wake up in the morning and see how much people like you?'"

But what is so striking, said Whitman, is that the overwhelming majority of feedback on eBay is positive. That's interesting. People don't usually write Wal-Mart managers to compliment them on a fabulous purchase. But when you are part of a community that you feel ownership in, it is different. You have a stake. "The highest number of feedback we have is well over 250,000 positive comments, and you can see each one," said Whitman. "You can see the entire history of each buyer and seller, and we have introduced the ability to rebut . . . You cannot be anonymous on eBay. If you are not willing to say who you are, you should not be saying it. And it became the norm of the community really fast . . . We are not running an exchange—we are running a community." Indeed, with 105 million registered users from 190 countries trading more than $35 billion in products annually, eBay is actually a self-governing nation-state—the V.R.e., the Virtual Republic of eBay.

And how is it governed? The philosophy of eBay, said Whitman, is "Let's make a small number of rules, really enforce them, and then create an environment in which people can fulfill their own potential. There is something going on here besides buying and selling goods." Even allowing for corporate boosterism, Whitman's essential message is really worth contemplating: "People will say that 'eBay restored my faith in humanity'—contrary to the world where people are cheating and don't give people the benefit of the doubt. I hear that twice a week . . . eBay offers the little guy, who's disenfranchised, an opportunity to compete on a totally level playing field. We have a disproportionate share of wheelchairs and disabled and minorities, [because] on eBay people don't know who you are. You are only as good as your product and feedback."

Whitman recalled that one day she got an e-mail from a couple in Orlando who were coming to an "eBay Live" event at which she was speaking. These are big revival meeting–conventions of eBay sellers. They asked if they could come backstage to meet Whitman after her speech. "So after the keynote," she recalled, "they come back to my green room, and in comes mom and dad and a seventeen-year-old boy in a wheelchair—very disabled with cerebral palsy. They tell me, 'Kyle is very disabled and can't go to school, [but] he built an eBay business and last year my husband and I quit our jobs, and now we help him—we have made more money on eBay than we ever made on our jobs.' And then they added the most incredible thing. They said, 'On eBay, Kyle is not disabled.'"

Whitman told me that at another "eBay Live" event a young man came up to her, a big power seller on eBay, and said that thanks to his eBay business he had been able to buy a house and a car, hire people, and be his own boss. But the best part, said Whitman, was that the young man added, "I am so excited about eBay, because I did not graduate from college and was sort of disowned by my family, and I am now the hit of my family. I am a successful entrepreneur."

"It's this blend of economic opportunity and validation" that makes eBay tick, concluded Whitman. Those validated become transparent as good partners, because bad validation is an option for the whole community.

Bottom line: eBay didn't just create an online market. It created a self-governing community—*a context*—where anyone, from the severely handicapped to the head of the SEC, could come and achieve his or her potential and be validated as a good and trustworthy person by the whole community. That kind of self-esteem and validation is the best, most effective way of producing dehumiliation and redignification. To the extent that America can collaborate with regions like the Arab-Muslim world to produce contexts where young people can succeed, can achieve their full potential on a level playing field, can get validation and respect from achievements in this world—and not from martyrdom to get into the next world—we can help foster more young people with more dreams than memories.

INDIA

If you want to see this same process at work in a less virtual community, study the second largest Muslim country in the world. The largest Muslim country in the world is Indonesia and the second largest is not Saudi Arabia, Iran, Egypt, or Pakistan. It is India. With some 150 million Muslims, India has more Muslims than Pakistan. But here is an interesting statistic from 9/11: There are no Indian Muslims that we know of in al-Qaeda and there are no Indian Muslims in America's Guantánamo Bay post-9/11 prison camp. And no Indian Muslims have been found fighting alongside the jihadists in Iraq. Why is that? Why do we not read about Indian Muslims, who are a minority in a vast Hindu-dominated land, blaming America for all their problems and wanting to fly airplanes into the Taj Mahal or the British embassy? Lord knows, Indian Muslims have their grievances about access to capital and political representation. And interreligious violence has occasionally flared up in India, with disastrous consequences. I am certain that out of 150 million Muslims in India, a few will one day find their way to al-Qaeda—if it can happen with some American Muslims, it can happen with Indian Muslims. But this is not the norm. Why?

The answer is context—and in particular the secular, free-market, democratic context of India, heavily influenced by a tradition of nonviolence and Hindu tolerance. M. J. Akbar, the Muslim editor of the *Asian Age*, a national Indian English-language daily primarily funded by non-Muslim Indians, put it to me this way: "I'll give you a quiz question: Which is the only large Muslim community to enjoy sustained democracy for the last fifty years? The Muslims of India. I am not going to exaggerate Muslim good fortune in India. There are tensions, economic discrimination, and provocations, like the destruction of the mosque at Ayodhya [by Hindu nationalists in 1992]. But the fact is, the Indian Constitution is secular and provides a real opportunity for economic advancement of any community that can offer talent. That's why a growing Muslim middle class here is moving up and generally doesn't manifest the strands of deep anger you find in many nondemocratic Muslim states."

Where Islam is embedded in authoritarian societies, it tends to become the vehicle of angry protest—Egypt, Syria, Saudi Arabia, Pakistan. But where Islam is embedded in a pluralistic democratic society—Turkey or India, for instance—those with a more progressive outlook have a chance to get a better hearing for their interpretation and a democratic forum where they can fight for their ideas on a more equal footing. On November 15, 2003, the two main synagogues of Istanbul were hit by some fringe suicide bombers. I happened to be in Istanbul a few months later, when they were reopened. Several things struck me. To begin with, the chief rabbi appeared at the ceremony, hand in hand with the top Muslim cleric of Istanbul and the local mayor, while crowds in the street threw red carnations on them both. Second, the prime minister of Turkey, Recep Tayyip Erdogan, who comes from an Islamic party, paid a visit to the chief rabbi in his office—the first time a Turkish prime minister had ever called on the chief rabbi. Lastly, the father of one of the suicide bombers told the Turkish newspaper *Zaman*, "We cannot understand why this child had done the thing he had done . . . First let us meet with the chief rabbi of our Jewish brothers. Let me hug him. Let me kiss his hands and flowing robe. Let me apologize in the name of my son and offer my condolences for the deaths . . . We will be damned if we do not reconcile with them."

Different context, different narrative, different imagination.

I am keenly aware of the imperfections of Indian democracy, starting with the oppressive caste system. Nevertheless, to have sustained a functioning democracy with all its flaws for more than fifty years in a country of over one billion people, who speak scores of different languages, is something of a miracle and a great source of stability for the world. Two of India's presidents have been Muslims, and its current president, A.P.J. Abdul Kalam, is both a Muslim and the father of the Indian nuclear missile program. While a Muslim woman sits on India's Supreme Court, no Muslim woman is allowed even to drive a car in Saudi Arabia. Indian Muslims, including women, have been governors of many Indian states, and the wealthiest man in India today, high on the Forbes list of global billionaires, is an Indian Muslim: Azim Premji, the chairman of Wipro, one of India's most important technology companies. I was in India shortly after the United States invaded Afghanistan in late 2001, when Indian television carried a debate between the country's leading female movie star and parliamentarian—Shabana Azmi, a Muslim woman— and the imam of New Delhi's biggest mosque. The imam had called on Indian Muslims to go to Afghanistan and join the jihad against America, and Azmi ripped into him, live on Indian TV, basically telling the cleric to go take a hike. She told him to go to Kandahar and join the Taliban and leave the rest of India's Muslims alone. How did she get away with that? Easy. As a Muslim woman she lived in a context that empowered and protected her to speak her mind—even to a leading cleric.

Different context, different narrative, different imagination.

This is not all that complicated: Give young people a context where they can translate a positive imagination into reality, give them a context in which someone with a grievance can have it adjudicated in a court of law without having to bribe the judge with a goat, give them a context in which they can pursue an entrepreneurial idea and become the richest or the most creative or most respected people in their own country, no matter what their background, give them a context in which any complaint or idea can be published in the newspaper, give them a context in which anyone can run for office—and guess what? They usually don't want to blow up the world. They usually want to be part of it.

A South Asian Muslim friend of mine once told me this story: His Indian Muslim family split in 1948, with half going to Pakistan and half staying in Mumbai. When he got older, he asked his father one day why the Indian half of the family seemed to be doing better than the Pakistani half. His father said to him, "Son, when a Muslim grows up in India and he sees a man living in a big mansion high on a hill, he says, 'Father, one day, I will be that man.' And when a Muslim grows up in Pakistan and sees a man living in a big mansion high on a hill, he says, 'Father, one day I will kill that man.'" When you have a pathway to be the Man or the Woman, you tend to focus on the path and on achieving your dreams. When you have no pathway, you tend to focus on your wrath and on nursing your memories.

India only twenty years ago, before the triple convergence, was known as a country of snake charmers, poor people, and Mother Teresa. Today its image has been recalibrated. Now it is also seen as a country of brainy people and computer wizards. Atul Vashistha, CEO of the outsourcing consulting firm NeoIT, often appears in the American media to defend outsourcing. He told me this story: "One day I had a problem with my HP printer—the printing was very slow. I was trying to figure out the problem. So I call HP tech support. This guy answers and takes all my personal information down. From his voice it is clear he is somewhere in India. So I start asking where he is and how the weather is. We're having a nice chat. So after he is helping me for about ten or fifteen minutes he says, 'Sir, do you mind if I say something to you?' I said, 'Sure.' I figured he was going to tell me something else I was doing wrong with my computer and was trying to be polite about it. And instead he says, 'Sir, I was very proud to hear you on Voice of America. You did a good job . . .' I had just been on a VOA show about the backlash against globalization and outsourcing. I was one of three invited guests. There was a union official, an economist, and myself. I defended outsourcing and this guy heard it."

Remember: In the flat world you don't get just your humiliation dished out to you fiber-optically. *You also get your pride dished out to you fiber-optically.* An Indian help-line operator suddenly knows, in real time, all about how one of his compatriots is representing India half a world away, and it makes him feel better about himself.

The French Revolution, the American Revolution, the Indian democracy, and even eBay are all based on social contracts whose dominant feature is that authority comes from the bottom up, and people can and do feel self-empowered to improve their lot. People living in such contexts tend to spend their time focusing on what to do next, not on whom to blame next.

THE CURSE OF OIL

Nothing has contributed more to retarding the emergence of a democratic context in places like Venezuela, Nigeria, Saudi Arabia, and Iran than the curse of oil. As long as the monarchs and dictators who run these oil states can get rich by drilling their natural resources—as opposed to drilling the natural talents and energy of their people—they can stay in office forever. They can use oil money to monopolize all the instruments of power—army, police, and intelligence—and never have to introduce real transparency or power sharing. All they have to do is capture and hold the oil tap. They never have to tax their people, so the relationship between ruler and ruled is highly distorted. *Without taxation, there is no representation.* The rulers don't really have to pay attention to the people or explain how they are spending their money—because they have not raised that money through taxes. That is why countries focused on tapping their oil wells always have weak or nonexistent institutions. Countries focused on tapping their people have to focus on developing real institutions, property rights, rule of law, independent courts, modern education, foreign trade, foreign investment, freedom of thought, and scientific inquiry to get the most out of their men and women. In an essay in *Foreign Affairs* called "Saving Iraq from Its Oil" (July–August 2004), development economists Nancy Birdsall and Arvind Subramanian point out that "34 less-developed countries now boast significant oil and natural gas resources that constitute at least 30 percent of their total export revenue. Despite their riches, however, 12 of these countries' annual per capita income remains below $1,500 . . . Moreover, two-thirds of the 34 countries are not democratic, and of those that are, only three score in the top half of Freedom House's world rankings of political freedom."

In other words, imagination is also a product of necessity—when the context you are living in simply does not allow you to indulge in certain escapist or radical fantasies, you don't. Look where the most creative innovation is happening in the Arab-Muslim world today. It is in the places with little or no oil. As I noted earlier, Bahrain was one of the first Arab Gulf states to discover oil and was *the* first Arab Gulf state to run out of oil. And today it is the first Arab Gulf state to develop comprehensive labor reform for developing the skills of its own workers, the first to sign a free-trade agreement with the United States, and the first to hold a free and fair election, in which women could both run and vote. And which countries in that same region are paralyzed or actually rolling back reforms? Saudi Arabia and Iran, which are awash in oil money. On December 9, 2004, at a time when crude oil prices had soared to near $50 a barrel, *The Economist* did a special report from Iran, in which it noted, "Without oil at its present sky-high price, Iran's economy would be in wretched straits. Oil provides about half the government's revenue and at least 80% of export earnings. But, once again under the influence of zealots in parliament, the oil cash is being spent on boosting wasteful subsidies rather than on much-needed development and new technology."

It is worthy of note that Jordan began upgrading its education system and privatizing, modernizing, and deregulating its economy starting in 1989—precisely when oil prices were way down and it could no longer rely on handouts from the Gulf oil states. In 1999, when Jordan signed its free-trade agreement with the United States, its exports to America totaled $13 million. In 2004, Jordan exported over $1 billion of goods to America—things Jordanians made with their hands. The Jordanian government has also installed computers and broadband Internet in every school. Most important, in 2004, Jordan announced a reform of its education requirements for mosque prayer leaders. Traditionally, high school students in Jordan took an exam for college entrance, and those who did the best became doctors and engineers. Those who did the worst became mosque preachers. In 2004, Jordan decided to gradually phase in a new system. Henceforth, to become a mosque prayer leader, a young man will first have to get a B.A. in some other subject, and can study Islamic law only as a graduate degree—in order to encourage more young men of talent to go into the clergy and weed out those who were just "failing" into it. That is an important change in context that should pay dividends over time in the narratives that young Jordanians are nurtured upon in their mosques. "We had to go through a crisis to accept the need for reform," said Jordan's minister of planning, Bassem Awadallah.

There is no mother of invention like necessity, and only when falling oil prices force the leaders in the Middle East to change their contexts will they reform. People don't change when you tell them they should. They change when they tell themselves they must. Or as Johns Hopkins foreign affairs professor Michael Mandelbaum puts it, "People don't change when you tell them there is a better option. They change when they conclude that they have no other option." Give me $10-a-barrel oil, and I will give you political and economic reform from Moscow to Riyadh to Iran. If America and its allies will not collaborate in bringing down the price of crude oil, their aspirations for reform in all these areas will be stillborn.

There is another factor to consider here. When you have to make things with your hands and then trade with others in order to flourish, not just dig an oil well in your own backyard, it inevitably broadens imagination and increases tolerance and trust. It is no accident that Muslim countries make up 20 percent of the world's population but account for only 4 percent of world trade. When countries don't make things anyone else wants, they trade less, and less trade means less exchange of ideas and openness to the world. The most open, tolerant cities in the Muslim world today are its trading centers—Beirut, Istanbul, Jakarta, Dubai, Bahrain. The most open, tolerant cities in China are Hong Kong and Shanghai. The most closed cities in the world are in central Saudi Arabia, where no Christians, Hindus, Jews, or other non-Muslims are allowed to express their religions in public or build a house of worship, and, in the case of Mecca, even enter. Religions are the smelters and founders of imagination. The more any religion's imagination—Hindu, Christian, Jewish, Muslim, Buddhist—is shaped in an isolated bubble,

or in a dark cave, the more its imagination is likely to sail off in dangerous directions. People who are connected to the world and exposed to
different cultures and perspectives are far more likely to develop the
imagination of 11/9. People who are feeling disconnected, for whom personal freedom and fulfillment are a utopian fantasy, are more likely to
develop the imagination of 9/11.

JUST ONE GOOD EXAMPLE

Stanley Fischer, the former deputy managing director of the IMF, once
remarked to me, "One good example is worth a thousand theories." I
believe that is true. Indeed, people do not change only when they must:
They also change when they see that others—*like themselves*—have
changed and flourished. Or as Michael Mandelbaum also points out,
"People change as a result of what they notice, not just what they are
told"—especially when what they notice is someone just like them doing
well. As I pointed out earlier, there is only one Arab company that developed a world-class business strong enough to get itself listed on the
Nasdaq, and that was Aramex. Every Jordanian, every Arab, should know
and take pride in the Aramex story, the way every American knows the
Apple and Microsoft and Dell stories. It is the example that is worth a
thousand theories. It should be the role model of a self-empowered Arab
company, run by Arab brainpower and entrepreneurship, succeeding on
the world stage and enriching its own workers at the same time.

When Fadi Ghandour took Aramex public again in 2005, this time in
Dubai, some four hundred Aramex employees from all over the Arab
world who had stock options divided $14 million. I will never forget Fadi
telling me how proud these employees were—some of them managers,
some of them just delivery drivers. This windfall was going to enable
them to buy homes or send their kids to better schools. Imagine the dignity that these people feel when they come back to their families and
neighborhoods and tell everyone that they are going to build a new
house because the world-class *Arab* company they work for has gone

public. Imagine how much dignity they feel when they see themselves getting ahead by succeeding in the flat world—not in the traditional Middle Eastern way by inheritance, by selling land, or by getting a government contract, but by working for a real company, an Arab company. Just as it is no accident that there are no Indian Muslims in al-Qaeda, it is no accident that the three thousand Arab employees of Aramex want to deliver only packages that help economies grow and Arab people flourish—not suicide bombs.

Speaking of the Aramex employees with stock options, Ghandour said, "They all feel like owners. A lot of them came up to me and said, 'Thank you, but I want to invest my options back in the company and be an investor in the new IPO.'"

Give me just one hundred more examples like Aramex, and I will start to give you a different context—and narrative.

FROM UNTOUCHABLES TO UNTOUCHABLES

And while you are at it, give me one hundred Abraham Georges as well—individuals who step out of their context and set a different example can have such a huge impact on the imagination of so many others. One day in February 2004, I was resting in my hotel room in Bangalore when the phone rang. It was a young Indian woman who said she was attending a private journalism school on the outskirts of the city and wanted to know if I would come by and meet with her class. I've learned over the years that these sorts of accidental invitations often lead to interesting encounters, so I said, "What the heck, sure. I'll come." Two days later I drove ninety minutes from downtown Bangalore to an open field in which stood a lonely journalism school and dormitory. I was met at the door by a handsome middle-aged Indian man named Abraham George. Born in Kerala, George served in the Indian Army, while his mother immigrated to the United States and went to work for NASA. George followed her, went on to study at NYU, started a software firm that specialized in international finance, sold it in 1998, and decided to come back to India and use his American-made fortune to try to change India from the bottom—the absolute bottom—up.

One thing George learned from his time in the United States was that without more responsible Indian newspapers and journalists, the country could never improve its governance. So he started a journalism school. As we sat in his office sipping juice, it quickly became apparent to me, though, that as proud as he was of his little journalism school, he was even more proud of the elementary school he had started in a village outside Bangalore populated by India's lowest caste, the untouchables, who are not supposed to even get near Indians of a higher caste for fear that they will pollute the very air they breathe. George wanted to prove that if you gave these untouchable children access to the same technologies and solid education that have enabled other pockets of India to plug in and play with the flat world, they could do the same. The more he talked about the school, the more I wanted to see it and not talk journalism. So as soon as I finished speaking to his journalism students, we hopped into his jeep, along with his principal, Lalita Law, and set out on a two-hour drive to the Shanti Bhavan school, which, as I explained in Chapter 15, was located about ten miles and ten centuries from the outskirts of Bangalore. The word "wretched" does not even begin to describe the living conditions in the villages around the school.

When we eventually reached the school complex, though, we found neatly painted buildings, surrounded by some grass and flowers, a total contrast to the nearby hamlets. The first classroom we walked into had twenty untouchable kids at computers working on Excel and Microsoft Word. Next door, another class was practicing typing on a computer typing program. I loudly asked the teacher who was the fastest typist in the class. She pointed to an eight-year-old girl with a smile that could have melted a glacier.

"I want to race you," I said to her. All her classmates gathered round. I crunched myself into a tiny seat in the computer stall next to her, and we each proceeded to type the same phrase over and over, seeing who could do more in a minute. "Who's winning?" I shouted. Her classmates shouted her name back and cheered her on. I quickly surrendered to her gleeful laugh.

The selection process to get into Shanti Bhavan is based on whether a child is below the poverty line and the parents are willing to send him or her to a boarding school. Shortly before I arrived, the students had taken the California Achievement Tests. "We are giving them English education so they can go anywhere in India and anywhere in the world for higher education," said Law. "Our goal is to give them a world-class education so they can aspire to careers and professions that would have been totally beyond their reach and have been so for generations . . . Around here, their names will always give them away as untouchables. But if they go somewhere else, and if they are really polished, with proper education and social graces, they can break this barrier."

Then they can become *my* kind of untouchables—young people who one day can be special or specialized or adaptable.

Looking at these kids, George said, "When we talk about the poor, so often it is talk about getting them off the streets or getting them a job, so they don't starve. But we never talk about getting excellence for the poor. My thought was that we can deal with the issue of inequality if they could break out of all the barriers imposed upon them. If one is successful, they will carry one thousand with them."

After listening to George, my mind drifted back to only four months earlier, in the fall of 2003, when I had been in the West Bank filming another documentary about the Arab-Israeli conflict. As a part of that project, I went to Ramallah and interviewed three young Palestinian militants who were members of Yasser Arafat's paramilitary Tanzim organization. What was so striking about the interview were the mood swings of these young men from suicidal despair to dreamy aspirations. When I asked one of the three, Mohammed Motev, what was the worst thing about living in the context of Israeli occupation, he said the checkpoints. "When a soldier asks me to take off my clothes in front of the girls. It's a great humiliation to me . . . to take off my shirt and my pants and turn around and all the girls are standing there." It is one reason, he said, that all Palestinian young people today are just suicide bombers in waiting. He called them "martyrs in waiting," while his two friends nodded in assent. They warned me that if Israel tried to kill Yasser Arafat, who was then still alive (and was a leader who knew how to stimulate only memories, not dreams), they would turn the whole area into a living "hell." To underscore this point, Motev took out his wallet and showed me a picture of Arafat. But what caught my eye was the picture of a young girl next to it.

"Who's that?" I asked. That was his girlfriend, he explained, slightly red-faced. So there was his wallet—Yasser Arafat on one page, whom he was ready to die for, and his girlfriend on the other, whom he wanted to live for. A few minutes later, one of his colleagues, Anas Assaf, became emotional. He was the only one in college, an engineering student at Bir Zeit University near Ramallah. After breathing fire about also being willing to die for Arafat, he began waxing eloquent about how much he wanted to go to the University of Memphis, where his uncle lived, "to study engineering." Unfortunately, he said, he could not get a visa into the United States now. Like his colleague, Assaf was ready to die for Yasser Arafat, but he wanted to live for the University of Memphis.

These were good young men, not terrorists. But their role models were all angry men, and these young men spent a lot of their time imagining how to unleash their anger, not realizing their potential. Abraham George, by contrast, produced a different context and a different set of teacher role models for those untouchable children in his school, and together they planted in his students the seeds of a very different imagination. We must have more Abraham Georges—everywhere—by the thousands: people who gaze upon a classroom of untouchable kids and not only see the greatness in each of them but, more important, get them to see the greatness in themselves while endowing them with the tools to bring that out.

After our little typing race at the Shanti Bhavan school, I went around the classroom and asked all the children—most of whom had been in school, and out of a life of open sewers, for only three years—what they wanted to be when they grew up. These were eight-year-old Indian kids whose parents were untouchables. It was one of the most moving experiences of my life. Their answers were as follows: "an astronaut," "a doctor," "a pediatrician," "a poetess," "physics and chemistry," "a scientist and an astronaut," "a surgeon," "a detective," "an author."

All dreamers in action—not martyrs in waiting.

L et me close with one last point. My own daughter went off to college in the fall of 2004, and my wife and I dropped her off on a warm September day. The sun was shining. Our daughter was full of excitement. But I can honestly say it was one of the saddest days of my life. And it wasn't just the dad-and-mom-dropping-their-eldest-child-off-at-school thing. No, something else bothered me. It was the sense that I was dropping my daughter off into a world that was so much more dangerous than the one she had been born into. I felt like I could still promise my daughter her bedroom back, but I couldn't promise her the world—not in the carefree way that I had explored it when I was her age. That really bothered me. Still does.

The flattening of the world, as I have tried to demonstrate in this book, has presented us with new opportunities, new challenges, new partners, but also, alas, new dangers, particularly as Americans. It is imperative that we find the right balance among all of these. It is imperative that we be the best global citizens that we can be—because in a flat world, if you don't visit a bad neighborhood, it might visit you. And it is imperative that while we remain vigilant to the new threats, we do not let them paralyze us. Most of all, though, it is imperative that we nurture more people with the imaginations of Abraham George and Fadi Ghandour. The more people with the imagination of 11/9, the better chance we have of staving off another 9/11. I refuse to settle for a world that gets smaller in the wrong sense, in the sense that there are fewer and fewer places an American can go without a second thought and fewer and fewer foreigners feeling comfortable about coming to America.

To put it another way, the greatest dangers we Americans face are an excess of protectionism—excessive fears of another 9/11 that prompt us to wall ourselves in, in search of personal security—and excessive fears of competing in a world of 11/9 that prompt us to wall ourselves off, in search of economic security. Either one would be a disaster for us and for the world.

Yes, I have said a lot about how economic competition in the flat world will be more intense and involve more players. We Americans will have to work harder, run faster, and become smarter to make sure that more of us are able to connect and compete, collaborate and innovate on the flat-world platform—and derive all the benefits it has to offer. But remember: *the most important competition is now with yourself*—making sure that you are always striving to get the most out of your own imagination, and then acting on it.

I can't tell any other society or culture what to say to its own children, but I can tell you what I say to my own: The world is being flattened. I didn't start it and you can't stop it, except at a great cost to human development and your own future. But we can tilt it, and shape it, for better or for worse. If it is to be for better, not for worse, then you and your generation must not live in fear of either the terrorists or tomorrow, of either al-Qaeda or Infosys. You can flourish in this flat world, but it does take the right imagination and the right motivation. While your lives have been powerfully shaped by 9/11, the world needs you to be forever the generation of 11/9—the generation of strategic optimists, the generation with more dreams than memories, the generation that wakes up each morning and not only imagines that things can be better but also acts on that imagination every day.

ACKNOWLEDGMENTS

In 1999 I published a book on globalization called *The Lexus and the Olive Tree*. The phenomenon we call globalization was just taking off then, and *The Lexus and the Olive Tree* was one of the early attempts to put a frame around it. This book is not meant to replace *The Lexus and the Olive Tree* but rather to build on it and push the arguments forward as the world has evolved.

I am deeply grateful to the publisher of *The New York Times* and chairman of the New York Times Company, Arthur Sulzberger Jr., for granting me a leave of absence to be able to undertake this book, and to Gail Collins, editorial page editor of *The New York Times*, for supporting that leave and this whole project. It is a privilege to work for such a great newspaper. It was Arthur and Gail who pushed me to try my hand at documentaries for the Discovery Times Channel, which took me to India and stimulated this whole book. Thanks in that regard also go to Billy Campbell of the Discovery Channel for his enthusiastic backing of that Indian documentary, and to Ken Levis, Ann Derry, and Stephen Reverand for helping to bring it off. Without Discovery the show would not have happened.

I never could have written this book, though, without some wonderful tutors from the worlds of technology, business, and politics. A few individuals must be singled out for particular thanks. I never would have broken the code of the flat world without the help of Nandan Nilekani, CEO of the Indian technology company Infosys, who was the first to point out to me how the playing field was being leveled. Vivek Paul, president of the Indian technology company Wipro, really took me inside the business of the flat world and deciphered it all for me—time and time again. Joel Cawley, the head of IBM's strategic planning team, helped me connect so many of the dots between technology and business and politics on Planet Flat—connections I never would have made without him. Craig Mundie, chief technology officer of Microsoft, walked me through the technological evolutions that made the flat world possible and helped ensure that in writing about them I would not fall flat on my face. He was a tireless and demanding tutor. Paul Romer, the Stanford University economist who has done so much good work on the new economy, took the time to read the book in draft and brought both his humanity and his intellect to several chapters. Marc Andreessen, one of the cofounders of Netscape; Michael Dell of Dell Inc.; Sir John Rose, chief executive of Rolls-Royce; and Bill Gates of Microsoft were very generous in commenting on certain sections. My inventor friend Dan Simpkins was enormously helpful in walking this novice through his complex universe. Michael Sandel's always challenging questions stimulated me to write a whole chapter—"The Great Sorting Out." And Yaron Ezrahi, for the fourth book in a row, let me bounce countless ideas off his razor-sharp mind. The same was true for David Rothkopf. None of them is responsible for any mistakes, only for insights. I am truly in their debt.

So many other people shared with me their valuable time and commented on different parts of this book. I want to thank in particular Allen Adamson, Graham Allison, Alex and Jocelyn Attal, Jim Barksdale, Craig Barrett, Brian Behlendorf, Katie Belding, Jagdish Bhagwati, Sergey Brin, Bill Brody, Mitchell Caplan, Bill Carrico, John Chambers, Nayan Chanda, G. Wayne Clough, Alan Cohen, Maureen Conway, Rich DeMillo, Lamees El-Hadidy, Rahm Emanuel, Mike Eskew, Judy Estrin, Diana Farrell, Joel Finkelstein, Carly Fiorina, Frank Fukuyama, Merrick Furst, Jeff Garten, Fadi Ghandour, Bill Greer, Jill Greer, Ken Greer, Promod Haque, Steve Holmes, Dan Honig, Scott Hyten, Shirley Ann Jackson, P. V. Kannan, Alan Kotz, Gary and Laura Lauder, Robert Lawrence, Jerry Lehrman, Rick Levin, Joshua Levine, Will Marshall, Walt Mossberg, Moisés Naím, David Neeleman, Larry Page, Carlota Perez, Jim Perkowski, Thomas Pickering, Jamie Popkin, Clyde Prestowitz, Glenn Prickett, Saritha Rai, Jerry Rao, Rajesh Rao, Bill Ritz, Eric Schmidt, H. Lee Scott Jr., Dov Seidman, Terry Semel, Amartya Sen, Dinakar Singh, Eric Stern, Larry Summers, Jeff Ulin, Atul Vashistha, Philip Verleger Jr., Jeff Wacker, William Wertz, Meg Whitman, Irving Wladawsky-Berger, Bob Wright, Jerry Yang, and Ernesto Zedillo. And special thanks to my soul mates and constant intellectual companions Michael Mandelbaum and Stephen P. Cohen. Sharing ideas with them is one of the joys of my life. A special thanks to John Doerr and Herbert Allen Jr., who each gave me the opportunity to road-test this book on some of their very demanding and critical colleagues. Thanks too to Jill Priluck for her excellent fact-checking.

As always, my wife, Ann, was my first editor, critic, and all-around supporter. Without her help and intellectual input this book never would have happened. I am so lucky to have her as my partner. And thanks too to my daughters Orly and Natalie for putting up with another year of Dad closeted away in his office for long hours, and to my dear mother, Margaret Friedman, for asking every day when my book would be done. Max and Eli Bucksbaum provided valuable encouragement in the early hours of the morning in Aspen. And my sisters Shelley and Jane have always been in my corner.

I am blessed to have had the same literary agent, Esther Newberg, and publisher, Jonathan Galassi, for four books, and the same line editor, Paul Elie, for the last three. Paul's work was absolutely indispensable in the first and second editions of this book. This team is simply the best in the business. I was also blessed, while writing this book, to have the most talented and loyal assistant, Maya Gorman.

This book is dedicated to three very special people in my life: My mother- and father-in-law, Matt and Kay Bucksbaum, and my oldest childhood friend, Ron Soskin.

INDEX

ABC, 45
Abdul Kalam, A.P.J., 624
Abell, Pete, 156
Abizaid, Gen. John, 39
Accenture Ltd., 34, 240
Acción, 495
accounting, 12–15, 194, 216
Accounting Today, 14
ACM Siggraph, 369
activism, social and political, 489–92, 504–12
Adamson, Allen, 209–10
adaptability, 293–97, 304–23
Addison, Craig, 589
Adobe Photoshop, 107, 219, 305
Aetna Health Care, 301
Afghanistan, 59, 559, 564, 600, 602; bin
  Laden in, 614, 615; U.S. invasion of, 229,
  624
AFL-CIO, 258
Africa, 212, 410, 412, 413, 538, 539, 545,
  552, 562, 576; disease in, 539–44;
  manufacturing in, 273
African-Americans, 299, 341, 396–97, 567
Agere, 583
agriculture, environmental issues in, 508–9
Ahern, Bertie, 420
AIDS, *see* HIV-AIDS
Airborne Express, 450–53
Airbus Industries, 227, 247
Airman Flight School, 611
Air National Guard, 45, 46, 117
Airspace, 185, 194
AJAX (asynchronous JavaScript and XML),
  88
Akbar, M. J., 623
al-Arabiya news channel, 569

Ali, Ali Abdul Aziz, 610
Alibaba.com, 447
al-Jazeera television network, 564
Allen, George, 506
Allen, Jay, 158
Allison, Graham, 603
alogoholics, 272
Alps, 582
al-Qaeda, 8, 239, 483, 550, 558–59,
  595–603, 604, 610–11, 613, 622, 630
Al-Rashed, Abdel Rahman, 569
Al-Riyadh (newspaper), 424
Al-Sharq Al-Awsat (newspaper), 556, 567,
  569–70
al-Shehhi, Marwan, 559
Al-Sudairi, Turki, 424
al-Zarqawi, Abu Musab, 565
Amazon.com, 71, 74, 82, 88, 94, 182, 301,
  306, 447
Amazon rain forests, 576
ambition, 354–65
American Academy of Sciences, 351
American Airlines Flight 11, 615
American Association for the Advancement
  of Science, 340
American Chamber of Commerce; in
  China, 141, 337; in Egypt, 405; in Japan,
  247
American Diplomat Project, 302
American Express, 6, 200, 444, 592
American Indians, 131, 446
Americanization, cultural, 477–79
American Revolution, 625
America Online (AOL), 57, 60, 70, 95, 111,
  248, 376, 598
Amin, Idi, 425

AMR Research, 156
Anandan, P., 216–17
anchored jobs, 282
Andersen, Espen, 302
Anderson, Nate, 524–25
Anderson, Stuart, 349–50
Andreessen, Marc, 64–69, 76, 97, 99, 100, 269
Angola, 416
animation, 481–82
Annie Wright School, 356
Annunziata, Robert, 74
Answers.com, 123
anti-Americanism, 549–51
antiglobalization movement, 546–50
AOL, see America Online
Apache, 93–94, 97, 98, 100–105, 486
Apple Computer, 55–58, 275, 316, 398, 458, 629; iPod, 71, 119, 178, 181, 318, 327, 390, 399, 447, 458, 485, 486, 515, 516; iTunes, 119, 190; Macintosh, 66, 68, 290, 318
Arab Human Development Report, 561, 564
Arab News, 424
Arabs, 9, 390, 411, 423–26, 507, 508, 555–70, 627, 628
Aramex, 449–54, 629
Aratani, Lori, 521–23
Arce, Albert, 125
ARC Electronics, 73
Archibald, Nick, 114, 116
Architectural Digest, 289
Ardolino, Bill, 45–46
Argentina, 338, 407, 416, 446
Arguello, Mike, 97, 354–56
Arizona, University of, 314
Army, U.S., 247, 598; Central Command, 596
Arrow, 583
arstechnica.com, 524
Artoc Group for Investment and Development, 487
Arulselvan, Muthukrishnan, 212–13
Aryabhatta, 213
Asian Media Information and Communication Centre (AMIC), 479–80
ASIMCO Technologies, 137, 139, 143, 145, 147–48
Askey, 583
Associated Press, 42, 190, 255, 272, 337, 340, 562
Association of University Technology Managers, 332

Asustek, 583
asynchronous JavaScript and XML (AJAX), 88
AT&T, 6, 73, 74, 247; Bell Labs, 136, 341
Atef, Mohammed, 611
Athens Olympics, 338
Atlanta Olympics, 326
Atta, Mohammed, 390, 559, 560, 611, 615
Attal, Alex, 381
AU Optronics, 583
Auras, 582
Australia, 6, 16, 122, 164, 218, 415, 602
Austria, 415, 607
automobile industry, 29, 271; energy-saving technology in, 577–78; in India, 274–75; offshoring in, 144–48; supply chain in, 172
Avis, 591, 592
Awadallah, Bassem, 628
Azmi, Shabana, 624

Baader-Meinhof Gang, 559–60
Backstreet Boys, 485
Bahrain, 411, 422, 425, 506–8, 627, 628
Baker, Dolly, 36–37
Baker, James A., III, 51–52, 443
Baker, Stephen, 300
Bakkar cartoon series, 405
Bakó, József, 442–43
Baldwin family, 107
Baltimore, David, 395–96
Baltimore Orioles, 298
Bambery, Zoe, 522
BancoSol, 495
Banerjee, Indrajit, 479–81
Bangladesh, 410, 419
BankBoston, 331
bankruptcy, 414, 416
Barksdale, Jim, 63–66, 69–70
Barnes & Noble, 71
Barrett, Craig, 211, 212, 361–62, 371–73
basketball, 120, 125, 303, 337–39, 395
Battelle, John, 47
battellemedia.com, 47
Baxter International, 418
BBC, 95, 118, 311, 517
Beesley, Angela, 122
Behlendorf, Brian, 97–102, 105, 112–13
Beijing College of Foreign Affairs, 575
Beijing Municipal Bureau of Commerce, 572
Belding, Brian, 534–35
Belding, Katie, 534
Belgium, 122, 567

benefits, portable, 383–86
Benioff, Marc, 88–90
Berlin Wall, fall of, 51–55, 58, 59, 66, 79, 211–12, 225, 408, 447, 479, 548, 607–8
Berners-Lee, Tim, 60–62, 99
Berry, Justin, 482–83
Best Buy, 141
BeyondCore, 446
Bhagwati, Jagdish, 271
Bible, the, 51
Bigari, Steven, 42
Bill and Melinda Gates Foundation, 540–44
Billings, Sam, 295–97
Billpoint, 86
Bina, Eric, 64, 100
bin Laden, Osama, 59, 311, 517, 550, 560, 564–68, 602, 603, 609–14
Bin Tefla, Sa'd, 568
biodiversity, 509
biological renaissance, 297
bioscience, 287
Birdsall, Nancy, 626
BitTorrent, 95–96, 191
BlackBerry, 83, 249, 303, 446, 518
Bleha, Thomas, 363, 364
Blinder, Alan, 280–81, 299, 309
blogging, 47, 94, 96, 117–19, 237, 446, 486, 492, 502, 521, 523–28
Bloomberg news organization, 18
Bluetooth, 515
BMW, 458
Boeing Aircraft Corporation, 82, 199, 226–28, 247
Boeshart, Pat, 445
Bombardier, 358
Bomis.com, 121
Boomer, L. Gary, 14–15
Borelli, Wendy, 522
Boston College International Study Center, 350
Boston Globe, 46
Boucher, Richard, 591
Bradley, Bill, 228
Brazil, 54, 122, 140, 278, 444, 487, 581
Brezhnev, Leonid, 376
Brickwork, 31–32
Brin, Sergey, 177, 180, 390
Britain, 9, 122, 246, 270, 275, 422, 448, 474, 480, 611; automobile industry in, 198, 246; economic reform in, 409, 430; GDP of, 417; India and, 53, 222, 422, 425; Microsoft research center in, 367; Muslims in, 562; offshoring by, 583; steel

industry in, 598; terrorists in, 598; university enrollments in, 347
British Airways, 198, 591, 592
broadband, 363–64
Brody, Bill, 187–88, 365–66, 390
Brooke, Jim, 185–86
Brookings Institution, 391
Brown v. Board of Education (1954), 341
browsers, 60, 62–72, 77; see also specific browsers
Bryant, Kobe, 125
Buddhists, 628
Buffett, Jimmy, 535
Bureau of Labor Statistics (BLS), 345
Burkino Faso, 415
Burns, Nick, 39
Bush, George W., 45, 117, 292–30, 311, 352, 363–64, 370–71, 382, 529, 550, 578, 616–18
Business Monthly, 405–6
business startup costs, 413–16
Business Web, 87–92, 112, 303
BusinessWeek, 140, 141, 150, 172, 188, 191, 274, 284, 300, 494

California, University of; Berkeley, 99, 101, 105, 327; Los Angeles, 315; Santa Cruz, 391
California gold rush, 113
California Institute of Technology (Caltech), 98, 396
Calle, Luis de la, 407
Cambodia, 177, 425, 496–501
Cambridge University, 224, 275
camera phones, 196–97, 207, 524, 534–36
cameras, digital, 189, 289–90, 471–72
Cameroon, 415
Canada, 164, 169, 173, 218, 292–93, 404, 415, 418, 489, 574; gold mining in, 113–16
Cancer Vex, 77
capital markets, 332–33
CapitalOne, 389
Caplan, Mitchell H., 455–56
Caribou Coffee, 299
Carnegie Endowment for International Peace, 617
Carnegie Mellon University, 105, 127, 369
Carrier, 29
cartoon animation, 481–82
Castaneda, Jorge, 428–29
Caterpillar, 146, 148
CAT scans, 16, 30, 42

Cawley, Joel, 69, 86, 93, 303, 313, 447
CBS, 44, 95, 117, 332
CCI, 582
Celestica, 311
cell phones, 120, 186, 194, 196–97, 207, 214, 250, 327, 453, 504, 515–20; 534–36; cheap, 274; Internet access by, 363; text messaging on, 521–23
Center for American Progress, 364
Central European University, 442
Central Intelligence Agency (CIA), 39, 390
Central Liberal Truth, The (Harrison), 421
Cerf, Vint, 61
CERN, 60
Chambers, John, 419–20
Chanda, Nayan, 547, 569
Chaplin, Charlie, 217, 299
Chechnya, 569, 601, 602
Chen, Vicki, 286
Chen Shui-bian, 590
Cherukuri, Satyam, 30
Chicago, University of, 315, 422
Chicago Sun-Times, 46
Chile, 411, 444
Chi Mei Optoelectronics, 583
China, 30, 81, 110, 113, 122, 167, 177, 181, 211–14, 243, 339, 375, 398–400, 403–5, 407, 433, 447–49, 570, 596, 628; American Chamber of Commerce in, 141, 337; basketball in, 295, 338; capital markets in, 283, 333; cell phones in, 214, 274, 535; censorship in, 449; Central Bank of, 404; Communist revolution in, 602; Cultural Revolution in, 368, 425; culture of, 422, 424–25; disease in, 540, 545; economic reforms in, 408–10; education in, 319–20, 349, 361, 365–68, 397, 430–32; eighteenth-century, 11; energy consumption in, 297, 571–77; engineers in, 136, 345, 347–48, 379; enrollment in American universities of students from, 223–25, 347; environmental issues in, 297, 512; and fall of Berlin Wall, 54; foreign direct investment in, 418; IBM and, 245; immigrants from, 390; India and, 379; innovation in, 273, 274, 353, 369–71; intangibles of economic development in, 426–32; internship applicants from, 286; job competition with, 278, 327; manufacturing in, 21, 137–51, 273–74, 276–77, 303, 392, 398–400, 403, 443, 461, 581–83, 587, 588; middle class in, 547, 550; opening of, 58; outsourcing to, 32–36,

136, 221, 280, 336–37; podcasting in, 584–86; political stability of, 334; poverty in, 410, 437; rural population of, 258, 538, 539; scientists in, 345; Taiwan and, 585, 586, 588–91; trade policy and, 247, 266–71, 276–77; in Wal-Mart supply chain, 158, 163–66, 206; work ethic in, 358; work flow to, 89; zippies in, 223–25
China Airlines, 584–85
China Business Weekly, 164
China People's Daily, 142
Chinese Century, The (Shenkar), 140
Chittagong University, 494
Christians, 596, 628
Churchill, Winston, 533
Cisco Systems, 30, 66, 192, 207, 419
Citibank, 275, 552
Citigroup, 13
City Journal, 562
Civil War, 569
Claremont College, 286
Clark, Jim, 64, 65
Clinton, Bill, 10, 48, 252, 269, 284, 294, 341, 549
Clough, G. Wayne, 324–27, 367, 371
CNETNews.com, 75
CNN, 45, 327, 332, 591
Coast Guard, U.S., 20
Cobden, Richard, 580
Coca-Cola Corporation, 29, 487
Cohen, Alan, 93–94, 194
Cold War, 53, 211, 226, 259, 343, 374–78, 382
CollabNet, 98, 112–13
collaboration, 285–87; in education, 329, 501–3; in innovation, 110, 112–16, 254–55, 458, 504–5; trust in, 334
collaborative planning, forecasting, and replenishment (CPFR), 160
Collapse (Diamond), 571
Colombia, 415
Columbia University, 224, 271, 342, 351; Business School, 514
Columbus, Christopher, 3–5, 7, 9, 32
Commerce Department, U.S., 48, 146, 617
commercial contracts, enforcement of, 414, 415
commoditization, 304–7, 473
communism, 59, 369, 375, 409, 424, 428; collapse of, 52–55, 212
Communist Manifesto (Marx and Engels), 233–36

community-developed software, 93–112;
    free software movement, 97, 105–7, 219;
    intellectual commons, 96–105, 119
Compal, 582
Companhia Siderúrgica Nacional, 487
complexity, explaining, 288–90
compression technologies, 226
Compuserve, 57
Computer Associates, 103
computer games, 217–20, 481–82
Computerworld, 160
Concurrent Versions System, 102
Confederation of Indian Industry, 53, 592
Conference Board, 142
Congo, Democratic Republic of, 415
Congress, U.S., 124, 344, 362–63, 377, 380,
    385–86, 448, 578
connectivity, social downsides of, 515–30
Conservation International (CI), 443, 508,
    510, 576
Converse shoe company, 431
Conway, Maureen, 463, 464
core competencies, 461
Corning Glass, 264
Corporate Library, 74
Corus, 487
Cosby, Bill, 396–97
Costa Rica, 582
Costco Wholesale, 250–52, 257, 468
Council on Competitiveness National
    Innovation Summit, 370
Council of Economic Advisers, 230
Cowell, Simon, 356
CPFR, 160
C++, 134
Craigslist, 287
Cray supercomputers, 68
credit histories, 414, 415
Cronkite, Walter, 117
CSFB, 275
C2C (customer-to-customer) transactions, 85
Cuba, 76–77
culture, 420–26; Americanization of,
    477–79; local, preservation of, 478–86
Cummins, 146, 148
curiosity quotient (CQ), 313–15, 371
customer-to-customer (C2C) transactions, 85
Customs Service, U.S., 170
Czech Republic, 415

Daily News and Analysis, 312
DaimlerChrysler, 147
Daley-Harris, Sam, 494

Dallas Mavericks, 120
Dalrymple, Theodore, 562
Darbee, Peter, 579
Darfon, 583
Darfur, 492
Darwin, Charles, 357
Das, Tarun, 53
data-entry businesses, 497–500
David, Paul A., 206
Davidson, Malcolm, 356–57
Davis, Shannon, 40–41
Davis, Vicki, 501–3
Davos World Economic Forum (1999),
    71–72, 487
Dean, Howard, 119, 504–5
Death of a Salesman (Miller), 257, 279
Degner, Alan, 241
Dell, Michael, 299, 418, 583, 587
Dell Computer, 22, 34, 140, 155, 243–44,
    275, 288, 292, 418, 510, 580–88, 596, 629;
    Merge facility, 584; order management
    system, 580–81; socially responsible
    manufacturing practices of, 510–11;
    supplier logistics centers (SLCs), 581
Deloitte Consulting, 240
Delta Airlines, 25, 27, 591, 592
Delta Electronics, 583
DeMillo, Rich, 327–29
DeMint, Jim, 330
Democratic Party, 230, 241, 252, 258, 390,
    394, 448, 504–5
Deng Xiaoping, 138, 139, 409–10
Denmark, 415
deregulation, 252
desegregation, 341
DHC, 34
DHL, 449–50
Diamond, Jared, 571
Dictionary.com, 122
Digital Divide Data, 498–501
digital technology, 56, 58, 69–70, 187, 188
digital photography, 189, 298–90, 471–72
Dillon, Sam, 347
Discovery Times, 5, 263
disease, 538–46
disempowerment, 546–55
Disney Corporation, 77–78
DoCoMo, 195–97
Doerr, John, 62, 65, 77, 287, 379
Doing Business in 2004 (IFC), 413–14, 416
Dollar, David, 410
Dominican Republic, 415
Donaldson Company, Inc., 276

dot-com boom and bust, 70–72, 93, 126, 132, 133, 219, 228, 327, 451, 456
Dow Jones, 18
Drake, Jack, 283
DreamWorks SKG, 192–93
Dropload, 502
DSL, 303
Dubai, 411, 422, 426, 451
Duke University, Master of Engineering Management Program, 347–48
Dunn, Debra, 511
Dutkiewicz, Rafal, 359

East Germany, 52; see also Berlin Wall, fall of
East Timor, 602
eBay, 47, 74, 85, 89, 171, 238, 303, 483, 619–22
Eckroth, Joseph R., Jr., 155–56
e-commerce, 85–86, 269, 593–94
ecommerce-guide.com, 85
Economist, The, 271, 573, 627
Edison, Thomas, 61
eDonkey, 191
education, 212–13, 308–9, 313, 323–29, 343, 349–61, 365–66, 386–88, 408, 419, 430; collaboration in, 329, 501–3; curiosity and passion for, 313–15; instant messaging and, 521–23; in liberal arts, 316–20; lifelong, 383, 388–90; in mathematics, 302; parenting and, 394–98
Education, U.S. Department of, 353, 354
Education Week, 212, 349
Egypt, 403–6, 426–27, 487, 622, 623
Ehlers, Vern, 362–63
Einstein, Albert, 441
El-Adidy, Lamees, 404–5
Electric Boat, 20
Electronic Business Asia magazine, 589
Electronic Data Systems Corporation (EDS), 288–93; Systems Management Center (SMC), 291, 295
Electronics Industry Code of Conduct, 511
Ellsworth, John, 255
Ellsworth, Justin M., 255
Elpida, 582
El Salvador, 415
e-mail, 79–83, 119, 519, 528
Emanuel, Rahm, 252–53
employability, 383–90; see also jobs
employment laws, 333, 383–84, 412, 416
empowerment, 58, 92, 482, 541; education and, 343

E. M. Warburg, Pincus & Company, 74
Encarta, 94, 122
Encyclopedia Britannica, 122
Endeavor, 495–96
End of History and the Last Man, The (Fukuyama), 429
End of Runway Services, 174
Energy, U.S. Department of, 362
energy consumption, 297, 570–79; social entrepreneurship and, 490–91
energy independence, 382
Engels, Friedrich, 233–35
engineers, 217; education of, 324–26, 352, 361, 419; U.S. shortage of, 343–48
Enron, 229, 332, 465
environment, 478, 508–11; activists and, 490–92, 510, 512–14; energy consumption and, 570–73, 575–69; middle-class jobs and, 297
Environmental Defense, 490
Epson, 3
Erdogan, Recept Tayyip, 623
Eriksen Translations Inc., 191
Ernst & Young, 192, 444
Eskew, Mike, 170, 173–75
ESPN, 338
Estée Lauder, 89
Ethernet, 78
ethics, corporate, 334–35, 465–67
Ethiopia, 414
E*Trade, 107, 393, 455, 456
European Community, 417
European Organization for Nuclear Research, 60
European Union (EU), 54, 142, 417
Evoca, 502
Excel, 322
explainers, 288–90
extensible markup language (XML), 83, 86
Exxon, 17
Ezrahi, Yaron, 483, 484, 551, 568, 598

Facebook, 118, 523, 528
Face the Nation, 45
fascism, 558
Fast Company, 113–16
fax machines, 56–58
fclimo.hu, 443
Featherstone, Liza, 252
Federal Bureau of Investigation (FBI), 390
Federal Express, 62, 148, 167, 449, 450
Federal-Mogul Corporation, 145
Federal Reserve, 143

Feinstein, John, 338–39
Ferdinand, King of Spain, 4
Ferreyros, Alfredo, 443
Fertik, Michael, 529
fiber-optic cable, 56, 72–76, 126–28, 132, 187, 189, 207, 226, 231
file-sharing technology, 190–91
file transfer protocols (FTP), 67, 498
financial services, online, 322, 455–57
Financial Times, 47, 105, 283, 487, 506
Finland, 364, 416
Fiorina, Carly, 187, 207–8, 232
Firefox, 111
Fischer, Stanley, 629
Flat Classroom Project, 502–3
Flextronics, 511
Flickr, 492, 523
Florida Today, 343
Food and Drug Administration (FDA), 252–53, 286
football, 120–21
footprints, electronic, 184, 528–29
Forbes, 425, 624
Ford, Henry, 91
Ford, Rollin, 159–62
Ford Motor Company, 172
Foreign Affairs, 363, 626–27
Forrester Research, Inc., 40
Fortune 500 corporations, 386, 446
Foster, Dick, 332, 333
Foxconn, 582, 583
Foxwoods, 20
Frachon, 516
Fractal Graphics, 115
Fractint, 98
France, 285–86, 364, 407, 417, 418, 487, 515–16
Frankfurter Allgemeine Seitung, 403
Franklin, Benjamin, 521
Franklin, James M., 115
FreeBSD, 486
Freedom Forum First Amendment Center, 123
Freedom House, 559, 627
freelancers, 191, 303, 446, 470
Freeman, Howard, 289–90
Freeman, Richard B., 212
free software movement, 95, 105–7, 219
free trade, 4, 23–65, 569; see also North American Free Trade Agreement
French Revolution, 625
Friendster, 523
FTP (file transfer protocol), 67, 498

Fudan University, 335–36
Fujitsu, 583
Fukushima, Glen, 247
Fukuyama, Francis, 429
Furman, Jason, 251
Furst, Merrick, 327–29
futurists, 288

Gabr, Mohammed Shafik, 487
Gagarin, Yuri, 377
Ganguly, Deepak, 481–82
Gardels, Nathan, 487
Gartner Group, 293
Gates, Bill, 57, 59, 71–72, 225, 258, 365, 379, 399, 453, 540–44, 557
GeekCorps, 107
G-8 industrialized nations, 214, 548, 550
Gemtek, 583
General Electric (GE), 6, 30, 34, 118, 128–29, 133, 209, 591, 592, 595
General Motors (GM), 147, 243, 432
General Public License (GPL), 106
geogreenism, 577–79
George III, King of England, 521
George Washington University, 449
Georgia Institute of Technology, 324–29, 367, 371; College of Computing, 327–28
Germany, 246, 333, 403, 418–19, 430, 449, 452, 459, 460, 515, 568, 582; culture of, 425; education in, 347, 359; GDP of, 417; industrialization and modernization of, 558; internship applicants from, 286; radicals in, 559–60; see also Berlin Wall, fall of
Gerstner, Lou, 381
Ghana, 415
Ghandour, Ali, 449
Ghandour, Fadi, 449–54, 457, 460
Gimp, 107
Glaser, Mark, 118
Glass, David, 157–60
Glenn, John, 344
Global Competitiveness Report, 431–32
Global Crossing, 74, 128
Global Distribution Alliance, 452
Global Edge, 29
Global Insight, 276
Global Viewpoint magazine, 487
global warming, 382
glocalization, 420–26
Glocer, Tom, 17–20
GNU, 106
Goldcorp Challenge, 113–16

Goldin, Claudia, 387
Goldman Sachs, 3, 128, 300
Goodger, Ben, 111–12
Goodman, Allan E., 331
Goodman, Sara, 522
Google, 6, 47, 71, 90, 176–85, 219, 229, 237, 248, 269, 271, 272, 287–88, 301, 332, 372, 446, 482, 550, 523, 528, 529; in China, 449; Earth, 506–8; Video, 502; YouTube purchased by, 119
Gopalakrishnan, S. "Kris," 288
Gorbachev, Mikhail, 55, 409
Gore, Al, 311, 312
Gorman, Maya, 31
governance, 343, 408–9; corporate, 323, 465–67
Government Accounting Office (GAO), 344
GO Web server, 102
GPS (global positioning system), 515
Grace T.H.W. Group, 589
Grameen Bank, 493–95
Grand Challenges in Global Health, 542–43
Granofsky, Rena, 160–61
graphic facilitation, 553
Great Depression, 9
Great Society, 374, 375
Green Building Council, 513
Green New Deal, 578–79
Greer, Bill, 304–7
Greer, Jill, 469, 533
Greer, Ken, 257, 469–74, 533
Growing Stars, 43
Grunwald Associates, 119
Guardian, 118
Guatemala, 415
gun laws, 533–34
Gutenberg, Johann, 49, 56

Hadjimichael, Bita, 412
Haifa University, 598
Haiti, 415, 419
Hamad bin Issa al-Khalifa, King of Bahrain, 507
Hamas, 600, 601
Hamburg-Harburg, Technical University of, 559
Hammer, Michael, 250, 616
Hanafin, Mary, 419
Hang Zhou, 192
Hannstar Display, 583
Haque, Promod, 134, 534

Harney, Mary, 417
Harrison, Lawrence E., 421
Harvard University, 54, 127, 212, 214, 224, 233, 247, 301, 383, 387, 391, 496, 603; Business School, 154, 381, 446; Crimson, 497–98
Hastert, Dennis, 230
health care, 250, 283; portability of benefits, 383–87; poverty and lack of, 274, 538–44
HealthScribe, 130
Hebrew University, 551
Helsinki, University of, 106
Herbert, Bob, 395
Heritage Foundation, 146
Hewlett-Packard (HP), 3, 34, 187, 207–8, 232, 243, 275, 327, 625; Bank of India and, 462–64; patents registered by, 561; PocketPC, 185; poverty alleviation collaboration of, 553–55; socially responsible manufacturing practices of, 510–11; UPS and, 169, 170; videoconferencing suite designed by, 193; Wal-Mart and, 152
Heymath.com, 275
Higglytown Heroes (TV series), 78–79
high concept, high touch abilities, 320–23
Hill & Knowlton, 208, 469
Hindu, The (newspaper), 551
Hindus, 53, 425, 480, 623, 628
Hindustan Aeronautics, 227
Hispanics, 353
Hitachi, 583
Hitler, Adolf, 444, 558
HIV-AIDS, 538–40
Ho Chi Minh, 559
Hockenstein, Jeremy, 496–501
Holmes, Steve, 169
Homeland Security, U.S. Department of, 347, 390
homesourcing, 37–38
Honeywell, 26
Hong Kong, 6, 358, 415; University of, 121
horizontalization, 206–10
HotWired, 100
Houston Rockets, 120, 485
HOW (Seidman), 467
Howard Hughes Foundation, 335
Howstuffworks.com, 190
HTML (hypertext markup language), 62, 67, 82, 84
HTTP (Hyper Text Transfer Protocol), 62, 67, 82, 84
Hubbert, Jürgen, 147

human genome, mapping of, 287
Hungary, 442–45, 607–8
Hunter, Dick, 581, 583–84
Hyatt, 89
hypertext markup language, see HTML
Hyper Text Transfer Protocol, see HTTP
Hyten, Scott, 77–79

IAYF (information at your fingertips), 57
IBM, 3, 59, 80, 83, 86, 89, 93, 193, 288,
    290, 303, 313, 318, 338, 371, 447, 457,
    463, 609; business consulting services of,
    461–62; community-developed software
    and, 97, 108, 254; India and, 30, 129;
    Netscape and, 66, 69; open-sourcing
    and, 93–94, 102–4; PCs, 55–58; sale of
    Personal Computing Division by, 244–45;
    socially responsible manufacturing
    practices of, 510–11; Wikipedia's
    references to, 124
ideation, 305
Idei, Nobuyuki, 230
Illinois, University of, 64, 100
Illustrator, 305
immigrants, 390, 411, 425; educational
    attainment of, 386
InDCjournal.com, 45
India, 3, 8, 11–32, 113, 126–31, 243, 279,
    312, 321, 339, 365, 371, 399, 410, 433,
    446, 622–26; accounting in, 12–15; Bank
    of, 462–64; bankruptcy in, 414, 416;
    capital markets in, 333; caste system in,
    278; Center for Policy Research, 551;
    China and, 379; culture of, 422, 425,
    479–82; customer call centers in, 5,
    21–28, 42, 263, 299, 355, 376, 389,
    428–29, 461, 593–94; delivery firms in,
    450; disease in, 540; economic reforms
    in, 409, 434–37; education in, 212–13,
    319–20, 347–48, 355, 397, 430; energy
    consumption in, 297, 574–76, 578;
    environmental issues in, 297; and fall of
    Berlin Wall, 53–54; fiber-optic cable
    connecting U.S. and, 74, 126–29, 131–33;
    homesourcing versus outsourcing to, 38;
    immigrants from, 390; Indiana and,
    240–43; innovation in, 216–17, 273–75;
    Institutes of Management, 127; Institutes
    of Technology (IIT), 127–28, 136;
    intangibles of economic development
    in, 426–27; internships in, 285–86; job
    competition with, 278, 282, 291, 296, 327;
    manufacturing in, 273, 583; medical

transcription in, 130–31; middle class in,
    275, 538, 550; offshoring to, 583; online
    tutoring in, 42–43; opening of, 58; open-
    sourcing in, 107; outsourcing from,
    443–45; Pakistan and, 585, 591–95;
    personal remote assistants in, 31–32;
    politics in, 551–52; poverty in, 274, 410,
    436, 437, 538–39, 552–53; radiologists in,
    16; R&D in, 30; Reuters in, 17–20; Rolls-
    Royce in, 459, 460; rural population of,
    538, 539, 542, 547, 553–55; social
    entrepreneurs and, 496–98; software
    development in, 5, 30, 35, 128–30;
    synthesizing in, 288; trade policy and,
    150, 266, 267, 270–77; and Y2K computer
    crisis, 131–36; zippies in, 215–23
India's Globalization (Nayar), 434–37
Indonesia, 311, 413–14, 422, 545, 555, 576,
    588, 622
Industrial Revolution, 9, 49, 234, 420
Infineon, 582
influenza pandemics, 545–46
Infocus Tech, 611, 612
information at your fingertips (IAYF), 57
in-forming, 176–85, 187, 198, 204
Infosys, 5–7, 28, 132, 135, 167, 263, 264,
    271, 280, 286, 288, 300, 330
infrastructure, 343, 363–65, 408
innovation, 216, 273–75, 293, 331, 340, 342;
    collaborative, 110, 112–16, 254–55, 458,
    504–5; education and, 343, 365, 368–72;
    funding of, 332–33; trust and, 334
insolvency, resolution of, 416
in-sourcing, 167–75, 187, 197–98, 204
instant messaging (IM), 421–23
Institute of International Education, 213,
    331, 346
Institute of Medicine, 351
Intel, 29, 30, 107, 211, 271, 361, 371,
    418, 582; International Science and
    Engineering Fair, 349; Itanium processor,
    189; Science Talent Search, 349
intellectual commons, 96–97
intellectual property protection, 253–55,
    333, 343
intelligent design, 357
International Economy, The, 431
International Finance Corporation (IFC),
    412–17
International Herald Tribune, 487, 589
International Labor Organization (ILO),
    562
International Math Olympiad, 349

International Monetary Fund (IMF), 214, 548, 550
International Telecommunications Union (ITU), 364
Internet, 16, 17, 56–58, 60–62, 78–79, 92, 201, 207, 231, 236, 237, 239, 299, 346, 351, 403, 482, 516, 519, 536; activism and, 489, 491, 492, 506–8; Arabs and access to, 565; banking on, 463; broadband access to, 363–64; browsers, 60, 62–72, 77; in China, 35, 151, 366, 369; digitization and, 70–71, 187–88; and Electronics Industry Code of Conduct, 511; empowerment through, 58, 541; fiber-optic cables and, 73–76, 131; human contact versus, 256; in India, 218–19, 274; in Jordan, 453, 627; mathematicians and, 301; parcel delivery management and tracking on, 171, 173, 174, 453; phone calls via, 191–92, 214, 453, 479; real estate sales on, 237–38; routers for, 419; search engines, 176–85, 271–73, 287 (see also Google); small businesses and, 442–47; social downsides of, 523–30; social entrepreneurship and, 500–501; sports and, 120–21; 338; synthesizing tools on, 287–88; terrorist use of, 596–604, 611; total global usage of, 229; tutoring via, 42–43; uploading to, 93–126; wireless connectivity to, 185–87, 194–97; worker training programs on, 390; work flow and, 78–89; see also dot-com boom and bust; specific companies
Internet Engineering Task Force, 101
internetnews.com, 89
interpersonal skills, 299
Iran, 382, 390, 450, 474, 500, 576, 589, 622, 627
Iran-Iraq War, 450
Iraq, 38–40, 118, 569, 589, 626; U.S. war in, 210, 229, 255, 296, 450, 549, 565, 597, 601, 602, 614, 622
Ireland, 140, 243, 417–20, 433, 437, 581, 583
Isabella, Queen of Spain, 4
Islam, see Muslims
Islamic Studies and Research Center, 564
Islamists, 557, 560, 597
Islamo-Leninists, 559–60, 565–66, 595
Israel, 16, 311, 364, 371, 390, 483, 567, 585, 598; Arab conflict with, 450, 508, 556, 569, 597

Italy, 275, 446, 459, 550, 560
Ive, Jonathan, 458

Jackson, Janet, 182
Jackson, Jesse, 396–97
Jackson, Shirley Ann, 342–43, 399
JadooWorks, 481–82
Jahjah, Dyab Abou, 567
Janaagraha, 552
Japan, 6, 122, 164, 177, 211, 227, 245, 277, 363, 366, 407, 429, 459, 480, 481, 576, 585; American Chamber of Commerce in, 247; automobile industry in, 29; bankruptcy in, 416; broadband Internet access in, 364; China and, 32–36, 143, 574, 588–89; culture of, 422, 425; education in, 365; energy consumption in, 571, 573, 574; External Trade Organization (JETRO), 143, 588; in global supply chains, 582, 588, 589; immigrants from, 390; offshoring by, 266, 582–83; post–World War II, 53, 150, 269–70; radicals in, 560; research and development in, 363; Wal-Mart and, 165–66; wireless technology in, 185–86, 195–97; work flow to, 82
Jarrett, James, 418
Java, 134
JavaScript, 87
J.C. Penney, 141
J.C. Williams Group Ltd., 160
JetBlue Airways Corporation, 36–38, 609
Jet Propulsion Laboratory, 98
Jews, 239, 311, 596, 602, 623, 628
Jiang Mianheng, 589
Jiang Zemin, 589
Jihad.com, 312
jobs, 273; mass-production, 361; middle-class, 282–307
Jobs, Steve, 55, 59, 316–18, 399, 458
Jockey International, 168–69
John, Elton, 282
John, Princeton, 42–43
John, Priscilla, 43
Johns Hopkins University, 16, 136, 187–88, 365, 366, 390, 628
Johnson, Charles, 117
Johnson, Lyndon B., 374
Johnson, Paul, 424–25
Joint Chiefs of Staff, 38
Jordan, 411, 449–54, 500, 627–28
Jordan, Michael, 282
JPEG, 85

Judaism, see Jews
Juhaiman movement, 424
Jurvetson, Steve, 297
Juster, Ken, 88, 89
just-in-time supply chain, 160, 545

Kahn, Bob, 61
Kai Fu Li, 181, 367–68
Kalbag, Sachin, 312
Kanagawa, Treaty of (1854), 165
Kannan, P. V., 215–16, 358
Karatnycky, Adrian, 559
Kasparov, Garry, 322
Katz, Larry, 387
Kazaa, 191
Kellner, Peter, 495
Kelly, Kevin, 95–96, 205
Kennedy, John F., 123, 341, 343, 377, 382, 388, 399, 505
Kennedy, Robert F., 123
Kernan, Joe, 241
Kerry, John, 251
Khalifa family, 506
Khalsa, Gurujot Singh, 131
Khomeini, Ayatollah, 568
Khosla, Vinod, 127
Khrushchev, Nikita, 376
Kirshnakumar, N., 592
Kiuchi, Masao, 166
Klamath Communications, 209
Klausner, Rick, 543
Klein, Michael, 412
Kleiner Perkins Caulfield & Byers, 62
Kletzer, Lori, 391–93
Kmart, 159, 468
Knight, Bob, 339
Koenig, Josh, 119
Kohlberg Kravis Roberts, 490
Konica Minolta Technologies, 202
Koo, Richard C., 358
Koon, Tracy, 371–72
Korea, see North Korea; South Korea
Kraemer, Harry, Jr., 408
Kray, Art, 410
Krupp, Fred, 490–91
Kuehn, Kurt, 171
Kulkarni, Ashish, 481
Kulkarni, Vivek, 31–32, 593
Kurtz, Howard, 117
Kuwait, 445–46, 567

labor markets, flexibility of, 333, 383, 418–29
Landes, David, 421–23

Landor Associates, 209
Laos, 498–99, 501
Law, Lalita, 538–39
Lawrence, Robert, 383, 391
Laytonsville Elementary School, 315
leadership, 343, 379–82
Lebanon, 340, 449, 479, 489
LEED (Leadership in Energy and Environmental Design), 513
left-brain skills, 320–23
Leighton, Tom, 301
Lenin, V. I., 558, 559
Leninists, Islamic, see Islamo-Leninists
Lenovo, 244–45
Leonard, Andrew, 100, 102
Leonardo da Vinci, 316
Leopold, Aldo, 576
leveraging, 290–93
Levin, Richard C., 335
Levine, Joshua S., 393
Levitt, Arthur, 619
Lexis/Nexis, 332
Lexus and the Olive Tree, The (Friedman), 9, 10, 190, 586
LG.Philips LCD, 583
liberal arts, 316–20
lifetime employability, 381–90
Lih, Andrew, 121–22
Lindsay, Julie, 501–3
Linux, 105–8, 111, 355
Linux Journal, 313
Litan, Robert E., 391–93
Lite-Form, 445
Liteon, 583
literacy, 353–54
Lithuania, 338
Lloyd, Mark, 364
local, globalization of, 477–86
localized jobs, 282, 298–304
London Daily Telegraph, 574
London Spectator, 562
Longitudes 04, 154
Los Angeles Lakers, 125
Los Angeles Police Department, 567
Los Angeles Times, 38
Loughry, Marcia, 288–89, 294–97
LRN, 334, 465–67
Lu, Justin, 89
Lucent Technologies, 29, 74, 135–36, 189
Luft, Gai, 577
lump of labor theory, 266
Luxembourg, 417
Lynx, 100

Ma, Mary, 245
Macedonia, 416
macroeconomic reform, 408–10, 415
Madden, Mark, 44
Madonna, 282
Mahon, Karen, 255
Mail Boxes, Etc., 170
malaria, 538, 541
Malaysia, 122, 140, 243, 357, 422, 446, 461,
    563, 576, 581–85, 588, 601, 611
Mali, 106, 108
Mallaby, Sebastian, 251
Mandelbaum, Michael, 136, 376, 382, 628,
    629
Mankiw, N. Gregory, 230
Manpower Development and Training
    program, 377
Mao Zedong, 139, 424, 602
Maqbool Bin Ali Sultan, 44
Marshall, Will, 384–85
Marshall Plan, 53
Martin, Charles M., 141
Marx, Karl, 233–36, 358–59
Marx, Tzvi, 604
Marxism-Leninism, 558, 560
mash-ups, 287
Massachusetts Institute of Technology
    (MIT), 106, 115, 136, 152, 301, 331, 341,
    355, 369, 398
mathematicians, 300–302
Mattel Inc., 155
Maxim magazine, 306
McCaw Cellular, 64
McColly Real Estate, 237
McCool, Rob, 100
McCue, Mike, 74–75
McDonald's Corporation, 40–42, 226, 305,
    508–11, 548, 553, 586, 590–91, 593
McEwen, Rob, 113–16
McGill University, 434
McGregor, James, 337
MCI, 74
McKinsey & Company, 32, 332, 496–97
McKinsey Quarterly, 275, 432
Medicaid, 252, 383
Medicare, 383
Medline, 188
Meghna, C. M., 24
Mehta, Pratap Bhanu, 551
mentoring, entrepreneurial, 495–96
Mercedes Car Group, 147
Merrill Lynch, 114, 615
Messman, Jack, 105

Mexico, 21, 138, 140, 164, 271, 394, 403–4,
    407, 411, 415, 583; Center of Research for
    Development, 433; Central Bank of, 404;
    economic reforms in, 408–9; intangibles
    of economic development in, 426–33
microcredit, 493–94
micromultinationals, 461
Microsoft, 3, 56, 57, 71, 80, 82, 87, 93,
    94, 189, 225, 253, 269, 275, 365, 629;
    Business Web and, 90, 91; in China, 34,
    181, 367–70; community-developed
    software and, 97, 107–12; Dell and, 584;
    headquarters of, 372; in India, 22,
    216–17; Internet Explorer, 68, 70, 111;
    in Jordan, 453; Moviemaker, 478, 485;
    MSN, 95; MSN Search, 179, 184, 528;
    Office, 90, 107, 109, 219; and open-
    sourcing, 93–94, 107, 111, 378; Research
    Asia, 367–69; search engine optimizing
    for, 271, 272; Windows, 29, 55–57, 60,
    68, 77, 80, 92, 107, 108, 122, 187, 219,
    264, 296, 318, 485; Word, 82, 83, 110,
    219; Xbox, 369
middle class, 275, 374–76, 548, 550, 586;
    jobs for, 282–307
Mikeladze family, 356–57
Miller, George, 390
MindTree, 465–67, 592
mining, 113–16
Minneapolis Star Tribune, 276
Minnesota, University of, School of Public
    Health, 545
Minnesota Conceal and Carry Law,
    533–34
Minow, Nell, 74
MIPS (millions of instructions per second),
    188
Mitsubishi, 227
Mitsuishi, Tamon, 195–96
Mobility, 583
modeling, 304
modems, 56–58
Modern Times (movie), 299
Moguls, 422
Mohammad, Mahathir, 563
Mohammed, Khalid Sheikh, 609–10
Mohegan Sun, 20
Monday Morning, 238
Monde, Le, 516
Mondragon, 359
Mongolia, 500
Monier, Louis, 47
Montenegro, 416

Moore's Law, 519
More magazine, 306
Morgan Stanley, 69, 143
Mormons, 37, 612
Morocco, 411, 555
morphing, 306
Morris Air, 37, 612
Mosaic Web browser, 64, 76, 97
Motorola, 195, 583
MOUSE.org, 504
Moussaoui, Zacarias, 611–12
Mozilla, 111
MphasiS, 12, 320, 399
MP3 player, 45–46, 119
MRIs, 16
MSI, 582
MSNBC.com, 118
M-System, 583
Muhammad, 403, 560–61
Mullis, Ina, 350–51
multinational corporations, 243–46, 444,
    461, 489; see also specific companies
multipurpose devices, 202
Mundie, Craig J., 56–59, 82–83, 93, 109,
    189, 253, 364–65
Munteanu, Andrei, 350
Murrow, Edward R., 117
Music for America, 119
Muslims, 9, 59, 239, 311, 404–5, 422–25,
    506, 555–70, 596, 611, 630; in India, 422,
    622–25, 630; oil and, 627–29; terrorists,
    556–61, 569–70 (see also al-Qaeda)
Mussolini, Benito, 558
Myers, Gen. Richard, 38
MySpace, 502, 503, 523, 524, 525, 527, 528
MySQL, 486

Naipaul, V. S., 320
Namitha, Koyampurath, 42–43
Nanya, 582
Napster, 76, 190
Naqvi, Mujteba, 580
Nasdaq, 244, 332, 451, 629
Nation, The, 119, 505
National Academy of Engineering, 351
National Academy of Sciences, 362
National Aeronautics and Space
    Administration (NASA), 291, 343–44
National Assessment of Adult Literacy, 353
National Association of Realtors, 348
National Basketball Association (NBA), 125,
    337–39, 485
National Cancer Institute, 543

National Center for Supercomputing
    Applications (NCSA), 64, 100
National Center on Education and the
    Economy, 316, 359
National Commission on Mathematics and
    Science Teaching for the Twenty-first
    Century, 344
National Enquirer, 526
National Football League (NFL), 120–21
National Foundation for American Policy,
    349
National Guard, 45, 46, 117
National Innovation Initiative (NII), 370
National Institutes of Health (NIH), 282,
    335
National Journal, 364
National Review, 535, 559
National Science Board (NSB), 344–47
National Science Foundation (NSF), 229,
    343, 362, 380
National Security Agency, 301
NATO, 39
Natural Resources Defense Council
    (NRDC), 490, 512–13, 579
Naval Historical Center, 165
navigational skills, 310–13
Navy, U.S., 20, 573
Nazis, 560
Nayar, Baldev Raj, 434–37
NBC, 45, 123; Nightly News, 521
NEC, 583
Neeleman, David, 37–38, 609, 612–13
Nehru, Jawaharlal, 53, 127
Neland, Glenn E., 588–89
NeoIT, 625
neo-Nazis, 483
Netherlands, 9, 122, 416, 487
NetMeeting, 219
Netscape, 62–70, 76, 77, 79, 80, 94, 111,
    174, 187, 204, 205, 269
New Deal, 371; Green, 578–79
New Frontier, 375
newspapers: impact of Internet on, 237; see
    also specific newspapers
Newsweek, 122
New Yorker, The, 443
New York Review of Books, The, 95
New York Stock Exchange (NYSE), 332, 372
New York Times, The, 46, 76–77, 90, 117,
    125, 185, 198, 250, 304, 313, 347, 353,
    393, 403, 490, 614–15; Beijing Bureau,
    535; Book Review, 95; Magazine, 120,
    511–12; Washington Bureau, 280

New York University, 251
New Zealand, 415, 446, 536
Nickelodeon magazine, 306
Nielsen/NetRatings, 229
Nieman Marcus, 468
Nigeria, 415, 555, 626
Nike, 168, 169
Nikon, 174
Nilekani, Nandan, 4–8, 11, 28, 167, 280,
    281, 286, 300, 330, 448, 595, 613
9/11, 8, 229, 239, 345, 549, 556, 564, 599,
    601, 607–19, 622, 628; airlines and, 393;
    Bush urges consumption after, 340;
    exodus from New York following, 602–3;
    Islamo-Leninism and, 559, 565; middle-
    class Arabs and, 566; response of ordinary
    people to challenge of, 78; visa issuance
    after, 347
Nixon, Richard M., 382, 505
Nobel Prize, 308, 320, 493, 398
Nokia, 207
Nomura Research Institute, 358
non-governmental organizations (NGOs),
    490–91, 501, 499, 550–55
Nordstrom, 468
North American Free Trade Agreement
    (NAFTA), 230, 394, 404, 407, 427, 428,
    431, 433
North Carolina Agricultural and Technical
    State University, 610
North Korea, 375, 410, 585, 586, 589
North Texas, University of, 294
Northwest Venture Partners, 134, 534
Norton Utilities, 584
Norway, 364, 415
Norwegian School of Management, 302
Novell, 80, 105; Netware, 295
Nuclear Regulatory Commission, 341
Nuclear Terrorism (Allison), 603
nuclear weapons, 585, 591; terrorists and,
    588–603

O'Bannon, Frank, 241
Office Depot, 509
offshoring, 137–51, 187, 264,
    276–77
Ogilvy & Mather, 208
Ohio Pilot Store, 611
Ohio State University, 140
Ohmae, Kenichi, 32–33, 140
oil, 570–78, 626–29
O'Keefe, Sean, 344
Oklahoma, University of, 120

Oklahoma Center for the Advancement of
    Science and Technology (OCAST),
    331–32
Old Left, 549
"old middle" jobs, 282
Olympic Games, 294, 326, 337–39
Oman, 44, 415
openknowledge.org, 105
OpenOffice.org, 107–9
open protocols, 67
open-sourcing, 94, 238, 485; *see also*
    community-developed software
Opsware Inc., 76, 270
Oracle, 94
orchestration, 285–87
Oregon, University of, 120
O'Reilly, Tim, 125
Organization for Economic Co-operation
    and Development (OECD), 347
Organization of Petroleum Exporting
    Countries (OPEC), 575
Ortiz, Guillermo, 404
Osterholm, Michael T., 545–46
O'Sullivan, Fran, 245
Otellini, Paul, 271
Outlook, 219
Outlook magazine, 215
outsourcing, 38, 40, 187, 264, 321–22, 446,
    454, 463; of business process, 290–93; to
    Cambodia, 496–500; to China, 32–36,
    136, 221, 280, 336–37; collaboration in,
    286; digital technology and, 473; for
    growth, 464–67; to India, 3–8, 12–32, 35,
    38, 42–43, 126–36, 218–23, 266, 354,
    388, 592–93; of middle-class jobs, 282; to
    past, 280; to Russia, 226–28; to Uruguay,
    443–45
Oxford University, 224
Ozzie, Ray, 87, 90

Pacific Design, 583
Pacific Gas & Electric, 579
Page, Larry, 179
Paine, Thomas, 521
Paine Webber, 143
Pakistan, 53, 59, 410, 415, 427, 450, 500,
    585, 589, 591–94, 609, 610, 622–25;
    Islamist militants in, 597
Palestinians, 454, 556, 597
Palmer, Doug, 445–46
Palmisano, Sam, 254–55, 371
PalmPilot, 107, 184, 194, 518
Panama, 414, 416

pandemics, 544–46
Pan Yue, 577
Papa John's pizza, 168
parenting, 394–99
passion quotient (PQ), 313–15, 371
Pasteur, Louis, 136
patents, 30, 254, 363, 561
Paul, Vivek, 30, 132, 276–79, 333, 461, 547, 591–93
PayPal, 85–86, 119, 171, 583
PCs, 11, 66–70, 130, 131, 181, 189, 217, 254, 294, 300, 303, 318; in China, 245; in India, 219; Internet and, 57, 60, 64, 70, 77, 80, 207; introduction of, 55, 90, 92; modeling on, 304; networking of, 58; Windows-enabled, 55–57; wireless, 185–86; work flow and, 79–81, 84, 88, 187, 203
Pearl, Danny, 597
Pearlstein, Steven, 358–59
Peking University, 335
pensions, 383–84
Pentagon, 39
people skills, 285–87
Perella Weinberg Partners, 490
Perez, Carlota, 286, 297
Perkowski, Jack, 137, 139, 143–48
Perot, Ross, 290
Perry, Commodore Matthew Calbraith, 165, 166
personal computers, see PCs
personaldemocracy.com, 505
personal digital assistants (PDAs), 154, 188, 191, 192; see also PalmPilot
personalizing, 298–99
personal remote assistants, 31–32
Peru, 413, 416, 443, 520
Pfizer, 20
pharmaceutical industry, 252–53
Philippines, 415, 461, 582, 583, 588
photography, 289, 470–71; digital, 289–90, 471–74
PHP, 486
Physical Review, 363
Pickering, Thomas R., 226–28
Pink, Daniel, 320–23
Piusten, Bessy, 43
Pizza Hut, 3
Playboy magazine, 163
Plow & Hearth, 171
podcasting, 94, 96, 119, 484–86, 492, 521, 523
Poland, 358, 359

politics, electoral, 504–5
Politics of Diplomacy, The (Baker), 52
Pol Pot, 559
Ponemon Institute, 529
POP, 67
populism, 547–48, 551–52
Portman, Rob, 43
Portugal, 4, 416
postponement business strategy, 154–55
poverty, 274, 409, 412–13, 415, 538–44; alleviation of, 434, 436, 437, 493–94, 551–55
Powell, Colin, 248–49, 595
Powers, Pat, 149
PQ, 313–15, 371
Premji, Azim, 624
Price, Jo Ann, 395
Prickett, Glenn, 509, 510, 576
Princeton University, 280, 299
privacy, loss of, 184
Private Sector in Development, The (Klein and Hadjmichael), 412
Procter & Gamble, 162, 444
productivity, 207–9; outsourcing and, 354, 412
Program for International Student Assessment, 351
Progressive Policy Institute (PPI), 384–86
Pro-Growth Progressive, The (Sperling), 294
property rights, 416
protectionism, 265, 330, 446, 448
Protime Consulting, 89
Puerto Rico, 338

Qatar, 39, 411, 564, 566
QSRweb.com, 41
Quanta, 582
Quark, 305
Qusti, Raid, 424
Qwest, 190

Rabi, Isidor I., 308
Raby, Art, 237
radio frequency identification microchips (RFID), 161–62, 194
Rainbow/PUSH Coalition & Citizenship Education Fund, 396
Rajan, Raghuram, 275
Raju, B. Ramalinga, 445, 447
Ramanathan, Ramesh, 552
Ramanujam, Srinivasa, 213
Rao, Jaithirth "Jerry," 12–15, 91–92, 132, 370, 399, 422, 593

Rao, Rajesh, 29, 217–23
Rasch, Mark, 529
Rasiej, Andrew, 374, 504–6
RateMyTeachers.com, 119
Rather, Dan, 45, 46
Reagan, Ronald, 55, 59
real estate business on, 237–38
Red Army Faction, 560
Red Brigades, 560
Red Hat, 108
Reed College, 316–18
Reference.com, 123
reform, economic, 408–20, 429, 432,
   434–37; culture and, 420–26
renewable energy, 297
Rensselaer Polytechnic Institute, 340,
   341
Republican Party, 241, 258, 362, 371, 380,
   394, 448, 504, 617
Reputation Defender, 529
research and development (R&D), 29–30,
   109, 460; funding of, 343, 362–63;
   universities and, 330–31
Resilient Enterprise (Sheffi), 154
Reuters, 17–21
Reynolds, Glenn, 47
Reynolds, Jerry, 172
RFID (radio frequency identification
   microchips), 161–62, 194
RFID Journal, 161
Ricardo, David, 263–64, 272–73, 284
Ride, Sally, 557
right-brain skills, 320–23
Robinson, Shane, 193
Rogers, Will, 433
Rolls-Royce, 198, 246–47, 420, 458–60
Romania, 304, 340, 446
Romer, Paul, 203–4, 207, 267, 268, 373,
   387, 441
Rooney, Hilarie, 315
Roosevelt, Franklin D., 505
Rose, John, 198, 246–47, 420, 458–60
Rosen, Daniel H., 431–32
Rosenfeld, Jaeson, 497
Ross, Blake, 111
Rothkopf, David, 48, 280, 617
Rottenberg, Linda, 495
routers, 419
Rove, Karl, 505
Rowling, J. K., 282
Royal Jordanian Airlines, 449
Rozman, Gabriel, 444
RSS, 502

Rubio, Luis, 433
Rumsfeld, Donald, 600
Rushdie, Salman, 567–68
Russia, 30, 104, 126, 164, 211–12, 224, 247,
   248, 266, 371, 461, 548, 603; Chechnya
   and, 600, 601; Communist, see Soviet
   Union; economic reforms in, 408; energy
   consumption in, 297, 575; HP in, 243;
   immigrants from, 390; oil reserves of, 574;
   outsourcing to, 226–27, 355; work flow
   to, 82

Sachs, Jeffrey, 342
Saks Fifth Avenue, 468
Salem, Ali, 564
Salesforce.com, 87–89, 112
Salon.com, 100, 102, 162, 252
Samsonite, 583
Samsung, 582, 583
Samuelson, Paul A., 398
Sandel, Michael J., 233–36, 240
Sanmina-SCI, 511
Santana, Joe, 294
Sanyo, 164, 583
SAP, 34, 112
Sarnoff R&D firm, 30
SARS, 545
Satanic Verses, The (Rushdie), 567–68
Sathini, A., 584
Satyam Computer Services, 445
Saudi Arabia, 59, 258, 564, 610, 622–24;
   culture of, 423–26; oil in, 382, 568, 576,
   626, 627; terrorism in, 565, 569
Saving Free Trade (Lawrence and Litan),
   391
Schacht, Henry, 74, 135–36, 189
Schaltz, James R., 301
Schieffer, Bob, 45, 46, 48
Schiesel, Seth, 125
Schirrmacher, Frank, 403
Schleifer, Abdallah, 560
Schlesinger, David, 20–21
Schmidt, Britney, 314
Schmidt, Eric, 178, 183
Schroeder, Gerhard, 246
Schultz, Howard, 454
Science and Economic Indicators, 344–46
Science Foundation Ireland, 419
scientists: education of, 351–53, 361, 419;
   shortage in U.S. of, 343–47
Scott, H. Lee, Jr., 164
SDI, 583
Seagate, 583

search engines, 176–85, 271; optimizing, 271–73, 287; *see also* Google
Searls, Doc, 313–14
Sears Roebuck & Company, 159, 164
Second Life, 523
Securities and Exchange Commission (SEC), 332, 619, 622
segregation, 341; de facto, 360
Segrest Farms, 169
Seidman, Dov, 334, 465–69, 525, 528–30
Seigenthaler, John, 123–24, 239
Seiyu, 165–67
Selling Women Short (Featherstone), 252
Sen, Amartya, 54, 320
Sengupta, Arijit, 446
SEOs, 272
September 11 terrorist attacks, *see* 9/11
Serbia, 416
Services over the Internet protocol (SoIP), 192
Set America Free Coalition, 577
Severe Acute Respiratory Syndrome (SARS), 545
Sharp, 583
Sheffi, Yossi, 152–55
Shenkar, Oded, 140
Shockley, William, 61–62
Shum, Harry, 368, 369
Siemens, 358; Business Services, 294
Sierra Leone, 416
Sifry, Micah L., 47–48, 119, 125, 505–6
Silicon Graphics, 64
Simon & Schuster, 129
simple mail transfer protocol (SMTP), 67, 81
simple object access protocol (SOAP), 83
Simplo, 583
Simpson, O. J., 567
Singapore, 6, 275, 350, 416, 460, 480, 583, 588
Singh, Dinakar, 128, 244, 375, 426
Singh, Manmohan, 53, 130, 409, 547
SITE Institute, 601
60 Minutes, 45
Skype Technologies, 191–92, 214, 502
Slate magazine, 120
SlideMaster Photo-Imaging, 289
small businesses, 303–4, 442–47
Smart Modular, 583
Smith, Adam, 230
SMS (short message service), 521
SMTP (simple mail transfer protocol), 67, 81

SOAP (simple object access protocol), 83
social activism, 489–92, 504–12
social entrepreneurs, 489–501, 512–14
social networking, 502–3
Social Security, 371, 383
Soh, Felix, 480
SoIP (Services over the Internet protocol), 192
Solectron, 511
Solow, Robert, 206
Somaiah, Nitu, 25
Sony Corporation, 34, 89, 165, 230, 583
Sorbonne, 480
Soto, Hernando de, 413, 416
SourceForge.net, 107
South Africa, 104, 243
South Korea, 34, 213, 345, 358, 445, 446, 481, 561, 582, 583, 585; broadband Internet access in, 364, 374; energy consumption in, 575; in global supply chains, 588; immigrants from, 390
Southwest Airlines, 37, 201–3, 208, 612
Soviet Union, 53, 224, 343, 376; collapse of, 51–55, 59, 212, 409, 538, 549; education in, 212, 213; space program of, 341, 343, 375, 377, 382; *see also* Russia
Spain, 4, 154, 459, 460, 565, 598; Muslim, 425, 569
specialization, 282, 293
Sperling, Gene, 284, 294
Spiegel, Der, 398, 577
Spitzer, Eliot, 19, 332
sports, 120, 125, 303, 337–39, 395
SportsCenter, 338
spreadsheet software, 57
Sputnik, 341, 343, 375, 377
Sri Lanka, 222, 492
SSL, 67
Stallman, Richard, 106
Stanford University, 66, 105, 111, 179, 203, 247, 267, 316–18, 369, 373, 387, 446
Stanton, Jeff, 522
Starbucks, 269, 509, 455
Star Wars movies, 482
State Department, U.S., 248, 347, 591
steel industry, 487
Steinberg, Hattie M., 397
Steiner, Peter, 443
Stengel, Richard, 521
stepforth.com, 82
Stern, Eric, 351–53
Sternad, Ken, 175
Steyn, Mark, 535

Stone, Linda, 516, 520
StopTXU.com, 490
storage devices, 188–90
Straits Times, The, 480
Straw, Jack, 249
Stross, Randall, 111
suburbanization, 360
Sudan, 535, 574, 576
Sundaram, Natarajan, 463
Sunder, Sophie, 25
Sun Microsystems, 68, 94, 108–9, 127
Sunrex, 583
supply chains, 151–66, 204–6, 246, 253,
    584–85; environmental issues and,
    508–11; geopolitics and, 585–93; impact
    of digital technology on, 472; in-sourcing
    and, 165–75, 197–98; localized
    components of, 304; management of,
    458–59; orchestration of, 286; pandemics
    and, 544, 545; for small businesses, 447;
    terrorist, 595–98, 603
Supreme Court, U.S., 341
sustainability, 297, 571
Sutter, John, 113
Suzuki, 274
Swainson, John, 103–4
Sweden, 122, 450
Switzerland, 60, 427
synthesizing, 287–88, 316, 458
Syracuse University, 522
Syria, 415, 427, 589, 623

Taiwan, 243, 345, 351, 358, 363, 427, 461,
    581–83, 588–91
Taliban, 624
Tambopata Research Center, 520
Target, 141, 251, 468
Targus, 583
Tas, Jeroen, 13
Task Force on the Future of American
    Innovation, 362
Tata, Ratan, 274
Tata Consultancy Services Ltd. (TCS), 133,
    215, 240, 443–45
Tata Motors, 274
Tata Steel, 487
tax policies, 343
Taylor Wall & Associates, 115, 116
TCP/IP (transmission control protocol/
    Internet protocol), 67, 82, 84
TCS Iberoamerica, 444
Teac, 583
technological determinism, 535–36

Technorati.com, 118, 523
TechRepublic.com, 293–94
Telecommunications Act (1996), 73, 74, 128
teleconferencing, video, *see*
    videoconferencing
Tellme Networks, 75
Tenba, 583
terrorism, 516, 555–61, 569–70; nuclear,
    603; *see also* al-Qaeda; 9/11
Texas Instruments, 3, 30, 128, 130
Texas Pacific Group, 490
Thailand, 140, 415, 479, 583
Tharrington, Jeannie, 162
Thatcher, Margaret, 409, 430
thinkport.org, 302
3rd Generation User Interfaces, 193
3D Studio Max, 219
3M Corporation, 3, 479
Thurow, Shari, 272
Tiananmen Square massacre, 535
Tian Xu, 335
Timberlake, Justin, 182
Time magazine, 61, 399, 458, 521
Timm, David, 276
TiVo, 182
tolerance, culture of, 424–25
Tolstoy, Vladimir, 192
Toodou.com, 484–86
Torvalds, Linus, 106
Toshiba, 168, 583
Toyota, 358
Trade, Growth, and Poverty (Dollar and
    Kray), 410
trade policies, 43–44, 247, 264–69, 276–77,
    343, 446, 448–49, 628; *see also* free trade
Trade Representative, U.S. Office of
    (USTR), 247
transmission control protocol/Internet
    protocol (TCP/IP), 67, 82, 84
Trends in International Mathematics and
    Science Study, 350
Tropiano, Laurie, 461–62
trust, creation of, 334–35
Tsinghua University, 225, 369
Tucker, Marc, 316, 319, 359–61
Tufts University, 421
Tunisia, 415
Turkey, 422, 432, 450, 623
tutoring, online, 42–43
Twain, Mark, 530
24/7 Customer, 21–26, 28, 215
TXU Corporation, 490–91, 521
Tyco, 229

Ubiquity magazine, 302
UBS, 44
Uganda, 425
Ugarte, Jose, 359
Ukraine, 446
Unabomber, 596
Unilever, 305
United Arab Emirates, 414
United Kingdom, *see* Britain
United Nations, 248, 376, 499;
    Development Program, 561; Security
    Council, 574
United Parcel Service (UPS), 154, 167–75,
    197, 302, 304, 453, 585
United Press International, 20
United States, 122, 173, 222, 229–30, 411,
    446, 459, 498–99; activism in, 489–91,
    505–6; Afghanistan and, 59, 229, 624;
    ambition level in, 354–59; automobile
    industry in, 147, 172, 271; broadband
    Internet access in, 363–64; business
    startups in, 432; capital markets in,
    332–33; China and, 143, 145–50, 247,
    283, 428–30; in Cold War, 343, 374–76,
    382; credit registries in, 415; crisis in
    science and technology in, 340–48, 382;
    culture of, 422; education in, 42–43, 119,
    212, 213, 313–19, 324–29, 348–61,
    365–67, 501–3, 521–23; energy
    consumption in, 573–79; flexibility of
    economy of, 330; global supply chains
    of, 589–90; immigrants to, 390, 480;
    innovation-generating institutions
    in, 330–31; Institute of Peace, 598;
    intellectual property protection in, 254,
    333; Iraq war, 210, 229, 255, 296, 450,
    549, 565, 597, 601, 602, 614, 622; Ireland
    and, 418; Japan and, 165, 247–48; labor
    market flexibility in, 333, 383, 419;
    manufacturing in, 164; Mexico and,
    404, 433 (*see also* North American Free
    Trade Agreement); multinationals
    headquartered in, 243 (*see also specific
    companies*); national highway system in,
    75; offshoring by, 582–83; openness of,
    333; outsourcing to, 460; party politics
    in, 257–58; Physics Team, 349;
    political leadership in, 379–82; political
    stability of, 334; post–World War II, 339;
    productivity gains in, 206–7; radicals in,
    559; terrorists and, 556, 599–600 (*see also*
    al Qaeda; 9/11); trade policies of, 43–44,
    247, 263–69, 276–77, 448–49, 628; video

game industry in, 218, 220; visas for
    entry into, 215–16, 223–24, 350; wage
    stagnation in, 283–84, work flow to,
    82–83
United Technologies, 592
Unix, 66, 486
Unnikrisan, Anney, 28
uploading, 93–126, 187, 197, 204, 478–79,
    595; of content, 121–24; innovation
    and, 112–16; of news and commentary,
    117–21; of software, 94, 96–112; of
    videos, *see* YouTube
Uruguay, 443–46
USAID, 421
USA Today, 123–24, 237
U.S.-China Business Council, 149
USI, 583

Vajpayee, Ata Bihari, 593
Vanderbilt University, 123
Vashistha, Atul, 625
Venezuela, 382, 416, 575, 626
venture capital, 297, 287, 332
Verleger, Phillip K., Jr., 576, 577
versatilists, 293–97, 389
videoconferencing, 43–44, 192–93, 226
video games, 125, 193, 218, 220, 457–58
Vietnam, 104, 140, 273; war in, 20
Vioxx, 253
Virtual Caliphate, 596, 597
virtual private network (VPN), 220
Virtual Tax Room (VTR), 13
Visa credit cards, 580
Voice of America (VOA), 625
Voice over Internet Protocol (VoIP), 191–92,
    214, 453, 479, 502
Volex, 583
Volpi, Mike, 192
Volvo, 358
Vora family, 356
VPN, 220

Wacker, Jeff, 288, 292
wage insurance, 391–93
Waitman, Claudia, 191
Wales, Jimmy, 121–22, 124
Wallis, William, 506
Wall Street Journal, The, 127, 495, 597
Wal-Mart, 141, 151–66, 169, 194, 205–6,
    250–52, 468, 510, 544, 573
Walsh, Patrick, 187–88
Walton, Sam, 156–59, 163, 164, 252
Wang, Gary, 484–86

Wang, Winston, 589
Warburg Pincus, 74
Ward, Steve, 245
Warrior, Padmasree, 195
Washington Post, The, 46, 117, 251, 337, 358, 521, 529
Washington University, 224
Watanabe, Osamu, 143, 588
Watson, Rob, 512
Wealth and Poverty of Nations, The (Landes), 421
Weather Underground, 559
Web browsers, 60, 62–72, 77; *see also* Netscape
Webcams, 483
Web-delivered services, 87–89
WebSphere, 104
Wee Theng Tan, 349
Weimann, Gabriel, 598–601
Welch, Jack, 129
Wen Jiabao, 379
Wertz, William, 156
Western Electric, 74
Westinghouse science competition, 351
Westwood Schools, 501–3
Whirlpool, 358
Whitehurst, Grover J., 354
Whitman, Meg, 85–86, 619–21
Whole New Mind, A (Pink), 320–23
Wi-Fi, 504
Wikipedia, 64, 94, 96, 121–24, 313
Wild Brain, 77–79, 82
Wilder, C. John, 490
Wilkinson, Amy M., 43
Will, George, 521
Williams, Brian, 521
Williams, Candace Lee, 614–15
Williams, Robin, 312
Wince-Smith, Deborah, 370
Win Liu, 34
Winnebago Indians, 446
Winnick, Gary, 74
Winthrop, Elizabeth, 518
Wipro Technologies, 30, 128, 129, 132, 133, 135, 276, 278, 333, 389, 461, 547, 592, 593, 624
Wired magazine, 95, 111, 205
wireless technology, 185–87, 194–97
Wistron, 582
Wladawsky-Berger, Irving, 193, 609
word processing, 57
workers, lifetime employability of, 381–90

work flow software, 56, 77–92, 174, 198, 203, 219, 226, 231, 580
World Bank, 214, 410, 412, 492, 501, 548, 573
WorldCom, 229
World Learning, 107
World Trade Organization (WTO), 122, 137–39, 144, 149, 214, 429, 432, 548, 549, 572
World War I, 9, 568, 576
World War II, 9
World Wide Web, 9, 60–63, 67, 82, 92, 99–100; navigating, 310–13; *see also* Internet
Wozniak, Steve, 55
WPP, 208–9
Wrighton, Mark, 224–25
Wu Qidi, 366

Xia Deren, 34–36
XML, 83, 86
X-rays, 79, 82–83
Xu Jun, 163–64

Yahoo!, 71, 89, 179, 182–84, 255, 269, 271, 301, 365, 500, 528, 537; Groups, 523
YaleGlobal Online, 118, 121, 434, 547, 569, 599
Yale University, 128, 224, 335–36, 351–52, 529
Yamani, Ahmed Zaki, 568
Yang, Jerry, 179, 183–84, 365, 537, 548
Yang Yuanqing, 245
Yao Ming, 485
Yiting Liu, 224
Young & Rubicam, 208
Yousif, Mahmood al-, 507
YouTube, 119–21, 468, 492, 502, 504, 521, 523, 538
Y2K computer crisis, 131–38
Yunus, Muhammad, 493–94

Zaman, 623
Zara, 154
Zaun, Todd, 186, 197
Zawahiri, Ayman al-, 558, 560, 611, 614
Zayat, Taha, 405–6
Zedillo, Ernesto, 394, 409, 430, 431
Zee TV, 480
Zhao, Michael, 572
Zimbabwe, 430
zippies, 214–23, 264